I0138223

THE BOOK OF THE INDIANS

OF NORTH AMERICA

SAGOYEWATHA alias **RED-JACKET**

Chief of the Senecas

Annin Smith & Co's Lith.[y]

THE

BOOK OF THE INDIANS

OF

NORTH AMERICA:

COMPRISING

DETAILS IN THE LIVES OF ABOUT FIVE HUNDRED CHIEFS AND OTHERS,

THE MOST DISTINGUISHED AMONG THEM.

ALSO,

A HISTORY OF THEIR WARS; THEIR MANNERS AND CUSTOMS; SPEECHES OF ORATORS, &c., FROM THEIR FIRST BEING KNOWN TO EUROPEANS TO THE PRESENT TIME.

EXHIBITING ALSO AN ANALYSIS OF THE MOST DISTINGUISHED AUTHORS WHO HAVE WRITTEN UPON THE GREAT QUESTION OF THE

FIRST PEOPLING OF AMERICA.

They waste us, aye, like April snow,
In the warm noon we shrink away;
And fast they follow as we go
Towards the setting day,
Till they shall fill the land, and we
Are driven into the western sea

BRYANT.

BY SAMUEL G. DRAKE,
Member of the New-Hampshire Historical Society.

Boston:

PUBLISHED BY JOSIAH DRAKE,
AT THE ANTIQUARIAN BOOKSTORE, 56 CORNHILL.
1833.

THE BOOK OF THE INDIANS OF NORTH AMERICA

By Samuel G. Drake

As Published in 1833

Trade Paperback ISBN: 1-58218-094-6
Hardcover ISBN: 1-58218-132-2
eBook ISBN: 1-58218-093-8

Digital Scanning and Publishing is a leader in the electronic republication of historical books and documents. We publish many of our titles as eBooks, as well as traditional hardcover and trade paper editions. DSI is committed to bringing many traditional and little known books back to life, retaining the look and feel of the original work.

First DSI Printing: March 2001

Published by DIGITAL SCANNING, INC.
Scituate, MA 02066
www.digitalscanning.com

PREFACE.

ACCURACY, and minuteness of detail, where the subject seemed to require it, have been our land-mark throughout this laborious performance. We say laborious; but were all readers antiquarians, even so much need not have been said. Although we have been very minute, in numerous instances, in our lives of chiefs, yet there are many others in which we gladly would have been more so, if materials could, at the time of writing, have been had. However, we do not presume that we arrogate to ourselves too much, when we promise to give the reader a much greater amount of Indian history, than he can elsewhere find in any separate work.

The merits or demerits of INDIAN BIOGRAPHY rest solely upon its author, whose various cares and avocations, could they be known to the critical reader, would cause him to be sparing of his criticisms. We call this the second edition, although we have treated the subject under a new arrangement, and varied the title-page a little. The method of books and chapters was adopted, mainly for the benefit of combining history with biography; and it was thought it would be quite as convenient for reference. Besides containing all of the first edition, which was important, this will be found to contain, in addition, twice as much new matter.

Many names of the same persons and places will appear spelt differently in various parts of the work; but this our plan could not obviate, because we wished to preserve the orthography of each author from whom we extracted, in that particular. Except in quotations, we did intend to have been uniform; but we are aware that we have not been entirely so, from several causes, which are unnecessary to be named here.

It was not expected that a work of this kind would meet with a ready sale; but such was the case, and the very favorable reception with which the first edition met, was the cause of the early appearance of this.

In general, the notes give due credit to all such as have assisted the author in any way in his work. This observation is intended for the living; and for their kindnesses they now have this public acknowledgment of thanks. As to the works of deceased authors, we have made use of them as public property, taking care always to cite them, except where the same facts were common to many.

There is no work before the public upon this subject, unless, indeed, some juvenile performances be so considered, recently published in New York. Those we have not particularly examined.

CONTENTS

BOOK I.
INTRODUCTION .

CHAPTER I .

CHAPTER II.

CHAPTER III.

BOOK II .
BIOGRAPHY AND HISTORY OF THE NORTHERN OR NEW ENGLAND INDIANS.

CHAPTER I.

CHAPTER II.

CONTENTS

CONTENTS

BOOK III . BIOGRAPHY AND HISTORY OF THE NEW ENGLAND INDIANS CONTINUED.

CHAPTER I.

CHAPTER II.

CHAPTER III.

LIVES OF PHILIP'S CHIEF CAPTAINS.

CONTENTS

CONTENTS

CHAPTER VIII.

CHAPTER IX .

BOOK IV.
BIOGRAPHY AND HISTORY OF THE SOUTHERN INDIANS.

CHAPTER I.

CONTENTS

CONTENTS

CHAPTER V.

BOOK V.
BIOGRAPHY AND HISTORY OF THE IROQUOIS OR FIVE NATIONS, AND OTHER NEIGHBOR INGNATIONS OF THE WEST .

CHAPTER I.

CHAPTER II.

CHAPTER III.

CONTENTS

CONTENTS

LIST OF THE ENGRAVINGS.

All of the above portraits may be relied upon as good likenesses, except that of *Philip*, and we know nothing to the contrary but that is also; but we rather believe the figure given for his, a representation of any New England chief of his times. The dress, however, corresponds with all descriptions of him which we have seen.

BOOK I.

INTRODUCTION.

CHAPTER I.

Origin of the name Indian.—Why applied to the people found in America.—Ancient authors supposed to have referred to America in their writings—Theopompus—Voyage of Hanno—Diodorus Siculus—Plato—Aristotle—Seneca.

THE name *Indian* was erroneously applied to the original man of America* by its first discoverers. The hope of arriving at the East Indies by sailing west caused the discovery of America. When the islands and continent were at first discovered, Columbus, and many after him, supposed that they had arrived at the eastern shore of the continent of India, and hence the people they met with were called *Indians*. The error was not discovered until the name had so obtained, that it could not well be changed. It is true that it matters but little to us by what name the indigenes of a country are known, and especially those of America, in as far as the name is seldom used among us but in application to the aboriginal Americans. But with the people of Europe it is not so unimportant. Situated between the two countries, India and America, the same name for the inhabitants of both must, at first, have produced considerable inconvenience. Therefore, in a historical point of view, the error is, at least, as much to be deplored as that the name of the continent itself should have been derived from *Americus* instead of *Columbus*.

It has been the practice of almost every writer, who has written about the indigenes of a country, to give some wild theories of others, concerning their origin, and to close his account with his own; which generally has been more visionary, if possible, than those of his predecessors. Long, laborious, and, we may add, useless disquisitions have been daily laid before the world, from the discovery of America by Columbus to the present time, to endeavor to explain by what means the inhabitants got from the old to the new world. To act, therefore, in unison with many of our predecessors, we will begin as far back as they have done, and so shall commence with Theopompus and others, from whose writings it is alleged that the ancients had knowledge of America, and hence peopled it.

Theopompus, a learned historian and orator, who flourished in the time of *Alexander* the Great, in a book entitled *Thaumasia*, gives a sort of dialogue between *Midas* the Phrygian and *Silenus*. The book itself is lost, but

* So named from *Vespucius Americus*, a Florentine, who made a discovery of some part of the coast of South America in 1499 two years after *Cabot* had explored the coast of North America; but *Americus* had the fortune to confer his name upon both.

Strabo refers to it, and *Ælianus* has given us the substance of the dialogue, which follows. After much conversation, *Silenus* said to *Midas*, that Europe, Asia and Africa were but islands surrounded on all sides by the sea; but that there was a continent situated beyond these, which was of immense dimensions, even without limits; and that it was so luxuriant, as to produce animals of prodigious magnitude, and men grew to double the height of themselves, and that they lived to a far greater age;* that they had many great cities; and their usages and laws were different from ours; that in one city there was more than a million of inhabitants; that gold and silver were there in vast quantities.† This is but an abstract from *Ælianus's* extract, but contains all of it that can be said to refer to a country west of Europe and Africa.‡ Ælian or Ælianus lived about A. D. 200—230.

Hanno flourished when the Carthaginians were in their greatest prosperity, but the exact time is unknown. Some place his times 40, and others 140, years before the founding of Rome, which would be about 800 years before our era.§ He was an officer of great enterprise, having sailed around and explored the coast of Africa, set out from the Pillars of Hercules, now called the Straits of Gibraltar, and sailed westward 30 days. Hence it is inferred by many, that he must have visited America, or some of its islands. He wrote a book, which he entitled *Periplus*, giving an account of his voyages, which was translated and published about 1533, in Greek.‖

Many, and not without tolerably good reasons, believe that an island or continent existed in the Atlantic Ocean about this period, but which disappeared afterwards.

Diodorus Siculus says that some "Phœnicians were cast upon a most fertile island opposite to Africa." Of this, he says, they kept the most studied secrecy, which was doubtless occasioned by their jealousy of the advantage the discovery might be to the neighboring nations, and which they wished to secure wholly to themselves. *Diodorus Siculus* lived about 100 years before *Christ*. Islands lying west of Europe and Africa are certainly mentioned by *Homer* and *Horace*. They were called *Atlantides*, and were supposed to be about 10000 furlongs from Africa.

---

* *Buffon* and *Raynal* either had not read this story, or they did not believe it to have been America; for they taught that all animals degenerated here. Many of the first adventurers to the coasts of unknown countries reported them inhabited by giants. *Swift* wrote *Gulliver's* Travels to bring such accounts into ridicule. How well he succeeded is evident from a comparison of books of voyages and travels before and after his time. *Dubartas* has this passage:—

> "Our fearless sailors, in far voyages
> (More led by gain's hope than their compasses),
> On th' Indian shore have sometime noted some
> Whose bodies covered two broad acres room;
> And in the South Sea they have also seen
> Some like high-topped and huge-armed treen;
> And other some, whose monstrous backs did bea.
> Two mighty wheels, with whirling spokes, that were
> Much like the winged and wide-spreading sails
> Of any wind-mill turned with merry gales."
>
> *Divine Weeks*, p. 117, ed. 4to, 1613.

† Ælian, Variar. Historiar. lib. iii. chap. viii.

‡ Since the text was written, there has come into my hands a copy of a translation of Ælian's work, "in Englishe (as well according to the truth of the Greeke texte, as of the Latine), by *Abraham Fleming*." London, 1576, 4to. It differs not materially from the above, which is given from a French version of it.

§ Encyclopædia Perthensis.

‖ The best account of *Hanno* and his voyages, with which we are acquainted, is to be found in *Mariana's* Hist. of. Spain, vol. i. 93, 109, 119, 122, 133, and 150, ed. Paris, 1725, 5 vols. 4to.

Here existed the poets' fabled Elysian fields. But to be more particular with *Diodorus*, we will let him speak for himself. "After having passed the islands which lie beyond the Herculean Strait, we will speak of those which lie much farther into the ocean. Towards Africa, and to the west of it, is an immense island in the broad sea, many days' sail from Lybia. Its soil is very fertile, and its surface variegated with mountains and valleys. Its coasts are indented with many navigable rivers, and its fields are well cultivated; delicious gardens, and various kinds of plants and trees." He finally sets it down as the finest country known, where the inhabitants have spacious dwellings, and every thing in the greatest plenty- To say the least of this account of *Diodorus*, it corresponds very well with that given of the Mexicans when first known to the Spaniards, but perhaps it will compare as well with the Canaries.

Plato's account has more weight, perhaps, than any of the ancients. He lived about 400 years before the Christian era. A part of his account is as follows: "In those first times [time of its being first known], the Atlantic was a most broad island, and there were extant most powerful kings in it, who, with joint forces, appointed to occupy Asia and Europe: And so a most grievous war was carried on; in which the Athenians, with the common consent of the Greeks, opposed themselves, and they became the conquerors. But that Atlantic island, by a flood and earthquake, was indeed suddenly destroyed, and so that warlike people were swallowed up." He adds, in another place, "An island in the mouth of the sea, in the passage to those straits, called the Pillars of *Hercules*, did exist; and that island was greater and larger than Lybia and Asia; from which there was an easy passage over to other islands, and from those islands to that continent, which is situated out of that region."* "*Neptune* settled in this island, from whose son, Atlas, its name was derived, and divided it among his ten sons. To the youngest fell the extremity of the island, called *Gadir*, which, in the language of the country signifies *fertile* or *abounding in sheep*. The descendants of Neptune reigned here, from father to son, for a great number of generations in the order of primogeniture, during the space of 9000 years. They also possessed several other islands; and, passing into Europe and Africa, subdued all Lybia as far as Egypt, and all Europe to Asia Minor. At length the island sunk under water; and for a long time afterwards the sea thereabouts was full of rocks and shelves."† This account, although mixed with fable, cannot, we think, be entirely rejected; and that the ancients had knowledge of countries westward of Europe appears as plain and as well authenticated as any passage of history of that period.

Aristotle, or the author of a book which is generally attributed to him,‡ speaks of an island beyond the Straits of Gibraltar; but the passage savors something of hearsay, and is as follows: "Some say that, beyond the Pillars of *Hercules*, the Carthaginians have found a very fertile island, but without inhabitants, full of forests, navigable rivers and fruit in abundance. It is several days' voyage from the main land. Some Carthaginians, charmed by the fertility of the country, thought to marry and settle there; but some say that the government of Carthage forbid the settlement upon pain of death, from the fear that it would increase in power so as to deprive the mother country of her possessions there." If *Aristotle* had uttered this as a prediction, that such a thing would take

* America known to the Ancients, 10, 8vo, Boston, 1773.

† Encyclopædia Perthensis, Art. ATLANTIS.

‡ De mirabil, auscultat. Opera, vol. i. *Voltaire* says of this book, "On en fesait honneur aux Carthaginois, et on citait un livre d'Aristote qu'il n'a pas composé." *Essai sur les Mœurs et l'esprit des nations*, chap. cxlv. p. 703. vol. iv. of his works. Edit Paris, 1817, in 8vo.

place in regard to some future nation, no one, perhaps, would have called him a false prophet, for the American revolution would have been its fulfilment. This philosopher lived about 384 years before *Christ*.

Seneca lived about the commencement of the vulgar era. He wrote tragedies, and in one of them occurs this passage:—

"Venient annis
Sæcula seris, quibus oceanus
Vincula rerum laxet, et ingens
Pateat tellus, Typhisque novos
Detegat orbes; nec sit terris
Ultima Thule."

Medea, Act 3. v. 375.

This is nearer prophecy, and may be rendered in English thus: "The time will come when the ocean will loosen the chains of nature, and we shall behold a vast country. A new Typhis shall discover new worlds: Thule shall no longer be considered the last country of the known world."

Not only these passages from the ancient authors have been cited and *re*-cited by moderns, but many more, though less to the point, to show that, in some way or other, America must have been peopled from some of the eastern continents. Almost every country has claimed the honor of having been its first discoverer, and hence the father or mother of the Indians. But since the recent discoveries in the north, writers upon the subject say but little about getting over inhabitants from Europe, Asia, or Africa through the difficult way of the Atlantic seas and islands, as it is much easier to pass them over the narrow channels of the north in canoes, or upon the ice. *Grotius, C. Mather, Hubbard,* and after them *Robertson,* are glad to meet with so easy a method of solving a question which they consider as having puzzled their predecessors so much.

CHAPTER II.

Of modern Theorists upon the peopling of America.—St. Gregory.—Herrera. —T.Morton.—Williamson.—Wood.—Josselyn.—Thorowgood.—Adair.— R. Williams.—C. Mather—Hubbard.—Robertson.—Smith.—Voltaire.— Mitchel.—M'Culloh.—Lord Kaim.—Swinton.—Cabrera.

St. *Gregory*, who flourished in the 7th century, in an epistle to St. *Clement*, said that beyond the ocean there was another world.*

Herrera argues, that the new world could not have been known to the ancients; and that what *Seneca* has said was not true. For that *God* had kept it hid from the old world, giving them no certain knowledge of it; and that, in the secrecy and incomprehensibility of his providence, he has been pleased to give it to the Castilian nation. That Seneca's prediction (if so it may be considered) was a false one, because he said that a new world would be discovered in the north, and that it was found in the west.† *Herrera* wrote about 1598,‡ before which time little knowl-

* "S. Gregoire sur l'epistre de S. Clement, dit que passé l'ocean, il y a vn autre mond." (*Herrera*, I Decade, 2.) This is the whole passage.

† Ibid, 3.

‡ He died 27 Mar. 1625, at the age of about 66 years. His name was *Tordesillas Antonio de Herrera*—one of the best Spanish historians. His history of the voyages to, and settlement of America is very minute and very valuable. The original in Spanish is very rare. *Acosta's* translation (into French) 3 v. 4to, 1660, is also scarce and valuable. It is this we cite.

edge was obtained of North America. This may account for his impeachment of *Seneca's* prophecy.

Thomas Morton, who came to New England in 1622, published in 1637 an account of its natural history, with much other curious matter. In speaking upon the peopling of America, he thinks it altogether out of the question to suppose that it was peopled by the Tartars from the north, because "a people, once settled, must be removed by compulsion, or else tempted thereunto in hopes of better fortunes, upon commendations of the place unto which they should be drawn to remove. And if it may be thought that these people came over the frozen sea, then would it be by compulsion. If so, then by whom, or when? Or what part of this main continent may be thought to border upon the country of the Tartars? It is yet unknown; and it is not like that a people well enough at ease, will, of their own accord, undertake to travel over a sea of ice, considering how many difficulties they shall encounter with. As, 1st, whether there be any land at the end of their unknown way, no land being in view; then want of food to sustain life in the mean time upon that sea of ice. Or how shall they do for fuel, to keep them at night from freezing to death? which will not be had in such a place. But it may perhaps be granted, that the natives of this country might originally come of the scattered Trojans; for after that *Brutus*, who was the fourth from *Eneas*, left Latium upon the conflict held with the Latins (where, although he gave them a great overthrow, to the slaughter of their grand captain and many others of the heroes of Latium, yet he held it more safely to depart unto some other place and people, than, by staying, to run the hazard of an unquiet life or doubtful conquest; which, as history maketh mention, he performed.) This people was dispersed, there is no question, but the people that lived with him, by reason of their conversation with the Grecians and Latins, had a mixed language, that participated of both."* This is the main ground of *Morton*, but he says much more upon the subject; as that the similarity of the languages of the Indians to the Greek and Roman is very great. From the examples he gives, we presume he knew as little about the Indian languages as Dr. *Mather, Adair*, and *Boudinot*, who thought them almost to coincide with the Hebrew. Though *Morton* thinks it very improbable that the Tartars came over by the north from Asia, because they could not see land beyond the ice, yet he finds no difficulty in getting them across the wide Atlantic, although he allows them no compass. That the Indians have a Latin origin he thinks evident, because he fancied he heard among their words *Pasco-pan*, and hence thinks, without doubt, their ancestors were acquainted with the god *Pan*.†

Dr. *Williamson*‡ says, "It can hardly be questioned that the Indians of South America are descended from a class of the Hindoos, in the southern parts of Asia." That they could not have come from the north, because the South American Indians are unlike those of the north. This seems to clash with the more rational views of Father *Venegas*. § He writes as follows: "Of all the parts of America hitherto discovered the Californians lie nearest to Asia. We are acquainted with the mode of writing in all the eastern nations. We can distinguish between the characters of the Japanese, the Chinese, the Chinese Tartars, the Mogul Tartars, and other nations extending as far as the Bay of Kamschathka; and learned dissertations on them, by Mr. *Boyer*, are to be found in the acts of the imperial academy of sciences at Petersburg. What discovery

* New Canaan, book i. pages 17 and 18. † Ibid. 18.

‡ In his Hist. N. Carolina, i. 216.

§ Hist. California, i. 60. His work was published at Madrid in 1758.

would it be to meet with any of these characters, or others like them, among the American Indians nearest to Asia! But as to the Californians, if ever they were possessed of any invention to perpetuate their memoirs, they have entirely lost it; and all that is now found among them, amounts to no more than some obscure oral traditions, probably more and more adulterated by a long succession of time. They have not so much as retained any knowledge of the particular country from which they emigrated." This is the account of one who lived many years among the Indians of California.

Mr. *William Wood*,* who left New England in 1633,† after a short stay, says, "Of their language, which is only peculiar to themselves, not inclining to any of the refined tongues: Some have thought they might be of the dispersed Jews, because some of their words be near unto the Hebrew; but by the same rule, they may conclude them to be some of the gleanings of all nations, because they have words which sound after the Greek, Latin, French, and other tongues."‡

Mr. *John Josselyn*, who resided some time in N. England, from the year 1638, says, "The Mohawks are about 500: their speech a dialect of the Tartars (as also is the Turkish tongue)."§ In another work,|| he says, "N. England is by some affirmed to be an island, bounded on the north with the River of Canada (so called from Monsieur Cane), on the south with the River Monhegan or *Hudson's* River, so called, because he was the first that discovered it. Some will have America to be an island, which out of question must needs be, if there be a north-east passage found out into the South Sea. It contains 1152400000 acres. The discovery of the north-west passage (which lies within the River of Canada) was undertaken with the help of some Protestant Frenchmen, which left Canada, and retired to Boston about the year 1669. The north-east people of America, that is, N. England, &c., are judged to be Tartars, called Samoades, being alike in complexion, shape, habit and manners." We have given here a larger extract than the immediate subject required, because we would let the reader enjoy his curiosity, as well as we ours, in seeing how people understood things in that day. *Barlow*, looking but a small distance beyond those times, with great elegance says,—

"In those blank periods, where no man can trace
The gleams of thought that first illumed his race,
His errors, twined with science, took their birth,
And forged their fetters for this child of earth.
And when, as oft, he dared expand his view,
And work with nature on the line she drew,
Some monster, gendered in his fears, unmanned
His opening soul, and marred the works he planned.
Fear, the first passion of his helpless state,
Redoubles all the woes that round him wait,
Blocks nature's path, and sends him wandering wide,
Without a guardian, and without a guide."
Columbiad, ix. 137, &c.

Rev. *Thomas Thorowgood* published a small quarto, in 1652,¶ to prove that the Indians were the Jews, who had been "lost in the world for the space

---

* The author of a work entitled *New England's Prospect*, published in London, 1634, in 4to. It is a very rare, and, in some respects, a curious and valuable work.

Prospect, 51.

Ibid. 112. ed. 1764.

§ His account of two voyages to N. England, printed London, 1673, page 124.

|| N. Eng. Rarities, 4, 5, printed London, 1672.

¶ Its title commences, "*Digitus Dei: New Discoveries, with sure Arguments to prove*," &c.

of near 200 years." But whoever has read *Adair* or *Boudinot*, has, beside a good deal that is irrational, read all that in *Thorowgood* can be termed rational.

Rev. *Roger Williams* was, at one time, as appears from *Thorowgood's* work,* of the same opinion. Being written to for his opinion of the origin of the natives, "he kindly answers to those letters from Salem in N. Eng. 20th of the 10th month, more than 10 yeers since, in *hœc verba*." That they did not come into America from the N. East, as some had imagined, he thought evident for these reasons: 1. their ancestors affirm they came from the S. West, and return thence when they die: 2. because they "separate their women in a little wigwam by themselves in their feminine seasons:" and 3. "beside their god *Kuttand* to the S. West, they hold that *Nanawitnawit*† (a god over head) made the heavens and the earth; and some tast of affinity with the Hebrew I have found."

Dr. *Cotton Mather* is an author of such singular qualities, that we almost hesitate to name him, lest we be thought without seriousness in so weighty a matter. But we will assure, the reader, that he is an author with whom we would in no wise part; and if sometimes we appear not serious in our introduction of him, what is of more importance, we believe *him* really to be so. And we are persuaded that we should not be pardoned did we not allow him to speak upon the matter before us.

He says, "It should not pass without remark, that *three* most memorable things which have borne a very great aspect upon *human affairs*, did, near the same time, namely, at the conclusion of the *fifteenth*, and the beginning of the *sixteenth*, century, arise unto the world: the first was the *Resurrection of Literature*; the second was the opening of *America*; the third was the *Reformation of Religion*." Thus far we have an instructive view of the subject, calculated to lead to the conclusion that, in the dark ages, when literature was neglected and forgotten, discoveries might have been also, and hence the knowledge of America lost for a time. The reader must now summon his gravity. "But," this author continues, "as probably the *Devil*, seducing the first inhabitants of America into it, therein aimed at the having of them and their posterity out of the sound of the *silver trumpets* of the gospel, then to be heard through the Roman empire.‡ If the *Devil* had any expectation, that, by the peopling of America, he should utterly deprive any Europeans of the two benefits, *literature and religion*, which dawned upon the miserable world, (one just *before*, the other just *after*,) the first famed navigation hither, 'tis to be hoped he will be disappointed of that expectation."§ The learned doctor, having forgotten what he had written in his first book, or wishing to inculcate his doctrine more firmly, nearly repeats a passage which he had at first given, in a distant part of his work;|| but, there being considerable

* Pages 5 and 6.

† *Getannitowit* is *god* in Delaware.—*Heckewelder*.

‡ This, we apprehend, is not entirely original with our author, but borders upon plagiarism. *Ward*, the celebrated author of the *"Simple Cobler of Aggawam,"* say of the Irish, "These Irish (anciently called *anthropophagi*, man-eaters) have a tradition among them, that when the Devil showed our Saviour all the kingdoms of the earth, and their glory, that he would not show him Ireland, but reserved it for himself. It is, probably, true; for he hath kept it ever since for his own peculiar: the *old fox* foresaw it would eclipse the glory of all the rest: he thought it wisdom to keep the land for a Boggards for his unclean spirits employed in this hemisphere, and the people to do his son and heir (the Pope) that service for which *Lewis* the XI kept his Barbor Oliver, which makes them so bloodthirsty."—*Simple Cobler*, 86, 87. Why so much gall is poured out upon the poor Irish, we cannot satisfactorily account. The circumstance of his writing in the time of *Cromwell* will explain a part, if not the whole, of the enigma. He was the first minister of Ipswich, Mass. but was born and died in England.

§ Magnalia Christ. Amer. b. i.

|| Ibid. b. iii.

addition, we recite it: "The natives of the country now possessed by the Newenglanders, had been forlorn and wretched *heathen* ever since their first herding here; and though we know not *when* or *how* these Indians first became inhabitants of this mighty continent, yet we may guess that probably the *Devil* decoyed those miserable salvages hither, in hopes that the gospel of the Lord Jesus Christ would never come here to destroy or disturb his absolute empire over them. But our Eliot was in such ill terms with the *Devil*, as to alarm him with sounding the *silver trumpets* of heaven in his territories, and make some noble and zealous attempts towards outing him of ancient possessions here. There were, I think, 20 several *nations* (if I may call them so) of Indians upon that spot of ground which fell under the influence of our *Three United Colonies*; and our *Eliot* was willing to rescue as many of them as he could from that old usurping *landlord* of America, who is, *by the wrath of God*, the prince of this world." In several places he is decided in the opinion that Indians are Scythians, and is confirmed in the opinion, on meeting with this passage of *Julius Cæsar*: "*Difficilius Invenire quam interficere*," which he thus renders, "It is harder to find them than to foil them." At least, this is a happy application of the passage. *Cæsar* was speaking of the Scythians, and our historian applies the passage in speaking of the sudden attacks of the Indians, and their agility in hiding themselves from pursuit.* Dr. Mather wrote at the close of the seventeenth century, and his famous book, *Magnalia Christi Americana*, was published in 1702.

Adair, who resided 40 years (he says) among the southern Indians, previous to 1775, published a huge quarto upon their origin, history, &c. He tortures every custom and usage into a like one of the Jews, and almost every word in their language into a Hebrew one of the same meaning.

Dr. *Boudinot*, in his book called "The Star in the West," has followed up the theory of Adair, with such certainty, as he thinks, as that the "long lost ten tribes of Israel" are clearly identified in the American Indians. Such theories have gained many supporters. It is of much higher antiquity than *Adair*, and was treated as such visionary speculations should be by authors as far back as the historian *Hubbard*.

Hubbard, who wrote about 1680, has this, among other passages: "If any observation be made of their manners and dispositions, it's easier to say from what nations they did not, than from whom they did, derive their original. Doubtless their conjecture, who fancy them to be descended from the ten tribes of the Israelites, carried captive by *Salamaneser* and *Esarhaddon*, hath the least show of reason of any other, there being no footsteps to be observed of their propinquity to them more than to any other of the tribes of the earth, either as to their language or manners."† This author is one of the best historians of his times; and, generally, he writes with as much discernment upon other matters as upon this.

That because the natives of one country and those of another, and each unknown to the other, have some customs and practices in common, it has been urged by some, and not a few, that they must have had a common origin; but this, in our apprehension, does not necessarily follow. Who will pretend that different people, when placed under similar circumstances, will not have similar wants, and hence similar actions? that like wants will not prompt like exertions? and like causes produce *not* like effects? This mode of reasoning we think sufficient to show, that, although the Indians may have some customs in common with the Scythians, the Tartars, Chinese, Hindoos, Welsh, and indeed every other nation, still, the former, for any reason we can see to the contrary, have

* See Magnalia, b. vii.

† Hist. N. England, 27.

as good right to claim to themselves priority of origin as either or all of the latter.

Dr. *Robertson* should have proved that people of color produce others of no color, and the contrary, before he said, "We know with infallible certainty, that all the human race spring from the same source,"* meaning *Adam*. He founds this broad assertion upon the false notion that, to admit any other would be an inroad upon the verity of the holy Scriptures. Now, in our view of the subject, we leave them equally inviolate in assuming a very different ground;† namely, that all habitable parts of the world may have been peopled at the same time, and by different races of men. That it *is* so peopled, we *know*: that it *was* so peopled as far back as we have an account, we see no reason to disbelieve. Hence, when it *was not* so is as futile to inquire, as it would be impossible to conceive of the annihilation of space. When a new country was discovered, much inquiry was made to ascertain from whence came the inhabitants found upon it—not even asking whence came the other animals. The answer to us is plain. Man, the other animals, trees and plants of every kind, were placed there by the supreme directing hand, which carries on every operation of nature by fixed and undeviating laws. This, it must be plain to every ready, is, at least, as reconcilable to the Bible as the theory of *Robertson*, which is that of *Grotius*,‡ and all those who have followed them.

When it has been given in, at least by all who have thought upon the subject, that climate does not change the complexion of the human race, to hold up the idea still that all must have sprung from the same source, (*Adam*,) only reminds us of our grandmothers, who to this day laugh at us when we tell them that the earth is a globe. Who, we ask, will argue that the negro changes his color by living among us, or changing his latitude? Who have ever become negroes by living in their country or among them? Has the Indian ever changed his complexion by living in London? Do those change which adopt our manners and customs, and are surrounded by us? Until these questions can be answered in the affirmative, we discard altogether that *unitarian* system of peopling the world. We would indeed prefer *Ovid's* method:—

> "Ponere duritiem cœpere, suumque rigorem;
> Mollirique mora, mollitaque ducere formam.
> Mox ubi creverunt, naturaque mitior illis
> Contigit," &c. &c.
>
> *Metamor.* lib. i. fab. xi.

That is, *Deucalion* and *Pyrrha* performed the office by traveling over the country and picking up stones, which, as they cast them over their heads, became young people as they struck the earth.

We mean not to be understood that the exterior of the skin of people is not changed by climate, for this is very evident; but that the children of persons would be any lighter or darker, whose residence is in a climate different from that in which they were born, is what we deny, as in the former case. As astonishing as it may appear to the succinct reasoner, it is no less true, that Dr. Samuel Stanhope Smith has put forth an octavo book of more than 400 pages to prove the *unity*, as he expresses it, "of the human race," that is, that all were originally descended from one man. His reasoning is of this tenor: "The American and European

* Hist. America, book iv.

† Why talk of a theory's clashing with holy writ, and say nothing of the certainty of the sciences of geography, astronomy, geology, &c.?

‡ He died in 1645, æt. 62.

sailor reside equally at the pole, and under the equator." Then, in a triumphant air, he demands—"Why then should we, without necessity, assume the hypothesis that originally there existed different species of the human kind?"* What kind of argument is contained here we leave the reader to make out; and again, when he would prove that all the human family are of the same tribe, he says that negro slaves at the south, who live in white families, are gradually found to conform in features to the whites with whom they live!† Astonishing! and we wonder who, if any, knew this beside the author. Again, and we have done with our extraordinary philosopher. He is positive that deformed or disfigured persons will, in process of time, produce offspring marked in the same way. That is, if a man practise flattening his nose, his offspring will have a flatter nose than he would have had, had his progenitor not flattened his; and so, if this offspring repeat the process, his offspring will have a less prominent nose; and so on, until the nose be driven entirely into or off the face! In this, certainly, our author has taken quite a roundabout way to vanquish or put to flight a nose. We wish he could tell us how many ages or generations it would take to make this formidable conquest. Now, for any reason we can see to the contrary, it would be a much less tedious business to cut off a member at once, and thus accomplish the business in a short period; for to wait several generations for a fashion seems more novel than the fashion itself, and, to say the least, is as incompatible with human nature as the fashion itself. A man must be monstrously blind to his prejudices, to maintain a doctrine like this. As well might he argue that colts would be tailless because it has long been the practice to shorten the tails of horses, of both sexes; but we have never heard that colts' tails are in the least affected by this practice which has been performed on the horse so long.‡ Certainly, if ever, we should think it time to discover something of it! Nor have we ever heard that a female child has ever been born with its ears bored, although its ancestors have endured the painful operation for many generations;—and here we shall close our examination of Mr. *Smith's* 400 pages.§

Another theory, almost as wild, and quite as ridiculous, respecting the animals of America, seems here to present itself. We have reference to the well known assertions of *Buffon* and *Raynal*,|| two philosophers who were an honor to the times of *Franklin*, which are, that man and other animals in America degenerate.¶ This has been met in such a masterly manner by Mr. *Jefferson*,** that to repeat any thing here would be entirely out of place, since it has been so often copied into works on both sides of the Atlantic. It may even be found in some of the best English Encyclopædias.††

---

* Smith on Complexion, N. Brunswick, N. J. 1810, p. 11. † Ibid. 170, 171.

‡ The author pleads not guilty to the charge of plagiarism; for it was not until some months after the text was written, that he knew that even this idea had occurred to any one. He has since read an extract very similar, in Dr. Lawrence's valuable Lectures on Zoology, &c.

§ On reflection, we have thought our remarks rather pointed, as Mr. *Smith* is not a living author; but what called them forth must be their apology.

|| After speaking of the effect of the climate of the old world in producing man and other animals in perfection, he adds, "Combien, au contraire, la nature paro t avoir négligé nouveau mond! Les hommes y sont moins forts, moins courageux; sans barbe et sans poil," &c. *Histoire Philos. des deux Indes*, viii. 210. Ed. Geneva, 1781, 12 vols. 8vo.

¶ *Voltaire* does not say quite as much, but says this: "La nature enfin avait donné aux Americanes beaucoup moins d'industrie qu'aux hommes de l'ancien monde. Toutes ces causes ensemble ont pu nuire beaucoup à la population." [*Œuvres*, iv. 19.] This is, however, only in reference to the Indians.

** In his Notes on Virginia, Quer. vii. †† Perthensis, i. 637. (Art. AMER. § 38.)

*Smith** does not deal fairly with a passage of *Voltaire*, relating to the peopling of America; as he takes only a part of a sentence to comment upon. Perhaps he thought it as much as he was capable of managing.† The complete sentence to which we refer we translate as follows: "There are found men and animals all over the habitable earth: who has put them upon it? We have already said, it is he who has made the grass grow in the fields; and we should be no more surprised to find in America men, than we should to find flies."‡ We can discover no contradiction between this passage and another in a distant part of the same work; and which seems more like the passage Mr. *Smith* has cited: "Some do not wish to believe that the caterpillars and the snails of one part of the world should be originally from another part: wherefore be astonished, then, that there should be in America some kinds of animals, and some races of men like our own?"§

Voltaire has written upon the subject in a manner that will always be attracting, however much or little credence may be allowed to what he has written. We will, therefore, extract an entire article wherein he engages more professedly upon the question than in other parts of his works, in which he has rather incidentally spoken upon it. The chapter is as follows:|| "Since many fail not to make systems upon the manner in which America has been peopled, it is left only for us to say, that he who created flies in those regions, created man there also. However pleasant it may be to dispute, it cannot be denied that the Supreme Being, who lives in all nature,¶ has created about the 48 two-legged animals without feathers, the color of whose skin is a mixture of white and carnation, with long beards approaching to red; about the line, in Africa and its islands, negroes without beards; and in the same latitude, other negroes with beards, some of them having wool and some hair on their heads; and among them other animals quite white, having neither hair nor wool, but a kind of white silk. It does not very clearly appear what should have prevented *God* from placing on another continent animals of the same species, of a copper color, in the same latitude in which, in Africa and Asia, they are found black; or even from making them without beards in the very same latitude in which others possess them. To what lengths are we carried by the rage for systems joined with the tyranny of prejudice! We see these animals; it is agreed that *God* has had the power to place them where they are; yet it is not agreed that he *has* so placed them. The same persons who readily admit that the *beavers* of Canada are of Canadian origin, assert that the men must have come there in boats, and that Mexico must have been peopled by some of the descendants of *Magog*. As well might it be said, that, if there be men in the moon, they must have been taken there by *Astolpho* on his hippogriff, when he went to fetch *Roland's* senses, which were corked up in a bottle. If America had been discovered in his time, and there had then been men in Europe *systematic* enough to have advanced, with the Jesuit *Lafitau*,** that the Caribbees descended from the inhabitants of Caria, and the Hurons from the Jews, he would have done well to have brought back the bottle containing the wits of these reasoners,

---

* *Samuel Smith*, who published a history of New Jersey, in 1765, printed at Burlington.

† See Hist. N. J. 8.

‡ Essai sur les Mœurs et l'Esprit des Nations. (Œuvres, iv. 18.)

§ Ibid. 708.

|| Œuvres, t. vii. 197, 198.

¶ Will the reader of this call *Voltaire* an atheist?

** He wrote a history of the savages of America, and maintained that the Caribbee language was radically Hebrew.

which he would doubtless have found in the moon, along with those of *Angelica's* lover. The first thing done when an inhabited island is discovered in the Indian Ocean, or in the South Sea, is to inquire, Whence came these people? but as for the trees and the tortoises, *they* are, without any hesitation, pronounced to be indigenous; as if it were more difficult for nature to make men than to make tortoises. One thing, however, which seems to countenance this system, is, that there is scarcely an island in the eastern or western ocean, which does not contain jugglers, quacks, knaves and fools. This, it is probable, gave rise to the opinion, that these animals are of the same race with ourselves."

Some account of what the Indians themselves have said upon the subject of their origin may be very naturally looked for in this place. Their notions in this respect can no more be relied upon than the fabled stories of the gods in ancient mythology. Indeed, their accounts of primitive inhabitants do not agree beyond their own neighborhood, and often disagree with themselves at different times. Some say their ancestors came from the north, others from the north-west, others from the east, and others from the west; some from the regions of the air, and some from under the earth. Hence that to raise any theory upon any thing coming from them upon the subject, would show only that the theorist himself was as ignorant as his informants. We might as well ask the forest trees how they came planted upon the soil in which they grow. Not that the Indians are unintelligent in other affairs, any further than the necessary consequence growing out of their situation implies; nor are they less so than many who have written upon their history.

> "Since, then, the wisest are as dull as we,
> In one grave maxim let us all agree—
> Nature ne'er meant her secrets should be found,
> And man's a riddle, which man can't expound!"
>
> *Paine's Ruling Passion.*

The different notions of the Indians will be best gathered from their lives in their proper places in the following work.

Dr. *S. L. Mitchel,* of New York, a man who writes learnedly, if not wisely, on almost every subject, has, in his opinion, like hundreds before him, set the great question, *How was America peopled?* at rest. He has no doubt but the Indians, in the first place, are of the same color originally as the north-eastern nations of Asia, and hence sprung from them. What time he settles them in the country he does not tell us, but gets them into Greenland about the year 8 or 900. Thinks he saw the Scandinavians as far as the shores of the St. Lawrence, but what time this was he does not say. He must of course make these people the builders of the mounds scattered all over the western country. After all, we apprehend the doctor would have short time for his emigrants to do all that nature and art have done touching these matters. In the first place, it is evident that many ages passed away from the time these tumuli were began until they were finished: 2d, a multitude of ages must have passed since the use for which they were reared has been known; for trees of the age of 200 years grow from the ruins of others which must have had as great age: and, 3d, no Indian nation or tribe has the least tradition concerning them.* This could not have happened had the ancestors of the present Indians been the erectors of them, in the nature of things.†

The observation of an author in Dr. *Rees's* Encyclopædia,‡ although

* Or none but such as are at variance with all history and rationality.
† Archæologia Americana, i 325, 326, 341, &c.
‡ Art. AMERICA.

saying no more than has been already said in our synopsis, is, nevertheless, so happy, that we should not feel clear to omit it:—"As to those who pretend that the human race has only of late found its way into America, by crossing the sea at Kamschatka, or the Straits of Tschutski, either upon the fields of ice or in canoes, they do not consider that this opinion, besides that it is extremely difficult of comprehension, has not the least tendency to diminish the prodigy; for it would be surprising indeed that one half of our planet should have remained without inhabitants during thousands of years, while the other half was peopled. What renders this opinion less probable is, that America is supposed in it to have had animals, since we cannot bring those species of animals from the old world which do not exist in it, as those of the tapir, the glama, and the tajactu. Neither can we admit of the recent organization of matter for the western hemisphere; because, independently of the accumulated difficulties in this hypothesis, and which can by no means be solved, we shall observe, that the fossil bones discovered in so many parts of America, and at such small depths, prove that certain species of animals, so far from having been recently organized, have been annihilated a long while ago."

Before we had known, that, if we were in error, it was in the company of philosophers, such as we have in this chapter introduced to our readers, we felt a hesitancy in avowing our opinions upon a matter of so great moment. But, after all, as it is only matter of honest opinion, no one should be intolerant, although he may be allowed to make himself and even his friends merry at our expense. When, in the days of *Chrysostom*, some ventured to assert their opinions of the rotundity of the earth, that learned father "did laugh at them."* And, when science shall have progressed sufficiently, (if it be possible,) to settle this question, there is a possibility that the *Chrysostoms* of these days will not have the same excuse for their infidelity. But as it is a day of prodigies, there is some danger of treating lightly even the most seemingly absurd conjectures. We therefore feel very safe, and more especially as it required considerable hardihood to laugh even at the theory of the late Mr. *Symmes*.

When we lately took up a book entitled "*Researches, Philosophical and Antiquarian, concerning the Aboriginal History of America*, by J. H. M'CULLOH, Jr. M. D."† we did think, from the imposing appearance of it, that some new matters on the subject had been discovered: and more especially when we read in the preface, that "his first object was to explain the origin of the men and animals of America, so far as that question is involved with the apparent physical impediments that have so long kept the subject in total obscurity." Now, with what success this has been done, to do the author justice, he shall speak for himself, and the reader then may judge for himself.

"Before we attempt to explain in what manner the men and animals of America reached this continent, it is necessary to ascertain, if possible, the circumstances of their original creation; for upon this essential particular depends the great interest of our present investigation. [We are not able to discover that he has said any thing further upon it.] It must be evident that we can arrive at no satisfactory conclusion, if it be doubtful whether the Creator of the universe made man and the animals but in one locality, from whence they were dispersed over the earth; or whether he created them in each of those various situations where we now find them living. So far as this inquiry respects mankind, there can be no

---

* See Acosta's Hist. E. and W. Indies, p. 1. ed. London, 1604.

† Published at Baltimore, 1829, in 8vo.

reasonable ground to doubt the one origin of the species. This fact may be proved both physically and morally. [If the reader can discover any thing that amounts to proof in what follows, he will have made a discovery that we could not.] That man, notwithstanding all the diversities of their appearance, are but of one species, is a truth now universally admitted by every physiological naturalist. [That is, notwithstanding a negro be black, an Indian brown, a European white, still, they are all men. And then follows a quotation from Dr. *Lawrence** to corroborate the fact that men are all of one species.] It is true, this physiologist does not admit that the human species had their origin but from one pair; for he observes, the same species might have been created at the same time in very different parts of the earth. But when we have analyzed the moral history of mankind, to which Mr. *Lawrence* seems to have paid little attention, [and if our author has done it, we would thank him to show us where we can find it,] we find such strongly marked analogies in abstract matters existing among nations the most widely separated from each other, that we cannot doubt there has been a time, when the whole human family have intimately participated in one common system of things, whether it be of truth or of error, of science or of prejudice. [This does not at all agree with what he says afterwards, 'We have been unable to discern any traces of Asiatic or of European civilization in America prior to the discovery of Columbus.' And again: 'In comparing the barbarian nations of America with those of the eastern continent, we perceive no points of resemblance between them, in their moral institutions or in their habits, that are not apparently founded in the necessities of human life.' If, then, there is no affinity, other than what would accidentally happen from similar circumstances, wherefore this prating about *'strongly-marked analogies,'* &c. just copied.] As respects the origin of animals, [we have given his best proofs of the origin of man and their transportation to America,] the subject is much more refractory. We find them living all over the surface of the earth, and suited by their physical conformity to a great variety of climates and peculiar localities. Every one will admit the impossibility of ascertaining the history of their original creation from the mere natural history of the animals themselves." Now, as "refractory" as this subject is, we did not expect to see it fathered off upon a miracle, because this was the easy and convenient manner in which the superstitious of every age accounted for every thing which they at once could not comprehend. And we do not expect, when it is gravely announced, that a discovery in any science is to be shown, that the undertaker is going to tell us it is accomplished by a miracle, and that, therefore, "he knows not why he should be called upon to answer objections," &c.

As it would be tedious to the reader, as well as incompatible with our plan, to quote larger from Mr. *M'Culloh's* book, we shall finish with him after a few remarks.

We do not object to the capacity of the ark for all animals, but we do object to its introduction in the question undertaken by Mr. *M'Culloh*; for every child knows that affair to have been miraculous; and if any part of the question depended upon the truth or falsity of a miracle, why plague the world with a book of some 500 pages, merely to promulgate such a belief, when a sentence would be all that is required? No one, that admits an overruling power, or the existence of God, will doubt of his ability to create a myriad of men, animals, and all matter, by a breath; or that an ark ten feet square could contain, comfortably, ten

---

* The celebrated author of Lectures on *Physiology, Zoology, and the Natural History of Man.*

thousand men, as well as one of the dimensions given in scripture to contain what that did. Therefore, if one in these days should make a book expressly to explain the cause of the different lengths of days, or the changes of the seasons, and find, after he had written a vast deal, that he could in no wise unravel the mystery, and, to close his account, declares it was all a miracle, such an author would be precisely in the predicament of Mr. *M'Culloh.*

We do not pretend that the subject can be pursued with the certainty of mathematical calculations; and so long as it is contended that the whole species of man spring from one pair, so long will the subject admit of controversy: therefore it makes but little or no difference whether the inhabitants are got into America by the north or the south, the east or the west, as it regards the main question. For it is very certain that, if there were but one pair originally, and these placed upon a certain spot, all other places where people are now found must have been settled by people from the primitive spot, who found their way thither, some how or other, and it is very unimportant how, as we have just observed.

Lord *Kaim*, a writer of great good sense, has not omitted to say something upon this subject.* He very judiciously asks those who maintain that America was peopled from Kamskatka, whether the inhabitants of that region speak the same language with their American neighbors on the opposite shores. That they do not, he observes, is fully confirmed by recent accounts from thence; and "whence we may conclude, with great certainty, that the latter are not a colony of the former."† We have confirmation upon confirmation, that these nations speak languages entirely different; and for the satisfaction of the curious, we will give a short vocabulary of words in both, with the English against them.

English.	*Kamskadale.*	*Aléoutean.* ‡
God	Nionstichtchitch	Aghogoch.
Father	Iskh	Athan.
Mother	Nas-kh	Anaan.
Son	Pa-atch	L'laan.
Daughter	Souguing	Aschkinn
Brother	Ktchidsch	Koyota.
Sister	Kos-Khou	Angün.
Husband	Skoch	Ougünn.
Woman	Skoua-aou	A -yagar.
Girl	Kh-tchitchou	Ougeghilikinn.
Young boy	Pahatch	Auckthok.
Child	Pahatchitch	Ouskolik.
A man	Ouskaams	Toyoch.
The people	Kouaskou.	
Persons	Ouskaamsit.	
The head	T-Khousa	Kamgha.
The face	Koua-agh	Soghimaginn.
The nose	Kaankang	Aughosinn.
The nostrils	Kaanga	Gouakik.
The eye	Nanit	Thack.

* See his *"Sketches of the History of Man,"* a work which he published in 1774, at Edinburgh, in 2 vols. 4to.

† Vol. ii. 71.

‡ The Aléouteans inhabit the chain of islands which stretch from the N. W. point of America into the neighborhood of Kamskatka. It must be remembered that these names are in the French orthography, being taken from a French translation of *Billings's* voyage into those regions, from 1785 to 1794.

After observing that "there are several cogent arguments to evince that the Americans are not descended from any people in the north of Asia, or in the north of Europe," Lord *Kaim* continues,—"I venture still further; which is, to conjecture, that America has not been peopled from any part of the old world." But although this last conjecture is in unison with those of many others, yet his lordship is greatly out in some of the proofs which he adduces in its support. As we have no ground on which to controvert this opinion, we may be excused from examining its proofs; but this we will observe, that Lord *Kaim* is in the same error about the beardlessness of the Americans as some other learned Europeans.

The learned Dr. *Swinton*,* in a dissertation upon the peopling of America,† after stating the different opinions of various authors who have advocated in favor of the "dispersed people," the Phœnicians, and other eastern nations, observes, "that, therefore, the Americans in general were descended from some people who inhabited a country not so far distant from them as Egypt and Phœnicia, our readers will, as we apprehend, readily admit. Now, no country can be pitched upon so proper and convenient for this purpose as the north-eastern part of Asia, particularly Great Tartary, Siberia, and more especially the peninsula of Kamtschatka. That probably was the tract through which many Tartarian colonies passed into America, and peopled the most considerable part of the new world."

This, it is not to be denied, is the most rational way of getting inhabitants into America, if it must be allowed that it was peopled from the "old world." But it is not quite so easy to account for the existence of equatorial animals in America, when all authors agree that they never could have passed that way, as they could not have survived the coldness of the climate, at any season of the year. Moreover, the vocabulary we have given, if it prove any thing, proves that either the inhabitants of North America did not come in from the north-west, or that, if they did, some unknown cause must have, for ages, suspended all communication between the emigrants and their ancestors upon the neighboring shores of Asia.

In 1822, there appeared in London a work which attracted some attention, as most works have upon similar subjects. It was entitled, "Description of the ruins of an ancient city, discovered near Palenque, in the kingdom of Guatemala, in Spanish America: translated from the original manuscript report of Capt. *Don Antonio Del Rio*: followed by a critical investigation and research into the *History of the Americans*, by Dr. *Paul Felix Cabrera*, of the city of New Guatemala."

Capt. *Del Rio* was ordered by the Spanish king, in the year 1786, to make an examination of whatever ruins he might find, which he accordingly did. From the manuscript he left, which afterwards fell into the hands of Dr. *Cabrera*, his work was composed, and is that part of the work which concerns us in our view of systems or conjectures concerning the peopling of America. We shall be short with this author, as his system differs very little from some which we have already sketched. He is very confident that he has settled the question how South America received its inhabitants, namely, from the Phœnicians, who sailed across the Atlantic Ocean, and that the ruined city described by Capt. *Del Rio* was built by the first adventurers.

Dr. *Cabrera* calls any system, which, in his view, does not harmonize

* Dr. *John Swinton*, the eminent author of many parts of the *Ancient Universal History*. He died in 1777, aged 74.

† Universal History, xx. 162, 163.— See *Malone's* edition of *Boswell's Life Dr. Johnson*, v. 271. ed. in 5 v. 12mo. London, 1821.

with the Scriptures, an innovation upon the "holy Catholic religion;" and rather than resort to any such, he says, "It is better to believe his [God's] works miraculous, than endeavor to make an ostentatious display of our talents by the cunning invention of new systems, in attributing them to natural causes."* The same reasoning will apply in this case as in a former. If we are to attribute every thing to miracles, wherefore the necessity of investigation? These authors are fond of investigating matters in their way, but are displeased if others take the same liberty. And should we follow an author in his theories, who cuts the whole business short by declaring all to be a miracle, when he can no longer grope in the labyrinth of his own forming, our reader would be just in condemning such waste of time. When every thing which we cannot at first sight understand or comprehend must not be inquired into, from superstitious doubts, then and there will be fixed the bounds of all science; *but*, as Lord *Byron* said upon another occasion, *not till then.*

"If it be allowed (says Dr. LAWRENCE)† that all men are of the same species, it does not follow that they are all descended from the same family. We have no data for determining this point: it could indeed only be settled by a knowledge of facts, which have long ago been involved in the impenetrable darkness of antiquity." That climate has nothing to do with the complexion, he offers the following in proof:

"The establishments of the Europeans in Asia and America have now subsisted about three centuries. *Vasquez De Gama* landed at Calicut in 1498; and the Portuguese empire in India was founded in the beginning of the following century. Brazil was discovered and taken possession of by the same nation in the very first year of the sixteenth century. Towards the end of the 15th, and the beginning of the 16th century, *Columbus, Cortez,* and *Pizarro*, subjugated for the Spaniards the West Indian islands, with the empires of Mexico and Peru. Sir *Walter Ralegh* planted an English colony in Virginia in 1584; and the French settlement of Canada has rather a later date. The colonists have, in no instance, approached to the natives of these countries: and their descendants, where the blood has been kept pure, have, at this time, the same characters as native Europeans."‡

The eminent antiquary, *De Witt Clinton*,§ supposed that the ancient works found in this country were similar to those supposed to be Roman by *Pennant* in Wales. He adds, "The Danes, as well as the nations which erected our fortifications, were in all probability of Scythian origin. According to *Pliny*, the name of Scythian was common to all the nations living in the north of Asia and Europe."§

CHAPTER III.

Manners and Customs of the Indians, as illustrated by Anecdotes, Narratives, &c.

Wit.—AN Ottaway chief, known to the French by the name of *White-john*, was a great drunkard. Count *Frontenac* asked him what he thought brandy to be made of; he replied that it must be made of hearts and tongues—"For," said he, "when I have drunken plentifully of it, my heart

* Page 30.

† Lectures on Zoology, &c. 442. ed. 8vo. Salem, 1828. ‡ Ibid. 464, 465.

§ *A Memoir on the Antiquities of the Western Parts of the State of N. York*, pages 9, 10. 8vo. Albany, 1818.

is a thousand strong, and I can talk, too, with astonishing freedom and rapidity."*

Honor.—A chief of the Five Nations, who fought on the side of the English in the French wars, chanced to meet in battle his own father, who was fighting on the side of the French. Just as he was about to deal a deadly blow upon his head, he discovered who he was, and said to him, "You have once given me life, and now I give it to you. Let me meet you no more; for I have paid the debt I owed you."†

Recklessness.—In Connecticut River, about "200 miles from Long Island Sound, is a narrow of 5 yards only, formed by two shelving mountains of solid rock. Through this chasm are compelled to pass all the waters which in the time of the floods bury the northern country." [This is now called *Turner's* Falls, from the great fight he had there with the Indians in Philip's war.] It is a frightful passage of about 400 yards in length. No boat, or, as my author expresses it, "no living creature, was ever known to pass through this narrow, except an Indian woman." This woman had undertaken to cross the river just above, and although she had the god Bacchus by her side, yet Neptune prevailed in spite of their united efforts, and the canoe was hurried down the frightful gulf. While this Indian woman was thus hurrying to certain destruction, as she had every reason to expect, she seized upon her bottle of rum, and did not take it from her mouth until the last drop was quaffed. She was marvellously preserved, and was actually picked up several miles below, floating in the canoe, still quite drunk. When it was known what she had done, and being asked how she dared to drink so much rum with the prospect of certain death before her, she answered that she knew it was too much for one time, but she was unwilling that any of it should be lost.‡

Justice.—A missionary residing among a certain tribe of Indians, was one day, after he had been preaching to them, invited by their chief to visit his wigwam. After having been kindly entertained, and being about to depart, the chief took him by the hand and said, "I have very bad squaw. She had two little children. One she loved well, the other she hated. In a cold night, when I was gone hunting in the woods, she shut it out of the wigwam, and it froze to death. What must be done with her?" The missionary replied, "She must be hanged." "Ah!" said the chief, "go, then, and hang your God, whom you make just like her."

Revenge. —"An Indian, in Chatauque county, New York, a stout man, known by the name of the *Devil's-ramrod*, lately had a rencounter with a white man, in which he came off second best. Mortified at the result, he twice jumped into a neighboring creek to drown himself, but was dragged out by the people present. He made a third attempt, and succeeded."§

Magnanimity.—A hunter, in his wanderings for game, fell among the back settlements of Virginia, and by reason of the inclemency of the weather, was induced to seek refuge at the house of a planter, whom he met at his door. Admission was refused him. Being both hungry and thirsty, he asked for a morsel of bread and a cup of water, but was answered in every case, "No! you shall have nothing here! *Get you gone, you Indian dog!*" It happened, in process of time, that this same planter lost himself in the woods, and, after a fatiguing day's travel, he came to an Indian's cabin, into which he was welcomed. On inquiring the way, and the distance to the white settlements, being told by the Indian that he could not go in the night, and being kindly offered lodging and victuals, he gladly refreshed and reposed himself in the Indian's cabin. In the morning, he conducted him through the wilderness, agreeably to

* Universal Museum for 1763.
† Ibid.
‡ Peters's Hist. Connecticut.
§ Niles's Regr. xx. 368.

his promise the night before, until they came in sight of the habitations of the whites. As he was about to take his leave of the planter, he looked him full in the face, and asked him if he did not know him. Horror-struck at finding himself thus in the power of a man he had so inhumanly treated, and dumb with shame on thinking of the manner it was requited, he began at length to make excuses, and beg a thousand pardons, when the Indian interrupted him, and said, "When you see poor Indians fainting for a cup of cold water, don't say again, 'Get you gone, you Indian dog!'" He then dismissed him to return to his friends. My author adds, "It is not difficult to say, which of these two had the best claim to the name of Christian."*

Deception.—The captain of a vessel, having a desire to make a present to a lady of some fine oranges which he had just brought from "the sugar islands," gave them to an Indian in his employ to carry to her. Lest he should not perform the office punctually, he wrote a letter to her, to be taken along with the present, that she might detect the bearer, if he should fail to deliver the whole of what he was intrusted with. The Indian, during the journey, reflected how he should refresh himself with the oranges, and not be found out. Not having any apprehension of the manner of communication by writing, he concluded that it was only necessary to keep his design secret from the letter itself, supposing that would tell of him if he did not; he therefore laid it upon the ground, and rolled a large stone upon it, and retired to some distance, where he regaled himself with several of the oranges, and then proceeded on his journey. On delivering the remainder and the letter to the lady, she asked him where the rest of the oranges were; he said he had delivered all; she told him that the letter said there were several more sent; to which he answered that the letter lied, and she must not believe it. But he was soon confronted in his falsehood, and, begging forgiveness of the offence, was pardoned.†

Shrewdness.—As Governor Joseph *Dudley* of Massachusetts was superintending some of his workmen, he took notice of an able-bodied Indian, who, half naked, would come and look on, as a pastime, to see his men work. The governor took occasion one day to ask him *why he did not work and get some clothes, wherewith to cover himself.* The Indian answered by asking him *why he did not work.* The governor, pointing with his finger to his head, said, "*I work head work,* and so have no need to work with my hands as you should." The Indian then said he would work if any one would employ him. The governor told him he wanted a calf killed, and that, if he would go and do it, he would give him a shilling. He accepted the offer, and went immediately and killed the calf, and then went sauntering about as before. The governor, on observing what he had done, asked him why he did not dress the calf before he left it. The Indian answered, "*No, no, Coponoh;* that was not in the bargain: I was to have a shilling for killing him. *Am he no dead, Coponoh?* [governor.]" The governor, seeing himself thus outwitted, told him to dress it, and he would give him another shilling.

This done, and in possession of two shillings, the Indian goes directly to a grog-shop for rum. After a short stay, he returned to the governor, and told him he had given him a bad shilling piece, and presented a brass one to be exchanged. The governor, thinking possibly it might have been the case, gave him another. It was not long before he returned a second time with another brass shilling to be exchanged; the governor was now convinced of his knavery, but, not caring to make words at the time, gave him another; and thus the fellow got four shillings for one.

---

* Carey's Museum, vi. 40.

† Uring's Voyage to N. England in 1709, 8vo. London, 1726.

The governor determined to have the rogue corrected for his abuse, and, meeting with him soon after, told him he must take a letter to Boston for him [and gave him a half a crown for the service.*] The letter was directed to the keeper of bridewell, ordering him to give the bearer so many lashes; but, mistrusting that all was not exactly agreeable, and meeting a servant of the governor on the road, ordered him, in the name of his master, to carry the letter immediately, as he was in haste to return. The consequence was, this servant got egregiously whipped. When the governor learned what had taken place, he felt no little chagrin at being thus twice outwitted by the Indian.

He did not see the fellow for some time after this, but at length, falling in with him, asked him by what means he had cheated and deceived him so many times. Taking the governor again in his own play, he answered, pointing with his finger to his head, "*Head work, Coponoh, head work!*" The governor was now so well pleased that he forgave the whole offence.†

Equality.—An Indian chief, on being asked whether his people were free, answered, "Why not, since I myself am free, although their king?"‡

Matrimony.—"An aged Indian, who for many years had spent much time among the white people, both in Pennsylvania and New Jersey, one day, about the year 1770, observed that the Indians had not only a much easier way of getting a wife than the whites, but also a more certain way of getting a good one. 'For,' said he in broken English, 'white man court—court—may be one whole year!—may be two years before he marry! Well—may be then he get very good wife—but may be not—may be very cross! Well, now suppose cross! scold so soon as get awake in the morning! scold all day!—scold until sleep!—all one—he must keep him!—White people have law forbidding throw away wife he be ever so cross—must keep him always! Well, how does Indian do? Indian, when he see industrious squaw, he like, he go to him, place his two fore fingers close aside each other, make two like one—then look squaw in the face—see him smile—this is all one he say yes!—so he take him home—no danger he be cross! No, no—squaw know too well what Indian do if he cross! throw him away and take another!—Squaw love to eat meat—no husband no meat. Squaw do every thing to please husband, he do every thing to please squaw—live happy.' "§

Toleration.—In the year 1791, two Creek chiefs accompanied an American to England, where, as usual, they attracted great attention, and many flocked around them, as well to learn their ideas of certain things as to behold "the savages." Being asked their opinion of religion, or of what religion they were, one made answer, that they had no priests in their country, or established religion, for they thought, that, upon a subject where there was no possibility of people's agreeing in opinion, and as it was altogether matter of *mere* opinion, "it was best that every one should paddle his canoe his own way." Here is a volume of instruction in a short answer of a savage!

A recruiting officer, engaged in the service of the United States' government in the time of the Western Indian wars, (about 1790,) wrote thus to a friend: "Where I am, the recruiting business goes on heavily; none but the refuse of creation to be picked up; gallows-looking fellows, (like Sir John Falstaff's regiment,) who only enlist with a design to desert; and, when collected, will, I fear, be pronounced

> So worn, so wasted, so despised a crew,
> As even Indians might with pity view."

---

* A sentence added in a version of this anecdote in *Carey's Museum*, vi. 204.
† Uring, *ut supra*. 120. ‡ *Carey's Museum*, vi. 482.
§ Heckewelder's Hist. Ind. Nations.

Justice.—A white trader sold a quantity of powder to an Indian, and imposed upon him by making him believe it was a grain which grew like wheat, by sowing it upon the ground. He was greatly elated by the prospect, not only of raising his own powder, but of being able to supply others, and thereby becoming immensely rich. Having prepared his ground with great care, he sowed his powder with the utmost exactness in the spring. Month after month passed away, but his powder did not even sprout, and winter came before he was satisfied that he had been deceived. He said nothing; but some time after, when the trader had forgotten the trick, the same Indian succeeded in getting credit of him to a large amount. The time set for payment having expired, he sought out the Indian at his residence, and demanded payment for his goods. The Indian heard his demand with great complaisance; then, looking him shrewdly in the eye, said, "*Me pay you when my powder grow.*" This was enough. The guilty white man quickly retraced his steps, satisfied, we apprehend, to balance his account with the chagrin he had received.

Hunting.—The Indians had methods to catch game which served them extremely well. We will give here an anecdote of one of their snares *catching a pilgrim*, and then explain, by an engraving, their fence traps.

The same month in which the Mayflower brought over the fathers, November, 1620, to the shores of Plimouth, several of them ranged about the woods near by to learn what the country contained. Having wandered farther than they were apprised, in their endeavor to return, they say, "We were shrewdly puzzled, and lost our way. As we wandered, we came to a tree, where a young sprit was bowed down over a bow, and some acorns strewed underneath. *Stephen Hopkins* said, it had been to catch some deer. So, as we were looking at it, *William Bradford* being in the rear, when he came looking also upon it, and as he went about, it gave a sudden jerk up, and he was immediately caught up by the legs. It was (they continue) a very pretty device, made with a rope of their own making, [of bark or some kind of roots probably,] and having a noose as artificially made as any roper in England can make, and as like ours as can be; which we brought away with us."*

* Mourt's Relation.

Greatness of Mind, a Narrative.—*Silòuee* was a Cherokee chief, and was introduced by Mr. *Jefferson*, to illustrate the observation in his Notes on Virginia, that the Indian "is affectionate to his children, careful of them, and indulgent in the extreme; that his affections comprehend his other connections, weakening, as with us, from circle to circle, as they recede from the centre; that his friendships are strong and faithful to the uttermost extremity." "A remarkable instance of this appeared in the case of the late Col. *Byrd*,* who was sent to the Cherokee nation to transact some business with them. It happened that some of our disorderly people had just killed one or two of that nation. It was therefore proposed in the council of the Cherokees, that Col. *Byrd* should be put to death, in revenge for the loss of their countrymen. Among them was a chief called *Silòuee*, who, on some former occasion, had contracted an acquaintance and friendship with Col. *Byrd*. He came to him every night in his tent, and told him not to be afraid, they should not kill him. After many days' deliberation, however, the determination was contrary to *Silòuee's* expectation, that *Byrd* should be put to death, and some warriors were despatched as executioners. *Silòuee* attended them; and when they entered the tent, he threw himself between them and *Byrd*, and said to the warriors, '*This man is my friend: before you get at him, you must kill me!*' On which they returned, and the council respected the principle so much, as to recede from their determination."

A more impolitic and barbarous measure, perhaps, never entered the heart of man, than that of offering a reward for human scalps. This was done by Virginia. It is true the government of Virginia was not alone in this criminal business, but that betters not her case. The door of enormity being thus opened, it was easy to have foreseen, that many men upon the frontiers, "of bad lives and worse principles," says an intelligent writer,† stood ready to step in. As the event proved, many friendly Indians were *murdered*, and the government *defrauded*. It was at the news of a murder of this description that Col. *Byrd* was seized.

Preaching against Practice.—*John Simon* was a Sogkonate, who, about the year 1700, was a settled minister to that tribe. He was a man of strong mind, generally temperate, but sometimes remiss in the latter particular. The following anecdote is told as characteristic of his notions of justice. *Simon*, on account of his deportment, was created justice of the peace, and when difficulties occurred involving any of his people, he sat with the English justice to aid in making up judgment. It happened that *Simon's* squaw, with some others, had committed some offence. Justice *Almy* and *Simon*, in making up their minds, estimated the amount of the offence differently; *Almy* thought each should receive *eight* or *ten* stripes, but *Simon* said, "*No, four or five are enough—Poor Indians are ignorant, and it is not Christian-like to punish so hardly, those who are ignorant, as those who have knowledge.*" Simon's judgment prevailed. When Mr. *Almy* asked *John* how many his wife should receive, he said, "*Double, because she had knowledge to have done better*;" but Col. *Almy*, out of regard to *John's* feelings, wholly remitted his wife's punishment. *John* looked very serious, and made no reply while in presence of the court, but, on the first fit opportunity, remonstrated very severely against his judgment; and said to him, "*To what purpose do we preach a religion of justice, if we do unrighteousness in judgment.*"

---

* Perhaps the same mentioned by *Oldmixon*, (i. 283.) in speaking of the Indian powwows; one of whom he says, "very lately conjured a shower of rain for Col. *Byrd's* plantation in a time of drouth, for two bottles of rum," and of which Mr. *Oldmixon* says, "had we not found this in an author who was on the spot, we should have rejected it as a fable."

† Dr. *Burnaby*.

BOOK II.

BIOGRAPHY AND HISTORY OF THE NORTHERN OR NEW ENGLAND INDIANS.

" 'Tis good to muse on nations passed away,
Forever from the land we call our own."

AMOYDEN.

CHAPTER I

An account of such as have been carried away by the early voyagers.—Donacona—Agona—Tasquantum, or Squanto—Dehamda—Skettwarroes—Assacumet—Manida—Pechmo—Monopet—Pekenimne—Sakaweston—Epanow—Manawet—Wanape—Coneconam.

THE first voyagers to a country were anxious to confirm the truth of their accounts, and therefore took from their newly-discovered lands whatever seemed best suited to the objects in view. The inhabitants of America carried off by Europeans were not, perhaps, in any instance, taken away merely for this object, but that they might, in time, learn from them the value of the country from whence they came. Besides those forcibly carried away, there were many who went through overpersuasion, and ignorance both of the distance and usage they should meet in a land of strangers; which was not always as it should have been, and hence such as were ill used, if they ever returned to their own country, were prepared to be revenged on any strangers of the same color, that chanced to come among them.

There were three natives presented to Henry VII. by *Sebastian Cabot*, in 1502, which he had taken from Newfoundland. What were their names, or what became of them, we are not informed; but from the notice of historians, we learn that, when found, "they were clothed with the skins of beasts, and lived on raw flesh; but after two years, [residence in England,] were seen in the king's court clothed like Englishmen, and could not be discerned from Englishmen."* These were the first Indians ever seen in England.† They were brought to the English court "in their country habit," and "spoke a language never heard before out of their own country."‡

The French discovered the River St. Lawrence in 1508, and the captain of the ship who made the discovery, carried several natives to Paris, which were the first ever seen in France. What were their names, or even how many they were in number, is not set down in the accounts of this voyage. The name of this captain was *Thomas Aubert*.§

John Verazzini, in the service of France, in 1524, sailed along the American coast, and landed in several places. At one place, which we judge to be some part of the coast of Connecticut, "20 of his men landed, and went about two leagues up into the country. The inhabitants fled before them, but they caught an old woman who had hid herself in the high grass, with a young woman about 18 years of age. The old woman carried a child on her back, and had, besides, two little boys with her. The young woman, too, carried three children of her own sex. Seeing themselves discovered, they began to shriek, and the old one gave them to understand, by signs, that the men were fled to the woods. They offered her something to eat, which she accepted, but the maiden refused it. This girl, who was tall and well shaped, they were desirous of taking along with them, but as she made a violent outcry, they contented themselves with taking a boy away with them."|| The name of NEW FRANCE was given to North America in this voyage. In another voyage here, *Verazzini* was killed and eaten by the Indians.

Donacona, a chief upon the River St. Croix, was met with, in 1535, by the voyager *James Cartier*, who was well received and kindly treated by him and his people; to repay which, *Cartier*, "partly by stratagem and partly by force," carried him to France, where he soon after died.¶ Notwithstanding, *Cartier* was in the country five years after, where he found *Agona*, the successor of *Donacona*, and exchanged presents with him, probably reconciling him by some plausible account of the absence of *Donacona*.

Tasquantum, or *Tisquantum*, was one of the five natives carried from the coast of New England, in 1605, by Capt. *George Waymouth*, who had been sent out to discover a north-west passage. This Indian was known afterwards to the settlers of Plimouth, by whom he was generally called

---

* Rapin's *Hist. England*, i. 685. ed. fol.

† This is upon the authority of *Berkely*. Instead of *England*, however, he says *Europe*; but, by saying the six, which *Columbus* had before taken from St. Salvador, made their escape, he shows his superficial knowledge of those affairs. Hear *Herrera*:—

"*En suitte de cela*, [*that is, after Columbus had replied to the king's letter about a second voyage*,] *il* [*Columbus*] *partit pour aller à Barcelone auec sept Indiens, parce que les autres estoient morts en chemin. Il fit porter aueque luy des perroquets verds, et de rouges, et d'autres choses dignes d'admiration qui n'auoient iamais esté veues en Espagne.*" Hist. des Indes Occident. i. 102. Ed. 1660, 3 tomes, 4to. See also *Harris, Voyages*, ii. 15. ed. 1764, 2 v. fol.; *Robertson, America*, i. 94. ed. 1778, 4to.

‡ Berkely's *Naval Hist. Brit.* 268. ed. 1756. fol. and Harris, *Voyages*, ii. 191.

§ Forster, 432. || Ibid. 434, 435. ¶ Ibid. 440—442.

'Squanto or *'Squantum*, by abbreviation. The names of the other four were *Manida*, *Skettwarroes*, *Dehamda** and *Assacumet*.

Sir *Ferdinando Gorges* says, *Waymouth*, "falling short of his course, [in seeking the N. W. passage,] happened into a river on the coast of America, called *Pemmaquid*, from whence he brought five of the natives." "And it so pleased our great God, that" *Waymouth*, on his return to England, "came into the harbor of Plymouth, where I then commanded." Three† of whose natives, namely, *Manida*, *Skettwarroes* and *Tasquantum*, "I seized upon. They were all of one nation, but of several parts, and several families. This accident must be acknowledged the means, under God, of putting on foot and giving life to all our plantations."

Paying great attention to these natives, he soon understood enough by them about the country from whence they came to establish a belief that it was of great value; not perhaps making due allowance for its being their *home*. And Sir *Ferdinando* adds, "After I had those people sometimes in my custody, I observed in them an inclination to follow the example of the better sort; and in all their carriages, manifest shows of great civility, far from the rudeness of our common people. And the longer I conversed with them, the better hope they gave me of those parts where they did inhabit, as proper for our uses; especially when I found what goodly rivers, stately islands, and safe harbors, those parts abounded with, being the special marks I leveled at as the only want our nation met with in all their navigations along that coast. And having kept them full three years, I made them able to set me down what great rivers ran up into the land, what men of note were seated on them, what power they were of, how allied, what enemies they had," &c.

Thus having gained a knowledge of the country, Sir *Ferdinando* got ready "a ship furnished with men and all necessaries" for a voyage to America, and sent as her captain Mr. *Henry Challoung*,‡ with whom he also sent two of his Indians. The names of these were *Assacumet* and *Manida*. *Chalons*, having been taken sick in the beginning of the voyage, altered his course, and lost some time in the West Indies. After being able to proceed northward, he departed from Porto Rico, and was soon after taken by a Spanish fleet, and carried into Spain, "where their ship and goods were confiscate, themselves made prisoners, the voyage overthrown, and both my natives lost." One, however, *Assacumet*, was afterwards recovered, if not the other. This voyage of *Chalons* was in 1606.

It appears that the Lord Chief Justice *Popham*§ had agreed to send a vessel to the aid of *Chalons*, which was accordingly done before the news of his being taken was known in England. For Sir *Ferdinando Gorges* says, "It pleased the lord chief justice, according to his promise, to despatch Capt. [*Martin*] *Prin* from Bristol, with hope to have found

---

* Although *Gorges* does not say *Dehamda* was one brought at this time, it is evident that he was, because, so far as we can discover, there were no other natives, at this time in England, but these five.

† It seems, from this part of his narrative, that he had but three of them, but, from subsequent passages, it appears he had them all. See also *America painted to the Life*.

‡ *Challons*, by some. *Gorges* has him, sometimes, *Chalowns*, *Chalon*, &c.

§ The same who presided at the trial of Sir W. *Ralegh* and his associates, in 1603. See *Prince's Worthies of Devon*, 672, 673. *Fuller*, in his *Worthies of England*, ii. 284, says, "Travelers owed their safety to this judge's severity many years after his death, which happened Anno Domini 16**," thinking, no doubt, he had much enlightened his reader by definitely stating that Sir *John Popham* died some time within a *hundred* years. The severity referred to has reference to his importuning King *James* not to pardon so many robbers and thieves, which, he said, tended to render the judges contemptible, and "which made him more sparing afterward."

Capt. *Challounge*;" "but not hearing by any means what became of him, after he had made a perfect discovery of all those rivers and harbors," "brings with him the most exact discovery of that coast that ever came to my hands since, and, indeed, he was the best able to perform it of any I met withal to this present, [time,] which, with his relation of the country, wrought such an impression in the lord chief justice, and us all that were his associates, that (notwithstanding our first disaster) we set up our resolutions to follow it with effect."

Dehamda and *Skettwarroes* were with *Prin** in this voyage, and were, without doubt, his most efficient aids in surveying the coast. It appears from *Gorges*, that *Dehamda* was sent by the chief justice, who we suppose had considered him his property,† and *Skettwarroes* by himself. They returned again to England with *Prin*.

The next year, 1607, these two natives piloted the first New England colony to the mouth of Sagadahock River, since the Kennebeck. They left England 30 May, and did not arrive here until 8 August following. "As soon as the president had taken notice of the place, and given order for landing the provisions, he despatched away Captain *Gilbert*, with *Skitwarres* his guide, for the thorough discovery of the rivers and habitations of the natives, by whom he was brought to several of them, where he found civil entertainment, and kind respects, far from brutish or savage natures, so as they suddenly became familiar friends, especially by the means of *Dehamda* and *Skitwarrers*." "So as the president was earnestly intreated by *Sassenow, Aberemet*, and others, the principal Sagamores, (as they call their great lords,) to go to the Bashabas, who it seems was their king." They were prevented, however, by adverse weather, from that journey, and thus the promise to do so was unintentionally broken, "much to the grief of those Sagamores that were to attend him. The Bashebas, notwithstanding, hearing of his misfortune, sent his own son to visit him, and to beat a trade with him for furs."

Several sad and melancholy accidents conspired to put an end to this first colony of New England. The first was the loss of their storehouse, containing most of their supplies, by fire, in the winter following, and another was the death of Lord *Popham*. It consisted of 100 men, and its beginning was auspicious; but these calamities, together with the death of their president, broke down their resolutions. So many discouragements, notwithstanding a ship with supplies had arrived, determined them to abandon the country, which they did in the spring.‡ What became of *Dehamda* and *Skettwarroes* there is no mention, but they probably remained in the country with their friends, unless the passage which we shall hereafter extract, be construed to mean differently.§

To return to *Tisquantum*. There is some disagreement in the narratives of the cotemporary writers in respect to this chief, which shows, either that some of them are in error, or that there were two of the same name—one carried away by *Waymouth*, and the other by *Hunt*. From a critical examination of the accounts, it is believed there was but one, and

---

* *Gorges*, one of the main springs of these transactions, who wrote the account we give, makes no mention of any other captain accompanying him; yet Dr. *Holmes's* authorities, *Annals*, i 125, led him to record *Thomas Hanam* as the performer of this voyage. And a writer of 1622 says, *Hanam*, or, as he calls him, *Haman*, went commander, and *Prinne* master. See 2 *Col. Mass. Hist. Soc.* ix. 3. This agrees with the account of *Gorges* the younger.

† He had probably been given to him by Sir *Ferdinando*.

‡ They had "seated themselves in a peninsula, which is at the mouth of this river, [Sagadahock,] where they built a fortress to defend themselves from their enemies, which they named *St. George*." *America painted to the Life*, by *Ferd. Gorges, Esq.* p. 19.

§ See life *Massasoit*.

that he was carried away by *Waymouth*, as Sir *Ferdinando Gorges* relates, whose account we have given above.* It is impossible that Sir *Ferdinando* should have been mistaken in the names of those he received from *Waymouth*. The names of those carried off by *Hunt* are not given, or but few of them, nor were they kidnapped until nine years after *Waymouth's* voyage. It is, therefore, possible that *Squantum*, having returned home from the service of Gorges, went again to England with some other person, or perhaps even with *Hunt*. But we are inclined to think that there was but one of the name, and his being carried away an error of inadvertence.

Patuxet, afterward called *Plimouth*, was the place of residence of *Squantum*, who, it is said, was the only person that escaped the great plague of which we shall particularly speak in the life of *Massasoit*; where, at the same time, we shall take up again the life of *Squantum*, whose history is so intimately connected with it.

It was in 1611 that Captain *Edward Harlow*† was sent "to discover an Ile supposed about Cape Cod," who "falling with Monagigan, they found onely Cape Cod no Ile but the maine; there [at Monhigon Island] they detained three Saluages aboord them, called *Pechmo, Monopet* and *Pekenimne*, but *Pechmo* leapt ouerboard, and got away; and not long after, with his cousorts, cut their Boat from their sterne, got her on shore, and so filled her with sand, and guarded her with bowes and arrowes, the English lost her."‡

This exploit of *Pechmo* is as truly brave as it was daring. To have got under the stern of a ship, in the face of armed men, and at the same time to have succeeded in his design of cutting away and carrying off their boat, was an act as bold and daring, to say the least, as that performed in the harbor of Tripoli by our countryman *Decatur*.

From Monhigon *Harlow*, proceeding southward, fell in with an island called then by the Indians *Nohono*. From this place "they tooke *Sakaweston*, that after he had lived many years in England, went a soldier to the wars of Bohemia."§ Whether he ever returned, we are not told. From this island they proceeded to Capawick, since called *Capoge*, [Martha's Vineyard.] Here "they tooke Coneconam and *Epenow*," and "so, with fiue Saluages, they returned for England."

Epenow, or, as some wrote, *Epanow*, seems to have been much such a character as *Pechmo*—artful, cunning, bold and daring. Sir *Ferdinando Gorges* is evidently erroneous in part of his statement about this native, in as far as it relates to his having been brought away by *Hunt*. For *Harlow's* voyage was in 1611. and *Epanow* was sent over to Cape Cod with Captain Hobson, in 1614, some months before *Hunt* left.

As it is peculiarly gratifying to the writer to hear such old venerable writers as *Smith, Gorges*, &c. speak, the reader perhaps would not pardon him were he to withhold what the intimate acquaintance of the interesting *Epanow* says of him. Hear, then, Sir *Ferdinando*:—

"While I was laboring by what means I might best continue life in my languishing hopes, there comes one Henry *Harley*|| unto me, bringing with him a native of the Island of Capawick, a place seated to the southward of Cape Cod, whose name was *Epenewe*, a person of goodly stature, strong and well proportioned. This man was taken upon the main, [by

* It is plain, from *Prince, Chron.* 134, that his authors had confounded the names of these Indians one with another.

† Sir *Ferd. Gorges* is probably wrong in calling him *Henry Harley*.

‡ Capt. Smith's *Gen. Hist. N. Eng.*

§ Ibid.

|| Perhaps not the Capt. *Harlow* before mentioned, though *Prince* thinks *Gorges* means him.

force,] with some 29* others by a ship of London that endeavored to sell them for slaves in Spaine, but being understood that they were Americans, and being found to be unapt for their uses, they would not meddle with them, this being one of them they refused, wherein they exprest more worth than those that brought them to the market, who could not but known that our nation was at that time in travel for setling of Christian colonies upon that continent, it being an act much tending to our prejudice, when we came into that part of the countries, as it shall further appear. How Capt. *Harley* came to be possessed of this savage, I know not, but I understood by others how he had been shown in London for a wonder. It is true (as I have said) he was a goodly man, of a brave aspect, stout and sober in his demeanor, and had learned so much English as to bid those that wondered at him, WELCOME, WELCOME; this being the last and best use they could make of him, that was now grown out of the people's wonder. The captain, falling further into his familiarity, found him to be of acquaintance and friendship with those subject to the Bashaba, whom the captain well knew, being himself one of the plantation, sent over by the lord chief justice, [*Popham,*] and by that means understood much of his language, found out the place of his birth," &c.

Before proceeding with the history of *Epanow,* the account of Capt. *Thomas Hunt's* voyage should be related; because it is said that it was chiefly owing to his perfidy that the Indians of New England were become so hostile to the voyagers. Nevertheless, it is plain, that (as we have already said) *Hunt* did not commit his depredations until after Epanow had escaped out of the hands of the English. Capt. *John Smith* was in company with *Hunt,* and we will hear him relate the whole transaction. After stating that they arrived at Monhigon in April, 1614;† spent a long time in trying to catch whales without success; and as "for gold, it was rather the master's device to get a voyage, that projected it;" that for trifles they got "near 11000 beaver skins, 100 martin, and as many otters, the most of them within the distance of 20 leagues," and his own departure for Europe, Capt. *Smith* proceeds:—

"The other ship staid to fit herself for Spain with the dry fish, which was sold at Malaga at 4 rials the quintal, each hundred weight two quintals and a half.—But one *Thomas Hunt,* the master of this ship, (when I was gone,) thinking to prevent that intent I had to make there a plantation, thereby to keep this abounding country still in obscurity, that only he and some few merchants more might enjoy wholly the benefit of the trade, and profit of this country, betrayed four-and-twenty of those poor salvages aboard his ship, and most dishonestly and inhumanly, for their kind usage of me and all our men, carried them with him to Malaga; and there, for a little private gain, sold these silly salvages for rials of eight; but this vile act kept him ever after from any more employment to those parts."

F. Gorges the younger is rather confused in his account of *Hunt's* voyage, as well as the elder. But the former intimates that it was on account of *Hunt's* selling the Indians he took as slaves, the news of which having got into England before *Epanow* was sent out, caused this Indian to make his escape, and consequently the overthrow of the voyage; whereas the latter, Sir *Ferdinando,* does not attribute it to that. We will now hear him again upon this interesting subject:—

---

* If in this he refers to those taken by *Hunt,* as I suppose, he sets the number higher than others. His grandson, *F. Gorges,* in *America Painted,* &c., says 24 was the number seized by *Hunt.*

† Smith had an Indian named *Tantum* with him in this voyage, whom he set on shore at Cape Cod.

"*The reasons of my undertaking the employment for the island of Capawick.*

"At the time this new savage [*Epanow*] came unto me, I had recovered *Assacumet*, one of the natives I sent with Capt. *Chalownes* in his unhappy employment, with whom I lodged *Epenaw*, who at the first hardly understood one the other's speech, till after a while; I perceived the difference was no more than that as ours is between the northern and southern people, so that I was a little eased in the use I made of my old servant, whom I engaged to give account of what he learned by conference between themselves, and he as faithfully performed it."

There seems but little doubt that *Epanow* and *Assacumet* had contrived a plan of escape before they left England, and also, by finding out what the English most valued, and assuring them that it was in abundance to be had at a certain place in their own country, prevailed upon them, or by this pretended discovery were the means of the voyage being undertaken, of which we are now to speak. Still, as will be seen, Sir *Ferdinando* does not speak as though he had been quite so handsomely duped by his cunning man of the woods. Gold, it has been said, was the valuable commodity to which *Epanow* was to pilot the English. *Gorges* proceeds:—

"They [Capt. *Hobson* and those who accompanied him] set sail in June, in Anno 1614, being fully instructed how to demean themselves in every kind, carrying with them *Epenow, Assacomet* and *Wanape*,* another native of those parts sent me out of the Isle of Wight,† for my better information in the parts of the country of his knowledge: when as it pleased God that they were arrived upon the coast, they were piloted from place to place, by the natives themselves, as well as their hearts could desire. And coming to the harbor where *Epenow* was to make good his undertaking, [to point out the gold mine, no doubt,] the principal inhabitants of the place came aboard; some of them being his brothers, others his near cousins, [or relatives,] who, after they had communed together, and were kindly entertained by the captain, departed in their canoes, promising the next morning to come aboard again, and bring some trade with them. But *Epenow* privately (as it appeared) had contracted with his friends, how he might make his escape without performing what he had undertaken, being in truth no more than he had told me he was to do though with loss of his life. For otherwise, if it were found that he had discovered the secrets of his country,‡ he was sure to have his brains knockt out as soon as he came ashore;§ for that cause I gave the captain strict charge to endeavor by all means to prevent his escaping from them. And for the more surety, I gave order to have three gentlemen of my own kindred to be ever at hand with him; clothing him with long garments, fitly to be laid hold on, if occasion should require. Notwithstanding all this, his friends being all come at the time appointed with 20 canoes, and lying at a certain distance with their bows ready, the captain calls to them to come aboard; but they not

---

* Doubtless the same called by others *Manawet*, who, it would seem from Mr. *Hubbard*, (Hist. N. Eng. 39.) died before *Epanow* escaped, "soon after the ship's arrival."

† How he came there, we are at a loss to determine, unless natives were carried off, of whom no mention is made. This was unquestionably the case, for when it came to be a common thing for vessels to bring home Indians, no mention, of course, would be made, especially if they went voluntarily, as, no doubt, many did.

‡ The *secrets* of the sandy island Capoge, or the neighboring shores of Cape Cod, whatever they are now, existed only in faith of such sanguine minds as Sir *Ferdinando* and his adherents.

§ We need no better display of the craft of *Epanow*, or proof of his cunning in deep plots.

moving, he speaks to *Epenow* to come unto him, where he was in the forecastle of the ship, he being then in the waste of the ship, between the two gentlemen that had him in guard; starts suddenly from them, and coming to the captain, calls to his friends in English to come aboard, in the interim slips himself overboard: And although he were taken hold of by one of the company, yet, being a strong and heavy man, could not be stayed, and was no sooner in the water, but the natives, [his friends in the boats,] sent such a shower of arrows, and came withal desperately so near the ship, that they carried him away in despight of all the musquetteers aboard, who were, for the number, as good as our nation did afford. And thus were my hopes of that particular [voyage] made void, and frustrate."

From the whole of this narration it is evident that *Epanow* was forcibly retained, if not forcibly carried off, by the English. And some relate* that he attacked Capt. *Dermer* and his men, supposing they had come to seize and carry him back to England. It is more probable, we think, that he meant to be revenged for his late captivity, and, according to real Indian custom, resolved that the first whites should atone for it, either with their life or liberty. *Gorges* does not tell us what his brave "musquetteers" did when *Epanow* escaped, but from other sources we learn that they fired upon his liberators, killing and wounding some, but how many, they could only conjecture. But there is no room for conjecture about the damage sustained on the part of the ship's crew, for it is distinctly stated that when they received the "shower of arrows," Capt. *Hobson* and many of his men were wounded.† And *Smith*‡ says, "So well he had contrived his businesse, as many reported he intended to have surprised the ship; but seeing it could not be effected to his liking, before them all he leaped ouer boord."

We next meet with *Epanow* in 1619. Capt. *Thomas Dormer*, or *Dermer*, in the employ of Sir *F. Gorges*, met with him at Capoge, the place where, five years before, he made his escape from Capt. *Hobson*. *Gorges* writes, "This savage, speaking some English, laughed at his owne escape, and reported the story of it. Mr. *Dormer* told him he came from me, and was one of my servants, and that I was much grieved he had been so ill used as to be forced to steal away. This savage was so cunning, that, after he had questioned him about me, and all he knew belonged unto me, conceived he was come on purpose to betray him; and [so] conspired with some of his fellows to take the captain; thereupon they laid hands upon him. But he being a brave, stout gentleman, drew his sword and freed himself, but not without 14 wounds. This disaster forced him to make all possible haste to Virginia, to be cured of his wounds. At the second return [he having just come from there] he had the misfortune to fall sick and die, of the infirmity many of our nation are subject unto at their first coming into those parts."

The ship's crew being at the same time on shore, a fight ensued, in which some of *Epanow's* company were slain. "This is the last time," says a writer in the Historical Collections, "that the soil of Martha's Vineyard was stained with human blood; for from that day to the present [1807] no Indian has been killed by a white man, nor white man by an Indian."

In relation to the fight which *Dermer* and his men had with the Indians at the Vineyard, *Morton*§ relates that the English went on shore to trade with them, when they were assaulted and all the men slain but one that kept the boat. "But the [captain] himself got on board very sore

* Belknap, Amer. Biog. i. 362.
† Smith's New Eng.
‡ Ibid.
§ N. Eng. Memorial, 58, 59.

wounded, and they had cut off his head upon the cuddy of the boat, had not his man rescued him with a sword, and so they got him away." Squanto was with Capt. *Dermer* at this time, as will be seen in the life of *Massasoit.*

We may have occasion, in another chapter, to extend our notices upon several matters related in this.

CHAPTER II.

Of the natives known to the first settlers of Plimouth.—Samoset—Squanto— MASSASOIT—*Iyanough—Aspinet—Cauneconam*—CAUNBITANT—WITTUWAMET—PEKSUOT—HOBOMOK—*Tokamahamon—Obbatinewat*—NAMEPASHAMET—*Squaw-Sachem of Massachusetts—Webcowet.*

Welcome Englishmen! Welcome Englishmen! are words so inseparably associated with the name of *Samoset*, that we can never hear the one without the pleasing recollection of the other. These were the first accents our pilgrim fathers heard on the American strand, from any native. We mean intelligible accents, for when they were attacked at Namskeket, on their first arrival, they heard only the frightful war-whoop.

The first time Indians were seen by the pilgrims, was upon 15th Nov. 1620. "They espied 5 or 6 people, with a dog, coming towards them, who were savages; who, when they saw them, ran into the woods, and whistled the dog after them."* And though the English ran towards them, when the Indians perceived it "they ran away might and main," and the English "could not come near them." Soon after this, *Morton* says the Indians "got all the powaws in the country, who, for three days together, in a horid and devilish maner did curse and execrate them with their conjurations, which assembly and service they held in a dark and dismal swamp. Behold how Satan labored to hinder the gospel from coming into New England!"

It was on Friday, 16th March, 1621, that *Samoset* suddenly appeared at Plimouth, and, says *Mourt*, "He very boldly came all alone, and along the houses, strait to the rendezvous, where we intercepted him, not suffering him to go in, as undoubtedly he would, out of his boldness." He was naked, "only a leather about his waist, with a fringe about a span long." The weather was very cold, and this author adds, "We cast a horsman's coat about him." To reward them for their hospitality, *Samoset* gave them whatever information they desired. "He had, say they, learned some broken English amongst the Englishmen that came to fish at Monhiggon, and knew by name the most of the captains, commanders and masters, that usually come [there.] He was a man free in speech, so far as he could express his mind, and of seemly carriage. We questioned him of many things: he was the first savage we could meet withal. He said he was not of those parts, but of Moratiggon, and one of the sagamores or lords thereof: had been 8 months in these parts, it

* *Relation or Journal of a Plantation settled at Plymouth, in N. E.*, usually cited *Mourt's Relation*. It was, no doubt, written by several of the company, or the writer was assisted by several. *Mourt* seems to have been the publisher. I have no scruple but that the suggestion of Judge *Daris* is correct, viz. that *Richard Gardner* was the principal author. About the early settlement of any country, there never was a more important document. It was printed in 1622, and is now reprinted in the *Mass. Hist. Col.*

lying hence [to the eastward] a day's sail with a great wind, and 5 days by land. He discoursed of the whole country, and of every province, and of their sagamores, and their number of men, and strength." "He had a bow and two arrows, the one headed, and the other unheaded. He was a tall, strait man; the hair of his head black, long behind, only short before; none on his face at all. He asked some beer, but we gave him strong water and biscuit, and butter, and cheese, and pudding, and a piece of a mallard; all which he liked well." "He told us the place where we now live is called Patuxet, and that about 4 years ago all the inhabitants died of an extraordinary plague, and there is neither man, woman, nor child remaining, as indeed we have found none; so as there is none to hinder our possession, or lay claim unto it. All the afternoon we spent in communication with him. We would gladly been rid of him at night, but he was not willing to go this night. Then we thought to carry him on ship-board, wherewith he was well content, and went into the shallop; but the wind was high and water scant, that it could not return back. We lodged [with him] that night at *Stephen Hopkins'* house, and watched him."

Thus, through the means of this innocent Indian, was a correspondence happily begun. He left Plimouth the next morning, to return to *Massasoit,* who, he said, was a sachem having under him 60 men. The English having left some tools exposed in the woods, on finding that they were missing, rightly judged the Indians had taken them. They complained of this to *Samoset* in rather a threatening air. "We willed him (say they) that they should be brought again, otherwise we would right ourselves." When he left them "he promised within a night or two to come again," and bring some of *Massasoit's* men to trade with them in beaver skins. As good as his word, *Samoset* came the next Sunday, "and brought with him 5 other tall, proper men. They had every man a deer's skin on him; and the principal of them had a wild cat's skin, or such like, on one arm. They had most of them long hosen up to their groins, close made; and aboue their groins, to their waist, another leather: they were altogether like the Irish trousers. They are of complexion like our English gipsies; no hair, or very little on their faces; on their heads long hair to their shoulders, only cut before; some trussed up before with a feather, broadwise like a fan; another a fox tail hanging out." The English had charged *Samoset* not to let any who came with him bring their arms; these, therefore, left "their bows and arrows a quarter of a mile from our town. We gave them entertainment as we thought was fitting them. They did eat liberally of our English victuals;" and appeared very friendly; "sang and danced after their manner, like anticks." "Some of them had their faces painted black, from the forehead to the chin, four or five fingers broad: others after other fashions, as they liked. They brought three or four skins, but we would not truck with them all that day, but wished them to bring more, and we would truck for all; which they promised within a night or two, and would leave these behind them, though we were not willing they should; and they brought all our tools again, which were taken in the woods, in our absence. So, because of the day, [Sunday,] we dismissed them so soon as we could. But *Samoset,* our first acquaintance, either was sick, or feigned himself so, and would not go with them, and stayed with us till Wednesday morning. Then we sent him to them, to know the reason they came not according to their words; and we give him a hat, a pair of stockings and shoes, a shirt, and a piece of cloth to tie about his waist."

Samoset returned again, the next day, bringing with him *Squanto,* mentioned in the last chapter. He was "the only native (says MOURT'S RE-

LATION) of Patuxet, where we now inhabit, who was one of the 20 [or 24] captives, that by *Hunt* were carried away, and had been in England, and dwelt in Cornhill with master *John Slaine*, a merchant, and could speak a little English, with three others." They brought a few articles for trade, but the more important news "that their great sagamore, MASSASOYT, was hard by," whose introduction to them accordingly followed.

In June, 1621, a boy, *John Billington*, having been lost in the woods, several English, with *Squanto* and *Tokamahamon*, undertook a voyage to Nauset in search for him. *Squanto* was their interpreter; "the other, *Tokamahamon*, a special friend." The weather was fair when they set out, "but ere they had been long at sea, there arose a storm of wind and rain, with much lightning and thunder, insomuch that a [water] spout arose not far from them." However, they escaped danger, and arrived at night at Cummaquid. Here they met with some Indians, who informed them that the boy was at Nauset. These Indians treated them with great kindness, inviting them on shore to eat with them.

Iyanough was sachem of this place, and these were his men. "They brought us to their sachim, (says *Mourt*,) or governor, whom they call *Iyanough*," who then appeared about 26 years of age, "but very personable, gentle, courteous, and fair conditioned, indeed, not like a savage, save for his attire. His entertainment was answerable to his parts, and his cheer plentiful and various." Thus is portrayed the amiable character, *Iyanough*, by those who knew him. We can add but little of him except his wretched fate. The severity executed upon *Wittuwamet* and *Peksuot* caused such consternation and dread of the English among many, that they forsook their wonted habitations, fled into swamps, and lived in unhealthy places, in a state of starvation, until many died with diseases which they had thus contracted. Among such victims were *Iyanough, Aspinet, Coneconam*, and many more. Hence the English supposed they were in *Peksuot's* conspiracy, as will be more particularly related hereafter.

While the English were with *Iyanough* at Cummaquid, they relate that there was an old woman, whom they judged to be no less than 100 years old, who came to see them, because she had never seen English, "yet (say they) [she] could not behold us without breaking forth into great passion, weeping and crying excessively." They inquired the reason of it, and were told that she had three sons, "who, when master *Hunt* was in these parts, went aboard his ship to trade with him, and he carried them captives into Spain." *Squanto* being present, who was carried away at the same time, was acquainted with the circumstances, and thus the English became knowing to her distress, and told her they were sorry, that *Hunt* was a bad man, but that all the other English were well disposed, and would never injure her. They then gave her a few trinkets, which considerably appeased her.

Our voyagers now proceed to Nauset, accompanied by *Iyanough* and two of his men. *Aspinet* was the sachem of this place, to whom *Squanto* was sent, *Iyanough* and his men having gone before.* *Squanto* having informed *Aspinet* that his English friends had come for the boy, he "came (they relate) with a great train, and brought the boy with him," one carrying him through the water.

At this time, *Aspinet* had in his company "not less than an hundred;" half of whom attended the boy to the boat, and the rest "stood aloof," with their bows and arrows, looking on. *Aspinet* delivered up the boy in a formal manner, "behung with beads, and made peace with us; we

---

* This was the place where an attack was made on the English on their first arrival, which caused them to be much on their guard at this time.

bestowing a knife on him, and likewise on another, that first entertained the boy, and brought him thither."

Iyanough did not accompany the expedition in their return from Nauset, but went home by land, and was ready to entertain the company on their return. From contrary winds and a want of fresh water, the voyagers were obliged to touch again at Cummaquid. "There (say they) we met again with *Iyanough*, and the most of his town." "He, being still willing to gratify us, took a rundlet, and led our men in the dark a great way for water, but could find none good, yet brought such as there was on his neck with them. In the meantime the women joined hand in hand, singing and dancing before the shallop;* the men also showing all the kindness they could, *Iyanough* himself taking a bracelet from about his neck, and hanging it about one of us."

They were not able to get out of the harbor of Cummaquid from baffling winds and tides, which *Iyanough* seeing, the next morning he ran along the shore after them, and they took him into their shallop and returned with him to his town, where he entertained them in a manner not inferior to what he had done before. They now succeeded in getting water, and shortly after returned home in safety.

While at Nauset, the English heard that *Massasoit* had been attacked and carried off by the Narragansets, which led to the expedition of *Standish* and *Allerton* against *Caunbitant*, as will be found related in his life.

About this time, six sachems of the neighboring country had their fidelity tested, by being called upon to sign a treaty subjecting themselves to King *James*, as will be found, also, in that life. But to return again to *Aspinet*, and other sachems of Cape Cod.

By the improvidence of a company settled at Wessaguscus, under the direction of Mr. *Thomas Weston*, in 1622, they had been brought to the very brink of starvation in the winter of that year. In fact, the Plimouth people were but very little better off; and but for the kindness of the Indians, the worst of consequences might have ensued to both these infant colonies.

As the winter progressed, the two colonies entered into articles of agreement to go on a trading voyage among the Indians of Cape Cod to buy corn, and whatever else might conduce to their livelihood. *Squanto* was pilot in this expedition, but he died before it was accomplished, and the record of his death stands thus in WINSLOW'S RELATION:—

"But here, [at Manamoyk, since Chatham,] though they had determined to make a second essay, [to pass within the shoals of Cape Cod,] yet God had otherwise disposed, who struck *Tisquantum* with sickness,† insomuch as he there died; which crossed their southward trading, and the more, because the master's sufficiency was much doubted, and the season very tempestuous, and not fit to go upon discovery, having no guide to direct them."

Thus died the famous *Squanto*, or *Tasquantum*, in December, 1622. To him the pilgrims were greatly indebted, although he often, through extreme folly and shortsightedness, gave them, as well as himself and others, a great deal of trouble, as in the life of *Massasoit* and *Hobomok* will appear.

---

* It was a custom with most Indian nations to dance when strangers came among them. Baron *Lahontan* says it was the manner of the Iroquois to dance "lorsque les étrangers passent dans leur pa s, ou que leurs ennemis envoient des ambassadeurs pour faire des propositions de paix." *Memoires de L'Amerique*, ii. 110.

† His disorder was a fever, "bleeding much at the nose, which the Indians reckon a fatal symptom." He desired the governor would pray for him, that he might go to the Englishmen's God, "bequeathing his things to sundry of his English friends, as remembrances of his love; of whom we have a great loss." *Prince out of Bradford.*

Thus, at the commencement of the voyage, the pilot was taken away by death, and the expedition came near being abandoned. However, before *Squanto* died, he succeeded in introducing his friends to the sachem of Manamoick and his people, where they were received and entertained in a manner that would do honor to any people in any age. It is the more worthy of remark, as none of the English had ever been there before, and were utter strangers to them. After they had refreshed them "with store of venison and other victuals, which they brought them in great abundance," they sold them "8 *hogsheads of corn and beans, though the people were but few.*"

From Manamoick they proceeded to Massachusetts, but could do nothing there, as Mr. *Weston's* men had ruined the market by giving "as much for a quart of corn, as we used to do for a beaver's skin."* Therefore they returned again to Cape Cod, to Nauset, "where the sachem *Aspinet* used the governor very kindly, and where they bought 8 or 10 hogsheads of corn and beans: also at a place called *Mattachiest,* where they had like kind entertainment and corn also." While here, a violent storm drove on shore, and so damaged their pinnace, that they could not get their corn on board the ship; so they made a stack of it, and secured it from the weather, by covering it with mats and sedge. *Aspinet* was desired to watch and keep wild animals from destroying it, until they could send for it. Also, not to suffer their boat to be concerned with; all this he faithfully did, and the governor returned home by land, "receiving great kindness from the Indians by the way."

Some time after, *Standish* went to bring the corn left at Nauset, and, as usual, gets himself into difficulty with the Indians. One of *Aspinet's* men happening to come to one of *Standish's* boats, which being left entirely without guard, he took out a few trinkets, such as "beads, scissors, and other trifles," which when the English captain found out, "he took certain of his company with him, and went to the sachem, telling him what had happened, and requiring the same again, or the party that stole them," *"or else he would revenge it on them before his departure,"* and so departed for the night, "*refusing whatsoever kindness they offered.*" However, the next morning, *Aspinet,* attended by many of his men, went to the English, "in a stately manner," and restored all the "trifles;" for the exposing of which the English deserved ten times as much reprehension as the man for taking them.

Squanto being the only person that escaped the great sickness at Patuxet, inquirers for an account of that calamity will very reasonably expect to find it in a history of his life. We therefore will relate all that is known of it, not elsewhere to be noticed in our progress. The extent of its ravages, as near as we can judge, was from Narraganset Bay, to Kennebeck, or perhaps Penobscot, and was supposed to hare commenced about 1617, and the length of its duration seems to have been between two and three years, as it was nearly abated in 1619. The Indians gave a frightful account of it; saying that they died so fast "that the living were not able to bury the dead." When the English arrived in the country, their bones were thick upon the ground in many places. This they looked upon as a great providence, inasmuch as it had destroyed "multitudes of the barbarous heathen to make way for the chosen people of God."

"Some had expired in fight,—the brands
Still rusted in their bony hands,—
In plague and famine some!"
CAMPBELL

* At this time, there was a great sickness among the Massachusett Indians, "not unlike the plague, if not the same." No particulars of it are recorded.

2

All wars and disasters in those days were thought to be preceded by some strange natural appearance; or, as appeared to them, unnatural appearance or phenomenon; hence the appearance of a comet, in 1618, was considered by some the precursor of this pestilence.*

We will give here, from a curious work,† in the language of the author, an interesting passage, relating to this melancholy period, of the history of the people of *Massasoit*; in which he refers to *Squanto*. After relating the fate of a French ship's crew among the Wampanoags, as extracted in the life of *Massasoit*, in continuation of the account, he proceeds thus: "But contrary wise, [the Indians having said "they were so many that God could not kill them," when one of the Frenchmen rebuked them for their "wickedness," telling them God would destroy them,] in short time after, the hand of God fell heavily upon them, with such a mortall stroake, that they died on heaps, as they lay in their houses, and the living that were able to shift for themselves, would runne away and let them dy, and let their carkases ly above the ground without buriall. For in a place, where many inhabited, there hath been but one left alive, to tell what became of the rest; the living being (as it seems) not able to bury the dead. They were left for crowes, kites, and vermine to pray upon. And the bones and skulls upon the severall places of their habitations, made such a spectacle after my comming into those parts,‡ that as I travailed in that forrest nere the Massachussets, it seemed to me a new-found Golgotha."

Sir *Ferdinando Gorges*, as we have seen, was well acquainted with the coast of New England. After his design failed at Sagadahock, he tells us that he sent over a ship upon his own account, which was to leave a company under one *Vines*,§ to remain and trade in the country. These were his own servants, and he ordered "them to leave the ship and ship's company, for to follow their business in the usual place, (for I knew they would not be drawn to seek by any means,) by these, and the help of those natives formerly sent over, I come to be truly informed of so much as gave me assurance that in time I should want no undertakers, though as yet I was forced to hire men to stay there the winter quarter at extreme rates, and not without danger, for that the war|| had consumed the Bashaba, and the most of the great sagamores, with such men of action as followed them, and those that remained were sore afflicted with the plague; for that the country was in a manner left void of inhabitants. Notwithstanding, *Vines*, and the rest with him that lay in the cabins with those people that died, some more, some less, mightily, (blessed be God for it) not one of them ever felt their heads to ache while they stayed there." Here, although we are put in possession of several of the most important facts, yet our venerable author is deficient in one of the main particulars—I mean that of dates. Therefore we gain no further data

---

* The year 1618 seems to have been very fruitful in comets, "as therein no less than four were observed." I. *Mather's Discourse concerning Comets*, 108. Boston, 12mo. 1683. There may be seen a curious passage concerning the comet of 1618 in *Rushworth's Hist. Col.* of that year.

† New English Canaan, 23, by *Thomas Morton*, 4to. Amsterdam, 1637.

‡ Mr. *Morton* first came over in 1622. He settled near Weymouth. After great trouble and losses from those of a different religion, he was banished out of the country, and had his property seqestered, but soon after returned. He died in York, Me., 1646. If it be pretended that *Morton had no religion*, we say, "Judge not." He professed to have.

§ Mr. *Richard Vines*. *America painted to the Life*, by *Ferd. Gorges*, Esq. 4to. Lond. 1659.

|| A great war among the Indians at this time is mentioned by most of the first writers, but the particulars of it cannot be known. It seems to have been between the Tarratines and tribes to the west of Pascataqua.

as to the time or continuance of this plague among the Indians; for Sir *Ferdinando* adds to the above, "and this course I held some years together, but nothing to my private profit," &c.

In Capt. *Smith's* account of New England, published in 1631, he has a passage about the plague, which is much like that we have given above from *Morton*. The ship cast away, he says, was a fishing vessel, and the man that they kept a prisoner, on telling them he feared his God would destroy them, their king made him stand on the top of a hill, and collected his people about it that the man might see how numerous they were. When he had done this, he demanded of the Frenchman whether his God, that he told so much about, had so many men, and whether they could kill all those. On his assuring the king that he could, they derided him as before. Soon after, the plague carried off all of the Massachusetts, 5 or 600, leaving only 30, of whom 28 were killed by their neighbors, the other two escaping until the English came, to whom they gave their country. The English told the Indians that the disease was the plague. Capt. Smith says this account is second hand to him, and therefore begs to be excused if it be not true in all its particulars.

We have now come to one of the most interesting characters in Indian history.

MASSASOIT, chief of the Wampanoags, resided at a place called Pokanoket or Pawkunnawkut, by the Indians, which is now included in the town of Bristol, Rhode Island. He was a chief renowned more in peace than war, and was, as long as he lived, a friend to the English, notwithstanding they committed repeated usurpations upon his lands and liberties.

This chief's name has been written with great variation, as *Woosamequin, Asuhmequin, Oosamequen, Osamekin, Owsamequin, Ousamequine, Ussamequen, Wasamegin*, &c.; but the name by which he is generally known in history, is that with which we commence his life.* Mr. *Prince*, in his Annals, says of that name, "the printed accounts generally spell him *Massasoit*; Gov. *Bradford* writes him *Massasoyt*, and *Massasoyet*; but I find the ancient people, from their fathers in Plimouth colony, pronounced his name *Ma-sas-so-it*." Still we find no inclination to change a letter in the name of an old friend, which has been so long established; for if a writer suffer the spirit of innovation in himself, he knows not where to stop, and we pronounce him no *antiquary*.

It has often been thought strange, that so mild a sachem as *Massasoit* should have possessed so great a country, and our wonder has been increased when we consider, that Indian possessions are generally obtained by prowess and great personal courage. We know of none who could boast of such extensive dominions, where all were contented to consider themselves his friends and children. *Pontiac, Little-turtle, Tecumseh*, and many more that we could name, have swayed many tribes, but theirs was a temporary union, in an emergency of war. That *Massasoit* should be able to hold so many tribes together, without constant war, required qualities belonging only to few. That he was not a warrior no one will allow, when the testimony of *Annawon* is so distinct. For that great chief gave Capt. *Church* "an account of what mighty success he had had formerly, in the wars against many nations of Indians, when he served *Asuhmequin, Philip's* father."

The limits of his country towards the Nipmuks, or inland Indians, are

---

* Some have derived the name of *Massachusetts* from this chief, but that conjecture is not to be heeded. If any man knew, we may be allowed to suppose that *Roger Williams* did. He learned from the Indians themselves, *"that the Massachusetts were called so from the Blue Hills."* In the vocabulary of Indian words, by Rev. *John Cotton*, the definition of *Massachusett* is, "*an hill in the form of an arrow's head.*"

rather uncertain, but upon the east and west we are sure. It is evident, however, from the following extract, that, in 1647, the Nipmuks were rather uncertain about their sachem, and probably belonged at one time to *Massasoit* and at another to the Narragansets, &c., as circumstances favored. "The Nopnat [Nipnet, or Nipmuk] Indians having noe sachem of their own are at liberty; part of them, by their own choice, doe appertaine to the Narraganset sachem, and parte to the Mohegens."* And certainly, in 1660, those of Quabaog belonged to *Massasoit*, or *Wassamegin*, as he was then called, as will be evident from facts, to be found in the life of *Uncas*. He owned Cape Cod, and all that part of Massachusetts and Rhode Island between Narraganset and Massachusetts bays; extending inland between Pawtucket and Charles rivers, a distance not satisfactorily ascertained, as was said before, together with all the contiguous islands. It was filled with many tribes or nations, and all looking up to him, to sanction all their expeditions, and settle all their difficulties. And we may remark, further, with regard to the Nipmuks, that at one time they were his tributaries. And this seems the more probable, for in *Philip'* war there was a constant intercourse between them, and when any of his men made an escape, their course was directly into the country of the Nipmuks. No such intercourse subsisted between the Narragansets and either of these. But, on the contrary, when a messenger from the Narragansets arrived in the country of the Nipmuks, with the heads of some of the English, to show that they had joined in the war, he was at first fired upon, though afterwards, when two additional heads were brought, they were received.

Massasoit had several places of residence, but the principal was Mount Hope, or Pokanoket. The English early gave it the name of Mount Hope, but from what circumstance we have not learned. Some suppose the words *Mount Hope* corrupted from the Indian words *Mon-top*,† but with what reason we are not informed. Since we have thus early noticed the seat of the ancient chiefs, before proceeding with the life of the first of the Wampanoags, we will give a description of it. It appears to the best advantage from the village of Fall River, in the town of Troy, Massachusetts, from which it is distant about four miles. From this place, its top very much resembles the dome of the state-house in Boston, as seen from many places in the vicinity, at four or five miles' distance. Its height by admeasurement is said to be about 200 feet.‡ It is very steep on the side towards Pocasset, and its appearance is very regular. To its natural appearance a gentleman of Bristol has contributed to add materially, by placing upon its summit a circular summer-house, and this is a principal reason why it so much resembles the Massachusetts state-house. This mount, therefore, since some time previous to 1824, does not appear as in the days of *Massasoit*, and as it did to his early friends and visitors, *Winslow* and *Hamden*. It was sufficiently picturesque without such addition, as an immense stone§ originally formed its summit, and completed its domelike appearance. The octagonal summer-house being placed upon this, completes the cupola or turret. From this the view of Provi-

* Records of the U. Col. in *Hazard*, ii. 92.

† *Alden's* Collection of Epitaphs, iv. 685. President *Stiles*, in his notes to the second edition of CHURCH'S HIST. PHILIP'S WAR, p. 7, spells it *Mont-haup*, but it is not so in the text of either edition. Moreover, we have not been able to discover that *Mon-top* is derived from Indian words, and do not hesitate to pronounce it a corruption of the two English words commonly used in naming it.

‡ Yamoyden, 259.

§ By some, this has been called *Philip's chair*, and some modern book-makers have ventured to say it resembles that piece of furniture. We should be glad to know in what respect; having personally examined it, we can assure the reader that no such resemblance appeared to us.

Mount Hope.

dence, Warren, Bristol, and, indeed, the whole surrounding country, is very beautiful.

This eminence was known among the Narragansets by the name *Pokanoket*, which signified in their language *the wood or land on the other side of the water*, and to the Wampanoags by the name *Sowwams*. And it is worthy remark here, that *Kuequenáku* was the name of the place where Philadelphia now stands. Mr. *Heckewelder* says, it signified *the grove of the long pine trees*. There was a place in Middleborough, and another in Raynham, where he spent some part of particular seasons, perhaps the summer. The place in Raynham was near Fowling Pond, and he no doubt had many others.

Sir *Francis Drake* is the first, of whom we have any account, that set foot upon the shores of New England. This was in 1586, about seven years after he had taken possession, and named the same country New England, or New Albion, upon the western side of the continent. It is an error of long standing, that Prince *Charles* named the country New England, and it even now so stands upon the pages of history. But it is very clear that Sir *Francis* is justly entitled to the credit of it. American historians seem to have looked no further than *Prince* and *Robertson*, and hence assert that Capt. *Smith* named the country New England. We will now hear *Smith** on this matter. "New England is that part of America, in the Ocean sea, opposite to *Noua Albion*, in the South Sea, discovered by the most memorable Sir *Francis Drake*, in his voyage about the world, *in regard whereof, this is stiled New England*."

Capt. *Smith*, in 1614, made a survey of the coast of what is now New England, and because the country was already named New England, or, which is the same, New Albion, upon its western coast, he thought it most proper to stamp it anew upon the eastern. Therefore Capt. *Smith* neither takes to himself the honor of naming New England, as some writers of authority assert, nor does he give it to King *Charles*, as Dr. *Robertson* and many others, copying him, have done.

The noble and generous minded *Smith*, unlike *Americus*, would not permit or suffer his respected friend and contemporary to be deprived of any honor due to him in his day; and to which we may attribute the revival of the name New England in 1614.

It was upon some part of Cape Cod that the great circumnavigator landed. He was visited by the "king of the country," who submitted his territories to him, as *Hioh* had done on the western coast. After several days of mutual trade, and exchange of kindnesses, during which time the natives became greatly attached to Sir *Francis*, he departed for England. Whether the "king of the country" here mentioned were *Massasoit*, we have not the means of knowing, as our accounts do not give any name; but it was upon his dominions that this first landing was made, and we have therefore thought it proper to be thus particular, and which, we venture to predict, will not be unacceptable to our readers.

Smith landed in many places upon the shores of *Massasoit*, one of which places he named *Plimouth*, which happened to be the same which now bears that name.

Our accounts make Capt. *Bartholomew Gosnold* the next visitor to the shores of *Massasoit*, after Sir *Francis Drake*. His voyage was in 1602, and he was the first who came in a direct course from Old to New England.† He landed in the same place where Sir *Francis* did 16 years before.

---

* See his "Description of N. England," and the error may henceforth be dispensed with.

† The route had hitherto been by the Canaries and West India Islands, and a voyage to and from New England took up nearly a year's time.

We can know nothing of the early times of *Massasoit*. Our next visitor to his country, that we shall here notice, was Capt. *Thomas Dermer*. This was in May, 1619. He sailed for Monhigon; thence, in that month, for Virginia, in an open pinnace; consequently was obliged to keep close in shore. He found places which had been inhabited, but at that time contained none; and farther onward nearly all were dead, of a great sickness, which was then prevailing, but nearly abated. When he came to Plimouth, all were dead. From thence he traveled a day's journey into the country westward, to Namasket, now Middleborough. From this place he sent a messenger to visit *Massasoit*. In this expedition, he redeemed two Frenchmen from *Massasoit's* people, who had been cast away three years before.

But to be more particular with Capt. *Dermer*, we will hear him in his own manner, which is by a letter he wrote to *Samuel Purchase*, the compiler of the Pilgrimage, dated 27th Dec. 1619.

"When I arrived at my savage's [*Squanto's*] native country, (finding all dead,) I travelled alongst a day's journey, to a place called *Nummastaquyt*, where finding inhabitants, I despatched a messenger, a day's journey farther west, to Pocanokit, which bordereth on the sea; whence came to see me two kings, attended with a guard of 50 armed men, who being well satisfied with that my savage and I discoursed unto them, (being desirous or novelty,) gave me content in whatsoever I demanded; which I found that former relations were true. Here I redeemed a Frenchman, and afterwards another at Masstachusit, who three years since escaped shipwreck at the north-east of Cape Cod."*

We have mentioned his interview with *Massasoit*, which we supposed was one of the kings mentioned in the letter. *Quadequina* was no doubt the other.

In another letter, Mr. *Dermer* says the Indians would have killed him at Namasket, had not *Squanto* entreated hard for him. "Their desire of revenge (he adds) was occasioned by an Englishman, who, having many of them on board, made great slaughter of them with their murderers and small shot, when (as they say) they offered no injury on their parts."

Mr. *Thomas Morton*,† the author who made himself so merry at the expense of the pilgrims of Plimouth, has the following passage concerning these Frenchman:—"It fortuned some few yeares before the English came to inhabit at new Plimmouth in New England, that, upon some distast given in the Massachussets Bay, by Frenchmen, then trading there with the natives for beaver, they set upon the men, at such advantage, that they killed manie of them, burned their shipp, then riding at anchor by an island there, now called *Peddock's Island*, in memory of *Leonard Peddock* that landed there, (where many wilde anckies‡ haunted that time, which hee thought had bin tame,) distributing them unto five sachems which were lords of the severall territories adjoyning, they did keep them so long as they lived, only to sport themselves at them, and made these five Frenchmen fetch them wood and water, which is the generall worke they require of a servant. One of these five men outliving the rest, had learned so much of their language, as to rebuke them for their bloudy deede: saying that God would be angry with them for it; and that he would in his displeasure destroy them; but the salvages (it seems, boasting of their strength) replyed, and said, that they were so many that God could not kill them." This seems to be the same story, only differently told from that related above from *Smith*.

---

* This extract is in *Davis's* notes to *Morton*.

† In his *"New Canaan,"* 22, 23.

‡ Modern naturalists do not seem to have been acquainted with this animal!

Dec. 11, O. S. 1620. The pilgrims arrived at Plimouth, and possessed themselves of a portion of *Massasoit's* country. With the nature of their proceedings, he was at first unacquainted, and sent occasionally some of his men to observe their strange motions. Very few of these, however, were seen by the pilgrims. At length he sent one of his men, who had been some time with the English fishing vessels about the country of the Kennebeck, and had learned a little of their language, to observe more strictly what was progressing among the intruders at his place of Patuxet, which was now called Plimouth. This was in March, 1621, as before related.

We have, in speaking of *Samoset* and *Squanto*, observed that it was through the agency of the former that a knowledge was gained of *Massasoit*. It was upon 22 March, 1621, that they brought the welcome news to Plimouth, that their chief was near at hand;* "and they brought with them (say the pilgrims) some few skins to truck, and some red herrings, newly taken and dried, but not salted; and signified unto us, that their great sagamore, *Massasoit,* was hard by, with *Quadequina*, his brother. They could not well express in English what they would; but after an hour the king came to the top of an hill [supposed to be that now called *Watson's,* on the south side of Town-brook] over against us, and had in his train 60 men, that we could well behold them, and they us. We were not willing to send our governor to them, and they unwilling to come to us: so *Squanto* went again unto him, who brought word that we should send one to parley with him, which we did, which was *Edward Winslow*, to know his mind, and to signify the mind and will of our governor, which was to have trading and peace with him. We sent to the king a pair of knives, and a copper chain, with a jewel in it. To *Quadequina* we sent likewise a knife, and a jewel to hang in his ear, and withal a pot of strong water, a good quantity of biscuit, and some butter, which were all willingly accepted."

The Englishman then made a speech to him, about his king's love and goodness to him and his people, and that he accepted of him as his friend and ally. "He liked well of the speech, (say the English,) and heard it attentively, though the interpreters did not well express it. After he had eaten and drunk himself, and given the rest to his company, he looked

* *Mourt's* narrative is here continued from the last extract in p. 10, without any omission.

upon our messenger's sword and armor which he had on, with intimation of his desire to buy it; but, on the other side, our messenger showed his unwillingness to part with it. In the end he left him in the custody of *Quadequina*, his brother, and came over the brook, and some 20 men following him. We kept six or seven as hostages for our messenger."

As *Massasoit* proceeded to meet the English, they met him with six soldiers, who saluted each other. Several of his men were with him, but all left their bows and arrows behind. They were conducted to a new house which was partly finished, and a green rug was spread upon the floor, and several cushions for *Massasoit* and his chiefs to sit down upon. Then came the English governor, followed by a drummer and trumpeter and a few soldiers, and after kissing one another, all sat down. Some strong water being brought, the governor drank to *Massasoit,* who in his turn "drank a great draught, that made him sweat all the while after."

They now proceeded to make a treaty, which stipulated, that neither *Massasoit* nor any of his people should do hurt to the English, and that if they did they should be given up to be punished by them; and that if the English did any harm to him or any of his people, they, the English, would do the like to them. That if any did unjustly war against him, the English were to aid him, and he was to do the same in his turn, and by so doing King *James* would esteem him his friend and ally.

"All which (they say) the king seemed to like well, and it was applauded of his followers." And they add, "All the while he sat by the governor, he trembled for fear."

At this time he is described as "a very lusty man, in his best years, an able body, grave of countenance, and spare of speech; in his attire little or nothing differing from the rest of his followers, only in a great chain of white bone beads about his neck; and at it, behind his neck, hangs a little bag of tobacco, which he drank, and gave us to drink.* His face was painted with a sad red like murrey, and oiled both head and face, that he looked greasily. All his followers likewise were, in their faces, in part or in whole, painted, some black, some red, some yellow, and some white; some with crosses and other antic works; some had skins on them, and some naked; all strong, tall men in appearance. The king had in his bosom, hanging in a string, a great long knife. He marvelled much at our trumpet, and some of his men would sound it as well as they could. *Samoset* and *Squanto* stayed all night with us." *Massasoit* retired into the woods, about half a mile from the English, and there encamped at night with his men, women and children. Thus ended March 22d, 1621.

During his first visit to the English, he expressed great signs of fear, and during the treaty could not refrain from trembling.† Thus it is easy to see how much hand he had in making it, *but would that there had never been worse ones made.*

It was agreed that some of his people should come and plant near by, in a few days, and live there all summer. "That night we kept good watch, but there was no appearance of danger. The next morning divers of their people came over to us, hoping to get some victuals, as we imagined. Some of them told us the king would have some of us

* We have been asked what this drinking of tobacco means. We are confident it means smoking.

In the year 1646, we find this entry in the Plimouth records:—"*Anthony Thacher* and *George Pole* were chosen a comittee to draw vp an order concerneing disorderly drinkeing of tobacco." Rev. *Roger Williams* says, in his Key, "Generally all the men throughout the country have a tobacco-bag, with a pipe in it, hanging at their back."

† And, with this fact before him, the author of *"Tales of the Indians"* says, the treaty was made with *deliberation* and *cheerfulness* on the part of *Massasoit!*

come to see him. Capt. *Standish* and *Isaac Alderton* went venterously, who were welcomed of him after their manner. He gave them three or four ground nuts and some tobacco. We cannot yet conceive, (they continue,) but that he is willing to have peace with us; for they have seen our people sometimes alone two or three in the woods at work and fowling, when as they offered them no harm, as they might easily have done; and especially because he hath a potent adversary, the Narrohigansets,* that are at war with him, against whom he thinks we may be some strength to him; for our pieces are terrible unto them. This morning they stayed till 10 or 11 of the clock; and our governor bid them send the king's kettle, and filled it with peas, which pleased them well; and so they went their way." Thus ended the first visit of *Massasoit* to the pilgrims. We should here note that he ever after treated the English with kindness, and the peace now concluded was undisturbed for nearly 40 years. Not that any writing or articles of a treaty, of which he never had any adequate idea, was the cause of his friendly behavior, but it was the natural goodness of his heart.

The pilgrims report, that at this time he was at war with the Narragansets. But if this were the case, it could have been nothing more than some small skirmishing.

Meanwhile *Squanto* and *Samoset* remained with the English, instructing them how to live in their country; equal in all respects to *Robinson Crusoe's man Friday*, and had *De Foe* lived in that age he might have made as good a story from their history as he did from that of *Alexander* Selkirk.—"*Squanto* went to fish [a day or two after *Massasoit* left] for eels. At night he came home with as many as he could lift in one hand, which our people were glad of. They were fat and sweet. He trod them out with his feet, and so caught them with his hands, without any other instrument."

This *Squanto* became afterwards an important personage in Indian politics, and some of his manœuvres remind us of some managing politicians of our own times. In 1622, he forfeited his life by plotting to destroy that of *Massasoit*, as will be found related in the life of *Hobomok*. On that occasion, *Massasoit* went himself to Plimouth, "being much offended and enraged against *Tisquantum*;" but the governor succeeded in allaying his wrath for that time. Soon after, he sent a messenger to entreat the governor to consent to his death; the governor said he deserved death, but as he knew not how to get along without him in his intercourse with the Indians, he would spare him.

Determined in his purpose, *Massasoit* soon sent the same messenger again, accompanied by many others, who offered many beaver skins if *Tisquantum* might be given up to them. They demanded him in the name of *Massasoit*, as being one of his subjects, whom, (says *Winslow*,) by our first articles of peace, we could not retain. But out of respect to the English, they would not seize him without their consent. *Massasoit* had

* Few Indian names have been spelt more ways than this. From the nature of the Indian language, it is evident that no *r* should be used in it.—*Nahigonsik* and *Nantigansick, R. Williams*.—Nechegansitt, *Gookin*.—Nantyggansiks, *Callender*.—Nanohigganset, *Winslow's Good News from N. Eng.*—Nanhyganset, *Judge Johnson's Life of Gen. Greene*.—These are but few of the permutations without the *r*, and those with it are still more numerous.

The meaning of the name is still uncertain. Madam *Knight*, in her Journal, 22 and 23, says, at a place where she happened to put up for a night in that country, she heard some of the "town topers" disputing about the origin of the word *Narraganset*. "One said it was so named by Indians, because there grew a brier there of a prodigious height and bigness, who quoted an Indian of so barbarous a name for his author that she could not write it." Another said it meant a celebrated spring, which was very cold in summer, and "as hot as could be imagined in the winter."

sent his own knife to be used in cutting off his head and hands, which were to be brought to him.

Meantime *Squanto* came and delivered himself up to the governor, charging *Hobomok* with his overthrow, and telling him to deliver him or not to the messengers of *Massasoit,* as he thought fit. It seems from the narrative that, as the governor was about to do it, they grew impatient at the delay, and went off in a rage. The delay was occasioned by the appearance of a boat in the harbor, which the governor pretended might be that of an enemy, as there had been a rumor that the French had meditated breaking up the settlement of the English in this region. This, however, was doubtless only a pretence, and employed to wear out the patience of his unwelcome visitors. Hence that *Massasoit* should for some time after "seem to frown" on the English, as they complain, is certainly no wonder.

The next summer, in June or July, Massasoit was visited by several of the English, among whom was Mr. *Edward Winslow*, Mr. *Stephen Hopkins,* and *Squanto* as their interpreter. Their object was to find out his place of residence, in case they should have to call upon him for assistance; to keep good the friendly correspondence commenced at Plimouth; and especially to cause him to prevent his men from hanging about them, and living upon them, which was then considered very burdensome, as they had begun to grow short of provisions. That their visit might be acceptable, they took along, for a present, a trooper's red coat, with some lace upon it, and a copper chain; with these *Massasoit* was exceedingly well pleased. The chain, they told him, he must send as a signal, when any of his men wished to visit them, so that they might not be imposed upon by strangers.

When the English arrived at Pokanoket, *Massasoit* was absent, but was immediately sent for. Being informed that he was coming, the English began to prepare to shoot off their guns; this so frightened the women and children, that they ran away, and would not return until the interpreter assured them that they need not fear; and when *Massasoit* arrived, they saluted him by a discharge, at which he was very much elated; and "who, after their manner, (says one of the company,) kindly welcomed us, and took us into his house, and set us down by him, where, having delivered our message and presents, and having put the coat on his back, and the chain about his neck, he was not a little proud to behold himself, and his men also, to see their king so bravely attired."* A new treaty was now held with him, and he very good-naturedly assented to all that was desired. He then made a speech to his men, many of them being assembled to see the English, which, as near as they could learn its meaning, acquainted them with what course they might pursue in regard to the English. Among other things, he said, "*Am I not Massasoit, commander of the country about us? Is not such and such places mine, and the people of them? They shall take their skins to the English.*" This his people applauded. In his speech, "he named at least thirty places," over which he had control. "This being ended, he lighted tobacco for us, and fell to discoursing of England and of the king's majesty, marvelling that he should live without a wife." He seems to have been embittered against the French, and wished "us not to suffer them to come to Narraganset, for it was King *James's* country, and he was King *James's* man." He had no victuals at this time to give to the English, and night coming on, they retired to rest supperless. He had but one bed, if so it might be called, "being only planks laid a foot from the ground, and a thin mat

* *Mourt's Relation*, in *Col. Mass. Hist. Soc.*

upon them."* "He laid us on the bed with himself and his wife, they at the one end, and we at the other. Two more of his men, for want of room, pressed by and upon us; so that we were worse weary of our lodging than of our journey."

"The next day, many of their sachims or petty governors came to see us, and many of their men also. There they went to their manner of games for skins and knives." It is amusing to learn that the English tried to get a chance in this gambling affair. They say, "There we challenged them to shoot with them for skins," but they were too cunning for them, "only they desired to see one of us shoot at a mark; who shooting with hail shot, they wondered to see the mark so full of holes."

The next day, about one o'clock, *Massasoit* brought two large fishes and boiled them; but the pilgrims still thought their chance for refreshment very small, as "there were at least forty looking for a share in them;" but scanty as it was, it came very timely, as they had fasted two nights and a day. The English now left him, at which he was very sorrowful. "Very importunate he was (says our author) to have us stay with them longer. But we desired to keep the sabbath at home, and feared we should either be light-headed for want of sleep; for what with bad lodging, the savages' barbarous singing, (for they used to sing themselves asleep,) lice and fleas within doors, and musketoes without, we could hardly sleep all the time of our being there; we much fearing, that if we should stay any longer, we should not be able to recover home for want of strength. So that, on Friday morning, before sunrising, we took our leave, and departed, *Massasoyt* being both grieved and ashamed, that he could no better entertain us. And retaining *Tisquantum* to send from place to place to procure truck for us, and appointing another, called *Tokamahamon*, in his place, whom we had found faithful before and after upon all occasions."

This faithful servant, *Tokamahamon*, was in the famous "voyage to the kingdom of Nauset," and was conspicuous for his courage in the expedition against *Caunbitant*.

In 1623, *Massasoit* sent to his friends in Plimouth to inform them that he was very dangerously sick. Desiring to render him aid if possible, the governor despatched Mr. *Winslow* again, with some medicines and cordials, and *Hobbomok* as interpreter; "having one Master *John Hamden*, a gentleman of London, who then wintered with us, and desired much to see the country, for my consort."† In their way they found many of his subjects were gone to Pokanoket, it being their custom for all friends to attend on such occasions. "When we came thither (says Mr. *Winslow*) we found the house so full of men, as we could scarce get in, though they used their best diligence to make way for us. There were they in

---

* *La Salle* says (Expedition in America, p. 11.) of the Indians' beds in general, that "they are made up with some pieces of wood, upon which they lay skins full of wool or straw, but, for their covering, they use the finest sort of skins, or else mats finely wrought."

† Winslow's Relation. The Mr. *Hamden* mentioned, is supposed, by some, to be the celebrated *John Hamden*, famous in the time of *Charles* I., and who died of a wound received in an attempt to intercept Prince *Rupert*, near Oxford, while supporting the cause of the parliament. See *Ràpin's* England, ii. 477, and *Kennet*, iii. 137.

It would be highly gratifying, could the certainty of this matter be known; but, as yet, we must acknowledge that all is mere speculation. Nevertheless, we are pleased to meet with the names of such valued martyrs of liberty upon any page, and even though they should sometimes seem rather *mal apropos* to the case in hand. We cannot learn that any of *Hamden's* biographers have discovered that he visited America. Still there is a strong presumption that he was

"The village *Hampden*, that, with dauntless breast,
The little tyrant of his fields withstood,"
Gray's Elegy.

the midst of their charms for him, making such a hellish noise, as it distempered us that were well, and, therefore, unlike to ease him that was sick. About him were six or eight women, who chafed his arms, legs and thighs, to keep heat in him. When they had made an end of their charming, one told him that his friends, the English, were come to see him. Having understanding left, but his sight was wholly gone, he asked, *who was come*. They told him *Winsnow*, (for they cannot pronounce the letter *l*, but ordinarily n in the place thereof.)* He desired to speak with me. When I came to him, and they told him of it, he put forth his hand to me, which I took. Then he said twice, though very inwardly, *Keen Winsnow?* which is to say, *Art thou Winsnow?* I answered, *Ahhe*, that is, *Yes*. Then he doubled these words: *Matta neen wonckanet namen, Winsnow*! that is to say, *O Winslow, I shall never see thee again!*" But contrary to his own expectations, as well as all his friends, by the kind exertions of Mr. *Winslow*, he in a short time entirely recovered. This being a passage of great interest in the life of the great *Massasoit,* we will here go more into detail concerning it. When he had become able to speak, he desired Mr. *Winslow* to provide him a broth from some kind of fowl: "so (says he) I took a man with me, and made a shot at a couple of ducks, some sixscore paces off, and killed one, at which he wondered: so we returned forthwith, and dressed it, making more broth therewith, which he much desired; never did I see a man so low brought, recover in that measure in so short a time. The fowl being extraordinary fat, I told *Hobbamock* I must take off the top thereof, saying it would make him very sick again if he did eat it; this he acquainted *Massassowat* therewith, who would not be persuaded to it, though I pressed it very much, showing the strength thereof, and the weakness of his stomach, which could not possibly bear it. Notwithstanding, he made a gross meal of it, and ate as much as would well have satisfied a man in health." As *Winslow* had said, it made him very sick, and he vomited with such violence that it made the blood stream from his nose. This bleeding caused them great alarm, as it continued for four hours. When his nose ceased bleeding, he fell asleep, and did not awake for 6 or 8 hours more. After he awoke, Mr. *Winslow* washed his face "and supplied his beard and nose with a linnen cloth," when taking a quantity of water into his nose, by fiercely ejecting it, the blood began again to flow, and again his attendants thought he could not recover, but, to their great satisfaction, it soon stopped, and he gained strength rapidly.

For this attention of the English he was very grateful, and always believed that his preservation at this time was from the benefit received from Mr. *Winslow*. In his way on his visit to *Massasoit,* he broke a bottle containing some preparation, and, deeming it necessary to the sachem's recovery, wrote a letter to the governor of Plimouth for another, and some chickens, and giving him an account of his success thus far. The intention was no sooner made known to *Massasoit*, than one of his men was set off, at two o'clock at night, for Plimouth, who returned again with astonishing quickness. The chickens being alive, *Massasoit* was so pleased with them, and, being better, would not suffer them to be killed,

* Every people, and consequently every language, have their peculiarities. Baron *Lahontan*, *Memoires de la Amerique*, ii. 236, 237, says, "*Je dirai de la langue des Hurons and des Iroquois une chose assez curieuse, qui est qu'il ne s'y trouve point de lettres labiales; c'est a dire, de* b, f, m, p. *Cependant, cette langue des Hurons paroît être fort belle et de un son tout a fait beau; quoi qu'ils ne ferment jamais leurs lêvres en parlant.*" And "*J'ai passê quatre jours à vouloir faire prononcer à des Hurons les lettres labiales, mais je n'ai pû y réüssir, et je crois qu'en dix ans ils ne pourrout dire ces mots,* bon, fils, Monsieur, Pontchartrain; *car au lieu de dire* bon, *ils diroient* ouon, *au lieu de fils, ils prononceroient* rils; *au lieu de* monsieur, caounsieur, au lieu de Pontchartrain, Conchartrain." Hence it seems their languages are analogous.

and kept them, with the idea of raising more. While at *Massasoit's* residence, and just as they were about to depart, the sachem told *Hobomok* of a plot laid by some of his subordinate chiefs for the purpose of cutting off the two English plantations, which he charged him to acquaint the English with, which he did. *Massasoit* stated that he had been urged to join in it, or give his consent thereunto, but had always refused, and used his endeavors to prevent it. The particulars of the evils which that plot brought upon its authors will be found in the history of *Wittuwamet.*

At this time the English became more sensible of the real virtues of *Massasoit* than ever before. His great anxiety for the welfare of his people was manifested by his desiring Mr. *Winslow*, or, as *Winslow* himself expresses it, "He caused me to go from one to another, [in his village,] requesting me to wash their mouths also, [many of his people being sick at that time,] and give to each of them some of the same I gave him, saying they were good folk." An account of his character as given by *Hobomok* will be found in the life of that chief or paniese.

"Many whilst we were there (says *Winslow*) came to see him; some, by their report, from a place not less than 100 miles from thence."

In 1632, a short war was carried on between *Massasoit* and *Canonicus,* the sachem of the Narragansets, but the English interfering with a force under the spirited Capt. *Standish*, ended it with very little bloodshed. *Massasoit* expected a serious contest; and, as usual on such occasions, changed his name, and was ever after known by the name of *Owsamequin,* or *Ousamequin*. Our historical records furnish no particulars of his war with the Narragansets, further than we have stated.

We may infer from a letter written by *Roger Williams*, that some of Plimouth instigated *Massasoit*, or *Ousamequin*, as we should now call him, to lay claim to Providence, which gave that good man some trouble, because, in that case, his lands were considered as belonging to Plimouth, in whose jurisdiction he was not suffered to reside; and, moreover, he had bought and paid for all he possessed, of the Narraganset sachems. It was in 1635 that Mr *Williams* fled to that country, to avoid being seized and sent to England. He found that *Canonicus* and *Miantunnomoh* were at bitter enmity with *Ousamequin,* but by his great exertions he restored peace, without which he could not have been secure, in a border of the dominion of either. Ousamequin was well acquainted with Mr. *Williams,* whom he had often seen during his two years' residence at Plimouth, and was a great friend to him, and therefore he listened readily to his benevolent instructions; giving up the land in dispute between himself and the Narraganset sachems, which was the island now called Rhode Island, Prudence Island, and perhaps some others, together with Providence. "And (says Mr. *Williams)* I never denied him, nor *Meantinomy,* whatever they desired of me." Hence their love and attachment for him, for this is their own mode of living.

It appears that, before *Miantunnomoh's* reverses of fortune, he had, by some means or other, got possession of some of the dominions of *Ousamequin*. For at the meeting of the Commissioners of the United Colonies, in the autumn of 1643, they order, "That Plymouth labor by all due means to restore *Woosamequin* to his full liberties, in respect of any encroachments by the Nanohigganseтts, or any other natives; that so the properties of the Indians may be preserved to themselves, and that no one sagamore encroach upon the rest as of late: and that *Woosamequin* be reduced to those former terms and agreements between Plymouth and him."*

Under date 1638, Gov. *Winthrop* says, "*Owsamekin*, the sachem of

* Records of the U. Colonies.

Acoomemeck, on this side Connecticut, came to [him] the governor, and brought a present of 18 skins of beaver from himself and the sachems of Mohegan beyond Connecticut and Pakontuckett." They having heard that the English were about to make war upon them was the cause of their sending this present. The governor accepted it, and told *Ousamequin,* that if they had not wronged the English, nor assisted their enemies, they had nothing to fear; and, giving him a letter to the governor of Connecticut, dismissed him well satisfied.*

In 1649, *Ousamequin* sold to *Miles Standish,* and the other inhabitants of Duxbury, "a tract of land usually called *Saughtucket,"* seven miles square. This was Bridgewater. It had been before granted to them, only, however, in preëmption. They agreed to pay *Ousamequin* seven coats, of a yard and a half each, nine hatchets, eight hoes, twenty knives, four moose skins, and ten and a half yards of cotton cloth.

By a deed bearing date 9th March, 1653, *Ousamequin* and his son *Wamsitto,* [*Wamsutta,*] afterwards called *Alexander,* sold to the English of Plimouth "all those severall parcells of land lyeing on the south-easterly side of Sinkunke, alias Rehoboth, bounded by a little brooke of water called Moskituash westerly, and soe runing by a dead swamp eastward, and soe by marked trees as *Ousamequin* and *Wamsitto* directed, unto the great riuer, and all the meadow about the sides of both, and about the neck called Chachacust, also Papasquash neck, also the meadow from the bay to Keecomewett," &c. For this the consideration was "£35 sterling."

By a writing bearing date "this twenty-one of September, 1657," *Ousamequin* says, "I *Vssamequen* do by these presents ratify and allow the sale of a certain island called Chesewanocke, or Hogg Island, which my son *Wamsitta* sold to *Richard Smith,* of Portsmouth in R. I., with my consent, which deed of sale or bargain made the 7th of February in the year 1653, I do ratify, own and confirm."

In 1656, Mr. *Williams* says that *Ousamequin,* by one of his sachems, "was at daily feud with *Pumham* about the title and lordship of Warwick;" and that hostility was daily expected. But we are not informed that any thing serious took place.

This is the year in which it has been generally supposed that *Ousamequin* died, but it is an error of *Hutchinson's* transplanting from Mr. *Hubbard's* work into his own. That an error should flourish in so good a soil as that of the "History of the Colony of Massachusetts Bay," is no wonder; but it is a wonder that the "accurate *Hutchinson"* should set down that date, from that passage of the Indian Wars, which was evidently made without reflection. It being at that time thought a circumstance of no consequence.

That the sachem of Pokanoket should be scarcely known to our records between 1657 and 1661, a space of only about three years, as we have shown, is not very surprising, when we reflect that he was entirely subservient to the English, and nearly or quite all of his lands being before disposed of, or given up to them. This, therefore, is a plain reason why we do not meet with his name to deeds and other instruments. And, besides this consideration, another sachem was known to be associated with him at the former period, who seems to have acted as *Ousamequin's* representative.

He was alive in 1661, and as late in that year as September. Several months previous to this, *Oneko,* with about seventy men, fell upon a defenceless town within the dominions of *Ousamequin,* killing three persons and carrying away six others captive. He complained to the General

* *Journal,* i. 264.

Court of Massachusetts, which interfered in his behalf, and the matter was soon settled.*

From the "Relation" of Dr. I. *Mather*, it is clear that he lived until 1662. His words are, "*Alexander* being dead, [having died in 1662,] his brother *Philip*, of late cursed memory, rose up in his stead, and he was no sooner styled sachem, but immediately, in the year 1662, there were vehement suspicions of his bloody treachery against the English."†

Whether he had more than two sons, is not certain, although it is confidently believed that he had. It is probable that his family was large. A company of soldiers from Bridgewater, in a skirmish with *Philip*, took his sister, and killed a brother of *Ousamequin*, whose name was *Unkompoen*,‡ or *Akkompoin*.§ That he had another brother, called *Quadequina*, has been mentioned.

Gov. *Winthrop* gives the following anecdote of *Ousamequin*. As Mr. *Edward Winslow* was returning from a trading voyage southward, having left his vessel, he traveled home by land, and in the way stopped with his old friend *Massasoit*, who agreed to accompany him the rest of the way. In the mean time, *Ousamequin* sent one of his men forward to Plimouth, to surprise the people with the news of Mr. *Winslow's* death. By his manner of relating it, and the particular circumstances attending, no one doubted of its truth, and every one was grieved and mourned exceedingly at their great loss. But presently they were as much surprised at seeing him coming in company with *Ousamequin*. When it was known among the people that the sachem had sent this news to them, they demanded why he should thus deceive them. He replied that it was to make him the more welcome when he *did* return, and that this was a custom of his people.

One of the most renowned captains within the dominions of *Massasoit* was CAUNBITANT,|| whose residence was at a place called Mettapoiset, in the present town of Swansey. His character was much the same as that of the famous *Metacomet*. The English were always viewed by him as intruders and enemies of his race, and there is little doubt but he intended to wrest the country out of their hands on the first opportunity.

In August, 1621, *Caunbitant* was supposed to be in the interest of the Narragansets, and plotting with them to overthrow *Massasoit*; and, being at Namasket seeking "to draw the hearts of *Massasoyt's* subjects from him; speaking also disdainfully of us, storming at the peace between Nauset, Cummaquid and us, and at *Tisquantum*, the worker of it; also at Tokamahamon, and one *Hobomok*, (two Indians or Lemes, one of which he would treacherously have murdered a little before, being a special and trusty man of *Massasoyt's*,) *Tokamahamon* went to him, but the other two would not; yet put their lives in their hands, privately went to see if they could hear of their king, and, lodging at Namaschet, were discovered to *Coubatant*, who set a guard to beset the house, and took *Tisquantum*, (for he had said, if he were dead, the English had lost their tongue.) *Hobbamok* seeing that *Tisquantum* was taken, and *Coubatant* held [holding] a knife at his breast, being a strong and stout man, brake from them, and came to New Plimouth, full of fear and sorrow for *Tisquantum*, whom he thought to be slain."

Upon this the Plimouth people sent an expedition, under *Standish*, of 14 men,¶ "and *Hobbamok* for their guide, to revenge the supposed death

---

* Original *manuscript* documents. The particulars of these matters will be given at large, when we come to treat of the *life* of *Uncas*.

† Relation, 72. ‡ I. Mather, 44. § Church, 38, edit. 4to.

|| *Corbitant, Coubatant,* and *Conbitant,* were ways of writing his name also, by his cotemporaries.

¶ Ten, says the Relation.

of *Tisquantum* on *Coubatant* our bitter enemy, and to retain *Nepeof,* another sachem, or governor, who was of this confederacy, till we heard what was become of our friend *Massasoyt."*

After much toil, the little army arrived near the place they expected to find *Caunbitant.* "Before we came to the town (says the narrator) we sat down and eat such as our knapsacks afforded; that being done, we threw them aside, and all such things as might hinder us, and so went on and beset the house, according to our last resolution. Those that entered, demanded if *Coubatant* were not there; but fear had bereft the savages of speech. We charged them not to stir, for if *Coubatant* were not there, we would not meddle with them; if he were, we came principally for him, to be avenged on him for the supposed death of Tisquantum, and other matters: but howsoever, we would not at all hurt their women or children. Notwithstanding, some of them pressed out at a private door, and escaped, but with some wounds. At length perceiving our principal ends, they told us *Coubatant* was returned [home] with all his train, and that *Tisquantum* was yet living, and in the town; [then] offering some tobacco, [and] other, such as they had to eat."

In this hurley hurley, (as they call it,) two guns were fired "at random," to the great terror of all but *Squanto* and *Tokamahamon,* "who, though they knew not our end in coming, yet assured them [so frightened] of our honesty, [and] that we would not hurt them." The Indian boys, seeing the squaws protected, cried out, *Neensquaes! Neensquaes! that is, I am a squaw! I am a squaw!* and the women tried to screen themselves in *Hobomok's* presence, reminding him that he was their friend.

This attack upon a defenceless house was made at midnight, and must have been terrible, in an inconceivable degree, to its inmates, especially the sound of the English guns, which few, if any of them, had ever heard before. The relater proceeds: "But to be short, we kept them we had, and made them make a fire that we might see to search the house; in the meantime, *Hobbamok* gat on the top of the house, and called *Tisquantum* and *Tokamahamon."* They soon came, with some others with them, some armed and others naked. The English took away the bows and arrows from those that were armed, but promised to return them as soon as it was day, which they probably did.

They kept possession of the captured wigwam until daylight, when they released their prisoners, and marched into the town (as they call it) of the Namaskets. Here, it appears, *Squanto* had a house, to which they went, and took breakfast, and held a court afterward, from which they issued forth the following decree against *Caunbitant:*—

"Thither came all whose hearts were upright towards us, but all *Coubatant's* faction were fled away. There in the midst of them we manifested again our intendment, assuring them, that, although *Coubitant* had now escaped us, yet there was no place should secure him and his from us, if he continued his threatening us, and provoking others against us, who had kindly entertained him, and never intended evil towards him till he now so justly deserved it. Moreover, if *Massasoyt* did not return in safety from Narrohigganset, or if hereafter he should make any insurrection against him, or offer violence to *Tisquantum, Hobomok,* or any of *Massasoyt's* subjects, we would revenge it upon him, to the overthrow of him and his. As for those [who] were wounded, [how many is not mentioned,] we were sorry for it, though themselves procured it in not staying in the house at our command: yet, if they would return home with us, our surgeon should heal them. At this offer one man and a woman that were wounded went home with us, *Tisquantum* and many other known friends accompanying us, and offering all help that might be by carriage of any thing we had to ease us. So that by God's good providence we safely returned home the morrow night after we set forth."*

Notwithstanding these rough passages, *Caunbitant* became in appearance reconciled to the English, and on the 13th Sept. following went to Plimouth and signed a treaty of amity. It was through the intercession of *Massasoit* that he became again reconciled, but the English always doubted his sincerity, as most probably they had reason to. The treaty or submission was in these words:—

"Know all men by these presents, that we whose names are underwritten, do acknowledge ourselves to be the royal subjects of King *James*, king of Great Britain, France and Ireland, defender of the faith, &c. In witness whereof, and as a testimonial of the same, we have subscribed our names, or marks, as followeth:—

OHQUAMEHUD,	NATTAWAHUNT,	QUADAQUINA,
CAWNACOME,	CAUNBATANT,	HUTTMOIDEN,
OBBATINNUA,	CHIKKATABAK,	APANNOW."

Of some of these sachems nothing is known beyond this transaction, and of others very little.

Obbatinua is supposed to have been sachem of Shawmut, where Boston now stands.

Cawnacome and *Apannow* may be the same before spoken of as *Coneconam* and *Epanow*.† *Nattawahunt* we shall again meet with, under the name *Nashoonon*. *Coneconam* was sachem of *Manomet*, on Cape Cod.

When, in the winter of 1623, the English traversed the country to trade with the Indians for corn, they visited him among other chiefs; who, they say, "it seemed was of good respect, and authority, amongst the Indians. For whilst the governor was there, within night, in bitter cold weather, came two men from Manamoyck, before spoken of, and having set aside their bows and quivers, according to their manner, sat down by the fire, and took a pipe of tobacco, not using any words in that time, nor any other to them, but all remained silent, expecting when they would speak. At length they looked toward *Canacum;* and one of them made a short speech, and delivered a present to him, from his sachim, which was a basket of tobacco, and many beads, which the other received thankfully. After which he made a long speech to him," the meaning of which *Hobomok* said was, that two of their men fell out in a game, "for they use gaming as much as any where, and will play away all, even their skin from their backs, yea their wive's skins also," and one killed the other. That the murderer was a powow, "one of special note amongst them," and one whom they did not like to part with; yet they were threatened with war, if they did not kill the murderer. That, therefore, their sachem deferred acting until the advice of *Coneconam* was first obtained.

After consulting with this chief, and some of his head men, these messengers desired *Hobomok's* judgment upon the matter. With some deference he replied, that "he thought it was better that one should die than many, since he had deserved it;" "whereupon he passed the sentence of death upon him."

We shall have occasion again to notice this chief, at whose house the first act of a tragic scene was acted, which in its course brought ruin upon its projectors.

---

* From *Mourt, ut supra*, and signed only with the capital letter *A*, which is supposed to stand for *Isaac Allerton*, who accompanied Standish perhaps. From the use of the pronoun in the first person, the writer, whoever he was, must have been present.

† See chapter i. of b. ii.

When Mr. *Edward Winslow* and Mr. *John Hamden* went to visit *Massasoit* in his sickness, in 1623, they heard by some Indians, when near *Caunbitant's* residence, that *Massasoit* was really dead: they, therefore, though with much hesitation, ventured to his house, hoping they might treat with him, he being then thought the successor of *Massasoit*. But he was not at home. The squaw sachem, his wife, treated them with great kindness, and learning here that *Massasoit* was still alive, they made all haste to Pokanoket. When they returned, they staid all night with *Caunbitant,* at his house, who accompanied them there from *Massasoit's*.

Mr. *Winslow* gives the account in these words:—"That night, through the earnest request of *Conbatant,* who, till now, remained at Sowaams, or Puckanokick, we lodged with him at Mattapuyst. By the way, I had much conference with him, so likewise at his house, he being a notable politician, yet full of merry jests and squibs, and never better pleased than when the like are returned again upon him. Amongst other things he asked me, if in case *he* were thus dangerously sick, as *Massasoit* had been, and should send word thereof to Patuxet, for *maskiest,** [that is, physic,] whether their master governor would send it; and if he would, whether I would come therewith to him. To both which I answered, yea; whereat he gave me many joyful thanks." He then expressed his surprise that two Englishmen should adventure so far alone into their country, and asked them if they were not afraid. Mr. *Winslow* said, "where was true love, there was no fear." "But," said *Caunbitant, "if your love be such, and it bring forth such fruits, how cometh it to pass, that when we come to Patuxet, you stand upon your guard, with the mouth of your pieces presented towards us?"* Mr. *Winslow* told him that was a mark of respect, and that they received their best friends in that manner; but to this he shook his head, and answered, that he did not like such salutations.†

When *Caunbitant* saw his visiters crave a blessing before eating, and return thanks afterwards, he desired to know what it meant. "Hereupon I took occasion (says our author) to tell them of God's works of creation and preservation, of the laws and ordinances, especially of the ten commandments." They found no particular fault with the commandments, except the seventh, but said there were many inconveniences in that a man should be tied to one woman. About which they reasoned a good while.

When Mr. *Winslow* explained the goodness of God in bestowing on them all their comforts, and that for this reason they thanked and blessed him, "this all of them concluded to be very well; and said they believed almost all the same things, and that the same power that we call God they called *Kichtan."* "Here we remained only that night, but never had better entertainment amongst any of them."

What became of this chief is unknown. His name appearing no more in our records, leads us to suppose that he either fled his country on the murder of *Wittuwamet, Peksuot,* and others, or that he died about that time.

Wittuwamet was a Massachusetts chief, as was his companion *Peksuot,* but their particular residence has not been assigned. *Wittuwamet* was a desperate and bold fellow, and, like most other warriors, delighted in the blood of his enemies. It is not improbable but that he became exasperated against the English from the many abuses some of them had practised upon his countrymen. This will account, perhaps, for all the severity and malignity portrayed by the forefathers in his character.

* In Williams's Key, *Maskit* is translated, "Give me some physic."
† Good News from N. England, *Col. Mass. Hist. Soc.*

He was one of those, they say, who murdered some of the crew of the French ship, cast away upon Cape Cod, as we have before mentioned.

That *Wittuwamet, Peksuot,* and some other chiefs, intended to have freed their country of intruders in the year 1623, there can be no doubt, and in relating the rise, progress and termination of their league to effect this object, we shall, to avoid the charge of partiality, adhere closely to the record.

We have before, in speaking of *Caunecum*, or *Coneconam*, mentioned the voyage of the governor of Plimouth to that sachem's country to trade for corn; that was in January, 1623. Not being able to bring away all he obtained, Capt. *Miles Standish* was sent the next month to take it to Plimouth, also to purchase more at the same place, but he did not meet with very good reception, which led him to apprehend there was mischief at hand. And immediately after, while at *Coneconam's* house with two or three of his company, "in came two of the Massachusetts men. The chief of them was called *Wittuwamat*, a notable insulting villain, one who had formerly imbrued his hands in the blood of English and French, and had oft boasted of his own valor, and derided their weakness, especially because, as he said, they died crying, making sour faces, more like children than men. This villain took a dagger from about his neck, which he had gotten of Master *Weston's* people, and presented it to the sachem, [*Coneconam*,] and after made a long speech in an audacious manner, framing it in such sort as the captain, though he be the best linguist among us, could not gather any thing from it. The end of it was afterwards discovered to be as followeth. The Massachuseucks formerly concluded to ruinate Mr. *Weston's* colony; and thought themselves, being about 30 or 40 men, strong enough to execute the same: yet they durst not attempt it, till such time as they had gathered more strength to themselves, to make their party good against us at Plimouth; concluding that if we remained, though they had no other arguments to use against us, yet we would never leave the death of our countrymen unrevenged; and therefore their safety could not be without the overthrow of both plantations. To this end they had formerly solicited this sachem, as also the other, called *Ianough*, and many others, to assist them; and now again came to prosecute the same; and since there was so fair an opportunity offered by the captain's presence, they thought best to make sure of him and his company."

Coneconam, after this speech, treated *Standish* with neglect, and was very partial to *Wittuwamet*, which much increased the jealousy of the former. These Indians meantime contrived to kill *Standish*, having employed a "lusty Indian of Paomet" to execute the plan. The weather was severely cold, and *Standish* lodged on shore at night, and this was the time he was to have been killed. But the extreme coldness of the night kept him from sleeping, and thus he avoided assassination.

We have had occasion, in the life of *Massasoit*, to mention that that chief had been solicited to engage in this confederacy, and of his charging *Hobomok* to warn the English of it. The people of the places named at that time by *Massasoit*, as in the plot, were Nauset, Paomet, Succonet, Mattachiest, Manomet, Agowaywam, and the Island of Capawack. "Therefore, (says Mr. *Winslow* in his Relation,) as we respected the lives of our countrymen and our own safety, he advised us to kill the men of Massachuset, who were the authors of this intended mischief. And whereas we were wont to say, we would not strike a stroke till they first began, If, said he, [*Massasoit* to *Hobomok*,] upon this intelligence, they make that answer, tell them, when their countrymen at Wichaguscusset are killed, they not being able to defend themselves, that then it will be too late to recover their lives," and it would be with difficulty that they preserved their own; "and therefore he counselled, without delay, to take away the principals, and then the plot would cease."

Meanwhile *Weston's* men had fallen into a miserable and wretched condition; some, to procure a daily sustenance, became servants to the Indians, "fetching them wood and water, &c., and all for a meal's meat." Those who were thus degraded, were, of course, only a few who had abandoned themselves to riot and dissipation, but whose conduct had affected the well being of the whole, notwithstanding. Some of these wretches, in their extremities, had stolen corn from the Indians, on whose complaint they had been put in the stocks and whipped. This not giving the Indians satisfaction, one was hanged. This was in February, 1623.

About this capital punishment much has been written; some doubting the fact that any one was hanged, others that it was the real offender, &c. But in our opinion the facts are incontestable that one was hanged; but whether the one really guilty or not, is not quite so easily settled. The fact that one was hanged for another appears to have been of common notoriety, both in Old and New England, from shortly after the affair until the beginning of the next century.*

Mr. *Hubbard*† has this passage upon the affair:—"Certain it is, they [the Indians] were so provoked with their filching and stealing, that they threatened them, as the Philistines did *Samson's* father-in-law, after the loss of their corn; insomuch that the company, as some report, pretended, in way of satisfaction, to punish him that did the theft, but, in his stead, hanged a poor, decrepit old man, that was unserviceable to the company, [an old bed-rid weaver,‡] and burdensome to keep alive, which was the ground of the story with which the merry gentleman, that wrote the poem called HUDIBRAS, did, in his poetical fancy, make so much sport." And from the same author it appears that the circumstance was well known at Plimouth, but they pretended that the right person was hanged, or, in our author's own words, "as if the person hanged was really guilty of stealing, as may be were many of the rest, and if they were driven by necessity to content the Indians, at that time, to do justice, there being some of Mr. *Weston's* company living, it is possible it might be executed not on him that most deserved, but on him that could be best spared, or who was not like to live long if he had been let alone."

It will now be expected that we produce the passage of Hudibras. Here it is:—

"Though nice and dark the point appear,
(Quoth Ralph,) it may hold up, and clear.
That *Sinners* may supply the place
Of suffering *Saints*, is a plain *Case*.
Justice gives Sentence, many times,
On one Man for another's crimes.
Our Brethren of New England use
Choice Malefactors to excuse,
And *hang* the Guiltless in their stead,
Of whom the *Churches* have less need:
As lately't happen'd: In a town
There lived a *Cobbler*, and but one,
That out of Doctrine could cut *Use*,
And mend Men's *Lives*, as well as *Shoes*.
This precious Brother having slain,
In Times of *Peace*, an Indian,
(Not out of Malice, but mere Zeal.
Because he was an infidel,)
The mighty *Tottipottymoy*
Sent to our *Elders* an *Envoy*,

* See Col. N. H. Hist. Soc. iii. 148. and b. i. chap. iii. *ante*.
† Hist. N. Eng. 77.
‡ Col. N. H. Hist. Soc. iii. 148.

Complaining sorely of the Breach
Of League, held forth by Brother *Patch*,
Against the *Articles* in force,
Between both churches, his and ours,
For which he craved the *Saints* to render
Into his Hands, or hang th' *Offender:*
But they, maturely having weighed,
They had no more but him o' th' Trade,
(A Man that served them in a double
Capacity, to *Teach* and *Cobble*,)
Resolv'd to spare him; yet to do
The *Indian Hoghan Moghgan*, too,
Impartial Justice, in his stead, did
Hang an old Weaver that was Bed-rid.
Then wherefore may not you be skip'd,
And in your Room another Whipp'd?"

The following note was early printed to this passage:—"The history of the cobbler had been attested by persons of good credit, who were upon the place when it was done." Mr. *Butler* wrote this part of his Hudibras before 1663.

Thomas Morton, who was one of the company, though perhaps absent at the time, pretends that there was no plot of the Indians, and insinuates that the Plimoutheans caused all the trouble, and that their rashness caused the Indians to massacre some of their men, as we shall presently relate, from a book which Mr. *Morton* published.*

"Master *Weston's* plantation being settled at Wessaguscus, his servants, many of them lazy persons, that would use no endeavor to take the benefit of the country, some of them fell sick and died.

"One amongst the rest, an able-bodied man, that ranged the woods, to see what it would afford, lighted by accident on an Indian barn, and from thence did take a cap full of corn. The salvage owner of it, finding by the foot [track] some English had been there, came to the plantation, and made complaint after this manner. The chief commander of the company, on this occasion, called a Parliament of all his people, but those that were sick and ill at ease.† And wisely now they must consult, upon this huge complaint, that a privy [paltry] knife or string of beads would well enough have qualified: And *Edward Iohnson* was a special judge of this business. The fact was there in repetition, construction made, that it was fellony, and by the laws of England punished with death, and this in execution must be put for an example, and likewise to appease the salvage; when straightways one arose, moved as it were with some compassion, and said he could not well gainsay the former sentence; yet he had conceived, within the compass of his brain, an embrio, that was of special consequence to be delivered, and cherished, he said; that it would most aptly serve to pacify the salvage's complaint, and save the life of one that might (if need should be) stand them in some good stead; being young and strong, fit for resistance against an enemy, which might come unexpectedly, for any thing they knew.

"The oration made was liked of every one, and he intreated to show the means how this may be performed. Says he, you all agree that one must die, and one shall die. This young man's clothes we will take off, and put upon one that is old and impotent, a sickly person that cannot escape death; such is the disease on him confirmed, that die he must. Put the young man's clothes on this man, and let the sick person be hanged in the other's stead. Amen, says one, and so says many more. And this had like to have proved their final sentence; and being there

* Entitled New English Canaan, 4to. Amsterdam, 1637.

† Against this sentence, in the margin, is—"A poor complaint."

confirmed by act of Parliament to after ages for a precedent. But that one, with a ravenous voice, begun to croak and bellow for revenge, and put by that conclusive motion; alleging such deceits might be a means hereafter to exasperate the minds of the complaining salvages, and that, by his death, the salvages should see their zeal to justice, and, therefore, he should die. This was concluded; yet, nevertheless, a scruple was made; now to countermand this act did represent itself unto their minds, which was how they should do to get the man's good will: this was indeed a special obstacle: for without that (they all agreed) it would be dangerous, for any man to attempt the execution of it, lest mischief should befall them every man. He was a person that, in his wrath, did seem to be a second *Sampson,* able to beat out their brains with the jaw-bone of an ass: therefore they called the man, and by persuasion got him fast bound in jest, and then hanged him up hard by in good earnest, who, with a weapon, and at liberty, would have put all these wise judges of this Parliament to a pittiful *non plus,* (as it hath been credibly reported,) and made the chief judge of them all buckle to him."

This is an entire chapter of the NEW CANAAN, which, on account of its great rarity, we have given in full. In his next chapter Mr. *Morton* proceeds to narrate the circumstances of the "massacre" of *Wittuwamet, Peksuot,* and other Massachusetts Indians, and the consequences of it. But we shall now draw from the Plimouth historian, and afterwards use *Morton's* chapter as we find occasion.

Mr. *Winslow* says that Mr. *Weston's* men "knew not of this conspiracy of the Indians before his [*John Sanders,* their 'overseer'] going; neither was it known to any of us our return from Sowaams, or Puckanokick: at which time also another sachim, called *Wassapinewat,* brother to *Obtakiest,* the sachim of the Massachusets, who had formerly smarted for partaking with *Conbatant,* and fearing the like again, to purge himself, revealed the same thing," [as *Massasoit* had done.]

It was now the 23d March, 1623, "a yearly court day" at Plimouth, on which war was proclaimed, "in public court," against the Massachusetts Indians. "We came to this conclusion, (says *Winslow,*) that Captain *Standish* should take so many men, as he thought sufficient to make his party good against all the Indians in the Massachusetts Bay; and as because, as all men know that have to do with them in that kind, it is impossible to deal with them upon open defiance, but to take them in such traps as they lay for others; therefore he should pretend trade as at other times: but first go to the English, [at Wessaguscus,] and acquaint them with the plot, and the end of their own coming, that, comparing it with their own carriages towards them, he might better judge of the certainty of it, and more fitly take opportunity to revenge the same: but should forbare, if it were possible, till such time as he could make sure *Wittuwamat,* that bloody and bold villain before spoken of; whose head he had order to bring with him, that he might be a warning and terror to all that disposition."

We will now hear a word of what Mr. *Morton* has to say upon this transaction. "After the end of that Parliament, [which ended in the hanging of one,*] some of the plantation there, about three persons, went to live with *Checatawback* and his company, and had very good quarter, for all the former quarrel with the Plimouth planters.† They are not like *Will Sommers,*‡ to take one for another. There they purposed to stay until Master *Weston's* arrival: But the Plimouth men intending no good

* As mentioned in our last extract from this author.
† Referring, it is supposed, to the quarrel with *Caunbitant.*
‡ The person who proposed hanging a sick man instead of the real offender.

to him, (as appeared by the consequence,) came in the mean time to Wessaguscus, and there pretended to feast the salvages of those parts, bringing with them pork, and things for the purpose, which they set before the salvages. They eat thereof without suspicion of any mischief, [and] who were taken upon a watchword given, and with their own knives (hanging about their necks) were, by the Plimouth planters, stabbed and slain. One of which was hanged up there, after the slaughter."* When this came to the knowledge of *Chikataubut's* people, they murdered the three English who had taken up their residence with them, as they lay asleep, in revenge for the murder of their countrymen.†

After *Standish* was ready to proceed against *Wittuwamet*, but before he set out, one arrived from Wessaguscus almost famished,‡ and gave the people of Plimouth a lamentable account of the situation of his fellows; that not the least of their calamities was their being insulted by the Indians, "whose boldness increased abundantly; insomuch as the victuals they got, they [the Indians] would take it out of their pots, and eat [it] before their faces," and that if they tried to prevent them, they would hold a knife at their breasts: And to satisfy them, they had hanged one of their company: "That they had sold their clothes for corn, and were ready to starve both with cold and hunger also, because they could not endure to get victuals by reason of their nakedness."

This truly was a wretched picture of the first colony of Massachusetts, the knowledge of which (says *Winslow*) "gave us good encouragement to proceed in our intendments." Accordingly, the next day, *Standish,* with *Hobomok* and eight Englishmen, set out upon the expedition. His taking so few men shows how a few English guns were yet feared by the Indians. Nevertheless, the historians would have us understand that *Standish* would take no more, because he would not have the Indians mistrust that he came to fight them; and they would insinuate that it was owing to his great valor.

When *Standish* arrived at Wessaguscus, he found the people scattered about, apprehending no danger whatever, engaged in their ordinary affairs. When he told them of the danger they were in from the Indians. they said "they feared not the Indians, but lived, and suffered them to lodge with them, not having sword or gun, or needing the same." *Standish* now informed them of the plot, which was the first intimation, it appears, they had of it. He ordered them to call in their men, and enjoined secrecy of his intended massacre. But it seems from *Winslow's* Relation, that the Indians got word of it, or mistrusted his design; probably some of the Wessaguscus men warned them of it, who did not believe there was any plot.

Meantime, an Indian came to trade, and afterwards went away in friendship. *Standish,* more sagacious than the rest, said he saw treachery in his eye, and suspected his end in coming there was discovered.

---

* New English Canaan, 111. † Ibid.

‡ His name was *Phinehas Prat.* An Indian followed him to kill him, but, by losing the direct path, the Indian missed him. In 1662, the general court of Massachusetts, in answer to a petition of *Phinehas Prat,* then of Charlestown, which was accompanied "with a narrative of the straights and hardships that the first planters of this colony underwent in their endeavors to plant themselves at Plimouth, and since, whereof he was one, the court judgeth it meet to grant him 300 acres of land, where it is to be had, not hindering a plantation." *MS. among the files in our state-house.*

I have not been able to discover the narrative of Prat, after long search. Mr. *Hubbard* probably used it in compiling his Hist. of New England.

At the court, 3 May, 1665, land was ordered to be laid out for *Prat,* "in the wilderness on the east of Merrimack River, near the upper end of Nacook Brook, on the southeast of it. *Court Files, ut supra.*

Prat married, in Plimouth, a daughter of *Cuthbert Cuthbertson,* in 1630. See 2 *Col. Hist. Soc.* vii. 122.

Shortly after, *Peksuot*, "who was a paniese,* being a man of a notable spirit," came to *Hobomok*, and told him, *He understood the captain was come to kill him and the rest of the Indians there.* "Tell him, (said *Peksuot,)* we know it, but fear him not, neither will we shun him; but let him begin when he dare[s], he will not take us unawares."

The Indians now, as we might expect, began to prepare to meet the danger, and the English say many of them came divers times into their presence, and "would whet and sharpen the point of their knives," "and use many other insulting gestures and speeches. Amongst the rest, *Wittuwamat* bragged of the excellency of his knife. On the end of the handle there was pictured a woman's face; but, said he, *I have another at home, wherewith I have killed both French and English, and that hath a man's face on it; and by and by these two must marry.*" To this he added, HINNAIM NAMEN, HINNAIM MICHEN, MATTA CUTS: that is, *By and by it should see, and by and by it should eat, but not speak.* "Also *Pecksuot*, (continues *Winslow*,) being a man of greater stature than the captain, told him though he were a great captain, yet he was but a little man: *and*, said he, *though I be no sachem, yet I am a man of great strength and courage.* These things the captain observed, yet bare with patience for the present."

It will be seen, in what we have related, as well as what we are about to add, that *Thomas Morton's* account, in some of the main facts, agrees with that of *Winslow*. From the latter it appears that *Standish*, after considerable manœuvring, could get advantage over but few of the Indians. At length, having got *Peksuot* and *Wittuwamat* "both together, with another man, and a youth of some eighteen years of age, which was brother to *Wittuwamat*, and, villain like, trod in his steps, daily putting many tricks upon the weaker sort of men, and having about as many of his own company in a room with them, gave the word to his men, and, the door being fast shut, began himself with *Pecksuot*, and, *snatching his own knife from his neck*, though with much struggling, *and killed him therewith*—the point whereof he had made as sharp as a needle, and ground the back also to an edge. *Wittuwamat* and the other man *the rest killed, and took the youth, whom the* captain caused to be hanged" [up there.†]

We could now wish this bloody tale were finished, but we have promised to keep close to the record. Mr. Winslow continues, "*But it is incredible how many wounds these two panieses received before they died, not making any fearful noise, but catching at their weapons, and striving to the last.*

"*Hobbamock* stood by all this time,‡ and meddled not, observing how our men demeaned themselves in this action." After the affray was ended, he said to *Standish*, "Yesterday *Pecksuot* bragged of his own strength and stature, said, though you were a great captain, yet you were

---

* "The Panieses are men of great courage and wisedome, and to these also the Deuill appeareth more familiarly than to others, and, as wee conceiue, maketh couenant with them to preserue them from death by wounds with arrows, knives, hatchets, &c." *Winslow's Relation*. Did *Charlevoix* (Voyage dans l'Amerique) mistake "Panis" [Paniese] for a nation of Indians? In speaking of the origin of calumet, some told him that it was given by the sun to *Panis*, a nation upon the Missouri. Perhaps his opinion was strengthened from seeing them blow the smoke towards the sun upon important occasions.

† New English Canaan, 111.

‡ This, we suppose, is the affair to which President *Allen* alludes, in his American Biography, (2d ed) when he says, "he [*Hobomok*] fought bravely by his [*Standish's*] side, in 1623." If standing and looking on be fighting, then did *Hobomok fight bravely* on this occasion.

but a little man; but to-day I see you are big enough to lay him on the ground."

Standish now sent to a company of *Weston's* men, and ordered them to kill the Indians that were among them. *They killed two.* Himself with some of his men *killed another,* at another place. As they were pursuing this business, intending to kill all they could lay hands upon, "through the negligence of one man, an Indian escaped, who discovered [disclosed] and crossed their proceedings."

Joined by some of Mr. *Weston's* men, *Standish* discovered a few Indians, and pursued them. *Standish* gained a hill which the Indians also strove to occupy, and who, after shooting a few arrows, fled. "Whereupon *Hobbamock* cast off his coat, and being a known paniese, theirs being now killed, chased them so fast, as our people were not able to hold way with him." One who made a stand to shoot *Standish* had his arm broken by a shot, which is all the advantage claimed by the English. The Indians got into a swamp, and after some bravadoing on both sides, the parties separated. After assisting the settlers of Wessaguscus to leave the place, the English returned to Plimouth, taking along the head of *Wittuwamet,* which they set up in their fort.

Meanwhile the Indian that followed *Prat* from Wessaguscus, as he returned from Manomet, called at Plimouth in a friendly manner, and was there seized and put in irons. Being asked if he knew the head of *Wittuwamat,* said he did, and "looked piteously" upon it. "Then he confessed the plot," and said his sachem, *Obtakiest,* had been drawn into it by the importunity of all the people. He denied any hand in it himself, and begged his life might be spared. Said he was not a Massachuset, but only resided as a stranger among them. *Hobomok* "also gave a good report of him, and besought for him; but was bribed so to do it." They finally concluded to spare him, "the rather, because we desired he might carry a message to *Obtakiest.*" The message they charged him with was this, that they had never intended to deal so with him, until they were forced to it by their treachery, and, therefore, they might thank themselves for their own overthrow; and as he had now began, if he persisted in his course, "his country should not hold him;" that he should forthwith send to Plimouth "the three Englishmen he had, and not kill them."*

The English heard nothing from *Obtakiest* for a long time; at length he sent a woman to them, (probably no man would venture,) to tell them he was sorry that the English were killed, before he heard from them, also that he wished for peace, but none of his men durst come to treat about it. The English learned from this woman, that he was in great consternation, "having forsaken his dwelling, and daily removed from place to place, expecting when we would take further vengeance on him." The terror was now general among them, and many, as we have elsewhere said, died through fear and want. To this dismal narrative Mr. *Winslow* adds, "And certainly it is strange to hear how many of late have, and still daily die amongst them; neither is there any likelihood it will easily cease; because through fear they set little or no corn, which is the staff of life, and without which they cannot long preserve health and strength."

These affairs call for no commentary, that must accompany every mind through every step of the relation. It would be weakness, as ap-

* *Morton,* in his *New Canaan,* 111, says, these three men went to reside with *Chikataubut;* hence *Morton* very reasonably suggests, that if the Plimouth people intended the men of Wessaguscus any good, why did they not first see that all of them were out of danger, before beginning war?

4

pears to us, to attempt a vindication of the rash conduct of the English. Amid their sufferings, some poor Indians resolved to attempt to appease the wrath of the English governor by presents. Four set out by water in a boat for Plimouth, but by accident were overset, and three of them were drowned; the other returned back.

When Mr. *Robinson*, the father of the Plimouth church, heard how his people had conducted in this affair with the Indians, he wrote to them, to consider of the disposition of Capt. *Standish*, "who was of a warm temper," but he hoped the Lord had sent him among them for a good end, if they used him as they ought. "He doubted," he said, "whether there was not wanting that tenderness of the life of man, made after God's image," which was so necessary; and above all, that "it would have been happy if they had converted some before they had killed any."

The reader has now passed through a period of Indian history of much interest; wherein he will doubtless have found much to admire, and more that he could have wished otherwise. Our business, however, we will here remind him, is that of a dealer in facts altogether, and he must take them, dry as they are, without any labored commentaries from us. Although we have had occasion to introduce *Hobomok* several times, yet there remain transactions of considerable interest in his life yet to be noticed.

Hobomok, or *Hobbamock*, was a great paniese or war captain among the Wampanoags, as we have already had occasion to observe. He came to Plimouth about the end of July, 1621, and continued with the English as long as he lived. He was a principal means of the lasting friendship of *Massasoit*, which *Morton* says, he "much furthered; and that he was a proper lusty young man, and one that was in account among the Indians in those parts for his valor." He was of the greatest service in learning them how to cultivate such fruits as were peculiar to the country, such as corn, beans, &c. The account of his mission to *Massasoit*, to learn the truth of a report that the Narragansets had made war upon him, and his interruption and trouble from *Caunbitant* are already related.

Being a favorite of *Massasoit*, and one of his chief captains, the pilgrims found that they need not apprehend any treachery on his part, as *Hobomok* was so completely in their interest, and also in that of the great sachem, that he would advise them if any thing evil were on foot against them. What strengthened them in this opinion was the following circumstance. The Massachusetts Indians had for some time been inviting the English into their country to trade for furs. When, in March, 1622, they began to make ready for the voyage, *Hobomok* "told us, (says *Winslow*,) that he feared the Massachusetts, or Massachuseuks, for they so called the people of that place, were joined in confederacy with the Nanohigganneuks, a people of Nanohigganset, and that they, therefore, would take this opportunity to cut off Capt. *Standish* and his company abroad; but howsoever, in the meantime, it was to be feared, [he said,] that the Nanohigganeuks would assault the town at home; giving many reasons for his jealousy; as also that *Tisquantum* was in the confederacy, who, [he said,] we should find, would use many persuasions to draw us from our shallops to the Indians' houses for their better advantage."

Nevertheless, they proceeded on their voyage, and when they had turned the point called the *Gurnet's Nose*, a false messenger came running into Plimouth town, apparently in a great fright, out of breath, and bleeding from a wound in his face. He told them that *Caunbitant*, with many of the Narragansets, and he believed *Massasoit* with them, were coming to destroy the English. No one doubted of his sincerity, and the first thought of the people was to bring back their military leader, who had just gone in the boat with *Hobomok*. A piece of cannon was immediately discharged, which, to their great joy, soon caused the boat to return, not having got out of hearing. They had no sooner arrived, than *Hobomok* told them there was no truth in the report, and said it was a plot of *Squanto*, who was then with them, and even one of those in the boat; that he knew *Massasoit* would not undertake such an enterprise without consulting him. *Hobomok* was confident, because he was himself a great chief, and one of *Massasoit's* counsellors. *Squanto* denied all knowledge of any plot, and thus ended the affair. The English, however, seemed well satisfied that *Squanto* had laid this shallow plot to set them against *Massasoit*, thinking they would destroy him, by which means he expected to become chief sachem himself; and this seems the more probable, as *Massasoit* was for some time irreconcilable because they withheld him from him, when he had forfeited his life, as in our narration has been set forth. But entirely to satisfy the English, *Hobomok* sent his wife to Pokanoket privately to gain exact intelligence, and her return only verified what her husband had said.

"Thus by degrees (continues *Winslow*) we began to discover *Tisquantum*, whose ends were only to make himself great in the eyes of his countrymen, by means of his nearness and favor with us; not caring who fell, so he stood. In general, his course was, to persuade them he could lead us to peace or war at his pleasure; and would oft threaten the Indians, sending them word, in a private manner, we were intended shortly to kill them, that thereby he might get gifts to himself, to work their peace, insomuch as they had him in greater esteem than many of their sachems: yea, they themselves sought to him, who promised them peace in respect of us; yea, and protection also, so as they would resort to him. So that whereas divers were wont to rely on *Massassowat* for protection, and resort to his abode, now they began to leave him, and seek after *Tisquantum*. But when we understood his dealings, we certified all the Indians of our ignorance and innocency therein; assuring them, till they begun with us, they should have no cause to fear: and if any hereafter should raise any such reports, they should punish them as liars, and seekers of their and our disturbance; which gave the Indians good satisfaction on all sides." "For these and the like abuses, the governor sharply reproved him, yet was he so necessary and profitable an instrument, as at that time we could not miss him."

To the end that he might possess his countrymen with great fear of the English, *Tisquantum* told them the English kept the plague buried in their store-house, and that they could send it, at any time, and to any place, to destroy whatever persons or people they would, though they themselves stirred not out of doors. Among the rest, he had made *Hobomok* believe this tale, who asked the English if it were true, and being informed that it was not, it exploded like his other impostures.

There is but little doubt, that *Squanto* was in the interest of *Caunbitant*, and lived among the English as a spy, while *Hobomok* was honestly, as he pretended, a strong friend to them; but for some time it was nearly impossible for them to know which was their best friend, as each seemed emulous to outvie the other in good offices. They were, however, at this time satisfied; for, *Hobomok's* wife having told *Massasoit* what had happened, and that it was one of *Squanto*'s men that gave the alarm, satisfied him that that sagamore had caused it, and he therefore demanded him of the English, that he might put him to death, according to their law, as has been related. But the English, regarding the benefit resulting to them from saving his life, more than keeping inviolate the treaty before made with *Massasoit*, evaded the demand, and thus *Squanto* was permitted to escape.

Hobomok was greatly beloved by *Massasoit*, notwithstanding he became a professed Christian, and *Massasoit* was always opposed to the English religion himself. It has been told in the life of the great *Massasoit*, how valuable was the agency of *Hobomok*, in faithfully revealing the mischievous plot of *Caunbitant*, which terminated in the death of *Wittuwamet* and *Peksuot*. He was the pilot of the English when they visited *Massasoit* in his sickness, whom before their arrival they considered dead, which caused great manifestations of grief in *Hobomok*. He often exclaimed, as they were on their way, "*Neen womasu Sagimus, neen womasu Sagimus*, &c.," which is, "My loving Sachem, my loving Sachem! many have I known, but never any like thee." Then, turning to Mr. Winslow, said, "While you live you will never see his like among the Indians; that he was no liar, nor bloody and cruel like other Indians. In anger and passion he was soon reclaimed; easy to be reconciled towards such as had offended him; that his reason was such as to cause him to receive advice of mean men; and that he governed his people better with few blows, than others did with many."

In the division of the land at Plimouth among the inhabitants, *Hobomok* received a lot as his share, on which he resided after the English manner, and died a Christian among them. The year of his death does not appear, but was previous to 1642.

It has already been mentioned that the pilgrims made a voyage to Massachusetts in the autumn of 1621. It was in this voyage that they became acquainted with the fame of *Nanepashemet*. The English had heard that the Indians in the Massachusetts had threatened them, and they went (says *Mourt*) "partly to see the country, partly to make peace with them, and partly to procure their truck."

Squanto was pilot in this voyage. They went ashore in the bottom of the bay, and landed under a cliff which some* have supposed was what has been since called Copp's Hill,† now the north part of Boston. This was on 20th Sept. 1621. They saw no Indians until some time after they went ashore, but found a parcel of lobsters which they had collected, with which they refreshed themselves. Soon after, as they were proceeding on an excursion, "they met a woman coming for her lobsters." They told her what they had done, and paid her for them. She told them where to find Indians, and *Squanto* went to them to prepare them for meeting with the English.

Obbatinewat now received the voyagers. This sachem (if he be the same) had made peace with the English at Plimouth only seven days previous, as we have had occasion to say before. He told them he was sachem of the place, and was subject to *Massasoit*; and that he dared not remain long in any place, from fear of the Tarratines, who were "wont to come at harvest and take away their corn, and many times kill them." Also that *Squaw-Sachem* of Massachusetts was his enemy. This *Squaw-Sachem*,‡ as we believe, was chief of those inland Indians since denominated the Nipnets, or Nipmucks, and lived at this time near Wachuset Mountain. The English intended§ to have visited her at this

* Dr. *Belknap* appears to have been the first who suggested this. See his Biog. ii. 224.

† We had supposed this eminence to have been so called from a copse or clump of trees, which for a long time remained upon it, after it became known to the whites; but *Shaw, Descrip. Boston*, 67, says it was named from one *Copp*, a shoemaker. And *Snow, Hist. Boston*, 105, says *William Copp* was the proprietor of "a *portion* of the hill."

‡ "Sachems or sagamores,—which are but one and the same title,—the first more usual with the southward, the other with the northward Indians, to express the title of him that hath the chief command of a place or people." Hist. N. E. 60.

§ Mr. *Shattuck* (Hist. Concord, 2) says she was visited at this time by these voyagers,

time, but found the distance too great to proceed. They received the greatest kindness from all the Indians they met with, and mentioned that of *Obbatinewat* in particular. And they say, "We told him of divers sachims that had acknowledged themselves to be King *James* his men, *and if he also would submit himself,** we would be his safeguard from his enemies, which he did."

At another place, "Having gone three miles, in arms, up in the country, we came (say they) to a place where corn had been newly gathered, a house pulled down, and the people gone. A mile from hence, *Nanepashemet*, their king, in his life-time had lived.† His house was not like others, but a scaffold was largely built, with poles and planks, some six foot from [the] ground, and the house upon that, being situated on the top of a hill. Not far from hence, in a bottom, we came to a fort," built by *Nanepashemet*. It was made with "poles some 30 or 40 foot long, stuck in the ground, as thick as they could be set one by another, and with these they enclosed a ring some 40 or 50 foot over. A trench, breast high, was digged on each side.‡ One way there was to get into it with a bridge. In the midst of this palisado stood the frame of an house, wherein, being dead, he lay buried. About a mile from hence, we came to such another, but seated on the top of an hill. Here *Nanepashemet* was killed, none dwelling in it since the time of his death."

According to Mr. *Lewis*, *Nanepashemet* was killed about the year 1619, and his widow, who was *Squaw-Sachem* before named, continued the government.§ He left five children,|| four of whose names we gather from the interesting History of Lynn; viz. 1. *Montowampate*, called by the English *Sagamore James*. He was sachem of Saugus. 2. *Abigail*, a daughter. 3. *Wonohaquaham*, called *Sagamore John*, sachem of *Winnesimet*. 4. *Winnepurkitt*, called *Sagamore George*, or *George Rumneymarsh*, the successor of *Montowampate* at Saugus. Of most of these we shall speak in detail hereafter.

Squaw-Sachem, according to the authority last mentioned, was the spouse of *Wappacowet*,¶ or *Webcowit*, in 1635. She and her husband, four years after, 1639, deeded to *Jotham Gibbones* "the reversion of all that parcel of land which lies against the ponds of Mystic, together with the said ponds, all which we reserved from Charlestown and Cambridge, late called Newtown, after the death of me, the said *Squaw-Sachem*." The consideration was, "the many kindnesses and benefits we have received from the hands of Capt. *Edward Gibbones*, of Boston."

The SQUA-SACHEM'S *mark*

WEBCOWIT'S *mark*

Webcowit was a powwow priest, or magical physician, and was considered next in importance to *Nanepashemet* among the subjects of that chief, after his death; as a matter of course, his widow took him to her bed. It does not appear, that he was either much respected or thought much of; especially by his wife, as in the above extract from their deed,

---

but I am not able to arrive at any such conclusion from any source of information in my possession.

* It does not seem from this that he is the same who before had submitted at Plimouth, as Mr. *Prince* supposes.

† Mr. *Shattuck*, in his valuable *Hist. Concord*, says, this "was in Medford, near Mystic Pond."

‡ Might not, then, the western mounds have been formed by Indians?

§ Hist. Lynn, 16.

|| *Shattuck*, ib. who fixes her residence at Concord; she, doubtless, had several places of residence.

¶ His name is spelt *Webcowits* to MS. deed in my possession, and in Mr. *Shattuck's* MSS. *Wibbacowitts*, as appears from his History.

no provision seems to have been made for him after her death, if he outlived her. At all events, we may conclude, without hazard we think, that if breeches had been in fashion among Indians, the wife of *Webcowit* would have been accountable for the article in this case.

In 1643, Massachusetts covenanted with "*Wassamequin, Nashoonon, Kutchamaquin, Massaconomet* and *Squaw-Sachem*,"* to the end that mutual benefit might accrue to each party. The sachems put themselves under the government of the English, agreeing to observe their laws, in as far as they should be made to understand them. For this confidence and concession of their persons and lands into their hands, the English on their part agreed to extend the same protection to them and their people as to their English subjects.†

What had become of *Webcowet* at this time does not appear; perhaps he was off powwowing, or at home, doing the ordinary labor of the household. We hear of him, however, four years after, (1647,) "taking an active part" in the endeavors made by the English to Christianize his countrymen. "He asked the English why some of them had been 27 years in the land, and never taught them to know God till then. Had you done it sooner, (said he,) we might have known much of God by this time, and much sin might have been prevented, but now some of us are grown [too] old in sin." The English said they repented of their neglect; but recollecting themselves answered, "You were not willing to heare till now," and that God had not turned their hearts till then.‡

Of the sachems who made the covenant above named, the first we suppose to have been *Massasoit*, on the part of the *Wampanoags*, who at this time was, perhaps, among the Nipmuks; *Nashoonon*, a Nipmuk chief, with whom *Massasoit* now resided. His residence was near what was since Magus Hill in Worcester county. He was probably at Plimouth 13 Sept., 1621, where he signed a treaty with eight others, as we have set down in the life of *Caunbitant*. His name is there spelt *Nattawahunt*. In *Winthrop's* Journal, it is *Nashacowam*, and we suppose he was father of *Nassowanno*, mentioned by *Whitney*.§ *Kutchamaquin* was sachem of Dorchester and vicinity, and *Massaconomet* was *Mascononomo*.

CHAPTER III.

*Some account of the Massachusetts—Geography of their country—*CHIKATAUBUT— WAMPATUCK—*his war with the Mohawks*—MASCONONOMO— CANONICUS—*Geography of the Narraganset country—Account of that Nation—Roger Williams*—MONTOWAMPATE—*Small-pox distresses the Indians* — WONOHAQUAHAM — WINNEPURKIT — MANATAHQUA — SCITTERYGUSSET— NATTAHATTAWANTS— WAHGUMACUT— JACK-STRAW— JAMES.

NOT long before the settlement of Plimouth, the Massachusetts had been a great people, but were greatly reduced at this time; partly from the great plague, of which we have already spoken, and subsequently from their wars with the Tarratines. Of this war none but the scanty records of the first settlers are to be had, and in them few particulars are preserved;

* In the *History of the Narraganset Country,* these names are written *Wassamegun, Nashawanon, Cutshamacke, Massanomell,* and *Squa-Sachem.* See 3 *Col. Mass. Hist. Soc.* i. 212.

† See Gookin's *MS. Hist. Praying Indians.*

‡ Hist. Concord, 25.

§ Hist. Worcester Co. 174.

of this, too, we have written in a previous chapter.* Therefore it will not be expected that ever a complete account of the territories and power of the Massachusetts can be given; broken down as they were at the time they became known to the Europeans; for we have seen that their sachems, when first visited by the Plimouth people, were shifting for their lives—not daring to lodge a second night in the same place, from their fear of the Tarratines. Hence, if these Indians had existed as an independent tribe, their history was long since swept away "in gloomy tempests," and obscured in "a night of clouds," and nothing but a meagre tradition remained. For some time after the country was settled, they would fly for protection from the Tarratines to the houses of the English.

It is said by Mr. *Gookin*, that "their chief sachem held dominion over many other petty governors; as those of Weechagaskas, Neponsitt, Punkapaog, Nonantum, Nashaway, some of the Nipmuck people, as far as Pokomtakuke, as the old men of Massachusetts affirmed. This people could, in former times, arm for war about 3000 men, as the old Indians declare. They were in hostility very often with the Narragansitts; but held amity, for the most part, with the Pawkunnawkutts."† Near the mouth of Charles River "used to be the general rendezvous of all the Indians, both on the south and north side of the country."‡ *Hutchinson*§ says, "That circle which now makes the harbors of Boston and Charlestown, round by Malden, Chelsea, Nantasket, Hingham, Weymouth, Braintree, and Dorchester, was the capital of a great sachem,|| much revered by all the plantations round about. The tradition is, that this sachem had his principal seat upon a small hill, or rising upland, in the midst of a body of salt marsh in the township of Dorchester, near to a place called Squantum."¶ Hence it will be observed, that among the accounts of the earliest writers, the dominions of the different sachems were considered as comprehended within very different limits; a kind of general idea, therefore, can only be had of the extent of their possessions. It is evident that the Massachusetts were either subject to the Narragansetts, or in alliance with them; for when the latter were at war with the Pequots, *Chikataubut* and *Sagamore John* both went with many men to aid *Canonicus*, who had sent for them. This war began in 1632, and ended in 1635, to the advantage of the Pequots.

We shall now proceed to speak of the chiefs agreeably to our plan.

Chikataubut, or *Chikkatabak*, in English,—a *house-a-fire*, was a sachem of considerable note, and generally supposed to have had dominion over the Massachusetts Indians. *Thomas Morton* mentions him in his NEW CANAAN, as sachem of Passonagesit, (about Weymouth,) and says his mother was buried there. I need make no comments upon the authority, or warn the reader concerning the stories of *Morton*, as this is done in almost every book, early and late, about New England; but shall relate the following from him.

In the first settling of Plimouth, some of the company, in wandering about upon discovery, came upon an Indian grave, which was that of the mother of *Chikataubut*. Over the body a stake was set in the ground, and two huge bear-skins, sewed together, spread over it; these the English

* This war was caused, says Mr. *Hubbard*, "upon the account of some treachery" on the part of the western tribes, i. e. the tribes west of the Merrimack. *Hist. New Eng.* 30.

† 1 Col. Mass. Hist. Soc. i. 148.

‡ Hist. N. Eng. 32.

§ From *Neal's Hist. N. Eng.*, probably, which see.

|| It will be a good while before the present possessors of the country can boast of such a capital.

¶ Hist. Mass. i. 460. And here it was, I suppose, that the Plimouth people landed in their voyage to Massachusetts before spoken of, and from *Squanto* who was with them it received its name.

took away. When this came to the knowledge of *Chikataubut*, he complained to his people, and demanded immediate vengeance. When they were assembled, he thus harangued them: "When last the glorious light of all the sky was underneath this globe, and birds grew silent, I began to settle, as my custom is, to take repose. Before mine eyes were fast closed, me tho't I saw a vision, at which my spirit was much troubled, and trembling at that doleful sight, a spirit cried aloud, 'Behold! my son, whom I have cherished; see the paps that gave thee suck, the hands that clasped thee warm, and fed thee oft; canst thou forget to take revenge of those wild people, that hath my monument defaced in a despiteful manner; disdaining our ancient antiquities, and honorable customs. See now the sachem's grave lies like unto the common people, of ignoble race defaced. Thy mother doth complain, implores thy aid against this thievish people new come hither; if this be suffered, I shall not rest in quiet within my everlasting habitation.' "*

Battle was the unanimous resolve, and the English were watched, and followed from place to place, until at length, as some were going ashore in a boat, they fell upon them, but gained no advantage. After maintaining the fight for some time, and being driven from tree to tree, the chief captain was wounded in the arm, and the whole took to flight. This action caused the natives about Plimouth to look upon the English as invincible, and this was the reason why peace was so long maintained between them.

Mourt's Relation goes far to establish the main facts in the above account. It says, "We brought sundry of the prettiest things away with us, and covered the corpse up again," and, "there was variety of opinions amongst us about the embalmed person," but no mention of the bear-skins.

From the agreement of the different accounts, there is but little doubt, that the English were attacked at Namskekit, in consequence of their depredations upon the graves, corn, &c. of the Indians.

In 1621, *Chikataubut*, with eight other sachems, acknowledged, by a written instrument, themselves the subjects of King *James*. About ten years after this, when Boston was settled, he visited Governor *Winthrop*, and presented him with a hogshead of corn. Many of "his sannops and squaws" came with him, but were most of them sent away, "after they had all dined," although it thundered and rained, and the governor urged their stay; *Chikataubut* probably feared they would be burdensome. At this time he wore English clothes, and sat at the governor's table, "where he behaved himself as soberly, &c. as an Englishman." Not long after, he called on Governor *Winthrop*, and desired to buy clothes for himself; the governor informed him that "English sagamores did not use to truck;† but he called his tailor, and gave him order to make him a suit of clothes; whereupon he gave the governor two large skins of coat beaver." In a few days his clothes were ready, and the governor "put him into a very good new suit from head to foot, and after, he set meat before them; but he would not eat till the governor had given thanks, and after meat he desired him to do the like, and so departed."

June 14, 1631, at a court, *Chikataubut* was ordered to pay a small skin of beaver, to satisfy for one of his men's having killed a pig, which he complied with. A man by the name of *Plastowe*, and some others, having stolen corn from him, the same year, the court, Sept. 27, ordered that *Plastowe* should restore "two-fold," and lose his title of gentleman, and

* If this be fiction, a modern compiler has deceived some of his readers. The article in the *Analectic Magazine* may have been his source of information, but the original may be seen in *Morton's New Canaan*, 106 and 107.

† However true this might have been of the governor, at least, we think, he should not have used the plural.

pay £5. This I suppose they deemed equivalent to four-fold. His accomplices were whipped, to *the same amount*. The next year we find him engaged with other sachems in an expedition against the Pequots. The same year two of his men were convicted of assaulting some persons of Dorchester in their houses. "They were put in the bilboes," and himself required to beat them, which he did.*

The small-pox was very prevalent among the Indians in 1633, in which year, some time in November, *Chikataubut* died.

The residence of the family of *Chikataubut* was at Tehticut, now included in Middleborough. He was in obedience to *Massasoit*, and, like other chiefs, had various places of resort, to suit the different seasons of the year; sometimes at Wessaguscusset, sometimes at Neponset, and especially upon that part of Namasket† called Tehticut. This was truly a river of sagamores. Its abundant stores of fish, in the spring, drew them from all parts of the realm of the chief sachem.

In deeds, given by the Indians, the place of their residence is generally mentioned, and from what we shall recite in the progress of this article, it will be seen that the same chief has different residences assigned to him.

August 5, 1665, Quincy, then Braintree, was deeded by a son of *Chikataubut*, in these terms:—

‡"To all Indian people to whom these presents shall come; *Wampatuck*, alias *Josiah Sagamore*, of Massathusetts, in Newengland, the son of *Chickatabut* deceased, sendeth greeting. Know yoo that the said *Wampatuck*, being of full age and power, according to the order and custom of the natives, hath, with the consent of his wise men, viz. *Squamog*, his brother *Daniel*, and *Old Hahatun*, and *William Mananiomott, Job Nassott, Manuntago, William Nahanton*§" "For divers goods and valuable reasons therunto; and in special for" £21 10s. in hand. It was subscribed and witnessed thus:—

JOSIAH, *alias* WAMPATUCK, *his* IO *marke.*
DANIEL SQUAMOG, *and a mark.*
OLD NAHATUN, *and a mark.*
WILLIAM MANUNION, *and a mark.*
JOB NOISTENNS.
ROBERT, *alias* MAMUNTAGO, *and a mark.*
WILLIAM HAHATUN.

In presence of
THOMAS KEYAHGUNSSON, *and a mark* O
JOSEPH MANUNION, *his* I —*mark.*
THOMAS WEYMOUS, *his* O *mark.*

There is a quit-claim deed from "*Charles Josias*, alias *Josias Wampatuck*, grandson of *Chikataubut*, dated in 1695, of Boston and the adjacent country, and the islands in the harbor, to the "proprietated inhabitants of the town of Boston," to be seen among the Suffolk records.|| *Wampatuck* says, or some one *for* him, "Forasmuch as I am informed, and well assured from several ancient Indians, as well those of my council as others, that, upon the first coming of the English to sit down and settle in those

* "The most usual custom amongst them in exercising punishments, is for the sachem either to beat, or whip, or put to death with his own hand, to which the common sort most quietly submit." *Williams*.

† Namaùasuck signified in their language fishes, and some early wrote Namascheuck.

‡ History of Quincy by Rev. Mr. *Whitney*, taken from the original in the possession of the Hon. *J. Q. Adams*.

§ *Nahaton*, or *Ahaton*, and the same sometimes written *Nehoiden*. See *Worthington's Hist. Dedham*, 21. He sold lands upon Charles River in 1680. *ib.*

|| Printed at length in *Snow's Hist. Boston*, 389, et cet.

parts of New England, my above-named grandfather, *Chikataubut*, by and with the advice of his council, for encouragement thereof moving, did give, grant, sell, alienate, and confirm unto the English planters," the lands above named.

Josias, or *Josiah Wampatuck*, was sachem of Mattakeesett,* and, from the deeds which he gave, must have been the owner of much of the lands southward of Boston. In 1653, he sold to *Timothy Hatherly, James Cudworth, Joseph Tilden, Humphrey Turner, William Hatch, John Hoare,* and *James Torrey*, a large tract of land in the vicinity of Accord Pond and North River.

In 1662, he sold Pachage Neck, [now called *Ptchade*,] "lying between Namassakett riuer and a brook falling into Teticutt riuer, viz. the most westerly of the three small brookes that do fall into the said riuer;" likewise all the meadow upon said three brooks, for £21. Also, another tract bounded by Plimouth and Duxbury on one side, and Bridgewater on the other, extending to the great pond Mattakeeset; provided it included not the 1000 acres given to his son and *George Wampey*, about those ponds. This deed was witnessed by *George Wampey* and *John Wampowes*.

After the death of his father, *Josias* was often called *Josias Chikataubut*. In the PLIMOUTH RECORDS we find this notice, but without date: "Memorandum, that *Josias Chickabutt* and his wife doe owne the whole necke of Punkateesett to beloing vnto Plymouth men," &c.

In 1668, "*Josias Chickatabutt*, sachem of Namassakeesett," sold to *Robert Studson* of Scituate, a tract of land called Nanumackeuitt, for a "valuable consideration," as the deed expresses it. This tract was bounded on the east by Scituate.

Josias had a son *Jeremy*; and "*Charles Josiah*, son of *Jeremy*, was the last of the race."† Of *Josiah*, Mr. *Gookin* gives us important information. In the year 1669, "the war having now continued between the Maquas and our Indians, about six years, divers Indians, our neighbors, united their forces together, and made an army of about 6 or 700 men, and marched into the Maquas' country, to take revenge of them. This enterprise was contrived and undertaken without the privity, and contrary to the advice of their English friends. Mr. *Eliot* and myself, in particular, dissuaded them, and gave them several reasons against it, but they would not hear us." Five of the Christian Indians went out with them, and but one only returned alive. "The chiefest general in this expedition was the principal sachem of Massachusetts, named *Josiah*, alias *Chekatabutt*, a wise and stout man, of middle age, but a very vicious person. He had considerable knowledge in the Christian religion; and sometime, when he was younger, seemed to profess it for a time;—for he was bred up by his uncle, *Kuchamakin*, who was the first sachem and his people to whom Mr. *Eliot* preached."‡

This army arrived at the Mohawk fort after a journey of about 200 miles; when, upon besieging it some time, and having some of their men killed in sallies, and sundry others sick, they gave up the siege and retreated. Meanwhile the Mohawks pursued them, got in their front, and, from an ambush, attacked them in a defile, and a great fight ensued. Finally the Mohawks were put to flight by the extraordinary bravery and prowess of *Chikataubut* and his captains. But what was most calamitous in this disastrous expedition, was, the loss of the great chief *Chikataubut*, who, after performing prodigies of valor, was killed in repelling the Mohawks in their last attack, with almost all his captains.§ This was a severe

* *Deane's Hist. Scituate*, 144.

† Ibid. *Squamaug* was a brother of *Josiah*, and ruled "as sachem during the minority" of Jeremy. Dr. *Harris, Hist. Dorchester*, 16, 17.

‡ 1 Col. Mass. Hist. Soc. i. 166.

§ Ibid. 167.

stroke to these Indians, and they suffered much from chagrin on their return home. The Mohawks considered themselves their masters, and although a peace was brought about between them, by the mediation of the English and Dutch on each side, yet the Massachusetts and others often suffered from their incursions.

A chief of much the same importance as *Chikataubut* and his sons, was *Masconònomo*, or *Masconomo*, sachem of Agawam, since called *Ipswich*. When the fleet which brought over the colony that settled Boston, in 1630, anchored near Cape Ann, he welcomed them to his shores, and spent some time on board one of the ships.*

On the 28th June, 1638, *Masconònomet*† executed a deed of "all his lands in Ipswich," to *John Winthrop*, jr., for the sum of £20.‡

At a court in July, 1631, it was ordered, that "the sagamore of Agawam is banished from coming into any Englishman's house for a year, under penalty of ten beaver-skins."§ The next year, or about that time, the Tarratines came out with great force against *Masconònomo*; he having, "as was usually said, treacherously killed some of those Tarratine families." || From Mr. *Cobbet's* account, it appears that they came against the English, who, but for an Indian, named *Robin*, would have been cut off, as the able men at this time, belonging to Ipswich, did not exceed 30; and most of these were from home on the day the attack was to have been made. *Robin*, having by some means found out their intentions, went to *John Perkins*,¶ and told him on such a day four Tarratines would come and invite the English to trade, "and draw them down the hill to the water side," when 40 canoes full of armed Indians would be ready, under "the brow of the hill," to fall upon them. It turned out as *Robin* had reported; but the Indians were frightened off by a false show of numbers, an old drum, and a few guns, without effecting their object.**

We hear no more of him until 1643, when, at a court held in Boston, "*Cutshamekin* and *Squaw-Sachem, Masconomo, Nashacowam* and *Wassamagin*,†† two sachems near the great hill to the west, called *Wachusett*, came into the court, and, according to their former tender to the governor, desired to be received under our protection‡‡ and government, upon the same terms that *Pumham* and *Sacononoco* were. So we causing them to understand the articles, and all the ten commandments of God, and they freely assenting to all,§§ they were solemnly received, and then presented the court with twenty-six fathom of wampum, and the court gave each of them a coat of two yards of cloth, and their dinner; and to them and their men, every one of them, a cup of sac at their departure; so they took leave, and went away very joyful."|| || Tradition says that Agawam, in Ipswich, was his place of residence, and that his bones were early found there; that his squaw for some time survived him, and had a piece of land that she could not dispose of, or that none were allowed to purchase.¶¶

We have too long delayed the biography of a chief early known both

---

* Hist. N. England.

† This is doubtless the most correct spelling of his name. It is scarce spelt twice alike in the MS. records.

‡ Records of Gen. Court, v. 381. § Prince, 357. || *Hubbard's N. E.* 145.

¶ Quarter-master, "living then in a little hut upon his father's island on this side of Jeofry's Neck." *MS. Narrative.*

** *Cobbet's MS. Narrative.* †† *Ousamequin*, or *Massasoit.*

‡‡ They desired this from their great fear of the Mohawks, it is said.

§§ The articles which they subscribed, will be seen at large when the *Manuscript Hist. of the Praying Indians, by Daniel Gookin*, shall be published. They do not read precisely as rendered by *Winthrop*.

|| || Winthrop's Journal. ¶¶ MS. Hist. of Newbury, by J. *Coffin*.

in Plimouth and Massachusetts, which seemed necessary to preserve the continuity of our history—*Canonicus*,* the great sachem of the Narragansets. He was contemporary with *Miantunnomoh*, who was his nephew. We know not the time of his birth, but a son of his was at Boston in 1631, the next year after it was settled. But the time of his death is minutely recorded by Governor *Winthrop*, in his "Journal," thus: "June 4, 1647. *Canonicus*, the great sachem of Narraganset, died, a very old man." He is generally supposed to have been about 85 years of age when he died.

He is mentioned with great respect by Rev. *Roger Williams*,† in the year 1654. After observing that *many hundreds* of the English were witnesses to the friendly disposition of the Narragansets, he says, "Their late famous long-lived *Caunonicus* so lived and died, and in the same most honorable manner and solemnity, (in their way,) as *you* laid to sleep *your* prudent peace-maker, Mr. *Winthrop*, did they honor this their prudent and peaceable prince; yea, through all their towns and countries how frequently do many, and oft times, our Englishmen travel alone with safety and loving kindness?"

It will be proper in this place to give some general account of the country and nation of our chief. The bounds of Narraganset were, as described in the times of the sachems,‡ "Pautuckit River, Quenebage [Quabaog] and Nipmuck," northerly; "westerly by a brook called Wequapaug, not far§ from Paquatuck River; southerly by the sea, or main ocean; and easterly by the Nanhiganset Bay, wherein lieth many islands, by deeds bought of the Nanhiganset sachems." Coweesett and Niantick, though sometimes applied to this country, were names only of places within it. According to Mr. *Gookin*, "the territory of their sachem extended about 30 or 40 miles from Sekunk River and Narragansitt Bay, including Rhode Island and other islands in that bay." Pawcatuck River separated them from the Pequots. This nation, under *Canonicus*, had, in 1642, arrived at the zenith of its greatness, and was supposed to contain a population of *thirty thousand*. This estimate was by *Richard Smith*, jr., who, with his father, lived in their country.

A census of those calling themselves a remnant of the Narragansets, taken Feb. 1832, was 315; only seven of whom were unmixed. The Indians themselves make their number 364.||

Of the early times of this nation, some of the first English inhabitants learned from the old Indians, that they had, previous to their arrival, a sachem named *Tashtassuck*, and their encomiums upon his wisdom and valor were much the same as the Delawares reported of their great chief *Tamany*; that since, there had not been his equal, &c. *Tashtassuck* had but two children, a son and daughter; these he joined in marriage, because he could find none worthy of them out of his family. The product of this marriage was four sons, of whom *Canonicus* was the oldest.¶

When Mr. *John Oldham* was killed near Block Island, and an investigation set on foot by the English to ascertain the murderers, they were fully satisfied that *Canonicus* and *Miantunnomoh* had no hand in the affair, but that "the six other Narraganset sachems had." It is no wonder that he

---

* This spelling does not convey the true pronunciation of the name; other spellings will be noticed in the course of his biography. Its sound approached so near the Latin word canonicus, that it became confounded with it.

† Manuscript letter to the governor of Massachusetts.

‡ See 3 Col. Mass. Hist. Soc. i. 210.

§ Four or five miles, says *Gookin*.

|| MS. letter of Rev. Mr. *Ely*.

¶ Hutchinson, i. 458, who met with this account in MS.; but we do not give implicit credit to it, as, at best, it is tradition.

should have taken great offence at the conduct of the English concerning the death of *Miantunnomoh*. The Warwick settlers considered it a great piece of injustice, and Mr. *Samuel Gorton* wrote a letter for *Canonicus* to the government of Massachusetts, notifying them that he had resolved to be revenged upon the Mohegans. Upon this the English despatched messengers to Narraganset to inquire of *Canonicus* whether he authorized the letter. He treated them with great coldness, and would not admit them into his wigwam for the space of two hours after their arrival, although it was exceedingly rainy. When they were admitted, he frowned upon them, and gave them answers foreign to the purpose, and referred them to *Pessacus*. This was a very cold reception, compared with that which the messengers received when sent to him for information respecting the death of Mr *Oldham*. "They returned with acceptance and good success of their business; observing in the sachem much state, great command of his men, and marvellous wisdom in his answers; and in the carriage of the whole treaty, clearing himself and his neighbors of the murder, and offering revenge of it, yet upon very safe and wary conditions."

This sachem is said to have governed in great harmony with his nephew. "The chiefest government in the country is divided between a younger sachem, *Miantunnomu*, and an elder sachem, *Caunaunacus*, of about fourscore years old,* this young man's uncle; and their agreement in the government is remarkable. The old sachem will not be offended at what the young sachem doth; and the young sachem will not do what he conceives will displease his uncle."† With this passage before him, Mr. *Durfee* versifies as follows, in his poem called *Whatcheer*:—

"Two mighty chiefs, one cautious, wise, and old,
One young, and strong, and terrible in fight,
All Narraganset and Coweset hold;
One lodge they build—one counsel fire they light."

"At a meeting of the commissioners of the United Colonies at Boston, vij Sept., 1643," it was agreed that Massachusetts, in behalf of the other colonies, "give *Conoonacus* and the Nanohiggunsets to understand, that from time to time" they have taken notice of their violation of the covenant between them, notwithstanding the great manifestations of their love to them by the English; that they had concurred with *Miantunnomoh* in his late mischievous plots, by which he had intended "to root out the body of the English" from the country, by gifts and allurements to other Indians; and that he had invaded *Uncas*, contrary to the "tripartie covenant" between himself. *Uncas* and Connecticut. Therefore, knowing "how peaceable *Conanacus* and *Mascus*, the late father of *Myantenomo*, governed that great people," they ascribed the late "tumults and outbreakings" to the malicious, rash and ambitious spirit of *Miantunnomoh* more than to "any affected way of their own."

Notwithstanding, *Miantunnomoh* being now put to death, the English and their confederate Indian sachems, namely, "Vncus, sagamore of the Mohegins, and his people, *Woosamequine* and his people, *Sacanocoe* and his people, *Pumham* and his people, were disposed, they said, still to have peace with the Narragansets; but should expect a more faithful observance of their agreement than they had shown hitherto." This determination was to be immediately laid before them, and a prompt answer demanded.

We have yet to go a step back to relate some matters of much interest in the history of this chief. It is related by Mr. *Edward Winslow*, in his "Good News from New England,"‡ that in February, 1622, O. S. *Canon-*

* This was written about 1643.
† Col. R. I. Hist. Soc. vol. i.
‡ 1 Col. Mass. Hist. Soc. viii.

icus sent into Plimouth, by one of his men, a bundle of arrows, bound with a rattlesnake's skin, and there left them, and retired. The Narragansets, who were reported at this time "many thousand strong," hearing of the weakness of the English, "began, (says the above-named author,) to breath forth many threats against us," although they had the last summer "desired and obtained peace with us."—"Insomuch as the common talk of our neighbor Indians on all sides was of the preparation they made to come against us." They were now emboldened from the circumstance that the English had just added to their numbers, but not to their arms nor provisions. The ship Fortune had, not long before, landed 35 persons at Plimouth, and the Narragansets seem to have been well informed of all the circumstances. This, (says Mr. *Winslow*,) "occasioned them to slight and brave us with so many threats as they did. At length came one of them to us, who was sent by *Conaucus*, their chief sachem or king, accompanied with one *Tokamahamon*, a friendly Indian. This messenger inquired for *Tisquantum*, our interpreter, who not being at home, seemed rather to be glad than sorry; and leaving for him a bundle of new arrows, lapped in a rattlesnake's skin, desired to depart with all expedition."

When *Squanto* was made acquainted with the circumstance, he told the English that it was a challenge for war. Governor *Bradford* took the rattlesnake's skin, and filled it with powder and shot, and returned it to *Canonicus*; at the same time instructing the messenger to bid him defiance, and invite him to a trial of strength. The messenger, and his insulting carriage, had the desired effect upon *Canonicus*, for he would not receive the skin, and it was cast out of every community of the Indians, until it at last was returned to Plimouth, and all its contents. This was a demonstration that he was awed into silence and respect of the English.

In a grave assembly, upon a certain occasion, *Canonicus* thus addressed *Roger Williams*: "I have never suffered any wrong to be offered to the English since they landed, nor never will;" and often repeated the word *Wunnaunewayean*. "If the Englishman speak true, if he mean truly, then shall I go to my grave in peace, and hope that the English and my posterity shall live in love and peace together."

When Mr. *Williams* said he hoped he had no cause to question the Englishmen's wunnaumwa onck, that is, faithfulness, having long been acquainted with it, *Canonicus* took a stick, and, breaking it into ten pieces, related ten instances wherein they had proved false; laying down a piece at each instance. Mr. *Williams* satisfied him that he was mistaken in some of them, and as to others he agreed to intercede with the governor, who, he doubted not, would make satisfaction for them.

In 1635, Rev. *Roger Williams* found *Canonicus* and *Miantunnomoh* carrying on a bloody war against the Wampanoags. By his intercession an end was put to it, and all the sachems grew much into his favor; especially *Canonicus*, whose "heart (he says) was stirred up to love me as his son to his last gasp." He sold the Island of Rhode Island to *William Coddington, Roger Williams,* and others. A son of *Canonicus*, named *Mriksah*, is named by *Williams* as inheriting his father's spirit.* This son is also called *Meika*, who, after his father's death, was chief sachem of the Narragansets, and was said to have been his eldest son. Many particulars of him will be found in our progress onward.

At the time of the Pequot war, much pains was taken to secure the friendship of *Canonicus* more firmly. Mr. *Williams* wrote to Governor *Winthrop* concerning him as follows: "Sir, if any thing be sent to the princes, I find *Canounicus* would gladly accept of a box of eight or ten pounds of sugar, and indeed he told me he would thank Mr. Governor for

* Manuscript letter.

a box full." In another letter which Mr. *Williams* sent to the same by *Miantunnomoh* himself, he says, "I am bold to request a word of advice of you concerning a proposition made by *Caunounicus* and *Miantunnomu* to me some half year since. *Caunounicus* gave an island in this bay to Mr. *Oldham*, by name *Chibachuwese*, upon condition, as it should seem, that he would dwell there near unto them." The death of Mr. *Oldham*, it appears, prevented his accepting it, and they offered it to Mr. *Williams* upon the same conditions; but he first desired to know whether in so doing it would be perfectly agreeable to Massachusetts, and that he had no idea of accepting, without paying the chiefs for it: said he told them "once and again, that for the present he mind not to remove; but if he had it, would give them satisfaction for it, and build a little house and put in some swine, as understanding the place to have store of fish and good feeding for swine." When *Miantunnomoh* heard that some of the Massachusetts men thought of occupying some of the islands, *Canonicus*, he says, desired he would accept of half of it, "it being spectacle-wise, and between a mile or two in circuit;" but Mr. *Williams* wrote to inform them that, if be had any, he desired the whole. This was not long before the Pequot war, which probably put a stop to further negotiation upon the subject.

There was another chief of the same name, in Philip's war, which Mr. *Hubbard* denominates "the great sachem of the Narragansets," and who, "distrusting the proffers of the English, was slain in the woods by the Mohawks, his squaw surrendering herself: by this means her life was spared."

In 1632, a war broke out between the Narragansets and the Pequots, on account of disputed right to the lands between Paucatuck River and Wecapaug Brook.* It was a tract of considerable consequence, being about ten miles wide, and fifteen or twenty long. *Canonicus* drew along with him, besides his own men, several of the Massachusetts sagamores. This was maintained with ferocity and various success, until 1635, when the Pequots were driven from it, but who, it would seem, considered themselves but little worsted; for *Canonicus*, doubting his ability to hold possession long, and ashamed to have it retaken from him, made a present of it to one of his captains, who had fought heroically in conquering it; but he never held possession. The name of this captain was *Sochoso*, a Pequot, who had deserted from them and espoused the cause of *Canonicus*, who made him a chief.

It is said that, in the war between *Uncas* and *Miantunnomoh*, two of the sons of *Canonicus* fought on the side of *Miantunnomoh*, and were wounded when he was taken prisoner at Sachem's Plain.

Canonicus has been the subject of a poem which was published at Boston, in 1803.† Among the tolerable passages are the following:—

"A mighty prince, of venerable age,
  A peerless warrior, but of peace the friend;
His breast a treasury of maxims sage—
  His arm, a host—to punish or defend."

Canonicus, at the age of 84 years, is made to announce his approaching dissolution to his people thus:—

* "The natives are very exact and punctual in the bounds of their lands, belonging to this or that prince or people, even to a river, brook, &c. And I have known them make bargain and sale amongst themselves, for a small piece, or quantity of ground; notwithstanding a sinful opinion amongst many, that Christians have right to heathen's lands." *R. Williams*.

† By *John Lathrop*, A. M. in 8vo.

"I die.—My friends, you have no cause to grieve:
To abler hands my regal power I leave.
Our god commands—to fertile realms I haste,
Compared with which your gardens are a waste.
There in full bloom eternal spring abides,
And swarming fishes glide through azure tides;
Continual sunshine gilds the cloudless skies,
No mists conceal Keesuckquand from our eyes."

About 1642, a son of *Canonicus* died, at which his grief was very great; insomuch that, "having buried his son, he burned his own palace, and all his goods in it, to a great value, in solemn remembrance of his son."

Like other men ignorant of science, *Canonicus* was superstitious, and was greatly in fear of the English, chiefly, perhaps, from a belief in their ability to hurt him by enchantment, which belief very probably was occasioned by the story that *Squanto* circulated, of which, in a previous chapter, we have spoken. When *Roger Williams* fled into his country, he at first viewed him with distrust, and would only frown upon him; at length he accused him, as well as the other English, of sending the plague among the Indians; but, as we have said before, he soon became reconciled to him, gave him lands, and even protected him. They became mutual helps to each other, and, but for animosities among the English themselves, it may be fair to conclude, friendship would have continued with the Narragansets through several generations.

Our attention is now called to consider the lives of several sachems, who, though of less notoriety than the one of which we have just taken a view, will be found by no means wanting in interest.

Montowampate, sagamore of Lynn and Marblehead, was known more generally among the whites as *Sagamore James*. He was son of *Nanepashemet*, and brother of *Wonohaquaham* and *Winnepurkitt*.* He died in 1633, of the small-pox, "with most of his people. It is said that these two promised, if ever they recovered, to live with the English, and serve their God."† The histories of those times give a melancholy picture of the distresses caused by the small-pox among the "wretched natives." "There are," says *Mather*, "some old planters surviving to this day, who helped to bury the dead Indians; even whole families of them all dead at once. In one of the wigwams they found a poor infant sucking at the breast of the dead mother."‡ The same author observes that, before the disease began, the Indians had begun to quarrel with the English about the bounds of their lands, "but God ended the controversy by sending the small-pox among the Indians at Saugus, who were before that time exceedingly numerous."

We have mentioned another of the family of *Nanepashemet*, also a sachem. This was *Wonohaquaham*, called by the English *Sagamore John*, of Winisimet. His residence was at what was then called *Rumneymarsh*, part of which is now in Chelsea and part in Saugus.* As early as 1631, he had cause to complain that some of the English settlers had burnt two of his wigwams. "Which wigwams," says Governor *Dudley*,|| "were not inhabited, but stood in a place convenient for their shelter, when, upon occasion, they should travel that way." The court, upon examination, found that a servant of Sir *R. Saltonstall* had been the means of the mischief, whose master was ordered to make satisfaction, "which he did by seven yards of cloth, and that his servant pay him, at the end of his time, fifty shillings sterling."¶ *Sagamore John* died at

* Lewis's Hist. Lynn, 16, 17.
† Hist. of New England, 195.
‡ Relation, &c. 23.
|| Letter to the Countess of Lincoln, in Col. Mass. Hist. Soc.
¶ Prince's Chronology.

Winisimet, in 1633, of the small-pox.* He desired to become acquainted with the Englishmen's God, in his sickness, and requested them to take his two sons and instruct them in Christianity, which they did.†

Winnepurkitt,‡ who married a daughter of *Passaconaway*, makes considerable figure also in our Indian annals. He was born about 1616, and succeeded *Montowampate* at his death, in 1633. The English called him *George Rumneymarsh*, and at one time he was proprietor of Deer Island, in Boston harbor. "In the latter part of his life, he went to Barbadoes. It is supposed that he was carried there with the prisoners who were sold for slaves, at the end of *Philip's* war. He died soon after his return, in 1684, at the house of *Muminquash*, aged 68 years." *Ahawayetsquaine*, daughter of *Poquanum*, is also mentioned as his wife, by whom he had several children.§

Manatahqua, called also *Black-william*, was a sachem, and proprietor of Nahant, when the adjacent country was settled by the whites. His father lived at Swampscot, and was also a sagamore, but probably was dead before the English settled in the country.‖ A traveller in this then¶ wilderness world, thus notices *William*, and his possessing Nahant. "One *Black-william*, an *Indian Duke*, out of his generosity gave this place in general to the plantation of Saugus, so that no other can appropriate it to himself." He was a great friend to the whites, but his friendship was repaid, as was that of many others of that and even much later times. There was a man by the name of *Walter Bagnall*, nicknamed *Great Wot*, "a wicked fellow," who had much wronged the Indians,** killed near the mouth of Saco River, probably by some of those whom he had defrauded. This was in October, 1631. As some vessels were upon the eastern coast in search of pirates, in January, 1633, they put in at Richmond's Island, where they fell in with *Black-william*. This was the place where *Bagnall* had been killed about two years before, but whether he had any thing to do with it, does not appear, nor do I find that any one, even his murderers, pretended he was any way implicated; but out of revenge for *Bagnall's* death, these pirate hunters hanged *Black-william*. On the contrary, it was particularly mentioned†† that *Bagnall* was killed by *Squidrayset* and his men, some Indians belonging to that part of the country.

This *Squidrayset*, or *Scitterygusset*, for whose act *Manatahqua* suffered, was the first sachem who deeded land in Falmouth, Maine. A creek near the mouth of Presumpscot River perpetuates his name to this day. Mr. *Willis* supposes he was sachem of the Aucocisco tribe, who inhabited between the Androscoggin and Saco rivers; and that from Aucocisco comes Casco.‡‡ There can be but little doubt that *Bagnall* deserved his fate,§§ if any deserve such; but the other was the act of white men, and we leave the reader to draw the parallel between the two: perhaps he will inquire, *Were the murderers* of MANATAHQUA *brought to justice*? All we can answer is, *The records are silent*. Perhaps it was considered an *offset* to the murder of *Bagnall*.

Nattahattawants, in the year 1642, sold to *Simon Willard*, in behalf of "Mr. *Winthrop*, Mr. *Dudley*, Mr. *Nowell*, and Mr. *Alden*," a large tract

---

* History of New England, 195, 650.

† Wonder-working Providence.

‡ Spelt also *Winnaperket*.

§ Hist. Lynn.

‖ Hist. N. Eng.

¶ 1633. *William Wood*, author of *New Eng. Prospect*.

** Winthrop's Journal, i. 62, 63.

†† Winthrop, ib.

‡‡ Col. Maine Hist. Soc. i. 68.

§§ He had in about three years, by extortion, as we infer from *Winthrop*, accumulated about £400 from among the Indians. See Journal *ut supra*.

of land upon both sides Concord River. "Mr. *Winthrop*, our present governor, 1260 acres, Mr. *Dudley*, 1500 acres, on the S. E. side of the river, Mr. *Nowell*, 500 acres, and Mr. *Allen*, 500 acres, on the N. E. side of the river, and in consideration hereof the said *Simon* giueth to the said *Nattahattawants* six fadom of waompampege, one wastcoat, and one breeches, and the said Nattahattawants doth covenant and bind himself, that hee nor any other Indians shall set traps within this ground, so as any cattle might recieve hurt thereby, and what cattle shall receive hurt by this meanes, hee shall be lyable to make it good." [In the deed, *Nattahattawants* is called sachem of that land.]

Witnessed by three whites. *The mark of* ● NATAHATTAWANTS. *The mark of* ● WINNIPIN, *an Indian that traded for him.**

The name of this chief, as appears from documents copied by Mr. *Shattuck*,† was understood *Tahattawan, Tahattawants, Attawan, Attawanee,* and *Ahatawanee*. He was sachem of Musketaquid, since Concord, and a supporter and propagator of Christianity among his people, and an honest and upright man. The celebrated *Waban* married his eldest daughter. *John Tahattawan* was his son, who lived at Nashoba, where he was chief ruler of the praying Indians—a deserving Indian. He died about 1670. His widow was daughter of *John*, sagamore of Patucket, upon the Merrimack, who married *Oonamog*, another ruler of the praying Indians, of Marlborough. Her only son by *Tahattawan*‡ was killed by some white ruffians, who came upon them while in their wigwams, and his mother was badly wounded at the same time. Of this affair we shall have occasion elsewhere to be more particular. *Naanashquaw*, another daughter, married *Naanishcow*, called *John Thomas*, who died at Natick, aged 110 years.

We know very little of a sachem of the name of *Wahgumacut*,§ except that he lived upon Connecticut River, and came to Boston in 1631, with a request to the governor "to have some English to plant in his country;" and as an inducement said he would "find them corn, and give them, yearly, 80 skins of beaver." The governor, however, dismissed him without giving him any encouragement; doubting, it seems, the reality of his friendship. But it is more probable that he was sincere, as he was at this time in great fear of the Pequots, and judged that if some of the English would reside with him, he should be able to maintain his country.

There accompanied *Wahgumacut* to Boston an Indian named *Jack-*

---

* Suffolk Records of Deeds, vol. i. No. 34. † Hist. Concord, Mass. *passim* chap. i.

‡ Mr. *Gookin* writes this name *Tohatooner*, that of the father *Tanattawarre*. *MS.* Hist. Praying Indians, 105.

§ *Wahginnacut*, according to Mr. *Savage's* reading of *Winthrop*. Our text is according to *Prince*, who also used *Winthrop* in MS. It is truly diverting to see how the author of *Tales of the Indians* has displayed his invention upon the passage in *Winthrop's Journal* bringing to our knowledge this chief. We will give the passage of *Winthrop*, that the reader may judge whether great ignorance, or misrepresentation "of set purpose" be chargeable to him. "He [Gov. *Winthrop*] discovered after [*Wahginnacut* was gone,] that the said sagamore is a very treacherous man, and at war with the *Pekoath* (a far greater sagamore.") Now, every child that has read about the Indians, it seems to us, ought to know that the meaning of *Pekoath* was mistaken by the governor, and no more meant a chief than the *Massasoits* meant what the Plimouth people first supposed it to mean. In the one case, the name of a tribe was mistaken for that of a chief, and in the other the chief for the tribe. Mistakes of this kind were not uncommon before our fathers became acquainted with the country. *Winthrop* says, too, the Mohawks was a great sachem. Now, who ever thought there was a chief of that name?

straw,* who was his interpreter.† We have labored to find some further particulars of him, but all that we can ascertain with certainty, is, that he had lived some time in England with Sir *Walter Ralegh*.‡ How Sir *Walter* came by him, does not satisfactorily appear. Captains *Amidas* and *Barlow* sailed to America in his employ, and on their return carried over

* Probably so named from the Maidstone minister, who flourished in *Wat Tyler's* rebellion, and whose real name was *John Ball*, but afterwards nick-named *Jack Straw*. He became chaplain to *Wat's* army, they having let him out of prison. A text which he made great use of in preaching to his liberators was this:—

When Adam dalfe and Eve span,
Who was then a gentleman?

This we apprehend was construed, *Down with the nobility!* See *Rapin's Eng.* i. 457. In *Kennet*, i. 247, *John Wraw* is called *Jack Straw*. He was beheaded.

† *Sagamore John* was also with him.

‡ "The imputation of the first bringing in of tobacco into England lies on this heroic knight." *Winstanley's Worthies*, 259. "Besides the consumption of the purse, and impairing of our inward parts, the immoderate, vain and phantastical abuse of the hellish weed, corrupteth the natural sweetness of the breath, stupifieth the brain; and indeed is so prejudicial to the general esteem of our country." Ibid. 211. Whether *Jack-straw* were the servant who acted a part in the often-told anecdote of Sir *Walter Ralegh's* smoking tobacco, on its first being taken to England, we shall not presume to assert, but for the sake of the anecdote we will admit the fact; it is variously related, but is said to be, in substance, as follows. At one time, it was so very unpopular to use tobacco in any way in England, that many who had got attached to it, used it only privately. Sir *Walter* was smoking in his study, at a certain time, and, being thirsty, called to his servant to bring him a tankard of beer. *Jack* hastily obeyed the summons, and Sir *Walter*, forgetting to cease smoking, was in the act of spouting a volume of smoke from his mouth when his servant entered. *Jack*, seeing his master smoking prodigiously at the mouth, thought no other but he was all on fire inside, having never seen such a phenomenon in all England before; dashed the quart of liquor at once in his face, and ran out screaming, "Massa's a fire! Massa's a fire!"

Having dismissed the servant, every one might reasonably expect a few words concerning his master. Sir *Walter Ralegh* may truly be said to have lived in an age fruitful in great and worthy characters. Capt. *John Smith* comes to our notice through his agency, and the renowned first English circumnavigator was his cotemporary. He, like the last named, was born in the county of Devonshire, in 1552, in the parish of Budley. Sir *Humphrey Gilbert*, so well known in our annals, was his half brother, his father having married Sir *Humphrey's* mother, a widow,* by whom he had *Walter*, a fourth son.† The great successes and discoveries of the celebrated admiral Sir *Francis Drake*, gave a new impetus to the English nation in maritime affairs, and consequent thereupon was the settlement of North America; as great an era, to say the least, as was ever recorded in history. No one shone more conspicuous in those undertakings than Sir *Walter Ralegh*. After persevering a long time, he established a colony in Virginia, in 1607. He was a man of great valor and address, and a favorite with the great Queen *Elizabeth*, the promoter of his undertakings, one of whose "maids of honor" he married. In this affair some charge him with having first dishonored that lady, and was for a time under the queen's displeasure in consequence, but marrying her restored him to favor. The city of Ralegh in Virginia was so named by his direction. He was conspicuous with *Drake* and *Howard* in the destruction of the Spanish armada in 1588. On the death of the queen, he was imprisoned almost 13 years in the tower of London, upon the charge of treason. It was during his imprisonment that he wrote his great and learned work, the History of the World. The alleged crime of treason has long since been viewed by all the world as without foundation, and the punishment of *Ralegh* reflects all its blackness upon the character of *James* I. The ground of the charge was, that *Ralegh* and others were in a conspiracy against the king, and were designing to place on the throne *Arabella Stewart*.‡ He was never pardoned, although the king set him at liberty, and permitted him to go on an expedition to South America in search of a gold mine of which he had gained some intimations in a previous visit to those countries. His attempt to find gold failed, but he took the town of St. Thomas, and established in it a garrison. This was a depredation, as Spain and England were then at peace, but *Ralegh* had the king's commission. The Spanish ambassador complained

* "Of *Otho Gilbert*, of Compton, Esq." *Polwhele's Hist. Devon*, ii. 219.

† Stith, Hist. Virginia, 7. Second son, says Mr. *Polwhele*, Devon, ii. 219.

‡ Rapin's Eng. ii. 161.

two natives from Virginia, whose names were *Wanchese* and *Manteo*.* It is barely possible that one of these was afterwards *Jack-straw*.

A Nipmuck Indian, of no small note in his time, it may in the next place be proper to notice.

James Printer, or *James-the-printer*, was the son of *Naoas*, brother of *Tukapewillin*† and *Anaweakin*. When a child, he was instructed at the Indian charity school, at Cambridge. In 1659, he was put apprentice to *Samuel Green*, to learn the printer's business;‡ and he is spoken of as having run away from his master in 1675. If, after an apprenticeship of 16 years, one could not leave his master without the charge of absconding, at least, both the master and apprentice should be pitied. In relation to this matter, Mr. *Hubbard* says,§ "He had attained some skill in printing, and might have attained more, had he not, like a false villain, ran away from his master before his time was out." And the same author observes that the name printer was superadded to distinguish him from others named *James*.

Dr. *I. Mather* || has this record of *James-printer*. "July 8, [1676.] Whereas the council at Boston had lately emitted a declaration, signifying, that such Indians as did, within 14 days, come in to the English, might hope for mercy, divers of them did this day return from among the Nipmucks. Among others, *James*, an Indian, who could not only read and write, but had learned the art of printing, notwithstanding his apostasy, did venture himself upon the mercy and truth of the English declaration, which he had seen and read, promising for the future to venture his life against the common enemy. He and the other now come in, affirm that very many of the Indians are dead since this war began; and that more have died by the hand of God, in respect of diseases, fluxes and fevers, which have been amongst them, than have been killed with the sword." Mr. Thomas says,¶ it was owing to the amor patriœ of *James-printer* that he left his master and joined in *Philip's* war. But how much *amor*

loudly against the transaction, and the miserable *James*, to extricate himself, and appease the Spanish king, ordered *Ralegh* to be seized on his return, who, upon the old charge of treason, was sentenced to be beheaded, which was executed upon him 29th Oct. 1618.* "I shall only hint," says Dr. *Polwhele*,† "that the execution of this great man, whom *James* was advised to sacrifice to the advancement of the peace with Spain, hath left an indelible stain on the memory of that misguided monarch." It appears from another account‡ that Sir *Walter*, on arriving at the mouth of the Oronoko, was taken "desperately sick," and sent forward a company under one of his captains in search of the gold mine. That they were met by the Spaniards, who attacked them, and that this was the cause of their assaulting St. Thomas, and being obliged to descend the river without effecting the object they were upon.

The following circumstance respecting the celebrated History of the World, not being generally known, cannot but be acceptable to the reader. The first volume (which is what we have of it) was published before he was imprisoned the last time. Just before his execution, he sent for the publisher of it. When he came, Sir *Walter* took him by the hand, and, "after some discourse, askt him how that work of his sold. Mr. *Burre* [the name of the publisher] returned this answer, that it had sold so slowly that it had undone him. At which words of his, Sir *Walter Ralegh*, stepping to his desk, reaches his other part of his history to Mr. *Burre*, which he had brought down to the times he lived in; clapping his hand on his breast, he took the other unprinted part of his works into his hand, with a sigh, saying, 'Ah, my friend, hath the first part undone thee, the second volume shall undo no more; this ungrateful world is unworthy of it.' When, immediately going to the fire-side, threw it in, and set his foot on it till it was consumed."§

* See *Cayley's* Life Sir *W. Ralegh*, i. 70. ed. Lond. 1816, 2 vols. 8vo.

† Some author of Indian tales might delight himself for a long time in ringing changes on this Indian preacher's name, without inventing any new ones; for it is not, as I remember, spelt twice alike in our authorities.

‡ Thomas, Hist. Printing. § Narrative, 96. || Brief Hist. 89.

¶ Hist. Printing, i. 290.

* Tindal's notes in Rapin, ii. 195. † Hist. Devonshire, i. 259.

‡ Winstanley, Worthies, 256. § Ibid. 257

vatricæ he must have had to have kept him an apprentice 16 years is not mentioned.

It was in 1685 that the second edition of the famous Indian Bible was completed. From the following testimony of Mr. *Eliot* will be seen how much the success of that undertaking was considered to depend on *James-the-printer*. In 1683, in writing to the Hon. *Robert Boyle* at London, Mr. *Eliot* says, "I desire to see it done before I die, and I am so deep in years, that I cannot expect to live long; besides, we have but one man, viz. the *Indian Printer*, that is able to compose the sheets, and correct the press with understanding." In another, from the same to the same, dated a year after, he says, "Our slow progress needeth an apology. We have been much hindered by the sickness the last year. Our workmen have been all sick, and we have but few hands, (at printing,) one Englishman, and a boy, and one Indian," &c.

This Indian was undoubtedly *James-the-printer*. And Mr. *Thomas* adds, "Some of *James's* descendants were not long since living in Grafton; they bore the surname of *Printer*."*

There was an Indian named *Job Nesutan*, who was also concerned in the first edition of the Indian Bible. He was a valiant soldier, and went with the English of Massachusetts, in the first expedition to Mount Hope, where he was slain in battle. "He was a very good linguist in the English tongue, and was Mr. *Eliot's* assistant and interpreter in his translation of the Bible and other books in the Indian language."†

In a letter of the commissioners of the U.C. of N. England, to the corporation in England, we find this postscript.—"Two of the Indian youths formerly brought up to read and write, are put apprentice; the one to a carpenter, the other to Mr. *Green* the printer, who take their trades and follow their business very well." *James-the-printer* was probably one of these. *Nesutan*, we presume, was only an interpreter. The above-mentioned letter was dated 10th Sept. 1660.

In 1698, *James* was teacher to five Indian families at Hassinammisco.‡ In 1709, he seems to have got through with his apprenticeship, and to have had some interest in carrying on the printing business. For, in the title pages of the Indian and English Psalter, printed in that year, is this imprint: "BOSTON, N. E. *Upprinthomunne au* B. GREEN, & J. PRINTER, *wutche guhtiantamwe Chapanukke ut New England*, &c. 1709."

We shall now pass to notice a Massachusetts sachem, who, like too many others, does not appear to the best advantage; nevertheless, we doubt not but as much so as he deserves, as by the sequel will he seen. We mean

Kutchmakin, known also by several other names, or variations of the same name; as *Kutshamaquin, Cutshamoquen, Cutchamokin*, and many more, as, in different parts of our work, extracts will necessarily show. He was one of those sachems who, in 1643—4, signed a submission to the English, as has been mentioned in a preceding chapter.

In 1636, *Kutshamakin* sold to the people of Dorchester, Uncataquisset, being the part of that town since called Milton. This, it appears, was at some period his residence. Though he was a sachem under *Woosamequin*, yet, like *Caunbitant*, he was opposed to the settlement of the English in his country. He soon, however, became reconciled to it, and became a Christian. When Mr. *Eliot* desired to know why he was opposed to

---

* Hist. Printing, 292, 293. † Gookin, *Hist. Praying Indians.*

‡ Information from Mr. *E. Tuckerman*, Jr.—Hassinammisco, Hassanamesit, &c. signified a *place of stones*. Thomas, *ut supra*.

his people's becoming Christians, he said, then they would pay him no tribute.

When the English of Massachusetts sent to *Canonicus*, to inquire into the cause of the murder of *John Oldham, Kutshamakin* accompanied them as interpreter, fighter, or whatever was required of him.

As no satisfaction could be had of the Pequots, for the murder of Mr. *Oldham*, it was resolved, in 1636, to send an army into their country "to fight with them," if what, in the opinion of the English, as a recompense, were not to be obtained without. The armament consisted of about 90 men. These first went to Block Island, where they saw a few Indians before they landed, who, after shooting a few arrows, which wounded two of the English, fled. The Indians had here "two plantations, three miles in sunder, and about 60 wigwams, some very large and fair, and above 200 acres of corn." This the English destroyed, "staved seven canoes," and after two days spent in this business, and hunting for Indians without success, sailed to the main land, where *Kutshamakin* performed his part in hastening on the Pequot calamity. Having waylaid one of that nation, he shot and scalped him. The scalp he sent to *Canonicus,* who sent it about among all his sachem friends; thus expressing his approbation of the murder, and willingness to engage his friends to fight for the English. As a further proof of his approval of the act, he not only thanked the English, but gave *Kutshamakin* four fathom of wampum.

Capt. *Lion Gardener* gives us some particulars of this affair, which are very valuable for the light they throw on this part of our early transactions with the Pequots. The affair we have just mentioned happened immediately after *Endicott, Turner* and *Underhill* arrived at Saybrook, from Block Island. Capt. *Gardener* then commanded the fort, who spoke to them as follows of their undertaking: "You come hither to raise these wasps about my ears, and then you will take wing and flee away." It so came to pass; and although he was much opposed to their going, yet they went, agreeably to their instructions. *Gardener* instructed them how to proceed, to avoid being surprised, but the Indians played them a handsome trick, as in the sequel will be heard.

On coming to the Pequot town, they inquired for the sachem,* wishing to parley with him: his people said "he was from home, but within three hours he would come; and so from three to six, and thence to nine, there came none." But the Indians came fearlessly, in great numbers, and spoke to them, through the interpreter, *Kutshamakin,* for some time. This delay was a stratagem which succeeded well; for they rightly guessed that the English had come to injure them in their persons, or property, or both. Therefore, while some were entertaining the English with words, others carried off their effects and hid them. When they had done this, a signal was given, and all the Indians ran away. The English then fell to burning and destroying every thing they could meet with. *Gardener* had sent some of his men with the others, who were unaccountably left on shore when the others reëmbarked, and were pursued, and two of them wounded by the Indians.

"The Bay-men killed not a man, save that one, *Kichomiquim,* an Indian sachem of the Bay, killed a Pequit; and thus began the war between the Indians and us, in these parts."† The Pequots henceforth used every means to kill the English, and many were taken by them, and some tortured in their manner. "Thus far," adds *Gardener,* "I had

---

* *Sassacus,* says *Winthrop,* (i. 194.) but being told he was gone to Long Island, the general demanded to see "the other sachem, &c." which was doubtless *Mononotto.*

† 3 *Col. Hist. Soc.* iii. 141, &c.

written in a book, that all men and posterity might know how and why so many honest men had their blood shed, yea, and some flayed alive, others cut in pieces, and some roasted alive, only because *Kichamokin*, a Bay Indian, killed one Pequot."

To say the least of our author, he had the best possible means *to be correctly informed* of these matters, and we know not that he had any motive to misrepresent them.

Governor *Winthrop* mentions, under date 1646, that Mr. *Eliot* lectured constantly "one week at the wigwam of one *Wabon*, a new sachem near Watertown mill, and the other the next week in the wigwam of *Cutshamekin*, near Dorchester mill." We shall have occasion in another chapter to speak of *Kutshamakin.*

In 1648, *Cutchamekin*, as he was then called, and *Jojeuny* appear as witnesses to a deed made by another Indian called *Cato*, alias *Goodman. Lane* and *Griffin* were the grantees "in behalf of the rest of the people of Sudbury." The tract of land sold adjoined Sudbury, and was five miles square; for which *Cato* received five pounds. *Jojeuny* was brother to *Cato.**

CHAPTER IV.

MIANTUNNOMOH —*His relations—Aids the English in destroying the Pequots —Sells Rhode Island—Anecdote—His difficulties with the English—Visits Boston—His Magnanimity and Independence—Charged with a conspiracy against the whites—Ably repels it*—WAIANDANCE *becomes his secret enemy—His speech to Waiandance and his people—His war with Uncas —His capture and Death—Circumstances of his execution—Participation of the whites therein—Impartial view of that affair—Traditions*—NINIGRET *—His connections and marriage—His wars with Uncas*—MEXAM, *alias* MEXANO—*Ninigret's speech to the English commissioners—Perfidy of Kutshamakin—Affair of Cuttaquin and Uncas—Difficulties about tribute —Character of Ascassassotick—Ninigret plots to cut off the English —Design frustrated by Waiandance—Account of this chief—Ninigret visits the Dutch—Accused by the English of plotting with them—Ably defends himself—Particulars of the affair—Notices of various other Indians—War between Ninigret and Ascassassotick—Participation of Ninigret and his people in Philip's war—Present condition of his descendants —Further account of Pessacus—His speech—Killed by the Mohawks.*

Miantunnomoh† was the son of a chief called *Mascus*, nephew of *Canonicus*, brother or brother-in-law to *Ninigret*,‡ and brother of *Otash*. And from a manuscript§ among the papers of the late Dr. *Trumbull*, it appears that *Mossup*, or *Mosipe*,|| and *Canjanaquond*¶ were also his brothers.

---

* Suffolk Reg. Deeds. There is no name signed to the deed, but in the place thereof, is the picture of some four-legged animal drawn on his back.

† This spelling is according to *Winthrop*: we prefer *Williams's* method, as more correct, which is *Miantunnomu*; but having employed the former in our first edition, it is retained in this. It is, however, oftener written *Myantonimo* now, which only shows another pronunciation. The accent is usually upon the penultimate syllable. See *Callender's Cent. Discourse*, page 1.

‡ MSS. of *R. Williams*.

§ Now published in the *Col. Mass. Hist. Soc.*

|| Called also *Cussusquench*, or *Sucquaneh*, and *Paticus*; that is, *Pessacus*. He "was killed by the Moqui, [Mohawks,] in the wilderness, about 20 miles above Pisataqua, in his travel eastward, in the time of the Indian wars, and other Indians with him, and were buried by order of Major *Waldron*." 3 *Col. Mas. Hist. Soc.*

¶ "Receaued this First of July, 1659, of Majr. *Humfrey Aderton, [Atherton,]* and

"This *Miantonimo,*" says Mr. *Hubbard,* "was a very good personage, [that is, well made,] of tall stature, subtil and cunning in his contrivements, as well as haughty in his designs."*

As early as 1632, this chief came with his wife to Boston, where he staid two nights. He was then known by the name of *Mecumeh.* While here he went to church with the English, and in the mean while, some of his men, twelve of whom had accompanied him, it seems, broke into a house, and committed a theft. Complaint was made to the English governor, who "told the sachem of it, and with some difficulty caused him to make one of his sannaps† beat them." The authors of the mischief were immediately sent out of town, but *Miantunnomoh* and the others, the governor took to his house, "and made much of them."‡

The English seem always to have been more favorably inclined towards other tribes than to the Narragansets, as appears from the stand they took in the wars between them and their enemies. And so long as other tribes succeeded against them, the English were idle spectators; but whenever the scale turned in their favor, they were not slow to intercede.

In the Life of *Canonicus,* the part *Miantunnomoh* exercised in the government of the great nation of the Narragansets is related.

In 1634, Captains *Stone* and *Norton* were killed by the Pequots, and in 1636, Mr. *John Oldham,* by the Indians "near Block Island." *Miantunnomoh* did all in his power to assist in apprehending the murderers, and was at much pains and trouble in furnishing the English with facts relative thereto, from time to time. And when it was told at Boston that there was a cessation of hostilities between the Narragansets and Pequots, *Miantunnomoh* was immediately ordered to appear there, which he did without delay, and agreed to assist them in a war against the Pequots; without whose aid and concurrence, the English would hardly have dared to engage in a war against them at that time.

Early in 1637, to show the governor of Massachusetts that he kept his promise, of warring against the Pequots, *Miantunnomoh* sent by some of his men a Pequot's hand. The war with them now commenced, and though of short duration, destroyed them to such a degree, that they appeared no more as a nation. One hundred of the Narragansets joined themselves with the English in its accomplishment, and received a part of the prisoners as slaves for their services.§ When the war was over, *Miantunnomoh* still adhered to the English, and seized upon such of the Pequots as had made their escape from bondage, and returned them to their English masters; gave up to them his claim of Block Island, and other places where the English had found Pequots, and which they considered as belonging to them by right of conquest.

Rev. *Samuel Gorton* and his associates purchased Shaomet, afterwards called Warwick, from the Earl of Warwick, of *Miantunnornoh,* but as *Gorton* could do nothing right in the eyes of the Puritans of Massachusetts, *Pumham* was instigated to claim said tract of country; and, although a sachem under *Miantunnomoh,*|| did not hesitate, when supported by the

---

the rest of his friends, the sume of 75 pounds in Wampam peag wth seueral other things as gratuity for certaine lands giuen ye said Majr. *Aderton* and his friends, as may appeare by two seuerall deeds of gift. I say receaued by me.

COGINAQUAN *His mark."*
MS. Documents.

* *Hist. New Eng.* 446. † A name the sachems gave their attendants.

‡ *Winthrop's* Journal. § *Miantunnomoh* received eighty. *Mather's Relation,* 39.

|| "The law of the Indians in all America is that the inferior sachems and subjects shall plant and remove at the pleasure of the highest and supreme sachems." *Roger Williams.* This is authority, and we need no other commontary on the arbitrary proceedings of the court of Massachusetts.

English, to assert his claim as chief sachem. And the government of Massachusetts, to give to their interference the appearance of disinterestedness, which it would seem, from their own vindication, they thought there was a chance to doubt, "Send for the foresaid sachems, [who had complained of Mr. *Gorton* and others, through the instigation of the English,] and upon examination find, both by English and Indian testimony, that *Miantonomo* was only a usurper, and had no title to the foresaid lands."* This is against the testimony of every record, and could no more have been believed *then,* than that *Philip* was not sachem of Pokanoket. In all cases of purchase, in those times, the chief sachem's grant was valid, and maintained, in almost every instance, by the purchaser or grantee. It was customary, generally, to make the inferior sachems, and sometimes all their men, presents, but it was by no means a law. The chief sachems often permitted those under them to dispose of lands also, without being called to account. This was precisely the situation of things in the Warwick controversy, of which we shall have occasion again to speak, when we come to the life of *Pumham.*

In March, 1637, *Miantunnomoh,* with four other sachems, sold to *William Coddington* and others, the island now called Rhode Island,† also most of the others in Narraganset bay, "for the full payment of 40 fathom of white peag, to be equally divided" between them. Hence *Miantunnomoh* received eight fathom. He was to "have ten coats and twenty hoes to give to the present inhabitants, that they shall remove themselves from the island before next winter."

On a time previous to 1643, *Roger Williams* delivered a discourse to some Indians at their residence, as he was passing through their country. *Miantunnomoh* was present, and seemed inclined to believe in Christianity. Mr. *Williams,* being much fatigued, retired to rest, while *Miantunnomoh* and others remained to converse upon what they had heard. One said to the chief, "Our fathers have told us that our souls go to the south-west;" *Miantunnomoh* rejoined, "How do you know your souls go to the south-west? did you ever see a soul go that way?" (Still he was rather inclined to believe, as Mr. *Williams* had just said, that they go up to heaven or down to hell.) The other added, "When did he (meaning *Williams*) ever see a soul go up to heaven or down to hell?"

---

* In *manuscript* on file, at the state house, Boston.

† From the same *manuscript document.* The deed of this purchase, a copy of which is in my possession, is dated 24th March, and runs thus: "We, *Canonicas* and *Meantinomie,* the two chief sachems of Naragansets, by virtue of our general command of this Bay, as also the particular subjecting of the dead sachems of Aquednick, Kitackamucknut, themselves and lands unto us, have sold unto Mr. *Coddington* and his friends * * the great Island of Aquidnick, lying from hence [Providence] eastward * * also the marshes, grass upon Qunnonigat and the rest of the islands in the bay, excepting Chabatewece, formerly sold unto Mr. *Winthrop,* the now Gov. of Mass. and Mr. *Williams* of Providence, also the grass upon the rivers and coves about Kitackamuckqut, and from thence to Paupasquat."

"*The mark of* [mark] CONONICUS.
[mark] YOTNESH, [OTASH, *brother of* MIANTUNNOMOH.]
The mark of [mark] MEANTINOMIE.
The mark of [mark] ASOTAMNET.
The mark of [mark] MEIHAMMOH, CANONICUS *his son.*

"This witnesseth that I, *Wanamatanamet,* the present sachem of the island, have received five fathom of wampum and consent to the contents.
The mark of [mark] WANAMATANAMET.

"Memorandum. I, *Osemequon,* freely consent" that they may "make use of any grass or trees on the main land on Pocasicke side," having receiued five fathom of wampum also. *The mark of* [mark] OSAMEQUEN.

We have given the above anecdote, which is thought a good illustration of the mind of man under the influence of a superstitious or prejudiced education.

When it was reported, in 1640, that *Miantunnomoh* was plotting to cut off the English, as will be found mentioned in the account of *Ninigret,* and several English were sent to him to know the truth of the matter, he would not talk with them through a Pequot interpreter, because he was then at war with that nation. In other respects he complied with their wishes and treated them respectfully, agreeing to come to Boston, for the gratification of the government, if they would allow Mr. *Williams* to accompany him. This they would not consent to, and yet he came, agreeably to their desires. We shall presently see who acted best the part of civilized men in this affair. He had refused to use a Pequot interpreter for good reasons, but when he was at Boston, and surrounded by armed men, he was obliged to submit. "The governor being as resolute as he, refused to use any other interpreter, thinking it a dishonor to us to give so much way to them!" The great wisdom of the government now displayed itself in the person of Gov. *Thomas Dudley*. It is not to be expected but that *Miantunnomoh* should resent their proceedings; for to the above insult they added others; "would show him no countenance nor admit him to dine at our table, as formerly he had done, till he had acknowledged his failing, &c., which he readily did."* By their own folly, the English had made themselves jealous of a powerful chief, and they appear ever ready afterwards to credit evil reports of him.

That an independent chief should be obliged to conform to transitory notions upon such an occasion, is absolutely ridiculous; and the justness of the following remark from him was enough to have shamed good men into their senses. He said, "*When your people come to me they are permitted to use their own fashions, and I expect the same liberty when I come to you.*"

In 1642, Connecticut became very suspicious of *Miantunnomoh,* and urged Massachusetts to join them in a war against him. Their fears no doubt grew out of the consideration of the probable issue of a war with Uncas in his favor, which was now on the point of breaking out. Even Massachusetts did not think their suspicious well founded; yet, according to their request, they sent to *Miantunnomoh,* who, as usual, gave them satisfactory answers, and, agreeably to their request, came again to Boston. Two days were employed by the court of Massachusetts in deliberating with him, and we are astonished at the wisdom of the great chief, even as reported by his enemies.

That a simple man of nature, who never knew courts or law, should cause such acknowledgments as follow, from the *civilized* and *wise,* will always be contemplated with intense admiration. "When he came," says *Winthrop,* "the court was assembled, and before his admission, we considered how to treat with him, for we knew him to be a very subtle man." When he was admitted, "he was set down at the lower end of the table, over against the governor," but would not at any time speak upon business unless some of his counsellors were present; saying, "he would have them present, that they might bear witness with him, at his return home, of all his sayings." The same author further says, "In all his answers he was very deliberate, and showed good understanding in the principles of justice and equity, and ingenuity withal."

He now asked for his accusers, urging, that if they could not establish their allegations, they ought to suffer what he expected to, if they did;

---

* *Winthrop's Journal.*

but the court said *they knew of none*, that is, they knew not whom they were, and therefore gave no credit to the reports until they had advised him according to a former agreement. He then said, "If you did not give credit to it, why then did you disarm the Indians?" Massachusetts having just then disarmed some of the Merrimacks under some pretence. "He gave divers reasons," says Gov. *Winthrop*,* "why we should hold him free of any such conspiracy, and why we should conceive it was a report raised by *Uncas*, &c. and therefore offered to meet *Uncas*, and would prove to his face his treachery against the English, &c., and told us he would come to us at any time," although he said some had tried to dissuade him, saying that the English would put him to death, yet he feared nothing, as he was innocent of the charges against him.†

The punishment due to those who had raised the accusations, bore heavily upon his breast, and "he put it to our consideration what damage it had been to him, in that he was forced to keep his men at home, and not suffer them to go forth on hunting, &c., till he had given the English satisfaction." After two days spent in talk, the council issued to the satisfaction of the English.

During the council, a table was set by itself for the Indians, which *Miantunnomoh* appears not to have liked, and "would not eat, until some food had been sent him from that of the governor's."

That wisdom seems to have dictated to Massachusetts, in her answer to Connecticut, must be acknowledged; but as justice to *Miantunnomoh* abundantly demanded such decision, credit in this case is due only to them, as to him who does a good act because it was his interest so to do. They urged Connecticut not to commence war alone, "alleging how dishonorable it would be to us all, that, while we were upon treaty with the Indians, they should make war upon them; for they would account their act as our own, seeing we had formerly professed to the Indians, that we were all as one; and in our last message to *Miantunnomoh*, had remembered him again of the same, and he had answered that he did so account us. Upon receipt of this our answer, they forbare to enter into a war, but (it seemed) unwillingly, and as not well pleased with us." The main considerations which caused Massachusetts to decide against war was, "That all those informations [furnished by Connecticut] might arise from a false ground, and out of the enmity which was between the Narraganset and Mohigan" sachems. This was no doubt one of the real causes, and had *Miantunnomoh* overcome *Uncas*, the English would, from policy, as gladly have leagued with him as with the latter, for it was constantly pleaded in those days, that their safety must depend on a union with some of the most powerful tribes.

There can be no doubt, on fairly examining the case, that *Uncas* used many arts, to influence the English in his favor, and against his enemy. In the progress of the war between the two great chiefs, the English acted precisely as the Indians have been always said to do—stood aloof, and watched the scale of victory, determined to join the conquerors: and we will here digress for a moment, to introduce a character, more fully to illustrate the cause of the operations of the English against the chief of the Narragansets.

Miantunnomoh had a wretched enemy in *Waiandance*, a Long Island sachem, who had assisted in the destruction of the Pequots, at their last retreat. He revealed the plots and plans of *Miantunnomoh*; and, says

---

* See book iii. chap. vii.

† Here, the reader may with propriety exclaim, was another *Michael Servetus:*—"*Pourquoy, Messeigneurs, je demande que mon faulx accusateur soit* puni pœna talionis," &c. Roscoe's *Leo* X. iv. 457.

Lion Gardener, "he told me many years ago," as all the plots of the Narragansets had been discovered, they now concluded to let the English alone until they had destroyed *Uncas* and himself, then, with the assistance of the Mohawks, "and Indians beyond the Dutch, and all the northern and eastern Indians, would easily destroy us, man and mother's son."

Mr. *Gardener* next relates that he met with *Miantunnomoh* at Meanticut, *Waiandance's* country, on the east end of Long Island. That *Miantunnomoh* was there, as *Waiandance* said, to break up the intercourse with those Indians. There were others with *Miantunnomoh*, and what they said to *Waiandance* was as follows:—

"*You must give no more wampum to the English, for they are no sachems, nor none of their children shall be in their place if they die. They have no tribute given them. There is but one king in England, who is over them all, and if you should send him 100,000 fathom of wampum, he would not give you a knife for it, nor thank you.*" Then said *Waiandance*, "They will come and kill us all, as they did the Pequits;" but replied the Narragansets, "*No, the Pequots gave them wampum and beaver, which they loved so well, but they sent it them again, and killed them because they had killed an Englishman; but you have killed none, therefore give them nothing.*"

Some time after Miantunnomoh went again "with a troop of men to the same place, and, instead of receiving presents as formerly, he gave presents to *Waiandance* and his people, and made the following speech:—

"*Brothers, we must be one as the English are, or we shall soon all be destroyed. You know our fathers had plenty of deer and skins, and our plains were full of deer and of turkeys, and our coves and rivers were full of fish. But, brothers, since these English have seized upon our country, they cut down the grass with scythes, and the trees with axes. Their cows and horses eat up the grass, and their hogs spoil our beds of clams; and finally we shall starve to death! therefore, stand not in your own light, I beseech you, but resolve with us to act like men. All the sachems both to the east and west have joined with us, and we are all resolved to fall upon them, at a day appointed, and therefore I have come secretly to you, because you can persuade the Indians to do what you will. Brothers, I will send over 50 Indians to Manisses, and 30 to you from thence, and take an 100 of Southampton Indians with an 100 of your own here. And, when you see the three fires that will be made at the end of 40 days hence, in a clear night, then act as we act, and the next day fall on and kill men, women and children; but no cows; they must be killed as we need them for provisions, till the deer come again.*"

To this speech all the old men said, "*Wurregen*," i. e. "IT IS WELL." But this great plot, if the account given by *Waiandance* be true, was by him brought to the knowledge of the English, and so failed. "And the plotter," says *Gardener*, "next spring after, did as *Ahab* did at Ramoth-Gilead.—So he to Mohegan,* and there had his fall."†

The war brought on between *Uncas* and *Miantunnomoh* was not within the jurisdiction of the English, nor is it to be expected that they could with certainty determine the justness of its cause. The broil had long existed, but the open rupture was brought on by *Uncas*' making war upon *Sequasson*, one of the sachems under *Miantunnomoh*. The English accounts say, (and we have no other,) that about 1000 warriors were raised by *Miantunnomoh*, who came upon Uncas unprepared, having only about 400 men; yet, after an obstinate battle, in which many were killed

* This goes to show that *Miantunnomoh* was not killed above Hartford, as *Winthrop* states; for the country at some distance from the mouth of Pequot River was called *Mohegan*. It probably included Windsor.

† 3 *Col. Mas. Hist. Soc.* iii. 155.

on both sides, the Narragansets were put to flight, and *Miantunnomoh* taken prisoner; that he endeavored to save himself by flight, but having on a coat of mail, was known from the rest, and seized by two* of his own men, who hoped by their treachery to save their own lives. Whereupon they immediately delivered him up to the conqueror. *Uncas* slew them both instantly; probably with his own hand. This specimen of his *bravery* must have had a salutary effect on all such as afterwards chanced to think of acting the part of traitors in their wars; at least among the Narragansets.

Being brought before *Uncas*, he remained without speaking a word, until *Uncas* spoke to him, and said, "*If you had taken me, I would have besought you for my life.*" He then took his prisoner to Hartford, and at his request left him a prisoner with the English, until the mind of the United Colonies should be known as to what disposition should be made of him.

The sorrowful part of the tale is yet to be told. The commissioners of the United Colonies having convened at Boston, "taking into serious consideration, they say, what was safest and best to be done, were all of opinion that it would not be safe to set him at liberty, neither had we sufficient ground for us to put him to death."† The awful design of putting to death *their friend* they had not yet fixed upon, but calling to their aid in council, "*five of the most judicious elders,*" "*they* all agreed that *he ought to be put to death.*" This was the final decision, and, to complete the deed of darkness, secrecy was enjoined upon all. And their determination was to be made known to *Uncas* privately, with direction that he should execute him within his own jurisdiction and without torture.

We will now go to the record, which will enable us to judge of the justness of this matter. When the English had determined that *Uncas* should execute *Miantunnomoh, Uncas* was ordered to be sent for to Hartford, "with some considerable number of his best and trustiest men," to take him to a place for execution, "carrying him into the next part of his own government, and there put him to death: provided that some discreet and faithful persons of the English accompany them, and see the execution, for our more full satisfaction; and that the English meddle not with the head or body at all."‡

The commissioners, at the same time, ordered "that Hartford- furnish Uncas with a competent strength of English to defend him against any present fury or assault, of the Nanohiggunsetts or any other." And "that in case *Uncas* shall refuse to execute justice upon *Myantenomo,* that then *Myantenomo* be sent by sea to the Massachusetts, there to be kept in safe durance till the commissioners may consider further how to dispose of him."‡

Here then we see fully developed the real state of the case. The Mohegans had by accident captured *Miantunnomoh,* after which event they were more in fear of his nation than before; which proves beyond doubt, that they would never have dared to put him to death, had they not been promised the protection of the English.

No one can read this account without being reminded of the fate of *Napoleon.* We do not say that the English of New England dreaded the power of *Miantunnomoh* as *much* as those of Old England did that of *Napoleon* afterwards; but that both were sacrificed in consequence of the

---

* In the records, (*Hazard,* ii. 48.) but one person is mentioned as having taken *Miantunnomoh,* whose name was *Tantoqueson,* and there he is called a Mohegan captain. That therefore the Narragansets tried to kill him; came upon him once in the night, and dangerously wounded him, as he lay in his wigwam asleep. See *note* in the *Life of Ninigret.*

† *Winthrop,* ii. 131. ‡ Records of the U. Colonies.

fears of those into whose power the fortune of wars cast them, will not, we presume, be denied.

When the determination of the commissioners and *elders* was made known to *Uncas*, he "readily undertook the execution, and taking *Miantunnomoh* along with him, in the way between Hartford and Windsor, (where *Uncas* hath some men dwell,) *Uncas*' brother, following after *Miantunnomoh*, clave his head with an hatchet."* Mather says, they "very fairly cut off his head."†

Dr. *Trumbull*‡ records an account of cannibalism, at this time, which we ought to caution the reader against receiving as true history, as it no doubt rests on the authority of tradition, which is wont to transfér even the transactions of one continent to another. It is this:—"*Uncas* cut out a large piece of his shoulder, and ate it in savage triumph;" saying, "'it was the sweetest meat he ever ate; it made his heart strong.'"§

We are now certain that what Dr. *Trumbull* has given us as unquestionable history, from a "manuscript of Mr. *Hyde*," is only tradition. Having been put in possession of a copy of that manuscript,|| we deem it highly important that it should be laid before the world, that its true weight may be considered by all who would be correctly informed in this important transaction.

By way of preliminary to his communication, Mr. *Hyde* says, "The following facts being communicated to me from some the ancient fathers of this town, who were contemporary with *Uncas*," &c. "That before the settlement of Norwich, the sachem of the Narraganset tribe [*Miantunnomoh*] had a personal quarrel with *Uncas*, and proclaimed war with the Moheg[an]s: and marched with an army of 900 fighting men, equipped with bows and arrows and hatchets. *Uncas* be[ing] informed by spies of their march towards his seat, Uncas called his warriors together, about 600, stout, hard men, light of foot, and skilled in the use of the bow; and, upon a conference, *Uncas* told his men that it would not do to let ye Narragansets come to their town, but they must go and meet them. Accordingly, they marched, and about three miles, on a large plain, the armies met, and both halted within bow-shot. A parley was sounded, and gallant *Uncas* proposed a conference with the Narraganset sachem, who agreed. And being met, *Uncas* saith to his enemy word[s] to this effect: '*You have got a number of brave men with you, and so have I. A'nt it a pity that such brave men should be killed for a quarrel between you and I? Only come like a man, as you pretend to be, and we will fight it out. If you kill me, my men shall be yours; but if I kill you, your men shall be mine.*' Upon which the Narraganset sachem replied: '*My men came to fight, and they shall fight.*'

---

* *Winthrop's Journal*, ii. 134. As to the place of *Miantunnomoh's* execution, *Winthrop* seems to have been in a mistake. It is not very likely that he was taken in the opposite direction, from *Uncas's* own country, as Windsor was from Hartford. It is also unlikely that *Uncas* had *men dwell* so far from his country upon the Thames.

A gentleman who lately visited his sepulchre, says the wandering Indians have made a heap of stones upon his grave. It is a well-known custom of the race, to add to a monumental pile of the dead whenever they pass by it. See *3 Col. Mass. Hist. Soc.* iii. 135. and *Jefferson's Notes*. ☞ Some wretchedly ignorant neighbors to this sacred pile (whites I suppose) have not long since taken stones from it to make wall! but enough remain to mark the spot. It is in the east part of Norwich. *Cols. Ibid.*

† Magnalia. ‡ History of Connecticut, i. 135.

§ That this is tradition, may be inferred from the circumstance of an *eminently* obscure writer's publishing nearly the same story, which he says, in his book, took place upon the death of *Philip. Oneko,* he says, cut out a pound of *Philip's* bleeding body and ate it. The book is by *one Henry Trumbull,* and purports to be a history of the discovery of America, the Indian wars, &c. The reader will find it about stalls by the street side, but rarely in a respectable book-store. It has been forced through many editions, but there is scarce a word of true history in it.

|| By Rev. *Wm. Ely* of Connecticut.

"*Uncas* having before told his men, that if his enemy should refuse to fight him, he would fall down, and then they were to discharge their artillery [arrows] on them, and fall right on them as fast as they could;" this was done, and the Mohegans rushed upon *Miantunnomoh's* army "like lions," put them to flight, and killed "a number on the spot." They "pursued the rest, driving some down ledges of rocks." The foremost of *Uncas's* men got ahead of *Miantunnomoh*, and impeded his flight, drawing him back as they passed him, "to give *Uncas* opportunity to take him himself."

"In the pursuit, at a place now called *Sachem's Plain*, *Uncas* took him by the shoulder. He then set down, knowing *Uncas*. *Uncas* then gave a whoop, and his men returned to him; and in a council then held, 'twas concluded by them, that *Uncas*, with a guard, should carry said sachem to Hartford, to the governor and magistrates, (it being before the charter,) to advise what they should do with him." "*Uncas* was told by them, as there was no war with the English and Narragansets, it was not proper for them to intermeddle, in the affair, and advised him to take his own way. Accordingly, they brought said Narraganset sachem back to the same spot of ground where he was took: where *Uncas* killed him, and cut out a large piece of his shoulder, roasted, and eat it; and said, '*It was the sweetest meel* he ever eat; it made him have strong hart.*' There they bury him, and made a pillar, which I have seen but a few years since."

This communication was in the form of a letter, and dated at Norwich, 9 Oct. 1769, and signed *Richard Hide*. The just remark of Mr. *Ely* upon it I cannot withhold, in justice to my subject.

"The above '*Manuscript of Mr. Hyde*,' as a *tradition*, is a valuable paper, and worthy of preservation; yet, being written 125 years after the event which it describes, it is surprising that Dr. *Trumbull* should have inserted it, in his History of Connecticut, in its principal particulars, as matter of fact."†

In the proceedings of the commissioners of the United Colonies, the main facts in reference to the death of *Miantunnomoh*, contained in the above account, are corroborated. The records of the commissioners say, that *Uncas*, before the battle, told *Miantunnomoh*, that he had many ways sought his life, and now, if he dared, he would fight him in single combat; but that *Miantunnomoh* "presuming upon his numbers of men, would have nothing but a battle."‡

It does not appear from these records, that *Uncas* had any idea of putting *Miantunnomoh* to death, but to extort a great price from his countrymen, for his ransom. That a large amount in wampum was collected for this purpose, appears certain, but before it was paid, *Uncas* received the decision of the English, and then pretended that he had made no such agreement, or that the quantity or quality was not as agreed upon, as will more at length be seen in the life of *Uncas*. We come now to.

Ninigret, often called *Ninicraft*, and sometimes *Nenekunat*,§ *Niniglud*, *Nenegxelett*, and written almost as many other ways as times mentioned, by some early writers. *Janemo* was the first name by which he was known to the English. He was generally styled sachem of the Nianticks, a tribe of the Narragansets, whose principal residence was at Wekapaug, now Westerly, in Rhode Island. He was cousin to *Miantunnomoh*,|| and

* *Trumbull* says *meat*, but the MS. is plain, and means *meal*.
† Manuscript letter, 1 Mar. 1833.
‡ See *Hazard's* Historical Collections, ii. 7, 10.
§ So written by *Roger Williams*.
|| Prince says he was *uncle* to *Miantunnomoh*, (*Chronology*, ii. 59.) but that could not have been.

is commonly mentioned in history as the chief sachem of the Nianticks, which always made a part of the great nation of the Narragansets. *Ninigret* married a sister of *Cashawashett*, otherwise called *Harmon Garret*, who was his uncle.

The relation in which the Nianticks stood to the Narragansets is plain, from the representation given by *Miantunnomoh* to the government of Massachusetts, in 1642. In treating with him, at that time, Gov. *Winthrop* says, "Some difficulty we had, to bring him to desert the Nianticks, if we had just cause of war with them. They were," he said, "as his own flesh, being allied by continual intermarriages, &c. But at last he condescended, that if they should do us wrong, as he could not draw them to give us satisfaction for, nor himself could satisfy, as if it were for blood, &c. then he would leave them to us."

In 1637, "*Miantunnomoh* came to Boston. The governor, deputy and treasurer treated with him, and they parted upon fair terms." "We gave him leave to right himself for the wrongs which *Janemoh* and *Wequash Cook* had done him; and, for the wrong they had done us, we would right ourselves, in our own time."* Hence it appears that at this period they were not so closely allied as they were afterwards.

The next year, *Janemo* was complained of by the Long Island Indians, who paid tribute to the English, that he had committed some robberies upon them. Capt. *Mason* was sent from Connecticut with seven men to require satisfaction. *Janemo* went immediately to the English, and the matter was amicably settled.†

When it was rumored that *Miantunnomoh* was plotting to cut off the English, and using his endeavors to unite other tribes in the enterprise, the English sent deputies to him, to learn the truth of the report, as will be found elsewhere fully stated. The deputies were well satisfied with the carriage of *Miantunnomoh,* but "*Janemoh,* the Niantick sachem, carried himself proudly, and refused to come to us, or to yield to any thing; only, he said, he would not harm us, except we invaded him."‡ Thus we cannot but form an exalted opinion of *Ninigret* in the person of *Janemo*.

We hear little of *Ninigret* until after the death of *Miantunnomoh*. In 1644, the Narragansets and Nianticks united against the Mohegans, and for some time obliged *Uncas* to confine himself and men to his fort.

This affair probably took place early in the spring, and we have elsewhere given all the particulars of it, both authentic and traditionary. It appears, by a letter from *Tho. Peters*, addressed to Gov. *Winthrop*, written about the time, that there had been some hard fighting; and that the Mohegans had been sadly beaten by the Narragansets. Mr. *Peters* writes:—

"I, with your son, [*John Winthrop* of Con.,] were at *Uncas*' fort, where I dressed seventeen men, and left plasters to dress seventeen more, who were wounded in *Uncas*' brother's wigwam before we came. Two captains and one common soldier were buried, and since we came thence two captains and one common man more, are dead also, most of which are wounded with bullets. *Uncas* and his brother told me, the Narragansets had 30 guns which won them the day, else would not care a rush for them. They drew *Uncas'* forces out by a wile, of 40 appearing only, but a thousand [lay hid] in ambush, who pursued *Uncas*' men into their own land, where the battle was fought *vario marte*, till God put fresh spirit into the Moheagues, and so drave the Narragansets back again." So it seems that *Uncas* had been taken in his own play. The letter goes on:—" 'T would pity your hearts to see them [*Uncas'* men] lie, like so many new circumcised Sechemites, in their blood. Sir, whatever information

* *Winthrop's Journal,* i. 243. † Ibid. 267. ‡ Ibid. ii. 8.

you have, I dare boldly say, the Narragansets first brake the contract they made with the English last year, for I helped to cure one *Tantiquieson*, a Moheague captain, who first fingered [laid hands on] *Miantinomio*. Some cunning squaws of Narraganset led two of them to *Tantiquieson's* wigwam, where, in the night, they struck him on the breast through the coat with an hatchet, and had he not fenced it with his arm, no hope could be had of his life," &c.*

"The English thought it their concern," says Dr. *I. Mather*,† "not to suffer him to be swallowed up by those adversaries, since he had, (though for his own ends,) approved himself faithful to the English from time to time." An army was accordingly raised for the relief of *Uncas*. "But as they were just marching out of Boston, many of the principal Narraganset Indians, viz. *Pessecus, Mexano*,‡ and *Witawash*, sagamores, and *Awasequin*, deputy for the Nianticks; these, with a large train, came to Boston, suing for peace, being willing to submit to what terms the English should see cause to impose upon them. It was demanded of them that they should defray the charges they had put the English to,§ and that the sachems should send their sons to be kept as hostages in the hands of the English, until such time as the money should be paid." After remarking that from this time the Narragansets harbored venom in their hearts against the English, Mr. *Mather* proceeds:—"In the first place, they endeavored to play *legerdemain* in their sending hostages; for, instead of sachems' children, they thought to send some other, and to make the English believe that those base *papooses* were of a royal progeny; but they had those to deal with, who were too wise to be so eluded. After the expected hostages were in the hands of the English, the Narragansets, notwithstanding that, were slow in the performance of what they stood engaged for. And when, upon an impartial discharge of the debt, their hostages were restored to them, they became more backward than formerly, until they were, by hostile preparations, again and again terrified into better obedience. At last, Capt. *Atherton*, of Dorchester, was sent with a small party‖ of English soldiers to demand what was due. He at first entered into the wigwam, where old *Ninigret* resided, with only two or three soldiers, appointing the rest by degrees to follow him, two or three dropping in at once; when his small company were come about him, the Indians in the mean time supposing that there had been many more behind, he caught the sachem by the hair of his head, and setting a pistol to his breast, protesting whoever escaped he should surely die, if he did not forthwith comply with what was required. Hereupon a great trembling and consternation surprised the Indians; albeit, multitudes of them were then present, with spiked arrows at their bow-strings ready to let fly. The event was, the Indians submitted, and not one drop of blood was shed."¶ This, it must be confessed, was a high-handed proceeding.

"Some space after that, *Ninigret* was raising new trouble against us,

---

* *Winthrop's Jour.* ii. 380, 381.

† Relation, 58.

‡ The editor of *Johnson's* Wonder-working Providence, in *Col. Mass. Hist. Soc.* makes a great mistake in noting this chief as Miantunnomoh. Mriksah, Mixanno, *Meika*, &c. are names of the same person, who was the eldest son of *Canonicus*. After the death of his father, he was chief sachem of the Narragansets. He married a sister of *Ninigret*, who was "a woman of great power," and no other than the famous *Quaiapen*, at one time called *Matantuck*, from which, probably, was derived *Magnus*. By some writers mistaking him for *Miantunnomoh*, an error has spread, that has occasioned much confusion in accounts of their genealogy.

§ A yearly tribute in wampum was agreed upon. *Manuscript* Narrative of the Rev. *T. Cobbet*, which places the affair in 1645.

‖ Twenty, says a MS. document among our *state papers*.

¶ Relation of the Troubles, &c. 4to, 1677.

amongst his Nianticks and other Indians; but upon the speedy sending up of Capt. *Davis*, with a party of horse to reduce him to the former peace, who, upon the news of the captain's approach, was put into such a panic fear, that he durst not come out of his wigwam to treat with the captain, till secured of his life by him, which he was, if he quietly yielded to his message, about which he was sent from the Bay. To which he freely consenting, that storm was graciously blown over."*

Thus having, through these extracts, summarily glanced at some prominent passages in the life of *Ninigret,* we will now go more into particulars.

The case of the Narragansets, at the period of the treaty before spoken of, had become rather desperate; two years having passed since they agreed to pay 2000 fathom of "good white wampum," as a remuneration for the trouble and damage they had caused the English and Mohegans, and they were now pressed to fulfil their engagements. *Ninigret,* then called Janemo, was not at Boston at that time, but *Aumsaaquen* was his deputy, and signed the treaty then made, with *Pessacus* and others. At their meeting, in July, 1647, *Pessacus* and others, chiefs of the Narragansets and Nianticks, were sent to by the English commissioners, as will be found in the life of *Pessacus*. Being warned to come to Boston, *Pessacus*, not being willing to get any further into trouble by being obliged to sign whatever articles the English might draw up, feigned himself sick, and told the messengers he had agreed to leave all the business to *Ninigret*. This seems to have been well understood, and we shall next see with what grace *Ninigret* acted his part with the commissioners, at Boston. Their record runs thus:—

"August 3d, [1647,] *Ninegratt*, with some of the Nyantick Indians and two of *Pessack's* men, came to Boston, and desiring Mr. *John Winthrop,* that came from Pequatt plantation, might be present, they were admitted. The commissioners asked *Ninegratt* for whom he came, whither as a publick person on the behalf of *Pessack's* and the rest of the Narragansets' confederates, or only for himself as a particular sagamore? He at first answered that he had spoken with *Pessack*, but had no such commission from him;" and said there had not been so good understanding between them as he desired; but from Mr. *Winthrop's* testimony, and the answer *Thos. Stanton* and *Benedict Arnold* brought from *Pessacus,* and also the testimony of *Pessacus'* two men, "it appeared to the commissioners that whatever formality might be wanting in *Pessack's* expressions to *Ninegratt*, yet *Pessack* had fully engaged himself to stand to whatsoever *Ninegratt* should conclude." Therefore they proceeded to demand of him why the wampum had not been paid, and why the covenant had not been observed in other particulars. *Ninigret* pretended he did not know what covenants had been made. He was then reminded that his deputy executed the covenant, and that a copy was carried into his country, and his ignorance of it was no excuse for him, for Mr. *Williams* was at all times ready to explain it, if he had taken the pains to request it of him. "There could, therefore, be no truth in his answere."

Ninigret next demanded, "*For what are the Narragansets to pay so much wampum? I know not that they are indebted to the English!*" The commissioners then repeated the old charges—the breach of covenant, ill treating messengers, and what he had said himself to the English messengers, namely, that he knew the English would try to bring about a peace at their meeting at Hartford, but he was resolved on war, nor would he inquire who began it—that if the English did not withdraw their men from assisting *Uncas,* he would kill them and their cattle, &c.

---

* *Cobbet's* MS. Narrative.

According to the records of the commissioners, *Ninigret* did not deny these charges with a very good face. He said, however, their messengers provoked him to say what he did.

In order to waive the criminating discourse, *Ninigret* called for documents; or wished the English to make a statement of their account against him, that he might know "how the reckoninge stood." The English answered that they had received of *Pessacus* 170 *fathom of wampum* at one time:—Afterwards *some kettles* and about 15 *fathom more,* "which beinge a *contemptible some,* was refused." As to the kettles, they said, "The Narraganset messengers had sould them to Mr. *Shrimpton,** a brasier in Boston," for a shilling a pound. Their weight was 285 *lbs.*, (not altogether so *contemptible* as one might be led to imagine,) which came to 14£. 5*s*., and the wampum to 4£. 4*s*. 6*d*.† Of the amount in Mr. *Shrimpton's* hands, the messengers took up 1£. probably to defray their necessary expenses while at Boston. The remainder an Englishman attached to satisfy "for goods stollen from him by a Narraganset Indian."

Ninigret said the attachment was not valid, "for that neither the kettles nor wampum did belonge to *Pessacks* himself, nor to the Indian that had stollen the goods," and therefore must be deducted from the amount now due. "The commissioners thought it not fit to press the attachment," but reckoned the kettles and wampum at 70 fathom, and acknowledged the receipt of 240 fathom, [in all,] besides a parcel sent by *Ninigret* himself to the governor; and though this was sent as a present, yet, as it was not accepted by the governor, they left it to *Ninigret* to say whether it should be now so considered, or whether it should be taken in payment of the debt. *Ninigret* said the governor should do as he pleased about it. It was then inquired how much he had sent; (it being deposited in *Cutshamokin's* hands, as we have elsewhere stated;) he said he had sent 30 fathom of black, and 45 of white, in value together 105 fathom. *Cutshamokin* was sent for to state what he had received in trust. He had produced two girdles, "with a string of wampum, all which himself rated at 45 fathom, affirming he had received no more, except 8s. which he had used, and would repay. He was brought before *Ninigret* and questioned, as there appeared a great difference in their accounts. "He at first persisted, says our record, and added to his lyes, but was at last convinced [confronted] by *Ninigret,* and his messengers who then brought the present, and besides *Cutshamokin* had sent him at the same time 10 fathom as a present also. It still remained to be settled whether this wampum should be received as a part of the debt, or as a present, and *Ninigret* was urged to say how it should be. With great magnanimity he answered:—

"*My tongue shall not belie my heart. Whether the debt be paid or not, I intended it as a present to the governor.*"

It is unpleasant to contrast the characters of the two chiefs, *Cutshamokin* and *Ninigret,* because the former had long had the *advantage* of a civilized neighborhood, and the latter was from the depths of the forest, where he saw an Englishman but seldom. We could say much upon it, but as it is thought by many that such disquisitions are unprofitable, we decline going into them here.

What we have related seems to have finished the business of the day, and doubtless the shades of night were very welcome to *Cutshamokin.* The next day, *Ninigret* came into court, with the deputies of *Pessacus,* and spoke to the following effect:—

* *Samuel Shrimpton,* probably, who bought a house and lands of *Ephraim Turner,* brasier, situated in Boston, in 1671.

† Hence 4£. 4*s*. 6*d*.÷15=5*s*. $7\frac{3}{5}$*d*.=value of a fathom of wampum in 1647.

"Before I came here I expected the burden had been thrown upon me, Pessacus not having done what he agreed to do. However, I have considered upon the treaty of 1645, and am resolved to give the English satisfaction in all things. I will send some of my men immediately to Narraganset and Niantick, to raise the wampum now due to them, and hope to hear what they will do in three days. In ten days I think the wampum will arrive, and I will stay here until it comes. I will tell this to the Narraganset confederates. But if there should not enough at this time be raised, I desire some forbearance as to time, as I assure you that the remainder shall be shortly paid, and you shall see me true to the English, henceforth."

This speech gave the commissioners great satisfaction, and they proceeded to other business.

The messengers sent out by *Ninigret* did not return so soon as was expected, but on the 16 August, notice was given of their arrival; sadly, however, to the disappointment of the commissioners, for they brought only 200 fathom of wampum. The feelings of the court were somewhat changed, and they rather sternly demanded "what the reason was, that, so much being due, so little was brought, and from whom this 200 fathom came." *Ninigret* answered that *he* was disappointed that more had not been brought, but said, if he had been at home more would have been obtained: that 100 fathom was sent by *Pessacus*, and the other 100 by his people.

The commissioners say, that "not thinking it meet to begin a present war, if satisfaction, (though with a little forbearance, may be had otherwise,)" told *Ninigret*, that since he had said the wampum would have been gathered and paid if he had been at home himself, they would now give him 20 days to go and get it in; and if he could not procure enough by 500 fathom, still they would not molest him until "next spring planting time." That as so much was still due, they would reckon the present before mentioned, but if they did not bring 1000 fathom in twenty days, the commissioners would send no more messengers into his country, "but take course to right themselves." That if they were "forced to seek satisfaction by arms, he and his confederates must not expect to make their peace, as lately they had done, by a little wampum. In the mean time, though for breach of covenants they might put their hostages to death, yet the commissioners would forthwith deliver the children to *Ninigret*,* expecting from him the more care to see engagements fully satisfied. And if they find him real in his performance, they will charge all former neglects upon *Pessacus*," and "in such case they expect from *Ninigret* his best assistance, when he shall be required to recover the whole remainder from him. All which *Ninigret* cheerfully accepted, and promised to perform accordingly."

Notwithstanding all their promises, the Narragansets had not discharged their debt at the end of two years more, though in that time they had paid about 1100 fathom of wampum. At their meeting this year, 1649, at Boston, "the commissioners were minded of the continued complaint of *Uncas*" against the Narragansets, that they were "still vndermining his peace and seeking his ruine," and had lately endeavored "to bring in the Mowhaukes vppon him," which failing, they next tried to take away his life by witchcraft. A Narraganset Indian, named *Cuttaquin*, "in an English vessel, in Mohegan River, ran a sword into his breast, wherby nee receeved, to all appearance, a mortal wound, which murtherus acte

---

* Glad, no doubt, to rid themselves of the expense of keeping them; for it must be remembered, that the English took them upon the condition that they should support them at their own expense.

the assalant then confessed hee was, for a considerable sum of wampum, by the Narragansett and Nianticke sachems, hired to attempt."

Meanwhile *Ninigret*, understanding what was to be urged against him, appeared suddenly at Boston before the commissioners. The old catalogue of delinquencies was read over to him, with several new ones appended. As it respected *Cuttaquin's* attempt upon the life of *Uncas, Ninigret* said that neither he nor *Pessacus* had any hand in it, but that "he [Cuttaquin] was drawn thereunto by torture from the Mohegans;" "but he was told, that the assailant, before he came into the hands of the Mohegans, presently after the fact was committed, layed the charge upon him, with the rest, which he confirmed, the day following, to Capt. *Mason,* in the presence of the English that were in the bark with him, and often reiterated it at Hartford, though since he hath dénied it: that he was presented to *Uncas* under the notion of one appertaining to *Vssamequin*, whereby he was acknowledged as his friend, and no provocation given him." *Cuttaquin* had affirmed, it was said, that his desperate condition caused him to attempt the life of *Uncas*, "through his great engagement to the said sachems, having received a considerable quantity of wampum, which he had spent, who otherwise would have taken away his life."

The judgment of the court was, that the sachems were guilty, and we next find them engaged in settling the old account of wampum. *Ninigret* had got the commissioners debited more than they at first were willing to allow. They say that it appeared by the auditor's account, that no more than 1529½ fathom hath been credited, "nor could *Ninigret* by any evidence make any more to appear, only he alleged that about 600 fathom was paid by measure which he accounted by tale, wherein there was considerable difference. The commissioners, not willing to adhere to any strict terms in that particular, (and though by agreement it was to be paid by measure and not by tale,) were willing to allow 62 fathom and half in that respect, so that there remains due 408 fathom. But *Ninigret* persisting in his former affirmation, and not endeavored to give any reasonable satisfaction to the commissioners in the premises, a small inconsiderable parcel of beaver being all that was tendered to them, though they understood he was better provided." They therefore gave him to understand that they were altogether dissatisfied, and that he might go his own way, as they were determined to protect *Uncas* according to their treaty with him.

The commissioners now expressed the opinion among themselves, that affairs looked rather turbulent, and advised that each colony should hold itself in readiness to act as circumstances might require, "which they the rather present to consideration, from an information they received since their sitting, of a marriage shortly intended betwixt *Ninigret's* daughter, and a brother or brother's son of *Sassaquas,* the malignant, furious Pequot, whereby probably their aims are to gather together, and reunite the scattered conquered Pequates into one body, and set them up again as a distinct nation, which hath always been witnessed against by the English, and may hazard the peace of the colonies."

The four years next succeeding are full of events, but as they happened chiefly among the Indians themselves, it is very difficult to learn the particulars. *Ninigret* claimed dominion of the Indians of a part of Long Island, as did his predecessors; but those Indians, seeing the English domineering over the Narragansets, became altogether independent of them, and even waged wars upon them.

Ascassasotick was at this period the chief of those Indians, a warlike and courageous chief, but as treacherous and barbarous as he was brave. These islanders had from the time of the Pequot troubles been protected by the English, which much increased their insolence. Not only had *Ninigret*, and the rest of the Narragansets, suffered from his insults, but the Mohegans had also, as we shall more fully make appear hereafter.

When the English commissioners had met at Hartford in 1650, *Uncas* came with a complaint to them, "that the Mohansick sachem, in Long Island, had killed som of his men; bewitched diuers others and himself also,* and desired the commissioners that hee might be righted therin. But because the said sachem of Long Island was not there to answer for himself," several Englishmen were appointed to examine into it, and if they found him guilty to let him know that they "will bring trouble upon themselves."

At the same meeting an order was passed, "that 20 men well armed be sent out of the jurisdiction of the Massachusetts to *Pessicus*, to demand the said wampum, [then in arrears,] which is 308 fathom;" but in case they could not get the wampum, they were ordered "to take the same, or the vallew therof, in the best and most suitable goods they can find." Or, if they could not find enough to satisfy all demands, they were ordered to seize and "bring away either *Pessacus* or his children, or such other considerable sachem or persons, as they prize, and may more probably bow them to reason."

From *Pessacus*, they were ordered to go to *Ninigret*, and inform him that the commissioners had heard "*that he had given his daughter in marriage to Sasecos his brother, who gathers Pequots under him, as if either he would become their sachem, or again possess the Pequot country,*" which was contrary to "engagements," and what they would not allow, and he must inform them whether it were so. To inform him also that *Wequash Cook* "complains of sundry wrongs." And that, as to his hunting in the Pequot country, to inform him he had no right to do so, as that country belonged to the English. The termination of this expedition, in which Ninigret was taken "by the hair," has been previously mentioned in our extract from Dr. *Mather*.

We have in the life of *Miantunnomoh* given some account of the acts of a chief called *Waiandance*, especially relating to the disorganization of the plans of that great chief. We come, in this place, to a parallel act in relation to *Ninigret*. About a year after the death of *Miantunnomoh, Ninigret* undertook to organize a plan for expatriating the English; and sent a messenger to *Waiandance*, the Long Island sachem, to engage him in it. Instead of listening to his message, *Waiandance* seized upon *Ninigret's* messenger, bound him, and sent him to Capt. *Gardener* at Saybrook fort. From thence he was sent, under a guard of 10 men, for Hartford. But they were wind-bound in their passage, and were obliged to put in to Shelter Island, where an old sachem lived, who was *Waiandance's* elder brother. Here they let *Ninigret's* ambassador escape, and thus he had knowledge that his plan was overthrown.

Since we have here introduced the sachem *Waiandance*, we will add the account of his last acts and death. One *William Hammond* being killed "by a giant-like Indian" near New York, about 1637, Capt. Gardener told *Waiandance* that he must kill that Indian; but this being against the advice of the great sachem, his brother, he declined it, and told the captain that that Indian was a mighty great man, and no man dared meddle with him, and that he had many friends. Some time after, he killed another, one *Thomas Farrington*, and in the mean time, *Waiandance's* brother having died, he undertook his execution, which he accomplished. This was his last act in the service of the English; "for in the time of a great mortality among them, he died, but it was by poison; also two

* This was doubtless as true as were most of his charges against the Narragansets.

thirds of the Indians upon Long Island died, else the Narragansets had not made such havoc here as they have."

Ninigret passed the winter of 1652—3 among the Dutch of New-York. This caused the English great suspicion, especially as they were enemies to the Dutch at that time; and several sagamores who resided near the Dutch had reported that the Dutch governor was trying to hire them to cut off the English; consequently, there was a special meeting of the English commissioners at Boston, in April, 1653, occasioned by a rumor that the Narragansets had leagued with the Dutch to break up the English settlements. Whereupon a letter was sent by them to their agent at Narraganset, *Thomas Stanton*, containing "divers queries," by him to be interpreted "to *Ninegrett, Pessicus* and *Meeksam*, three of the chiefest Narraganset sachems," and their answers to be immediately obtained and reported to the commissioners.

The questions to be put to the sachems were in substance as follows:—1. Whether the Dutch had engaged them* to fight against the English.—2. Whether the Dutch governor did not endeavor such a conspiracy.—3. Whether they had not received arms and munitions of war from the Dutch.—4. What other Indians are engaged in the plot.—5. Whether, contrary to their engagement, they were resolved to fight against the English.—6. If they are so resolved, *what they think the English will do*.—7. Whether they had not better be true to the English.—8. Similar to the first.—9. What were their grounds of war against the English.—10. Whether they had not better come or send messengers to treat with the English.—11. Whether they had hired the Mohawks to help them.

"The answare of the sachems, viz. *Nimigrett, Pessecus* and *Mixam*, vnto the queries and letters sent by the messengers, Sarjeant Waite and Sarjeant *John Barrell*, the 18th of the second month, 1653."

Mexam seems to have been the first that answered; and of the first query he said:—

"*I speak unfeignedly, from my heart, and say, without dissimulation, that I know of no such plot against the English, my friends; implicating either the Dutch governor or any other person. Though I be poor, it is not goods, guns, powder nor shot, that shall draw me to such a plot as this against the English, my friends.*† *If the Dutch governor had made known any such intention to me, I would have told it, without delay, to the English, my friends. With respect to your second question, I answer, No. What do the English sachems, my friends, think of us?—do they think we should prefer goods, guns, powder and shot, before our lives? our means of living? both of us and ours? As to the 4th query, I speak from my heart, and say, I know of no such plot by the Dutch governor. There may come false news and reports against us; let them say what they will, they are false. It is unnecessary to say more. But in answer to the 10th query I will say, It is just messengers should be sent to treat with the English sachems, but as for myself, I am old, and cannot travel two days together, but a man shall be sent to speak with the sachems. I have sent to Mr.* Smith, *and* Voll‡ *his man, to speak to Mr.* Brown,

---

* The third person singular, *he*, is used throughout, in the original, as it was supposed by the propounders that each chief would be questioned separately.

† Every one must be forcibly reminded of the answer given by one of our revolutionary worthies, *Joseph Reed*, Esq., to a British agent, on reading this answer of the chief *Mexam*, though not under circumstances exactly similar. Mr. *Reed* was promised a fortune if he would exert himself on the side of the king. Viewing it in the light of a bribe, he replied: "*I am not worth purchasing, but, such as I am, the king of Great Britain is not rich enough to do it.*" Dr. *Gordon's* America, iii. 172. ed. London, 4 vols. 8 vo. 1788.

‡ *Vallentine Whitman*, an interpreter, elsewhere named.

and to say to him, that I love the English sachems, and all Englishmen in the Bay: And desire Mr. Brown *to tell the sachems of the Bay, that the child that is now born, or that is to be born in time to come, shall see no war made by us against the English."*

Pessacus spoke to this purpose:—

"*I am very thankful to these two men that came from the Massachusetts, and to you Thomas, and to you Poll,* and to you Mr. Smith, you that are come so far as from the Bay to bring us this message, and to inform us of these things we knew not of before. As for the governor of the Dutch, we are loath to invent any falsehood of him, though we be far from him, to please the English, or any others that bring these reports. For what I speak with my mouth I speak from my heart. The Dutch governor did never propound any such thing unto us. Do you think we are mad? and that we have forgotten our writing that we had in the Bay, which doth bind us to the English, our friends, in a way of friendship? Shall we throw away that writing and ourselves too? Have we not reason in us? How can the Dutch shelter us, being so remote, against the power of the English, our friends—we living close by the doors of the English, our friends? We do profess, we abhor such things."*

Lastly, we come to the chief actor in this affair, *Ninigret*. He takes up each query in order, and answers it, which, for brevity's sake, we will give in a little more condensed form, omitting nothing, however, that can in any degree add to our acquaintance with the great chief. He thus commences:—

"*I utterly deny that there has been any agreement made between the Dutch governor and myself, to fight against the English. I did never hear the Dutchmen say they would go and fight against the English; neither did I hear the Indians say they would join with them. But, while I was there at the Indian wigwams, there came some Indians that told me there was a ship come in from Holland, which did report the English and Dutch were fighting together in their own country, and there were several other ships coming with ammunition to fight against the English here, and that there would be a great blow given to the English when they came. But this I had from the Indians, and how true it is I cannot tell. I know not of any wrong the English have done me, therefore* WHY *should I fight against them? Why do the English sachems ask me the same questions over and over again? Do they think we are mad—and would, for a few guns and swords, sell our lives, and the lives of our wives and children? As to their tenth question, it being indifferently spoken, whether I may go or send, though I know nothing myself, wherein I have wronged the English, to prevent* MY *going; yet, as I said before, it being left to my choice, that is, it being indifferent to the commissioners, whether I will send some one to speak with them, I will send."*†

To the letters which the English messengers carried to the sachems, *Mexam* and *Pessacus* said, "*We desire there may be no mistake, but that we may be understood, and that there may be a true understanding on both sides. We desire to know where you had this news, that there was such a league made betwixt the Dutch and us, and also to know our accusers.*"

Ninigret, though of the most importance in this affair, is last mentioned in the records, and his answer to the letter brought him by the commissioners is as follows:—

---

* So printed in *Hazard*, but probably means the same as *Voll*; *V*, in the latter case, having been taken for *P*. We have known such instances.

† The preceding sentence of our text, the author of *Tales of the Indians* thinks, "would puzzle the most *mystifying* politician of modern times." Indeed! What! a Philadelphia *lawyer?* Really, we cannot conceive that it ought in the least to puzzle even a *Boston lawyer*. If a puzzle exist any where, we apprehend it is in some *mystifying* word.

"*You are kindly welcome to us, and I kindly thank the sachems of Massachusetts that they should think of me as one of the sachems worthy to be inquired of concerning this matter. Had any of the other sachems been at the Dutch, I should have feared their folly might have done some hurt, one way or other, but* THEY *have not been there. I am the man. I have been there myself. I alone am answerable for what I have done. And, as I have already declared, I do utterly deny and protest that I know of no such plot as has been apprehended. What is the story of these great rumors that I hear at Pocatocke—that I should be cut off, and that the English had a quarrel against me? I know of no such cause at all for my part. Is it because I went thither to take physic for my health? or what is the cause? I found no such entertainment from the Dutch governor, when I was there, as to give me any encouragement to stir me up to such a league against the English, my friends. It was winter time, and I stood, a great part of a winter day, knocking at the governor's door, and he would neither open it, nor suffer others to open it, to let me in. I was not wont to find such carriage from the English, my friends.*"

Not long after the return of the English messengers, who brought the above relation of their mission, *Awashaw* arrived at Boston, as "messenger" of *Ninigret, Pessacus* and *Mexam,* with "three or four" others. An inquisition was immediately held over him, and, from his *cross*-examination, we gather the following answers:—

"Ninigret *told me that he went to the Dutch to be cured of his disease, hearing there was a Frenchman there that could cure him; and Mr.* John Winthrop *knew of his going. He carried 30 fathom of wampum, gave the doctor 10, and the Dutch governor 15, who, in lieu thereof, gave him coats with sleeves, but not one gun, though the Indians there gave him two guns. That, while* Ninigret *was there, he crossed Hudson's River, and there an Indian told him about the arrival of the Dutch ships. As to the corn sent to the Dutch by* Ninigret, *it was only to pay his passage, the Dutch having brought him home in a vessel. Five men went with* Ninigret. *Four came home with him in the vessel, and one came by land before. One of his company was a Mohegan, and one a Conecticott Indian, who lived on the other side of Hudson's River. A canoe was furnished with 60 fathom of wampum, after* Ninigret's *return from Monhatoes, to be sent there to pay for the two guns, but six fathom of it was to have been paid to the doctor, which was then due to him. There were in it, also, two raccoon coats, and two beaver skins, and seven Indians to go with it. They and the canoe were captured by* Uncas."

An Indian named *Newcom-Matuxes,* sometimes of Rhode Island," was one that accompanied *Awashaw.* "One *John Lightfoot,* of Boston," said *Matuxes* told him, in Dutch, (he had lived among them at Southhold, and learned their language,) that the Dutchmen would "cut off" the English of Long Island. "*Newcom* also confesseth [to him] that *Ninigret* said that he heard that some ships were to come from Holland to the Monhattoes to cut off the English." "That an Indian told him that the Dutch would come against the English, and cut them off, but they would save the women and children and guns, for themselves. But Capt. *Simkins* and the said *Lightfoot* do both affirm that the said *Newcom* told them that the Dutchmen *told him,* as before [stated,] though he now puts it off, and saith an *Indian* told him so." Simkins affirmed also that *Newcom* told him that if he would go and serve the Dutch, they would give him a 100£ a year.

On examining *Newcom,* the commissioners gave it as their opinion that he was guilty of perfidy, and that they should not have let him escape without punishment, but for his being considered as an ambassador. They, therefore, desired *Awashaw* to inform *Ninigret* of it, that he might send him to them again, "the better to clear himself." This we apprehend was not done. *Awashaw* next notified the court that he had not done with them, "whereupon he was sent for to speak what he had further to propound." He demanded how they came by their information "of all these things touching *Ninigret*." They said from several Indians, *particularly* "the Monheage Indian and the Narraganset Indian, which were both taken by *Uncas* his men, who had confessed the plot before Mr. Haines at Hartford." Awashaw also demanded restitution of the wampum taken by Uncas. The commissioners told him that they had not as yet understood of the truth of that action, but when they had thoroughly examined it, he should have an *answer*.

So, all this legislating was about *Ninigret's going* to the Dutch; for as to a plot there appears no evidence or any; but when *Uncas* had committed a great depredation upon *Ninigret*, why—"that altered the case"—they must inquire into it, which doubtless was all right so far, but if a like complaint had been preferred against *Ninigret* by *Uncas*, we have reason to think it would have been forthwith "inquired into," at least, without an *if*.

A story, it cannot be called evidence, told by *Uncas*, relating to *Ninigret's* visit to the Dutch, is recorded by the commissioners, and which, if it amount to any thing, goes to prove himself guilty, and is indeed an acknowledgment of his own perfidy in taking *Ninigret's* boat and goods as charged by *Awashaw*. It is as follows:—

"*Uncas*, the Mohegan sachem, came lately to Mr. *Hains*' house at Hartford, and informed him that *Ninnigrett*, sachem of the Niantick Narragansetts, went this winter to the Monhatoes" and made a league with the Dutch governor, and for a large present of wampum received 20 guns and a great box of powder and bullets. *Ninigret* told him of the great injuries he had sustained from *Uncas* and the English. That on the other side of Hudson's River, *Ninigret* had a conference with a great many Indian sagamores, and desired their aid to cut off the Mohegans and English. Also, that, about two years since, *Ninigret* "sent to the Monheage sachem, and gave him a present of wampum, pressing him to procure a man skilful in magic workings, and an artist in poisoning, and send unto him; and he should receive more one hundredth fathom of wampum, which was to have been conveyed to the Monheage sachem, and the powaugh at the return of him that was to bring the poison. *Uncas* having intelligence of these things, caused a narrow watch to be set, by sea and land, for the apprehending of those persons; and accordingly took them returning in a canoe to the number of seven: whereof four of them were Narragansets, two strangers and one Pequatt. This was done in his absence, while he was with Mr. *Haines*, at Conecticott, and carried by those of his men that took them to Mohegen. Being there examined, two of them, the [Wampeage*] sachem's brother, and one Narraganset freely confessed the whole plot formerly expressed, and that one of their company was that powaugh and prisoner, pointing out the man. Upon this, his men in a rage slew him, fearing, as he said, least he should make an escape, or otherwise do either mischief to *Uncas* or the English, in case they should carry him with the rest before them, to Conecticott to be further examined. And being brought to Conecticott before Mr. *Haines*, and examined, did assert these particulars."

An Indian squaw also informed "an inhabitant of Wethersfield, that the Dutch and Indians generally were" confederating to cut off the English, and that election day, [1654,] was the time set, "because then it is apprehended the plantations will be left naked and unable to defend themselves, the strength of the English colonies being gathered from the

* See declaration onward in the records, (*Haz.* ii. 222.)

several towns. And the aforesaid squaw advised the said inhabitants to acquaint the rest of the English with it, desiring they would remember how dear their slighting of her former information of the Pequots coming upon the English cost them."*

It would seem, from a careful examination of the records, that something had been suggested either by the Dutch or Indians, about "cutting off the English," which justice to *Ninigret* requires us to state, might have been the case without *his* knowledge or participation. For, the testimony of the messengers of "nine Indian sagamores who live about the Monhatoes" no how implicates him, and, therefore, cannot be taken into account, any more than what an Indian named *Ronnessoke* told *Nicholas Tanner*, as interpreted by another Indian called *Addam*; the latter, though relating to *Ninigret's* visit, was only a hearsay affair. *Ronnessoke* was a sagamore of Long Island.

Addam also interpreted the story of another Indian, called *Powanege*, "who saith he came from the Indians who dwell over the river, over against the Monhatoes, where the plot is a working, that was this: that the Dutchmen asked the Indians whether they would leave them at the last cast, or stand up with them. And told the Indians they should fear nothing, and not be discouraged because the plot was discovered," &c.

Addam the interpreter had also a story to tell. He said, "this spring [1653, O. S.] the Dutch governor went to Fort Aurania, [since Albany,] and first went to a place called *Ackicksack*, [Hackinsack,] a great place of Indians, from thence to Monnesick, [Minisink,] thence to Opingona, thence to Warranoke, thence to Fort Aurania: And so far he went in his own person. From thence he sent to Pocomtock, [Deerfield, on the Connecticut,] and he carried with him many note of sewan, that is, bags of wampam, and delivered them to the sagamores of the places, and they were to distribute them amongst their men; and withal he carried powder, shot, cloth, lead and guns; and told them he would get all the great Indians under him, and the English should have the scum of the Indians, and he would have those sagamores with their men to cut off the English, and to be at his command whenever he had use of them, and he was to find them powder and shot till he had need of them. Further, he sent one Govert, a Dutchman, to Marsey, on Long Island, to *Nittanahom*, the sagamore, to assist him and to do for him what he would have [him] do: But the sagamore told him he would have nothing to [do] with it: whereupon Govert gave the sagamore a great kettle to be silent. *Nittanaham* told him he had but 20 men, and the English had never done him wrong, [and] he had no cause to fight against them. Further, he saith that *Ninnegrett*, the fiscal,† and the Dutch governor were up two days in a close room, with other sagamores; and there was no speaking with any of them except when they came for a coal of fire,‡

* Referring to an affair of 1637, which Dr. *I. Mather* relates as follows: "In the interim, [while Capt. *Mason* was protecting Saybrook fort,] many of the Pequods went to a place now called *Wethersfield* on Connecticut River, and having confederated with the Indians of that place, (as it was generally thought,) they laid in ambush for the English people of that place, and divers of them going to their labor in a large field adjoining to the town, were set upon by the Indians. Nine of the English were slain upon the place, and some horses, and two young women were taken captive." *Relation of the Troubles*, &c. 26.—Dr. *Trumbull* says this happened in April. *Hist. Con.* i. 77.

The cause of this act of the Pequots, according to *Winthrop*, i. 260, was this. An Indian called *Sequin* had given the English lands at Wethersfield, that he might live by them and be protected from other Indians. But when he came there, and had set down his wigwam, the English drove him away by force. And hence it was supposed that he had plotted their destruction, as above related, with the Pequots.

† A Dutch officer, whose duty is similar to that of treasurer among the English.

‡ To light their pipes, doubtless—the Dutch agreeing well, in the particular of smoking, with the Indians.

or the like. And much sewan was seen at that time in *Ninnegret's* hand, and he carried none away with him;" and that *Ronnesseoke* told him that the governor bid him fly for his life, for the plot was now discovered.

Nevertheless, as for any positive testimony that *Ninigret* was plotting against the English, there is none. That he was in a room to avoid company, while his physician was attending him, is very probable.

In a long letter, dated 26th May, 1653, which the governor of New Amsterdam, *Peter Stuyvesant*, wrote to the English, is the following passage:—"It is in part true, as your worships conclude, that, about January, there came a strange Indian from the north, called *Ninnigrett*, commander of the Narragansets. But he came hither with a pass from Mr. *John Winthrop*. Upon which pass, as we remember, the occasion of his coming was expressed, namely, to be cured and healed; and if, upon the other side of the river, there hath been any assembly or meeting of the Indians, or of their sagamores, we know not [of it.] We heard that he hath been upon Long Island, about Nayacke, where he hath been for the most part of the winter, and hath had several Indians with him, but what he hath negotiated with them remains to us unknown: only this we know, that what your worships lay unto our charge are false reports, and feigned informations."

The war with *Ascassasôtic*, of which we shall give all the particulars in our possession, was the next affair of any considerable moment in the life of *Ninigret*.

In 1654, the government of Rhode Island communicated to Massachusetts, that the last summer *Ninigret*, without any cause, "that he doth so much as allege, fell upon the Long Island Indians, our friends and tributaries," and killed many of them, and took others prisoners, and would not restore them. "This summer he hath made two assaults upon them; in one whereof he killed a man and woman, that lived upon the land of the English, and within one of their townships; and another Indian, that kept the cows of the English." He had drawn many of the foreign Indians down from Connecticut and Hudson Rivers, who rendezvoused upon Winthrop's Island, where they killed some of his cattle.* This war began in 1653, and continued "several years."†

The commissioners of the United Colonies seemed blind to all complaints against *Uncas;* but the Narragansets were watched and harassed without ceasing. Wherever we meet with an unpublished document of those times, the fact is very apparent. The chief of the writers of the history of that period copy from the records of the United Colonies, which accounts for their making out a good case for the English and Mohegans. The spirit which actuated the grave commissioners is easily discovered, and I need only refer my readers to the case of *Miantunnomoh*. Desperate errors require others, oftentimes still more desperate, until the first appear small compared with the magnitude of the last! It is all along discoverable, that those venerable records are made up from one kind of evidence, and that when a Narraganset appeared in his own defence, so many of his enemies stood ready to give him the lie, that his indignant spirit could not stoop to contradict or parley with them; and thus his assumed guilt passed on for history. The long-silenced and borne-down friend of the Indians of Moosehausic,‡ no longer sleeps. Amidst his toils and perils, he found time to raise his pen in their defence; and though his letters for a season slept with him, they are now awaking at the voice of day.

When the English had resolved, in 1654, to send a force against the Narragansets, because they had had difficulties and wars with *Ascassasô-*

---

* *Manuscript* documents. † *Wood's* Hist. Long Island. ‡ Providence.

tic, as we have related, Mr. *Williams* expressed his views of the matter in a letter to the governor of Massachusetts as follows:—"The cause and root of all the present mischiefs is the pride of two barbarians, *Ascassasôtick,* the Long Island sachem, and Nenekunat of the Narigenset. The former is proud and foolish, the latter is proud and fierce. I have not seen him these many years, yet, from their sober men, I hear he pleads, 1st. that *Ascassasôtick,* a very inferior sachem, (bearing himself upon the English,) hath slain three or four of his people, and since that sent him challenges and darings to fight and mend himself. 2d. He, *Nenekunat* consulted by solemn messengers, with the chief of the English governors, Maj. *Endicot,* then governor of the Massachusetts, who sent him an implicit consent to right himself: upon which they all plead that the English have just occasion of displeasure. 3d. After he had taken revenge upon the Long Islanders, and brought away about 14 captives, (divers of them chief women,) yet he restored them all again, upon the mediation and desire of the English. 4th. After this peace [was] made, the Long Islanders pretending to visit *Nenekunat* at Block Island, slaughtered of his Narragansets near 30 persons, at midnight; two of them of great note, especially *Wepiteammock's* son, to whom *Nenekunat* was uncle. 5th. In the prosecution of this war, although he had drawn down the inlanders to his assistance, yet, upon protestation of the English against his proceedings, he retreated and dissolved his army."*

The great Indian apostle looked not so much into these particulars, being entirely engaged in the cause of the praying Indians; but yet we occasionally meet with him, and will here introduce him, as an evidence against the proceeding of *Uncas,* and his friends the commissioners:

"The case of the Nipmuk Indians, so far as by the best and most credible intelligence, I have understood, presented to the honored general court, [of Massachusetts,] 1. *Uncas* his men, at unawares, set upon an unarmed poor people, and slew eight persons, and carried captive twenty-four women and children. 2. Some of these were subjects to Massachusetts government, by being the subjects of *Josias.*† 3. They sued for relief to the worshipful governor and magistrates. 4. They were pleased to send, (by some Indians,) a commission to Capt. *Denison,* [of Stonington,] to demand these captives. 5. *Uncas* his answer was, (as I heard,) insolent. 6. They did not only abuse the women by filthiness, but have, since this demand, sold away (as I hear) some or all of those captives. 7. The poor bereaved Indians wait to see what you please to do. 8. You were pleased to tell them, you would present it to the free court, and they should expect their answer from them, which they now wait for. 9. *Nenecroft,* yea, all the Indians of the country, wait to see the issue of this matter."‡

This memorial is dated 12th May, 1659, and signed by *John Eliot;* from which it is evident there had been great delay in relieving those distressed by the haughty *Uncas.* And yet, whether he was caused to make remuneration in any way, we do not find.

In 1660, "the general court of Connecticut did, by their letters directed to the commissioners of the other colonies, this last summer, represent an intolerable affront done by the Narraganset Indians, and the same was now complained of by the English living at a new plantation at Mohegan, viz: that some Indians did, in the dead time of the night, shoot eight bullets into an English house, and fired the same; wherein five Englishmen were asleep. Of which insolency the Narraganset sachems have so far taken notice, as to send a slight excuse by Maj. *Atherton,* that

---

* From the *original letter, in manuscript,* among the files in our state-house.

† Son of *Chikataubut.*

‡ *Manuscript state paper.*

they did neither consent to nor allow of such practices, but make no tender of satisfaction."* But they asked the privilege to meet the commissioners at their next session, at which time they gave them to understand that satisfaction should be made. This could not have been other than a reasonable request, but it was not granted; and messengers were forthwith ordered to "repair to *Ninigret, Pessicus, Woquacanoose*, and the rest of the Narraganset sachems," to demand "at least four of the chief of them that shot into the English house." And in case they should not be delivered, to demand five hundred fathoms of wampum. They were directed, in particular, to "charge Ninigret with breach of covenant, and high neglect of their order, sent them by Maj. *Willard*, six years since, not to invade the Long Island Indians; and [that they] do account the surprising the Long Island Indians at Gull Island, and murdering of them, to be an insolent carriage to the English, and a barbarous and inhuman act." These are only a few of the most prominent charges, and five hundred and ninety-five† fathoms of wampum was the price demanded for them; and "the general court of Connecticut is desired and empowered to send a convenient company of men, under some discreet leader, to force satisfaction of the same above said, and the charges of recovering the same; and in case the persons be delivered, they shall be sent to Barbadoes,"‡ and sold for slaves.

It appears that the force sent by Connecticut could not collect the wampum, nor secure the offenders; but for the payment, condescended to take a mortgage of all the Narraganset country, with the provision that it should be void, if it were paid in four months. *Quissoquus*,§ *Neneglud*, and *Scuttup*, || signed the deed.

Ninigret did not engage with the other Narraganset chiefs, in *Philip's* war. Dr. *Mather*¶ calls him an "old crafty sachem, who had with some of his men withdrawn himself from the rest." He must at this time have been "an old sachem," for we meet with him as a chief, as early as 1632.

Although *Ninigret* was not personally engaged in *Philip's* war, still he must have suffered considerably from it; often being obliged to send his people to the English, to gratify some whim or caprice, and at other times to appear himself. On 10 Sept. 1675, eight of his men came as ambassadors to Boston, "having a certificate from Capt. *Smith*,"** who owned a large estate in Narraganset. After having finished their business, they received a pass from the authorities to return to their own country. This certificate or pass was fastened to a staff and carried by one in front of the rest. As they were going out of Boston "a back way," two men met them, and seized upon him that carried the pass. These men were brothers, who had *had* a brother killed by *Philip's* men some time before. This Indian they accused of killing him, and in court swore to his identity, and he was in a few days hanged.††

Notwithstanding these affairs, another embassy was soon after sent to Boston. On the 15 Sept. "the authority of Boston sent a party" to order *Ninigret* to appear there in person, to give an account of his sheltering

* Record of the United Colonies, in *Hazard*.

† The additional ninety-five was for another offence, viz. "for the insolencies committed at Mr. *Brewster's*, in killing an Indian servant at Mrs. *Brewster's* feet, to her great affrightment, and stealing corn, &c., and other affronts." *Hazard*, ii. 433.

‡ Records of the United Colonies, in Hazard.

§ The same called *Quequegunent*, the son of *Magnus*. *Newcom* and *Awashars* were witnesses. The deed itself may be seen on file among our *State Papers*.

|| Grandson of *Canonicus*, son of *Magnus*, and brother of *Quequegunent*.

¶ Brief History, 20.

** Capt. *Richard Smith*, probably, who settled quite early in that country. We find him there 15 years before this.

†† Present State, &c., 14.

Quaiapen, the squaw-sachem of Narraganset. He sent word that he would come, "provided he might be safely returned back." Mr. *Smith,* "living near him, offered himself, wife and children, and estate, as hostages" for his safe return, and the embassy forthwith departed for Boston. A son,* however, of *Ninigret,* was deputed prime minister, "he himself being very aged."

Capt. *Smith* accompanied them, and when they came to Roxbury they were met by a company of English soldiers, whose martial appearance so frightened them, that, had it not been for the presence of Mr. *Smith,* they would have escaped as from an enemy.

They remained at Boston several days, until "by degrees they came to this agreement: That they were to deliver the squaw-sachem within so many days at Boston; and the league of peace was then by them confirmed, which was much to the general satisfaction; but many had hard thoughts of them, fearing they will at last prove treacherous."†

Ninigret was opposed to Christianity; not perhaps so much from a disbelief of it, as from a dislike of the practices of those who professed it. When Mr. *Mayhew* desired *Ninigret* to allow him to preach to his people, the sagacious chief "bid him go and make the English good first, and chid Mr. *Mayhew* for hindering him from his business and labor."‡

There were other Niantick sachems of this name, who succeeded Ninigret.

According to the author of the "Memoir of the Mohegans§," one would suppose he was alive in 1716, as that writer himself *supposed*; but if the anecdote there given be true, it related doubtless to *Charles* Ninigret, who, I suppose, was his son. He is mentioned by *Mason*, in his history of the Pequot war, as having received a part of the goods taken from Capt. *Stone*, at the time he was killed by the Pequots, in 1634. The time of his death has not been ascertained.

The burying-places of the family of *Ninigret* are in Charlestown, R. I. It is said that the old chief was buried at a place called Burying Hill, "a mile from the street." A stone in one of the places of interment has this inscription:—

"*Here leth the Body of George, the son of Charles Ninigret, King of the Natives, and of Hannah his Wife. Died Decembr. ye.22, 1732: aged 6 mo.*"

"*George*, the last king, was brother of *Mary Sachem*, who is now, [1832,] sole heir to the crown. *Mary* does not know her age; but from data given by her husband, *John Harry*, she must be about 66. Her mother's father was *George Ninigret. Thomas* his son was the next king. *Esther*, sister of *Thomas. George*, the brother of *Mary* above named, and the last king crowned, died aged about 20 years. *George* was son of *Esther. Mary* has daughters, but no sons."||

On a division of the captive Pequots, in 1637, *Ninigret* was to have twenty, "when he should satisfy for a mare of *Eltweed*¶ *Pomroye's* killed by his men." This remained unsettled in 1659, a space of twenty-two years. This debt *certainly was outlawed! Poquin*, or *Poquoiam*, was the name of the man who killed the mare.**

He was a Pequot, and brother-in-law to *Miantunnomoh*, and was among those captives assigned to him at their final dispersion, when the Pequot war was ended; at which time *Pomeroy* states "all sorts of horses were at an high price." *Miantunnomoh* had agreed to pay the demand, but his death prevented him. *Ninigret* was called upon, as he inherited a considerable part of *Miantunnomoh's* estate, especially his part of the

* Probably *Catapazat*.

† Present State, *ut supra*.

‡ Douglas's Summary, ii, 118.

§ In 1 *Col. Mass. Hist. Soc.* ix. 83.

|| MS. communication of Rev. *Wm. Ely*.

¶ Familiarly called *Elty*, probably from *Eltwood*.

** Hazard, ii. 188, 189.

Pequots, of whom *Poquoiam* was one. He was afterwards called a Niantick and *brother* to *Ninigret.**

Pessacus, often mentioned in the preceding pages, though under a variety of names, was born about 1623, and, consequently, was about 20 years of age when his brother, *Miantunnomoh*, was killed.† The same arbitrary course, as we have seen already in the present chapter, was pursued towards him by the English, as had been before to *Miantunnomoh*, and still continued towards *Ninigret*, and other Narraganset chiefs. Mr. *Cobbet*‡ makes this record of him: "In the year 1645, proud *Pessacus* with his Narragansets, with whom *Ninigret* and his Niantigs join; so as to provoke the English to a just war against them. And, accordingly, forces were sent from all the towns to meet at Boston, and did so, and had a party of fifty horse to go with them under Mr. *Leveret*, as the captain of the horse." *Edward Gibbons* was commander in chief, and Mr. *Thompson*, pastor of the church in Braintree, "was to sound the silver trumpet along with his army."§ But they were met by deputies from *Pessacus* and the other chiefs, and an accommodation took place, as mentioned in the account of *Ninigret*.

The commissioners, having met at New Haven in Sept. 1646, expected, according to the treaty made at Boston with the Narragansets, as particularized in the life of *Uncas*, that they would now meet them here to settle the remaining difficulties with that chief. But the time having nearly expired, and none appearing, "the commissioners did seriously consider what course should be taken with them. They called to minde their breach of couenant in all the articles, that when aboue 1300 fadome of wampan was due they sent, as if they would put a scorne vpon the [English,] 20 fathome, and a few old kettles." The Narragansets said it was owing to the backwardness of the Nianticks that the wampum had not been paid, and the Nianticks laid it to the Narragansets. One hundred fathom had been sent to the governor of Massachusetts as a present by the Nianticks, they promising "to send what was due to the colonies uery speedily," but he would not accept of it. He told them they might leave it with *Cuchamakin*, and when they had performed the rest of their agreement, "he would consider of it." The commissioners had understood, that, in the mean time, the Narraganset sachems had raised wampum among their men, "and by good euidence it appeared, that by presents of wampum, they are practisinge with the Mohawkes, and with the Indyans in those parts, to engage them in some designe against the English and *Vncus*." Therefore, "the commissioners haue a cleare way open to right themselues, accordinge to iustice by war; yet to shew how highly they prize peace with all men, and particularly to manifest their forbearance and long sufferinge to these barbarians, it was agreede, that first the forementioned present should be returned," and then a declaration of war to follow.

At the same court, complaint was brought against the people of *Pessacus* by "Mr. *Pelham* on behalf of *Richard Woody* and Mr. *Pincham*," [*Pinchon*,] that they had committed sundry thefts. Mr. *Brown*, on behalf of *Wm. Smith* of Rehoboth, preferred a similar charge; but the Indians having no knowledge of the procedure, it was suspended.

Thus the Narragansets were suffered to remain unmolested until the next year, and we do not hear that the story about their hiring the Mohawks and others to assist them against *Uncas* and the English, turned out to be any thing else but a sort of bugbear, probably invented by the

* See Hazard, ii. 152.

† MS. letter, subscribed with the mark of the sachem *Pumham*, on file at our capital, (Mass.)

‡ MS. Narrative.

§ Mather's Relation, and Hazard.

Mohegans. "One principall cause of the comissioners meetinge together at this time, [26 July, 1647,] being," say the records, "to consider what course should be held with the Narraganset Indyans;" the charges being at this time much the same as at the previous meeting. It was therefore ordered that *Thomas Stanton, Benedict Arnold,* and Sergeant *Waite* should be sent to *Pessacks, Nenegrate* and *Webetamuk,* to know why they had not paid the wampum as they agreed, and why they did not come to New Haven; and that now they might meet *Uncas* at Boston; and therefore were advised to attend there without delay; but "yf they refuse or delay, they intend to send no more," and they must abide the consequences. When the English messengers had delivered their message to *Pessacus,* he spoke to them as, follows:—

"*The reason I did not meet the English sachems at New Haven last year, is, they did not notify me. It is true I have broken my covenant these two years, and that now is, and constantly has been, the grief of my spirit. And the reason I do not meet them now at Boston is because I am sick. If I were but pretty well I would go. I have sent my mind in full to Ninigret, and what he does I will abide by. I have sent* Powpynamett *and* Pomumsks *to go and hear, and testify that I have betrusted my full mind with* Nenegratt. *You know well, however, that when I made that covenant two years ago, I did it in fear of the army that I did see; and though the English kept their covenant with me, yet they were ready to go to Narraganset and kill me, and the commissioners said they would do it, if I did not sign what they had written."*

Moyanno, another chief, said he had confided the business with *Ninigret* last spring, and would now abide by whatever he should do.

When the English messengers returned and made known what had been done, the commissioners said that *Pessacus*' speech contained "seuerall passages of vntruth and guile, and [they] were vnsatisfyed."

What measures the English took "to right themselues,"' or whether any, immediately, is not very distinctly stated; but the next year, 1648, there were some military movements of the English towards his country, occasioned by the non-payment of the tribute, and some other less important matters. *Pessacus,* having knowledge of their approach, fled to R. Island. "*Ninicraft* entertained them courteously, (there they staid the Lord's day,) and came back with them to Mr. *Williams',* and then *Pessacus* and *Canonicus*' son, being delivered of their fear, came to them; and being demanded about hiring the Mohawks against *Uncas,* they solemnly denied it; only they confessed, that the Mohawks, being a great sachem, and their ancient friend, and being come so near them, they sent some 20 fathom of wampum for him to tread upon, as the manner of Indians is."* The matter seems to have rested here; *Pessacus,* as usual, having promised what was desired.

This chief was killed by the Mohawks, as we have stated in the life of Canonicus. His life was a scene of almost perpetual troubles. As late as September, 1668, his name stands first among others of his nation, in a complaint sent to them by Massachusetts. The messengers sent with it were *Rich*[d]. *Wayt, Capt. W Wright* and Capt. *Sam*[l]. *Mosely*; and it was in terms thus:—

"Whereas Capt. *Wm. Hudson* and *John Viall* of Boston, in the name of themselves and others, proprietors of lands and farms in the Narraganset country, have complained unto us, [the court of Mass.,] of the great insolencies and injuries offered unto them and their people by several, as burning their hay, killing sundry horses, and in special manner, about one month since, forced some of their people from their labors in mowing

* *Winthrop's Journal.*

grass upon their own land, and assaulted others in the high way, as they rode about their occasions; by throwing many stones at them and their horses, and beating their horses as they rode upon them," &c. The remonstrance then goes on warning them to desist, or otherwise they might expect severity. Had *Mosely* been as well known then among the Indians, as he was afterwards, his presence would doubtless have been enough to have caused quietness, as perhaps it did even at this time.

CHAPTER V.

"So swift and black a storm behind them low'rd,
On wings of fear thro' dismal wastes they soar'd.
Destruction of the Pequots."

Uncas—*His character—Connections—Geography of the Mohegan country—General account of that nation—Uncas joins the English against the Pequots—Captures a chief at Sachem's Head—Visits Boston—His speech to Gov. Winthrop—Specimen of the Mohegan language—Sequasson—The war between Uncas and Miantunnomoh—Examination of its cause—The Narragansets determine to avenge their sachem's death—Forces raised to protect Uncas—Pessacus—Great distress of Uncas—Timely relief from Connecticut—Treaty of 1645—Frequent complaints against Uncas—Wequash—Obechickwod—Woosamequin.*

Uncas, sachem of the Mohegans, of whom we have already had occasion to say considerable, has left no very favorable character upon record. His life is a series of changes, without any of those brilliant acts of magnanimity, which throw a veil over numerous errors. Mr. *Gookin* gives us this character of him in the year 1674: (Mr. *James Fitch* having been sent about this time to preach among the Mohegans:) "I am apt to fear, says he, that a great obstruction unto his labors is in the sachem of those Indians, whose name is *Unkas*; an old and wicked, wilful man, a drunkard, and otherwise very vicious; who hath always been an opposer and underminer of praying to God."* Nevertheless, the charitable Mr. *Hubbard*, when he wrote his Narrative, seems to have had some hopes that he was a Christian, with about the same grounds, nay better, perhaps, than those on which Bishop *Warburton* declared *Pope* to be such.

Uncas lived to a great age. He was a sachem before the Pequot wars, and was alive in 1680. At this time, Mr. *Hubbard* makes this remark upon him: "He is alive and well, and may probably live to see all his enemies buried before him."†

From an epitaph on one of his sons, copied in the Historical Collections, we do not infer, as the writer there seems to have done, "that the race of *Uncas*" was "obnoxious in collonial history;" but rather attribute it to some waggish Englishman, who had no other design than that of making sport for himself and others. It is upon his tomb-stone, and is as follows:

Here lies the body of *Sunseeto*
Own son to Uncas grandson to *Oneko*‡
Who were the famous sachems of MOHEGAN
But now they are all dead I think it is *werheegen*."§

The connections of *Uncas* were somewhat numerous, and the names of several of them will be found as we proceed with his life, and elsewhere. *Oneko* his son was the most noted of them.

Uncas was originally a Pequot, and one of the 26 war captains of that famous but ill-fated nation. Upon some intestine commotions, he revolted against his sachem, and set up for himself. This took place about the time that nation became known to the English, perhaps in 1634 or 5.

By the revolt of *Uncas,* the Pequot territories became divided, and that part called *Moheag*, or *Mohegan*, fell generally under his dominion, and extended from near the Connecticut River on the south to a space of disputed country on the north, next the Narragansets. By a recurrence to our account of the dominions of the Pequots and Narragansets, a pretty clear idea may be had of all three.

This sachem seems early to have courted the favor of the English, which it is reasonable to suppose was occasioned by the fear he was in from his potent and warlike neighbors, both on the north and on the south. In May, 1637, he was prevailed upon to join the English in their war upon the Pequots. Knowing the relation in which he stood to them, the English at first were nearly as afraid of *Uncas* and his men, as they were of the Pequots. But when, on the 15 of the same month, they had arrived at Saybrook fort, a circumstance happened that tended much to remove their suspicions, and is related by Dr. *Mather* as follows: "Some of *Uncas* his men being then at Saybrook, in order to assisting the English against the Pequots, espied seven Indians, and slily encompassing them, slew five of them, and took one prisoner, and brought him to the English fort, which was great satisfaction and encouragement to the English; who, before that exploit, had many fears touching the fidelity of the Moheag Indians. He whom they took prisoner was a perfidious villain, one that could speak English well, having in times past lived in the fort,

---

* 1 *Col. Mass. Hist. Soc.* i. 208. Moheek, since *Montville*, Ct., about 10 miles north of New London, is the place "where *Unkas*, and his sons, and *Wanuho*, are sachems." *Ibid*.

† Hist. New. Eng. 464.—"Although he be a friend to the English, yet he and all his men continue pagans still," 1676. Dr. *I. Mather,* Brief Hist. 45.

‡ The writer or sculptor no doubt meant the contrary of this, if indeed he may be said to have meant any thing.

§ A genuine Indian word, and, as it is used here, means, simply, *well*. "Then they bid me stir my instep, to see if that were frozen: I did so. When they saw that, they said that was *wurregen*." *Stockwell's Nar. of his Captivity among the Indians in* 1677.

and knowing all the English there, had been at the slaughtering of all the English that were slaughtered thereabouts. He was a continual spy about the fort, informing *Sassacus* of what he could learn. When this bloody traitor was executed, his limbs were by violence pulled from one another, and burned to ashes. Some of the Indian executioners barbarously taking his flesh, they gave it to one another, and did eat it, withal singing about the fire."*

Notwithstanding, both Uncas and *Miantunnomoh* were accused of harboring fugitive Pequots, after the Mystic fight, as our accounts will abundantly prove. It is true they had agreed not to harbor them, but perhaps the philanthropist will not judge them harder for erring on the score of mercy, than their English friends for their strictly religious perseverance in revenge.

A traditionary story of *Uncas* pursuing, overtaking, and executing a Pequot sachem, as given in the Historical Collections, may not be unqualifiedly true. It was after Mystic fight, and is as follows: Most of the English forces pursued the fugitives by water, westward, while some followed by land with *Uncas* and his Indians. At a point of land in Guilford, they came upon a great Pequot sachem, and a few of his men. Knowing they were pursued, they had gone into an adjacent peninsula, "hoping their pursuers would have passed by them. But *Uncas* knew Indian's craft, and ordered some of his men to search that point. The Pequots perceiving that they were pursued, swam over the mouth of the harbor, which is narrow. But they were waylaid, and taken as they landed. The sachem was sentenced to be shot to death. *Uncas* shot him with an arrow, cut off his head, and stuck it up in the crotch of a large oak tree near the harbor, where the skull remained for a great many years."† This was the origin of SACHEM'S HEAD, by which name the harbor of Guilford is well known to coasters.

Dr. *Mather* records the expedition of the English, but makes no mention of *Uncas*. He says, they set out from Saybrook fort, and "sailed westward in pursuit of the Pequots, who were fled that way. Sailing along to the westward of Mononowuttuck, the wind not answering their desires, they cast anchor." "Some scattering Pequots were then taken and slain, as also the Pequot sachem, before expressed,‡ had his head cut off, whence that place did bear the name of SACHEM'S HEAD."§

Uncas's fear of the Pequots was doubtless the cause of his hostility to them; and when he saw them vanquished, he probably began to relent his unprovoked severity towards his countrymen, many of whom were his near relations; and this may account for his endeavors to screen some of them from their more vindictive enemies. The next spring after the war, "*Unkus*, alias *Okoco,* the Monahegan sachem in the twist of Pequod River, came to Boston with 37 men. He came from Connecticut with Mr. *Haynes,* and tendered the governor a present of 20 fathom of wampum. This was at court, and it was thought fit by the council to refuse it, till he had given satisfaction about the Pequots he kept, &c. Upon this he was much dejected, and made account we would have killed him; but, two days after, having received good satisfaction of his innocency, &c. and he promising to submit to the order of the English, touching the Pequots he had, and the differences between the Naragansetts and him, we accepted his present. And about half an hour after, he came to the governor," and made the following speech. Laying his hand upon his breast, he said,

"*This heart is not mine, but yours. I have no men: they are all yours.*

* Relation of the Troubles, &c. 46.
† Hist. *Guilford*, in 1 *Col. Mass. Hist.* Soc. 100.
‡ His name is not mentioned.
§ Relation, 49.

Command me any difficult thing, I will do it. I will not believe any Indians' words against the English. If any man shall kill an Englishman, I will put him to death, were he never so dear to me."

"So the governor gave him a fair red coat, and defrayed his and his men's diet, and gave them corn to relieve them homeward, and a letter of protection to all men, &c. and he departed very joyful."*

For the gratification of the curious, we give, from Dr. *Edwards's* "Observations on the Muhkekaneew [Mohegan] Language," the Lord's prayer in that dialect. "*Nogh-nuh, ne spummuck oi-e-on, taugh mau-weh wneh wtu-ko-se-auk ne-an-ne an-nu-woi-e-on. Taugh ne aun-chu-wut-am-mun wa-weh-tu-seek ma-weh noh pum-meh. Ne ae-noi-hit-teeh mau-weh aw-au-neek noh hkey oie-cheek, ne aun-chu-wut-am-mun, ne au-noi-hit-teet neek spum-muk oie-cheek. Men-e-nau-nuh noo-nooh wuh-ham-auk tquogh nuh uh-huy-u-tam-auk ngum-mau-weh. Ohq-u-ut-a-mou-we-nau-nuh au-neh mu-ma-choi-e-au-keh he anneh ohq-u-ut-a-mou-woi-e-auk num-peh neek mu-ma-cheh an-neh-o-quau-keet. Cheen hqu-uk-quau-cheh-si-u-keh an-neh-e-henau-nuh. Pan-nee-weh htou-we-nau-nuh neen maum-teh-keh. Ke-ah ng-weh-cheh kwi-ou-wau-weh mau-weh noh pum-meh; kt-an-woi; es-tah aw-aun w-tin-noi-yu-wun ne au-noi-e-yon; han-wee-weh ne kt-in-noi-een.*"

Uncas was said to have been engaged in all the wars against his countrymen, on the part of the English, during his life-time.† He shielded some of the infant settlements of Connecticut in times of troubles, especially Norwich. To the inhabitants of this town the Mohegans seemed more particularly attached, probably from the circumstance of some of its settlers having relieved them when besieged by *Ninigret*, as will be found related in the ensuing history. The remnant of the Mohegans, in 1768, was settled in the north-east corner of New London, about five miles south of Norwich; at which place they had a reservation.

The Mohegans had a burying-place called the Royal *burying-ground*, and this was set apart for the family of *Uncas*. It is close by the falls of the stream called Yantic River, in Norwich city; "a beautiful and romantic spot." The ground containing the grave of Uncas is at present owned by *C. Goddard*, Esq. of Norwich. This gentleman has, very laudably, caused an enclosure to be set about it.‡

When the commissioners of the United Colonies had met in 1643, complaint was made to them by *Uncas*, that *Miantunnomoh* had employed a Pequot to kill him, and that this Pequot was one of his own subjects. He shot *Uncas* with an arrow, and, not doubting but that he had accomplished his purpose, "fled to the Nanohiggansets, or their confederates," and proclaimed that he had killed him. "But when it was known *Vncas* was not dead, though wounded, the traitor was taught to say that *Uncus* had cut through his own arm with a flint, and hired the Pequot to say he had shot and killed him. *Myantinomo* being sent for by the governor of the Massachusetts upon another occasion, brought the Pequot with him: but when this disguise would not serve, and that the English out of his [the Pequot's] own mouth found him guilty, and would have sent him to *Uncus* his sagamore to be proceeded against, *Myantinomo* desired he might not be taken out of his hands, promising [that] he would send [him] himself to *Vncus* to be examined and punished; but, contrary to his promise, and fearing, as it appears, his own treachery might be discouered, he within a day or two cut off the Peacott's head, that he might tell no tales. After this some attempts were made to poison *Vncus*, and, as is reported, to take away his life by sorcery. That being discovered, some

* *Winthrop*, Jour. i. 265—6.

† MS. communication of Rev. *Mr. Ely*.

‡ 3 Col. Mass. Hist. Soc. iii. 135.

of *Sequasson's* company, an Indian sagamore allied to, and an intimate confederate with *Myantinomo*, shot at *Uncus* as he was going down Conectacatt River with a arrow or two. *Vncus*, according to the foresaid agreement," which was, in case of difficulty between them, that the English should be applied to as umpires, complained to them. They endeavored to bring about a peace between *Uncas* and *Sequasson*; but *Sequasson* would hear to no overtures of the kind, and intimated that he should be borne out in his resolution by *Miantunnomoh*. The result was the war of which we have given an account in the life of *Miantunnomoh*. We have also spoken there of the agency of the English in the affair of *Miantunnomoh's* death; but that no light may be withheld which can in any way reflect upon that important as well as melancholy event, we will give all that the commissioners have recorded in their records concerning it. But firstly, we should notice, that, after *Miantunnomoh* was taken prisoner, the Indians affirmed, (the adherents of *Uncas* doubtless,) that *Miantunnomoh* had engaged the Mohawks to join him in his wars, and that they were then encamped only a day's journey from the frontiers, waiting for him to attain his liberty. The record then proceeds:—

"These things being duly weighed and considered, the commissioners apparently see that *Vncus* cannot be safe while *Myantenomo* lives; but that, either by secret treachery or open force, his life will be still in danger. Wherefore they think he may justly put such a false and bloodthirsty enemy to death; but in his own jurisdiction, not in the English plantations. And advising that, in the manner of his death, all mercy and moderation be showed, contrary to the practice of the Indians who exercise tortures and cruelty. And *Vncus* having hitherto shown himself a friend to the English, and in this craving their advice; [therefore,] if the Nanohiggansitts Indians or others shall unjustly assault *Vncus* for this execution, upon notice and request the English promise to assist and protect him, as far as they may, against such violence."

We presume not to commentate upon this affair, but we would ask whether it does not appear as probable, that *Uncas* had concerted the plan with his Pequot subject for the destruction of *Miantunnomoh*, as that the latter had plotted for the destruction of the former. Else, why did *Miantunnomoh* put the Pequot to death? The commissioners do not say that the Pequot had by his confession any how implicated *Miantunnomoh*. Now, if this Pequot had been employed by him, it does not seem at all likely that he would have put him to death, especially as he had not accused him. And, on the other hand, if he had acknowledged himself guilty of attempting the life of his own sachem, that it might be charged upon others, it is to us a plain reason why *Miantunnomoh* should put him to death, being fully satisfied of his guilt upon his own confession. It may be concluded, therefore, that the plot against *Uncas* was of his own or his Pequot subject's planning. The Pequot's going over to *Miantunnomoh* for protection is no evidence of that chief's participation in his plot. And it is highly probable that, after they had left the English court, his crime was aggravated, in *Miantunnomoh's* view, by some new confession or discovery, which caused him to be forthwith executed.

As though well assured that the justness of their interference would be called in question, the commissioners shortly after added another clause to their records, as much in exoneration of their conduct as they could find words in which to express themselves. They argue that, "whereas *Uncas* was advised [by them] to take away the life of *Miantunnomoh* whose lawful captive he was, they [the Narragansets] may well understand that this is without violation of any covenant between them and us; for *Uncas* being in confederation with us, and one that hath diligently observed his covenants before mentioned, for aught we know, and requiring advice from us, upon serious consideration of the premises, viz. his treacherous and murderous disposition against *Uncas*, &c. and how great a disturber he hath been of the common peace of the whole country, we could not in respect of the justice of the case, safety of the country, and faithfulness of our friend, do otherwise than approve of the lawfulness of his death; which agreeing so well with the Indians' own manners, and concurring with the practice of other nations with whom we are acquainted; we persuaded ourselves, however his death may be grievous at present, yet the peaceable fruits of it will yield not only matter of safety to the Indians, but profit to all that inhabit this continent."

It is believed that the reader is now put in possession of every thing that the English could say for themselves, upon the execution of Mian-*tunnomoh*. He will therefore be able to decide, whether, as we have stated, their judgment was made up of one kind of evidence; and whether the Narragansets had any lawyers to advocate their cause before the commissioners.

After *Miantunnomoh* was executed, the Narragansets demanded satisfaction of *Uncas* for the money they had raised and paid for the redemption of their chief. This demand was through the English commissioners; who, when they were met, in Sept. 1644, deputed *Thomas Stanton* to notify both parties to appear before them, that they might decide upon the case according to the evidence which should be produced.

It appears that *Kienemo*,* the Niantick sachem, immediately deputed *Weetowisse*, a sachem, *Pawpiamet* and *Pummumshe*, captains, from the Narragansets, with two of their men, to maintain their action before the commissioners, and to complain of some insolences of *Uncas* besides.† On a full hearing, the commissioners say, that nothing was substantiated by them. "Though," they say, "several discourses had passed from *Uncas* and his men, that for such quantities of wampum and such parcels of other goods to a great value, there might have been some probability of sparing his life." Hence it appears that *Uncas* had actually entered upon a negotiation with the Narragansets, as in the life of *Miantunnomoh* has been stated; and it does not, it is thought, require but a slight acquaintance with the general drift of these affairs, to discern, that *Uncas* had encouraged the Narragansets to send wampum, that is, their money, giving them to understand that he would not be hard with them; in so far, that they had trusted to his generosity, and sent him a considerable amount. The very face of it shows clearly, that it was a trick of *Uncas* to leave the amount indefinitely stated, which gave him the chance, (that a knave will always seize upon,) to act according to the caprice of his own mind on any pretence afterwards.

The commissioners say that "no such parcels were brought," though, in a few lines after, in their records, we read: "And for that wampums and goods sent, [to *Uncas*,] as they were but *small parcels*, and scarce considerable for such a purpose," namely the redemption of their chief: and still, they add; "But *Uncas* denieth, and the Narraganset deputies did not alledge, much less prove that any ransom was agreed, nor so much as any treaty begun to redeem their imprisoned sachem." Therefore it appears quite clear that *Uncas* had all the English in his favor, who, to preserve his friendship, caressed and called him their friend; while, on the other hand, the agents from the Narragansets were frowned upon,

---

* The same afterwards called *Ninigret*. *Janemo* was doubtless the pronunciation, *J* being at that time pronounced ji; therefore *Jianemo* might have been sometimes understood *Kianemo*.

† The author of *Tales of the Indians* seems dismally confused in attempting to narrate these affairs, but see *Hazard*, ii. 25 and 26.

and no doubt labored under the disadvantage of not being personally known to the English.

As to the goods which *Uncas* had received, the commissioners say, "A part of them [were] disposed [of] by *Miantunnomoh* himself, to *Uncas'* counsellors and captains, for some favor, either past or hoped for, and part were given and sent to *Uncas*, and to his squaw for preserving his life so long, and using him courteously during his imprisonment."

Here ended this matter; but before the Narraganset deputies left the court, the English made them sign an agreement that they would not make war upon *Uncas*, "vntill after the next planting of corn." And even then, that they should give 30 days' notice to the English before commencing hostilities. Also that if "any of the Nayantick Pecotts should make any assault upon *Uncas* or any of his, they would deliver them up to the English to be punished according to their demerits. And that they would not use any means to procure the Mawhakes to come against *Uncas* during this truce." At the same time the English took due care to notify the Narraganset commissioners, by way of awing them into terms, that if they did molest the Mohegans, all the English would be upon them.

The date of this agreement, if so we may call it, is, "Hartford, the xviijth of September, 1644," and was signed by four Indians; one besides those named above, called *Chimough*.

That no passage might be left open for excuse, in case of war, it was also mentioned, that "proof of the ransom charged" must be made satisfactory to the English before war was begun.

The power of *Pessacus* and *Ninigret* at this time was much feared by the English, and they were ready to believe any reports of the hostile doings of the Narragansets, who, since the subjection of the Pequots, had made themselves masters of all their neighbors, except the English, as the Pequots had done before them. The Mohegans were also in great fear of them, as well after as before the death of *Miantunnomoh*; but for whose misfortune in being made a prisoner by a stratagem of *Uncas*, or his captains, the English might have seen far greater troubles from them than they did, judging from the known abilities of that great chief.

There was "a meeting extraordinary" of the commissioners of the United Colonies, in July 1645, at Boston, "concerning the French business, and the wars between *Pissicus* and *Vncus* being begun." Their first business was to despatch away messengers to request the appearance of the head men of the belligerents to appear themselves at Boston, or to send some of their chief men, that the difficulties between them might be settled.

These messengers, Sergeant *John Dames,* [*Davis*?] *Benedict Arnold,* and *Francis Smyth,* on their first arrival at Narraganset, were welcomed by the sachems, who offered them guides to conduct them to *Uncas;* but, either having understood their intentions, or judging from their appearance that the English messengers meant them no good, changed their deportment altogether, and in the mean time secretly despatched messengers to the Nianticks before them, giving them to understand what was going forward. After this, say the messengers, "there was nothing but proud and insolent passages [from *Ninigret.*] The Indian guides which they had brought with them from *Pumham* and *Sokakanoco* were, by frowns and threatening speeches, discouraged, and returned; no other guides could be obtained." The sachems said they knew, by what was done at Hartford last year, that the English would urge peace, "*but they were resolved, they said, to have no peace without Uncas his head.*" As to who began the war, they cared not, but they were resolved to continue it; that if the English did not withdraw their soldiers from *Uncas,* they should consider it a breach of former covenants, and would procure as many Mohawks as the English had soldiers to bring against them. They reviled *Uncas* for having wounded himself, and then charging it upon them, and said he was no friend of the English, but would now, if he durst, kill the English messengers, and lay that to them. Therefore, not being able to proceed, the English messengers returned to the Narragansets, and acquainted *Pessacus* of what had passed, desiring he would furnish them with guides; "he, (in scorn, as they apprehended it,) offered them an old Peacott squaw."

The messengers now thought themselves in danger of being massacred; "three Indians with hatchets standing behind the interpreter in a suspicious manner, while he was speaking with *Pessacus*, and the rest frowning and expressing much distemper in their countenance and carriage." So, without much loss of time, they began to retrace their steps. On leaving *Pessacus*, they told him they should lodge at an English trading house not far off that night, and if he wanted to send any word to the English, he might send to them. In the morning, he invited them to return, and said he would furnish them with guides to visit *Uncas*, but he would not suspend hostilities. Not daring to risk the journey, the messengers returned home. *Arnold*, the interpreter, testified that this was a true relation of what had passed, which is necessary to be borne in mind, as something may appear, as we proceed, impeaching the veracity of *Arnold*.

Meanwhile the commissioners set forth an armament to defend *Uncas*, at all hazards. To justify this movement, they declare, that, "considering the great provocations offered, and the necessity we should be put unto of making war upon the Narrohiggin, &c. and being also careful in a matter of so great weight and general concernment to see the way cleared and to give satisfaction to all the colonists, did think fit to advise with such of the magistrates and elders of the Massachusetts as were then at hand, and also with some of the chief military commanders there, who being assembled, it was then agreed: First, that our engagement bound us to aid and defend the Mohegan sachem. Secondly, that this aid could not be intended only to defend him and his, in his fort or habitation, but, (according to the common acceptation of such covenants or engagements considered with the ground or occasion thereof,) so to aid him as hee might be preserved in his liberty and estate. Thirdly, that this aid must be speedy, least he might be swallowed up in the mean time, and so come too late."

"According to the counsel and determination aforesaid, the commissioners, considering the present danger of *Uncas* the Mohegan sachem, (his fort having been divers times assaulted by a great army of the Narrohiggansets, &c.) agreed to have 40 soldiers sent with all expedition for his defense." Lieut. *Atherton* and Sergeant *John Davis* led this company, conducted by two of "*Cutchamakin's*" Indians as guides. *Atherton* was ordered not to make an "attempt upon the town otherwise than in Uncas' defence." Capt. *Mason* of Connecticut was to join him, and take the chief command. Forty men were ordered also from Connecticut, and 30 from New Haven under Lieut. *Sealy*. In their instructions to *Mason*, the commissioners say, "We so now aim at the protection of the Mohegans, that we would have no opportunity neglected to weaken the Narragansets and their confederates, in their number of men, their cane canoes, wigwams, wampum and goods. We look upon the Nianticks as the chief incendiaries and causes of the war, and should be glad they might first feel the smart of it." The Nianticks, therefore, were particularly to be had in view by *Mason*, and he was informed at the same time that Massachusetts and Plimouth were forthwith to send "another army to invade the Narragansets."

The commissioners now proceeded to make choice of a commander in chief of the two armies. Maj. *Edward Gibbons* was unanimously elected. In his instructions is this passage: "Whereas the scope and cause of this expedition is not only to aid the Mohegans, but to offend the Narragansets, Nianticks, and other their confederates." He was directed also to conclude a peace with them, if they desired it, provided it were made with special reference to damages, &c. And they say, "But withal, according to our engagements, you are to provide for *Uncas'* future safety, that his plantations be not invaded, that his men and squaws may attend their planting and fishing and other occasions without fear or injury, and *Vssamequine, Pomham, Sokakonoco, Cutchamakin,* and other Indians, friends or subjects to the English, be not molested," &c.

Soon after the death of *Miantunnomoh,* which was in September, 1643, his brother *Pessacus,* "the new sachem of Narraganset," then "a young man about 20," sent to Governor *Winthrop* of Massachusetts, as a present, an *otter coat,* a girdle of wampum, and some of that article besides, in value about £15. The messenger, named *Washose,** also a sachem, told the governor that his chief desired to continue in peace with the English; but that he was about to make war upon *Uncas,* to avenge the death of his brother, and hoped they would not interfere, nor aid *Uncas.* The governor said they wished to be at peace with all Indians, and that all Indians would be at peace among themselves, and that they must agree to this, or they could not accept their present. *Washose* said he was instructed no further than to make known his mission and leave the present, which he did, and returned to his own country. This was in Feb. 1644, N. S. Within the same month, the same messenger appeared again at Boston; and "his errand was, (says Gov. *Winthrop,*) that, seeing they, at our request, had set still this year, that now this next year we would grant their request, and suffer them to fight with *Onkus,* with many arguments." But he was answered, that the English would not allow such a proceeding, and if they persisted, all the English would fall upon them.

Planting time, and 30 days besides, had passed before the English sent an army to invade the Narragansets. *Pessacus* and the other chiefs had done all they could do to cause the English to remain neutral, but now determined to wait no longer, and hostile acts were committed on both sides.

The traditionary account of *Uncas's* being besieged in his fort by the Narragansets will very properly be looked for in this connection, as it has not only adorned many *tales of the Indians,* but has been seriously urged as truth in more imposing forms. What we are about to give is contained in a letter, dated at New Haven, 19 Sept. 1796, by *Wm. Leffingwell,* and directed *Dr. Trumbull.*

"At the time the Mohegan tribe of Indians were besieged by the Narraganset tribe, in a fort near the River Thames, between Norwich and New London, the provisions of the besieged being nearly exhausted, *Uncas,* their sachem, found means to inform the settlers at Saybrook of their distress, and the danger they would be in from the Narragansets, if the Mohegan tribe were cut off. Ensign *Thomas Leffingwell,* one of the first settlers there, loaded a canoe with beef, corn and peas, and in the night time paddled from Saybrook into the Thames, and had the address to get the whole into the fort of the besieged;—received a deed from *Uncas* of the town of Norwich, and made his escape that very night. In consequence of which, the besiegers, finding *Uncas* had procured relie., raised the siege, and the Mohegan tribe were saved, and have ever proved strict friends to the N. England settlers."†

---

* Perhaps the same as *Awashers.*

† Copied from the original, for the author, by Rev. *Wm. Ely,* who thus remarks upon

The above agrees very well with Mr. *Hyde's* account. "When *Uncas* and tribe were attacked by a potent enemy, and blocked up in their fort on a hill, by the side of the great river, and almost starved to death, Lieut. *Thos. Leffingwell,* Capt. *Benj. Brewster,* of said Norwich, and others, secretly carried their provision, in the night seasons, upon which the enemy raised the siege."* In consideration of which, "Uncas gave sundry donations of land," &c.†

At the congress of the commissioners at Boston, in 1645, above mentioned, it was ascertained that the present from *Pessacus* still remained among them, and therefore he might think it was probable that the English had complied with their desires, as they had not returned it. Lest this should be so understood, Capt. *Harding,* Mr. *Welborne* and *Benedict Arnold* were ordered and commissioned to repair to the Narraganset

---

it: "This tradition, from a highly respectable source, *Trumbull* states as history; yet, in some minor points, at least, it would seem obvious that the tradition could not have been strictly preserved for 150 years." *MS. letter.*

* Some very beautiful verses appeared several years since in the Connecticut Mirror, to which it seems the above had given rise. They were prefaced with the following among other observations: "In the neighborhood of Mohegan is a rude recess, environed by rocks, which still retains the name of the 'chair of *Uncas;*'" and that the people of *Uncus* were perishing with hunger when *Leffingwell* brought him relief. We give the following stanzas from it:—

"The monarch sat on his rocky throne,
Before him the waters lay;
His guards were shapeless columns of stone,
Their lofty helmets with moss o'ergrown,
And their spears of the bracken gray.

"His lamps were the fickle stars, that beamed
Through the veil of their midnight shroud,
And the reddening flashes that fitfully gleamed
When the distant fires of the war-dance streamed
Where his foes in frantic revel screamed
'Neath their canopy of cloud," &c.

"Behind him his leaguered forces lay
Withering in famine's blight,
And he knew, with the blush of the morning ray,
That *Philip* would summon his fierce array
On the core of the warrior's heart to prey,
And quench a nation's light.

"It comes! it comes!—that misty speck
Which over the waters moves!
It boasts no sail, nor mast, nor deck;
Yet dearer to him was that nameless wreck
Than the maid to him who loves," &c.

"The eye of the king with that rapture blazed
Which the soul in its rapture sends;
His prayer to the Spirit of good he raised,
And the shades of his buried fathers praised,
As toward his fort he wends.

"That king hath gone to his lowly grave!
He slumbers in dark decay;
And like the crest of the tossing wave,
Like the rush of the blast, from the mountain cave,
Like the groan of the murdered, with none to save,
His people have passed away," &c.

† MS. letter to Dr. *Trumbull* before cited and life of *Miantunnomoh.*

country, and to see, if possible, "*Piscus, Canownacus, Janemo,*" and other sachems, and to return the present before mentioned, and to inform them that the English were well aware of their beginning and prosecuting a war upon *Uncas*, and their "having wounded and slain divers of his men, seized many of his canoes, taken some prisoners, spoiled much of his corn," refused to treat with him, and threatened the English. Nevertheless, if they would come themselves forthwith to Boston, they should be heard and protected in their journey, but that none except themselves would be treated with, and if they refused to come, the English were prepared for war, and would proceed immediately against them.

Harding and *Welborne* proceeded to Providence, where *Arnold* was to join them. But he was not there, and they were informed that he dared not venture among the Narragansets. Whether he had been acting the *traitor* with them, or something quite as much to merit condemnation, we will leave the reader to judge from the relation. The two former, therefore, made use of Rev. Mr. *Williams* as interpreter in their business, but were reprimanded by the commissioners for it on their return. On going to the Narraganset sachems, and opening their business, it appeared that all they were ordered to charge them with was not true; or, at least, denied by them. These charges, it appears, had been preferred by *Arnold*, and sworn to upon oath. The chiefs said "that *Ianemo*, the Nyantick sachem, had been ill divers days, but had now sent six men to present his respects to the English, and to declare his assent and submission to what the Narrohiggenset sachems and the English should agree upon."

It was in the end agreed, that the chiefs, *Pessacus*, *Mexam*, and divers others, should proceed to Boston, agreeably to the desire of the English, which they did, in company with *Harding* and *Welborne*, who brought back the old present, and for which they also received the censure of the congress. They arrived at Boston just as the second levy of troops were marching out for their country, and thus the expedition was stayed until the result of a treaty should be made known.

It appeared, on a conference with the commissioners, that the sachems did not fully understand the nature of all the charges against them before leaving their country, and in justice to them it should be observed, that, so far as the record goes, their case appears to us the easiest to be defended of the three parties concerned. They told the commissioners of sundry charges they had against *Uncas*, but they said they could not hear them, for *Uncas* was not there to speak for himself; and that they had hindered his being notified of their coming. As to a breach of covenant, they maintained, for some time, that they had committed none, and that their treatment of the English had been misrepresented. "But, (says our record,) after a long debate and some priuate conferrence, they had with Serjeant *Cullicutt*, they acknowledged they had brooken promise or couenant in the afore menconed warrs, and offerred to make another truce with *Vncas*, either till next planting tyme, as they had done last yeare at Hartford, or for a yeare, or a yeare and a quarter."

They had been induced to make this admission, no doubt, by the persuasion of *Cullicut*, who, probably, was instructed to inform them that the safety of their country depended upon their compliance with the wishes of the English at this time. An army of soldiers was at that moment parading the streets, in all the pomposity of a modern training, which must have reminded them of the horrible destruction of their kindred at Mystic eight years before.

The proposition of a truce being objected to by the English, "one of the sachems offered a stick or a wand to the commissioners, expressing himself, that therewith they put the power and disposition of the war into their hands, and desired to know *what the English would require of them."* They were answered that the expenses and trouble they had caused the English were very great, "besides the damage *Vncas* had sustained; yet to show *their moderacon,* they would require of them but *twoo thousand* fathome of white wampon for their owne satisfaccon," but that they should restore to *Uncas* all the captives and canoes taken from him, and make restitution for all the corn they had spoiled. As for the last-mentioned offence, the sachems asserted there had been none such; for *it was not the manner of the Indians to destroy corn.*

This most excellent and indirect reproof must have had no small effect on those who heard it, as no doubt some of the actors as well as the advisers of the destruction of the Indians' corn, previous to and during the Pequot war, were now present: Block Island, and the fertile fields upon the shores of the Connecticut, must have magnified before their imaginations.

Considering, therefore, that this charge was merely imaginary, and that *Uncas* had taken and killed some of their people, the English *consented* that *Uncas "might"* restore such captives and canoes as he had taken from them. Finally, they agreed to pay the wampum, "crauing onely some ease in the manner and tymes of payment," and on the evening of *"the xxvijth of the 6 month,* (August,) 1645," articles to the following effect were signed by the principal Indians present:—

1. That the Narragansets and Nianticks had made war upon the Mohegans contrary to former treaties; that the English had sent messengers to them without success, which had made them prepare for war.
2. That chiefs duly authorized were now at Boston, and having acknowledged their breach of treaties, having "thereby not only endamaged Vncas, but had brought much charge and trouble vpon all the English colonies, which they confest were just they should satisfy."
3. That the sachems agree for their nations to pay to the English 2000 fathom "of good white wampum, or a third part of good black wampempeage, in four payments, namely," 500 fathom in 20 days, 500 in four months, 500 at or before next planting time, and 500 in two years, which the English agree to accept as full "satisfaccon."
4. That each party of the Indians was to restore to the other all things taken, and where canoes were destroyed, others "in the roome of them, full as good," were to be given in return. The English obligated themselves for *Uncas.*
5. That as many matters cannot be treated of on account of the absence of Uncas, they are to be deferred until the next meeting of the commissioners at Hartford, in Sept. 1646, where both parties should be heard.
6. The Narraganset and Niantick sachems bind themselves to keep peace with the English and their successors, "and with *Vncas* the Mohegan sachem and his men, with *Vssamequin,* Pomham, Sokaknooco, Cutchamakin, Shoanan,† Passaconaway,* and all others. And that, in case difficulties occur, they are to apply to the English.
7. They promise to deliver up to the English all fugitives who shall at any time be found among them; to pay a yearly tribute, "a month before Indian harvest, every year after this, at Boston," "for all such Pecotts as live amongst them," according to the treaty of 1638; "namely, one fathom of white wampum for each Pequot man, and half a fathom for each Peacott youth, and one hand length of wampum for each Peacott man-child; and if *Weekwash Cake‡* refuse to pay this tribute for any

* *Ousamequin.*

† Perhaps *Shoshanim,* or *Sholan.*

‡ *Wequash Cook.*

Peacotts with him, the Narrohigganset sagamores promise to assist the English against him;" and to yield up to the English the whole Pequot country.

8. The sachems promise to deliver four of their children into the hands of the English, "viz[t]. *Pissacus* his eldest sonn, the sonn of *Tassaquanawitt*, brother to *Pissacus*, *Awashanoe* his sonn, and *Ewangeso's* sonn, a Nyantick, to be kept as pledges or hostages," until the wampum should be all paid, and they had met *Uncas* at Hartford, and *Janemo* and *Wypetock** had signed these articles. As the children were to be sent for, *Witowash, Pomamse, Jawassoe*, and *Waughwamino* offered their persons as security for their delivery, which were accepted.

9. Both the securities and hostages were to be supported at the charge of the English.

10. That if any hostilities were committed while this treaty was making, and before its provisions were known, such acts not to be considered a violation thereof.

11. They agree not to sell any of their lands without the consent of the commissioners.

12. If any Pequots should be found among them who had murdered English, they were to be delivered to the English. Here follow the names, with a mark to each.

PESSECUS,
AUMSAAQUEN,† *deputy for the Nianticks*,
ABDAS,
POMMUSH,
CUTCHAMAKINS,
WEEKESANNO,
WITTOWASH.

We do not see *Mexam's* or *Mixanno's* name among the signers, although he is mentioned as being present, unless another name was then applied to him. There were four interpreters employed upon the occasion, namely, Serg. *Cullicut* and his Indian man, *Cutchamakin* and *Josias*.‡

From this time to the next meeting of the commissioners, the country seems not to have been much disturbed. In the mean time, however, Uncas, without any regard to the promise and obligations the English had laid themselves under for him, undertook to chastise a Narraganset sachem for some alleged offence. On opening their congress, at New Haven, letters from Mr. *Morton* and Mr. *Peters*, at Pequot, were read by the commissioners, giving accounts of *Uncas's* perfidy. The complainants were sent to, and informed that *Uncas* was shortly to be there, and that they should bring their proof in order to a trial.

Meanwhile *Uncas* came, who, after waiting a few days, and his accusers not appearing, was examined and dismissed. It appears that the English at Nameoke, since Saybrook, were the suffering party, as their neighborhood was the scene of *Uncas's* depredations. Of some of the charges he acknowledged himself guilty, especially of fighting *Neckwash* [Wequash] *Cooke* so near to the plantation at Pequot; although he alleged that some of the English there had encouraged *Wequash* to hunt upon his lands. He was informed that his brother had also been guilty of some offence, but neither the accuser nor the accused were present, and, therefore, it could not be acted upon. So, after a kind of *reprimand, Uncas* was dismissed, as we have just mentioned. But before he had left the

* *Wepiteamock*. † *Awasequin*.

‡ Son of *Chikataubut*, probably.

town, Mr. *Wm. Morton* arrived at court, with three Indians, to maintain the action against him; he was, therefore, called in, and a hearing was had, "but the commissioners founde noe cause to alter the former writinge giuen him." This was as regarded the affair with *Wequash.* Mr. *Morton* then produced a Pequot powwow, named *Wampushet,* who, he said, had charged *Uncas* with having hired him to do violence to another Indian, or to procure it to be done, which accordingly was effected, the Indian being wounded with a hatchet. This crime was at first laid to the charge of *Wequash,* as *Uncas* had intended. "But after [wards,] the Pequat's powow, troubled in conscience, could have no rest till he had discoured *Vncus* to be the author." He first related his guilt to *Robin,** an Indian servant of Mr. *Winthrop*; but, to the surprise of the whole court, *Wampushet,* the only witness, on being questioned through Mr. *Stanton,* the interpreter, told a story diametrically the reverse of what he had before stated. "He cleared *Vncus,* and cast the plot and guilt vpon *Neckwash Cooke* and *Robin*;" "and though the other two Pequats, whereof the one was *Robin's* brother, seemed much offended," and said *Uncas* had hired him to alter his charge, "yet he persisted, and said *Neckwash Cooke* and *Robin* had giuen him a payre of breeches, and promised him 25 fadome of wampum, to cast the plot upon *Vncus,* and that the English plantacon and Pequats knew it. The commissioners abhorring this diuillish falshoode, and advisinge Vncus, if he expected any favoure and respect from the English, to haue no hand in any such designes or vniust wayes."

Hence it appears that the court did not doubt much of the villany of *Uncas,* but, for reasons not required here to be named, he was treated as a fond parent often treats a disobedient child; reminded of the end to which such crimes lead; and seem to threaten chastisement in their words, while their deportment holds out quite different language.

At the congress of the United Colonies at Boston, in July, 1647, Mr. *John Winthrop* of Connecticut presented a petition, "in the name of many Pequatts," in the preamble of which *Casmamon* and *Obechiquod* are named, requesting that they might have liberty to dwell somewhere under the protection of the English, that they might appoint. They acknowledged that their sachems and people had done very ill against the English formerly, for which they had justly suffered, and been rightfully conquered by the English; but that they had had no hand, by consent or otherwise, in shedding the blood of the English, and that it was by the advice of *Necquash*† that they fled from their country, being promised by him that the English would not hurt them, if they did not join against them. The names of 62 craving pardon and protection were at the same time communicated.

In answer the commissioners say, that while *Wequash* lived he had made no mention of "such innocent Pequats, or from any other person since;" and on "enquiry from *Thomas Stanton,* from *Foxon,* one of *Uncus* his men, and at last by confession of the Pequats present, found that some of the petitioners were in Mistick fort in fight against the English, and fled away in the smoke," and that others were at other times in arms against the English and Mohegans, and, therefore, the ground of their petition was false and deceitful.

It appears that they had taken refuge under *Uncas,* who had promised

---

* His Indian name was *Casmamon,* perhaps the same as *Cassassinnamon,* or *Casasinemon,* &c.

† *Wequash,* the traitor. He became a noted praying Indian, after the Pequot war, and was supposed to have died by poison. Frequent mention will be found of him elsewhere in our work.

them good usage, which was probably on condition that they should pay him a tribute. They resided at this time at Namyok.

At the same court *Obechiquod* complained that *Uncas* had forcibly taken away his wife, and criminally obliged her to live with him. "*Foxon* being present, as *Uncas's* deputy, was questioned about this base and unsufferable outrage; he denied that *Uncas* either took or kept away *Obechiquod's* wife by force, and affirmed that [on] *Obechiquod's* withdrawing, with other Pequots, from *Uncas*, his wife refused to go with him; and that, among the Indians, it is usual when a wife so deserts her husband, another may take her. *Obechiquod* affirmed that *Uncas* had dealt criminally before, and still kept her against her will."

Though not satisfied in point of proof, the commissioners say, "Yet abhoring that lustful adulterous carriage of *Uncas*, as it is acknowledged and mittigated by *Foxon*," ordered that he should restore the wife, and that *Obechiquod* have liberty to settle under the protection of the English, where they should direct.*

Complaints at this time were as thick upon the head of *Uncas* as can well be conceived of, and still we do not imagine that half the crimes he was guilty of, are upon record. Another Indian named *Sanaps*, at the same time, complained that he had dealt in like manner with the wife of another chief, since dead; that he had taken away his corn and beans, and attempted his life also. The court say they found no proof, "first or last, of these charges," still, as to the corn and beans, "*Foxon* conceives *Uncas* seized it because *Sannop*, with a Pequot, in a disorderly manner withdrew himself from *Uncas*." Hence it seems not much evidence was required, as *Uncas's* deputy uniformly pleaded guilty; and the court could do no less than order that, on investigation, he should make restitution. As to *Sannop*, who was "no Pequot," but a "Connecticut Indian," he had liberty to live under the protection of the English also.

We pass now to the year 1651, omitting to notice some few events more or less connected with our subject, which, in another chapter, may properly pass under review.

Last year, *Thos. Stanton* had been ordered "to get an account of the number and names of the several Pequots living among the Narragansets, Nianticks, or Mohegan Indians, &c.; who, by an agreement made after the Pequot war, are justly tributaries to the English colonies, and to receive the tribute due for this last year." *Stanton* now appeared as interpreter, and with him came also *Uncas* and several of his men, *Wequash Cook* and some of "*Ninnacraft's*" men, "*Robert*, a Pequot, sometimes a servant to Mr. *Winthrop*, and some with him, and some Pequots living on Long Island." They at this time delivered 312 fathom of wampum. Of this *Uncas* brought 79, *Ninigret's* men 91, &c.

"This wampum being laid down, *Uncas* and others of the Pequots demanded why this tribute was required, how long it was to continue, and whether the children to be born hereafter were to pay it." They were answered that the tribute had been due yearly from the Pequots since 1638, on account of their murders, wars, &c. upon the English. "Wherefore the commissioners might have required both account and payment, as of a just debt, for time past, but are contented, if it be thankfully accepted, to remit what is past, accounting only from 1650, when *Thomas Stanton's* employment and salary began." Also that the tribute should end in ten years more, and that children hereafter born should be exempt. Hitherto all male children were taxed.

---

* This chief is the same, we believe, called in a later part of the records, (Hazard, ii. 413,) *Abbachickwood*. He was fined, with seven others, ten fathom of wampum for going to fight the Pocomptuck Indians with *Uncas*, in the summer of 1659.

The next matter with which we shall proceed has, in the life of *Ousamequin*, been merely glanced at, and reserved for this place, to which it more properly belongs.

We have now arrived to the year 1661, and it was in the spring of this year that a war broke out between *Uncas* and the old sachem before named. It seems very clear that the Wampanoags had been friendly to the Narragansets, for a long time previous, but, separated as they were from them, were not often involved in their troubles. They saw how *Uncas* was favored by the English, and were, therefore, careful to have nothing to do with the Mohegans, from whom they were still farther removed. Of the rise, progress and termination of their war upon the Quabaogs, a tribe of Nipmucks belonging to *Ousamequin*, the reader may gather the most important facts from some documents,* which we shall in the next place lay before him.

"MERCURIUS DE QUABACONK, or a declaration of the dealings of *Uncas* and the Mohegin Indians, to certain Indians the inhabitants of Quabaconk, 21, 3d mo. 1661.

"About ten weeks since *Uncas'* son, accompanied with 70 Indians, set upon the Indians at Quabaconk, and slew three persons, and carried away six prisoners; among which were one squaw and her two children, whom when he had brought to the fort, *Uncas* dismissed the squaw, on conditions that she would go home and bring him £25 in peag, two guns and two blankets, for the release of herself and her children, which as yet she hath not done, being retained by the sagamore of Weshakeim, in hopes that their league with the English will free them.

"At the same time he carried away also, in stuff and money, to the value of £37, and at such time as *Uncas* received notice of the displeasure of the English in the Massachusetts by the worshipful Mr. *Winthrop*, he insolently laughed them to scorn, and professed that he would still go on as he had begun, and assay who dares to controll him. Moreover, four days since there came home a prisoner that escaped; two yet remaining, whom *Uncas* threatens, the one of them to kill, and the other to sell away as a slave, and still threatens to continue his war against them, notwithstanding any prohibition whatsoever; whose very threats are so terrible, that our Indians dare not wander far from the towns about the Indians for fear of surprise.

From the relation of
PAMBASSUA,
and testimony of
WASAMAGIN,
QUAQUEQUUNSET,
and others."

From this narrative it is very plain that *Uncas* cared very little for the displeasure of the English: it is plain, also, that he knew as well as they what kept them from dealing as severely with him as with the Narragansets, his neighbors. They must succumb to him, to keep him in a temper to aid in fighting their battles when called upon. Hence, when he had committed the grossest insults on other Indians, the wheels of justice often moved so slow, that they arrived not at their object until it had become quite another matter. It must, however, be considered that the English were very peculiarly situated—upon the very margin of an unknown wilderness, enclosed but on one side by Indians, whose chief business was war. They had destroyed the Pequots, but this only added

* In manuscript, and never before published.

to their fears, for they knew that revenge lurked still in the breasts of many, who only were waiting for an opportunity to gratify it; therefore, so long as one of the most numerous tribes could possibly be kept on their side, the English considered themselves in safety. They had made many missteps in their proceedings with the Indians, owing sometimes to one cause and sometimes to another, for which now there was no remedy; and it is doubtful whether, even at this day, if any set of men were to go into an unknown region and settle among wild men, that they would get along with them so much better than our fathers did with the Indians here, as some may have imagined. These are considerations which must be taken into account in estimating the "wrongs of the Indians." They seem the more necessary, in this place, for in the biography of *Uncas* there is as much, perhaps, to censure regarding the acts of the English, as in any other article of Indian history.

The narrative just recited being sent in to the court of Massachusetts, was referred to a select committee, who, on the 1 June, reported,

That letters should be sent to *Uncas,* signifying how sensible the court was of the injuries he had done them, by his outrage upon the Indians of Quabaconk, who lived under their sagamore *Wassamagin,* as set forth in the narrative. That, therefore, they now desired him to give up the captives and make restitution for all the goods taken from them, and to forbear for time to come all such unlawful acts. That if *Wassamagin* or his subjects had or should do him or his subjects any wrong, the English would, upon due proof, cause recompense to be made. Also that Uncas be given to understand and assured, that if he refuse to comply with the request, they were then resolved to right the injuries upon him and his, and for all costs they might be put to in the service. "That for the encouragement and safety of the sayd *Wassamagin* and his subjects, there be by order of Major *Willard* three or four armed men, well accomodate in all respects, with a proporcon of powder, bulletts and match sent from Lancaster to Quabaconk vnto the sayd *Wassamagin,* there to stay a night or two, and to shoote of their musquets so often, and in such wise, as the major shall direct, to terrifie the enemies of *Wassamagin,* and so to return home again." To inform *Wassamagin* and his subjects that the authorities of Massachusetts would esteem it an acknowledgment of their regard, if they would permit them to have the captives to be recovered from *Uncas,* to bring them up in a proper manner, that they might be serviceable to their friends, &c. Also, "aduice and require *Wassamagin* and his men to be verie carefull of iniuring or any ways prouoking of *Vncas,* or any of his men, as he will answer our displeasure therein, and incurr due punishment for the same." That if *Uncas* committed any other hostile acts, he must complain to them, &c.* Thus Ousamequin was as much threatened as *Uncas.*

Matters seem to have remained thus until the meeting of the commissioners in September following; when, in due course, the business was called up, and acted upon as follows:—

"Vpon complaint made to the comissionars of the Massachusetts against *Vnkas,* this following message was sent to him:—

"*Vncas,* wee haue receiued information and complaint from the generall court of the Massachusetts of youer hostile invading of *Wosamequin* and the Indians of Quabakutt, whoe are and longe haue bine subjects to the English, killing some and carrying away others; spoyling theire goods to the vallue of 33lb. as they allege." That he had done this contrary to his covenants, and had taken no notice of the demands of the Massachusetts, though some time since they had ordered him to deliver up the captives,

* Here ends our MSS. relating to this affair.

make remuneration, &c. And to which he had returned no answer; "which," continues the letter, "seemes to bee an insolent and proud carriage of youers. We cannot but wonder att it, and must beare witness against it." He was, as before, required to return the captives, &c., and give reasons for his operations; and if he neglected to do so, the Massachusetts were at liberty to right themselves.

In the mean time, as we apprehend, a letter from *Uncas* was received, written by Capt. *Mason*, which was as follows:—

"Wheras there was a warrant sent from the court of Boston, dated in my last to *Vncas*, sachem of Mohegen, wherin it was declared vpon the complaint of *Wesamequen*,* a sachem subject to the Massachusetts, that the said *Vncas* had offered great violence to theire subjects at Quabauk, killing some and taking others captiue; which warrant came not to *Uncas*, not aboue 20 daies before these presents, who, being summoned by Major *John Mason*, in full scope of the said warrant, wherein he was deeply charged if he did not return the captiues, and £33 damage, then the Massachusetts would recouer it by force of armes, which to him was uery grieuous: professing he was altogether ignorant that they were subjects belonging to the Massachusetts; and further said that they were none of *Wesamequen's* men, but belonging to *Onopequin*, his deadly enemie, whoe was there borne; one of the men then taken was his own cousin, who had formerly fought against him in his own person; and yett sett him att libertie; and further saith that all the captiues were sent home. Alsoe that *Wesamequin*['s] son, and diuers of his men had fought against him diuers times. This he desired might bee returned as his answare to the comissioners.

"*Allexander* allis *Wamsutta*, sachem of Sowamsett, being now att Plymouth, hee challenged Quabauke Indians to belong to him; and further said that hee did warr against *Vncas* this summer on that account.†

Signed by

JOHN MASON."

The particulars of the issue of these troubles were not recorded, and the presumption is, that *Uncas* complied with the reasonable requests of the English, and the old peaceable *Ousamequin*, being unwilling to get into difficulty, put up with the result without avenging his wrongs. His son, *Wamsutta*, as will be seen, about this time found himself involved in difficulties nearer home, which probably prevented him from continuing the war against *Uncas*, had he been otherwise disposed.

* By this it would seem that *Massasoit* had, for some time, resided among the Nipmucks. He had, probably, given up Pokanoket to his sons.

† It seems always to have been uncertain to whom the Nipmucks belonged. *Roger Williams* says, in 1668, "That all the Neepmucks were unquestionably subject to the Nanhigonset sachems, and, in a special manner, to *Mejksah*, the son of *Caunounicus*, and late husband to this old *Squaw-Sachem*, now only surviving. I have abundant and daily proof of it," &c. MS. *letter*. See life *Massasoit*, b. ii. chap. ii.

At one time, *Kutshamakin* claimed some of the Nipmucks, or consented to be made a tool of by some of them, for some private end. But Mr. *Pynchon* said they would not own him as a sachem any longer "than the sun shined upon him." Had they belonged to him, Massachusetts must have owned them, which would have involved them in much difficulty in 1648, by reason of several murders among them.

CHAPTER VI.

*Of the Pequot nation—Geography of their country—*SASSACUS, *their first chief, known to the English—War—The cause of it—*WEQUASH—*Canonicus and Miantunnomoh accused of harboring fugitive Pequots—Sassamon—*MONONOTTO—*Otash*—CASSASSINNAMON.

IT is said by Mr. *Hubbard*,* that the Pequots,† "being a more fierce, cruel and warlike people than the rest of the Indians, came down out of the more inland parts of the continent, and by force seized upon one of the goodliest places near the sea, and became a terror to all their neighbors." The time of their emigration is unknown. They made all the other tribes "stand in awe, though fewer in number than the Narragansets, that bordered next upon them."‡

Their country, according to Mr. *Gookin*,§ "the English of Connecticut jurisdiction, doth now, [1674,] for the most part, possess." Their dominion, or that of their chief sachem, was, according to the same author, "over divers petty sagamores; as over part of Long Island, over the Mohegans, and over the sagamores of Quinapeake, [now New Haven,] yea, over all the people that dwelt upon Connecticut River, and over some of the most southerly inhabitants of the Nipmuck country, about Quinabaag." The principal seat of the sagamores was near the mouth of Pequot River, now called the Thames, where New London stands. "These Pequots, as old Indians relate, could in former times, raise 4000 men fit for war."|| The first great chief of this nation, known to the English, was *Sassacus*, whose name was a terror to all the neighboring tribes of Indians. From the fruitful letters of the Rev. *Roger Williams*, we learn that he had a brother by the name of *Puppompoges*, whose residence was at Monahiganick, probably Mohegan. Although *Sassacus's* principal residence was upon the Thames, yet, in his highest prosperity, he had under him no less than 26 sachems, and his dominions were from Narraganset Bay to Hudson's River, in the direction of the sea-coast. Long Island was also under him, and his authority was undisputed far into the country.

About the time the English had determined on the subjugation of the Pequots, *Roger Williams* wrote to Governor *Winthrop* of Massachusetts, giving him important directions how they should proceed to advantage, and what was very important then, gave the following rude draft of their country:—

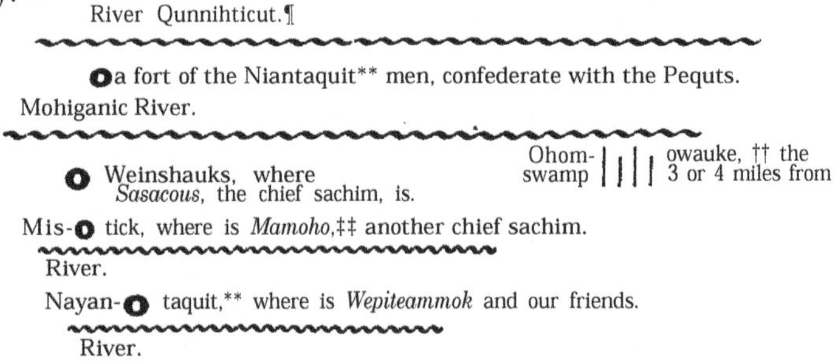

River Qunnihticut.¶

~~~~~~~~~~~~~~~~~~~~~~~~~~~~~~~

O a fort of the Niantaquit** men, confederate with the Pequts.

Mohiganic River.

~~~~~~~~~~~~~~~~~~~~~~~~~~~~~~~

O Weinshauks, where *Sasacous*, the chief sachim, is. Ohom- | | | owauke, †† the swamp | | | 3 or 4 miles from

Mis-O tick, where is *Mamoho*,‡‡ another chief sachim.

~~~~~~~~~~~~~~~~~~~~~~

River.

Nayan-O taquit,** where is *Wepiteammok* and our friends.

~~~~~~~~~~~~~~~~~~~~~~

River.

* Narrative, i. 116.
† We believe this name meant *Gray foxes*, hence Gray-fox Indians, or Pequots.
‡ Hist. New England, 33.
§ See his *Collections* in 1 Col. Mass. Hist. Soc. i. 147.
|| Ib *Same letter.*
¶ Connecticut. ** Niantick. †† A name signifying an *Owl's nest.*
‡‡ Probably *Mononotto.*

In the same letter, Mr. *Williams* urges the necessity of employing faithful guides for the English forces; "as shall be best liked of [to] be taken along to direct, especially two Pequts; viz. *Wequash*, [whose name signified a swan,] and *Wuttackquiackommin*, valiant men, especially the latter, who have lived these three or four years with the Nanhiggonticks, and know every pass and passage amongst them, who desire armor to enter their houses."

The Pequots having, for a long time, exercised their power without restraint among their countrymen, according to the custom of savage nations, which was a *right* always assumed by the strongest, and yet too much the case with those nations calling themselves civilized, extended, therefore, the same carriage towards the English as to the rest of their neighbors—killing such as came in their way, who refused a compliance with their demands. Captains *Stone, Norton* and *Oldham*, were successively murdered by them, in and about Connecticut River. The English could get no satisfaction of them, and being assured of the assistance of the Narragansets, determined to subdue them. Early in the summer of 1637, forces from Connecticut, under Captain *John Mason*, and from Massachusetts, under Captain *Israel Stoughton*, were sent on this design. A part of the Massachusetts forces only, under Captain *Underhill*, who was before stationed at Saybrook fort, shared in the taking of the strong fort of *Sassacus*. This fort was situated upon an eminence in the present town of Groton, Connecticut. The English arrived in its vicinity on the 25th of May; and on the 26th, before day, with about 500 Indians, encompassed it, and began a furious attack. The Mohegans and Narragansets discovered great fear on approaching the fort, and could not believe that the English would dare to attack it. When they came to the foot of the hill on which it was situated, Captain *Mason* was apprehensive of being abandoned by them, and, making a halt, sent for *Uncas*, who led the Mohegans, and *Wequash*, their pilot, who was a fugitive Pequot chief,* and urged them not to desert him, but to follow him at any distance they pleased. These Indians had all along told the English they dared not fight the Pequots, but boasted how *they* themselves would fight. *Mason* told them now they should see whether Englishmen would fight or not. Notwithstanding their boastings, they could not overcome the terror which the name of *Sassacus* had inspired in them, and they kept at a safe distance, until the fight was over; but assisted considerably in repelling the attacks of the Pequots, in the retreat from the fort;—for the Pequots, on recovering from their consternation, collected in a considerable body, and fought the confederates for many miles.

The English had but 77 men, which were divided into two companies, one led by *Mason*, and the other by *Underhill*. The Indians were all within their fort, asleep in their wigwams, and the barking of a dog was the first notice they had of the approach of the enemy, yet very few knew the cause of the alarm, until met by the naked swords of the foe. The fort had two entrances at opposite points, into which each party of English were led, sword in hand. "*Wanux! wanux!*"† was the cry of *Sassacus's* men; and such was their surprise, that they made very feeble resistance. Having only their own missile weapons, they could do nothing at hand to hand, with the English broad-swords. They were pursued

* The same, it is believed, elsewhere called *Waquash Cook*; "which *Wequash*, (says Dr. I. *Mather*,) was by birth a sachem of that place, [where *Sassacus* lived,] but upon some disgust received, he went from the Pequots to the Narragansets, and became a chief captain under *Miantunnomoh*." Relation, 74.

† *Allen's* History of the Pequot War. It signified, *Englishmen! Englishmen!* In *Mason's* history, it is written *Owanux*. *Allen* merely copied from *Mason*, with a few such variations.

from wigwam to wigwam, and slaughtered in every secret place. Women and children were cut to pieces, while endeavoring to hide themselves in and under their beds. At length fire was set in the mats that covered the wigwams, which furiously spread over the whole fort, and the dead and dying were together consumed. A part of the English had formed a circumference upon the outside, and shot such as attempted to fly. Many ascended the pickets to escape the flames, but were shot down by those stationed for that purpose. About 600 persons were supposed to have perished in this fight; or perhaps I should say, massacre.* There were but two English killed, and about 20 wounded. *Sassacus* himself was in another fort, and being informed of the ravages of the English, destroyed his habitations, and, with about 80 others, fled to the Mohawks, who treacherously beheaded him.

Notwithstanding the great slaughter at Mistick, there were great numbers of Pequots in the country, and were hunted from swamp to swamp, and their numbers thinned continually, until a remnant promised to appear no more as a nation.

The English, under Captain *Stoughton,* came into Pequot River about a fortnight after the Mistick fight, and assisted in the work of their extermination. After his arrival in the enemy's country, he wrote to the governor of Massachusetts, as follows:—"By this pinnace, you shall receive 48 or 50 women and children, unless there stay any here to be helpful, &c. Concerning which, there is one, I formerly mentioned, that is the fairest and largest that I saw amongst them, to whom I have given a coate to cloathe her. It is my desire to have her for a servant, if it may stand with your good liking, else not. There is a little squaw that steward *Culacut* desireth, to whom he hath given a coate. Lieut. *Davenport* also desireth one, to wit, a small one, that hath three strokes upon her stomach, thus:— ||| +. He desireth her, if it will stand with your good liking. *Sosomon,* the Indian, desireth a young little squaw, which I know not.

"At present, Mr. *Haynes,* Mr. *Ludlo,* Captain *Mason,* and 30 men are with us in Pequot River, and we shall the next week joine in seeing what we can do against *Sassacus,* and another great sagamore, *Monowattuck,* [*Mononotto.*] Here is yet good work to be done, and how dear it will cost is unknown. *Sassacus* is resolved to sell his life, and so the other with their company, as dear as they can."†

Perhaps it will be judged that *Stoughton* was looking more after the profit arising from the sale of captives, than for warriors to fight with. Indeed, *Mason's* account does not give him much credit.

There was a manifest disposition on the part of *Uncas, Canonicus, Miantunnomoh* and *Ninigret,* and perhaps other chiefs, to screen the poor, denounced and flying Pequots, who had escaped the flames and swords of the English in their war with them. Part of a correspondence about these sachems' harboring them, between *R. Williams* and the governor of Massachusetts, is preserved in the Massachusetts Collections; from which it appears that Massachusetts had requested Mr. *Williams* to explain to the chiefs the consequences to be depended upon, if they did not strictly observe their agreement in regard to the fugitive Pequots. *Otash*‡ carried to Mr. *Williams* a letter from the Massachusetts governor upon this subject. After he had obeyed its contents, as far as he was able, he answered, that he went with *Otash* "to the Nanhiggonticks, and having got *Canounicus* and *Miantunnomu,* with their council, together, I acquainted them

* "It was supposed," says *Mather,* "that no less than 500 or 600 Pequot souls were brought down to hell that day." *Relation,* 47. We in charity suppose that by hell the doctor only meant death.

† Manuscript letter of Captain *Stoughton,* on file among our state papers.

‡ *Yotaash,* Mr. *Williams* writes his name.

faithfully with the contents of your letter, *both grievances and threatenings*; and to demonstrate, I produced the copy of the league, (which Mr. [Sir *Henry*] *Vane* sent me,) and, with breaking of a straw in two or three places, I showed them what they had done."

These chiefs gave Mr. *Williams* to understand, that when Mr. Governor understood what they had to say, he would be satisfied with their conduct; that they did not wish to make trouble, but they "*could relate many particulars wherein the English had broken their promises*," since the war.

In regard to some squaws that had escaped from the English, *Canonicus* said he had not seen any, but heard of some, and immediately ordered them to be carried back again, and had not since heard of them, but would now have the country searched for them, to satisfy the governor.

Miantunnomoh said he had never heard of but six, nor saw but four of them; which being brought to him, he was angry, and asked those who brought them, why they did not carry them to Mr. *Williams*, that he might convey them to the English. They told him the squaws were lame, and could not go; upon which *Miantunnomoh* sent to Mr. *Williams* to come and take them. Mr. *Williams* could not attend to it, and in his turn ordered *Miantunnomoh* to do it, who said he was busy and could not; "as indeed he was, (says *Williams*,) in a strange kind of solemnity, wherein the sachims eat nothing but at night, and all the natives round about the country were feasted." In the mean time the squaws escaped.

Miantunnomoh said he was sorry that the governor should think he wanted these squaws, for he did not. Mr. *Williams* told him he knew of his sending for one. Of this charge he fairly cleared himself, saying, the one sent for was not for himself, but for *Sassamun*,* who was lying lame at his house; that *Sassamun* fell in there in his way to Pequt, whither he had been sent by the governor. The squaw he wanted was a sachem's daughter, who had been a particular friend of *Miantunnomoh* during his life-time; therefore, in kindness to his dead friend, he wished to ransom her.

Moreover, *Miantunnomoh* said, he and his people were true "to the English in life or death," and but for which, he said, *Okase* [*Unkus*] and his Mohiganeucks had long since proved false, as he still feared they would. For, he said, they had never found a Pequot, and added, "*Chenock ejuse wetompatimucks?*" that is, "Did ever friends deal so with friends?" Mr. Williams requiring more particular explanation, *Miantunnomoh* proceeded:—

"My brother, *Yotaash*, had seized upon *Puttaquppuunck, Quame*, and 20 Pequots, and 60 squaws; they killed three and bound the rest, whom they watched all night. Then they sent for the English, and delivered them in the morning to them. I came by land, according to promise, with 200 men, killing 10 Pequots by the way. I desired to see the great sachem, *Puttaquppuunck*, whom my brother had taken, who was now in the English houses, but the English thrust at me with a pike many times, that I durst not come near the door."

Mr. *Williams* told him they did not know him, else they would not; but *Miantunnomoh* answered, "All my company were disheartened, and they all, and *Cutshamoquene*, desired to be gone." Besides, he said, "two of my men, *Wagonckwhut*† and *Maunamoh* [*Meihamoh*] were their guides to Sesquankit, from the river's mouth." Upon which, Mr. *Williams* adds to the governor: "Sir, I dare not stir coals, but I saw them too much disregarded by many."

* Probably the same mentioned afterwards. He might have been the famous *John Sassamon*, or his brother *Rowland*.

† Perhaps *Wahgumacut*, or *Wahginnacut*.

Mr. *Williams* told the sachems "they received Pequts and wampom without Mr. Governor's consent. *Cannounicus* replied, that although he and *Miantunnomu* had paid many hundred fathom of wampum to their soldiers, as Mr. Governor did, yet he had not received one yard of beads nor a Pequt. Nor, saith *Miantunnomu*, did I, but one small present from four women of Long Island, which were no Pequts, but of that isle, being afraid, desired to put themselves under my protection."

The Pequot war has generally been looked upon with regret, by all good men, since. To exterminate a people before they had any opportunity to become enlightened, that is, to be made acquainted with the reason of other usages towards their fellow beings than those in which they had been brought up, is a great cause of lamentation; and if it proves any thing, it proves that great ignorance and barbarism lurked in the hearts of their exterminators. We do not mean to exclude by this remark the great body of the present inhabitants of the earth from the charge of such barbarism.

In the records of the United Colonies for the year 1647, it is mentioned that "Mr. *John Winthrop* making claim to a great quantity of land at Niantic by purchase from the Indians, gave in to the commissioners a petition in those words:—'Whereas I had the land of Niantick by a deed of gift and purchase from the sachem [Sassacus] before the [Pequot] wars, I desire the commissioners will be pleased to confirm it unto me, and clear it from any claim of English and Indians according to the equity of the case.' " *Winthrop* had no writing from *Sassacus*, and full ten years had elapsed since the transaction, but *Fromatush*, *Wamberquaske* and *Antuppo* testified some time after, that "upon their knowledge before the wars were against the Pequots, *Sassacus* their sachem of Niantic did call them and all his men together, and told that he was resolved to give his country to the governor's son of the Massachusetts, who lived then at Pattaquassat alias Connecticut River's mouth, and all his men declared themselves willing therewith. Thereupon he went to him to Pattaquassets, and when he came back he told them he had granted all his country to him the said governor's son, and said he was his good friend, and he hoped he would send some English thither some time hereafter. Moreover, he told him he had received coats from him for it, which they saw him bring home." This was not said by those Indians themselves, but several English *said they heard them say so.* The commissioners, however, set aside his claim with considerable appearance of independence.

Dr. *Dwight* thus closes his poem upon the destruction of the Pequots:—

"Indulge, my native land, indulge the tear
That steals, impassioned, o'er a nation's doom.
To me, each twig from Adam's stock is near,
And sorrows fall upon an Indian's tomb."

Greenfield Hill, p. 104, 105.

Another, already mentioned, and the next in consequence to *Sassacus*, was *Mononotto*. *Hubbard* calls him a "noted Indian," whose wife and children fell into the hands of the English, and as "it was known to be by her mediation that two English maids, (that were taken away from Weathersfield, upon Connecticut River,) were saved from death, in requittal of whose pity and humanity, the life of herself and children was not only granted her, but she was in special recommended to the care of Gov. *Winthrop*, of Massachusetts." *Mononotto* fled with *Sassacus* to the Mohawks, for protection, with several more chiefs. He was not killed by them as *Sassacus* was, but escaped from them wounded, and probably died by the hands of his English enemies. He is thus mentioned by Gov. *Wolcott,* in his poem upon *Winthrop's* agency, &c.

"'Prince *Mononotto* sees his squadrons fly,
And on our general having fixed his eye,
Rage and revenge his spirits quickening,
He set a mortal arrow in the string.' "

The first troubles with the Pequots have already been noticed. It was among the people of *Mononotto,* that the English caused the blood of a Pequot to flow. Some English had been killed, but there is no more to excuse the murder of a Pequot than an Englishman. The English had injured the Indians of Block Island all in their power, which it seems did not satisfy them, and they next undertook to make spoil upon them in their own country upon Connecticut River. "As they were sailing up the river, says Dr. I. *Mather,* many of the Pequots on both sides of the river called to them, desirous to know what was their end in coming thither."* They answered, that they desired to speak with *Sassacus;* being told that *Sassacus* had gone to Long Island, they then demanded that *Mononotto* should appear, and they pretended he was from home also. However, they went on shore, and demanded the murderers of Capt. *Stone,* and were told that if they would wait they would send for them, and that *Mononotto* would come in the mean time. But very wisely, the Pequots, meanwhile, "transported their goods, women and children to another place."† One of them then told the English that *Mononotto* would not come. Then the English began to do what mischief they could to them, and a skirmish followed, wherein one Indian was killed, and an Englishman was wounded."‡

The name of *Mononotto's* wife appears to have been *Wincumbone.* She should not be overlooked in speaking of *Mononotto,* as she was instrumental in saving the life of an Englishman, as disinterestedly as *Pocahontas* saved that of Capt. *Smith.* Some English had gone to trade with the Pequots, and to recover some horses which they had stolen, or picked up on their lands. Two of the English went on shore, and one went into the sachem's wigwam and demanded the horses. The Indians within slily absented themselves, and *Wincumbone,* knowing their intention, told him to fly, for the Indians were making preparations to kill him. He barely escaped to the boat, being followed by a crowd to the shore.

Cassassinnamon was a noted Pequot chief, of whom we have some account as early as 1659. In that year a difficulty arose about the limits of Southerton, since called Stonington, in Connecticut, and several English were sent to settle the difficulty, which was concerning the location of Wekapauge. "For to help us, (they say,) to understand where Wekapauge is, we desired some Poquatucke Indians to go with us." *Cassassinnamon* was one who assisted. They told the English that "*Cashawasset,* (the governor of Wekapauge,) did charge them that they should not go any further than the east side of a little swamp, near the east end of the first great pond, where they did pitch down a stake, and told us, [the English,] that *Cashawasset* said that that very place was Wekapauge; said that *he* said it and not them; and if they should say that Wekapauge did go any further, *Cashawasset* would be angry." *Cashawasset* after this had confirmed to him and those under him, 8000 acres of land in the Pequot country, with the provision that they continued subjects of Mas-

* Relation, 44. † Ibid.
‡ Ibid. Capt. *Lion Gardener,* who had some men in this affair, gives quite a different account. See life of *Kutshamoquin,* alias *Kutshamakin.*

sachusetts, and should "not sell or alienate the said lands, or any part thereof, to any English man or men, without the court's approbation."

The neck of land called *Quinicuntauge* was claimed by both parties, but *Cassassinnamon* said that when a whale was some time before cast ashore there, no one disputed *Cashawasset's* claim to it, which it is believed settled the question: *Cashawasset* was known generally by the name of *Harmon Garret.**

We next meet with Cassassinnamon in Philip's war, in which he commanded a company of Pequots, and accompanied Capt. *Denison* in his successful career, and was present at the capture of *Canonchet.*†

In November, 1651, *Cassassinnamon* and eight others executed a sort of an agreement "with the townsmen of Pequot," afterward called *New London.* What kind of *agreement* it was we are not told. His name was subscribed *Casesymamon.* Among the other names we see *Obbachickwood, Neesouweêgun* alias *Daniel, Cutchámaquin* and *Mahmawámbam. Cassassinnamon,* it is said, signed "in his own behalf and the behalf of the rest of Nameeag Indians."‡

---

* Several manuscript documents.
† *Hubbard.*
‡ 1 *Col. Mass. Hist. Soc.* x. 101.

BOOK III.

BIOGRAPHY AND HISTORY OF THE NEW ENGLAND INDIANS CONTINUED.

CHAPTER I.

Events which led to the war with Philip—Life of ALEXANDER *alias* WAMSUTTA*—He and Metacom, his younger brother, receive English names—* WEETAMOO *his wife—Early events in her life—*PETANANUET, *her second husband—Account of him—Weetamoo's latter career and death—Ninigret—Death of Alexander—*JOHN SASSAMON*—His country and connections—Becomes a christian—Schoolmaster—Minister—Settles at Assawomset—*FELIX *marries his daughter—Sassamon discovers the plots of Philip—Is murdered—Proceedings against the murderers—They are condemned and executed—Names of the jury who sat at their trial—No Indians among the jurors—Some are consulted.*

Alexander was the English name of the elder son of *Massasoit.* His real name appears at first to have been *Mooanam,* and afterwards *Wamsutta,* and lastly *Alexander.* The name of *Mooanam* he bore as early as 1639; in 1641 we find him noticed under the name *Wamsutta.* About the year 1656, he and his younger brother, *Metacomet,* or rather *Pometacom,* were brought to the court of Plimouth, and being solicitous to receive English names, the governor called the elder *Alexander,* and the younger *Philip,* probably from the two Macedonian heroes, which, on being explained to them, might have flattered their vanities; and which was probably the intention of the governor.

Alexander appears pretty early to have set up for himself, as will be seen in the course of this chapter; occasioned, perhaps, by his marrying a female sachem of very considerable authority, and in great esteem among her neighbors.

Namumpum, afterwards called *Weetamoo,* squaw-sachem of Pocasset, was the wife *Alexander*; and who, as says an anonymous writer,* was more willing to join *Philip* when he began war upon the English, being persuaded by him that they had poisoned her husband. This author calls her "as potent a prince as any round about her, and hath as much corn, land, and men, at her command."

Alexander having, in 1653, sold a tract of the territory acquired by his wife, as has been related in the life of *Massasoit,* about six years after, *Wetamo* came to Plimouth, and the following account of her business is contained in the records.

"I, *Namumpum,* of Pokeesett, hauing, in open court, June last, fifty-nine, [1659,] before the governour and majestrates, surrendered up all that right and title of such lands as *Woosamequin* and *Wamsetta* sould to the

* Of a work entitled, *Present State of New England,* &c. p. 3. fol. 1676. This work has just been republished, with notes, at the Antiquarian Bookstore, Boston.

purchasers; as appeeres by deeds giuen vnder theire hands, as alsoe the said *Namumpum* promise to remoue the Indians of from those lands; and alsoe att the same court the said *Wamsutta* promised *Namumpum* the third part of the pay, as is expressed in the deed of which payment *Namumpum* haue receiued of *John Cooke*, this 6 of Oct. 1659: these particulars as followeth: item;

20 *yards blew trading cloth,*
2 *yards red cotton,*
2 *paire of shooes, 2 paire stockings,*
6 *broade hoes and 1 axe;*

And doe acknowledge receiued by me, NAMUMPUM."

Witnessed by *Squabsen, Wahatunchquatt*, and two English.

Thus this land affair seems to have been amicably settled; but the same year of *Alexander's* death, whether before or after we are not assured, *Namumpum* appeared at Plimouth, and complained that *Wamsutta* had sold some of her land without her consent. "The court agreed to doe what they could in conuenient time for her relief."

We apprehend there was some little difficulty between Alexander and his wife about this time, especially if her complaint were before his death, and we are rather of the opinion that it was, for it was June when her complaint was made, and we should assign a little later date for the death of her husband; and therefore all difficulty was settled in his death.

What time she deeded land to *John Sanford* and *John Archer*, we are not informed, but it was probably about the beginning of 1662. It was a deed of gift, and appears to have been only deeded to them to prevent her husband's selling it; but these men, it seems, attempted to hold the land in violation of their promise; however, being a woman of preserverance, she so managed the matter, that in the year 1668, she found witnesses who deposed to the true meaning of the deed, and thus was, we presume, restored to her rightful possessions.

Since we have been thus particular in acquainting the reader with the wife of *Wamsutta*, we will, before proceeding with our account of the husband, say all that we have to say of the interesting *Weetamoo*.

Soon after the death of *Alexander*, we find *Namumpum*, or *Weetamoo*, associated with another husband, named *Petonowowet*. He was well known to the English, and went by the familiar name of *Ben*. Now, unless we can manufacture the name *Peter Nunnuit* out of *Peto-now-owet*,* we must allow her to have had a third husband in 1675. We, however, are pretty well satisfied that these two names are, as they appear to be, one and the same name.

This husband of *Weetamoo* does not appear to have been of so much importance as her first, *Wamsutta;* and as he only appears occasionally in the crowd, we are of opinion that she took good care in taking a second husband, and fixed upon one that she was better able to manage than she was the determined *Wamsutta*.

On the 8 May, 1673, *Tatamomock, Petonowowett*, and *William* alias *Ijasocke,* sold to *Nathaniel Paine* of Rehoboth, and *Hugh Cole* of Swansey, a lot of land in Swansey, near Mattapoiset, and Showamet neck, for £35 5*s*. *Weetamoo, Phillip* alias *Wagusoke*, and *Steven* alias *Nucano,* were the Indian witnesses.

About the same time, one *Piowant* was intruded upon by some others claiming his lands, or otherwise molesting him, and the business seems to have undergone a legal scrutiny; in this affair both *Weetamoo* and her husband appear upon our records. They testify that the tract of land

* We have met with this spelling, *Petananuet*, which approaches still nearer

bounded by a small river or brook called *Mastucksett,* which compasseth said tract to Assonett River, and so to Taunton River, [by trees, &c.] hath for many years been in the possession of *Piowant.* The place of the bounds on Taunton River was called *Chippascuitt,* which was a little south of Mastucksett. *Pantauset, Quanowin, Nescanoo,* and *Panowwin,* testified the same.

It does not appear that *Peta-nan-u-et* was at all concerned in *Philip's* war against the English, but, on the contrary, forsook his wife and joined them against her. Under such a leader as *Church,* he must have been employed against his countrymen with great advantage. At the time he came over to the English, he no doubt expected his wife would do the same, as she gave *Church* to understand as much. After the war he was honored with a command over the prisoners, who were permitted to reside in the country between Sepecan and Dartmouth. *Numpus,* or *Nompash,* and *Isaac* were also in the same office.

After Mr. *Church* left *Awashonks*' council, a few days before the war broke out, he met with both *Weetamoo* and her husband at Pocasset. He first met with the husband, *Petananuet,* who had just arrived in a canoe from *Philip's* head quarters at Mount Hope. He told *Church* there would certainly be war, for that *Philip* had held a war dance of several weeks, and had entertained the young men from all parts of the country. He said, also, that *Philip* expected to be sent for to Plimouth, about *Sassamon's* death, knowing himself guilty of contriving that murder. *Petananuet* further said, that he saw Mr. *James Brown* of Swansey, and Mr. *Samuel Gorton,* who was an interpreter, and two other men that brought a letter from the governor of Plimouth to *Philip. Philip's* young warriors, he said, would have killed Mr. *Brown,* but *Philip* told them they must not, for his father had charged him to show kindness to him; but to satisfy them, told them, that on the next Sunday, when the English had gone to meeting, they might plunder their houses, and afterwards kill their cattle.

Meanwhile *Weetamoo* was at her camp just back from Pocasset shore, on the high hill a little to the north of what is now Howland's ferry, and *Petananuet* requested Mr. *Church* to go up and see her. He did so, and found her in rather a melancholy mood, all her men having left her and gone to *Philip's* war dance, much, she said, against her will.

Church, elated with his success at *Awashonks*' camp, and thinking both "queens" secured to the English interest, hastened to Plimouth to give the governor an account of his discoveries.—This was a day big to *Philip;* he immediately took measures to reclaim *Wetamore,* and had nearly drawn off *Awashonks* with the vivid hopes of conquest and booty.

Weetamoo could no longer remain neutral; the idea still harrowed upon her mind, that the authorities of Plimouth had poisoned her former husband,* and was now sure that they had seducéd her present one; therefore, from the power of such arguments, when urged by the artful *Philip,* there was no escape or resistance. Hence his fortune became her own, and she moved with him from place to place about her dominions, in the country of Pocasset, until the 30 July, when all the Wampanoags escaped out of a swamp, and retired into the country of the Nipmuks. From this time *Weetamoo's* operations become so blended with those of her allies that the life of *Philip* takes up the narration.

When, by intestine divisions, the power of *Philip* was destroyed among the Nipmucks, *Weetamoo* seems to have been deserted by almost all her followers, and, like *Philip,* she sought refuge again in her own country. It was upon the 6 August, 1676, when she arrived upon the western bank of Tehticut River in Mettapoiset, where, as was then supposed, she

* Present State of N. E.

was drowned by accident, in attempting to cross the river to Pocasset, at the same point she had crossed the year before, in her flight with *Philip*.

Her company consisted now of no more than 26 men, whereas, in the beginning of the war they amounted to 300; and she was considered by the English "next unto *Philip* in respect of the mischief that hath been done."* The English at Taunton were notified by a deserter of her situation, who offered to lead any that would go, in a way that they might easily surprise her and her company. Accordingly, 20 men volunteered upon this enterprise, and succeeded in capturing all but *Weetamoo,* "who," as Mr. *Hubbard* expresses,† "intending to make an escape from the danger, attempted to get over a river or arm of the sea near by, upon a raft, or some pieces of broken wood; but whether tired and spent with swimming, or starved with cold and hunger, she was found stark naked in Metapoiset, not far from the water side, which made some think she was first half drowned, and so ended her wretched life." "Her head being cut off and set upon a pole in Taunton, was known by some Indians then prisoners, which set them into a horrible lamentation." Mr. *Mather* improves upon this passage, giving it in a style more to suit the taste of the times: "They made a most horid and diabolical lamentation, crying out that it was their queen's head."

The authors of Yamoyden thus represent *Philip* escaping from the cold grasp of the ghostly form of *Weetamoo:*—

"As from the water's depths she came,
With dripping locks and bloated frame,
Wild her discolored arms she threw
To grasp him; and, as swift he flew,
Her hollow scream he heard behind
Come mingling with the howling wind:
'Why fly from *Wetamoe*? she died
Bearing the war-axe on thy side.'"

It does not seem from all we can discover that *Weetamoo* went with *Philip* into the Nipmuck country, or, if she did, she soon returned among the Narragansets. For the English early took measures to cause the Narragansets to deliver her up to them. They agreed to do this, as will be found related in the life of *Ninigret.*

In this connection it should be noted, that the time expired, in which *Ninigret* was to deliver up *Weetamoo*, some time previous to the great fight in Narraganset, and hence this was seized upon, as one pretext for invading the Narragansets. And moreover, it was said, that if she were taken by that formidable army of a 1000 men, "her lands would more than pay all the charge" the English had been at in the whole war.

Weetamoo, it is presumed, left *Ninigret* and joined the hostile Narragansets and the Wampanoags in their strong fort, some time previous to the English expedition. And it was about this time that she connected herself with the Narraganset chief *Quinnapin*, as will be found related in his life. She is mentioned by some writers as *Philip's* kinswoman, which seems to have been the case in a two-fold manner: first from her being sister to his wife, and secondly from her marrying *Alexander,* his brother. To return to *Wamsutta.*

A lasting and permanent interest will always be felt, and peculiar feelings associated with the name of this chief. Not on account of a career of battles, devastations or murders, for there were few of these,‡ but there is left for us to relate the melancholy account of his death. Mr.

* *I. Mather.* † Narrative, 103 and 109.

‡ In 1661, he was forced into a war with *Uncas*, the account of which, properly belonging to the life of that chief, will be found there related.

Hubbard's account of this event is in the hands of almost every reader, and cited by every writer upon our early history, and hence is extensively known as by him related. Dr. *I. Mather* agrees very nearly in his account with Mr. *Hubbard*, but being more minute, and rarely to be met with, we give it entire:—

"In A. D. 1662, Plimouth colony was in some danger of being involved in trouble by the Wampanoag Indians. After *Massasoit* was dead, his two sons, called *Wamsutta* and *Metacomet*, came to the court at Plimouth, pretending high respect for the English, and, therefore, desired English names might be imposed on them, whereupon the court there named *Wamsutta*, the elder brother, *Alexander*, and *Metacomet*, the younger brother, *Philip*. This *Alexander, Philip's* immediate predecessor, was not so faithful and friendly to the English as his father had been. For some of Boston, having been occasionally at Narraganset, wrote to Mr. *Prince*, who was then governor of Plimouth, that *Alexander* was contriving mischief against the English, and that he had solicited the Narragansets to engage with him in his designed rebellion. Hereupon, Capt. *Willet*, who lived near to Mount Hope, the place where *Alexander* did reside, was appointed to speak with him, and to desire him to attend the next court in Plimouth, for their satisfaction, and his own vindication. He seemed to take the message in good part, professing that the Narragansets, whom, he said, were his enemies, had put an abuse upon him, and he readily promised to attend at the next court. But when the day for his appearance was come, instead of that, he at that very time went over to the Narragansets, his pretended enemies, which, compared with other circumstances, caused the gentlemen at Plimouth to suspect there was more of truth in the information given, than at first they were aware of. Wherefore the governor and magistrates there ordered Major *Winslow*, (who is since, and at this day [1677] governor of that colony,) to take a party of men, and fetch down *Alexander*. The major considering that *semper nocuit deferre paratis*, he took but 10 armed men with him from Marshfield, intending to have taken more at the towns that lay nearer Mount Hope. But Divine Providence so ordered, as that when they were about the midway between Plimouth and Bridgewater,* observing an hunting house, they rode up to it, and there did they find *Alexander* and many of his men† well armed, but their guns standing together without the house. The major, with his small party, possessed themselves of the Indians' arms, and beset the house; then did he go in amongst them, acquainting the sachem with the reason of his coming in such a way; desiring *Alexander* with his interpreter to walk out with him, who did so a little distance from the house, and then understood what commission the major had received concerning him. The proud sachem fell into a raging passion at this surprise, saying the governor had no reason to credit rumors, or to send for him in such a way, nor would he go to Plimouth, but when he saw cause. It was replied to him, that his breach of word touching appearance at Plimouth court, and, instead thereof, going at the same time to his pretended enemies, augmented jealousies concerning him. In fine, the major told him, that his order was to bring him to Plimouth, and that, by the help of God, he would do it, or else he would die on the place; also declaring to him 'that if he would submit,

* Within six miles of the English towns. *Hubbard*, 10, (Edition, 1677.) *Massasoit*, and likewise *Philip*, used to have temporary residences in eligible places for fishing, at various sites between the two bays, Narraganset and Massachusetts, as at Raynnam, Namasket, Titicut, [in Middleborough,] and Munponset Pond in Halifax. At which of these places he was, we cannot, with certainty, decide: that at Halifax would, perhaps, agree best with Mr. *Hubbard's* account.

† Eighty, says *Hubbard*, 6.

he might expect respective usage, but if he once more denied to go, he should never stir from the ground whereon he stood; and with a pistol at the sachem's breast, required that his next words should be a positive and clear answer to what was demanded. Hereupon his interpreter, a discreet Indian, brother to *John Sausaman*,* being sensible of *Alexander's* passionate disposition, entreated that he might speak a few words to the sachem before he gave his answer. The prudent discourse of this Indian prevailed so far as that *Alexander* yielded to go, only requesting that he might go like a sachem, with his men attending him, which, although there was some hazard in it, they being many, and the English but a few, was granted to him. The weather being hot, the major offered him an horse to ride on, but his squaw and divers Indian women being in company, he refused, saying he could go on foot as well as they, entreating only that there might be a complying with their pace, which was done. And resting several times by the way, *Alexander* and his Indians were refreshed by the English. No other discourse happening while they were upon their march, but what was pleasant and amicable. The major sent a man before, to entreat that as many of the magistrates of that colony as could would meet at Duxbury. Wherefore having there had some treaty with *Alexander*, not willing to commit him to prison, they entreated Major *Winslow* to receive him to his house, until the governor, who then lived at Eastham, could come up. Accordingly, he and his train were courteously entertained by the major. And albeit, not so much as an angry word passed between them whilst at Marshfield; yet proud *Alexander*, vexing and fretting in his spirit, that such a check was given him, he suddenly fell sick of a fever. He was then nursed as a choice friend. Mr. *Fuller*, the physician, coming providentially thither at that time, the sachem and his men earnestly desired that he would administer to him, which he was unwilling to do, but by their importunity was prevailed with to do the best he could to help him, and therefore gave him a portion of working physic, which the Indians thought did him good. But his distemper afterwards prevailing, they entreated† to dismiss him, in order to a return home, which upon engagement of appearance at the next court was granted to him. Soon after his being returned home he died."‡

Thus ends Dr. *Mather's* "relation" of the short reign of *Alexander*. And although by a document lately published by Judge *Davis* of Boston, which sets the conduct of the English in a very favorable light, yet it is very difficult to conceive how Mr. *Mather* and Mr. *Hubbard* could have been altogether deceived in their information. (We mean in respect to the treatment *Alexander* received at the hands of his captors.) They both wrote at the same time, and at different places, and neither knew what the other had written. Of this we are confident, if, as we are assured, there was, at this time, rather a misunderstanding between these two reverend authors.

It now only remains that we make such extracts from the above-mentioned document as will exhibit all the evidence on the side of the English. There is to be seen, in the library of the Massachusetts Historical Society, a manuscript paper, headed "*Narative de Alexandro*." This

---

* He had a brother by the name of *Roland*.

† "Entreating those that held him prisoner, that he might have liberty to return home, promising to return again if he recovered, and to send his son as hostage till he could so do. On that consideration, he was fairly dismissed, but died before he got half way home."— *Hubbard*.

‡ It is a pity that such an able historian as Grahame should not have been in possession of other authorities upon this matter than those who have copied from the above. See his *Hist. N. America*, i. 401.

paper contains an account of the transaction, drawn up by the authorities of Plimouth, and Mr. *Mather's* and Mr. *Hubbard's* accounts are the substance of it. As the affair had caused much excitement, and, judging from the writers of that time, particularly the latter, some recrimination upon the conduct of the government of Plimouth, by some of the other English, who were more in the habit of using or recommending mild measures towards Indians than the Plimouth people appear to have been, seems to have been indulged. After thus premising, we will offer the document, which is a letter written by the Rev. *John Cotton*, of Plimouth, to Dr. *I. Mather*, and now printed by Judge *Davis*, in his edition of *Morton's* Memorial. There is no date to it, at least the editor gives none; but if it were written in answer to one from Mr. *Mather* to him, desiring information on that head, dated 21st April, 1677,* we may conclude it was about this time; but Mr. *Mather's* "Relation" would not lead us to suppose that he was in possession of such information, and, therefore, he either was not in possession of it when he published his account, or that he had other testimony which invalidated it.

The letter begins, "Major *Bradford*, [who was with Mr. *Winslow* when *Alexander* was surprised,] confidently assures me, that in the narrative *de Alexandro* there are many mistakes, and, fearing lest you should, through misinformation, print some mistakes on that subject, from his mouth I this write. Reports being here that *Alexander* was plotting or privy to plots, against the English, authority sent to him to come down. He came not. Whereupon Major *Winslow* was sent to fetch him. Major *Bradford*, with some others, went with him. At Munponset River, a place not many miles hence, they found *Alexander* with about eight men and sundry squaws. He was there about getting canoes. He and his men were at breakfast under their shelter, their guns being without. They saw the English coming, but continued eating; and Mr. *Winslow* telling their business, *Alexander*, freely and readily, without the least hesitancy, consented to go, giving his reason why he came not to the court before, viz.; because he waited for Captain *Willet's* return from the Dutch, being desirous to speak with him first. They brought him to Mr. *Collier's* that day, and Governor *Prince* living remote, at Eastham, those few magistrates who were at hand issued the matter peaceably, and immediately dismissed *Alexander* to return home, which he did part of the way; but, in two or three days after, he returned and went to Major *Winslow's* house, intending thence to travel into the *bay* and so home; but, at the major's house, he was taken very sick, and was, by water, conveyed to Major *Bradford's*, and thence carried upon the shoulders of his men to Tethquet River, and thence in canoes home, and, about two or three days after, died."

Thus it is evident that there is error somewhere, and it would be very satisfactory if we could erase it from our history; but, at present, we are able only to agitate it, and wait for the further discovery of documents before *Alexander's* true history can be given; and to suspend judgment, although some may readily decide that the evidence is in favor of the old printed accounts. It is the business of a historian, where a point is in dispute, to exhibit existing evidence, and let the reader make up his own judgment.

We are able, from the first extract given upon this head, to limit the time of his sachemship to a portion of the year 1662.

It will have appeared already, that enough had transpired to inflame the minds of the Indians, and especially that of the sachem *Philip*, if, indeed, the evidence adduced be considered valid, regarding the blama-

* See his Memorial, 288.

bleness of the English. Nevertheless, our next step onward will more fully develop the causes of *Philip's* deep-rooted animosities.

We come now to speak of *John Sassamon*, who deserves a particular notice; more especially as, from several manuscripts, we are able not only to correct some important errors in former histories, but to give a more minute account of a character which must always be noticed in entering upon the study of this part of our history. Not that he would otherwise demand more notice than many of his brethren almost silently passed over, but for his agency in bringing about a war, the interest of which increases in proportion as time carries us from its period.

John Sassamon was a subject of *Philip*, an unstable-minded fellow; and, living in the neighborhood* of the English, became a convert to Christianity, learned their language, and was able to read and write, and had translated some of the Bible into Indian. Being rather insinuating and artful, he was employed to teach his countrymen at Natick, in the capacity of a schoolmaster. How long before the war this was, is not mentioned, but must have been about 1660, as he was *Philip's* secretary, or interpreter, in 1662, and this was after he had become a Christian. He left the English, from some dislike, and went to reside with *Alexander*, and afterwards with *Philip*, who, it appears, employed him on account of his learning. Always restless, *Sassamon* did not remain long with *Philip* before he returned again to the English; "and he manifested such evident signs of repentance, as that he was, after his return from pagan *Philip*, reconciled to the praying Indians and baptized, and received, as a member, into one of the Indian churches; yea, and employed as an instructer amongst them every Lord's day."†

Previous to the war, we presume in the winter of 1672, *Sassamon* was sent to preach to the Namaskets,‡ and other Indians of Middleborough, who, at this time, were very numerous. The famous *Watuspaquin* was then the chief of this region, and who appears to have been disposed to encourage the new religion taught by *Sassamon*. For, in 1674, he gave him a tract of land near his own residence to induce him to remain among his people. The deed of gift of this land was, no doubt, drawn by *Sassamon*, and is in these words:—

"Know all men by these presents, that I, *Old Watuspaquin*, doe graunt vnto *John Sassamon*, allies *Wassasoman*, 27 acrees of land for a home lott at Assowamsett necke. This is my gift, giuen to him the said *John Sassamon*, by me the said *Watuspaquin*, in Anno 1673, [or 1674, if between 1 Jan. and 25 March.]

OLD WATUSPAQUIN *his marke.*
WILLIAM TUSPAQUIN *his marke.*
Witness, alsoe, NANEHEUNT§ † *his marke.*"

As a further inducement for Sassamon to settle here, *Old Tuspaquin* and his son deeded to *Felix*, an Indian who married *Sassamon's* daughter, 58 and an half acres of land; as "a home lott," also. This deed was dated 11 March, 1673, O. S. which doubtless was done at the same time with the other. This daughter of *Sassamon* was called by the English

* "This *Sassamon* was by birth a Massachusett, his father and mother living in Dorchester, and they both died Christians."—*I. Mather.*

† *Mather's* Relation, 74.

‡ The inhabitants of the place call it *Nemasket*. In the records, it is almost always written *Namassakett.*

§ Spelt also *Memeheutt.*

name *Betty*,* but her original name was *Assowetough*. To his son-in-law, *Sassamon* gave his land, by a kind of will, which he wrote himself, not long before his death; probably about the time he became tired of his new situation, which we suppose was also about the time that he discovered the design of *Philip* and his captains to bring about their war of extermination.

Old Tuspaquin, as he called himself, and his son, not only confirmed *Sassamon's* will, but about the same time made a bequest themselves to his daughter, which, they say, was "with the consent of all the chieffe men of Assowamsett." This deed of gift from them was dated 23 Dec. 1673. It was of a neck of land at Assowamsett, called Nahteawamet. The names of some of the places which bounded this tract were Mashquomoh, a swamp, Sasonkususett, a pond, and another large pond called Chupipoggut. *Tobias, Old Thomas, Pohonoho,* and *Kankunuki*, were upon this deed as witnesses.

Felix served the English in Philip's war, and was living in 1679, in which year Governor *Winslow* ordered, "that all such lands as were formerly *John Sassamon's* in our collonie, shal be settled on *Felix* his son-in-law," and to remain his and his heirs "foreuer." *Felix's* wife survived him, and willed her land to a daughter, named *Mercy*. This was in 1696, and *Isacke Wanno* witnessed said will. There was at a later period an Indian preacher at Titicut† named *Thomas Felix*, perhaps a son of the former.‡ But to return to the more immediate subject of our discourse.

There was a *Sassaman*, or, as my manuscript has it, *Sosomon*, known to the English as early as 1637, but as we have no means of knowing how old *John Sassamon* was when he was murdered, it cannot be decided with probability, whether or not it were he. This *Sosomon*, as will be seen in the life of *Sassacus*, went with the English to fight the Pequots.

Sassamon acted as interpreter, witness or scribe, as the case required, on many occasions. When *Philip* and *Wootonekanuske,* his wife, sold, in 1664, Mattapoisett to *William Brenton, Sassamon* was a witness and interpreter. The same year he was *Philip's* agent "in settling the bounds of Acushenok, Coaksett, and places adjacent." Again, in 1665, he witnessed the receipt of £10 paid to *Philip* on account of settling the bounds the year before.

There was a *Rowland Sassamon*, who I suppose was the brother of *John*. His name appears but once in all the manuscript records I have met with, and then only as a witness, with his brother, to *Philip's* deed of Mattapoisett, above mentioned.

The name *Sassamon*, like most Indian names, is variously spelt, but the way it here appears is nearest as it was understood in his last years, judging from the records. But it was not so originally. *Woosansaman* was among the first modes of writing it.

This detail may appear dry to the general reader, but we must occasionally gratify our antiquarian friends. We now proceed in our narrative.

While living among the Namaskets, *Sassamon* learned what was going

---

* The English sometimes added her surname, and hence, in the account of Mr. *Bennet*, (1 *Col. Mass. Hist. Soc.* iii. 1.) *Betty Sasemore*. The noted place now called *Betty's Neck*, in Middleborough, was named from her. In 1793, there were eight families of Indians there.

† *Cotuhticut, Ketchiquut, Tehticut, Keketticut, Keticut, Teightaquid, Tetehquet*, are spellings of this name in the various books and records I have consulted.

‡ *Backus's* Middleborough, in 1 *Col. Mass. Hist. Soc.* iii. 150.

forward among his countrymen, and, when he was convinced that their design was blood, goes immediately to Plimouth, and communicates his discovery to the governor. "Nevertheless, his information," says Dr. *I. Mather*,* "(because it had an Indian original, and one can hardly believe them when they do speak the truth,) was not at first much regarded."

It may be noticed here, that at this time if any Indian appeared friendly, all Indians were so declaimed against, that scarcely any one among the English could be found that would allow that an Indian could be faithful or honest in any affair. And although some others besides *Sassamon* had intimated, and that rather strongly, that a "rising of the Indians" was at hand, still, as Dr. *Mather* observes, because Indians said so, little or no attention was paid to their advice. Notwithstanding, Mr. *Gookin*, in his MS. history,† says, that, previous to the war, none of the Christian Indians had "been *justly* charged, either with unfaithfulness or treachery towards the English." "But, on the contrary, some of them had discovered the treachery, particularly *Walcut*, the ruler of *Philip* before he began any act of hostility." In another place the same author says, that, in April, 1675, *Waban* "came to one of the magistrates on purpose, and informed him that he had ground to fear that sachem *Philip*, and other Indians his confederates, intended some mischief shortly." Again in May, about six weeks before the war, he came and said the same. Adding that *Philip's* men were only waiting for the trees to get leaved out, that they might prosecute their design with more effect. To return to *Sassamon*:

In the mean time, some circumstances happened that gave further grounds of suspicion, that war was meditated, and it was intended that messengers should be sent to *Philip*, to gain, if possible, the real state of the case. But before this was effected, much of the winter of 1674 had passed away, and the Rev. *Sassamon* still resided with the Namaskets, and others of his countrymen in that neighborhood. And notwithstanding he had enjoined the strictest secrecy upon his English friends at Plimouth, of what he had revealed, assuring them that if it came to *Philip's* knowledge, he should be immediately murdered by him, yet it by some means got to the chief's knowledge, and *Sassamon* was considered a traitor and an outlaw; and by the laws of the Indians, he had forfeited his life, and was doomed to suffer death. The manner of effecting it was of no consequence with them, so long as it was brought about, and it is probable that *Philip* had ordered any of his subjects who might meet with him, to kill him.

Early in the spring of 1675, *Sassamon* was missing, and, on search being made, his body was found in Assawomset Pond, in Middleborough‡ Those that killed him not caring to be known to the English, left his hat and gun upon the ice, that it might be supposed that he had drowned himself; but from several marks upon his body, and the fact that his neck was broken, it was evident he had been murdered.§ Several persons were suspected, and, upon the information of one called *Patuckson*,

---

* *Relation of the Troubles*, &c. 74.

† Not yet published. We are informed it soon will be. It will form a lasting monument of one of the best men of those days. The author was, as Mr. *Eliot* expresses himself, "a pillar in our Indian work." He died in 1687, aged 75.

‡ Some would like to know, perhaps, on what authority Mr. *Grahame* (*Hist. N. Amer.* i. 402.) states that *Sassamon's* body *was found in a field*.

§ *Gookin's* MS. Hist. of Christian Indians. This author says, "*Sasamand* was the first Christian martyr," and that "it is evident he suffered death upon the account of his Christian profession, and fidelity to the English."

*Tobias** one of *Philip's* counsellors, his son, and *Mattashinnamy*, were apprehended, tried by a jury, consisting of half Indians,† and in June, 1675, were all executed at Plimouth; "one of them before his execution confessing the murder," but the other two denied all knowledge of the act, to their last breath. The truth of their guilt may reasonably be called in question, if the circumstance of the bleeding of the dead body at the approach of the murderer, had any influence upon the jury. And we are fearful it was the case, for, if the most learned were misled by such hallucinations in those days, we are not to suppose that the more ignorant were free from them. Dr. *Increase Mather* wrote within two years of the affair, and he has this passage: "When *Tobias* (the suspected murderer) came near the dead body, it fell a bleeding on fresh, as if it had been newly slain; albeit, it was buried a considerable time before that."‡

Nothing of this part of the story is upon record among the manuscripts, as we can find, but still we do not question the authenticity of Dr. *Mather*, who, we believe, is the first that printed an account of it. Nor do the records of Plimouth notice *Sassamon* until some time after his death. The first record is in these words: "The court seeing cause to require the personal appearance of an Indian called *Tobias* before the court, to make further answer to such interrogatories as shall be required of him, in reference to the sudden and violent death of an Indian called *John Sassamon*, late deceased." This was in March, 1674, O. S.

It appears that *Tobias* was present, although it is not so stated, from the fact that *Tuspaquin* and his son *William* entered into bonds of £100 for the appearance of *Tobias* at the next court in June following. A mortgage of land was taken as security for the £100.

June having arrived, three instead of one are arraigned as the murderers of *Sassamon*. There was no intimation of any one but *Tobias* being guilty at the previous court. Now, *Wampapaquan*, the son of *Tobias*, and *Mattashunannamo*§ are arraigned with him, and the bill of indictment runs as follows: "For that being accused that they did with joynt consent vpon the 29 of January ann 1674, [or 1675, N. S.] att a place called *Assowamsett Pond*, wilfully and of sett purpose, and of mallice fore thought, and by force and armes, murder *John Sassamon*, an other Indian, by laying violent hands on him, and striking him, or twisting his necke vntill hee was dead; and to hyde and conceale this theire said murder, att the tyme and place aforesaid, did cast his dead body through a hole of the iyce into the said pond."

To this they pleaded "not guilty," and put themselves on trial, say the records. The jury, however, were not long in finding them guilty, which they express in these words: "Wee of the jury one and all, both English and Indians doe joyntly and with one consent agree upon a verdict."

Upon this they were immediately remanded to prison, "and from thence [taken] to the place of execution and there to be hanged by the head‖ vntill theire bodies are dead." Accordingly, *Tobias* and *Mattashun-*

* His Indian name was *Poggapanossoo*.

† *Mather's* Relation, 74. Judge *Davis* retains the same account, (*Morton's* Memorial, 289.) which we shall presently show to be erroneous.

‡ *Mather's* Relation, 75.

§ The same called *Mattashinnamy*. His name in the records is spelt four ways.

‖ This old phraseology reminds us of the French mode of expression, *couper le cou*, that is, to cut off the neck instead of the head; but the French say, *il sera pendu par son cou*, and so do modern hangmen, alias *jurists*, of our times.

annamo were executed on the 8 June, 1675. "But the said *Wampapaquan*, on some considerations was reprieued until a month be expired." He was, however, shot within the month.

It is an error that the jury that found them guilty was composed of half Indians; there were but four, while there were twelve Englishmen. We will again hear the record:—

"Itt was judged very expedient by the court, that, together with this English jury aboue named, some of the most indifferentest, grauest and sage Indians should be admitted to be with the said jury, and to healp to consult and aduice with, of, and concerning the premises: there names are as followeth, viz. one called by an English name *Hope*, and *Maskippague, Wannoo, George Wampye* and *Acanootus*; these fully concurred with the jury in theire verdict."

The names of the jurymen were *William Sabine, William Crocker, Edward Sturgis, William Brookes, Nath[l]. Winslow, John Wadsworth, Andrew Ringe, Robert Vixon, John Done, Jon[a]. Bangs, Jon[a]. Shaw* and *Benj[a]. Higgins.*

That nothing which can throw light upon this important affair be passed over, we will here add, from an exceeding scarce tract, the following particulars, although some parts of them are evidently erroneous: "About five or six years since, there was brought up, amongst others, at the college at Cambridge, (Mass.) an Indian, named *Sosomon*; who, after some time he had spent in preaching the gospel to Uncas, a sagamore Christian in his territories, was, by the authority of New Plimouth, sent to preach in like manner to King *Philip*, and his Indians. But King *Philip*, (heathen-like,) instead of receiving the gospel, would immediately have killed this *Sosomon*, but by the persuasion of some about him, did not do it, but sent him by the hands of three men to prison; who, as he was going to prison, exhorted and taught them in the Christian religion. They, not liking his discourse, immediately murthered him after a most barbarous manner. They, returning to King *Philip*, acquainted him with what they had done. About two or three months after this murther, being discovered to the authority of New Plimouth, *Josiah Winslow* being then governor of that colony, care was taken to find out the murtherers, who, upon search, were found and apprehended, and, after a fair trial, were all hanged. This so exasperated King *Philip*, that, from that day after, he studied to be revenged on the English—judging that the English authority had nothing to do to hang an Indian for killing another."*

* *Present State of New England*, by a merchant of Boston, *in respect to the present Bloody Indians Wars*, page 3. folio, London, 1676. [Since reprinted.]

PHILLIP alias **METACOMET** of Pokanoket.

Engraved from the original as Published by Church.

CHAPTER II.

Life of KING PHILIP*—His real name—The name of his wife—Makes frequent sales of his lands—Account of them—His first treaty at Plimouth—Expedition to Nantucket—Events of 1671—Begins the* WAR *of 1675—First acts of hostility—Swamp Fight at Pocasset—Narrowly escapes out of his own country—Is pursued by Oneko—Fight at Rehoboth Plain—Cuts off a company of English under Capt. Beers—Incidents—Fight at Sugar-loaf Hill, and destruction of Capt. Lathrop's company—Fights the English under Mosely—English raise 1500 men—Philip retires to Narraganset—Strongly fortifies himself in a great swamp—Description of his fortress—English march to attack him—The great Fight at Narraganset—Again flies his country—Visits the Mohawks—Ill-devised stratagem—Events of 1676—Returns again to his country—Reduced to a wretched condition—Is hunted by Church—His chief counsellor, Akkompoin, killed, and his sister captured—His wife and son fall into the hands of Church—Flies to Pokanoket—Is surprised and slain.—Specimen of the Wampanoag Language—Other curious matter.*

IN regard to the native or Indian name of *Philip,* it seems a mistake has always prevailed, in printed accounts. *Pometacom* gives as near its Indian sound as can be approached by our letters. The first syllable was dropped in familiar discourse, and hence, in a short time, no one imagined but what it had always been so; in nearly every original deed executed by him, which we have seen, and they are many, his name so appears. It is true that, in those of different years, it is spelt with some little variation, all which, however, conveyed very nearly the same sound. The variations are *Pumatacom, Pamatacom, Pometacome,* and *Pometacom*; the last of which prevails in the records.

We have another important discovery to communicate:* it is no other than the name of the wife of *Pometacom*—the innocent WOOTONEKANUSKE! This was the name of her who, with her little son, fell into the hands of Capt. *Church.* No wonder that *Philip* was "now ready to die," as some of his traitorous men told *Church,* and that "his heart was now ready to brake!" All that was dear to him was now swallowed up in the vortex! But they still lived, and this most harrowed his soul—lived for what? to serve as slaves in an unknown land! could it be otherwise than that madness should seize upon him, and despair torment him in every place? that in his sleep he should hear the anguishing cries and lamentations of *Wootonekanuske* and his son? But we must change the scene.

It seems as though, for many years before the war of 1675, *Pometacom,* and nearly all of his people sold off their lands as fast as purchasers presented themselves. They saw the prosperity of the English, and they were just such philosophers as are easily captivated by any show of ostentation. They were forsaking their manner of life, to which the proximity of the whites was a deadly poison, and were eager to obtain such things as their neighbors possessed; these were only to be obtained by parting with their lands. That the reader may form some idea of the

* The author feels a peculiar satisfaction that it has fallen to his lot to be the first to publish the real name of the great sachem of the Wampanoags, and also that of the sharer of his perils, *Wootonekanuske.*

2

rapidity with which the Indians' lands in Plimouth colony were disposed of, we add the following items:—

In a deed dated 23 June, 1664, "*William Brenton,* of Newport, R. I. merchant," "for a valuable consideration" paid by him, buys Matapoisett of *Philip.* This deed begins, "I, *Pumatacom* alias *Philip,* chief sachem of Mount Hope, Còwsumpsit and of all territories thereunto belonging." *Philip* and his wife both signed this deed, and *Tockomock, Wecopauhim,* Nesetaquason, Pompaquase, Aperniniate, Taquanksicke, Paquonack, Watapatahue, Aquetaquish, John Sassamon* the interpreter, *Rowland Sassamon,* and two Englishmen, signed as witnesses.

In 1665, he sold the country about Acushena, [now New Bedford,] and Coaxet, [now in Compton.] *Philip's* father having previously sold some of the same, £10 was now given him to prevent any claim from him, and to pay for his marking out the same.

John Woosansman [one of the names of *Sassamon*] witnessed this deed.

In 1667, *Philip* sells to *Constant Southworth,* and others, all the meadow lands from Dartmouth to Matapoisett, for which he had £15. Particular bounds to all tracts are mentioned in the deeds, but as they were generally or often stakes, trees, and heaps of stones, no one at this time can trace many of them.

The same year, for "£10 sterling," he sells to *Thos. Willet* and others, "all that tract of land lying between the Riuer Wanascottaquett and Cawatoquissett, being two miles long and one broad." *Pawsaquens,* one of *Philip's* counsellors, and *Tom* alias *Sawsuett,* an interpreter, were witnesses to the sale.

In 1668, "*Philip Pometacom,* and *Tatamumaque*† alias *Cashewashed,* sachems," for a "valuable consideration," sell to sundry English a tract of some square miles. A part of it was adjacent to Pokanoket. In describing it, Memenuckquage and Towansett neck are mentioned, which we conclude to be in Swansey. Besides two Englishmen, *Sompointeen,* alias *Tom,* and *Nananuntnew,* son of *Thomas Piants,* were witnesses to this sale.

The next year, the same sachems sell 500 acres in Swansey for £20. *Wanueo,* a counsellor, and *Tom,* the interpreter, were witnesses.

In 1668, *Philip* and *Uncompawen* laid claim to a part of New-meadows neck, alleging that it was not intended to be conveyed in a former deed, by *Ossamequin* and *Wamsutta,* to certain English, "although it appears, says the record, pretty clearly so expressed in said deed," "yet that peace and friendship may be continued," "Capt. *Willet,* Mr. *Brown* and *John Allen,* in the behalf of themselves and the rest," agree to give *Philip* and *Uncompawen* the sum of £11 in goods.

PHILIP NANUSKOOKE‡ *his* π *mark,*
VNCOMPAWEN *his* ✕ *mark.*

TOM SANSUWEST, *interpreter,*
And NIMROD.

The same year, we find the following record, which is doubly interesting, from the plan with which we are able to accompany it, drawn by Philip himself, who, no doubt, over urged to sell certain lands, contracts or agrees, by the following writing under his hand, that "this may inform

* Perhaps *Uncompoin.*

† Written in another deed, *Atunkamomake.* This deed was in the next year. It was of 500 acres of land, "more or lesse," in Swansey; and £20 the consideration. *Hugh Cole, Josias Winslow, John Coggeshall* and *Constant Southworth* were the purchasers, and *Wanueo,* a counsellor, one of the witnesses.

‡ This double name, we suppose, was meant to stand for the signature of himself and wife.

the honoured court [of Plimouth,] that I *Philip* ame willing to sell the land within this draught; but the Indians that are vpon it may liue vpon it still; but the land that is [waste]* may be sould, and *Wattachpoo* is of the same minde. I have sed downe all the principall names of the land wee are willing should bee sould."

"From Pacanaukett PHILLIP P *his marke.*"
the 24 of the 12 mo. 1668."

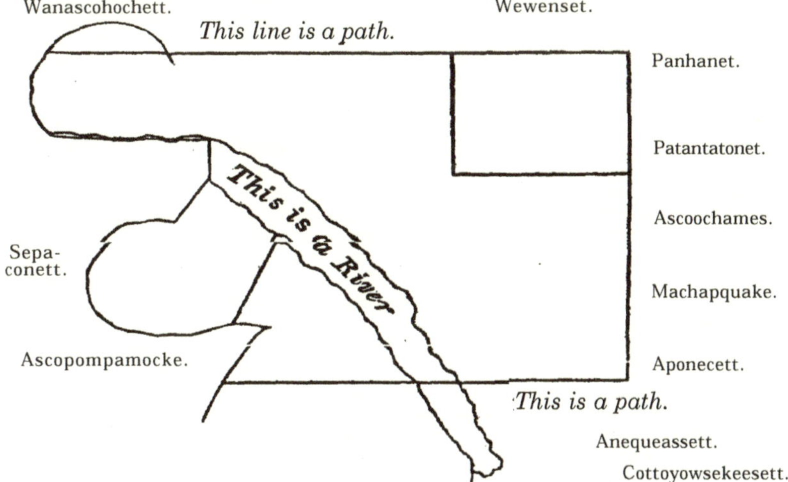

"Osamequen" having, "for valuable considerations," in the year 1641, sold to *John Brown* and *Edward Winslow* a tract of land eight miles square, situated on both sides of Palmer's River, *Philip*, in 1668, was required to sign a quit-claim of the same. This he did in presence of *Umptakisoke, Phillip*, and *Peebe*,† counsellors, *Sonconewhew, Phillip's* brother, and *Tom* the interpreter.

Also in 1669, for £10 "and another valuable and sufficient gratuity," he sells to *John Cook* of Akusenag in Dartmouth,‡ "one whole island nere the towne," called Nokatay.

The same year, *Philip* and *Tuspaquin* sell a considerable tract of land in Middleborough, for £13. *Thomas* the interpreter, *William*, the son of *Tuspaquin*, and *Benjamin Church*, were witnesses.

In 1671, *Philip* and "*Monjokam* of Mattapoisett," for £5, sell to *Hugh Cole*, of Swansey, shipwright, land lying near a place called *Acashewah*, in Dartmouth.

In 1672, *Philip* sold to *William Brenton* and others, of Taunton, a tract to the southward of that town, containing 12 square miles, for £143; and, a few days after, adjoining it, four square miles more, to *Constant Southworth.* Others were concerned in the sale of the larger tract, as is judged by the deeds being signed by *Nunkampahoonett, Umnathum,* alias *Nimrod, Cheemaughton*, and Capt. *Annawam*, besides one *Philip. Thomas*, alias *Sanksuit*, was among the witnesses. The sale of the last tract was witnessed

* So in the records.

† Called, in Mr. *Hubbard's* history, *Thebe*; he was afterwards killed at Swansey, in the beginning of the war.

‡ The place where *Cook* lived is now included in New Bedford.

by *Munashum*, alias *Nimrod, Woackompawhan*,* and Capt. *Annowan*, [*Annawon*.]

These are but a part of the sales of land by *Pometacom*. Many other chiefs sold very largely, particularly Watuspaquin and *Josias Wampatuck*.

We meet with a singular record of *Philip* previous to this time, the authorship of which we attribute to *John Sassamon*, and which, besides extending our knowledge of *Philip*, into his earlier times, serves to make us acquainted with *Sassamon's* acquirements in the language of the pilgrims.

"Know all men by these presents, that *Philip* haue giuen power vnto *Watuchpoo*† and *Sampson*‡ and theire brethren to hold and make sale of to whom they will by my consent, and they shall not haue itt without they be willing to lett it goe it shal be sol by my consent, but without my knowledge they cannot safely to: but with my consent there is none that can lay claime to that land which they haue marked out, it is theires foreuer, soe therefore none can safely purchase any otherwise but by *Watachpoo* and *Sampson* and their bretheren. PHILIP 1666."

At the court of Plimouth, 1673, "Mr. *Peter Talmon* of Rhode Iland complained against *Philip* allies *Wewasowanuett*, sachem of Mount Hope, brother or predecessor of *Pacanawkett* as heire adminnostrator or successor vnto his brother or predecessor *Wamsitta, Sopaquitt*,§ or *Alexander* deceased, in an action on the case, to the damage of £800 forfeiture of a bond of such a value, bearing date, June the 28th, 1661, giuen to the said *Peter Talman*, obliging him the said *Wamsitta* allies *Allexander* to make good to him, his heires and a deed of gift of a considerable track of land att Sapowett and places adjacent, as in the said deed is more particularly expressed; for want wherof the complainant is greatly damnifyed."

Whether the conduct of the people of Plimouth towards *Wamsutta*, *Pometacom's* elder brother, and other neighboring Indians, made them always suspicious of the chief sachem, as it had their neighbors before in the case of *Miantunnomoh*, or whether *Philip* were in reality "contriving mischief," the same year of his coming in chief sachem, remains a question, to this day, with those best acquainted with the history of those times.

The old benevolent sachem *Massasoit*, alias *Woosamequin*, having died in the winter of 1661–2, as we believe, and but few months after died also *Alexander*, *Philip's* elder brother and predecessor, *Philip* himself, by the order of succession, came to be chief of the Wampanoags.

Philip having by letter complained to the court of Plimouth of some injuries, at their October term, 1668, they say, "In answer unto a letter from *Philip*, the sachem of Pocanokett, &c., by way of petition requesting the court for justice against *Francis Wast*, [*West*,] for wrong done by him to one of his men about a gun taken from him by the said *Wast*; as also for wrong done unto some swine of the said Indian's. The court have ordered the case to be heard and determined by the selectmen of Taunton; and in case it be not by them ended, that it be referred unto the next March court at Plimouth to be ended." How the case turned we have not found. But for an Indian to gain his point at an English court, unless his case were an exceeding strong one, was, we apprehend, a rare occurrence.

---

* Probably "*Philip's* old uncle *Akkompoin*."

† Sometimes *Tukpoo*, by abbreviation. See a further account of him in the life of *Tatoson*.

‡ Many Indians bore the same English name. In 1671, there was a *Sampson* of Nobscussett, and another of Nauset.

§ That is, nicknamed *Alexander*, according to the French mode of expression; *ou par sobriquet Alexander*, as I imagine. Mr. *Hubbard* says of *Philip*, (Narrative, 10,) that, "for his ambitious and haughty spirit, [he was] nicknamed *King Philip*."

"He was no sooner styled sachem," says Dr. *I. Mather*,* "but immediately, in the year 1662, there were vehement suspicions of his bloody treachery against the English." This author wrote at the close of *Philip's* war, when very few could speak of Indians, without discovering great bitterness. Mr. *Morton*† is the first who mentions *Metacomet* in a printed work, which, being before any difficulty with him, is in a more becoming manner. "This year," (1662,) he observes, "upon occasion of some suspicion of some plot intended by the Indians against the English, *Philip*, the sachem of Pokanoket, otherwise called *Metacom*, made his appearance at the court held at Plimouth, August 6, did earnestly desire the continuance of that amity and friendship that hath formerly been between the governor of Plimouth and his deceased father and brother."

The court expressing their willingness to remain his friends, he signed the articles prepared by them, acknowledging himself a subject of the king of England, thus:—

"The *mark of* PHILLIP, *sachem of Pocanakett*,
The mark of ◁ VNCUMPOWETT, *vnkell to the aboue said sachem.*"

The following persons were present, and witnessed this act of *Philip*, and his great captain *Uncompoin*:—

"JOHN SASSAMON,
The mark ♏ of FRANCIS, *sachem* of *Nauset*,
The mark DI of NIMROD *alias* PUMPASA,
The mark ♑ of PUNCKQUANECK,
The mark [mark] of AQUETEQUESH."‡

Of the uneasiness and concern of the English at this period, at the hostile movements of *Philip*, Mr. *Hubbard*, we presume, was not informed; or so important an event would not have been omitted in his minute and valuable history. Mr. *Morton*, as we before stated, and Mr. *Mather* mention it, but neither of these, or any writer since, to this day, has made the matter appear in its true light, from their neglect to produce the names of those that appeared with the sachem.

For about nine years succeeding 1662, very little is recorded concerning *Philip*. During this time, he became more intimately acquainted with his English neighbors, learned their weakness and his own strength, which rather increased than diminished, until his fatal war of 1675. For, during this period, not only their additional numbers gained them power, but their arms were greatly strengthened by the English instruments of war put into their hands. *Roger Williams* had early brought the Narragansets into friendship with *Massasoit*, which alliance gained additional strength on the accession of the young *Metacomet*. And here we may look for a main cause of that war, although the death of *Alexander* is generally looked upon by the early historians, as almost the only one. The continual broils between the English and Narragansets, (we name the English first, as they were generally the aggressors,) could not be unknown to *Philip*; and if his countrymen were abused, he knew it. And what friend will see another abused, without feeling a glow of resentment in his breast? And who will wonder, if, when these abuses had followed each other, repetition upon repetition, for a series of years, that they should at last break out into open war? The Narraganset chiefs were

* Relation, 72.

† In his N. England's Memorial.

‡ From the Records in *manuscript*.

not conspicuous at the period of which we speak; there were several of them, but no one appears to have had a general command or ascendency over the rest; and there can be little doubt but that they unanimously reposed their cause in the hands of *Philip*. *Ninigret* was at this time grown old, and though, for many years after the murder of *Miantunnomoh*, he seems to have had the chief authority, yet pusillanimity was always rather a predominant trait in his character. His age had probably caused his withdrawal from the others, on their resolution to second *Philip*. *Canonchet* was at this period the most conspicuous; *Pumham* next; *Potok, Magnus*, the squaw-sachem, whose husband, *Mriksah*, had been dead several years; and lastly *Mattatoag*.

Before proceeding with later events, the following short narrative, illustrative of a peculiar custom, it will be proper to notice.

There is a tradition current at Nantucket, that, in the year 1665, an Indian named *John Gibbs* of that island had spoken something concerning a dead relative of *Philip*; and, as it was an observance or law among them, that whoever should speak evil of the dead should be put to death, *Philip* went there to execute this law upon *Gibbs*. He was, however, defeated in his design, for one of *Gibbs's* friends, understanding *Philip's* intention, ran to him and gave him notice of it, just in time for him to escape; not, however, without great exertions, for *Philip* came once in sight of him, after pursuing him some time among the English from house to house; but *Gibbs*, by leaping a bank, got out of sight, and so escaped. *Philip* would not leave the island until the English had ransomed *John* at the exorbitant price of nearly all the money upon the island.* *Gibbs* was a Christian Indian, and his Indian name was *Assasamoogh*. He was a preacher to his countrymen in 1674, at which time there were belonging to his church 30 members.

What grounds the English had in the spring of the year 1671, for suspecting that a plot was going forward for their destruction, cannot satisfactorily be ascertained; but it is evident there were some warlike preparations made by the great chief, which very much alarmed the English, as in the life of *Awashonks* we shall have occasion again to notice. Their suspicions were further confirmed when they sent to him to come to Taunton and make known the causes for his operations; as he discovered "shyness," and a reluctance to comply. At length, on the 10th of April, this year, he came to a place about four miles from Taunton, accompanied with a band of his warriors, attired, armed and painted as for a warlike expedition. From this place he sent messengers to Taunton, to invite the English to come and treat with him. The governor either was afraid to meet the chief, or thought it beneath his dignity to comply with his request, and therefore sent several persons, among whom was *Roger Williams*, to inform him of their determination, and their good disposition towards him, and to urge his attendance at Taunton. He agreed to go, and hostages were left in the hands of his warriors to warrant his safe return. On coming near the village with a few of his warriors, he made a stop, which appears to have been occasioned by the warlike parade of the English, many of whom were for immediately attacking him. These were the Plimouth people that recommended this rashness, but they were prevented by the commissioners from Massachusetts, who met here with the governor of Plimouth to confer with *Philip*.

---

* A friend of the author, now living at Nantucket, obligingly offered to furnish him with whatever could be found relating to the Indians of that place; it is presumed be could discover nothing, as he has not since been heard from. For some of what we have given above, see 1 *Col. Mass. Hist. Soc.* iii. 159, furnished for that work by Mr. *Zaccheus Macy*, whose ancestor, it is said, assisted in secreting *Assasamoogh*.

In the end it was agreed that a council should be held in the meeting-house, one side of which should be occupied by the Indians, and the other by the English. *Philip* had alleged that the English injured the planted lands of his people, but this, the English say, was in no wise sustained. He said his warlike preparations were not against the English, but the Narragansets, which the English also say was proved to his face to be false; and that this so confounded him, that he confessed the whole plot, and "that it was the naughtiness of his own heart that put him upon that rebellion, and nothing of any provocation from the English."* Therefore, with four of his counsellors, whose names were *Tavoser*, Capt. *Wispoke, Woonkaponehunt, [Unkompoin,]* and *Nimrod*, he signed a submission, and an engagement of friendship, which also stipulated that he should give up all the arms among his people, into the hands of the governor of Plimouth, to be kept as long as the government should "see reason."†

The English of Massachusetts, having acted as umpires in this affair, were looked to, by both parties, on the next cause of complaint. *Philip* having delivered the arms which himself and men had with them at Taunton,‡ promised to deliver the rest at Plimouth by a certain time. But they not being delivered according to agreement, and some other differences occurring, a messenger was sent to Boston from Plimouth, to make complaint; but *Philip,* perhaps, understanding what was intended, was quite as early at Boston in person;|| and, by his address, did not fail to be well received, and a favorable report of him was returned to Plimouth; and, at the same time, proposals that commissioners from all the United Colonies should meet *Philip* at Plimouth, where all difficulties where expected to be settled. This meeting took place the same year, September, 1671, where the issue of the meeting was very nearly the same as that at Taunton. "The conclusion was," says Mr. *Mather*,§ "*Philip* acknowledged his offence, and was appointed to give a sum of money to defray the charges which his insolent clamors had put the colony unto."

As usual, several articles were drawn up by the English, of what *Philip* was to submit to, to which we find the names of three only of his captains or counsellors, *Uncompaen*, who was his uncle,¶ *Wotokom* and *Samkama.*

Great stress in those days was laid on the Indians submitting themselves as "subject to his majesty the king of England." This they did only to get rid of the importunity of the English, as their course immediately afterwards invariably showed.

The articles which the government of Plimouth drew up at this time, for *Philip* to sign, were not so illiberal as might be imagined, were we not to produce some of them. Article second reads,—

"I [*Philip*] am willing, and do promise to pay unto the government of Plimouth £100, in such things as I have; but I would entreat the favor that I might have three years to pay it in, forasmuch as I cannot do it at present." And in article third, he promises "to send unto the governor, or whom he shall appoint, five wolves' heads, *if he can get them*; or as

* *Hubbard*, Indian Wars, 11, 1st edition.

† The articles of this treaty may be seen in *Hubbard, Mather* and *Hutchinson's* histories.

‡ Mather's Relation, 73.

§ Ibid.

|| Perhaps this was the time Mr. *Josselyn* saw *Philip* at Boston, richly caparisoned, as will hereafter be mentioned.

¶ Called by *Church, Akkompoin.*

many as he can procure, until they come to five wolves' heads yearly." These articles were dated* 29 Sept. 1671, and were signed by

The mark P *of* PHILLIP;
The mark T *of* WOHKOWPAHENITT;†
The mark V *of* WUTTAKOOSEEIM;
The mark T *of* SONKANUHOO;
The mark 2 *of* WOONASHUM, *alias* NIMROD;
The mark Y *of* WOOSPASUCK, *alias* CAPTAIN.

On the 3 Nov. following, *Philip* accompanied *Takanumma* to Plimouth, to make his submission, which he did, and acknowledged, by a writing, that he would adhere to the articles signed by *Philip* and the others, the 29 Sept. before. *Tokamona* was brother to *Awashonks*, and, at this time, was sachem of Seconet, or Saconett. He was afterwards killed by the Narragansets.‡

A general disarming of the neighboring Indians was undertaken during the spring and summer of 1671, and nothing but trouble could have been expected to follow.

That nothing may be omitted which can throw light upon this important era in the biography of *Philip*, we will lay before the reader all the unpublished information furnished by the records.§ Having met in June, 1671, "The court [of Plimouth] determins all the guns in our hands, that did belong to *Philip,* are justly forfeit; and do at the present order the dividing of them, to be kept at the several towns, according to their equal proportions, until October court next, and then to be at the court's dispose, as reason may appear to them, and then to belong unto the towns, if not otherwise disposed of by the court.

"That which the court grounds their judgment upon is,—For that at the treaty at Taunton, *Philip* and his council did acknowledge that they had been in a preparation for war against us; and that not grounded upon any injury sustained from us, nor provocation given by us, but from their naughty hearts, and because he had formerly violated and broken solemn covenants made and renewed to us; he then freely tendered, (not being in a capacity to be kept faithful by any other bonds,) to resign up all his English arms, for our future security in that respect. He failed greatly in the performance thereof, by secret[ly] conveying away, and carrying home several guns, that might and should have been then delivered, and not giving them up since, according to his engagement; nor so far as is in his power; as appears in that many guns are known still to be amongst the Indians that live by him, and [he] not so much as giving order to some of his men, that are under his immediate command, about the bringing in of their arms.

"In his endeavoring, since the treaty [at Taunton,] to render us odious to our neighbor colony by false reports, complaints and suggestions; and his refusing or avoiding a treaty with us concerning those and other matters that are justly offensive to us, notwithstanding his late engagement, as well as former, to submit to the king's authority, and the authority of this colony.

"It was also ordered by the court that the arms of the Indians of

* There is no date, but the year, set to any printed account. Mr. *Hubbard* by mistake omitted it, and those who have since written, have not given themselves the pleasure of recurring to the records.

† *Uncompoin.* ‡ See *Church,* 39.

§ Plimouth Colony Records, in *manuscript.*

Namassakett and Assowamsett, that were fetched in by Major *Winslow*, and those that were with him, are confiscated, and forfeit, from the said Indians, for the grounds above expressed; they being in a compliance with *Phillipe* in his late plot: And yet would neither by our governor's order, nor by *Phillipe's* desire, bring in their arms, as was engaged by the treaty; and the said guns are ordered by the court to the major and his company for their satisfaction, in that expedition.

"This court have agreed and voted" to send "some" forces to "Saconett to fetch in" the arms among the Indians there.

If then, therefore, these Indians had not already become hostile, no one would marvel had it now become the case. Bows and arrows were almost entirely out of use. Guns had so far superseded them, that undoubtedly many scarce could use them with effect, in procuring themselves game: Nor could it be expected otherwise, for the English had, by nearly 40 years' intercourse, rendered *their* arms far more necessary to the existence of the Indians than to their own: hence their unwillingness to part with them. *Philip*, it is said, directed the Middleborough Indians to give up their guns. His object in this was to pacify the English, judging that, when war should begin, these Indians would join the English, or at least many of them; and, therefore, it affected his cause but little which party possessed them; but not so with his immediate followers, as we have just seen in the record.

A council of war having convened at Plimouth, 23 August, 1671, the following, besides the matters already expressed, they took into consideration: *Philip's* "entertaining of many strange Indians, which might portend danger towards us. In special by his entertaining of divers Saconett Indians, professed enemies to this colony, and this against good counsel given him by his friends. The premises considered [the council] do unanimously agree and conclude, that the said *Phillip* hath violated [the] covenant plighted with this colony at Taunton in April last.

"2. It is unanimously agreed and concluded by the said council, that we are necessarily called to cause the said sachem to make his personal appearance to make his purgation, in reference to the premises; which, in case of his refusal, the council, according to what at present appears, do determin it necessary to endeavor his reducement by force; inasmuch as the controversy which hath seemed to lie more immediately between him and us, doth concern all the English plantations. It is, therefore, determined to state the case to our neighbor colonies of the Massachusetts and Rhode Island; and if, by their weighty advice to the contrary, we are not diverted from our present determinations, to signify unto them, that if they look upon themselves concerned to engage in the case with us against a common enemy, it shall be well accepted as a neighborly kindness; which we shall hold ourselves obliged to repay, when Providence may so dispose that we have opportunity.

"Accordingly, letters were despatched and sent from the council, one unto the said *Phillip* the said sachem, to require his personal appearance at Plymouth, on the 13th day of September next, in reference to the particulars above mentioned against him. This letter was sent by Mr. *James Walker*, one of the council, and he was ordered to request the company of Mr. *Roger Williams* and Mr. *James Brown*, to go with him at the delivery of the said letter. And another letter was sent to the governor and council of the Massachusetts by the hands of Mr. *John Freeman*, one of our magistrates, and a third was directed to the governor and council of Rhode Island, and sent by Mr. *Thomas Hinckley* and Mr. *Constant Southworth*, two other of our magistrates, who are ordered by our council with the letter, to unfold our present state of matters relating to the premises, and to certify them, also, more certainly of the time of the meeting together, in reference to engagement with the Indians, if there be a going forth, which will be on the 20 of September next.

"It was further ordered by the council, that those formerly pressed shall remain under the same impressment, until the next meeting of the said council, on the 13 day of Sept. next, and so also until the intended expedition is issued, unless they shall see cause to alter them, or add or detract from them, as occasion may require: And that all other matters remain as they were, in way of preparation to the said expedition, until we shall see the mind of God further by the particulars forenamed, improved for that purpose.

"It was further ordered by the council, that all the towns within this jurisdiction shall, in the interim, be solicitously careful to provide for their safety, by convenient watches and wardings, and carrying their arms to the meetings on the Lord's days, in such manner, as will best stand with their particulars, and the common safety.

"And in particular they order, that a guard shall be provided for the safety of the governor's person, during the time of the above-named troubles and expeditions.

"And the council were summoned by the president, [the governor of Plimouth,] to make their personal appearance at Plymouth, on the 13th day of Sept. next, to attend such further business as shall be then presented by providence, in reference to the premises. [Without any intermediate entry, the records proceed:]

"On the 13 Sept. 1671, the council of war appeared, according to their summons, but *Phillip* the sachem appeared not; but instead thereof repaired to the Massachusetts, and made complaint against us to divers of the gentlemen in place there; who wrote to our governor, by way of persuasion, to advise the council to a compliance with the said sachem, and tendered their help in the achieving thereof; declaring, in sum, that they resented not his offence so deeply as we did, and that they doubted whether the covenants and engagements that *Phillip* and his predecessors had plighted with us, would plainly import that he had subjected himself, and people, and country to us any further than as in a neighborly and friendly correspondency."

Thus, whether *Philip* had been able by misrepresentation to lead the court of Massachusetts into a conviction that his designs had not been fairly set forth by Plimouth, or whether it be more reasonable to conclude that that body were thoroughly acquainted with the whole grounds of complaint, and, therefore, considered Plimouth nearly as much in error as *Philip*, by assuming authority not belonging to them, is a case, we apprehend, not difficult to be settled by the reader. The record continues:—

"The council having deliberated upon the premises, despatched away letters, declaring their thankful acceptance of their kind proffer, and invited the commissioners of the Massachusetts and Connecticut, they [the latter] then being there in the Bay, [Boston,] and some other gentlemen to come to Plymouth and afford us their help: And, accordingly, on the 24 of Sept. 1671, Mr. *John Winthrop,* Gov. of Connecticut, Maj. Gen. *Leverett,* Mr. *Thos. Danforth,* Capt. *Wm. Davis,* with divers others, came to Plymouth, and had a fair and deliberate hearing of the controversy between our colony and the said sachem *Phillip*, he being personally present; there being also competent interpreters, both English and Indians. At which meeting it was proved by sufficient testimony to the conviction of the said *Phillip*, and satisfaction of all that audience, both [to] the said gentlemen and others, that he had broken his covenant made with our colony at Taunton in April last, in divers particulars: as also carried very unkindly unto us divers ways.

"1. In that he" had neglected to bring in his arms, although "competent time, yea his time enlarged" to do it in, as before stated.

"2. That he had carried insolently and proudly towards us on several occasions, in refusing to come down to our court (when sent for) to have speech with him, to procure a right understanding of matters in difference betwixt us."

This, to say the least, was a wretchedly sorry complaint. That an independent chief should refuse to obey his neighbors whenever they had a mind to command him, of the justness of whose mandates he was not to inquire, surely calls for no comment of ours. Besides, did *Philip* not do as he agreed at Taunton?—which was, that in case of future troubles, both parties should lay their complaints before Massachusetts, and abide by their decision?

The 3d charge is only a repetition of what was stated by the council of war, namely, harboring and abetting divers Indians not his own men, but "vagabonds, our professed enemies, who leaving their own sachem were harbored by him."

The 4th has likewise been stated, which contains the complaint of his going to Massachusetts, "with several of his council, endeavoring to insinuate himself into the magistrates, and to misrepresent matters unto them," which amounts to little else but an accusation against Massachusetts, as, from what has been before stated, it seems that the "gentlemen in place there" had, at least in part, been convinced that *Philip* was not so much in fault as their friends of Plimouth had pretended.*

"5. That he had shewed great incivility to divers of ours at several times; in special unto Mr. *James Brown*, who was sent by the court on special occasion, as a messenger unto him; and unto *Hugh Cole* at another time, &c.

"The gentlemen forenamed taking notice of the premises, having fully heard what the said *Phillip* could say for himself, having free liberty so to do without interruption, adjudged that he had done us a great deal of wrong and injury, (respecting the premises,) and also abused them by carrying lies and false stories to them, and so misrepresenting matters unto them; and they persuaded him to make an acknowledgment of his fault, and to seek for reconciliation, expressing themselves, that there is a great difference between what he asserted to the government in the Bay, and what he could now make out concerning his pretended wrongs; and such had been the wrong and damage that he had done and procured unto the colony, as ought not to be borne without competent reparation and satisfaction; yea, that he, by his insolencies, had (in probability) occasioned more mischief from the Indians amongst them, than had fallen out in many years before; they persuaded him, therefore, to humble himself unto the magistrates, and to amend his ways, if he expected peace; and that, if he went on in his refractory way, he must expect to smart for it."

The commissioners finally drew up the treaty of which we have before spoken, and *Philip* and his counsellors subscribed it; and thus ended the chief events of 1671.

Whether it were before this time, or between it and the war, that what we are about to relate took place, is not certain, but it probably belongs to the latter period. It is this:—The governor of Massachusetts sent an ambassador to *Philip*, to demand of him why he would make war upon

---

* Not a very high compliment to the authorities of Massachusetts; for it appears, if this were the case, *Philip* had succeeded in deceiving them in matters of which certainly they might have been correctly informed, as we should rather apprehend they were; having been present at Taunton, and heard both sides of the story afterwards.

the English, and requested him, at the same time, to enter into a treaty. The sachem made him this answer:—

"*Your governor is but a subject of King Charles* of England. I shall not treat with a subject. I shall treat of peace only with the king, my brother. When he comes, I am ready.*"†

This is literal, although we have changed the order of the words a little, and is worthy of a place upon the same page with the speech of the famous *Porus*, when taken captive by *Alexander*.‡

We meet with nothing of importance until the death of *Sassamon*, in 1674, the occasion of which was charged upon *Philip*, and was the cause of bringing about the war with him a year sooner than he had expected. This event prematurely discovered his intentions, which occasioned the partial recantation of the Narragansets, who, it is reported, were to furnish 4000 men, to be ready to fall upon the English in 1676. Concert, therefore, was wanting; and although nearly all the Narragansets ultimately joined against the English, yet the powerful effect of a general simultaneous movement was lost to the Indians. *Philip's* own people, many of whom were so disconcerted at the unexpected beginning of the war, continued some time to waver, doubting which side to show themselves in favor of; and it was only from their being without the vicinity of the English, or unprotected by them, that determined their course, which was, in almost all cases, in favor of *Philip*. Even the Praying Indians, had they been left to themselves, would, no doubt, many of them, have declared in his favor also, as many really did.

Until the execution of the three Indians, supposed to be the murderers of *Sassamon*, no hostility was committed by *Philip* or his warriors. About the time of their trial, he was said to be marching his men "up and down the country in arms," but when it was known that they were executed, he could no longer restrain his young men, who, upon the 24th of June, provoked the people of Swansey, by killing their cattle, and other injuries,§ until they were fired upon, which was a signal to commence the war, and what they had desired; for the superstitious notion prevailed among the Indians, that the party who fired the first gun would be conquered.‖ They had probably been made to believe this by the English themselves.

It was upon a fast day that this great drama was opened. As the peo-

---

* *Charles* II. whose reign was from 1660 to 1676.

† *Present State of N. Eng.* 68.

‡ The conqueror asked him how he would be treated, who, in two words, replied, "Like a king." Being asked if he had no other request to make, he said, "No. Every thing is comprehended in that." (*Plutarch's Life of Alexander*.) We could wish, in many cases, that the English conquerors had acted with as much magnanimity towards the Indians, as *Alexander* did towards those he overcame. *Porus* was treated as he had desired.

§ "In the mean time King *Philip* mustered up about 500 of his men, and arms them compleat; and had gotten about 8 or 900 of his neighboring *Indians*, and likewise arms them compleat; (i. e. guns, powder and bullets;) but how many he hath engaged to be of his party, is unknown to any among us. The last spring, several *Indians* were seen in small parties, about *Rehoboth* and *Swansey*, which not a little affrighted the inhabitants. Who demanding the reason of them, wherefore it was so? Answer was made, That they were only on their own defence, for they understood that the *English* intended to cut them off. About the 20th of *June* last, seven or eight of King *Philip's* men came to *Swansey* on the Lord's day, and would grind a hatchet at an inhabitant's house there; the master told them, it was the sabbath day, and their God would be very angry if he should let them do it. They returned this answer: They knew not who his God was, and that they would do it, for all him, or his God either. From thence they went to another house, and took away some victuals, but hurt no man. Immediately they met a man travelling on the road, kept him in custody a short time, then dismist him quietly; giving him this caution, that he should not work on his God's day, and that he should tell no lies." *Present State of N. Eng.* p. 8 and 9 of the new edition.

‖ Callendar.

ple were returning from meeting, they were fired upon by the Indians, when one was killed and two wounded. Two others, going for a surgeon, were killed on their way. In another part of the town, six others were killed the same day. Swansey was the next town to *Philip's* country, and his men were as well acquainted with all the walks of the English as they were themselves.

It is not supposed that *Philip* directed this attack, but, on the other hand, it has been said that it was against his wishes. But there can be no doubt of his hostility and great desire to rid his country of the white intruders; for had he not reason to say,

> "Exarsere ignes animo; subit ira, cadentem
> Ulcisci patriam, et sceleratas sumere pœnas"?

The die was cast. No other alternative appeared, but to ravage, burn and destroy as fast as was in his power. There had been no war for a long time, either among themselves or with the English, and, therefore, numerous young warriors from the neighboring tribes, entered into his cause with great ardor; eager to perform exploits, such as had been recounted to them by their sires, and such as they had long waited an opportunity to achieve. The time, they conceived, had now arrived, and their souls expanded in proportion to the greatness of the undertaking. To conquer the English! to lead captive their haughty lords! must have been to them thoughts of vast magnitude, and exhilarating in the highest degree.

Town after town fell before them, and when the English forces marched in one direction, they were burning and laying waste in another. A part of Taunton, Middleborough and Dartmouth, in the vicinity of Pocasset, upon Narraganset Bay, soon followed the destruction of Swansey, which was burnt immediately after the 24th of June, on being abandoned by the inhabitants.

Philip commanded in person upon Pocasset, where, upon the 18th of July, he was discovered in a "dismal swamp." He had retired to this place, which is adjacent to Taunton River, with the most of his Wampanoags, and such others as had joined him, to avoid falling in with the English army, which was now pursuing him. From their numbers, the English were nearly able to encompass the swamp, and the fate of *Philip* they now thought sealed. On arriving at its edge, a few of *Philip's* warriors showed themselves, and the English rushed in upon them with ardor, and by this feint were drawn far into an ambush, and "about 15 were slain." The leaves upon the trees were so thick, and the hour of the day so late, that a friend could not be distinguished from a foe, "whereby 'tis verily feared, that [the English themselves] did sometimes unhappily shoot Englishmen instead of Indians."* A retreat was now ordered, and, considering *Philip's* escape impossible, the most of the forces left the place, a few only remaining, "to starve out the enemy." That *Philip's* force was great at this time is certain, from the fact that a hundred wigwams were found near the edge of the swamp, newly constructed of green bark. In one of those the English found an old man, who informed them that *Philip* was there. He lost but few men in the encounter, though it is said, that he had a brother killed at this time.†

The idle notion of building a fort here to starve out *Philip*, was sufficiently censured by the historians of that day. For, as Capt. *Church*

---

* *Mather's* Brief Hist. War, 5.

† This is upon the authority of the anonymous author of the "*Present State*," &c. of which we shall elsewhere have occasion to take notice.

3

expresses it, *to build a fort for nothing to cover the people from nobody,** was rather a ridiculous idea. This observation he made upon a fort's being built upon Mount Hope neck, some time after every Indian had left that side of the country, and who, in fact, were laying waste the towns before mentioned.

The swamp where *Philip* was now confined, was upon a piece of country which projected into Taunton River, and was nearly seven miles in extent. After being guarded here 13 days, which, in the end, was greatly to his advantage, and afforded him sufficient time to provide canoes in which to make his escape, he passed the river with most of his men, and made good his retreat into the country upon Connecticut River. In effecting this retreat, an accident happened which deprived him of some of his choicest and bravest captains, as we shall proceed to relate.

About the 26 July, 1675, *Oneko,* with two of his brothers, and about 50 men, came to Boston, by direction of *Uncas*, and declared their desire to assist the English against the Wampanoags. A few English and three Naticks were added to their company, and immediately despatched, by way of Plimouth, to the enemy's country.† This circuitous route was taken, perhaps, that they might have their instructions immediately from the governor of that colony; Massachusetts, at that time, probably, supposing the war might be ended without their direct interference. This measure, as it proved, was very detrimental to the end in view; for if they had proceeded directly to Seekonk, they would have been there in season to have met *Philip* and his warriors in their flight from Pocasset. And this force, being joined with the other English forces, then in the vicinity, in all probability might have finished the war by a single fight with him. At least, his chance of escape would have been small, as he had to cross a large extent of clear and open country, where they must have been cut down in flight, or fought man to man. Whereas *Oneko* was encamped at some distance, having arrived late the night before, and some time was lost in rallying.‡ They overtook them, however, about 10 o'clock in the morning of the 1st of August, and a smart fight ensued. *Philip* having brought his best men into the rear, many of them were slain; among these was *Nimrod*, alias *Woonasham*, a great captain and counsellor, who had signed the treaty at Taunton, four years before.

From what cause the fight was suspended is unknown, though it would seem from some relations, that it was owing to *Oneko's* men, who, seeing themselves in possession of considerable plunder, fell to loading themselves with it, and thus gave *Philip* time to escape. From this view of the case, it would appear that the Mohegans were the chief actors in the offensive. It is said that the Naticks urged immediate and further pursuit, which did not take place, in consequence of the extreme heat of the weather: and thus the main body were permitted to escape.

Mr. *Newman*, of Rehoboth, gave an account of the affair in a letter, in which he said that "14 of the enemy's principal men were slain." He also mentioned, in terms of great respect, the Naticks and Mohegans under *Oneko*.§

Having now taken a position to annoy the back settlements of Massachusetts, his warriors fell vigorously to the work; one town after another,

---

* Hist. Philip's War, p. 6. ed. 4to.

† They were conducted by Quarter-master *Swift*, and a company of horse. The governor of Plimouth, understanding the route taken by these forces to be by way of Plimouth, immediately ordered them to Rehoboth, otherwise nothing would have been effected at this time against *Philip*.

‡ *Gookin's* MS. Hist. Praying Indians.

§ *Gookin*, ibid. *Oneko* was the oldest son and successor of *Uncas*, and, like his father, was opposed to Christianity.

and one company of soldiers after another, were swept off by them. A garrison being established at Northfield, Capt. *Richard Beers*, of Watertown,* with 36 men, was attacked while on their way to reinforce them, and 20 of the 36 were killed. *Robert Pepper*, of Roxbury, was taken captive, and the others effected their escape. *Philip's* men had the advantage of attacking them in a place of their own choosing, and their first fire was very destructive. *Beers* retreated with his men to a small eminence, and maintained the unequal fight until their ammunition was spent, at which time a cart containing ammunition fell into the hands of the Indians, and, the captain being killed, all who were able took to flight. The hill to which the English fled, at the beginning of the fight, was known afterwards by the name of *Beers's Mountain*.

Some time in the month of August, "King *Philip's* men had taken a young lad alive, about 14 years old, and bound him to a tree two nights and two days, intending to be merry with him the next day, and that they would roast him alive to make sport with him; but God, over night, touched the heart of one Indian, so that he came and loosed him, and bid him *run grande*, (i. e. run apace,) and by that means he escaped."†

About this time, some English found a single Indian, an old man, near Quabaog, whom they captured. As he would not give them any information respecting his countrymen, or, perhaps, such as they desired, they pronounced him worthy of death; so "they laid him down, *Cornelius*, the Dutchman, lifting up his sword to cut off his head, the Indian lifted up his hand between, so that his hand was first cut off, and partly his head, and the second blow finished the execution."‡

It was about this time, as the author of the "PRESENT STATE" relates, that "King *Philip*, now beginning to want money, having a coat made all of wampampeag, (i. e. Indian money,) cuts his coat to pieces and distributes it plentifully among the Nipmoog sachems and others, as well as to the eastward as southward and all round about."§

On the 18 Sept. Captain *Lothrop*, of Beverly, was sent from Hadley with about 88 men, to bring away the corn, grain, and other valuable articles, from Deerfield. Having loaded their teams and commenced their march homeward, they were attacked at a place called *Sugarloaf Hill*, where almost every man was slain. This company consisted of choice young men, the flower of Essex county.|| Eighteen of the men belonged to Deerfield.¶ Capt. *Mosely*, being not far off, upon a scout, was drawn to the scene of action by the report of the guns, and, having with him 70 men, charged the Indians with great resolution, although he computed their numbers at a 1000. He had two of his men killed and eleven wounded. The Indians dared him to begin the fight, and exultingly said to him, "*Come, Mosely, come, you seek Indians, you want Indians; here is Indians enough for you.*"** After continuing a fight with them, from eleven o'clock until almost night, he was obliged to retreat. The Indians cut open the bags of wheat and the feather-beds, and scattered their contents to the winds.** After *Mosely* had commenced a retreat, Major *Treat*, with 100 English and 60 Mohegans, came to his assistance. Their united forces obliged the Indians to retreat in their turn.†† The Indians were said

---

* Manuscript documents.

† Pres. State of N. Eng. &c. 12.

‡ Manuscript in library of Mass. Hist. Soc.

§ Pres. State, 13. If this were the case, *Philip* must have had an immense big coat—yea, even bigger than Dr. *Johnson's* great coat, as represented by *Boswell;* the side pockets of which, he said, were large enough each to contain one of the huge volumes of his folio dictionary!

|| *Hubbard's* Narrative.

¶ These were the teamsters.

** Manuscript letter, written at the time.

†† *I. Mather's* History of the War.

to have lost, in the various encounters, 96 men. It was a great oversight, that Captain *Lothrop* should have suffered his men to stroll about, while passing a dangerous defile. "Many of the soldiers having been so foolish and secure, as to put their arms in the carts, and step aside to gather grapes, which proved dear and deadly *grapes* to them."* The same author observes, "This was a black and fatal day, wherein there were eight persons made widows, and six-and-twenty children made fatherless, all in one little plantation and in one day; and above sixty persons buried in one dreadful grave!"

The Narragansets had not yet heartily engaged in the war, though there is no doubt but they stood pledged so to do. Therefore, having done all that could be expected upon the western frontier of Massachusetts, and concluding that his presence among his allies, the Narragansets, was necessary to keep them from abandoning his cause, *Philip* was next known to be in their country.

An army of 1500 English was raised by the three colonies, Massachusetts, Plimouth and Connecticut, for the purpose of breaking down the power of *Philip* among the Narragansets. They determined upon this course, as they had been assured that, in the spring, that nation would come with all their force upon them. It was not known that *Philip* was among them when this resolution was taken, and it was but a rumor that they had taken part with him. It was true, that they had promised to deliver up all the Wampanoags, who should flee to them, either alive or dead; but it is also true, that those who made this promise, had it not in their power to do it; being persons, chiefly in subordinate stations, who had no right or authority to bind any but themselves. And, therefore, as doubtless was foreseen by many, none of *Philip's* people were delivered up, although many were known to have been among them. Thus, in few words, have we exhibited the main grounds of the mighty expedition against the Narragansets in the winter of 1675.

Upon a small island, in an immense swamp, in South Kingston, Rhode Island, *Philip* had fortified himself, in a manner superior to what was common among his countrymen. Here he intended to pass the winter, with the chief of his friends. They had erected about 500 wigwams of a superior construction, in which was deposited a great store of provisions. Baskets and tubs of corn† were piled one upon another, about the inside of them, which rendered them bullet proof. It was supposed that about 3000 persons had here taken up their residence.

But, to be more particular upon the situation of "the scene of the destruction of the Narragansets," we will add as follows from the notes of a gentleman lately upon the spot, for the express purpose of gaining information. "What was called *The Island* is now an upland meadow, a few feet higher than the low meadow with which it is surrounded. The island, by my estimate, contains from three to four acres. One fourth of a mile west, is the Usquepaug; a small stream also at a short distance on the east." The celebrated island on which the fort was built is now in the farm of *J. G. Clark*, Esq. a descendant of *John Clark,* of R. I. and about 30 rods west of the line of the "Pettyswamscot Purchase." Water still surrounds it in wet seasons. It was cleared by the father of the present possessor about 1780, and although improved from that time to the present, charred corn and Indian implements are yet ploughed up.‡

---

* *I. Mather's* History of the War, 12.

† 500 bushels, says Dr. *I. Mather.* Hollow trees, cut off about the length of a barrel, were used by the Indian for tubs. In such they secured their corn and other grains.

‡ MS. communication of Rev. Mr. *Ely,* accompanied by a drawing of the island. Its shape is very similar to the shell of an oyster. Average rectangular lines through it measure, one 35 rods, another 20.

President *Stiles*, in his edition of CHURCH'S HISTORY OF PHILIP'S WAR, states that the Narraganset fort is seven miles nearly due west from the South Ferry. This agrees with data furnished by Mr. *Ely*, in stating the returning march of the English army. Pine and cedar were said to have been the former growth.* An oak 300 years old, standing upon the island, was cut down in 1782, two feet in diameter, 11 feet from the ground. From another, a bullet was cut out, surrounded by about 100 *annuli*, at the same time. The bullet was lodged there, no doubt, at the time of the fight. We will now return to our narrative of the expedition to this place in December, 1675.

After nearly a month from their setting out, the English army arrived in the Narraganset country, and made their head quarters about 18 miles from *Philip's* fort. They had been so long upon their march, that the Indians were well enough apprized of their approach, and had made the best arrangements in their power to withstand them. The army had already suffered much from the severity of the season, being obliged to encamp in the open field, and without tents to cover them!

The 19th of December, 1675, is a memorable day in the annals of New England. Cold, in the extreme,—the air filled with snow,—the English were obliged, from the low state of their provisions, to march to attack *Philip* in his fort. Treachery hastened his ruin. One of his men, by hope of reward, betrayed his country into their hands. This man had, probably, lived among the English, as he had an English name. He was called *Peter*,† and it was by accident that himself, with thirty-five others, had just before fallen into the hands of the fortunate Captain *Mosely*. No Englishman was acquainted with the situation of *Philip's* fort; and but for their pilot, *Peter*, there is very little probability that they could have even found, much less effected any thing against it. For it was one o'clock on that short day of the year, before they arrived within the vicinity of the swamp. There was but one point where it could be assailed with the least probability of success; and this was fortified by a kind of block-house, directly in front of the entrance, and had also flankers to cover a cross fire. Besides high palisades, an immense hedge of fallen trees, of nearly a rod in thickness, surrounded it, encompassing an area of about five acres. Between the fort and the main land was a body of water, over which a great tree had been felled, on which all must pass and repass, to and from it. On coming to this place, the English soldiers, as many as could pass upon the tree, which would not admit two abreast, rushed forward upon it, but were swept off in a moment by the fire of *Philip's* men. Still, the English soldiers, led by their captains, supplied the places of the slain. But again and again were they swept from the fatal avenue. Six captains and a great many men had fallen, and a partial, but momentary, recoil from the face of death took place.

Meanwhile, a handful, under the fortunate *Mosely*, had, as miraculous as it may seem, got within the fort. These were contending hand to hand with the Indians, and at fearful odds, when the cry of "*They run! they run*!" brought to their assistance a considerable body of their fellow soldiers. They were now enabled to drive the Indians from their main breastwork, and their slaughter became immense. Flying from wigwam to wigwam—men, women and children, indiscriminately, were hewn down and lay in heaps upon the snow. Being now masters of the fort, at the recommendation of Mr. *Church*,‡ General *Winslow* was about to

* Holmes's Annals, i. 376.

† The name of *Peter* among the Indians was so common, that it is, perhaps, past determination *who* this one was. Mr. *Hubbard* calls him a fugitive from the Narragansets.

‡ Afterwards the famous Colonel *Church*. He led the second party that entered the fort, and was badly wounded in the course of the fight.

quarter the army in it for the present, which offered comfortable habitations to the sick and wounded, besides a plentiful supply of provisions. But one of the captains* and a surgeon opposed the measure; probably from the apprehension that the woods was full of Indians, who would continue their attacks upon them, and drive them out in their turn. There was, doubtless, some reason for this, which was strengthened from the fact that many English were killed after they had possessed themselves of the fort, by those whom they had just dispossessed of it. Notwithstanding, had *Church's* advice been followed, perhaps many of the lives of the wounded would have been saved; for he was seldom out in his judgment, as his continued successes proved afterwards.

After fighting three hours, the English were obliged to march 18 miles, before the wounded could be dressed, and in a most horrid and boisterous night. Eighty English were killed in the fight, and 150 wounded, many of whom died afterwards. The English left the ground in considerable haste, leaving eight of their dead in the fort.

Philip, and such of his warriors as escaped unhurt, fled into a place of safety, until the enemy had retired; when they returned again to the fort. The English, no doubt, apprehended a pursuit, but *Philip*, not knowing their distressed situation, and, perhaps, judging of their loss from the few dead which they left behind, made no attempt to harass them in their retreat. Before the fight was over, many of the wigwams were set on fire. Into these, hundreds of innocent women and children had crowded themselves, and perished in the general conflagration! And, as a writer of that day expresses himself, "no man knoweth how many." The English learned afterwards, from some that fell into their hands, that in all about 700 perished.†

The sufferings of the English, after the fight, are almost without a parallel in history. The horrors of Moscow will not longer be remembered. The myriads of modern Europe, assembled there, bear but small proportion to the number of their countrymen, compared with that of the army of New England and theirs, at the fight in Narraganset.

Col. *Church*, then only a volunteer, was, in reality, the *Napoleon* in this fight. We will hear a few of his observations. "By this time, the English people in the fort had begun to set fire to the wigwams and houses, which Mr. *Church* labored hard to prevent; they told him they had orders from the general to burn them; he begged them to forbear until he had discoursed the general." Then, hastening to him, he urged, that "The wigwams were musket-proof, being all lined with baskets and tubs of grain, and other provisions, sufficient to supply the whole army until the spring of the year; and every wounded man might have a good warm house to lodge in; which, otherwise, would necessarily perish with the storms and cold. And, moreover, that the army had no other provision to trust unto or depend upon; that he knew that Plymouth forces had not

* Probably *Mosely*.

† There is printed in *Hutchinson's* Hist. Mass. i. 300. a letter which gives the particulars of the Narraganset fight. I have compared it with the original, and find it correct in the main particulars. He mistakes in ascribing it to Maj. *Bradford*, for it is signed by *James Oliver*, one of the Plimouth captains. *Hutchinson* copied from a copy, which was without signature. He omits a passage concerning Tift, or *Tiffe*, who, *Oliver* says, confirmed his narrative. That man had "married an Indian, a Wompanoag—he shot 20 times at us in the swamp—was taken at Providence, [by Captain *Fenner*,] Jan. 14th—brought to us the 16th—executed the 18th; a sad wretch. He never heard a sermon but once this 14 years; he never heard of the name of *Jesus Christ*. His father going to recall him, lost his head, and lies unburied." *Hubbard* says, (Narrative, 59.) that "he was condemned to die the death of a traitor, and traitors of those days were quartered. As to his religion, he was found as ignorant as an heathen, which, no doubt, caused the fewer tears to be shed at his funeral." A sorrowful record!

so much as one biscuit left." The general was for acceding to *Church's* proposition, but a captain and a doctor prevented it, as we have before observed; the former threatening to shoot the general's horse under him, if he attempted to march in, and the latter said, *Church* should bleed to death like a doge, before he would dress his wounds, if he gave such advice. *Church* then proceeds: "And, burning up all the houses and provisions in the fort, the army returned the same night in the storm and cold. And, I suppose, every one that is acquainted with the circumstances of that night's march, deeply laments the miseries that attended them; especially the wounded and dying men. But it mercifully came to pass that Capt. *Andrew Belcher* arrived at Mr. *Smith's,* [in Narraganset,] that very night from Boston, with a vessel loaden with provisions for the army, who must otherwise have perished for want."*

Soon after this, *Philip*, with many of his followers, left that part of the country, and resided in different places upon Connecticut River. Some report that he took up his residence near Albany, and that he solicited the Mohawks to aid him against the English, but without success.

The story of the foul stratagem said to have been resorted to by *Philip* for this object, is, if it be true, the deepest stain upon his character. According to one of the historians† of the war, it was reported at Boston, in the end of June or beginning of July, 1676, that "those Indians who are known by the name of Mauquawogs, (or Mohawks, i. e. man-eaters,) had lately fallen upon *Philip*, and killed 40 of his men. And if the variance between *Philip* and the Mauquawogs came to pass, as is commonly reported and apprehended, there was a marvellous finger of God in it. For we hear that *Philip* being this winter entertained in the Mohawks' country, made it his design to breed a quarrel between the English and them; to effect which, divers of our returned captives do report, that he resolved to kill some scattering Mohawks, and then to say that the English had done it; but one of these, whom he thought to have killed, was only wounded, and got away to his countrymen, giving them to understand that not the English, but *Philip*, had killed the men that were murdered; so that, instead of bringing the Mohawks upon the English, he brought them upon himself."

> "On human *plans* what *accidents* attend,
> Crowd every walk, and darken to the end!"
> *Power of Solitude.*‡

The author of the anonymous "LETTERS TO LONDON" has this passage§ concerning *Philip's* visit to the Mohawks. "King *Philip* and some of these northern Indians, being wandered up towards Albany, the Mohucks marched out very strong, in a warlike posture, upon them, putting them to flight, and pursuing them as far as Hassicke River, which is about two days' march from the east side of Hudson's River, to the north-east, killing divers, and bringing away some prisoners with great pride and triumph,

* "Our wounded men, (in number about 150,) being dressed, were sent into Rhode Island, as the best place for their accommodation; where, accordingly, they were kindly received by the governor, and others, only some churlish Quakers were not free to entertain them, until compelled by the governor. Of so inhumane, peevish and untoward a disposition are these *Nabals,* as not to vouchsafe civility to those that had ventured their lives, and received dangerous wounds in their defence." *A new and further Nar. &c. of the bloudy Ind. War, 2.*

† Dr. *I. Mather*, Brief Hist. 38.

‡ By *Joseph Story,* now the eminent Judge *Story*. The words in italics we have substituted for others.

§ In his third part, which he calls "A continued Account of the Bloudy Indian War, from March till August, 1676," page 13. fol. Lond. 1676.

which ill success on that side, where they did not expect any enemy, having lately endeavored to make up the ancient animosities, did very much daunt and discourage the said northern Indians, so that some hundreds came in and submitted themselves to the English at Plimouth colony, and *Philip* himself is run skulking away into some swamp with not above ten men attending him."

The various attacks and encounters he had with the English, from February to August, 1676, are so minutely recorded, and in so many works, that we will not enlarge upon them in this place.

When success no longer attended him, in the western parts of Massachusetts, those of his allies whom he had seduced into the war, upbraided and accused him of bringing all their misfortunes upon them; that they had no cause of war against the English, and had not engaged in it but for his solicitations; and many of the tribes scattered themselves in different directions. With all that would follow him, as a last retreat, *Philip* returned to Pokanoket.

The Pecomptuck or Deerfield Indians were among the first who abandoned his cause, and many of the other Nipmucks and Narragansets soon followed their example.

On the 11th of July, he attempted to surprise Taunton, but was repulsed.* His camp was now at Matapoiset. The English came upon him here, under Captain *Church*, who captured many of his people, but he escaped over Taunton River, as he had done a year before, but in the opposite direction, and screened himself once more in the woods of Pocasset. He used many stratagems to cut off Capt. *Church*, and seems to have watched and followed him from place to place, until the end of this month; but he was continually losing one company of his men after another. Some scouts ascertained that he, and many of his men, were at a certain place upon Taunton River, and, from appearances, were about to repass it. His camp was now at this place, and the chief of his warriors with him. Some soldiers from Bridgewater fell upon them here, on Sunday, July 30, and killed ten warriors; but *Philip*, having disguised himself, escaped.† His uncle, *Akkompoin*, was among the slain, and his own sister taken prisoner.

The late attempt by *Philip* upon Taunton had caused the people of Bridgewater to be more watchful, and some were continually on the scout. Some time in the day, Saturday, 29 July, four men, as they were ranging the woods, discovered one Indian, and, rightly judging there were more at hand, made all haste to inform the other inhabitants of Bridgewater of their discovery. *Comfort Willis* and *Joseph Edson* were "pressed" to go "post" to the governor of Plimouth, at Marshfield, who "went to Plimouth with them, the next day, [30 July,] to send Capt. *Church* with his company. And Capt. Church came with them to Monponset on the sabbath, and came no further that day, he told them he would meet them the next day." Here *Willis* and *Edson* left him, and arrived at home in the evening. Upon hearing of the arrival of *Church* in their neighborhood, 21 men "went out on Monday supposing to meet with Capt. *Church*; but they came upon the enemy and fought with them, and took 17 of them alive, and also much plunder. And they all returned, and not one of them fell by the enemy; and received no help from *Church*." This account is given from an old manuscript, but who its author was is not

---

* A captive negro made his escape from *Philip's* men, and gave notice of their intention; "whereupon the inhabitants stood upon their guard, and souldiers were timously sent in to them for their relief and defence." *Prevalency of Prayer*, 8.

† " 'Tis said that he had newly cut off his hair, that he might not be known." *Hubbard, Nar.* 101.

certain.* *Church's* account differs considerably from it. He says, that on the evening of the same day he and his company marched from Plimouth, "they heard a smart firing at a distance from them, but it being near night, and the firing of short continuance, they missed the place, and went into Bridgewater town."

On the 1 August, the intrepid *Church* came upon *Philip's* head quarters, killed and took about 130 of his people, *Philip* himself very narrowly escaping. Such was his precipitation, that he left all his wampum behind, and his wife and son fell into the hands of *Church.*

No sooner had the story of the destruction of the Indians begun to attract attention, (which, however, was not until a long time after they had been destroyed,) much inquiry was made concerning the fate of this son of the famous *Metacomet;* and it was not until considerable time had elapsed, that it was discovered that he was sold into slavery! It is gratifying to learn what did become of him, although it must cause pain in every humane breast; not more for the lot of young *Metacomet,* than for the wretched depravity of the minds of those who advised and executed the decree of slavery upon him.

Some of *Philip's* Indians, who now served under *Church,* said to him, "You have now made *Philip* ready to die; for you have made him as poor and miserable as he used to make the English. You have now killed or taken all his relations—that they believed he would soon have his head, and that this bout had almost broken his heart."

Church† relates this attack upon the flying chief as follows:—"Next morning, [after the skirmish in which *Akkompoin* was killed,] Capt. *Church* moved very early with his company, which was increased by many of Bridgewater that listed under him for that expedition, and, by their piloting, he soon came, very still, to the top of the great tree which the enemy had fallen across the river; and the captain spied an Indian sitting upon the stump of it, on the other side of the river, and he clapped his gun up, and had doubtless despatched him, but that one of his own Indians called hastily to him not to fire, for he believed it was one of his own men; upon which the Indian upon the stump looked about, and Capt. *Church's* Indian, seeing his face, perceived his mistake, for he knew him to be *Philip;* clapped up his gun and fired, but it was too late; for *Philip* immediately threw himself off the stump, leaped down a bank on the side of the river, and made his escape. Capt. *Church,* as soon as possible, got over the river, and scattered in quest of *Philip* and his company, but the enemy scattered and fled every way; but he picked up a considerable many of their women and children, among which were *Philip's* wife and son of about nine years old." The remainder of the day was spent in pursuing the flying *Philip,* who, with his Narragansets, was still formidable. They picked up many prisoners, from whom they learned the force of those of whom they were in pursuit. At night, *Church* was under obligation to return to his men he had left, but commissioned *Lightfoot,* captain, to lead a party on discovery. *Lightfoot* returned in the morning with good success, having made an important discovery and taken 13 prisoners. *Church* immediately set out to follow up their advantage. He soon came where they had made fires, and shortly after overtook their women and children. who "were faint and tired," and who informed them "that *Philip,* with a great number of the enemy, were a little before." It was almost sunset when they came near enough to observe them, and "*Philip* soon came to

---

* It is published by Mr. *Mitchel,* in his valuable account of Bridgewater, and supposed to have been written by *Comfort Willis,* named above. See 1 Col. Mass. Hist Soc. vii. 157.

† Hist. *Philip's* War, 38. ed. 4to.

a stop, and fell to breaking and chopping wood, to make fires; and a great noise they made." *Church*, concentrating his followers, formed them into a circle, and set down "without any noise or fire." Their prisoners showed great signs of fear, but were easily put in confidence by the conciliatory conduct of *Church*. Thus stood matters in *Church's* camp through the night of the 2 August, 1676. At dawn of day, he told his prisoners they must remain still where they were, until the fight was over, (for he now had every reason to expect a severe one shortly to follow,) "or, as soon as the firing ceased, they must follow the tracks of his company, and come to them. (An Indian is next to a bloodhound to follow a track.)"*

It being now light enough to make the onset, *Church* sent forward two soldiers to learn *Philip's* position. *Philip,* no less wary, had, at the same time, sent out two spies to see if any were in pursuit of him. The respective spies of the two famous chiefs gave the alarm to both camps at the same time; but, unhappily for *Philip,* his antagonist was prepared for the event, while he was not. "All fled at the first tidings, [of the spies,] left their kettles boiling, and meat roasting upon their wooden spits, and run into a swamp with no other breakfast, than what Capt. *Church,* afterwards treated them with." *Church* sent his lieutenant, Mr. *Isaac Howland,* on one side of the swamp, while himself ran upon the other, each with a small party, hoping, as the swamp was small, to prevent the escape of any. Expecting that when *Philip* should discover the English at the further extremity of the swamp, he would turn back in his own track, and so escape at the same place he entered, *Church* had, therefore, stationed an ambush to entrap him in such an event. But the wariness of *Philip* disappointed him. He, thinking that the English would pursue him into the swamp, had formed an ambush for them also, but was, in like manner, disappointed. He had, at the same time, sent forward a band of his warriors, who fell into the hands of *Church* and *Howland.* They, at first, attempted to fly, and then offered resistance; but *Church* ordered *Matthias*† to tell them the impracticability of such a step. He accordingly called to them, and said, "If *they fired one gun they were all dead! men."* This threat, with the presence of the English and Indians, so amazed them, that they suffered "the English to come and take the guns out of their hands, when they were both charged and cocked." Having secured these with a guard, armed with the guns just taken from them, *Church* presses through the swamp in search of *Philip,* towards the end at which that chief had entered. Having waited until he had no hopes of ensnaring Capt. *Church, Philip* now moved on after the company he had sent forward, and thus the two parties met. The English had the advantage of the first discovery, and, covered by trees, made the first fire. *Philip* stood his ground for a time, and maintained a desperate fight; but, a main body of his warriors having been captured, which, by this time, he began to apprehend, as they did not come to his aid, he, therefore, fled back to the point where he entered the swamp, and thus fell into a second ambush. Here the English were worsted, having one of their number slain, viz. *Thomas Lucas,*‡ of Plimouth: thus escaped, for a few days, *Philip* and some of his best captains, such as

---

* Hist. *Philip's* War, 39.

† One of *Church's* Indian soldiers, but of whom *he* makes no mention.

‡ An improvident fellow, given to intoxication, and, from *Church's* expression about his being killed, "not being so careful as he might have been," it leaves room to doubt whether he were not, at this time, under the effects of liquor. He had been often fined, and once whipped, for getting drunk, beating his wife and children, defaming the character of deceased magistrates, and other misdemeanors.

Tuspapin and Tabson. This was August the 3d, and *Philip's* numbers had decreased, since the 1st, 173, by the exertions of *Church.**

Philip, having now but few followers left, was driven from place to place, and lastly to his ancient seat near Pokanoket. The English, for a long time, had endeavored to kill him, but could not find him off his guard for he was always the first who was apprized of their approach. Having put to death one of his men† for advising him to make peace, his brother, fearing the same fate, deserted him, and gave Captain *Church* an account of his chief's situation, and offered to lead him to his camp. Early on Saturday morning, 12 Aug. *Church* came to the swamp where *Philip* was encamped, and, before he was discovered, had placed a guard about it, so as to encompass it, except a small place. He then ordered Captain Golding‡ to rush into the swamp, and fall upon *Philip* in his camp; which he immediately did – but was discovered as he approached, and, as usual, *Philip* was the first to fly. Having but just awaked from sleep, and having on but a part of his clothes, he fled with all his might. Coming directly upon an Englishman and an Indian, who composed a part of the ambush at the edge of the swamp, the Englishman's gun missed fire, but *Alderman,* the Indian, whose gun was loaded with two balls, "sent one through his heart, and another not above two inches from it. He fell upon his face in the mud and water, with his gun under him."

There were many reports in circulation of the particulars of this last great tragedy of the Wampanoag sachem, which occasioned, as in many other events, different accounts being handed down; but all of them which we have seen, though manifestly contradictory in some particulars, have, nevertheless, some facts of great importance. The following being exceedingly curious, we give the substance of it. Besides containing some additional facts, it serves to show one of the different reports. It is contained in a single sheet, in folio form, printed in London, 1677, and was licensed 4 Nov. of that year. Its title is, "THE WARR IN NEW ENGLAND VISIBLY ENDED. King PHILIP, that barbarous *Indian,* now Beheaded, and most of his Bloudy Adherents submitted to Mercy, the Rest fled far up into the Countrey, which hath given the Inhabitants Encouragement to prepare for their Settlement. Being a True and perfect Account brought in by *Caleb More,* Master of a vessel newly arrived from *Rhode Island."* Its substance is as follows: *Philip* had, when he began the war, 300 men, but when he was killed, 10 only remained of them. He was a "pestilent ringleader." The swamp in which he was killed, was "so loose, that our men sunk to the middle" in the mud. "By chance, the Indian guide and the [a] Plimouth man, being together, the guide espied an Indian, and bids the Plimouth man shoot, whose gun went not off, only flashed in the pan; with that the Indian looked about, and was going to shoot, but the Plimouth man prevented him, and shot the enemy through the body, dead, with a brace of bullets; and, approaching the place where he lay, upon search, it appeared to be King *Philip,* to their no small amazement and great joy. This seasonable prey was soon divided; they cut off his head and hands, and conveyed them to Rhode Island, and quartered his body, and hung it upon four trees. One Indian more of King *Philip's* company they then killed, and some of the rest they wounded. But the swamp being so thick and miry, they made their escape."

---

* *Church,* 41. In the account of *Tatoson, Church's* narrative is continued.
† Brother of *Alderman.*
‡ Capt. *Roger Goulden,* of R. I. Plimouth granted him 100 acres of land on Pocasset, in 1676, for his eminent services. *Plim. Records.*

Drawn by J. Neilson Eng. by A.B. Durand

SEAT OF KING PHILLIP

"Cold, with the beast he slew, he sleeps;
O'er him no filial spirit weeps;
* * * * * * *
Even that he lived, is for his conqueror's tongue;
By foes alone his death-song must be sung;
No chronicles but theirs shall tell
His mournful doom to future times;
May these upon his virtues dwell,
And in his fate forget his crimes."—*Sprague.*

The name of the man stationed with *Alderman* was *Caleb Cook,** who had shared in many of *Church's* hazardous expeditions before the present. Seeing that he could not have the honor of killing *Philip,* he was desirous if possible of having a memento of the mighty exploit. He therefore prevailed upon *Alderman* to exchange guns with him. This gun was kept in the family until the present century, when the late *Isaac Lothrop* Esq. of Plimouth obtained the lock of it from Mr. *Sylvanus Cook,* late of Kingston. *Sylvanus* was great-grandson of *Caleb.*† The stock and barrel of the gun are still retained by the descendants of the name of *Cook.*‡

We are able to add yet a little for the gratification of the curious: a lock shown in the library of the Mass. Hist. Soc. is said to be the same which *Alderman* used in shooting *Philip.* This *Alderman* was a subject of *Weetamoo.* In the commencement of this war, he went to the governor of Plimouth, and desired to remain in peace with the English, and immediately took up his residence upon an island, remote from the tribes engaged in the war. But after *Phililp* had returned to his own country, *Alderman,* upon some occasion, visited him. It was at this time that he learned the fate of his brother before spoken of; or his murder was actually committed while he was present. This caused his flight to the English, which he thought, probably, the last resort for vengeance. He "came down from thence, says *Church,* (where *Philip's* camp now was,) on to Sand Point over against *Trips,* and hollow'd, and made signs to be fetch'd over" to the island. He was immediately brought over, and gave the information desired. Capt. *Church* had but just arrived upon Rhode Island, and was about eight miles from the upper end, where *Alderman* landed. He had been at home but a few minutes, when "they spy'd two horsemen coming a great pace," and, as he prophesied, "they came with tydings." Major *Sanford* and Capt. *Golding* were the horsemen, "who immediately ask'd Capt. *Church what he would give to hear some news of Philip.* He reply'd, *That was what he wanted.*" The expedition was at once entered upon, and *Alderman* went as their pilot. But to return to the fall of *Philip:*—

"By this time," continues *Church,* "the enemy perceived they were waylaid on the east side of the swamp, tacked short about," and were led out of their dangerous situation by the great captain *Annawon.* "The man that had shot down *Philip* ran with all speed to Capt. *Church,* and informed him of his exploit, who commanded him to be silent about it, and let no man more know it until they had drove the swamp clean; but when they had drove the swamp through, and found the enemy had escaped, or at least the most of them, and the sun now up, and so the dew gone that they could not easily track them, the whole company met together at the place where the enemy's night shelter was, and then Capt.

* *Baylies,* in his N. Plimouth, ii. 168, says his name was *Francis,* but as he gives no authority, we adhere to older authority.

† This *Caleb Cook* was son of *Jacob* of Plimouth, and was born there, 29 Mar. 1651. He had two or more brothers; *Jacob,* born 14 May, 1653, and *Francis,* 5 Jan. 1663–4. Hence it is not probable that *Francis* was a soldier at this time, as he was only in his 13th year.

‡ *Col. Mass. Hist. Soc.* iv. 63.

Church gave them the news of *Philip's* death. Upon which the whole army* gave three loud huzzas. Capt. *Church* ordered his body to be pulled out of the mire on to the upland. So some of Capt. *Church's* Indians took hold of him by his stockings, and some by his small breeches, being otherwise naked, and drew him through the mud unto the upland; and a doleful, great, naked dirty beast, he looked like." (Now follows one of the most barbarous passages in the life of the excellent *Church*. As the word *excellent* may surprise some of my readers, I will add, *in as far as it is possible for a warrior to be so.*) Capt. *Church* then said, "*Forasmuch as he has caused many an Englishman's body to lie unburied and rot above ground, not one of his bones shall be buried!*"

With the great chief, fell five of his most trusty followers, one of whom was his chief captain's son,† and the very Indian who fired the first gun at the commencement of the war.

"*Philip* having one very remarkable hand, being much scarred, occasioned by the splitting of a pistol in it formerly, Capt. *Church* gave the head and that hand to *Alderman,* the Indian who shot him, to show to such gentlemen as would bestow gratuities upon him; and accordingly he got many a penny by it."‡

The barbarous usage of beheading and quartering traitors was now executed upon the fallen *Philip. Church,* "calling his old Indian executioner, bid him behead and quarter him. Accordingly, he came with his hatchet, and stood over him, but before he struck, he made a small speech, directing it to *Philip,"* saying, "*You have been a very great man, and have made many a man afraid of you; but so big as you be I will now chop your ass [arse] for you.*" He then proceeded to the execution of his orders.

His head was sent to Plimouth, where it was exposed upon a gibbet for 20 years, and one of his hands to Boston, where it was exhibited in savage triumph, and his mangled body was denied the right of sepulture.

Church and his company returned to the island the same day, and arrived with the prisoners at Plimouth two days after, namely, Tuesday, August 15, "ranging through all the woods in their way." They now "received their premium, which was 30 *shillings* per head," for all enemies killed or taken, "instead of all wages, and *Philip's* head went at the same price." This *amounted to only four and sixpence apiece,* "which was all the reward they had, except the honor of killing *Philip."*

During the bloody contest, the pious fathers wrestled long and often with their God, in prayer, that he would prosper their arms and deliver their enemies into their hands; and when, upon stated days of prayer, the Indians gained advantage, it was looked upon as a rebuke of Providence, and animated them to greater sincerity and fervor; and on the contrary, when their arms prevailed upon such days, it was viewed as an immediate interposition in their favor. The philosophic mind will be shocked at the expressions of some, very eminent in that day for piety and excellence of moral life. Dr. *Increase Mather,*§ in speaking of the efficacy of prayer, in bringing about the destruction of the Indians, says, "Nor could they [the English] cease crying to the Lord against *Philip,* until they had prayed the bullet into his heart." And in speaking of the slaughter of *Philip's* people, at Narraganset, he says, "We have heard of two-and-twenty Indian captains, slain all of them, and brought down to hell in

---

* Eighteen English and twenty-two Indians constituted his army a week before, but we know not how many were at the taking of *Philip,* though we may suppose about the same number. Hence this expedition cost the colony £9.

† Very probably a son of *Uncompoin,* or *Woonashum.*

‡ *Philip's* War.

§ In his "Prevalency of Prayer," page 10.

4

one day." Again, in speaking of a chief who had sneered at the English religion, and who had, "withal, added a most hideous blasphemy, immediately upon which a bullet took him in the head, and dashed out his brains, sending his cursed soul in a moment amongst the devils, and blasphemers in hell forever."*

These extracts are made with no other view than to show the habits of thinking in those times.

The low and vulgar epithets† sneeringly cast upon the Indians by their English contemporaries are not to be attributed to a single individual, but to the English in general.‡ It is too obvious that the early historians viewed the Indians as inferior beings, and some went so far as hardly to allow them to be human.

Like *Massasoit, Philip* always opposed the introduction of Christianity among his people. When Mr. *Eliot* urged upon him its great importance, he said he cared no more for the gospel than he did for a button upon his coat.§ This does not very well agree with the account of Mr. *Gookin,* respecting *Philip's* feelings upon religious matters; at least, it shows that there was a time when he was willing to listen to such men as the excellent and benevolent *Gookin.* In speaking of the Wampanoags, he says, "There are some that have hopes of their greatest and chiefest sachem, named *Philip,* living at Pawkunnawkutt. Some of his chief men, as I hear, stand well inclined to hear the gospel: and himself is a person of good understanding and knowledge in the best things. I have heard him speak very good words, arguing that his conscience is convicted: but yet, though his will is bowed to embrace *Jesus Christ,* his sensual and carnal lusts are strong bands to hold him fast under *Satan's* dominions."‖ And Dr. *Mather* adds, "It was not long, before the hand which now writes, [1700,] upon a certain occasion took off the jaw from the exposed skull of that blasphemous *leviathan;* and the renowned *Samuel Lee* hath since been a pastor to an English congregation, sounding and showing the praises of heaven, upon that very spot of ground, where *Philip* and his Indians were lately worshipping of the devil."¶

The error that *Philip* was grandson to *Massasoit,* is so well known to be such, that it would hardly seem to have required notice, but to inform the reader of its origin. The following passage from Mr. *Josselyn's* work** will, besides proving him to be the author of the error, at least the first writer that so denominates him, furnish some valuable information. Speaking of the Indians in general, he says, "Their beads are their money; of these, there are two sorts, blue beads and white beads; the first is their gold, the last their silver. These they work out of certain shells, so cunningly, that neither *Jew* nor *Devil* can counterfeit.†† They drill them and string them, and make many curious works with them, to

---

* Prevalency of Prayer, page 7.

† Such as *dogs, wolves, blood-hounds, demons, devils-incarnate, caitiffs, hell-hounds, fiends, monsters, beasts,* &c. Occasional quotations will show what authors have used these.

‡ The author of "*Indian Tales*" has fathered all he could think of upon Mr. *Hubbard.* He *may* be called upon to point out the passage in that valuable author's works where he has called one or *any* of the Indians "*hell-hounds.*" Such loose, gratuitous expressions will not do at the bar of history.

§ Magnalia.

‖ 1 *Col. Mass. Hist. Soc.* i. 200.

¶ Mr. *Lee* was taken by the French in a voyage to England, and carried into their country, where he died, in 1691. This event, it was thought, hastened his end. Perhaps the surviving natives did not attribute the disaster to his usurping their territory, and teaching a religion they could not believe; but might they not with equal propriety?

** Account of two Voyages to New England, 142, 143.

†† Of this he was misinformed. There was much spurious wampum, which became a subject of legislation. See *Hazard's Hist. Col.* vol. ii.

adorn the persons of their sagamores and principal men, and young women, as belts, girdles, tablets, borders for their women's hair, bracelets, necklaces, and links to hang in their ears. Prince *Philip,* a little before I came for England, [1671,] coming to Boston, had a coat on and buskins set thick with these beads, in pleasant wild works, and a broad belt of the same; his accoutrements were valued at £20. The English merchant giveth them 10s. a fathom for their white, and as much more, or near upon, for their blue beads." "The roytelet now of the Pocanakets is prince *Philip,* alias *Metacon,* the grandson of *Massasoit.*"*

In November, 1669, *Philip* sold to the selectmen of Dedham, the tract of land called *Woollommonuppogue* "within the town bounds, [of Dedham,] not yet purchased." What the full consideration paid to him was, we do not learn. In an order which he sent to them afterwards, he requests them "to pay to this bearer, for the use of King *Philip,* £5 5s. money, and £5 in trucking cloth, at money price." In a receipt signed by *Peter,* the following amount is named: "In reference to the payment of King *Philip* of Mount Hope, the full and just sum of £5 5s. in money, and twelve yards of trucking cloth, three pounds of powder, and as much lead as to make it up; which is in full satisfaction with £10 that he is to receive of *Nathaniel Pane.*"†

While Mrs. *Rowlandson* was a captive in the wilderness with the allies of *Philip,* she mentions meeting with him; and although she speaks often with bitterness of the Indians in general, yet of him nothing of that nature appears in her journal. The party she was with visited *Philip* on the west side of the Connecticut, about five miles above Northfield, then called *Squakeag.* Having arrived at the point of crossing, Mrs. *Rowlandson* says, "We must go over the river to *Philip's* crew. When I was in the canoe, I could not but be amazed at the numerous crew of pagans that were on the bank on the other side." She was much afraid they meant to kill her here, but, being assured to the contrary, become more resigned to her fate. "Then came one of them, (she says,) and gave me two spoonfuls of meal (to comfort me,) and another gave me half a pint of peas, which was worth more than many bushels at another time. Then I went to see King *Philip;* he bade me come in and sit down; and asked me whether I would smoke it; (a usual compliment now a days, among the saints and sinners;) but this no ways suited me."‡

"During my abode in this place, *Philip* spake to me to make a shirt for his boy, which I did; for which he gave me a shilling." "Afterward he asked me to make a cap for his boy, for which he invited me to dinner; I went, and he gave me a pancake, about as big as two fingers; it was made of parched wheat, beaten and fried in bears' grease; but I thought I never tasted pleasanter meat in my life."§

It is extremely gratifying to hear any testimony in favor of the humanity of men so near a state of nature. We speak not of this because such testimonies are few, for they are many, as it is unnecessary to apprize the reader of even a few pages in this book. To say the least of *Philip's* humanity, it was as great towards captives, so far as we have any knowledge, as was that of *any* of the English to the captive Indians.

As the Indians were returning from their recesses upon the Connecticut, (in what is now New Hampshire and Vermont,) towards Wachuset, "having indeed my life, (says Mrs. *Rowlandson,)* but little spirit, *Philip,* who was in the company, came up, and took me by the hand, and said,

* Account of two Voyages to New England, 146. He is also called grandson of *Massasoit,* in the work entitled *Present State of New England, in respect to the Indian War,* fol. London, 1676; the author of that work doubtless copied from *Josselyn.*

† MS. Documents among our state papers.

‡ *Narrative of her Captivity,* 38, 39.

§ Ibid. 40.

'*Two weeks more and you shall be mistress again.*' I asked him if he spoke true: he said, '*Yes, and quickly you shall come to your master** again,' who had been gone from us three weeks."†

In bringing our account of this truly great man towards a close, we must not forget to present the reader with a specimen of the language in which he spoke. The following is the Lord's prayer in Wampanoag:—

Noo-shun kes-uk-qut, qut-tian-at-am-unch koo-we-su-onk, kuk-ket-as-soo-tam-oonk pey-au-moo-utch, kut-te-nan-tam-oo-onk ne nai, ne-ya-ne ke-suk-qut kah oh-ke-it. As-sa-ma-i-in-ne-an ko-ko-ke-suk-o-da-e nut-as-e-suk-ok-ke pe-tuk-qun-neg. Kah ah-quo-an-tam-a-i-in-ne-an num-match-e-se-ong-an-on-ash, ne-wutch-e ne-na-wun wonk nut-ah-quo-an-tam-au-o-un-non-og nish-noh pasuk noo-na-mon-tuk-quoh-who-nan, kah ahque sag-kom-pa-gin-ne-an en qutch-e-het-tu-ong-a-nit, qut poh-qua-wus-sin-ne-an wutch match-i-tut.‡

Since we are upon curiosities, the following may very properly be added. There is to be seen in the library of the Mass. Hist. Society a large skimmer, which some have mistaken for a bowl, cut out of the root of ash, that will hold about two quarts. On this article is this historical inscription, in gilt letters: "*A trophy from the wigwam of King* Philip; *when he was slain in* 1676, *by* Richard; *presented by* Ebenezer Richard, *his grandson.*"§

CHAPTER III.

LIVES OF PHILIP'S CHIEF CAPTAINS.

"I am a man, and you are another."
Black-hawk's speech to President Jackson.

Nanuntenoo—*Reasons for his aiding Philip—His former name—Meets the English and Indians under Capt. Peirse—Fights and destroys his*

* *Quinnapin.* See his life. † Nar. of Mrs. *Rowlandson,* 63.
‡ *Eliot's* Indian Bible, Luke xi. 2—4.
§ No mention is made to whom, or when it was presented. It does not appear to us to be of such antiquity as its inscription pretends; and the truth of which may very

*whole company at Pawtucket—Incidents relating to that fight—Notice of Capt. Peirse—Nanuntenoo surprised and taken—His magnanimity—Speech to his captors—Is executed and his body burnt—Cassassinnamon—Catapazet—Monopoide—*ANNA WON—*His escape from the swamp when Philip was killed—Capt. Church sent out to capture him—Discovers his retreat—Takes him prisoner—His magnanimous behavior—His speech to Church—Presents him with Philip's ornaments—Description of them—Church takes Annawon to Plimouth, where he is put to death*—QUINNAPIN—*His connections and marriage—At the capture of Lancaster—Account of his wives—Weetamoo—He is taken and shot*—TUSPAQUIN—*His sales of lands—His operations in Philip's War—Surrenders himself, and is put to death—Reflections upon his executioners*—TATOSON—*Early notices of—Captures a garrison in Plimouth—Trial and execution of Keweenam—Totoson dies of a broken heart*—BARROW *cruelly murdered* — TYASKS.

Nanuntenoo, son of *Miantunnomoh*, "was chief sachem of all the Narragansets, and heir of all his father's pride and insolency, as well as of his malice against the English."* Notwithstanding this branding character, drawn by a contemporary, we need only look into the life of *Miantunnomoh*, to find excuse for "malice and insolency" tenfold more than was contained in the breast of *Nanuntenoo.*

The English had cut to pieces the women and children of his tribe, burned them to death in their wigwams, and left their mangled bodies bleaching in the wintry blast! The swamp fight of the 19 Dec. 1675, could not be forgotten! *Nanuntenoo* escaped from this scene, but we cannot doubt that he acquitted himself agreeably to the character we have of him.

The first name by which he was known to the English was *Canonchet.* He had been in Boston the October before the war, upon a treaty, at which time he received, among other presents, a silver-laced coat. Dr. *Mather* says, speaking of the Narragansets, "their great sachem called *Quanonchet*, was a principal ringleader in the Narraganset war, and had as great an interest and influence, as can be said of any among the Indians;"† and that, "when *he* was taken and slain, it was an amazing stroke to the enemy."‡

The name of *Canonchet* stands first to the treaty, to which we have just alluded, which was entered into at Boston, 18 Oct. 1675. By that treaty, the Narragansets agreed to deliver to the English in 10 days, "all and euery one of the said Indians, whether belonging vnto *Philip*, the Pocasset Sqva, or the Saconett Indians, Quabaug, Hadley, or any other sachems or people that haue bin or are in hostillitie with the English, or any of their allies or abettors."§ The names to the treaty are as follows:

"QUANANCHETT'S ✓ *mark, sachem in behalf of himself and* Conanacus *and the* Old Queen *and* Pomham *and* Quaunapeen, (seal)
MANATANNOO *counceller his* + ✝ *mark, and* Cannonacus *in his behalf*, (seal)
AHANMANPOWETT'S ✝ *mark, counceller and his* (seal)
CORNMAN, *cheiffe counceller to* Ninnegrett, *in his behalfe, and a seal* (S.)"

Witnesses.
RICHARD SMITH,
JAMES BROWNE,
SAMUEL GORTON, Jr.
Interpreters.
JOHN NOWHENETT'S ✕ *mark,*
Indian interpreter.

reasonably be questioned, in this particular, when the more glaring error of the name of the person said to have killed *Philip*, is staring us in the face.

* *Hubbard*, 67.—Mr. *Oldmixon* calls him "the mighty sachem of Narraganset."—*Brit. Empire.*

† *Brief Hist.* 26.

‡ *Prevalency of prayer*, 11.

§ It may be seen at large in *Hazard's Collections*, i. 536, 537.

The Indians having carried their whirlwind of war to the very doors of Plimouth, caused the sending out of Capt. *Peirce*, (or, as his name is uniformly in the records, *Peirse*,) to divert them from these ravages, and destroy as many of them as he was able. He had a large company, consisting of 70 men, 20 of whom were friendly Indians. With these, no doubt, *Peirse* thought himself safe against any power of the Indians in that region.

Meanwhile this most valiant chief captain of the Narragansets, *Nanuntenoo*, learning, we presume, by his spies, the direction the English were taking, assembled his warriors at a crossing place on Pawtucket River, at a point adjacent to a place since called *Attleborough-Gore*, and not far distant from Pawtucket falls. It is judged that *Nanuntenoo* was upon an expedition to attack Plimouth, or some of the adjacent towns, for his force was estimated at upwards of 300 men.

On arriving at this fatal place, some of *Nanuntenoo's* men showed themselves retiring, on the opposite side of the river. This stratagem succeeded,—*Peirse* followed.* No sooner was he upon the western side, than the warriors of *Nanuntenoo*, like an avalanche from a mountain, rushed down upon him; nor striving for coverts from which to fight, more than their foes, fought them face to face with the most determined bravery.

A part of *Nanuntenoo's* force remained on the east side of the river, to prevent the retreat of the English, which they most effectually did, as in the event will appear. When Capt. *Peirse* saw himself hemmed in by numbers on every side, he drew up his men upon the margin of the river, in two ranks, back to back,† and in this manner fought until nearly all his men were slain. *Peirse* had timely sent a messenger to Providence for assistance, and although the distance could not have been more than six or eight miles, from some inexplicable cause, no succor arrived; and Mr. *Hubbard*‡ adds, "As Solomon saith, a faithful messenger is as snow in harvest."

This dreadful fight was on Sunday, 26 March, 1676, when, as Dr. *Mather* says, "Capt. *Peirse* was slain and forty and nine English with him, and eight, (or more,) Indians, who did assist the English." The Rev. Mr. *Newman* of Rehoboth wrote a letter to Plimouth dated the day after the slaughter, in which he says, "52 of our English, and 11 Indians," were slain.§ The company was, no doubt, increased by some who volunteered as they marched through the country, or by such as were taken for pilots.

Nanuntenoo's victory was complete, but, as usual on such occasions, the English consoled themselves by making the loss of the Indians appear as large as possible. Dr. *Mather* says, that some Indians that were afterwards taken confessed they lost 140, which, no doubt, is not far from the truth.||

An Englishman, and perhaps the only one who escaped from this disastrous fight, was saved by one of the friendly Indians in this manner: The friendly Indian being taken for a Narraganset, as he was pursuing with an uplifted tomahawk the English soldier, no one interfered, seeing him pursue an unarmed Englishman at such great advantage. In this manner, covering themselves in the woods, they escaped.

A friendly Indian, being pursued by one of *Nanunenoo's* men, got behind the root of a fallen tree. Thus screened by the earth raised upon

* Dr. *Mather* (Brief Hist. 24.) says, "a small number of the enemy who in desperate subtlety ran away from them, and they went limping to make the English believe they were lame," and thus effected their object.

† *Deane's* Hist. Scituate, 121.

‡ Narrative, 64.

§ See the letter giving the names of the company in *Deane's* Scituate, 122, 123.

|| Mr. *Hubbard's* account is *the same.*

the roots, the Indian that pursued waited for him to run from his natural fort, knowing he would not dare to maintain it long. The other soon thought of an expedient, which was to make a port-hole in his breast work, which he easily did by digging through the dirt. When he had done this, he put his gun through, and shot his pursuer, then fled in perfect safety.

Another escaped in a manner very similar. In his flight he got behind a large rock. This afforded him a good shelter, but in the end he saw nothing but certain death, and the longer he held out the more misery he must suffer. In this deplorable situation, he bethought himself to try the following device. Putting his cap upon his gun, he raised it very gradually above the rock, as though to discover the position of his enemy: it had the desired effect—he fired upon it. The one behind the rock now rushed upon him, before he could reload his gun, and despatched him. Thus, as Mr. *Hubbard* says, "it is worth the noting, what faithfulness and courage some of the Christian Indians shewed in this fight." That this most excellent author did not approve of the severity exercised towards those who appeared friendly, is abundantly proved by his writings. In another place he says, "Possibly if some of the English had not been too shy in making use of such of them as were well affected to their interest, they never need have suffered so much from their enemies."

A notice may be reasonably expected of the unfortunate Capt. *William Peirse*, of Scituate. He was one of those adventurous spirits "who never knew fear," and who sought rather than shrunk from dangers. He was, like his great antagonist, in the Narraganset fight; and in 1673, when the government of Plimouth raised a force to go against the Dutch, who had encroached upon them in Connecticut, he was appointed ensign in one of the companies. He resided in several places before going to Plimouth. Mr. Deane, in his *History of Scituate*, gives a genealogical account of his family, from which we learn that he had a second wife, and several sons and daughters. Of what family he was, there is no mention.* He possessed considerable estate, and made his will on engaging in the war with the Indians.

The "sore defeat" of Capt. *Peirse*, and the tide of the Indians' successes about this time, caused the United Colonies to send out almost their whole strength.

Nanuntenoo came down from the country upon Connecticut River, early in March, for the purpose of collecting seed corn to plant such ground as the English had been driven from, and to effect any other object he might meet with. Whether he had effected the first-named object before falling in with *Peirse*, we are not able to state; but certain it is, that he was but few days after encamped very near the ground where the fight had been, and was there fallen upon at unawares, when but a few of his men were present, and there taken prisoner.

Nanuntenoo was nearly as much dreaded as *Philip* himself, and consequently his capture caused great rejoicing among his enemies, and re quires to be particularly related.

Four volunteer companies from Connecticut began their march into the enemy's country the next day after Pawtucket fight. Among the captains of these companies, *George Denison* of Southerton was the most conspicuous. The others were commanded by *James Avery, John Staunton,* and Major *Palms,* who also had the chief command. With these were

* In the *Records of Plimouth*, under date March, 1669, there is this entry:—"*Michel Peirse* of Scittuate" was presented at the court for vnseemly carriages towards *Sarah Nichols* of Scittuate," and "forasmuch as there appeared but one testimony to the p'sentment, and that the testimony was written and not read vnto the deponant, the court saw cause to remit the said p'sentment."

three companies of Indians; one led by *Oneko*, composed of Mohegans; one of Pequots, by *Cassasinnamon*; and the other of Nianticks, by *Catapazet*; in all about 80.

When this formidable army came near to *Nanuntenoo's* camp, on the first week in April, 1676, "they met with a stout Indian of the enemie's, whom they presently slew, and two old squaws," who informed them of the situation of *Nanuntenoo*. At the same time, their own scouts brought the same intelligence. The news of the enemy's approach reached the chief at the moment, says Mr. *Hubbard*, "that he was divertizing himself with the recital of Capt. *Pierce's* slaughter." But seven of his men were about him at the moment; the rest were probably in the neighborhood attending to their ordinary affairs. And although he had stationed two sentinels upon an adjacent hill, to give him timely notice if any appeared, their surprise was so great, at the sudden approach of the English, that, in their fright, they ran by their sachem's wigwam, "as if they wanted time to tell what they saw." Seeing this, the sachem sent a third, to learn the cause of the flight of the first, but he fled in the same manner; and lastly he sent two more, one of which, "either endued with more courage, or a better sense of his duty, informed him in great haste that all the English army was upon him: whereupon, having no time to consult, and but little to attempt an escape, and no means to defend himself, he began"* to fly with all speed. Running with great swiftness around the hill, to get out of sight upon the opposite side, he was distinguished by his wary pursuers, and they immediately followed him with that eagerness their important object was calculated to inspire.

The pursuers of the flying chief were *Catapazet* and his Nianticks, "and a few of the English lightest of foot." Seeing these were gaining upon him, he first cast off his blanket, then his silver-laced coat, and lastly his belt of peag. On seeing these, a doubt no longer remained of its being *Nanuntenoo,* which urged them, if possible, faster in the chase. There was in the company of *Catapazet*, one *Monopoide*, a Pequot, who outran all his companions, and who, gaining upon *Nanuntenoo*, as he fled upon the side of the river, obliged him to attempt to cross it sooner than he intended. Nevertheless, but for an accident in his passage, he would doubtless have effected his escape. As he was wading through the river, his foot slipped upon a stone, which brought his gun under water. Thus losing some time in recovering himself, and also the use of his gun, probably made him despair of escaping; for *Monopoide* came up and seized upon him, "within 30 rods of the river side."

Nanuntenoo, having made up his mind to surrender, made no resistance, although he was a man of great physical strength, of superior stature, and acknowledged bravery; and the one who seized upon him very ordinary in that respect. One of the first Englishmen that came up was Robert *Staunton*, a young man, who presumed to ask the captured chief some questions. He appeared at first to regard the young man with silent indignity, but at length, casting a disdainful look upon his youthful face, "this manly sachem" said, in broken English, "YOU MUCH CHILD! NO UNDERSTAND MATTERS OF WAR! LET YOUR BROTHER OR CHIEF COME, HIM I WILL ANSWER." And, adds Mr. Hubbard, he "was as good as his word: acting herein, as if, by a *Pythagorean* metempsychosis, some old Roman ghost had possessed the body

---

* This elegant passage of Mr. *Hubbard* brings to our mind that inimitable one of *Clavigero,* in his account of the woful days of the Mexicans: "They had neither arms to repel the multitude and fury of their enemies, strength to defend themselves, nor space to fight upon; the ground of the city was covered with dead bodies, and the water of every ditch and canal purpled with blood." *Hist. Mexico,* iii. 73.

of this western pagan. And, like *Attilius Regulus*,* he would not accept of his own life, when it was tendered him." This tender of life to *Nanuntenoo* was, no doubt, upon the condition of his obtaining the submission of his nation. He met the idea with indignation; and when the English told him that he should be put to death if he did not comply, in the most composed manner he replied, that killing him would not end the war. Some of his captors endeavored to reflect upon him, by telling him, that he had said *he would burn the English in their houses*, and that he had boasted, in defiance of his promise last made to the English, which was to deliver the Wampanoags to them, that *he would not deliver up a Wampanoag or the paring of a Wampanoag's nail.* To this he only replied. "OTHERS WERE AS FORWARD FOR THE WAR AS MYSELF, AND I DESIRE TO HEAR NO MORE ABOUT IT." Had the English not burned his people in their houses? Did they ever deliver up any that had committed depredations upon the Narragansets? No!—Who, then, will ask for an excuse for the magnanimous Nanuntenoo? So indignant was he at their conduct, that he would hear nothing about peace; "refusing to send an old counsellor of his to make any motion that way."

Under the eye of *Denison, Nanuntenoo* was taken to Stonington, where, by the "advice of the English commanders, he was shot." His head was cut off and carried to Hartford, and his body consumed by fire. The English prevailed upon some of each tribe of their allies, viz. Pequets, Mohegans and Nianticks, to be his executioners, "thereby the more firmly to engage the said Indians against the treacherous Narragansets."† "Herein," says another writer‡ of that day, "the English dealt wisely, for by this means the three Indian nations are become abominable to the other Indians." And a respectable writer§ of our own times says, "It may be pleasing to the reader to be informed" of the fate of *Nanuntenoo!*

When it was announced to the noble chief that he must be put to death, he was not in the least daunted, and all he is reported to have said is this:—

"I LIKE IT WELL; I SHALL DIE BEFORE MY HEART IS SOFT, OR HAVE SAID ANY THING UNWORTHY OF MYSELF." With *Nanuntenoo*, fell into the hands of the English 43 others.||

The author of the anonymous "*Letters to London*"¶ says the Indians were "commanded by that famous but very bloody and cruel sachem, *Quononshot*, otherwise called *Myantonomy*," whose "carriage was strangely proud and lofty after he was taken; being examined why he did foment that war, which would certainly be the destruction of him and all the heathen Indians in the country, &c., he would make no other reply to

---

* *Marcus Attilius Regulus*, a Roman consul and general, taken prisoner by the Carthaginians, 251 years B. C. They sent him to Rome to use his endeavors to effect a peace, by his solemn promise to return within a given period. The most excruciating tortures awaited him, should he not execute his mission according to his instructions. When arrived at Rome, he exhorted his countrymen to hold out, and maintain the war against the Carthaginians, stating their situation, and the great advantages that would accrue. He knew what would be his fate on returning to Carthage, and many a noble Roman besought him not to return, and thus sacrifice his life; but he would not break his promise, even with his barbarous enemies. This is what is meant by not accepting his own life when tendered him. He returned, and, if history be true, no Indian nation ever tortured a prisoner, beyond what the Carthaginians inflicted upon *Marcus Attilius Regulus*. See *Echard's Roman Hist.* i. 188-9.

† *Hubbard*. ‡ I. *Mather*. § *Deane*, Hist. Scituate, 124.

|| Manuscript letter in Hist. library. Both *Hubbard* and *Mather* say 44; perhaps they included *Nanuntenoo*.

¶ Elsewhere cited as *The Present State*, &c.

any interrogatories, but this: that he was born a prince, and if princes came to speak with him he would answer, but none present being such, he thought himself obliged, in honor, to hold his tongue;" and that he said he would rather die than remain a prisoner, and requested that *Oneko* might put him to death, as he was of equal rank. "Yet withall threatened, he had 2000 men, [who] would revenge his death severely. Wherefore our forces, fearing an escape, put the stoutest men to the sword, but preserved *Myantonomy* till they returned to Stoneington; where our Indian friends, and most of the English soldiers, declaring to the commanders their fear that the English should, upon conditions, release him, and that then he would, (though the English might have peace with him,) be very pernicious to those Indians that now assisted us, the said Indians, (on these considerations, and the mischiefs and murthers he had done during this war,) permitted to put him to death.* And that all might share in the glory of destroying so great a prince, and come under the obligation of fidelity, each to other, the Pequods shot him, the Mohegins cut off his head and quartered his body, and the Ninnicrofts men made the fire and burned his quarters, and, as a token of their love and fidelity to the English, presented his head to the council at Hartford!" This must close our notice of *Nanuntenoo*, in this place, and we hasten to speak of:

Annawon, a Wampanoag, and one of *Philip's* most famous counsellors and captains. He was his fast friend, and resisted as long as there was a beam of hope; and when at last every chance of success had failed, he gave himself up in the most heroic manner, as will appear in the following account.

At the swamp, when *Philip* was killed, he escaped with most of his men, as has been related, by his thoroughly understanding the situation of his enemies. "Perceiving (says *Church*) they were waylaid on the east side of the swamp, tacked short about. One of the enemy, who seemed to be a great surly old fellow, hallooed with a loud voice, and often called out, *I-oo-tash, I-oo-tash*. Captain *Church* called to his Indian *Peter*,† and asked him who that was that called so. He answered that it was old *Annawon, Philip's* great captain, calling on his soldiers to stand to it, and fight stoutly."

"Captain *Church* had been but little while at Plimouth, [after the death of *Philip*,] before a post from Rehoboth came to inform the governor that old *Annawon, Philip's* chief captain, was with his company ranging about their woods, and was very offensive and pernicious to Rehoboth and Swansey. Captain *Church* was immediately sent for again, and treated with to engage in one expedition more. He told them their encouragement was so poor, he feared his soldiers would be dull about going again. But being a hearty friend to the cause, he rallies again, goes to Mr. *Jabez Howland*, his old lieutenant, and some of his soldiers that used to go out with him, told them how the case was circumstanced, and that he had intelligence of old *Annawon's* walk and haunt, and wanted hands to hunt him. They did not want much entreating, but told him they would go with him as long as there was an Indian left in the woods. He moved and ranged through the woods to Pocasset."

In the early part of this expedition, some of Captain *Church's* Indian scouts captured a number of *Annawon's* company, but from whom they could learn nothing of the old chief, only that he did not lodge "twice in a place."

"Now a certain Indian soldier, that Captain *Church* had gained over to

---

* This seems to us the most probable account of the affair of all we have seen.

† The son of *Awashonks*, it is supposed.

be on his side, prayed that he might have liberty to go and fetch in his father, who, he said, was about four miles from that place, in a swamp, with no other than a young squaw. Captain *Church* inclined to go with him, thinking it might be in his way to gain some intelligence of *Annawon*; and so taking one Englishman and a few Indians with him, leaving the rest there, he went with his new soldier to look his father. When he came to the swamp, he bid the Indian go and see if he could find his father. He was no sooner gone, but Captain *Church* discovered a track coming down out of the woods, upon which he and his little company lay close, some on one side of the track, and some on the other. They heard the Indian soldier making a howling for his father, and at length somebody answered him; but while they were listening, they thought they heard somebody coming towards them. Presently they saw an old man coming up, with a gun on his shoulder, and a young woman following in the track which they lay by. They let them come between them, and then started up and laid hold of them both. Captain *Church* immediately examined them apart, telling them what they must trust to if they told false stories. He asked the young woman what company they came from last. She said from Captain *Annawon's*. He asked her how many were in company with him when she left him. She said 'fifty or sixty.' He asked her how many miles it was to the place where she left him. She said she did not understand miles, but he was up in Squannaconk swamp. The old man, who had been one of *Philip's* council, upon examination, gave exactly the same account." On being asked whether they could get there that night, answered, "If we go presently, and travel stoutly, we may get there by sunset." The old man said he was of *Annawon's* company, and that *Annawon* had sent him down to find some Indians that were gone down into Mount Hope neck to kill provisions. Captain *Church* let him know that that company were all his prisoners.

The Indian who bad been permitted to go after his father, now returned with him and another man. Captain *Church* was now at great loss what he should do. He was unwilling to miss of so good an opportunity of giving a finishing blow to the Indian power. He had, as himself says, but "half a dozen men beside himself," and yet was under the necessity of sending some one back to give Lieutenant *Howland*, whom he left at the old fort in Pocasset, notice, if he should proceed. But, without wasting time in pondering upon what course to pursue, he put the question to his men, "whether they would willingly go with him and give *Annawon* a visit." All answered in the affirmative, but reminded him "that they knew this Captain *Annawon* was a great soldier; that he had been a valiant captain under *Asuhmequin*, [*Woosamequin*,] *Philip's* father; and that he had been *Philip's* chieftain all this war." And they further told Captain Church, (and these men knew him well,) that he was "a very subtle man, of great resolution, and had often said that he would never be taken alive by the English."

They also reminded him that those with Annawon were "resolute fellows, some of *Philip's* chief soldiers," and very much feared that to make the attempt with such a handful of soldiers, would be hazardous in the extreme. But nothing could shake the resolution of Captain *Church*, who remarked to them, "that he had a long time sought for *Annawon*, but in vain," and doubted not in the least but Providence would protect them. All with one consent now desired to proceed.

A man by the name of *Cook*,* belonging to Plimouth, was the only Englishman in the company, except the captain. Captain *Church* asked Mr. *Cook* what his opinion of the undertaking was. He made no other

* *Caleb*, doubtless, who was present at the time *Philip* was killed.

reply than this: "I am never afraid of going any where when you are with me." The Indian who brought in his father informed Captain *Church*, that it was impossible for him to take his horse with him, which he had brought thus far. He therefore sent him and his father, with the horse, back to Lieutenant *Howland*, and ordered them to tell him to take his prisoners immediately to Taunton, and then to come out the next morning in the Rehoboth road, where, if alive, he hoped to meet him.

Things being thus settled, all were ready for the journey. Captain *Church* turned to the old man, whom he took with the young woman, and asked him whether he would be their pilot. He said, "You having given me my life, I 'am under obligations to serve you." They now marched for Squannaconk. In leading the way, this old man would travel so much faster than the rest, as sometimes to be nearly out of sight, and consequently might have escaped without fear of being recaptured, but he was true to his word, and would stop until his wearied followers came up.

Having travelled through swamps and thickets until the sun was setting, the pilot ordered a stop. The captain asked him if he had made any discovery. He said, "About that hour of the day, *Annawon* usually sent out his scouts to see if the coast was clear, and as soon as it began to grow dark the scouts returned, and then we may move securely." When it was sufficiently dark, and they were about to proceed, Captain *Church* asked the old man if he would take a gun and fight for him. He bowed very low, and said, "I pray you not to impose such a thing upon me as to fight against Captain *Annawon*, my old friend, but I will go along with you, and be helpful to you, and will lay hands on any man that shall offer to hurt you." They had proceeded but a short space, when they heard a noise, which they concluded to be the pounding of a mortar. This warned them that they were in the vicinity of *Annawon's* retreat. And here it will be very proper to give a description of it. It is situated in the south-easterly corner of Rehoboth, about eight miles from Taunton Green, a few rods from the road which leads to Providence, and on the south-easterly side of it. If a straight line were drawn from Taunton to Providence, it would pass very nearly over this place. Within the limits of an immense swamp of nearly 3000 acres, there is a small piece of upland, separated from the main only by a brook, which in some seasons is dry. This island, as we may call it, is nearly covered with an enormous rock, which to this day is called *Annawon's Rock*. Its south-east side presents an almost perpendicular precipice, and rises to the height of 25 or 30 feet. The north-west side is very sloping, and easy of ascent, being at an angle of not more than 35 or 40°. A more gloomy and hidden recess, even now, although the forest tree no longer waves over it, could hardly be found by any inhabitant of the wilderness.

When they arrived near the foot of the rock, Captain *Church*, with two of his Indian soldiers, crept to the top of it, from whence they could see distinctly the situation of the whole company, by the light of their fires. They were divided into three bodies, and lodged a short distance from one another. *Annawon's* camp was formed by felling a tree against the rock, with bushes set up on each side.

"He passed, in the heart of that ancient wood—
* * * * * * *
Nor paused, till the rock where a vaulted bed
Had been hewn of old for the kingly dead
Arose on his midnight way."
Mrs. Hemans's Sword of the Tomb.

With him lodged his son, and others of his principal men. Their guns were discovered standing and leaning against a stick resting on two crotches, safely covered from the weather by a mat. Over their fires were pots and kettles boiling, and meat roasting upon their spits. Captain *Church* was now at some loss how to proceed, seeing no possibility of getting down the rock without discovery, which would have been fatal. He therefore creeps silently back again to the foot of the rock, and asked the old man, their pilot, if there was no other way of coming at them. He answered, "No;" and said that himself and all others belonging to the company were ordered to come that way, and none could come any other without danger of being shot.

The fruitful mind of *Church* was no longer at loss, and the following stratagem was put in successful practice. He ordered the old man and the young woman to go forward, and lead the way, with their baskets upon their backs, and when *Annawon* should discover them, he would take no alarm, knowing them to be those he had lately sent forth upon discovery. "Captain *Church* and his handful of soldiers crept down also, under the shadow of those two and their baskets. The captain himself crept close behind the old man, with his hatchet in his hand, and stepped over the young man's head to the arms. The young Annawon discovering him, whipped his blanket over his head, and shrunk up in a heap. The old Captain *Annawon* started up on his breech, and cried out '*Howoh*!' which signified, 'Welcom.'"* All hope of escape was now fled forever, and he made no effort, but laid himself down again in perfect silence, while his captors secured the rest of the company. For he supposed the English were far more numerous than they were, and before he was undeceived, his company were all secured.

One circumstance much facilitated this daring project. It has been before mentioned that they heard the pounding of a mortar, on their approach. This continued during their descent down the rock. A squaw was pounding green dried corn for their supper, and when she ceased pounding, to turn the corn, they ceased to proceed, and when she pounded again, they moved. This was the reason they were not heard as they lowered themselves down, from crag to crag, supported by small bushes that grew from the seams of the rock. The pounded corn served afterwards for a supper to the captors.

Annawon would not have been taken at this time but for the treachery of those of his own company. And well may *their Lucan* exclaim, as did the *Roman*,

> "A race renowned, the world's victorious lords,
> Turned on themselves with their own hostile swords."—*Rowe.*

The two companies situated at a short distance from the rock knew not the fate of their captain, until those sent by *Church* announced it to them. And, to prevent their making resistance, they were told, that Capt. *Church* had encompassed them with his army, and that to make resistance would be immediate death; but if they all submitted peaceably, they should have good quarter. "Now they being old acquaintance, and many of them relations," readily consented: delivering up their guns and hatchets, they were all conducted to head quarters.

* It is a curious fact, that among the tribes of the west the same word is used to signify approbation: thus, when a speech had been made to some in that region, which pleased them, at the end of each paragraph they would exclaim, "*Hoah! Hoah!*"—*Weld's Travels in America.*

The fact becomes still more curious when we find the same word used yet farther west—even on the North-west Coast, and with very nearly the same signification. See *Dixon's Voyage*, 189, 4to. London, 1789. In this work it is spelt *Whoah.*

"Things being thus far settled, Captain *Church* asked *Annawon* what he had for supper, 'for,' said he, 'I am come to sup with you.'" *Annawon* replied, "*Taubut*," with a "big voice," and, looking around upon his women, ordered them to hasten and provide Capt. *Church* and his company some supper. He asked Capt. *Church* "whether he would eat cow beef or horse beef." *Church* said he would prefer cow beef. It was soon ready, and, by the aid of some salt he had in his pocket, he made a good meal. And here it should be told, that a small bag of salt (which he carried in his pocket) was the only provision he took with him upon this expedition.

When supper was over, Capt. *Church* set his men to watch, telling them if they would let him sleep two hours, they should sleep all the rest of the night, he not having slept any for 36 hours before; but after laying a half hour, and feeling no disposition to sleep, from the momentous cares upon his mind,—for, as Dr. *Young* says in the Revenge,

> "The dead alone, in such a night, can rest,—"

he looked to see if his watch were at their posts, but they were all fast asleep. *Annawon* felt no more like sleeping than *Church*, and they lay for some time looking one upon the other. *Church* spoke not to *Annawon*, because he could not speak Indian, and thought *Annawon* could not speak English, but it now appeared that he could, from a conversation they held together. *Church* had laid down with *Annawon* to prevent his escape, of which, however, he did not seem much afraid, for after they had laid a considerable time, *Annawon* got up and walked away out of sight, which *Church* considered was on a common occasion; but being gone some time, "he began to suspect some ill design." He therefore gathered all the guns close to himself, and lay as close as he possibly could under young *Annawon's* side, that if a shot should be made at him, it must endanger the life of young *Annawon* also. After laying a while in great suspense, he saw, by the light of the moon, *Annawon* coming with something in his hands. When he had got to Captain *Church*, he knelt down before him, and, after presenting him what he had brought, spoke in English as follows:—"*Great captain, you have killed* Philip, *and conquered his country. For I believe that I and my company are the last that war against the English, so suppose the war is ended by your means, and therefore these things belong unto you.*" He then took out of his pack a beautifully wrought belt, which belonged to *Philip*. It was nine inches in breadth, and of such length, as when put about the shoulders of Capt. *Church*, it reached to his ankles. This was considered, at that time, of great value, being embroidered all over with money, that is, wampumpeag,* of various colors, curiously wrought into figures of birds, beasts and flowers. A second belt, of no less exquisite workmanship, was next presented, which belonged also to *Philip*. This, that chief used to ornament his head with; from the back part of which flowed two flags, which decorated his back. A third was a smaller one, with a star upon the end of it, which he wore upon his breast. All three were edged with red hair, which, *Annawon* said, was got in the country of the Mohawks. These belts, or some of them, it is believed, remain at this day, the property of a family in Swansey. He next took from his pack two horns of glazed powder, and a red cloth blanket. These, it appears, were all that remained of the effects of the great chief. He told Capt. *Church* that those were *Philip's* royalties, which he was wont to adorn himself with, when he sat in state, and he thought himself happy in having an opportunity to present them to him.

* An Iroquois word, signifying *a muscle*. *Gordon's Hist.* Pennsylvania, page 598

The remainder of the night they spent in discourse, in which *Annawon* "gave an account of what mighty success he had had formerly in wars against many nations of Indians, when he served *Asuhmequin, Philip's* father."

Morning being come, they took up their march for Taunton. In the way they met Lieutenant *Howland*, according to appointment, at his no small surprise. They lodged at Taunton that night. The next day "Capt. *Church* took old *Annawon*, and half a dozen Indian soldiers, and his own men, and went to Rhode Island; the rest were sent to Plimouth, under Lieut. *Howland*.

Annawon, it is said, had confessed "that he had put to death several of the English, that had been taken alive; ten in one day, and could not deny but that some of them had been tortured;"* and therefore no mercy was to be expected from those into whose hands he had now fallen. His captor, Capt. *Church*, did not mean that he should have been put to death, and had entreated hard for him; but in his absence from Plimouth, not long after, he was remorselessly executed. We shall again have occasion to advert to the execution of *Annawon*, and shall now pass to consider the events in the life of a sachem of nearly equal interest.

Quinnapin was by birth a noble Narraganset, being the son of *Coginaquan*, otherwise *Conjanaquond*, who was nephew to *Canonicus*. Therefore *Miantunnomoh* was uncle to *Quinnapin*, and *Canonicus* was his great uncle.

We find his name spelled in almost every possible way, and for the amusement of the reader will offer a few of them—*Quanopin, Quonopin, Qunnapin, Quannopin, Quenoquin, Panoquin*, and *Quanepin*. His name has also been confounded with that of *Quaiapen*, the "old queen" of Narraganset.

In 1672, *Quinnapin* confirmed, by a writing, the sale of a tract of land previously granted by *Coginaquan*, his father.

This sachem took part with the Wampanoags in *Philip's* war, and from the punishment which the English executed upon him, on his falling into their hands, we may suppose he acted well his part in that war, although but little is recorded of him by the historians of that period. From Mrs. *Rowlandson's* account of him, we must conclude he was not wanting in attentions to the fair sex, as he had certainly three wives, one of whom was a sister of *Wootonekanuske*; consequently he was, according to the English method of calculating relationships, brother-in-law to the famous *Metacomet* himself.

Quinnapin was one of the chiefs who directed the attack on Lancaster, the 10 Feb. 1675, O. S., and he purchased Mrs. *Rowlandson* from a Narraganset Indian who had seized her when she came out of the garrison, among the captives of that place. And it was this circumstance which caused her to notice him in her Narrative.† *Wettimore*, whom she mentions in the following extract as his wife, we have said, was *Weetamoo*, the "queen of Pocasset."

In the winter of 1676, when the Narragansets were at such "great straits," from the loss of their provisions, in the great swamp fight, ("corn being two shillings a pint with them,") the English tried to bring about a peace with them; but their terms were too hard, or some other cause prevented. "*Canonchet* and *Panoquin* said they would fight it out, to the last man, rather than they would become servants to the English."‡ A truly noble resolution, and well worthy of the character we have of *Canonchet*.

---

* *Hubbard*, Nar. 108.

† Mr. *Willard's* edition of it, (p. 25.) Lancaster, 1828.

‡ *Hubbard*.

"My master (says Mrs. *Rowlandson*) had three squaws, living sometimes with one and sometimes with another. *Onux*, this old squaw at whose wigwam I was, and with whom my master [*Quinnapin*] had been these three weeks. Another was *Wettimore*, with whom I had lived and served all this while. A severe and proud dame she was; bestowing every day in dressing herself near as much time as any of the gentry of the land—powdering her hair and painting her face, going with her necklaces, with jewels in her ears, and bracelets upon her hands. When she had dressed herself, her work was to make girdles of wampum and beads. The third squaw [or wife] was a young one, by whom he had two papooses."*

While the Narragansets and Nipmucks were encamped at a place on Connecticut River at considerable distance above Northampton, perhaps near as far as Bellows Falls, Mrs. *Rowlandson* says, "My master's maid came home: she had been gone three weeks into the Narraganset country to fetch corn, where they had scored up some in the ground. *She brought home about a peck and a half of corn*"!

We shall relate, in the life of *Nepanet*, the mission of Mr. *Hoar* to *Philip's* quarters for the redemption of Mrs. *Rowlandson*. This was not long after Sudbury fight, and the Indians were preparing to commemorate it by a great dance, "which was carried on by eight of them, (as Mrs. *R.* relates,) four men and four squaws; my master and mistress [*Quinnapin* and *Weetamoo*] being two. He was dressed in his Holland shirt, with great stockings, his garters hung round with *shillings*, and had girdles of *wampom* upon his head and shoulders. She had a kearsey coat, covered with girdles of *wampom* from the loins upward. Her arms, from her elbows to her hands, were covered with bracelets; there were handfuls of necklaces about her neck, and several sorts of jewels in her ears. She had fine red stockings, and white shoes, her hair powdered, and her face painted red, that was always before black. And all the dancers were after the same manner. There were two others singing and knocking on a kettle for their music. They kept hopping up and down one after another, with a kettle of water in the midst, standing warm upon some embers, to drink of when they were dry. They held on till almost night, throwing out their *wampom* to the standers-by. At night I asked them again, if I should go home: they all as one said, No, except my husband would come for me. When we were lain down, my master went out of the wigwam, and by and by sent in an Indian called *James-the-printer*, who told Mr. *Hoar*, that my master would let me go home to-morrow, if he would let him have one pint of liquor. Then Mr. *Hoar* called his own Indians, *Tom* and *Peter*, and bid them all go and see if he would promise it before them three; and if he would he should have it, which he did, and had it. *Philip* smelling the business, called me to him, and asked me what I would give him, to tell me some good news, and to speak a good word for me, that I might go home to-morrow? I told him I could not tell what to give him, I would any thing I had, and asked him what he would have. He said two coats and 20 shillings in money, half a bushel of seed corn, and some tobacco. I thanked him for his love, but I knew that good news as well as that crafty fox. My master, after he had his drink, quickly came ranting into the wigwam again, and called for Mr. *Hoar*, drinking to him and saying *he was a good man*; and then again he would say, *Hang him a rogue*. Being almost drunk, he would drink to him, and yet presently say he should be hanged. Then he called for me; I trembled to hear him, and yet I was fain to go to him, and he drank to me, shewing no incivility. He was the first Indian I

---

* Narrative, 63, 64.

saw drunk, all the time I was among them. At last his squaw ran out, and he after her, round the wigwam, with his money jingling at his knees, but she escaped him; but having an old squaw, he ran to her,"* and troubled the others no more that night.

A day or two after, the sagamores had a council, or *general court*, as they called it, in which the giving up of Mrs. *R.* was debated. All seemed to consent for her to go except *Philip*, who would not come to the council. However, she was soon dismissed, and some who were at first opposed to her going, seemed now to rejoice at it. They shook her by the hand, and asked her to send them some tobacco, and some one thing and some another.

When the extensive system of war carried on by *Philip* was broken in the west by intestine bickerings, *Quinnapin* returned with *Philip* to his country of the Wampanoags. About the end of July, 1676, Captain *Church* learned by a captive squaw that *Quinnapin* and *Philip* were in a "great cedar swamp" near Aponaganset with "abundance of Indians." This news, together with a discovery the captain soon after made, induced him to leave that country without disturbing so formidable an enemy. Soon after, *Quinnapin* escaped from a company of Bridgewater men, who killed *Akkompoin*, as he and *Philip's* company were crossing Taunton River. The next day, *Church* pursued him, but he effected his escape.

Not long after this, he was taken, and, some considerable time after the war, was shot at Newport in R. Island. It appears that *Quinnapin* had had some difficulty with the R. Island people, who, some time before the war, had cast him into prison; but that by some means he had escaped, and become active in the war. He was reported "a young lusty sachem, and a very rogue."†

Tuspaquin, whose biography we shall next pursue, was one of *Philip's* most faithful captains, and sachem of Assawomset, as we have before had occasion to notice, in speaking of *John Sassamon*. His name in printed accounts differs but little, and is abbreviated from *Watuspaquin*. Also in our life of *Tatoson* it was necessary to speak of this chief. From a survey of the deeds which he executed of various large tracts of land, it is evident his sachemdom was very extensive. It will he necessary to glance at some of the conveyances of *Watuspaquin* for several reasons, the principal of which is, that the part he acted in the great drama of 1675 and 1676 may not be underrated. His conveyances to the Rev. *John Sassamon* and his family are already related.

On 9 Aug. 1667, "*Tuspequin*, otherwise called the *Black-sachem*," for £4, sells to *Henry Wood* of Plimouth his right and title to the land on the east side of "Namassakett" River,‡ bounded "on one end" by the pond called *Black-sachem's Pond*, or, in Indian, *Wanpawcutt*; on the other end, by a little pond called *Asnemscutt*. How much was included in the given bounds, is not mentioned, nor could we now by the description possibly tell how far said tract extended back from the river. With *Tuspaquin*, his wife, *Amey*, signed this deed, and it was witnessed only by two Englishmen.

On 17 July, 1669, *Tuspaquin* and his son *William* sell for £10 a tract or parcel of land near "Assowampsett," half a mile wide, and "in length from said ponds to Dartmouth path." Besides two English, *Samuel Henry, Daniel* and *Old Harry* were witnesses. *Experience Mitchell, Henry Sampson*, of Duxborough, *Thomas Little*, of Marshfield, and *Thomas Paine*, of Eastham, were the purchasers.

June 10, 1670, *Tuspaquin* and his son *William* sold for £6, to *Edward*

* Narrative, 73—75.

† Capt. *More's* account of "The Warr in N.E. visibly ended," &c.

‡ *Tuspaquin*, however, reserved the right "to gett ceder barke in the swamps."

Gray, "in the behalf of the court of Plimouth," "all that our meddow that lyeth in or neare the town of Middleberry," on the west side of a tract belonging to *John Alden* and *Constant Southworth*, "and is between Assowamsett Pond and Taunton path, being in three parsells vpon three brookes;" also another parcel on the other side of Taunton path. Witnessed by "*Amie*," the wife of *Tuspaquin*, and two English.

30 June, 1672, *Tuspaquin*, "sachem of *Namassakett*, and *Mantowapuct* alias *William* his son," sell to *Edward Gray* and *Josias Winslow*, lands on the easterly side of Assowamsett, to begin where Namasket River falleth out of the pond, and so south by the pond; thence by perishable bounds to *Tuspaquin's Pond*, and so home to the lands formerly sold to *Henry Wood*.

3 July, 1673, *Tuspaquin* and his son *William* sell to *Benjamin Church* of Duxborough, house carpenter, and *John Tompson* of Barnstable, lands about Middleborough, for which they paid him £15. It is described as "lying att and neare the township of Middleberry," bounded westerly by a river called *Monhiggen*, which runs into a pond called *Quisquasett*, and so by a cedar swamp to *Tuspaquin's* Pond; thence by *Henry Wood's* land to a place called *Pochaboquett*. Nahudset River is named as a northern boundary; and the two "places" called *Tuscomanest* and *Massapanoh* are also named, likewise a pond called *Sniptuett*, and a "river's mouth called *Tuppatuett* which runneth into a pond called *Quittuwashett*." Two English, *Sam Harry*, and *Joseph* of Namasket, were witnesses.

1 Nov. 1673, *William Watuspaquin, Assaweta, Tobias* and *Bewat*, for £10. sell to three English of Barnstable a tract of land bounded by Quetaquash Pond northerly, by Quetaquash River easterly, Snepetuitt Pond, &c.

14 May, 1675, the two *Tuspaquins*, father and son, "make over to *John Tompson, Constant Southworth*" and others, of Middleborough, "all that tract of land which we now have in possession, called commonly *Assowamsett* neck or necks, and places adjacent," as a security against the claims of others, &c. of other lands deeded at the same time; if, therefore, they are not disturbed in the possession of the former lands deeded, then they "are not to be outed of Assawamsett neck." *Pottawo*, alias *Daniel, Poyman, Pagatt*,* alias *Joseph*, were witnesses.

For the land deeded they received £33. "sterling." It consisted of uplands and meadows about the pond called *Ninipoket, Quiticus*,† &c., and, judging from the price paid, was, no doubt, a very large tract.

Thus are a few of the acts of *Watuspaquin* sketched previous to the war. We are now to trace his operations in quite another sphere. In our opinion, Mr. *Hubbard* was right in styling him "the next noted captain to *Philip*," but erroneously calls *Old Tuspaquin* "the Black-sachem's son." He does not appear to have known of the son *William*. Indeed, we hear nothing of him in the war, but it is probable he shared the fate of his father.

In the spring of 1676, *Tuspaquin* was marching from place to place with about 300 men, and was doubtless in high expectation of humbling the pride of his enemies, and, but for *Philip's* western disasters, occasioned by the disaffection of his Pocomptucks and others, his expectations might have been realized. It was doubtless under his direction that 19 buildings in Scituate were burnt on 20 April; and on the 8 May, had not a shower prevented, most, if not all, the houses in Bridgewater would have shared the same fate. *Tuspaquin* was known to have led his men

---

* Two names, probably; but in the MS, there is no comma between, as is often the case.

† *Titicut*, probably, now.

in this attack.* The inhabitants exerted themselves to repel the Indians, but, conscious of their strength, they maintained their ground until the next day, when they retreated. Notwithstanding the rain, they succeeded in burning 17 buildings before they decamped.

On 11 May, 1676, there were eleven houses and five barns burnt in Plimouth, and a few weeks after, seven houses more and two barns. These were probably such as were at a considerable distance from the village. and had chiefly been deserted. This "mischief" was attributed to *Tuspaquin* and his men.

About this time, *Benjamin Church* was commissioned by the government of Plimouth to lead parties in different directions over the colony; and from the time he commenced operations, the Indians found but few opportunities to do mischief in Plimouth colony.

Tuspaquin still kept his ground in the Assawomset country, and for a long time baffled all the skill Capt. *Church* was master of, who used every endeavor to take him prisoner. *Church* received his commission 24 July, 1676, and the same night set out on an expedition against *Tuspaquin*. His Indian scouts brought him before day upon a company of *Tuspaquin's* people in Middleborough, every one of whom fell into his hands. How many there were, *Church* does not say. He took them directly to Plimouth, "and disposed of them all," except "one *Jeffery*, who, proving very ingenious and faithful to him in informing where other parcels of the Indians harbored, Capt. *Church* promised him, that if he continued to be faithful to him, he should not be sold out of the country, but should be his waiting man, to take care of his horse, &c., and accordingly he served him faithfully as long as he lived."†

Thus strengthened by *Tuspaquin's* own men, *Church* pursued his successes with a manifold advantage. There was a small tribe residing near Munponset Pond, which was next captured without loss on either side, and there was henceforth scarcely a week passed wherein he did not captivate some of these people.

Not long after this, it was found that *Tuspaquin* had encamped about Assawomset, and Church set out on an expedition there; but finding *Old Tuspaquin* was ready for him at the neck between the two great ponds,‡ he was glad to make the best of his way on towards Acushnet and Dartmouth. As he was crossing Assawomset neck, a scout from *Tuspaquin's* camp fired upon him, but did him no injury.

Meanwhile the great *Annawon* having been surprised by the indefatigable *Church*, *Tuspaquin* saw no chance of holding out long; therefore appears afterwards only intent upon keeping out of the way of the English. This could not be long reasonably expected, as their scouts were ranging in every direction.

On 4 Sept. 1676, according to *Church's* account, *Tuspaquin's* company were encamped near Sippican, doing "great damage to the English in killing their cattle, horses and swine." The next day, *Church* and his rangers were in their neighborhood, and, after observing their situation, which was "sitting round their fires in a thick place of bruch,"§ in seeming safety, the captain "ordered every man to creep as he did; and surrounded them by creeping as near as they could, till they should be discovered, and then to run on upon them, and take them alive, if possible,

---

* Mr. *Hubbard* says, (Nar. 71.) the Indians were led by one *Tusguogen*, but we are satisfied *Tuspaquin* is meant.

† *Church*, Narrative, 31.

‡ Just below where *Sampson's* tavern now stands.

§ I suspect Mr. *Hubbard* mistakes the situation of this place, in saying it was "in Lakenham, upon Pocasset neck." *Church* is so unregarding of all geography, that it is quite uncertain where it was. If it were near Sippican, it was a long way from any part of Pocasset.

(for their prisoners were their pay.) They did so, taking every one that was at the fires, not one escaping. Upon examination, they agreed in their story, that they belonged to *Tispaquin*, who was gone with *John Bump* and one more to Agawom and Sipican to kill horses, and were not expected back in two or three days."* *Church* proceeds: "This same *Tispaquin* had been a great captain, and the Indians reported that he was such a great pouwau, [priest or conjurer,] that no bullet could enter him. Capt. *Church* said he would not have him killed, for there was a war broke out in the eastern part of the country, and he would have him saved to go with them to fight the eastern Indians. Agreeably, he left two old squaws of the prisoners, and bid them tarry there until their Captain *Tispaquin* returned, and to tell him, that *Church* had been there, and had taken his wife, children and company, and carried them down to Plymouth; and would spare all their lives, and his too, if he would come down to them and bring the other two that were with him, and they should be his soldiers, &c. Capt. *Church* then returned to Plymouth, leaving the old squaws well provided for, and bisket for *Tispaquin* when he returned."

This *Church* called laying a trap for *Tuspaquin*, and it turned out as he expected. We shall now see with what faith the English acted on this occasion. *Church* had assured him that, if he gave himself up, he should not be killed, but he was not at Plimouth when *Tuspaquin* came in, having gone to Boston on business for a few days; "but when he returned from Boston he found, to his grief, the heads of *Annawon, Tispaquin*, &c. cut off, which were the last of *Philip's* friends"!

It is true that those who were known to have been personally engaged in killing the English were, in the time of the greatest danger, cut off from pardon by a law; that time had now passed away, and, like many other laws of exigency, it should then have been considered a dead letter; leaving out of the case the faith and promise of their best servant, *Church*. View it, therefore, in any light, and nothing can be found to justify this flagrant inroad upon the promise of Captain *Church*. To give to the conduct of the Plimouth government a pretext for this murder, (a milder expression I cannot use,) Mr. *Hubbard* says, *Tuspaquin* having pretended that a bullet could not penetrate him, trial of his invulnerableness was resolved upon. So he was placed as a mark to shoot at, and "he fell down at the first shot"!

This was doubtless the end of numerous others, as we infer from the following passage in Dr. *Mather's* PREVALENCY OF PRAYER. He asks, "Where are the six Narraganset sachems, with all their captains and counsellors? Where are the Nipmuck sachems, with their captains and counsellors? Where is *Philip* and *Squaw-sachem* of Pocasset, with all their captains and counsellors? God do so to all the implacable enemies of Christ, and of his people in N. England"!! The next of *Philip's* captains, in our arrangement, is

Tatoson, also a great captain in the war of 1675. It seems rather uncertain whether he were a Narraganset or Wampanoag. He (or one bearing the same name) signed the treaty made with the Narragansets in the beginning of the war. It is quite certain that his residence afterwards was in Sandwich, since Rochester;† and when he signed the treaty just named, it is probable he was only among the Narragansets upon a mission or visit.

---

* By this it seems the place might have been as far off as Pocasset.

† On the right of the main road, as you pass from Matapoiset to Rochester village, and about two miles from the former, at a small distance from the road, is a kind of island in a miry swamp. Upon this, it is said, was *Tatoson's* camp. This island is connected by an isthmus to the main land.

We first meet with *Tatoson,** or, as his name is commonly printed, *Totoson,* in 1666, in the respectable company of Mr. Secretary *Morton* of Plimouth, and *Acanootus, Wannoo,* two "graue and sage Indians," and a number more, of whose characters we are not so well prepared to speak. Among this assemblage he is only conspicuous, however, as a witness to a deed of the lands upon *Weequancett* neck. Mr. *Morton's* name follows Tatoson's, on this instrument.

There was a general disarming of the Indians in 1671, as will be mentioned in the life of *Awashonks.* Among a great number ordered to appear at Plimouth the same year, to bind themselves more strongly in allegiance to the English, we find the name of *Tatoson,* or, as his name was then written, *Tautozen.* Also *Toby,* alias *Nauhnocomwit,*† and *Will,* alias *Washawanna.*

Tatoson was a son of the "noted *Sam Barrow,*" but of his own family, or whether he had any, we are not informed.

On the 12th of June, 1676, several Indians, who had been sent in by Bradford and *Church,* were "convented before the councell" at Plimouth; being "such of them as were accused of working vnsufferable mischeiffe vpon some of ours." Among them was one named Watukpoo, or, as he was often called, *Tukpoo.*‡ Against him, several charges were brought, such as his going off to the enemy, and trying to deceive the governor about the prospect of war; telling him that *Philip's* men had deserted him, and that he had only a few old men and boys remaining.

At this time were present three other Indians, whose names were *Woodcock, Quanapawhan* and *John-num.* The two first were accused by a squaw of destroying *Clark's* garrison at Eel River in Plimouth, and murdering the inhabitants. This had been done on the 12 March previous, and with such secrecy and effect, that the English knew not whom to accuse of it. Many supposed that *Watuspaquin* conducted the affair, and Mr. *Hubbard* charges it upon him without hesitation, but it is now quite certain that he had nothing to do with it, as in the sequel we shall show.

The two just mentioned, finding themselves detected, accused their fellow prisoner, *John-num.* It appears that *Num* not only owned himself guilty of this charge, but acknowledged, also, that he was concerned in the murder of "*Jacob Mitchel* and his wife, and *John Pope,*§ and soe centance of death was pronounced against them, which accordingly emediately was executed."

Before these were executed, they implicated a fourth, whose name was *Keweenam.* Although *Tatoson* commanded the company that put to death the people at *Clark's* garrison, yet *Keweenam* set the expedition on foot. He lived at Sandwich, and was probably one of *Tatoson's* men.

---

* So almost always in the MSS.

† Sometimes called *Toby Cole.* The same, we conclude, who joined *Philip* afterwards, and fell into the hands of Capt. *Church,* as did his mother, and many more at the same time.

‡ This Indian, whom we shall have occasion several times to mention, was not one of those sent in by *Bradford,* as appears from *Mather,* (Brief Hist. 40.) but they "informed that a bloudy Indian called *Tuckpoo,* (who the last summer murdered a man of Boston, at Namasket,) with about 20 Indians more, was at a place within 16 miles of Plimouth." Eight English and fourteen Indians succeeded in taking them all, and *Tuckpoo* was immediately executed.

§ The murder of these people is supposed to be referred to by Mr. *Hubbard* in his "Table." The passage follows: "In June, 1676, [1675?] a man and a woman were slain by the Indians; another woman was wounded and taken; but because she had kept an Indian child before, so much kindness was showed her, as that she was sent back, after they had dressed her wound; the Indians guarded her till she came within sight of the English." Mr. *Mitchel* informs us that the name of the wounded woman was *Dorothy Haywood.* See 1 *Col. Mass. Hist. Soc.* vii. 159.

However, on Saturday, the 11 March, he was at Mr. *William Clark's,* and observed how every part of the garrison was conditioned. He then went to his chief, *Tatoson,* and told him that it could be easily taken, as it was but slightly fortified; and that the next day, being Sunday, would be the proper time to execute their plan, as the residents would mostly be gone to meeting; "and in case they left a man at home, or so, they might soon dispatch him."

This intelligence was pleasing to *Tatoson,* and he found himself at the head of ten warriors the same day. Their names were as follows: *Woonashenah, Musquash, Wapanpowett, Tom,* "the son of *Tatoson's* brother," *Uttsooweest,* and *Tom Piant;* which, with the three before named, made up the whole company. Commencing their march before night, they arrived in the borders of Plimouth, where they lay concealed until the people had gone to public worship. About 10 o'clock in the morning, they came upon the garrison, which fell easily into their hands. After killing all they met with, they took what plunder they could carry, and burned the buildings; then again dispersed into the woods.

There were some of two other families in this garrison, mostly women and children. Three only were of Mr. *Clark's* family, but there were eight others belonging to the other two. Mrs. *Elizabeth Clark,** one of the heads of the family, was among the slain.†

Keweenam was beheaded, but how the other three were disposed of, we are not informed; it is very probable that the whole number suffered in due time. At the trial of *Keweenam* and the other three, some of them pleaded that the governor's proclamation was now their protection; from which it would seem that they had surrendered themselves. But there was none to plead their case, except their accusers, and they explained its things in their own way. The court said, "Forasmuch as the council had before this engaged to several Indians desirous to come in and tender themselves to mercy, that they should find favor in so doing: it was fully made known to such Indians as were then present, that the said engagement *was to be understood with exception* against such as by murder as above said had so acted, and not against such as killed his enemie in the field in a souldierlike way."

This kind of argument would answer among duelists, but when did the Indians agree to fight the English according to *their* rules of war? The former might with equal propriety demand that the English should conform to their manner, and not depend on their numbers, forts, and superior weapons.

Although the murder at *Clark's* garrison was one of those horrible acts in Indian warfare, which would justify the most rigid retaliation, still, as the English began the war, they had no right to expect but that it would be prosecuted by the Indians in all the ways at their command. On this ground the philanthropist will ever condemn the severity of the English.

When Capt. *Church* came upon *Philip* and a great number of his peo-

---

* "Who was the daughter of a godly father and mother, that came to N. England on the account of religion." "They also killed her sucking child, and knocked another child (who was about eight years old) in the head, supposing they had killed him, but afterwards he came to himself." I. *Mather,* Brief Hist. 24.

† We relate all that is to be found in the MS. records, but the author of the *Present State,* &c. furnishes the following valuable facts: "About this time, [his last date mentioned being 14 March,] one Mr. *Clark's* wife, children, and all his family, at his farm-house, two miles from Plimouth, were surprised and killed, except one boy, who was knockt down, and left for dead, but afterwards taken up and revived. The house they plundered of provision and goods to a great value; eight complete arms, 30l. [*lb.*] of powder, with an answerable quantity of lead for bullets, and 150l. in ready money; the said Mr. *Clark* himself narrowly escaping their cruelty, by being at that instant at a meeting."

ple, the 3d of August, 1676, "*Tispaquin, Totoson,* &c." prevented the entire destruction of some of them, by combating the English while their chief and others extricated themselves from a small swamp into which they had fled. "In this swamp skirmish Capt. *Church* with his two men which always ran by his side as his guard, met with three of the enemy, two of which surrendered themselves, and the captain's guard seized them; but the other, being a great stout surly fellow, with his two locks ty'd up with red, and a great rattlesnake's skin hanging to the back part of his head, (whom Capt. *Church* concluded to be *Totoson,)* ran from them into the swamp. Capt. *Church* in person pursued him close, till, coming pretty near up with him, presented his gun between his shoulders, but it missing fire, the Indian perceiving it, turned and presented at Capt. *Church,* and missing fire also, (their guns taking wet with the fog and dew of the morning,) but the Indian turning short for another run, his foot trip'd in a small grape-vine, and he fell flat on his face. Capt. *Church* was by this time up with him and struck the muzzle of his gun an inch and an half into the back part of his head, which dispatched him without another blow. But Capt. *Church* looking behind him saw *Totoson,* the Indian whom he tho't he had killed, come flying at him like a dragon; but this happened to be fair in sight of the guard that were set to keep the prisoners, who spying *Totoson* and others that were following him, in the very seasonable juncture made a shot upon them, and rescued their captain, though he was in no small danger from his friends' bullets, for some came so near him that he thought he felt the wind of them."* The celebrated *Church,* in the skirmishes he had in these two days, August 1 and 2, took and killed 173 Indians.

Little more than a month after the fall of *Philip, Church* surprised *Tatoson's* whole company, about 50 persons. He was the last that was left of the family of *Barrow;* and, says *Church,* "the wretch reflecting upon the miserable condition he had brought himself into, his heart became a stone within him, and he died. The old squaw [that *Church* had employed to persuade him to submit] flung a few leaves and brush over him—came into Sandwich, and gave this account of his death; and offered to show them where she left his body, but never had an opportunity, for she immediately fell sick and died also."

The fate of the father of *Barrow* does not so much excite sympathy, as does that of the son, but is one of those cases more calculated to arouse the fiercer passions. The old chief fell into the hands of Capt. *Church,* in one of his successful expeditions in the vicinity of Cape Cod. *Church* says, in his history, that he was "as noted a rogue as any among the enemy." Capt. *Church* told him that the government would not permit him to grant him quarter, "because of his inhuman murders and barbarities," and therefore ordered him to prepare for execution. "*Barrow* replied, that the sentence of death against him was just, and that indeed he was ashamed to live any longer, and desired no more favor, than to smoke a whiff of tobacco before his execution. When he had taken a few whiffs, he said, 'I am ready;' upon which one of Capt. *Church's* Indians sunk his hatchet into his brains."

Tiashq,† or *Tyasks,*‡ "was the next man to *Philip,*" says *Church*; there were others also said to be "next to him," and it may be all reconciled by supposing these chiefs as having the chief command over particular tribes. Mr. *Hubbard*§ says only this of the famous *Tiashq*: "In June last, [1676,] one *Tiashq,* a great captain of *Philip's,* his wife and child, or children, being taken, though he escaped himself at first, yet came since and surrendered himself." Dr. I. *Mather,* writing under date of 22

* Hist. *Philip's* War, 41. † *Hubbard, Mather.* ‡ *Church.* § Narrative, 106.

July, 1676, says it was "this week" that Capt. *Church* and his Indian soldiers fell upon *Tiashq* and his company. It appears therefore that Mr. *Hubbard* is in error, as the account given by *Church* corroborates that of *Mather,* who speaks thus of his operations: "It having been his manner when he taketh any Indians by a promise of favor to them, in case they acquit themselves well, to set them an hunting after more of these wolves, whereby the worst of them sometimes do singular good service in finding out the rest of their bloody fellows. In one of these skirmishes, *Tiashq, Philip's* chief captain, ran away leaving his gun behind him, and his squaw, who was taken."* These Indian soldiers, who performed this exploit, were forced upon it by *Church.* They had been seeking Indians about Aponaganset River, and discovered that a large company of them had just been gathering the apples at a deserted settlement on the east side of it. The English and Indians immediately pursued in their track.† "Traveling three miles or more, they came into the country road, where the track parted: one parcel steered towards the west end of the great cedar swamp, and the other to the east end. The captain halted and told his Indian souldiers that they had heard as well as he what some men had said at Plymouth about them,‡ &c., that now was a good opportunity for each party to prove themselves. The track being divided, they should follow one, and the English the other, being equal in number. The Indians declined the motion, and were not willing to move any where without him: said *they should not think themselves safe without him.* But the captain insisting upon it, they submitted. He gave the Indians their choice to follow which track they pleased. They replied, *They were light and able to travel, therefore if he pleased they would take the west track.* And appointing the ruins of *John Cook's* house at Cushnet§ for the place to meet at, each company set out briskly to try their fortunes."|| When the parties met, "they very remarkably found that the number that each company had taken and slain was equal. The Indians had killed three of the enemy, and taken 63 prisoners, as the English had done before them."¶ Both parties were much rejoiced at their successes, but the Indians told Capt. *Church* "that they had missed a brave opportunity by parting. They came upon a great town of the enemy, viz: Capt. *Tyasks'* company. (*Tyasks* was the next man to *Philip.*) They fired upon the enemy before they were discovered, and ran upon them with a shout. The men ran and left their wives and children, and many of them their guns. They took *Tyasks'* wife and son, and thought that if their captain and the English company had been with them they might have taken some hundreds of them, and now they determined not to part any more."** This transaction, in the opinion of Capt. *Church,* was a "remarkable providence," inasmuch, perhaps, as the equality of their successes prevented either party from boasting, or claiming superiority over the other. Nevertheless, *Church* adds,—"But the Indians had the fortune to take more arms than the English." It would add not a little, perhaps, to the gratification of the reader, could he know the name of the Indian captain in this far-famed exploit, or even that of one of his men; but at present they are hid alike from us and from him.

---

* Brief Hist. 42.

† *Church,* 33.

‡ The detestation in which the Indians were held by "some men," in many other places as well as in Plimouth, will often appear in this work. Such people could know nothing of human nature, and many would not have believed the Indians capable of good actions, though *one from the dead* had assured them to the contrary.

§ Abbreviated from Acushnet. See *Douglass,* Summary, i. 403. who writes it *Accushnot.* Thus many Indian names are changed. Instead of *Aponaganset,* we hear *Ponaganset,* and for *Asonet, Sonet,* &c. Cushnet is the river on which New Bedford and Fairhaven stand.

|| *Church,* 34.

¶ Ibid. 36.

** Ibid.

CHAPTER IV.

Chief women conspicuous in Philip's war—MAGNUS—*Her country and relations—Her capture and death*—AWASHONKS—*Is greatly annoyed in the events of 1671—Her men disarmed—Philip's endeavors to engage her against the English—Church prevents her—Is finally in the power of Philip—Reclaimed by Church—Some particulars of her family.*

ALTHOUGH, before we had finished the life of *Weetamoo,* we deemed it proper to have deferred it to this chapter, but as we had been led rather imperceptibly into many particulars concerning her in that place,* we could not break off our narrative without a greater impropriety than an omission here would have been, and shall therefore begin here with one of her cotemporaries, the bare facts in whose life are sufficient to maintain a high interest, we believe, in the mind of every reader.

Magnus was squaw-sachem of some part of the extensive country of the Narragansets, and was known by several names at different and the same times; as, *Old Queen, Sunk Squaw,*† *Quaiapen,* and *Matantuck.* She married *Mriksah,* or *Mexam,* a son of *Canonicus,* and was sister to *Ninigret.* She had two sons, *Scuttup* and *Quequaquenuct,* otherwise *Quequegunent,* called by the English *Gideon,* and a daughter named *Quinemiquet.* These two died young. *Gideon* was alive as late as 1661; *Scuttup,* and a sister also, in 1664. She was, in 1675, one "of the six present sachems of the whole Narraganset country."

In the beginning of *Philip's* war, the English army, to cause the Narragansets to fight for them, whom they had always abused and treated with contempt, since before the cutting off of *Miantunnomoh's* head, marched into their country, but could not meet with a single sachem of the nation. They fell in with a few of their people, who could not well secrete themselves, and who concluded a long treaty of mere verbosity, the import of which they could know but little, and doubtless cared less; for when the army left their country, they joined again in the war. The English caused four men to subscribe to their articles in the name, or in behalf of *Quaiapen* and the other chiefs, and took four others as hostages for their due fulfilment of those articles. Their names were *Wobequob, Weowchim, Pewkes,* and *Wenew,* who are said to have been "near kinsmen and choice friends" to the sachems.

We hear no more of her until the next year, when herself and a large company of her men were discovered by Major *Talcot,* on the 2 July, in Narraganset. The English scouts discovered them from a hill, having pitched their tents in a valley in the vicinity of a swamp, as was usually their custom. About 300 of the English, mounted upon fleet horses, divided into two squadrons, and fell upon them before they were aware of their approach, and made a great slaughter. The Mohegans and Pequots came upon them in the centre, while the horsemen beset them on each side, and thus prevented many from escaping into the swamp. When all were killed and taken within the encampment, Capt. *Newbury,* who commanded the horsemen, dismounted, and with his men rushed into the swamp, where, without resistance, they killed a hundred,

* Book iii. chap. 1.

† *Trumbull,* i. 347. from *Hubbard,* I suppose, i. 51. Female chiefs were called *saunks* by the Indians, which signified wife of the sachem; but writers, being ignorant of that fact, thought it a proper name of a particular person, and hence the appellations of *Snuke, Sunke, Snake,* &c. applied to *Magnus.*

and made many prisoners. In all, they killed and took 171* in this swamp fight, or rather massacre. Not an Englishman was hurt in the affair, and but one Mohegan killed, and one wounded, which we can hardly suppose was done by *Magnus's* people, as they made no resistance, but rather by themselves, in their fury mistaking one another. Ninety of the captives were put to death! among whom was *Magnus*.† The swamp where this affair took place is near the present town of Warwick, in Rhode Island.

We now approach affairs of great interest in our biographical history of the Indians.

Awashonks, squaw-sachem of Sogkonate,‡ was the wife of an Indian called *Tolony*, but of whom we learn very little. From her important standing among the Indians, few deserve a more particular attention; and we shall, therefore, go as minutely into her history as our documents will enable us.

The first notice we have of *Awashonks* is in 1671, when she entered into articles of agreement with the court of Plimouth as follows:—"In admitting that the court are in some measure satisfied with your voluntary coming in now at last, and submission of herself unto us; yet this *we expect* that she give some meet satisfaction for the charge and trouble she has put us upon by her too long standing out against the many tenders of peace we have made to her and her people. And that we yet see an intention to endeavor the reducement of such as have been the incendiaries of the trouble and disturbance of her people and ours. And as many of her people as shall give themselves and arms unto us, at the time appointed, shall receive no damage or hurt from us, which time appointed is ten days from the date hereof. Thus we may the better keep off such from her lands as may hereafter bring upon her and us the like trouble, and to regulate such as will not be governed by her, she having submitted her lands to the authority of the government. And that, if the lands and estates of such as we are necessitated to take arms against, will not defray the charge of the expedition, that she shall bear some due proportion of the charge. In witness whereof, and in testimony of the sachem, her agreement hereunto, she hath subscribed her hand in presence of *Samuel Barker* and *John Almey*.

Mark ╳ *of the squaw-sachem* AWASUNCKS;
the mark ╳ *of* TOTATOMET, *and* SOMAGAONET."

Witnessed at the same time by "TATTACOMMETT,
SAMPONCUT, *and*
TAMOUEESAM, *alias* JEFFERY."

Plimouth, 24 *July*, 1671.

The last-named witness appeared again, in the same capacity, 4 Sept. following, when "between 40 and 50 Indians, living near or in the town of Dartmouth, made a like submission." *Ashawanomuth, Noman, Marhorkum, James* and *John*, were other witnesses.

Awashonks was at Plimouth when the former articles were executed, from which it appears there was considerable alarm in Plimouth colony. There were about this time many other submissions of the Indians in different places. This step was taken to draw them from *Philip*, or at least to give a check to their joining with him, as he was now on the point

* Trumbull. 200, says *Cobbet's manuscript*; 240, Hubbard.

† Hubbard, Ind. Wars, i. 97, 98. I. Mather's Brief Hist. 39. Trumbull's Hist. Connecticut, i. 347.

‡ The point of land below Pocasset, and now chiefly included in the town of Compton, Rhode Island, and commonly called *Seconet*.

of attacking the English settlements, under a pretence of injury done him in his planting lands.

Not only the chiefs of tribes or clans subscribed articles, but all their men, that could be prevailed with, did the same. The August following, 42 of *Awashonks's* men signed a paper, approving what she had done, and binding themselves in like manner. Out of 42, we can give names of three only—*Totatomet, Tunuokum and Sausaman.*

It appears from the following letter from *Awashonks* to Gov. *Prince,* that those who submitted themselves, delivered up their arms to the English:—

"August 11, 1671, Honored sir, I have received a very great favor from your honor, in yours of the 7th instant, and as you are pleased to signify, that if I continue faithful to the agreement made with yourselves at Plimouth, I may expect all just favors from your honor. I am fully resolved, while I live, with all fidelity to stand to my engagement, and in a peaceable submission to your commands, according to the best of my poor ability. It is true, and I am very sensible thereof, that there are some Indians who do seek an advantage against me, for my submitting to his majesty's authority in your jurisdiction, but being conscious to myself of my integrity and real intentions of peace, I doubt not but you will afford me all due encouragement and protection. I had resolved to send in all my guns, being six in number, according to the intimation of my letter; but two of them were so large, the messengers were not able to carry them. I since proffered to leave them with Mr. *Barker*, but he not having any order to receive them, told me he conceived I might do well to send them to Mr. *Almy*, who is a person concerned in the jurisdiction, which I resolved to do; but since then an Indian, known by the name of *Broad-faced-will,* stole one of them out of the wigwam in the night, and is run away with it to Mount Hope; the other I think to send to Mr. *Almy*. A list of those that are obedient to me, and, I hope, and am persuaded, faithful to you, is here enclosed. Honored sir, I shall not trouble you further, but desiring your peace and prosperity, in which I look at my own to be included, I remain, your unfeigned servant, × AWASUNCKS."

This letter was very probably written by Mr. *Barker,* named in it.

October 20, 1671, Gov. Prince wrote to *Awashonks,* that he had received the list of names of her men and husband, that freely submitted themselves to his majesty's authority; and assured her that the English would befriend her on all just occasions; but intimates her disappointment and his own, that she had succeeded no better in procuring the submission of her subjects. "Though," he continued, "I fault not you, with any failing to endeavor, only to notice your good persuasions of them outwent their deserts, for aught yet appeareth. I could have wished they had been wiser for themselves, especially your two sons, that may probably succeed you in your government, and your brother also, who is so nearly tied unto you by nature. Do they think themselves so great as to disregard and affront his majesty's interest and authority here; and the amity of the English? Certainly, if they do, I think they did much disservice, and wish they would yet show themselves wiser, before it be too late." He closed by recommending her to send some of hers to the next court, to desire their arms, that her people might have the use of them in the approaching season. Desires her to let him hear from her and her husband.

On the 20 June, 1672, the following writing appears on record: "Wheras *Awashunckes,* squa-sachem, stand indebted vnto Mr. *John Almey* the sume of £25 to be paid in porke att three pence a pound, or peage att

16 peney, and 20 pole of stone wall att £4, which stone wall, or £4, is to be vnderstood to be prte of the fiue and twenty pound," therefore *Awashonks,* having failed to pay agreeably to her promise, agrees to set off land on the north side of "the Indian field," next Punkateesett, on the east line till it meets with "a great runing brooke," thence northerly to a fresh meadow, thence bounded to the river by a salt cove:—this "is mortgaged vnto the court of Plymouth" for the payment of said debt, which debt is to be paid 10 of February, 1672, O. S.

"*The mark* ✕ *of* AWASHUNKES."

To illustrate the connections and genealogy of the family of *Awashonks,* we give from the Records of Plimouth the following exceedingly valuable facts.

July 14, 1673. "Whereas *Mamaneway* [a son of *Awashonks*] hath by full and clear testimony proved to this court, in behalf of himself and brethren, the sons of *Toloney,* and a kinsman of theirs called *Anumpash,* [commonly written *Numposh,*] son to *Pokattawagg,* that they are the chief proprietors and sachems of Saconett, or places commonly so called; and yet it being also probable that *Tatuckamna* Awashunckes* and those of that kindred who are of the same stock, the more remote may have some right to lands there, as they are relations to the above said *Mamaneway,* &c. and have been long inhabitants of that place. This court adviseth that convenient proportions of land be settled on the above said *Tatacamana Awashanks,* &c. at Saconett aforesaid; concerning which, the above said *Mamaneway* and his brethren and kinsman who have proved their right to those lands do not or cannot agree, this court do appoint that some meet persons, by order of this court, shall repair to the place, and make settlement of the said lands by certain and known boundaries to intent that peace may be continued among the said Indians, and they may all be accommodated for their subsisting and payment of their debts in an orderly way."

The same year, we hear again of *Tokamona,* or, as he is then called, Totomonna, who, with his brother *Squamatt,* having endeavored to hinder the English from possessing some lands in Dartmouth, was, from some consideration, not named, induced to relinquish his right to them. And the next year, 1674, *Mamanawachy,* or, as his name was before written, *Mamaneway,* surrendered his right also. The rights of these Indians, it is said, had been sold by others.

We hear no more of *Awashonks* until about the commencement of *Philip's* war. The year before this war, Mr. *Benjamin Church,* afterwards the famous and well-known Col. *Church,* settled upon the peninsula of Sogkonate, in the midst of *Awashonks's* people. This peninsula is on the north-east side of Narraganset Bay, against the south-east end of the island of Rhode Island. Here he lived in the greatest friendship with these Indians, until the spring of the year 1675, when suddenly a war was talked of, and messengers were sent by *Philip* to *Awashonks,* to engage her in it. She so far listened to their persuasions, as to call her principal people together, and make a great dance; and because she respected Mr. *Church,* she sent privately for him also. *Church* took with him a man that well understood Indian, and went directly to the place appointed. Here "they found hundreds of Indians gathered together from all parts of her dominions. *Awashonks* herself, in a foaming sweat, was leading the dance;" but when it was announced that Mr. *Church* was come, she stopped short, and sat down; ordered her chiefs into her presence, and then invited Mr. *Church.* All being seated, she informed him that *Metacomet,* that is, *Philip,* had sent six of his men to urge her to join with him

* Or *Tokamona,* killed by the Narragansets, not long after, probably in 1674.

in prosecuting a war against the English. She said these messengers informed her that the *Umpames*,* that is, Plimouth men, were gathering a great army to invade his country, and wished to know of him if this were truly the case. He told her that it was entirely without foundation, for he had but just come from Plimouth, and no preparations of any kind were making, nor did he believe any thoughts of war were entertained by any of the head men there. "He asked her whether she thought he would have brought up his goods to settle in that place," if he in the least apprehended a war; at which she seemed somewhat convinced. *Awashonks* then ordered the six Pokanokets into their presence. These made an imposing appearance, having their faces painted, and their hair so cut as to represent a cock's comb; it being all shaved from each side of the head, left only a tuft upon the crown, which extended from the forehead to the occiput. They had powder-horns and shot-bags at their backs, which denoted warlike messengers of their nation. She now informed them of what Capt. *Church* had said. Upon which they discovered dissatisfaction, and a warm talk followed, but *Awashonks* soon put end to it; after which she told Mr. *Church* that *Philip* had told his messengers to tell her, that, unless she joined with him, he would send over some of his warriors, privately, to kill the cattle and burn the houses of the English, which they would think to be done by her men, and consequently would fall upon her.†

Mr. *Church* asked the Mount Hopes what they were going to do with the bullets in their possession, to which they scoffingly answered. "to shoot pigeons with." *Church* then told *Awashonks* that, if *Philip* were resolved on war, "her best way would be to knock those six Mount Hopes on the head, and shelter herself under the protection of the English." When they understood this, they were very silent, and it is to be lamented that so worthy a man as *Church* should be the first to recommend murder, and a lasting remembrance is due to the wisdom of *Awashonks,* that his unadvised counsel was not put in execution.

These six Pokanokets came over to Sogkonate with two of *Awashonks's* men, who seemed very favorably inclined to the measures of *Philip.* They expressed themselves with great indignation, at the rash advice of *Church.* Another of her men, called *Little-eyes,* one of her council, was so enraged, that he would then have taken *Church's* life, if he had not been prevented. His design was to get Mr. *Church* aside from the rest, under a pretence of private talk, and to have assassinated him when he was off his guard. But some of his friends, seeing through the artifice, prevented it.

The advice of *Church* was adopted, or that part which directed that *Awashonks* should immediately put herself under the protection of the English, and she desired him to go immediately and make the arrangement, to which he agreed. After kindly thanking him for his information and advice, she sent two of her men with him to his house, to guard him. These urged him to secure his goods, lest, in his absence, the enemy should come and destroy them; but he would not, because such a step might be thought a kind of preparation for hostilities; but told them, that in case hostilities were begun, they might convey his effects to a place of safety. He then proceeded to Plimouth, where he arrived 7 June, 1675.

In his way to Plimouth, he met, at Pocasset, the husband of *Weetamoo.* He was just returned from the neighborhood of Mount Hope, and confirmed all that had been said about Philip's intentions to begin a war. But before Mr. *Church* could return again to *Awashonks,* the war commenced,

* *Umpame* and *Apaum* were names of Plimouth.

† This may strengthen the belief that *Philip* put in practice a similar expedient to gain the Mohawks to his cause, as we have seen in his life.

and all communication was at an end. This was sorely regretted by *Church,* and the benevolent *Awashonks* was carried away in the tide of *Philip's* successes, which, as she was circumstanced, was her only alternative.

Mr. *Church* was wounded at the great swamp fight, 19 December following, and remained upon Rhode Island until about the middle of May, 1676. He now resolved to engage again in the war, and, taking passage in a sloop bound to Barnstable, arrived at Plimouth the first Tuesday in June. The governor and other officers of government were highly pleased to see him, and desired him to take the command of a company of men to be immediately sent out, to which he consented. We thus notice *Church's* proceeding, because it led to important matters connected with the history of *Awashonks.* Before he set out with the soldiers raised at Plimouth, it was agreed that he should first return to Rhode Island, for the purpose of raising other forces to be joined with them. In his return to the island, as he passed from Sogkonesset, now called *Wood's Hole,* to the island, and when he came against Sogkonate Point, some of the enemy were seen fishing upon the rocks. He was now in an open canoe, which he had hired at Sogkonesset, and two Indians to paddle it. He ordered them to go so near the rocks that he might speak with those upon them; being persuaded that if he could have an opportunity, he might still gain over the Sogkonates to the side of the English, for he knew they never had any real attachment to *Philip,* and were now in his interest only from necessity. They accordingly paddled towards them, who made signs for them to approach; but when they had got pretty near, they skulked away among the rocks, and could not be seen. The canoe then paddled off again, lest they should be fired upon; which when those among the rocks observed, they showed themselves again, and called to them to come ashore; and said they wished to speak with them. The Indians in the canoe answered them, but those on shore informed them that the waves dashed so upon the rocks that they could not understand a word they said. *Church* now made signs for two of them to go along upon the shore to a beach, where one could see a good space round, whether any others were near. Immediately two ran to the place, one without any arms, but the other had a lance. Knowing *Church* to be in the boat, they urged him to come on shore, and said they wanted to discourse with him. He told him that had the lance, that if he would carry it away at considerable distance, and leave it, he would. This he readily did. Mr. *Church* then went ashore, left one of his Indians to guard the canoe, and the other he stationed upon the beach to give notice if any should approach. He was surprised to find that *George* was one of them, a very good man, and the last Sogkonate he had spoken with, being one of those sent to guard him to his house, and to whom he had given charge of his goods when he undertook his mission to Plimouth. On being asked what he wanted that he called him ashore, answered, "that he took him for *Church,* as soon as he heard his voice in the canoe, and that he was glad to see him alive." He also told him that *Awashonks* was in a swamp about three miles off, and that she had left *Philip* and did not intend to return to him any more; and wished Mr. *Church* to stay while he should go and call her. This *Church* did not think prudent, but said he would come again and speak with *Awashonks,* and some other Indians that he should name. He therefore told *George* to notify *Awashonks,* her son *Peter,* their chief captain, and one *Nompash,* to meet him two days after at a certain rock, "at the lower end of Capt. *Richmond's* farm, which was a very noted place." It was provided that if that day should prove stormy, the next pleasant day should be improved. They parted with cordiality, *George* to carry the news to *Awashonks,* and *Church* for Newport.

On being made acquainted with *Church's* intention to visit those Indians, the government of Rhode Island marvelled much at his presumption, and would not give him any permit under their hands; assuring him that the Indians would kill him. They said also that it was madness on his part, after such signal services as he had done, to throw away his life in such a manner. Neither could any entreaties of friends alter his resolution, and he made ready for his departure. It was his intention to have taken with him one *Daniel Wilcox,** a man who well understood the Indian language, but the government utterly refused him; so that his whole retinue, in this important embassy, consisted only of himself, his own man, and the two Indians who conducted him from Sogkonesset. As an important item in his outfit, must be mentioned a *bottle of rum,* and a *roll of tobacco.*

The day appointed having arrived, after paddling about three miles, they came to the appointed rock, where the Indians were ready to receive them, and gave him their hands in token of friendship. They went back from the shore about fifty yards, for a convenient place for consultation, when all at once rose up from the high grass, a great many Indians, so that they were entirely encompassed. They were all armed with guns, spears and hatchets; faces painted and hair trimmed, in complete warlike array. If ever a man knew fear, we should apprehend it would discover itself upon an occasion like this. But, judging from his conduct, we should say he was one of those "who never felt fear."

As soon as he could be heard, Mr. *Church* told *Awashonks* that *George* had said that she desired to see him, about making peace with the English. She said, "Yes." Then, said Mr. *Church,* "it is customary when people meet to treat of peace, to lay aside their arms, and not to appear in such hostile form as your people do." At this there was much murmuring among them, and *Awashonks* asked him what arms they should lay aside. Seeing their displeasure, he said, only their guns, for form's sake. With one consent they then laid away their guns, and came and sat down. He then drew out his bottle of rum, and asked *Awashonks* whether she had lived so long up at Wachusett as to forget to drink *occapeches.* Then, drinking to her, he observed she watched him very narrowly to see whether he swallowed, and, on offering it to her, she wished him to drink again. He then told her there was no poison in it, and, pouring some into the palm of his hand, sipped it up. After he had taken a second hearty dram, *Awashonks* ventured to do likewise; then she passed it among her attendants. The tobacco was next passed round, and they began to talk. *Awashonks* wanted to know why he had not come, as he promised, the year before, observing that, if he had, she and her people had not joined with *Philip.* He told her he was prevented by the breaking out of the war, and mentioned that he made an attempt, notwithstanding, soon after he left her, and got as far as Punkatesse, when a multitude of enemies set upon him, and obliged him to retreat. A great murmur now arose among the warriors, and one, a fierce and gigantic fellow, raised his war club, with intention to have killed Mr. *Church,* but some laid hold on him and prevented him. They informed him that this fellow's brother was killed in the fight at Punkateese, and that he said it was *Church* that killed him, and he would now have his blood. *Church* told them to tell him that his brother began first, and that if he had done

---

* 1667, "*Daniel Willcockes* tooke the oath off fidelitie this court." *Plim. Rec.*
In 1642, one *Wilcox* set up a trading house in the Narraganset country. See *Callender's Cent. Discourse,* 38. If he were the same, it will well account for his being an interpreter.

as he had directed him, he would not have been hurt. The chief captain now ordered silence, telling them they should talk no more about old matters, which put an end to the tumult, and an agreement was soon concluded. *Awashonks* agreed to serve the English "in what way she was able," provided "Plimouth would firmly engage to her that she and all of her people, and their wives and children should have their lives spared, and none of them transported out of the country." This, *Church* told her he did not doubt in the least but Plimouth would consent to.

Things being thus matured, the chief captain stood up, and, after expressing the great respect he had for Mr. *Church,* said, "Sir, if you will please accept of me and my men, and will head us, we will fight for you, and will help you to *Philip's* head before the Indian corn be ripe." We do not expect that this chief pretended to possess the spirit of prophecy, but certainly he was a truer prophet than many who have made the pretension.

Mr. *Church* would have taken a few of the men with him, and gone directly through the woods to Plimouth; but *Awashonks* insisted that it would be very hazardous. He therefore agreed to return to the island and proceed by water, and so would take in some of their company at Sogkonate Point, which was accordingly brought about. And here it should be mentioned that the friendship, now renewed by the industry of Mr. *Church,* was never afterward broken. Many of these Indians always accompanied *Church* in his memorable expeditions, and rendered great service to the English. When *Philip's* war was over, *Church* went to reside again among them, and the greatest harmony always prevailed. But to return to the thread of our narrative:—

On returning to the island, Mr. *Church* "was at great pains and charge to get a vessel, but with unaccountable disappointments; sometimes by the falseness, and sometimes by the faint-heartedness of men that he bargained with, and sometimes by wind and weather, &c." he was hindered a long time. At length, Mr. *Anthony Low,* of Swansey, happening to put into the harbor, and although bound to the westward, on being made acquainted with Mr. *Church's* case, said he would run the venture of his vessel and cargo to wait upon him. But when they arrived at Sogkonate Point, although the Indians were there according to agreement waiting upon the rocks, they met with a contrary wind, and so rough a sea, that none but *Peter Awashonks* could get on board. This he did at great peril, having only an old broken canoe to get off in. The wind and rain now forced them up into Pocasset Sound, and they were obliged to bear away, and return round the north end of the island, to Newport.

Church now dismissed Mr. *Low,* as he viewed their effort against the will of Providence. He next drew up an account of what had passed, and despatched *Peter,* on the 9 July, by way of Sogkonate, to Plimouth.

Major *Bradford** having now arrived with an army at Pocasset, Mr.

* Out of a curious book we take the following note, as, besides giving us an interesting fact concerning the major, it contains others of value. It was written in 1697. At that time, some pretended that the age of people was much shorter in America than in Europe; which gave rise to what we are about to extract.—*Mary Brown* was the first-born of Newbury, Mass who married a *Godfry*; and, says our book, she "is yet alive, and is become the mother and grandmother of many children." "The mention of *Mary Brown,* brings to our mind an idle whimsey, as if persons born in New England would be short-lived; whereas, the natives live long. And a judgment concerning Englishmen, cannot well be made till 20 or 30 years hence. Capt. *Peregrine White,* born [on board the Mayflower] Nov. 1620, is yet alive, and like to live. [He died 7 years after, in 1704] Major *William Bradford* is more than 73 years old, and hath worn a bullet in his flesh above 20 of them, [which he doubtless received in *Philip's* war. He died aged 79.] *Elizabeth Alden,* (now *Paybody,* whose granddaughter is a mother,) Capt. *John Alden,* her brother, *Alexr. Standish,* and *John Howland,* have lived more than 70 years." S. Sewall's *New Heaven upon the New Earth,* 59, 60.

Church repaired to him, and told him of his transactions and engagements with *Awashonks*. *Bradford* directed him to go and inform her of his arrival, which he did. *Awashonks* doubtless now discovered much uneasiness and anxiety, but Mr. *Church* told her "that if she would be advised and observe order, she nor her people need not fear being hurt." He directed her to get all her people together, "lest, if they should be found straggling about, mischief might light on them;" and that the next day the army would march down into the neck to receive her. After begging him to consider the short time she had to collect them together, she promised to do the best she could, and he left her.

Accordingly, two days after, she met the army at Punkateese. *Awashonks* was now unnecessarily perplexed by the stern carriage of Major *Bradford*. For she expected her men would have been employed in the army; but instead of that, he "presently gave forth orders for *Awashonks*, and all her subjects, both men, women and children, to repair to Sandwich, and to be there upon peril, in six days." *Church* was also quite disconcerted by this unexpected order, but all reasoning or remonstrance was of no avail with the commander in chief. He told Mr. *Church* he would employ him if he chose, but as for the Indians, "he would not be concerned with them," and accordingly sent them off with a flag of truce, under the direction of *Jack Havens*, an Indian who had never been engaged in the war. Mr. *Church* told *Awashonks* not to be concerned, but it was best to obey orders, and he would shortly meet her at Sandwich.

According to promise, *Church* went by way of Plimouth to meet the Sogkonates. The governor of Plimouth was highly pleased at the account *Church* gave him of the Indians, and so much was he now satisfied of his superior abilities and skill, that he desired him to be commissioned in the country's service. He left Plimouth the same day with six attendants, among whom were Mr. *Jabez Howland*, and Mr. *Nathaniel Southworth*. They slept at Sandwich the first night, and here taking a few more men, agreeably to the governor's orders, proceeded to Agawam, a small river of Rochester, where they expected to meet the Indians. Some of his company now became discouraged, presuming, perhaps, the Indians were treacherous, and half of them returned home. When they came to Sippican River, which empties into Buzzard's Bay in Rochester, Mr. *Howland* was so fatigued that they were obliged to leave him, he being in years, and somewhat corpulent. *Church* left two more with him as a reserve, in case he should be obliged to retreat. They soon came to the shore of Buzzard's Bay, and, hearing a great noise at considerable distance from them, upon the bank, were presently in sight of a "vast company of Indians, of all ages and sexes, some on horseback, running races, some at foot-ball, some catching eels and flat fish in the water, some clamming, &c." They now had to find out what Indians these were, before they dared make themselves known to them. *Church* therefore halloed, and two Indians that were at a distance from the rest, rode up to him, to find out what the noise meant. They were very much surprised when they found themselves so near Englishmen, and turned their horses to run, but, *Church* making himself known to them, they gave him the desired information. He sent for *Jack Havens*, who immediately came. And when he had confirmed what the others had related, there arrived a large number of them on horseback, well armed. These treated the English very respectfully. *Church* then sent *Jack* to *Awashonks*, to inform her that he would sup with her that night, and lodge in her tent. In the mean time, the English returned with their friends they had left at Sippican. When they came to the Indian company, they "were immediately conducted to a shelter, open on one side, whither *Awashonks* and her chiefs soon came and paid their respects." When this had taken place, there were great shouts made by the "multitudes," which "made the heavens to ring." About sunset, "the *Netops** came running from all quarters, laden with the tops of dry pines, and the like combustible matter, making a huge pile thereof, near Mr. *Church's* shelter, on the open side thereof. But by this time supper was brought in, in three dishes, viz. a curious young bass in one dish, eels and flat fish in a second, and shell fish in a third;" but salt was wanting. When the supper was finished, "the mighty pile of pine knots and tops, &c. was fired, and all the Indians, great and small, gathered in a ring around it. *Awashonks,* with the eldest of her people, men and women mixed, kneeling down, made the first ring next the fire, and all the lusty stout men standing up made the next; and then all the rabble, in a confused crew, surrounded on the outside. Then the chief captain stepped in between the rings and the fire, with a spear in one hand, and a hatchet in the other, danced round the fire, and began to fight with it, making mention of all the several nations and companies of Indians in the country that were enemies to the English. And at naming of every particular tribe of Indians, he would draw out and fight a new fire-brand, and at his finishing his fight with each particular fire-brand, would bow to Mr. *Church* and thank him." When he had named over all the tribes at war with the English, he stuck his spear and hatchet in the ground, and left the ring, and then another stepped in, and acted over the same farce; trying to act with more fury than the first. After about a half a dozen had gone through with the performance, their chief captain stepped to Mr. *Church,* and told him "they were making soldiers for him, and what they had been doing was all one swearing of them." *Awashonks* and her chiefs next came and told him "that now they were all engaged to fight for the English." At this time *Awashonks* presented to Mr. *Church* a very fine gun. The next day, July 22, he selected a number of her men, and proceeded to Plimouth. A commission was given him, and, being joined with a number of English, volunteers, commenced a successful series of exploits, in which these Sogkonates bore a conspicuous part, but have never, since the days of *Church,* been any where noticed as they deserved.

It is said† that *Awashonks* had two sons; the youngest was *William Mommynewit,* who was put to a grammar school, and learned the Latin language, and was intended for college, but was prevented by being seized with the palsy. We have been able to extend the interesting memoir of the family of *Awashonks* in the early part of this article much beyond any before printed account; of *Tokamona* we have no printed notice, except what *Church*‡ incidentally mentions. Some of his Indian soldiers requested liberty to pursue the Narragansets and other enemy Indians, immediately after they had captured *Philip's* wife and son. "They said the Narragansets were great rogues, and they wanted to be revenged on them, for killing some of their relations; named *Tokkamona,* (*Awashonks's* brother,) and some others."

About 130 years ago, i. e. 1700, there were 100 Indian men of the Sogkonate tribe, and the general assembly appointed *Numpaus* their captain, who lived to be an old man, and died about 1748, after the taking of Cape Breton, 1745. At the commencement of the eighteenth century, they made quite a respectable religious congregation; had a meeting-house of

* Signifying *friends,* in Indian.

† *Col. Mass. Hist. Soc.*

‡ Hist. Philip's War, 39. It is usual to cite Capt. *Church* as the author or recorder of his own actions; it is so, although his son *Thomas* appears as the writer of the history. The truth is, the father dictated to the son, and corrected what appeared erroneous after the work was written.

their own, in which they were instructed by Rev. Mr. *Billings*, once a month, on Sundays. They had a steady preacher among themselves, whose name was *John Simon*, a man of a strong mind.

About 1750, a very distressing fever carried off many of this tribe, and in 1803 there were not above ten in Compton, their principal residence.

CHAPTER V.

A further account of chiefs conspicuous in Philip's war—PUMHAM—*Taken and slain*—*His son* QUAQUALH— CHICKON— SOCONONOCO— POTOCK—*His residence*—*Complaint against Wildbow's encroachments*—*Delivers himself up*—*Put to death*—STONE-WALL-JOHN—*A great captain*—*A mason*—*His men greatly annoy the English army in Narraganset*—*Kills several of them*—*They burn a garrison, and kill fifteen persons*—*A traffic in Indian prisoners*—*The burning of Rehoboth and Providence*—*John's discourse with Roger Williams*—*Is killed*—SAGAMORE JOHN—*Fate of* MATOONAS—*Put to death on Boston Common*—*His son hanged for murder*—MONOCO—*David*—*Andrew*—*James-the-printer*—OLD-JETHERO—SAGAMORE-SAM, *alias* SHOSHANIM—*Visited by Eliot in 1652*—*Anecdote*—PETER-JETHERO.

Pumham, it may be truly said, "was a mighty man of valor." Our history has several times heretofore brought him before us, and we shall now proceed to relate such facts concerning him as we have been able to collect. He was sachem of Shawomet, the country where the old squaw-sachem *Magnus* was taken and slain, as in her life we have shown.

This chief was brought into considerable difficulty by the English as early as 1645. In 1642, the Rev. *Samuel Gorton* took refuge in his country, and was kindly treated by him; and in January the next year, *Miantunnomoh* and *Canonicus* deeded to him Mishawomet, or Shaomet, which he afterward called *Warwick*, after the earl of that name. This settlement was grievous to the Puritan fathers of Massachusetts, as they soon showed by their resentment to *Miantunnomoh*; and here we cannot but discover the germ of all the subsequent disasters of that sachem. Mr. *Gorton* was kindly treated by him, as well as *Pumham*, until the latter was urged by Mr. *Gorton's* enemies to lay claim to the lands he had purchased of *Miantunnomoh*, whom the court of Massachusetts declared an usurper,* as in his life has been told.

By the letters of the unimpeachable *Roger Williams*, the above conclusions will appear evident. In 1656, he wrote to Massachusetts, showing them the wretched state Warwick was in from their difficulties with the Indians, as follows:—"Your wisdoms know the inhuman insultations of these wild creatures, and you may be pleased also to imagine, that they have not been sparing of your name as the patron of all their wickedness against our English men, women and children, and cattle, to the yearly damage of 60, 80 and 100£. The remedy is, (under God,) only your pleasure that *Pumham* shall come to an agreement with the town or colony."† Now it should be remembered, that when Warwick was purchased, *Pumham* and some other inferior sachems received presents for their particular interests in what was sold, agreeably to the laws and usages of the Indians.

The Plimouth people had their share in the Warwick controversy, having caused *Ousamaquin* to lay claim to the same place, or a sachem

* MS. *state paper*. † *Hutchinson's* papers, and *Hazard*.

who lived with him, named *Nawwashawsuck*; between whom and *Pumham* the quarrel ran so high that the former stabbed the latter.

The affairs of Warwick had been under consideration by the commissioners of the United Colonies for several years before this, and in 1649, they say, "Vppon a question betwixt the two collonies of the Massachusets and Plymouth, formerly propounded, and now again renewed by the commissioners of the Massachusetts, concerning a tract of land now or lately belonging to *Pamham* and *Saconoco,* two Indian sagamores who had submitted themselves and their people to the Massachusetts goverment, vppon part of which land som English, (besides the said Indians,) in anno 1643, were planted and settled." The decision was, that though the said tract of land fall within Plimouth bounds, it should henceforth belong to Massachusetts.

About 1646, we find the following record* of these chiefs:—"*Pomihom* and *Saconanoco* complaining to us [the court of Mass.] that many Indians dwelling 20 miles beyond them, (being friends and helpers to the Narragansetts in their present wars with *Uncas,*) are come upon their lands, and planted upon the same against their wills, they not being able of themselves to remove them, and therefore desire our counsel and help. We shall therefore advise them, if the deputies agree thereunto, to send a messenger to the sachem of those intruders to come to us to give an account of such his intention; and if he come to us, then to offer him protection upon the same terms that *Pumham* hath it, provided they satisfy *Uncas* for any injury they have done him. If he refuse to come, then we would have our messenger charge them to depart from *Pomham* and *Soconanocho* their lands, which also if they refuse, then we shall account them our enemies."*

Though, by the aid of the English, *Pumham* had been able to maintain a kind of independence for some years after the death of the chief sachem, yet he was among the first who espoused the cause of *Philip* in his war. The English army marched through his country, in their return from the attack on *Philip* and his confederates in Narraganset, in December, 1675. At this time a small fight took place between some of the English and a number of *Pumham's* men, under a chief whose name was *Quaqualh,* who gained some advantage of the English, wounding four of their men. The English, however, report that they killed five of the Indians. *Quaqualh* himself was wounded in the knee. At the same time they burnt *Pumham's* town,† which contained near 100 wigwams. The English were commanded by Capt. *Prentice.*‡

Pumham was not the chief captain in the fight at the great falls in the Connecticut, which took place 19 May, 1676, although we presume, from the known character of him, that he was the most conspicuous in it on the side of the Indians; being a man of vast physical powers and of extraordinary bravery. In this affair the English acted a most cowardly part, having every advantage of their enemy, who acquired credit upon the occasion, even at the time, from the historian. The English came upon them before day, while none were awake to give the alarm, and, "finding them secure indeed, yea, all asleep, without having any scouts abroad, so that our soldiers came and put their guns into their wigwams, before the Indians were aware of them, and made a great and notable slaughter amongst them."§ Many in their fright ran into the river, and were hurled

---

* In *manuscript,* among the papers on file in the secretary's office, Mass. without date.

† *Letter to London,* 58. 2d edition. This author has his name *Bumham.* There were many instances, at this time, of the use of *B* for *P.*

‡ *Hubbard,* Nar. 57.

§ I. *Mather,* 30.

down the falls,* some of whom, doubtless, were drowned. As soon as the English, who were led by Captains *Turner* and *Holioke,* had murdered the unresisting, and the Indians having begun to rally to oppose them, they fled in the greatest confusion, although they had "about an hundred and four score" men,† of whom but one was wounded when the flight began. This enhances the valor of the Indians, in our minds, especially as we read the following passage, in Mr. *Mather's* Brief History:—"In the mean while, a party of Indians from an island, (whose coming on shore might easily have been prevented, and the soldiers, before they set out from Hadley, were earnestly admonished to take care about that matter,) assaulted our men; yea, to the great dishonor of the English, a few Indians pursued our soldiers four or five miles, who were in number near twice as many as the enemy." In this flight Capt. *Turner* was killed, as he was crossing Green River. *Holioke* exerted himself with great bravery, and seems well calculated to oppose such a chief as *Pumham* was. We hear of no other bravery among the English in this massacre, but this passage concerning Holioke, which we are sorry is so sadly eclipsed, as appears by what follows. During the fight, some old persons, (whether men or women is not mentioned,) and children, had hid themselves under the bank of the river. Capt. *Holioke* discovered them, and with his own hands put five of them, "young and old," to death.‡ This English captain did not long survive his antagonist, for, by his great exertions in this fight, a fever was brought upon him, of which he died in September following, "about Boston."§

It would seem from the several accounts, that, although the English were sadly distressed in this fight, the Indians could never have repaired their loss; which, says the author of the PRESENT STATE, &c. was almost as much, nay, in some respects more considerable, than their lives." He continues, "We destroyed all their ammunition and provision, which we think they can hardly be so soon and easily recruited with, as possibly they may be with men. We likewise here demolished two forges they had to mend their arms, took away all their materials and tools, and drove many of them into the river, where they were drowned, and threw two great pigs of lead of theirs, (intended for making of bullets,) into the said river."||—"As our men were returning to Hadley, in a dangerous pass, which they were not sufficiently aware of, the skulking Indians, (out of the woods,) killed at one volley, the said captain, and eight-and-thirty of his men, but immediately after they had discharged, they fled."

In relating the capture and death of *Pumham*, Mr. *Hubbard* says,¶ "He was one of the stoutest and most valiant sachems that belonged to the Narragansets; whose courage and strength was so great that, after he had been mortally wounded in the fight, so as himself could not stand; yet catching hold of an Englishman that by accident came near him, had done him mischief, if he had not been presently rescued by one of his fellows." This was on 25 July, 1676. *Pumham*, with a few followers, had for some time secreted themselves in Dedham** woods, where it was suppposed they were "almost starved for want of victuals." In this sad

* We cannot agree with our friend Gen. *Hoyt,* that these falls should be named *Turner's Falls,* although we once thought it well enough. We would rather call them the *Massacre Falls,* IF, indeed, their Indian name cannot be recovered.

† I. *Mather,* 30. ‡ *Hubbard,* Nar. 88. § Ibid

|| Many of the Indians learned trades of the English, and in the wars turned their knowledge to good account. They had a forge in their fort at Narraganset, and the Indian blacksmith was killed when that was taken. The author of the *Present State,* &c. says, he was the only man amongst them that fitted their guns and arrow-heads; that among other houses they burnt his, demolished his forge, and carried away his tools.

¶ Narrative, 100. 4to. edition.

** *Woollummonuppogue* was its Indian name, or a part of it.

condition, they were fallen upon by the English under Capt. *Hunting*, who killed fifteen and took thirty-five of them without resistance.* They found here considerable plunder; "besides kettles, there was about half a bushel of wampumpeag, which the enemy lost, and twelve pounds of powder, which the captives say they had received from Albany but two days before."† A son of *Pumham* was among the captives, "a very likely youth," says *Hubbard*,‡ "and one whose countenance would have bespoke favor for him, had he not belonged to so bloody and barbarous an Indian as his father was." It would seem from this unfeeling account that he was put to death. Dr. *Mather* says he was carried prisoner to Boston. From the same author we must add to the revolting picture of the father's death. "This *Pumham*, after he was wounded so as that he could not stand upon his legs, and was thought to have been dead, made a shift, (as the soldiers were pursuing others,) to crawl a little out of the way, but was found again, and when an Englishman drew near to him, though he could not stand, he did, (like a beast,) in rage and revenge, get hold on the soldier's head, and had like to have killed him, had not another come in to his help, and rescued him out of the enraged dying hands of that bloody barbarian."†

A short time before this, a grandson of this chief was killed by a party under *Denison*,§ "who was also a sachem, and another sachem called *Chickon*."

Potok, a Narraganset chief, we may properly in the next place notice. None of his acts in *Philip's* war are recorded, at least none have come to our knowledge, but they could not have been inconsiderable, in the opinion of his enemies, as his life atoned for them. We find him first mentioned, on account of his opposition to the introduction of Christianity into his nation. When, in the beginning of *Philip's* war, the English army marched into the Narraganset country, to treat or fight with that nation, as they might be found inclined, *Potok* appeared as the principal chief. In the treaty which was concluded at that time, a condition was urged by him, "that the English should not send any among them to preach the gospel or call upon them to pray to God." But the English would not admit such an article; but if an article of this character had been urged on the other hand, we doubt whether there would have been any objection urged by the Indians. On this policy of the English *Roger Williams* should be heard, as, at this day even, we need no better commentary on the matter in hand. It is contained in a letter|| to the governor of Massachusetts, and is as follows:—"At my last departure for England, I was importuned by y[e] Narraganset sachems, and especially by *Nenecunat*, to present their petition to the high sachems of England, that they might not be forced from their religion; and, for not changing their religion, be invaded by war. For they said they were daily visited with threatenings by Indians, that came from about the Massachusetts; that if they would not pray, they should be destroyed by war." And again, in the same letter: "Are not all the English of this land, (generally,) a persecuted people from their native soil? and hath not the God of peace and Father of mercies made the natives more friendly in this than our native countrymen in our own land to us? have they not entred leagues of love, and to this day continued peaceable commerce with us? are not our families grown up in peace amongst them? Upon which I humbly ask how it can suit with Christian ingenuity, to take hold of some seeming occasions for their destruction."

* MS. Narrative of Rev. *T. Cobbet*.
† Mather's Brief Hist. 43.
‡ Narrative, *ut supra*.
§ Many write *Dennison*, but his own signature, in my possession, is as in the text.
|| In MS. dated Providence, 5:8: 1654.

We are able to fix the place of his residence in the vicinity of Point Judith. Our earliest notice of him is in 1661. In this year, *Potok,* with several other chiefs, complained to the court of Massachusetts, that "*Samuel Wildbow,* and others of his companie," claimed jurisdiction at Point Judith, in their country, and lands adjacent. They came on and possessed themselves forcibly, bringing their cattle and other effects with them.* What order the court took upon it does not appear. About the close of *Philip's* war, *Potok* came voluntarily to Rhode Island, no doubt with the view of making friends again with his enemies; but was sent to Boston, where, after answering all their inquiries, he was put to death without ceremony.

In the account carried to London by Capt. *More,* mentioned in the last chapter, is this notice of *Potok*:—"There is one *Potuck,* a mischievous Engine, and a Counsellour, taken formerly, said to be in Goal at Rhode-Island, is now sent to Boston, and there shot to death."

In the detail of the great Narraganset expedition of 1675, we have omitted to notice a by no means unimportant Indian captain.

Stone-wall-john, Stone-layer-john, and sometimes simply *Stone-wall,* were names by which his English friends knew him, and we have not discovered what was his Indian name. One writer of his time observes that he was called the *Stone-layer,* "for that, being an active, ingenious fellow, he had learned the mason's trade, and was of great use to the Indians in building their forts, &c." Hence we may hazard but little in the conjecture that he was the chief engineer in the erection of the great Narraganset fort, which has been described in the life of *Philip.* Although but little is known of him, he was doubtless one of the most distinguished Narraganset captains.

The first notice of *Stone-layer-john,* which we now remember, is contained in a letter of Capt. *Oliver,*† which he wrote while on his march with the English army to attack the fort, which we have just mentioned. He says, "Dec. 15 ca[me in] *John* a rogue, with a pretence of peace, and was dismissed with [this] errand: That we might speak with sachems. That evening, he not being gone a quarter of an hour, his company, that lay hid behind a hill of our quarters, killed two Salem men, and wounded a third within a mile of us, that he is dead. And at a house three mile off, where I had ten men, they killed two of them. Instantly Capt. *Mosely,* myself and Capt. *Gardner* were sent to fetch in Major *Appleton's* company, that kept three miles and a half off, and coming, they lay behind a stone wall, and fired on us in sight of the garrison, we killed the captain that killed one of the Salem men, and had his cap." Mr. *Hubbard* says, "A few desperate Indians, creeping under a stone-wall, fired twenty or thirty guns at *Mosely* in particular, a commander well known amongst them, but the rest of the company running down upon them, killed one of them and scattered the rest." Thus did the scouts from the main body of the Indians, under such captains as the *Stone-layer,* annoy the English in their march into their country. Immediately after these skirmishes, "they burnt *Jerry Bull's* house, and killed seventeen [persons.] Dec. 16, came that news. Dec. 17, came news that Connecticut forces were at Petaquamscut; killed four Indians and took six prisoners. That day we sold Capt. *Davenport* 47 Indians, young and old, for £80 in money."‡

How much *John* had to do in the devastations which had been perpetrated the previous season, is unknown, but we are told that he had no

* MS. documents.
† In manuscript. See an account of it in a note to the life of *Philip.*
‡ Capt. *Oliver's* MS. letter.

small agency in "the sacking of Providence,"* and Rehoboth also, without doubt. In the former about 30 houses† were burned, and in the latter place "near upon 40" houses and 30 barns.

Stone-wall-john was doubtless one who conversed with the Rev. Mr. *Williams* at the time Providence was burned. The substance of that conversation is related by our anonymous author, already cited, in these words:—"But indeed the reason that the inhabitants of the towns of Seaconick and Providence generally escaped with their lives, is not to be at tributed to any compassion or good nature of the Indians, (whose very mercies are inhumane cruelties,) but, [the author soon contradicts himself, as will be seen,] next to God's providence, to their own prudence in avoiding their fury, when they found themselves too weak, and unable to resist it, by a timely flight into Rhode Island, which now became the common *Zoar*, or place of refuge for the distressed; yet some remained till their coming to destroy the said towns; as in particular Mr. *Williams* at Providence, who, knowing several of the chief Indians that came to fire that town, discoursed with them a considerable time, who pretended, their greatest quarrel was against Plimouth; and as for what they attempted against the other colonies, they were constrained to it, by the spoil that was done them at Narraganset.‡ They told him, that when Captain *Pierce* engaged them near Mr. *Blackstone's*, they were bound for Plimouth. They gloried much in their success, promising themselves the conquest of the whole country, and rooting out of all the English. Mr. *Williams* reproved their confidence, minded them of their cruelties, and told them, that the Bay, viz. Boston, could yet spare 10,000 men; and, if they should destroy all them, yet it was not to be doubted, but our king would send as many every year from Old England, rather than they should share the country.§ They answered proudly, that they should be ready for them, or to that effect, but told Mr. *Williams* that he was a good man, and had been kind to them formerly, and therefore they would not hurt him."

This agrees well with Mr. *Hubbard's* account of the carriage of *John* at the time he went to the English army to talk about peace, already mentioned. His words are, "yet could the messenger, [*John*,] hardly forbear threatening, vaporing of their numbers and strength, adding, withal, that the English durst not fight them."

We have now to close the career of this Indian captain, for which it requires but a word, as he was killed on the 2 July, 1676, at the same time the old squaw-sachem *Quaiapen* and most of her people were fallen upon by Major *Talcot*, as we have related in a former chapter.

Many Indians bore the name of John, but when they were any ways conspicuous, some distinguishing prefix or affix was generally added, as we have seen in several instances in the preceding chapters. We have already given the life of one *Sagamore-john*, but another of that name, still more conspicuous, (for his treachery to his own nation,) here presents himself. This *Sagamore-john* was a Nipmuk sachem, and a traitor to his country. On the 27th of July, 1676, doubtless from a conviction of the hopelessness of his cause, he came to Boston, and threw himself on the mercy of the English. They pardoned him, as he enticed along with

* *Present State*, &c. 12.

† The building containing the records of R. I. was consumed at this time, and part of its contents. Some of them were saved by being thrown out of a window into some water. They bear to this time the marks of their immersion.—Oral information of N. *R. Staples*, Esq. of Providence.

‡ And who could ask for a better reason?

§ This was rather gasconading for so reverend a man! Had he lived since the revolutionary war, he would hardly have *meant* so, whatever he might have *said*.

him about 180 others. And, that he might have a stronger claim on their clemency, he seized *Matoonas*, and his son, against whom he knew the English to be greatly enraged, and delivered them up at the same time. On death's being immediately assigned as the lot of *Matoonas, Sagamore-john* requested that he might execute him with his own hands. To render still more horrid this story of blood, his request was granted; and he took *Matoonas* into the common, bound him to a tree, and there "shot him to death." To the above Dr. *Mather* adds,* "Thus did the Lord retaliate upon him the innocent blood which he had shed; as he had done, so God requited him."

Although much had been alleged against *John*, before he came in, afterwards the most favorable construction was put upon his conduct. Mr. *Hubbard* says, he "affirmed that he had never intended any mischief to the English at Brookfield, the last year, (near which village it seems his place was,) but that *Philip*, coming over night amongst them, he was forced, for fear of his own life, to join with them against the English."†

Matoonas was also a Nipmuk chief. A son of his was said to have murdered an Englishman in 1671, when "traveling along the road," which Mr. *Hubbard* says was "out of mere malice and spite," because he was "vexed in his mind that the design against the English, intended to begin in that year, did not take place." This son of *Matoonas* was hanged, and afterwards beheaded, and his head set upon a pole, where it was to be seen about six years after. The name of the murdered Englishman was *Zachary Smith*, a young man, who, as he was passing through Dedham, in the month of April, put up at the house of Mr. *Caleb Church*. About half an hour after he was gone, the next morning, three Indians passed the same way; who, as they passed by *Church's* house, behaved in a very insolent manner. They had been employed as laborers in Dorchester, and said they belonged to *Philip;* they left their masters under a suspicious pretence. The body of the murdered man was soon after found near the saw-mill in Dedham, and these Indians were apprehended, and one put to death, as is stated above.‡

Mr. *Hubbard* supposes that the father, "an old malicious villain," bore "an old grudge against them," on the account of the execution of his son. And the first mischief that was done in Massachusetts colony was charged to him; which was the killing of four or five persons at *Mendon,* a town upon Pawtucket River; and, says I. Mather, "had we *amended* our ways as we should have done, this misery would have been prevented."§

When old *Matoonas* was brought before the council of Massachusetts, he "confessed that he had rightly deserved death, and could expect no other." "He had often seemed to favor the praying Indians, and the Christian religion, but, like *Simon Magus*, by his after practice, discovered quickly that he had no part nor portion in that matter."||

The following horrible circumstance, according to an anonymous author,¶ took place at the execution of *Matoonas*:—"The executioners, (for there were many,) flung one end, [of a rope about his neck, by which they led him,] over a post, and so hoisted him up like a dog, three or four times, he being yet half alive and half dead; then came an Indian, a friend of his, and with his knife made a hole in his breast to his heart, and sucked out his heart-blood: being asked his reason therefor, his

---

* Brief History of the War, 43. † Narrative, 101. 4to edition.

‡ Manuscript documents, in the office of the secretary of the state of Massachusetts.

§ Brief Hist. 5. || *Hubbard*, 101.

¶ Of the *Letter to London*, 27, who makes no mention of the name of the Indian executed; but his account evidently relates to *Matoonas*.

answer, '*Umh, umh nu, me stronger as I was before. Me be so strong as me and he too, he be ver strong man fore he die.*' "

The author from whom we have made this extract is rather more of a savage than any one we have met with. Upon the above monstrous act he has this comment: "Thus with the dog-like death (good enough) of one poor heathen, was the people's rage laid, in some measure;" from which the reader will naturally infer that there was at this time a great thirst for blood amongst the English, which, it is too evident, was actually the case.

Our readers must ere this have become acquainted with the state of feeling towards the Indians, and consequently towards all those who ventured to raise their voice in commutation of severity towards them. At the time the *eleven* Indians were tried for their lives, the particulars of which we shall soon have occasion to relate, Mr. *Gookin* and Mr. *Eliot,* by singular perseverance, succeeded in clearing the most of them. The rage of the people was no longer confined to the rabble, as will be seen by the following passage from our anonymous author:—"But for Captain *Guggins*, why such a wise council as they should be so overborne by him, cannot be judged otherwise than because of his daily troubling them with his impertinences, and multitudinous speeches; insomuch, that it was told him on the bench by a very worthy person, Captain *Oliver*, there present, that he ought rather to be confined among his Indians, than to sit on the bench. His taking the Indians' part so much hath made him a by-word both among men and boys."*

While *Matoonas* belonged to the Christian Indians, his residence was at Pakachoog. Here he was made constable of the town.† On joining in the war, he led parties which committed several depredations. He joined the main body of the Nipmuks in the winter of 1675, when *James Quanapohit* was among them as a spy, who saw him arrive there with a train of followers, and take the lead in the war dances.‡ Doubtless *Quanapohit's* evidence drew forth the confessions which he made, and added to the severity exercised at his execution.

We have yet to notice a distinguished Nipmuk sachem, called

Monoco by his countrymen, but by the English, generally, *One-eyed-john*; as though deficient in the organs of vision, which probably was the case. He was, says an early writer, "a notable fellow," who, when *Philip's* war began, lived near Lancaster, and consequently was acquainted with every part of the town, which knowledge he improved to his advantage, on two occasions, in that war. On Sunday, 22 August, 1675, a man, his wife and two children were killed at that place.§ At this time the Hassanamesit praying Indians were placed at Marlborough by authority. No sooner was it known that a murder was committed at Lancaster, than not a few were wanting to charge it upon the Hassanamesits. Captain *Mosely,* who it seems was in the neighborhood, sent to their quarters, and found "much suspicion against *eleven* of them, for singing and dancing, and having bullets and slugs, and much powder hid in their baskets." For this *offence,* these eleven were sent to Boston, on suspicion, and there *tried.* "But upon trial, the said prisoners were all of them acquitted from the fact, and were either released, or else were, with others of that fort, sent for better security, and for preventing future trouble in the like kind, to some of the islands below Boston, towards Nan-

---

* *Letter to London*, 26.

† *Shattuck's* Hist. Concord, 31.

‡ 1 *Col. Mass. Hist. Soc.* vi. 206.

§ The above is Mr. *Hubbard's* account. Mr. *Willard,* in his excellent history of Lancaster, gives us the names of six, and says eight were killed. But in his enumeration I count *nine*; and *Gookin* says seven.

tasket."* Fifteen was the number brought down to Boston, but *eleven* or twelve only were suspected of the alleged offence. The others, among whom were *Abram Speen* and *John Choo*, were taken along and imprisoned, for no other reason but their being accidentally, at that time, at Marlborough, or the crime of being Indians. It appears some time had elapsed after the murder was committed, before they were sent down for trial, or more probably they were suffered to return home before being sent to Deer Island. For *Ephraim Turner* and *William Kent* were not sent up to find out where "they all were," and what answers they could get from those they should meet, until the beginning of October; at which time these eleven Indians were scattered in various directions, about their daily callings. And all the information *Turner* and *Kent* handed into court was, that they were thus dispersed. *Waban* and Mr. *John Watson*, who had been appointed to reside among those Indians, were the only persons questioned. What steps the court took upon this information, we are not informed, but they were about this time sent to Deer Island.

The names of these 12 Indians, concerning whom more particular inquiry may hereafter be made by the benevolent antiquary, it is thought should be given; especially as they may not elsewhere be preserved. They follow:—

Old-jethro and two sons, (Peter probably being one,) a *squaw*, (name not mentioned,) *James-the-printer, James Acompanet, Daniel Munups, John Cquasquaconet, John Asquenet, George Nonsequesewit, Thomas Mamuxonqua*, and *Joseph Watapacoson*.

After a trial of great vexation to these innocent Indians, *David*, the main witness against them, acknowledged he had perfidiously accused them; and at the same time, a prisoner was brought in, who testified that he knew *One-eyed-john* had committed the murder at Lancaster, and a short time after another was taken, who confirmed his testimony.

These Indians brought all these troubles upon themselves by reason of their attachment to the English. It was in their service that they discovered and captured *Andrew*, a brother of *David*, who, on being delivered to the soldiery, was shot by them with ferocious precipitancy. Therefore, when the Lancaster murder happened, Captain *Mosely*, having already sundry charges against *David*, held an inquisition upon him to make him confess relative to the Lancaster affair. The method taken to make him confess, (agreeably to the desire of his inquisitors,) was this: they bound him to a tree, and levelled guns at his breast. In this situation, to avert immediate death, as well as to be revenged for the death of his brother, he proceeded to accuse the eleven Indians before named. The result we have before stated. For thus falsely accusing his countrymen, and shooting at a boy who was looking after sheep at Marlborough, *David* was condemned to slavery, and accordingly sold.

James Acompanet was conspicuous at the trial, as one of the eleven, and "pleaded, in behalf of himself and the rest, that what *David* said against them, was to save his own life when bound to the tree," &c. *Acompanet*, says Mr. *Gookin*, "was a very understanding fellow."

Notwithstanding the two prisoners, taken at different times as we have mentioned, avowed that *Monoco* led the party that did the mischief, yet one* of the *eleven*, whom Mr. *Gookin* calls *Joseph Spoonant*, was, by a new jury, found guilty, and sold into foreign slavery. His Indian name was *Wattapacoson*.

Andrew's history is as follows: he had been gone for some time before the war, on a hunting voyage towards the lakes; and on his return home-

---

* *Gookin's MS. Hist. Praying Indians.*

ward, he fell in among *Philip's* men about Quabaog. This was about a month before the affair at Lancaster. The reason he staid among the hostile Indians is very obvious: he was afraid to venture into the vicinity of the whites, lest they should treat him as an enemy. But as his ill fortune fell out, he was found in the woods, by his countrymen of Marlborough, who conducted him to the English, by whom he was shot, as we have just related. The officer who presided over and directed this affair, would, no doubt, at any other time, have received a reward proportionate to the malignity of the offence. But in this horrid storm of war, many were suffered to transgress the laws with impunity.

We have yet to add a word concerning *Monoco*. When *Quanapohit* was out as a spy, *Monoco* kindly entertained him, on account of former acquaintance, not knowing his character. They had served together in their wars against the Mohawks. On 10 Feb. 1676, about 600 Indians fell upon Lancaster, and, after burning the town, carried the inhabitants into captivity. Among them was the family of Rev. Mr. *Rowlandson*. Mrs. *Rowlandson*, after her redemption, published an amusing account of the affair. *Monaco*, or *One-eyed-john*, it is said, was among the actors of this tragedy. On 13 March following, Groton was surprised. In this affair, too, *John Monoco* was principal; and on his own word we set him down as the destroyer of Medfield. After he had burned Groton, except one garrison house, he called to the captain in it, and told him he would burn in succession Chelmsford, Concord, Watertown, Cambridge, Charlestown, Roxbury and Boston. He boasted much of the men at his command; said he had 480 warriors; and added—"*What me will do.*" The report of this very much enraged the English, and occasioned his being entitled a "bragadocio" by the historian. At the close of *Philip's* war, with others, he gave himself up to Major *Waldron* at Cochecho; or, having come in there, at the request of *Peter-jethro*, to make peace, was seized and sent to Boston, where, in the language of Mr. *Hubbard*, he, "with a few more bragadocios like himself, *Sagamore-sam, Old-jethro,* and the sachem of Quabaog, [*Mautamp**], were taken by the English, and was seen, (not long before the writing of this,) marching towards the gallows, (through Boston streets, which he threatened to burn at his pleasure,) with a halter about his neck, with which he was hanged at the town's end, Sept. 26, in this present year, 1676."

It was reported, (no doubt by the Indians, to vex their enemies,) that Mrs. *Rowlandson* had married *Monaco*. "But," the author of the PRESENT STATE, &c. says, "it was soon contradicted," and, "that she appeared and behaved herself amongst them with so much courage and majestic gravity, that none durst offer any violence to her, but, on the contrary, (in their rude manner,) seemed to show her great respect."

In the above quotation from Mr. *Hubbard*, we have shown at what time several of the Nipmuk chiefs were put to death beside *Monaco*. *Old-jethro* was little less noted, though of quite a different character. His Indian name was *Tantamous*. He was present at the sale of Concord (Mass.) to the English, about which time he lived at Natick. In 1674, he was appointed a missionary to the Nipmuks living at Weshakim, since Sterling, but his stay there was short.† He and his family, (of about 12 persons,) were among those ordered to Deer Island, on the breaking out of the war the next year. Their residence then was at Nobscut Hill, near Sudbury. His spirit could not brook the indignity offered by those

---

* The same, probably, called *Mattawamppe,* who, in 1665, witnessed the sale of Brookfield, Mass., deeded at that time by a chief named *Shattoockquis*. *Mautamp* claimed an interest in said lands, and received part of the pay.—Rev. Mr. *Foot's Hist. Brookfield.*

† Mr. *Shattuck's* Hist. Concord, 30.

English who were sent to conduct the praying Indians to Boston, and in the night he escaped, with all his family, into his native wilds. His son *Peter* had been so long under the instruction of the English, that he had become almost one of them. He deserted his father's cause, and was the means of his being executed with the other Nipmuk sachems already mentioned. This occasioned Dr. *I. Mather* to say of him, "That abominable Indian, *Peter-jethro*, betrayed *his own father*, and other Indians of his special acquaintance, unto death." It seems he had been employed by the English for this purpose.

Sagamore-sam, sachem of Nashua, was a participant in the sufferings of those just named. He was one of those that sacked Lancaster, 10 Feb. 1676. His Indian name was at one time *Shoshanim*, but in *Philip's* war it appears to have been changed to *Uskatuhgun*; at least, if he be the same, it was so subscribed by *Peter-jethro*, when the letter was sent by the Indians to the English about the exchange of Mrs. *Rowlandson* and others, as will be found in the life of *Nepanet*. *Shoshanim* was successor to *Matthew*, who succeeded *Sholan*. This last-mentioned sachem is probably referred to by the author quoted in Mr. *Thorowgood's* curious book. In the summer of 1652, Rev. *John Eliot* intended to visit the Nashuas, in his evangelical capacity, but understanding there was war in that direction among the Indians, * delayed his journey for a time. The sachem of Nashua hearing of Mr. *Eliot's* intention, "took 20 men, armed after their manner," as his guard, with many others, and conducted him to his country. And my author adds, "this was a long journey into the wilderness of 60 miles: it proved very wet and tedious, so that he was not dry three or four days together, night nor day."† One of the Indians at this time asked Mr. *Eliot* why those who prayed to God among the English loved the Indians that prayed to God "more than their own brethren." The good man seemed some at a loss for an answer, and waved the subject by several scriptural quotations.

We may be incorrect in the supposition that the sachem who conducted Mr. *Eliot* on this occasion was *Sholan*, as perhaps *Passaconaway* would suit the time as well.

Another great and benevolent chief it would be proper to notice in this place, whose name was *Ashpelon*; but as he comes to our notice after *Philip's* war, we shall notice him in another chapter.

---

* In 1647, three Indians were killed between Quabaog and Springfield, by other Indians. The next year, five others were killed about midway between Quabaog and Lancaster.—*Winthrop's Journal*, (Savage's ed.) Such instances were common among the Indians.

† Sure Arguments to prove that the Jews inhabit now in America.—By *Thomas Thorowgood*, 4to. London, 1652. Sir *Roger L'Estrange* answered this book by another entitled, THE AMERICANS NO JEWS.

CHAPTER VI.

Friendly Indians—CAPTAIN AMOS—*Pursues Tatoson and Penachason—Escapes the slaughter at Pawtucket—Commands a company in the eastern war*—CAPTAIN LIGHTFOOT—*His services in Philip's war—In the eastern war*—KATTENANIT—*His services*—QUANNAPOHIT—*His important services as a spy*—MAUTAMP—*Monoco*—NEPANET—*Employed to treat with the enemy—Brings letters from them—Effects an exchange of prisoners*—PETER CONWAY— PETER EPHRAIM.

Amos, commonly called Captain *Amos*, was a Wampanoag, whose residence was about Cape Cod. We have no notice of him until *Philip's* war, at which time he was entirely devoted to the service of the English. After the Plimouth people had found that Tatoson was concerned in the destruction of *Clark's* garrison, they sought for some friendly Indians who would undertake to deliver him and his abettors into their hands. Captain *Amos* tendered his services, and was duly commissioned to prosecute the enterprise, and to take into that service any of his friends. Meantime, *Tatoson* had fled to Elizabeth Island, in company with *Penachason*, another chief who was also to be taken if he could be found. This *Penachason* was probably *Tatoson's* brother's son, sometimes called *Tom*, who, if the same, was also at the destroying of *Clark's* garrison. Yet the wily chiefs eluded the vigilance of Captain *Amos*, by flying from that region into the Nipmuks' country, where they joined *Philip*.

To encourage greater exertion on the part of the friendly Indians, to execute their commission, it was ordered, that in case they captured and brought in either *Tatoson* or *Penachason*, "they may expect for their reward, for each of them four coats, and a coat apiece for every other Indian that shall prove merchantable."

We have mentioned in a former chapter the horrid catastrophe of Captain *Peirse* and his men at Pawtucket. Captain *Amos* escaped that dreadful slaughter. He fought there with 20 of his warriors, and when Captain *Peirse* was shot down by a ball, which wounded him in the thigh, he stood by his side, and defended him as long as there was a gleam of hope. At length, seeing nearly all his friends slain, by great presence of mind he made his escape, by the following subtle stratagem:—*Nanuntenoo's* warriors had blackened their faces, which Captain *Amos* had observed, and by means of powder contrived to discolor his own unobserved by them. When he had done this, he managed, by a dexterous manœuver, to pass among the enemy for one of them, and by these means escaped.

What were Captain *Amos's* other acts in this war, if any, we have not learned; nor do we meet again with him until 1689. In that year, he went with Col. *Church* against the eastern Indians and French, in which expedition he also had the command of a company, *Church* arrived with his forces in Sept. at Casco, now Portland, and, having landed secretly under cover of the night, surprised, on the following morning, about four hundred Indians, who had come to destroy the place. Although the Indians did not receive much damage, yet, Gov. *Sullivan* says,* the whole eastern country was saved by the timely arrival of this expedition. In the fight at Casco, eight of the English were killed and many wounded. Two of Captain *Amos's* men were badly wounded, and *Sam Moses*, another friendly Indian, was killed. There was another Indian com-

* Hist. District of Maine, 102.

pany in this expedition, commanded by Captain *Daniel*, out of which one man was killed, who was of Yarmouth on Cape Cod.*

Lightfoot, of the tribe of the Sogkonates, distinguished in *Philip's* war, was also in the service under *Church* at Casco; a memorable expedition, on more than one account. One circumstance we will name, as it well nigh proved the ruin of the undertaking. When, on the following morning, after the arrival of the forces, the attack was begun, it was, to the inexpressible surprise of the English, found, that the bullets were much larger than the calibre of their guns. This was a most extraordinary and unaccountable occurrence, and great blame was chargeable somewhere. In this wretched dilemma, the fight having already begun, *Church* set some at work making the bullets into slugs, by which resort he was able to continue the fight. It being high water at the time, an estuary separated the battle-ground from the town. The bullets were to be carried to the army engaged, in buckets, after being hammered. When the first recruit of slugs was made up, Col. *Church* ran with it to the water's edge, and, not caring to venture himself to wade across, called to those on the other side to send some one to take it over to the army. None appeared but Lightfoot. This Indian dexterously repassed the estuary, with a quantity of powder upon his head, and a "kettle" of bullets in each hand, and thus the fight was maintained, and the enemy put to flight. In *Philip's* war, *Lightfoot's* exploits were doubtless very numerous, but few of them have come down to us. He volunteered to fight for the English, at *Awashonks's* great dance at Buzzard's Bay, already mentioned. When *Little-eyes* was taken at Cushnet, in 1676, Lightfoot was sent with him to what is now called Palmer's Island, near the mouth of Cushnet River, where he held him in guard, until he could be safely conducted to Plimouth. About the time *Akkompoin* was killed, and *Philip's* wife and son were taken, *Church* gave him a captain's commission, after which he made several successful expeditions.—We now pass to characters hitherto less known, though, perhaps, of more interest.

Very little was known of certain important characters among the friendly Indians of Massachusetts, which should have by no means been overlooked, until the discovery of Mr. *Gookin's* manuscript history of the praying Indians, not long since, and to which we have often referred already. We shall, therefore, devote the remainder of the present chapter to their history.

Job Kattenanit seems first to demand attention. He was a Christian Indian, and lived some time at Natick, but was at one time a preacher at Magunkog, and belonged originally, we believe, to Hassanamesit. However that may have been, it is certain he lived there in the beginning of *Philip's* war, when that chief's men made a descent upon the place, with the intention of carrying away those Christian Indians prisoners. *Job* made his escape from them at this time, and came in to the English at Mendon. He had still three children in the enemy's hands, and he was willing to run any venture to release them. He therefore applied for and obtained a pass, assuring him safety, provided that, in his return, he should fall into the hands of the English scouts. Besides liberating his children, considerable hopes were entertained, that he might be enabled to furnish information of the enemy. It unfortunately happened, that, before he had passed the frontier, he fell in with some English soldiers, who treated him as a prisoner, and an enemy, even taking from him his clothes and gun, sending him to the governor at Boston; "who, more to satisfy the clamors of the people than for any offence committed," assigned him to the common jail, where he suffered exceedingly; himself

* MS. letter of Capt. *Basset* of the expedition.

and many others being crowded into a narrow and filthy place. After about three weeks, he was taken out and sent to Deer Island. The clamors of the people were indeed high at this time, and many accused Major *Gookin*, who gave him the pass, as guilty of furnishing the enemy with intelligence.

After the Narraganset fight, 19 December, 1675, the English were very anxious to gain information relative to the position of the enemy, and accordingly instructed Major *Gookin* to use his endeavors to employ some friendly Indian spies; who, after considerable negotiation among those at Deer Island, engaged *Job* again, and *James Quannapohit*, alias *Quanapaug*. Their reward was to be *five* pounds apiece! They departed upon this service before day, the 30th of December, and, during their mission, behaved with great prudence, and brought valuable information to the English on their return; but which, from intestine bickerings among the English, turned to small account.

James Quannapohit returned 24th of Jan. following, nearly worn out and famished; having travelled about 80 miles in that cold season, upon snow-shoes, the snow being very deep. The information which he gave was written down by Major *Gookin*.* Among other matters, he stated that the enemy had taken up their quarters in different places, probably near Scattacook; and many others, including the Nipmuks, about Menumesse. The Narragansets had not yet joined *Philip* openly, but while *James* and *Job* were among the Nipmuks, messengers arrived from Narraganset which gave them much joy, for they expressed an ardent desire to join them and *Philip* in prosecuting the war. They said their loss in the great swamp fight was small. In three weeks, *James* learned, they would assault Lancaster, which accordingly came to pass, upon the very day which he said they intended it. He learned and thus divulged their plans to a great extent. A circumstance now occurred, which obliged him to make his escape, which was this: He found a friend and protector in *Mautamp*,† one of the Nipmuk chiefs, who, it seems, intended shortly to visit *Philip*; and insisted that *Quannapohit* should accompany him, and it was with no small difficulty he was able to elude the vigilant eye of *Mautamp*, and make his escape, which, however, was effected only by a cunning stratagem, as follows:—He told *Mautamp* that he had fought against *Philip* in the commencement of the war, and that *Philip* knew him, and that, unless he could go to him with some important trophy, Philip would not believe him, and would immediately kill him. And moreover *Tukapawillin* had privately told him that *Philip* had given out word that certain praying Indians should be sought after, and, if possible, seized and brought to him; for he wanted to put them to death in a cruel manner, with his own hands, and that he was one of them. He therefore told *Mautamp* that he would go, in the first place, and kill some English, and take their heads along with him, and then he should consider himself safe. This being consented to, he lost no time in retracing his steps to the frontiers of the English.

He mentions *Monoco*, or *One-eyed-john*, as a great captain among the enemy, who also treated him kindly, and entertained him in his wigwam during his stay there; they being old acquaintance, having served together in their wars against the Mohawks, ten years before.‡

And here also Mr. *Gookin* gives a favorable account of *Monoco*. *Philip* had ordered that the persons above named should be brought to him, if

---

* The same published in *Col. Mass. Hist. Soc.* 1. vi. 205—208.

† The same, probably, called Netaump, who was afterwards executed at Boston, at the same time with *Sagamore-sam*. See *Hubbard*, 35.

‡ Of this war we have given an account in b. 2. c. iii.

taken alive, "that he might put them to some tormenting death, *which had hitherto* been prevented by the care and kindness of a great captain among them, named *John-with-one-eye*, belonging to Nashua,* who had civilly treated and protected *James*, and entertained him at his wigwam, all the time of his being there."†

Job was requested to come away with *Quanapohit*, but saw no way of getting away his children, which was a main object with him. He knew, too, that *James* could give all the information they both possessed at that period, and not considering himself in imminent danger, preferred to tarry longer.

At Wanexit, or Manexit, they fell in with seven Indians, who took them and conveyed them about twenty miles, across the path leading to Connecticut, northward from Quabaog. These were some of the Quahmsits and Segunesits. At this place were three towns which contained about 300 warriors well armed. Here they were threatened with death, their mission being truly guessed. But going to the wigwam of *One-eyed-john*, or *Monoco*, he charged his gun and said, "I will kill whomsoever shall kill *Quanapohit*."‡ Some said he had killed one of *Philip's* counsellors at Mount Hope, and *Philip* had hired some to kill him; also *James Speen, Andrew Pitimy*, Captain *Hunter, Thomas Quanapohit*, and *Peter Ephraim*. On being ordered to visit *Philip*, "*Job* and he pretended to go out a hunting, killed three dear quickly, and perceiving they were dogged by some other Indians, went over a pond and lay in a swamp till before day, and when they had prayed together he ran away." *Job* was to return to the enemy, and tell them that *James* ran away because they had threatened to kill him. *Job*, not being particularly obnoxious to them, concluded to remain longer for the end of ransoming his children, as we have said.

He returned to the English in the night of the 9th of February, and said, as *James* had before, that on the next day Lancaster would be attacked, for he knew about four hundred of the enemy were already on their march. It resulted as *James* had foretold.

He further informed the English, that the enemy would shortly attack Medfield, Groton, Marlborough, and other places, and that the Narragansets had joined *Philip* and the Nipmuks.

While *James* was there, "a Narraganset brought to them one English head: they shot at him, and said the Narragansets were the English friends all last summer. Afterwards two messengers came with twelve heads, craving their assistance, they then accepted them."§

Before he left the enemy, he appointed a place of safety for his children, and sundry others of his friends, captured at Hassanamesit, where he would afterwards meet and conduct them to the English. He therefore petitioned the council for liberty to meet them, which was granted. But he now had new difficulties to encounter, owing to "the rude temper of those times," as one of the wise men of that age expressed it.|| Although both these men had acquitted themselves to the entire satisfaction of the authorities who sent them forth, yet the populace accused them of giving information to the enemy, and that they were secretly their advisers, or else they had not returned in safety; to appease which they were confined again to the island. This so interfered with the time set by *Job* to meet his children and friends, that great sufferings ensued to them, as well as to himself; and he knew not that ever he should have an opportunity to see his children again. But it much sooner happened, no doubt, than he expected, although in an indirect way. About the time he was

* Called sagamore of Nashua, in the *Cotton Manuscripts*.
† Hist. Praying Indians. ‡ Cotton Manuscripts. § Ibid.
|| Major *Daniel Gookin*, who was at least a hundred years in advance of that age.

sent to the island, a vote passed in the general court of Massachusetts, to raise an army of six hundred men, and Major *Thomas Savage* was applied to, to conduct them in the war. He refused, unless he could have some of the friendly Indians from the island for assistants. On a messenger being sent among them, six of their principal and bravest men volunteered in that service, among whom was *Job Kattenanit.* The army marched about the first of March, 1675, O. S. But when at Marlborough, *Job* got liberty of Major *Savage* and Major-general *Dennison,* to attempt the finding of his friends and children, whom he had appointed to meet near Hassanamesit. When it was known to Captain *Mosely,** he behaved himself very unbecoming towards the commanding officer, and nothing but his popularity with the army saved his reputation. Indeed, his conduct seems quite as reprehensible as that of a more modern Indian hunter in the Floridas, which all friends of humanity joined to condemn. *Mosely,* it appears, would place no confidence in any Indian, and doubtless thought he was acting for the best interests of the country. He urged that it was a most impolitic measure to suffer any Indian to go away at this time, knowing their natural treacherousness; and he doubted not but *Job* (although a tried friend) would inform the enemy of the approach of the army, which would frustrate all their designs. The great ascendency which this officer held in the army can best be understood by a simple statement of the fact, that Major *Savage* and General *Dennison* were obliged to send after *Job* before the soldiery would cease their clamors. Captain *Wadsworth* and Captain *Syll,* accompanied by *James Quannapohit,* went in pursuit with the utmost speed. But they did not overtake him, and he soon returned to the army without finding his friends; they, from fear of discovery, having changed their place, the time having been much longer than was set, and their consequent sufferings were indescribable.

We shall only add here concerning them, that they afterwards fell into the hands of a party of English, who treated them very ill, taking every thing from them. But when they were brought to Major *Savage,* he treated them kindly, and had them sent to Boston, all except four, who ran away from Marlborough, where they stopped for the night, from the fear of being murdered, some of the people so abused them. About two months after that, they were found and brought in by *Nepanet.* Finally, *Job* recovered all his children, and, marrying again, lived very happily. His wife was one of those which he had managed to deliver out of the hands of the enemy at such hazard and pains. She had, during their wanderings, nursed and kept alive his children, one, especially, which was very young.

When the Hassanamesits went off with the enemy, *James Quannapohit* was in the neighborhood with the English forces. Captain *Syll* sent out a scout, and *James* and *Elizer Pegin* accompanied. Seven of the enemy were soon discovered, one of whom was leading an English prisoner. They discovered the English scout, and fled. *James* and *Elizer* pursued them, and recovered the prisoner, whose name was *Christopher Muchin,* who had been taken from Marlborough. *James* also took one of the enemy's guns.†

The English having, by means of spies, as in the preceding life we have just stated, learned the state of feeling among their enemies, felt themselves prepared, as the spring of 1676 advanced, to make overtures to them for peace, or exchange of prisoners, or both, as they might be found inclined.

* It may be a question with some whether the captain meant, in the original documents, were *Mosely,* but I think I conjecture rightly.

† *Gookin's* MS. Hist. Christian Indians.

Tom Nepanet was fixed upon as plenipotentiary in this business. And, although unjustly suffering with many of his brethren upon a bleak island in Boston harbor, consented, at the imminent risk of his life, to proceed to meet the Indians in the western wilderness, in the service, and for the benefit, of those who had caused his sufferings.

Nepanet set out, April the 12th, 1676, to make overtures to the enemy for the release of prisoners, especially the family of Mr. *Rowlandson,* which was taken at Lancaster. He soon returned with a written answer from the enemy, saying, "*We no give answer by this one man, but if you like my answer sent one more man besides this one* Tom Nepanet, *and send with all true heart and with all your mind by two men; because you know and we know your heart great sorrowful with crying for your lost many many hundred man and all your house and all your land and woman child and cattle as all your thing that you have lost.*"

At the same time, and I conclude in the same letter, they wrote a few words to others as follows: "*Mr.* Rowlandson, *your wife and all your child is well but one dye. Your sister is well and her 3 child.*—John Kittell, *your wife and all your child is all well, and all them prisoners taken at Nashua is all well.*—

Mr. Rowlandson, *se your loving sister his hand* C Hanah.
And old Kettel *wif his hand* X
Brother Rowlandson, *pray send thre pound of Tobacco for me, if you can my loving husband pray send thre pound of tobacco for me.*

"*This writing by your enemies*—Samuel Uskattuhgun *and* Gunrashit, *two Indian sagamores.*"*

Mrs. *Rowlandson,* in her account of "The Sixteenth Remove," relates, that when they had waded over Baquaug† River, "Quickly there came up to us an Indian who informed them that I must go to Wachusect to my master, for there was a letter come from the council to the saggamores about redeeming the captives, and that there would be another in 14 days, and that I must be there ready."‡ This was doubtless after the letter just recorded had been sent to the English. "About two days after," Mrs. *R.* continues, "came a company of Indians to us, near 30, all on horseback. My heart skipt within me, thinking they had been Englishmen, at the first sight of them: For they were dressed in English apparel, with hats, white neck-cloths, and sashes about their waists, and ribbons upon their shoulders. But when they came near, there was a vast difference between the lovely faces of Christians, and the foul looks of those heathen, which much damped my spirits again."§

Having, after great distress, arrived at Wachuset, our authoress adds, "Then came *Tom* and *Peter* with the second letter from the council, about the captives." "I asked them how my husband did, and all my friends and acquaintance. They said they were well, but very melancholy." They brought her two biscuits and a pound of tobacco. The tobacco she gave to the Indians, and, when it was all gone, one threatened her because she had no more to give; probably not believing her. She told him when her husband came, she would give him some. "Hang him, rogue, says he, I will knock out his brains, if he comes here." "Again, at the same breath, they would say, if there should come an hundred without guns they would do them no hurt. So unstable and like madmen they were."|| There had been something talked about Mr. *Rowlandson's* going himself to ransom his wife, but she says she dared

---

* *Peter-jethro,* a Christian Indian, acted as scribe upon this occasion.

† Or Payquage, now Miller's River. Its confluence with the Connecticut is between Northfield and Montague.

‡ Narrative of her Captivity, 59. § Ibid. 60. || Ibid. 64, 65.

not send for him, "for there was little more trust to them than to the master they served."*

Nepanet learned by the enemy that they lost in the fight when Capt. *Pierse* was killed, "scores of their men that sabbath day."†

As they refused to treat with *Tom Nepanet* alone, *Peter Conway* was joined with him on a second expedition, as we have seen, which led to several others, to which some English ventured to add themselves, which resulted in the redemption of Mrs. *Rowlandson* and several others.

"When the letter was come, (says Mrs. *R.*,) the saggamores met to consult about the captives, and called me to them, to inquire how much my husband would give to redeem me: When I came and sat down among them, as I was wont to do, as their manner is: Then they bid me stand up, *and said they were the general court.* They bid me speak what I thought he would give. Now knowing that all that we had was destroyed by the Indians, I was in a great strait."‡ She ventured, however, to say £20, and *Tom* and *Peter* bore the offer to Boston.

Of their return the same writer proceeds: "On a sabbath day, the sun being about an hour high in the afternoon, came Mr. *John Hoar*, (the council permitting him, and his own forward spirit inclining him,) together with the two fore-mentioned Indians, *Tom* and *Peter,* with the third letter from the council. When they came near, I was abroad; they presently called me in, and bid me sit down, and not stir. Then they catched up their guns and away they ran, as if an enemy had been at hand, and the guns went off apace. I manifested some great trouble, and asked them what was the matter. I told them I thought they had killed the Englishman; (for they had in the mean time told me that an Englishman had come;) they said, *No, they shot over his horse, and under, and before his horse, and they pushed him this way and that way, at their pleasure,* SHOWING HIM WHAT THEY COULD DO."§

They would not at first suffer her to see Mr. *Hoar*, but when they had gratified their tantalizing whim sufficiently, she was permitted to see him. He brought her a pound of tobacco, which *she sold for nine shillings*. "The next morning, Mr. *Hoar* invited the saggamores to dinner; but when we went to get it ready, we found they had stolen the greatest part of the provisions Mr. *Hoar* had brought. And we may see the wonderful power of God, in that one passage, in that, when there was such a number of them together, and so greedy of a little good food, and no English there but Mr. *Hoar* and myself, that there they did not knock us on the head, and take what we had; there being not only some provision, but also trading cloth, a part of the 20 pounds agreed upon: But instead of doing us any mischief, they seemed to be ashamed of the fact, and said it was the *matchit* [bad] Indians that did it."||

It is now certain that this negotiation was the immediate cause of their final overthrow. For before this time the Pokanokets and Narragansets went hand in hand against their common enemy, and they were the most powerful tribes. This parleying with the English was so detestable to *Philip,* that a separation took place among these tribes in consequence, and he and the Narragansets separated themselves from the Nipmuks, and other inland tribes, and went off to their own country. This was the reason they were so easily subdued after this took place.

It was through *Nepanet's* means that a party of English, under Capt. *Henchman,* were enabled to surprise a body of his countrymen at Weshakom¶ Ponds near Lancaster, in May, 1676. Following in a track pointed

---

* Narrative, 64, 65. † Manuscripts of Rev. *J. Cotton.*
‡ Narrative, *ut supra*, 65. § Ibid. 71, 72. || Ibid. 72, 73.
¶ *Roger Williams* sets down sea as the definition of *Wechêcum.*

out by *Nepanet*, the Indians were fallen upon while fishing, and, being entirely unprepared, seven were killed, and 29 taken, chiefly women and children.

Peter-ephraim and *Andrew-pityme* were also two other considerably distinguished Nipmuk Indians. They rendered much service to the English in *Philip's* war. They went out in January, 1676, and brought in many of the Nipnets, who had endeavored to shelter themselves under *Uncas*. But, Mr. *Hubbard* observes, that *Uncas*, having "shabbed" them off, "they were, in the beginning of the winter, [1676,] brought in to Boston, many of them, by *Peter-ephraim* and *Andrew-pityme*." *Ephraim* commanded an Indian company, and had a commission from government. The news that many of the enemy were doing mischief about Rehoboth caused a party of English of Medfield to march out to their relief; *Ephraim* went with them, with his company, which consisted of 29. The snow being deep, the English soon grew discouraged, and returned, but Capt. *Ephraim* continued the march, and came upon a body of them, encamped, in the night. Early the next morning, he successfully surrounded them, and offered them quarter. "Eight resolute fellows refused, who were presently shot:" the others yielded, and were brought in, being in number 42. Other minor exploits of this Indian captain are recorded.

Thomas Quanapohit, called also *Rumney-marsh*, was a brother of *James*, and was also a Christian Indian. In the beginning of hostilities against *Philip*, Major *Gookin* received orders to raise a company of praying Indians to be employed against him. This company was immediately raised, and consisted of 52 men, who were conducted to Mount Hope by Capt. *Isaac Johnson*. *Quanapohit* was one of these. The officers under whom they served testified to their credit as faithful soldiers; yet many of the army, officers and men, tried all in their power to bring them into disrepute with the country. Such proceedings, we should naturally conclude, would tend much to dishearten those friendly Indians; but, on the contrary, they used every exertion to win the affections of their oppressors. *Quanapohit*, with the other two, received from government a reward for the scalps which they brought in. Though not exactly in order, yet it must be mentioned, that when *Thomas* was out, at or near Swansey, in the beginning of the war, he by accident had one of his hands shot off. He was one of the troopers, and carried a gun of remarkable length. The weather being excessively hot, his horse was very uneasy, being disturbed by flies, and struck the lock of the gun as the breech rested upon the ground, and caused it to go off, which horribly mangled the hand that held it; and, notwithstanding it was a long time in getting well, yet he rendered great service in the war afterward. The account of one signal exploit, having been preserved, shall here be related. While Capt. *Henchman* was in the enemy's country, he made an excursion from Hassanamesit to Packachoog, which lies about ten miles north-west from it. Meeting here with no enemy, he marched again for Hassanamesit; and having got a few miles on his way, discovered that he had lost a tin case, which contained his commission, and other instructions. He therefore despatched *Thomas* and two Englishmen in search of it. They made no discovery of the lost article until they came in sight of an old wigwam at Pachachoog, where, to their no small surprise, they discovered some of the enemy in possession of it. They were but a few rods from them, and being so few in number, that to have given them battle would have been desperate in the extreme, as neither of them was armed for such an occasion; stratagem, therefore, could only save them. The wigwam was situated upon an eminence; and some were standing in the door when they approached, who discovered them as soon as they came in sight. One presented his gun, but, the weather being stormy, it did not go off. At this moment our chief, looking back, called, and made many gestures, as though he were disposing of a large force to encompass them. At this manœuvre they all fled, being six in number, leaving our heroes to pursue their object. Thus their preservation was due to *Quanapohit*; and is the more to be admired, as they were in so far destitute of the means of defence. Capt. *Quanapohit* had but a pistol, and one of his men a gun without a flint, and the other no gun at all.*

CHAPTER VII.

*Of the Indians in New Hampshire and Maine previous to their wars with the whites—Dominions of the bashaba—Perishes in war—*PASSACONAWAY*—His dominions—His last speech to his people—His life—His daughter marries Winnapurket—Petitions the court of Massachusetts—Lands allotted to him—English send a force to disarm him—Their fears of his enmity unfounded—They seize and ill treat his son—He escapes—Passaconaway delivers his arms, and makes peace with the English—Traditions concerning—Life of* WANNALANCET*—His situation in Philip's war—Messengers and letters sent him by the English—Leaves his residence—His humanity—Fate of* JOSIAH NOUEL*—Wannalancet returns to his country—His lands seized in his absence—He again retires into the wilderness—Mosely destroys his village, &c.—Imprisoned for debt—Favors Christianity—A speech—*WEHANOWNOWIT, *sachem of New* Hampshire—ROBINHOOD—*His sales of land in Maine*—MONQUINE—KENNEBIS— ASSIMINASQUA — ABBIGADASSET— *Their residences and sales of land—Melancholy fate of* CHOCORUA.

SOME knowledge of the Indians eastward of the Massachusetts was very early obtained by Captain *John Smith*, which, however, was very general; as that they were divided into several tribes, each of which had their own sachem, or, as these more northern Indians pronounced that word, *sachemo*, which the English understood *sagamore*; and yet all the sachemos acknowledged subjection to one still greater, which they called *bashaba*.

Of the dominions of the bashaba, writers differ much in respect to their extent. Some suppose that his authority did not extend this side the Pascataqua, but it is evident that it did, from Captain *Smith's* account.† Wars and pestilence had greatly wasted the eastern Indians but a short time before the English settled in the country, and it was then difficult to determine the relation the tribes had stood in one to the other. As to the bashaba of Penobscot, tradition states that he was killed by the Tarratines, who lived still farther east, in a war which was at its height in 1615.

Passaconaway seems to have been a bashaba. He lived upon the

* *Gookin's* MS. Hist. Praying Indians.

† "The principal habitations I saw at northward, was Penobscot, who are in wars with the Terentines, their next northerly neighbors. Southerly up the rivers, and along the coast, we found Mecadacut, Segocket, Pemmaquid, Nusconcus, Sagadahock, Satquin, Aumaughcawgen and Kenabeca. To those belong the countries and people of Segotago, Pauhunlanuck, Pocopassum, Taughtanakagnet, Wabigganus, Nassaque, Masherosqueck, Wawrigwick, Moshoquen, Waccogo, Pasharanack, &c. To those are allied in confederacy, the countries of Aucocisco, Accominticus, Passataquak, Augawoam and Naemkeek, all these, for any thing I could perceive, differ little in language or any thing; though most of them be sagamos and lords of themselves, yet they hold the bashabes of Penobscot the chief and greatest amongst them." 3 *Col. Mass. Hist. Soc.* iii. 21, 22.

Merrimack River, at a place called *Pennakook*, and his dominions, at the period of the English settlements, were very extensive, even over the sachems living upon the Pascataqua and its branches. The Abenaques inhabited between the Pascataqua and Penobscot, and the residence of the chief sachem was upon Indian Island.* *Fluellen* and Captain *Sunday* were early known as chiefs among the Abenaques, and *Squando* at a later period; but of these we shall be more particular hereafter: the first sachem we should notice is *Passaconaway*. He "lived to a very great age; for," says my manuscript, "I saw him alive at Pawtucket, when he was about a hundred and twenty years old."† Before his death, he delivered the following speech to his children and friends: "*I am now going the way of all flesh, or ready to die, and not likely to see you ever meet together any more. I will now leave this word of counsel with you, that you may take heed how you quarrel with the English, for though you may do them much mischief, yet assuredly you will all be destroyed, and rooted off the earth if you do; for, I was as much an enemy to the English, at their first coming into these parts, as any one whatsoever, and did try all ways and means possible, to have destroyed them, at least to have prevented them settling down here, but I could no way effect it; therefore, I advise you never to contend with the English, nor make war with them.*" And Mr. *Hubbard* adds, "it is to be noted that this *Passaconawa* was the most noted powow and sorcerer of all the country."

A story of the marriage of a daughter of *Passaconaway*, in 1662, is thus related. *Winnepurket*, commonly called *George*, sachem of Saugus, made known to the chief of Pennakook, that he desired to marry his daughter, which, being agreeable to all parties, was soon consummated, at the residence of *Passaconaway*, and the hilarity was closed with a great feast. According to the usages of the chiefs, *Passaconaway* ordered a select number of his men to accompany the new-married couple to the dwelling of the husband. When they had arrived there, several days of feasting followed, for the entertainment of his friends, who could not be present at the consummation at the bride's father's, as well as for the escort; who, when this was ended, returned to Pennakook.

Some time after, the wife of *Winnepurket*, expressing a desire to visit her father's house and friends, was permitted to go, and a choice company conducted her. When she wished to return to her husband, her father, instead of conveying her as before, sent to the young sachem to come and take her away. He took this in high dudgeon, and sent his father-in-law this answer: "When she departed from me, I caused my men to escort her to your dwelling, as became a chief. She now having an intention to return to me, I did expect the same." The elder sachem was now in his turn angry, and returned an answer which only increased the difference; and it is believed that thus terminated the connection of the new husband and wife.‡

This same year, [1662,] we find the general court acting upon a petition of *Passaconaway*, or, as his name is spelt in the records themselves, *Papisseconeway*. The petition we have not met with, but from the answer given to it, we learn its nature. The court say: "In answer to the petition of *Papisseconeway*, this court judgeth it meete to graunt to

---

* *Williamson's* Hist. Maine, ii. 4.

† *Gookin's Hist. Praying Indians.* This history was drawn up during the year 1677, and how long before this the author saw him, is unknown; but there can be no doubt but he was dead some years before *Philip's* war. Nevertheless, with Mr. *Hubbard* and our text before him, the author of *Tales of the Indians* has made *Passaconaway* appear in the person of *Aspinquid*, in 1682, at Agamentacus in Maine.

‡ Deduced from facts in *Morton's N. Canaan.*

the said *Papisseconeway* and his men or associates about Naticot,* above Mr. *Brenton's* lands, where it is free, a mile and a half on either side Merremack Riuer in breadth, three miles on either side in length: provided he nor they do not alienate any part of this grant without leave and license from this court, first obtained."

Gov. *Winthrop* mentions this chief as early as 1632. One of his men, having gone with a white man into the country to trade, was killed by another Indian "dwelling near the Mohawks country, who fled away with his goods;" but it seems from the same account, that *Passaconaway* pursued and took the murderer. In 1642, there was great alarm throughout the English settlements from the belief that all the Indians in the country were about to make a general massacre of the whites. The government of Massachusetts took prompt measures "to strike a terror into the Indians." They therefore "sent men to *Cutshamekin,* at Braintree, to fetch him and his guns, bows, &c., which was done; and he came willingly: And being late in the night when they came to Boston, he was put into the prison; but the next morning, finding, upon examination of him and divers of his men, no ground of suspicion of his partaking in any such conspiracy, he was dismissed. Upon the warrant which went to Ipswich, Rowley and Newbury, to disarm *Passaconamy*, who lived by Merrimack, they sent forth 40 men armed the next day." These English were hindered from visiting the wigwam of *Passaconaway,* by rainy weather, "but they came to his son's and took him." This son we presume was *Wannalancet.* This they had orders to do; but for taking a squaw and her child, they had none, and were ordered to send them back again immediately. Fearing *Wannalancet's* escape, they "led him in a line, but he taking an opportunity, slipped his line and escaped from them, but one very indiscreetly made a shot at him, and missed him narrowly." These were called, then, "unwarranted proceedings," as we should say they very well might have been. The English now had some actual reason to fear that *Passaconaway* would resent this outrage, and therefore "sent *Cutshamekin* to him to let him know that what was done to his son and squaw was without order," and to invite him to a parley at Boston; also, "to show him the occasion whereupon we had sent to disarm all the Indians, and that when we should find that they were innocent of any such conspiracy, we would restore all their arms again." *Passaconaway* said when he should have his son and squaw returned safe, he would go and speak with them. The squaw was so much frightened, that she ran away into the woods, and was absent ten days. It seems that *Wannalancet* was soon liberated, as he within a short time went to the English, "and delivered up his guns, &c."† These were the circumstances to which *Miantunnomoh* alluded so happily afterwards.

At a court in Massachusetts in 1644, it is said, "*Passaconaway*, the Merrimack sachem, came in and submitted to our government, as *Pumham*, &c. had done before;" and the next year the same entry occurs again, with the addition of his son's submission also, "together with their lands and people."‡

This chief is supposed to have died about the same time with *Massasoit*, a sachem whom in many respects he seems to have much resembled.§

* Another version of *Nahum-keag.* † *Winthrop's Journal.* ‡ Ibid.

§ Among other stanzas in *Farmer* and *Moore's Collections*, the following very happily introduces *Passaconaway*:—

"Once did my throbbing bosom deep receive
The sketch, which one of *Passaconaway* drew.
Well may the muse his memory retrieve
From dark oblivion, and, with pencil true,
Retouch that picture strange, with tints and honors due."

He was often styled *the great sachem*, and, according to Mr. *Hubbard*, was considered a great powow or sorcerer among his people, and his fame in this respect was very extensive; and we know not that there was any thing that they thought him not able to perform: that he could cause a green leaf to grow in winter, trees to dance, and water to burn, seem to have been feats of common notoriety in his time. A sachem of nearly as much note was his son, already mentioned, named

Wannalancet, or *Wonolancet*, who, in obedience to the advice of his father, always kept peace with the English. He resided at an ancient seat of the sagamores, upon the Merrimack, called at that time *Naamkeke*, but from whence he withdrew, about six weeks before the war with *Philip*. Fearing that his movements might be hostile, the council of Massachusetts, in Sept. 1675, ordered that Lieut. *Thomas Henchman* of Chelmsford should send some messengers to find him, and persuade him of their friendship, and urge his return to his place of residence. With this order a letter was sent to Wannalancet at the same time, and are as follows: "It is ordered by the council that Lieut. *Thos. Henchman* do forthwith endeavor to procure by hire, one or two suitable Indians of Wamesit, to travel and seek to find out and speak with *Wannalancet* the sachem, and carry with them a writing from the council, being a safe conduct unto the said sachem, or any other principal men belonging to Natahook, Penagooge, or other people of those northern Indians, giving (not exceeding six persons) free liberty to come into the house of the said *Henchman*, where the council will appoint Capt. *Gookin* and Mr. *Eliot* to treat with them about terms of amity and peace between them and the English; and in case agreements and conclusions be not made to mutual satisfaction, then the said sachem and all others that accompany him shall have free liberty to return back again; and this offer the council are induced to make, because the said *Wannalancet* sachem, as they are informed, hath declared himself that the English never did any wrong to him, or his father *Passaconaway*, but always lived in amity, and that his father charged him so to do, and that said *Wannalancet* will not begin to do any wrong to the English." The following is the letter to *Wannalancet*:—

"This our writing or safe conduct doth declare, that the governor and council of Massachusetts do give you and every of you, provided you exceed not six persons, free liberty of coming unto and returning in safety from the house of Lieut. *T. Henchman* at Naamkeake, and there to treat with Capt. *Daniel Gookin* and Mr. *John Eliot*, whom you know, and [whom] we will fully empower to treat and conclude with you, upon such meet terms and articles of friendship, amity and subjection, as were formerly made and concluded between the English and old *Passaconaway*, your father, and his sons and people; and for this end we have sent these messengers [*blank in the MS.*] to convey these unto you, and to bring your answer, whom we desire you to treat kindly, and speedily to despatch them back to us with your answer. Dated in Boston, 1 Oct. 1675. Signed by order of the council. *John Leverett*, Govr.

Edwd. Rawson, Secr."

On the 3 May, 1676, *Thomas Kimbal* of Bradford was killed, and his wife and five children carried into the wilderness. From the circumstance that *Wannalancet* caused them to be sent home to their friends again, it would seem that they were taken by some of the enemy within his sachemdom, or by some over whom he had some control. From a manuscript written about the time,* we are able to make the following

* By Rev. *T. Cobbet* of Ipswich.

extract, which goes to show that *Wannalancet* was ever the friend of the English, and also his disposition to humane actions. Mr. *Cobbet* says, "though she, [Mrs. *Kimbal*,] and her sucking child were twice condemned by the Indians, and the fires ready made to burn them, yet, both times, saved by the request of one of their own grandees; and afterwards by the intercession of the sachem of Pennicook, stirred up thereunto by Major *Waldron*, was she and her five children, together with *Phillip Eastman* of Haverhill, taken captive when she and her children were, set at liberty, without ransom."

At the time *Wannalancet* forsook his residence, as we have just mentioned, several of the praying Indians, to avoid the war, went off with him, and when he delivered himself up afterwards to Maj. *Waldron*, they accompanied him, and delivered themselves up also. Some of these suffered capital punishment at Boston, and, it is to be feared, for charges which had no foundation in truth against them.

About the 19 Sept. 1676, the Indians fell upon Hatfield, burnt several houses and barns without the line of the town, wounded and killed about 12 persons, and carried off about 20 more into captivity. Most of the latter were women and children. This attack was supposed by some, at first, to have been made by a party of Mohawks, because it took place the next day after some of that nation had passed through the place with some Christian Indian prisoners, women and children, and a scalp, which it was afterwards found had been taken from the head of an Indian called *Josiah Nouel*, near Sudbury.* But it was found out soon after, by a white that escaped from his captivity, that the company of Indians that attacked Hatfield consisted of 23 men and four women, who were of the common enemy, but had for some time before been among the French about Quebeck, and that a second party, who just before separated from these, went towards the east, to fall upon some of the settlements upon the Merrimack. It appears that the fair promises of the English had before this induced the return of *Wannalancet* to Naamkeke, but who, finding that some lawless whites had, during his absence, taken possession of his grounds and planting, and consequently his chief means of subsistence were cut off, did, upon being visited by this party of the enemy, go off with them; but what was most astonishing in this affair, no mischief of any kind was committed at their going off, although it was in their power to have done the English great damage. All the whites attributed their escape to the influence of *Wannalancet*, to whom, no doubt, the credit was justly due.

Here, then, opens a fair field of reflection, in which "poor human nature," in her spontaneous growth and wild retreat, will be seen to flourish and bring forth fruits no less to be admired than any ever found in the cultivated garden of civilization.

We have still to relate another circumstance, which redounds as much to the honor and humanity of this sachem as any we have related. Some time after the letter had been sent to him, "there was a company of soldiers, about 100, sent under Capt. *Mosely*, to Pennagog, where it was reported there was a body of Indians; but it was a mistake, for there were not above 100 in all of the Pennagoog and Namkig Indians, whereof *Wannalancet* was chief. When the English drew nigh, whereof he had intelligence by scouts, they left their fort, and withdrew into the woods and swamps, where they had advantage and opportunity enough in ambushment to have slain many of the English soldiers, without any

* Nouel and *James Speen* were brothers-in-law. By his death four small children were left fatherless. He and *Speen* had been together but half an hour before, and by appointment were to have met again, but when Speen came to the place, he could find nothing of his friend.

great hazard to themselves; and several of the young Indians inclined to it. But the sachem *Wannalancet*, by his authority and wisdom restrained his men, and suffered not an Indian to appear or shoot a gun. They were very near the English, and yet, though they were provoked by the English, who burnt their wigwams, and destroyed some dried fish, yet not one gun was shot at any Englishman."* The facts in this affair were related by *Wannalancet* himself, and several of his men, after their return.

No mischief appears to have been done at the time that *Wannalancet* went away, and it is reasonable to suppose that he prevented the enemy with whom he went from doing any. Although he might not have been in any fear from the English, yet there were various causes, either of which were sufficient to induce him to leave this part of the country. A son of his lived with the French, or near them, in Canada, and many of his friends, and other relatives. While he withdrew from his place of residence, as has been mentioned, the English had taken possession of his planting ground, and so deprived him of means of living there.

He had acknowledged a belief in Christianity, and this was laid hold of by many to reproach the advocates of Christianizing the Indians.

In 1659, *Wannalansit* was thrown into prison for a debt of about £45. His people, who owned an island in Merrimack River, three miles above Pawtuckett Falls, containing 60 acres, half of which was under cultivation, relinquished it, to obtain his release. About 1670, he removed to Pawtuckett Falls, where, upon an eminence, he built a fort, and resided until *Philip's* war. He was about 55 years of age in 1674; always friendly to the English, but unwilling to be importuned about adopting their religion. When he had got to be very old, however, he submitted to their desires in that respect. Upon that occasion he is reported to have said, "*I must acknowledge I have all my days been used to pass in an old canoe, and now you exhort me to change and leave my old canoe, and embark in a new one, to which I have hitherto been unwilling, but now I yield up myself to your advice, and enter into a new canoe, and do engage to pray to God hereafter.*" After the war, *Wannalansit* went to the Rev. Mr. *Fisk* of Chelmsford, and inquired of him after the welfare of his former acquaintances, and whether the place had suffered much during the war. Mr. *Fisk* said they had been highly favored, and for which he thanked God. "Me next," said *Wannalanset*. This showed his consciousness of the great influence he had had in warding destruction from them.†

Rev[d]. *John Eliot* thus writes to the Hon. *Robert Boyle*‡ in England, in 1677:—"We had a sachem of the greatest blood in the country submitted to pray to God, a little before the wars: his name is *Wanalauncet*: in the time of the wars he fled, by reason of the wicked actings of some English youth, who causelessly and basely killed and wounded some of them. He was persuaded to come in again. But the English having plowed and sown with rye all their lands, they had but little corn to subsist by. A party of French Indians, (of whom some were of the kindred of this sachem's wife,) very lately fell upon this people, being but few and unarmed, and partly by persuasion, partly by force, carried them away. One, with his wife, child and kinswoman, who were of our praying Indians, made their escape, came in to the English, and discovered what was done. These things keep some in a continual disgust and jealousy of all the Indians."§

---

* *Gookin's* MS. Hist. † *Allen's* Hist. Chelmsford, 155, 159.

‡ For many years at the head of the Society for propagating the Gospel among the Indians. He was a great benefactor of N. England, and one of the founders of the Royal Society of London. He was by birth an Irishman, but settled finally at Oxford, Eng. He died in London, 1691, aged 64 years.

§ 1 *Col. Mass. Hist. Soc.* iii. 179.

It may be proper to add a word upon the name of the place which we have often mentioned in this life, as the same word, differently pronounced, was applied to a great many places by the Indians, and is the same word which Dr. *I. Mather* and some others made many believe was made up of two Hebrew words, to prove that the Indians were really the descendants of the dispersed Jews; but for which purpose, if we are not misinformed, any other Indian word would answer the same purpose. The doctor writes the name *Nahumkeik*, and adds that *Nahum* signifies *consolation*, and *keik* a *bosom*, or *heaven*; and hence the settlers of places bearing this name were seated in the bosom of consolation.* He points out this etymological analogy in speaking of the settlement of Salem, which was called by the Indians *Naumkeag, Namkeg, Naamhok, Naumkuk*, or something *a little* somewhat like it. A *sad bosome of consolation* did it prove in the days of *Tituba*, and even in Dr. *Mather's* own days. Though a digression, we shall, I doubt not, be pardoned for inserting here Dr. *C. Mather's* account of a curiosity at Amoskeag Falls, which he gave in a letter to London, and which afterwards appeared in the Philosophical Transactions:† "At a place called Amnuskeag, a little above the hideous‡ falls of Merimack River, there is a huge rock in the midst of the stream, on the top of which are a great number of pits, made exactly round, like barrels or hogsheads of different capacities, some so large as to hold several tuns. The natives know nothing of the time they were made; but the neighboring Indians have been wont to hide their provisions in them, in their wars with the Maquas; affirming, God had cut them out for that use for them. They seem plainly to be artificial." It could certainly have required no great sagacity to have supposed that one stone placed upon another in the water, so as to have been constantly rolled from side to side by the current, would, in time, occasion such cavities. One quite as remarkable we have seen near the source of this river, in its descent from the Franconia Mountains; also upon the Mohawk, a short distance below Little Falls. They may be seen as you pass upon the canal.

Early purchases of lands bring to our notice a host of Indians, many of whom, though sachems, but for such circumstances of trade, would never have come to our knowledge. There are some, however, of whom we shall in this chapter take notice, as such notices assist in enabling us to judge how the natives regarded their lands, and the territories of their neighboring countrymen.

Wehanownowit was a New Hampshire sachem, whose name has been considerably handled within a few years, from its being found to the much-talked-of deed conveying lands in New Hampshire to the Rev. *John Wheelwright*, and others, 3 April, 1638. If *Wehanownowit* were sachem of the tract said to have been by him conveyed, his "kingdom" was larger than some can boast of at this day who call themselves kings. It was to contain 30 miles square, and its boundaries were thus described: "lying and situate within three miles on the northerne side of y[e] River Meremoke, extending thirty miles along by the river from the sea side, and from the sayd river side to Pisscataqua Patents, 30 miles up into the countrey northwest, and so from the falls of Piscataqua to Oyster River, 30 miles square

---

* *Relation of the Troubles*, &c. 20. Dr. Increase Mather was the author of a great many works, chiefly sermons, many of which have become curious for their singularity, and some others valuable for the facts they contain. His sermons, like many others of that day, had very little meaning in them, and consequently are now forgotten. He was son of *Richard Mather*, preached in Boston above 60 years, died in 1723, aged 84 years. See *his life*, by his son, Dr. *Cotton Mather*, who was born 12 Feb. 1662—3, died 13 Feb. 1727—8, aged 65. See his life by *Samuel Mather*.

† Published in vol. v. of Jones's Abridgment, part ii. 164.

‡ We cannot say what they were in those days, but should expect to be laughed at if we should call them *hideous* at the present time.

every way." This deed has been shown to be a forgery. The original is in possession of Mr. *John Farmer*, of Concord, N. H.*

Tummadockyou was a son of *Wehanownowit*, and his name is also to the deed above mentioned; and another Indian, belonging to that tract of country, named *Watchenowet*: these both relinquished their title to, or concurred in the sale of said tract.

Robinhood† was the father of a more noted chief, whose Indian name was *Wohawa*, but commonly known among the English as *Hopehood*. His territories, as will appear, were upon the Kennebeck River in the first settlement of N. England.

Our first notice of *Robinhood* runs as follows: "Be it known"—"that I, *Ramegin*,‡ soe called by my Indian name, or *Robinhood*, soe called by English name, sagamore of Negusset, [or Neguasseag,] doe freely sell vnto *James Smith*,"—"part of my land, beginning att Merry-meeting Cove, and soe downward the maine riuer vnto a rocke, called *Winslowe's Rocke*, in the longe reach, and in breadth eastward ouer the little riuer, runinge through the great mersh, with the priuilidges [reserved to me] as hunting, fowlinge, fishing, and other games." *Smith* was to pay him or his heirs, on the 1 Nov. annually, "one peck of Indian corn." This deed bears date 8 May, 1648, and is signed and witnessed as follows:—§

NEGWINIS *his* ⊤ *mark.*	ROBINHOOD *his mark.*
SONGREEHOOD *his* ⊢ *mark*	MR. THOMAS △ *his mark.*
and two English.	PEWAZEGSAKE *his mark.*
	The mark of ROBIN.

The next year, 1649, he sold the island of Jeremysquam, on the east side of the Kennebeck, and in 1654 we find him selling his place of residence, which was in what is now Woolwich, to *Edward Bateman* and *John Brown*. In 1663, *Robinhood* is mentioned as one of the principal chiefs among the eastern Indians.||

In 1667, the inhabitants upon Connecticut River, about Hadley, sustained some injury from Indians, in their lands and domestic animals, and satisfaction therefor was demanded of *Robinhood*; at the same time threatening him with the utmost severity, if the like should be repeated. But whether his people were the perpetrators we are not told; but from the following facts it may be thought otherwise. "To promote amity with them, license was at length given to the traders in fur and in peltries, to sell unto *Indian friends guns and ammunition*."¶ Hence these *friends* could see no reason, afterwards, why arms were prohibited them, as we shall again have occasion to notice.

On the breaking out of *Philip's* war, *Robinhood* was in no wise inclined to join in it, and when a party of English was sent at that time to learn their feelings in that respect, he made a great dance, and by songs and shouts expressed his satisfaction that the English were disposed to maintain peace.

Monquine, "alias *Natahanada*, the son of old *Natawormett*, sagamore of Kennebeck River," sold to *William Bradford* and others, all the land on both sides of said river, "from Cussenocke upwards to Wesserunsicke."

* MS. communication of that gentleman.

† This name was adopted, I have no doubt, as it came something near the sound of his Indian name, as was the case in several instances which we have already recorded: the old English robber of that name, or fables concerning him, are among the first in the nursery. Even at this day, the curious adult will dispense with Mr. *Ritson's* collections of legends concerning him with peculiar regret.

‡ The same, I suppose, called in *Sullivan's* Hist. *Rogomok*.

§ From a *manuscript* copy of the original deed.

|| By *Josselyn*, who visited the country at this time. See his *Voyages*.

¶ *Williamson's Maine*, i. 428, from 3 *Mass. Rec.*

This sale bore date 8 August, 1648. The signature is "*Monquine*, alias *Dumhanada*." Then follows: "We, *Agodoademago*, the sonne of *Wasshemett*, and *Tassucke*, the brother of *Natahanada*, do consent freely unto the sale to *Bradford, Paddy*, and others."*

Kennebis was a sachem from whom it has been supposed that the Kennebeck River derived its name. But whether there were a line of sagamores of this name, from whom the river was so called, or whether sachems were so called from their living at a certain place upon it, is uncertain. It is certain, however, that there was one of this name residing there, contemporaneously with *Robinhood*, who, besides several others, deeded and redeeded the lands up and down in the country. He was sometimes associated in his sales with *Abbigadasset*, and sometimes with others. In 1649, he sold to *Christopher Lawson* all the land on the Kennebeck River up as high as Taconnet falls, now Winslow, which was the residence of the great chief *Essiminasqua*, or *Assiminasqua*, elsewhere mentioned. About the same time, he sold the same tract, or a part of it, to *Spencer* and *Clark*. The residence of *Kennebis* was upon Swan Island, "in a delightful situation, and that of *Abbigadasset* between a river of his name and the Kennebeck, upon the northern borders of Merry-meeting Bay."† Swan Island was purchased of *Abbigadasset* in 1667, by *Humphry Davie*, and afterwards claimed by Sir *John Davy*, a serjeant at law.‡

We shall proceed to notice here one, of another age, whose melancholy fate has long since commanded the attention of writers.

Some time previous to the settlement of Burton, N. H., that is, previous to 1766, there resided in that region a small tribe of Indians, among whom was one named

Chocorua, and he was the last of the primitives of those romantic scenes. This region was attracting to them on account of the beaver which were found in its pellucid waters, and its cragged cliffs afforded safe retreats to a plentiful game. It is handed to us by tradition, that *Chocorua* was the last of this region, and that he was murdered by a miserable white hunter, who, with others of his complexion, had wandered here in quest of game. This solitary man had retired to a neighboring mountain, and was there discovered and shot. The eminence to which it is said this Indian had retired, is the highest mountain in Burton, and commands a beautiful view of a great extent of surrounding country. One of the most superb engravings that has appeared in all our annuals, is that representing *Chocorua* in his last retreat.

It is a fact well known in all the neighboring parts of the country, that cattle cannot long survive in Burton, although there appears abundance of all that is necessary for their support. They lose their appetite, pine and die. It is said that *Chocorua* cursed the English before he expired, and the superstitious, to this day, attribute the disease of cattle to the curse of *Chocorua*. But a much more rational one, we apprehend, will be found in the affection of the waters by minerals.

---

* People of Plimouth.—*William Paddy* died at Boston. His gravestone was dug out of the rubbish under the old state-house in 1830.

† *Williamson*, i. 467.

‡ Ibid. 331.

CHAPTER VIII.

SQUANDO, *sachem of Saco—Attacks the town of Saco—Singular account of him by a cotemporary—The ill treatment of his wife a cause of war—His humanity in restoring a captive*—MADOKA WANDO—*Causes of his hostility*—ASSIMINASQUA —*His speech—Speech of* TARUMKIN—MUGG—*Is carried to Boston to execute a treaty—Is Madokawando's ambassador—Release of Thomas Cobbet—Madokawando's kindness to prisoners*—MOXUS *attacks Wells and is beaten off—Attacked the next year by the Indians under Madokawando and a company of Frenchmen—Are repulsed with great loss—Incidents of the siege—Mons. Casteins—A further account of Moxus*—WANUNGONET— ASSACOMBUIT—*Further account of Mugg—His death*—SYMON, ANDREW, JEOFFREY, PETER and JOSEPH—*Account of their depredations—Life of* KANKAMAGUS—*Treated with neglect—Flies his country—Becomes an enemy—Surprise of Dover and murder of Maj. Waldron*—MASANDOWET — WOROMBO—*His fort captured by Church—Kankamagus's wife and children taken*—HOPEHOOD—*Conspicuous in the massacre at Salmon Falls—His death*—MATTAHANDO— MEGUNNEWAY.

THE first chief which will here be properly noticed is *Squando*, a Tarratine, commonly called sagamore of Saco. He is mentioned with a good deal of singularity by the writers of his times. And we will here, by way of exordium, extract what Mr. *Mather*, in his BRIEF HISTORY, &c., says of him. "After this, [the burning of Casco,] they [the Indians] set upon Saco, where they slew 13 men, and at last burnt the town. A principal actor in the destruction of Saco was a strange *enthusiastical sagamore* called *Squando*, who, some years before, pretended that God appeared to him in the form of a tall man, in black clothes, declaring to him that he was God, and commanded him to leave his drinking of strong liquors, and to pray, and to keep sabbaths, and to go to hear the word preached; all which things the Indian did for some years, with great seeming devotion and conscience, observe. But the God which appeared to him said nothing to him about *Jesus Christ*; and therefore it is not to be marvelled at, that at last he discovered himself to be no otherwise than a child of him that was a murderer and a liar from the beginning." Mr. *Hubbard* says that he was "the chief actor or rather the beginner" of the eastern war of 1675—6; but rather contradicts the statement, as we apprehend, in the same paragraph, by attributing the *same cause* to the "rude and indiscrete act of some English seamen," who either for mischief overset a canoe in which was *Squando's* wife and child, or to see if young Indians could swim naturally like animals of the brute creation, as some had reported.* The child went to the bottom, but was saved from drowning by the mother's diving down and bringing it up, yet "within a while after the said child died." "The said *Squando*, father of the child, hath been so provoked thereat, that he hath ever since set himself to do all the mischief he can to the English." The whites did not believe that the death of the child was owing to its immersion; still we must allow the Indians to know as well as they. When the family of "old Mr. *Wakely*" was murdered, a young woman was carried away captive. *Squando* was the means of her being set at liberty. "She having been carried up and down the country, some hundreds of miles, as far as Narraganset fort, was, this last June, returned back to Major *Waldron's* by one *Squando*, the sagamore of Saco; a strange mixture of

* "They can swim naturally, striking their paws under their throat like a dog, and not spreading their arms as we do." *Josselyn's Voyage* to N. E. 142.

mercy and cruelty!" And the historian of Maine observes, that his "conduct exhibited at different times such traits of cruelty and compassion, as rendered his character difficult to be portrayed."

He was a great powwow, and acted in concert with *Madokawando*. These two chiefs "are said to be, by them that know them, a strange kind of moralized savages; grave and serious in their speech and carriage, and not without some show of a kind of religion, which no doubt but they have learned from the prince of darkness." In another place, Mr. *Hubbard* calls him an "enthusiastical, or rather diabolical miscreant." His abilities in war gained him this epithet.

Madokawando, of whom we have just made mention, was chief of the Penobscot tribe. He was the adopted son of a chief by the name of *Assiminasqua*. Some mischief had been done by the Androscoggin Indians in *Philip's* war, and the English, following the example of those whom they so much reprobated, retaliated on any Indians that fell in their way. *Madokawando* was not an enemy, nor do we learn that his people had committed any depredations, until after some English spoiled his corn, and otherwise did him damage.

Many of the eastern Indians had been kidnapped and sold for slaves, about the time *Philip's* war commenced. This, it will not be questioned, was enough to cause a war, without *Philip's* instigation, or the affront offered to the wife and child of *Squando*.

The English had prohibited the sale of arms and ammunition to the eastern Indians, as they had before to the western, as a means of lessening their power; provided they should declare themselves hostile: thus regarding their own safety, and totally disregarding whatever evils might accrue from the measure to the Indians. Knowing enough had been done to excite their resentment, agents were sent to parley with them, in the spring and summer of 1676, to hinder, if possible, their taking offence at these proceedings.

Meanwhile the Indians had complained to some friendly English of the outrage upon their friends, who were unacquainted with the circumstance, and hardly believed it; still, told the Indians, that if it were so, those kidnapped should be restored, and the perpetrators punished. But knowing the circumstance to be as they had represented, it is rather marvellous, that *Indians*, instead of at once retaliating, should hearken to unsatisfactory parleyings, as will appear.

When the English agents went to treat with them, or rather to excuse themselves for what they could not, or pretended they could not, amend, the Indians, in the course of the interview, said, "*We were driven from our corn last year by the people about Kennebeck, and many of us died. We had no powder and shot to kill venison and fowl with to prevent it. If you English were our friends, as you pretend you are, you would not suffer us to starve as we did.*"

"However, says Mr. *Hubbard*, the said agent, *making the best he could of a bad cause*, used all means to *pacify the complainants*." The great "*all means*" was, that they should try to get the Androscoggin Indians to *come and hold a treaty*! so that if the English could effect a treaty with them, then there would be a general peace with the eastern Indians. This talk, it was said, they received with joy. "Yet, adds the same author, still by one fatal accident or other, jealousies still seemed to increase in their minds, or else the former injuries began to boil afresh in their spirits, as not being easily digested," &c.

A meeting had been agreed upon at Totononnock, or Taconnet, and immediately after the meeting just mentioned a runner was sent down from thence, with word that *Squando* would be there with "divers Amonoscoggan sachems," *Mugg* being a messenger to him. Accordingly the English proceeded to Taconnet. On their arrival, they were honored with a salute, and conducted into the council house, where they found *Madokawando, Assiminasqua, Tarumkin, Hopehood, Mugg*, and many attendants. *Madokawando* was prime negotiator, and *Assiminasqua* chief speaker, who soon after proceeded to make a speech, and among other things said,—

"*It is not our custom when messengers come to treat of peace, to seize upon their persons, as sometimes the Mohawks do; yea, as the* English have done, *seizing upon fourteen Indians, our men, who went to treat with you—setting a guard over them, and taking away their guns. This is not all, but a second time you required our guns, and demanded us to come down unto you, or else you would kill us. This was the cause of our leaving both our fort and our corn, to our great loss.*"

This speech caused considerable embarrassment to the English, "yet to put the best construction might be, on such irregular actions, which could not well be justified, they told them, the persons who had so done* were not within the limits of their government, and therefore, though they could not call them to an account for so acting, yet they did utterly disallow thereof."† And to be as expeditious as possible, the English commissioners told these chiefs that they came to treat with the Androscoggins, and were sorry that *Squando* was not there. And it appears that, though the English reported a peace with the Penobscots, yet *Madokawando* and his coadjutors scarcely understood as much; and it is also evident that the business was hurried over as fast as possible by the English commissioners.

What had been said by Assiminasqua in the morning was merely preliminary, and it was his intention in the afternoon to enter more particularly into details; but the English cut the matter short, and proceeded to treat with such of the Androscoggins as were present. *Tarumkin* was their orator, and he spoke to this effect:—

"*I have been to the westward, where I have found many Indians unwilling to make peace; but for my own part, I am willing,*" which he confirmed by taking the English by the hand, as did seven or eight of his men, among whom were *Mugg* and *Robinhood's* son. The English had now, as they supposed, got matters into a regular train; but *Madokawando*, it appears, was not willing to leave things in quite so loose a manner, as it regarded his people. He therefore interrupted:—

"*What are we to do for powder and shot, when our corn is consumed? what shall we do for a winter's supply? Must we perish, or must we abandon our country, and fly to the French for protection?*"

The English replied that they would do what they could with the governor; "*some might be allowed them for necessity.*" *Madokawando* added: "*We have waited a great while already, and now we expect you will say yes or no.*" The English rejoined: "You say yourselves that many of the western Indians would not have peace, and, therefore, if we sell you powder, and you give it to the western men, what do we *but cut our own throats*? It is not in our power *without leave*, if you should wait ten years *more*, to let you have powder."

Here, as might reasonably have been expected, ended the negotiation, and massacres and bloodshed soon after desolated that part of the country.

At the close of the war of 1675 and 6, this sachem's people had among them about 60 English captives. When it was known to him that the English desired to treat about peace, he sent Mugg, one of his chiefs, to Pascataqua, to receive proposals; and, that he might meet with good ac-

* That is, those who had kidnapped their friends.

† *Hubbard*, part ii. 38.

ceptance, sent along with him a captive to his home. Gen. *Gendal*, of Massachusetts, being there, forced *Mugg* on board his vessel, and carried him to Boston, for which treacherous act an excuse was pleaded, that he was not vested with sufficient authority to treat with him. *Madokawando's* ambassador, being now in the power of the English, was obliged to agree to such terms as the English dictated.* It is no wonder, therefore, if the great chief soon appears again their enemy. Still, when *Mugg* was sent home, *Madokawando* agreed to the treaty, more readily, perhaps, as two armed vessels of the English conveyed him.

A son of Rev. *Thomas Cobbet* had been taken, and was among the Indians at Mount Desert. It so happened that his master had at that time sent him down to *Castein's* trading-house, to buy powder for him. *Mugg* took him by the hand, and told him he had been at his father's house, and had promised to send him home. *Madokawando* demanded a ransom, probably to satisfy the owner of the captive, "fearing to be killed by him, if he yielded him up without he were there to consent; for he was, he said, a desperate man, if crossed, and had *crambd*† two or three in that way." Being on board one of the vessels, and treated to some liquor, "he walked awhile to and again on the deck, and on a sudden made a stand, and said to Captain *Moore*, 'Well captain, since it is so, take this man: I freely give him up to you; carry him home to his friends.' "‡ A red coat was given to *Madokawando*, which gave him great satisfaction.

The historians of the war have all observed that the prisoners under *Madokawando* were remarkably well treated.

In February, 1677, Major *Waldron*, and Captain *Frost*, with a body of men, were sent into the eastern coast to observe the motions of the Indians, who still remained hostile. At Pemmaquid they were invited on shore to hold a treaty, but the English finding some weapons concealed among them, thought it a sufficient umbrage to treat them as enemies, and a considerable fight ensued, in which many of the Indians were killed, and several taken prisoners; among whom was a sister of *Madokawando*. He had no knowledge of the affair, having been gone for several months at a great distance into the country, on a hunting voyage.

We hear no more of *Madokawando*, until 1691. It will be found mentioned in the account of *Egeremet*, that in that year a treaty was made with him and other eastern chiefs. This was in November, and it was agreed by them, that, on the first of May following, they would deliver all the captives in their possession, at Wells. "But," says Dr. *Mather*,§ "as it was not upon the *firm land*, but in their *canoes* upon the *water*, that they signed and sealed this instrument; so, reader, we will be jealous that it will prove but a fluctuating and unstable sort of business; and that the Indians will *do a lie* as they used to do."

The time for the delivery of the captives having arrived, the English met at Wells to receive them, and to renew their treaty. They took care to be provided with an armed force, and to have the place of meeting at a strong place, which was *Storer's* garrison-house. But, as the author just cited observes, "The Indians being poor *musicians* for *keeping of time*, came not according to their articles." The reason of this we cannot explain, unless the warlike appearance of the English deterred them. After waiting a while, Captain *Converse* surprised some of them, and brought them in by force, and having reason to believe the Indians provoked by this time, immediately added 35 men to their force. These

---

* A treaty was signed 9th of Dec. 1676. Manuscript Nar. of Rev. T. Cobbet. I may be seen in *Hubbard's* Narrative.

† The Indian word for *killed*. *Wood's N. E. Prospect.*

‡ Manuscript Narrative, before cited.

§ Magnalia, ii. 529.

"were not come half an hour to *Storer's* house, on the 9th of June, 1691, nor had they got their *Indian weed* fairly lighted, into their mouths, before fierce *Moxus*, with 200 Indians, made an attack upon the garrison,"* but were repulsed and soon drew off. *Madokawando* was not here in person, but when he knew of the disaster of his chief captain, he said, "*My brother Moxus has missed it now, but I will go myself the next year, and have the dog Converse out of his hole.*"

The old chief was as good as his word, and appeared before the garrison 22 June, 1692. He was joined by *Burniff* and *Labrocre*, two French officers, with a body of their soldiers, and their united strength was estimated at about 500 men. They were so confident of success, that they agreed before the attack, how the prisoners and property should be divided. *Converse* had but 15 men, but fortunately there arrived two sloops with about as many more, and supplies, the day before the battle.

Madokawando's men had unwisely given notice of their approach, by firing upon some cattle they met in the woods, which running in wounded, gave the inhabitants time to fly to the garrison. *Madokawando* was not only seconded by the two French officers and a company of their men, as before observed, but *Moxus, Egeremet* and *Worombo* were also among them.

They began the attack before day, with great fierceness, but after continuing it for some time without success, they fell upon the vessels in the river; and here, although the river was not above twenty or thirty feet broad, yet they met with no better success than at the garrison. They tried many stratagems, and succeeded in setting fire to the sloops several times, by means of fire arrows, but it was extinguished without great damage. Tired of thus exposing themselves and throwing away their ammunition, they returned again to the garrison, resolving to practise a stratagem upon that, and thus ended the first day of the attack. They tried to persuade the English to surrender, but finding they could not prevail, made several desperate charges, in which they lost many. Beginning now to grow discouraged, they sent a flag to the garrison to effect a capitulation, but *Converse,* being a man of great resolution, replied, "that he wanted nothing but men to come and fight him." To which the bearer of the flag said, "*Being you are so stout, why don't you come and fight in the open field like a man, and not fight in a garrison like a squaw.*" This attempt proving ineffectual, they cast out many threats, one of which was, "We will cut you as small as tobacco, before to-morrow morning." The captain ordered them "to come on, for he wanted work."

Having nearly spent their ammunition, and general *Labrocre* being slain, they retired in the night, after two days' siege, leaving several of their dead, among whom was the general just named, who was shot through the head. They took one Englishman, named *John Diamond,* whom they tortured in a most barbarous manner. About the time of their retreating, they fired upon the sloops, and killed the only man lost by the vessels during the assault.

During the attack upon the vessels, among other stratagems, they prepared a breastwork upon wheels, and endeavored to bring it close to the edge of the river, which was within, perhaps, ten feet of them. When they had got it pretty near, one wheel sunk in the ground, and a French soldier, endeavoring to lift it out with his shoulder, was shot down; a second was also killed in the same attempt, and it was abandoned. They also built a raft in the creek above them, and placed on it an immense pile of combustibles, and, setting them on fire, floated it down

* Magnalia, ii. 529.

towards them. But when within a few rods of the sloops, the wind drove it on shore, and thus they were delivered from the most dangerous artifice of the whole. For it was said that, had it come down against them, they could not have saved themselves from the fury of its flames.

Madokawando lived several years after this, and is supposed to have died about 1698.

A daughter of his married the Baron *De Casteins*, by whom he had several children.*

Some have endeavored to ground an argument upon the similarity of the name of this chief to that of *Madock* the Welshman, that the eastern Indians were descended from a Welsh colony, who, in 1170, left that country, and were never heard of after. The *story* of some white Indians speaking Welsh, on the Missouri River, has gained supporters in former and latter periods.†

Moxus, or, as he was sometimes called, *Agamagus*, was also a noted Penobscot chief, and one of *Madokawando's* principal captains. We can add little concerning him, to what has already been said above. After that great sachem was dead, and the war between the French and English nations ceased, the eastern chiefs were ready to submit to terms. *Moxus* seems the successor of *Madokawando*, and when delegates were sent into the eastern country to make peace with the Indians, in 1699, his name stood first among the signers of the treaty.‡ He concluded another treaty with Gov. *Dudley*, in 1702. The next year, in company with *Wanungonet, Assacombuit*, and a number of French, he invested Captain

---

* A good deal has been said and written about Mons. *Casteins*, but generally without conveying much information. We will give here the original authority whence accounts have chiefly originated:—

"Le Baron de *Saint Casteins*, gentilhomme d'Oleron en Bearn, s'est rendu si re commandable parmi les Abenakis depuis vingt et tant d'années, vivans à la sauvage, qu'ils le regardent aujourd 'hui comme leur Dieu tutelaire. Il étoit autrefois officier de Carignan en Canada, mais dès que ce régiment fut cassé, il se jetta chez ces sauvages dont il avoit apris la langue. Il se maria à leur maniere, préférant les forêts de l'Acadie aux monts Pirenées dont son pa s est environné. Il vécut les premieres années avec eux d'une maniere à s'en faire estimer au-delà de tout ce qu'on peut dire. Ils le firent grand chef, qui est comme le souverain de la nation, et peu-à-peu il a travaillé à se faire une fortune dont tout autre que lui sauroit profiter, en retirant de ce pa s-là plus de deux ou trois cents mille écus qu'il a dans ses coffres en belle monnoie d'or. Cependant il ne s'en sert qu' à acheter des marchandises pour faire des presens à ses confréres les sauvages, qui lui font ensuite, au retour de leurs chasses, des presens de castors d'une triple valeur. Les gouverneurs généreaux de Canada le ménagent, et ceux de la Nouvelle Angleterre le craignent. Il a plusieurs filles et toutes mariées très avantageusement avec des François, aiant donne une riche dot à chacune. Il n' a jamais changé de femme,|| pour aprendre aux sauvages que Dieu n'aime point les hommes inconstans. On dit qu'il tâche de convertir ces pauvres peuples, mais que ses paroles ne produisant aucun fruit, il est done inutile que les Jésuites leur prêchent les véritez du christianisme cependant ces peres ne se rebutent pas, ils estiment que le baptême conféré à un enfant mourant, vaut dix fois la peine et le chagrin d'habiter avec ces peuples." *Memoires de l' Amerique par Lahontan*, ii. 29 and 30.

A son of *Casteins* was a sachem, and held in great esteem by his tribe, and, like his father, was a discreet and upright man. The English treated him very reprehensibly, and once took him prisoner and sent him to Boston, but he was soon released. His father had then retired to his estate in France.

† See Janson's *Stranger in America*, 270. ed. 4to. London, 1807; *Universal Magazine*, vol. xciii. 21; Dr. Southey's *Preface to his Madock*; Bouquet's Exped. *against Ohio Indians*, 69. ed. 4to. London, 1766; Ker's *Travels in America*, 167—172; Burk, *Hist. Virginia*, ii. 84. We may elsewhere devote a chapter to an examination of these accounts.

‡ Magnalia, ii. 543.

|| We do not apprehend that this amounts to a *denial* (as Mr. *Halket* reads it, Notes, 230,) that he had but one wife. His not *changing his wife* might be true also in the plural, if he had had several, as some authors state.

March in the fort at *Casco*. After using every endeavor to take it by assault, they had recourse to the following stratagem. They began at the water's edge to undermine it by digging, but were prevented by the timely arrival of an armed vessel under Captain *Southack*. They had taken a vessel and a great quantity of plunder. About 200 canoes were destroyed, and the vessel retaken. From which circumstance it may be inferred that their number was great.

Moxus was at Casco in 1713, to treat with the English, and at Georgetown, upon Arowsike Island, in 1717. There were seven other chiefs who attended also at the time and place last mentioned.

Mugg was a chief among the Androscoggins, and very conspicuous in the eastern war of 1676–7, into which he seems to have been brought by the same cause as *Madokawando,* already stated. He had been very friendly to the English, and had lived some time with them.

On the 12th Oct. 1676, he made an assault upon Black Point, now in Scarborough, with about 100 warriors. All the inhabitants being gathered into one fortified place upon that point, a few hands might have defended it against all the Indians on that side of the country.* While the captain of the garrison was gone out to hold a talk with *Mugg,* the people fled from the garrison, and took all their effects along with them. A few of his own servants, however, remained, who fell into the hands of the chief, who treated them kindly.

When *Francis Card* was a prisoner among his men, he told him "*that he had found out the way to burn Boston,*" and laughed much about the English, saying he would have all their vessels, fishing islands, and whole country, and bragged much about his great numbers. He was killed at Black Point, the same place where, the year before, he had had such good success, on 16 May. He had besieged the garrison three days, killed three men, and taken one captive. The celebrated *Symon,* who had done so much mischief in many places, was with him here. Lieutenant *Tippin,* who commanded the garrison, "made a successful shot upon an Indian, that was observed to be very busy and bold in the assault, who at that time was deemed to be *Symon,* the arch villain and incendiary of all the eastward Indians, but proved to be one almost as good as himself, who was called *Mogg.*"†

Symon, just named, was a troublesome fellow, who continued to create considerable alarm to the inhabitants upon the Merrimack River, in the vicinity of Newbury and Amesbury, about which part seems to have been his residence, as late as the month of July, 1677. On the 9th of July, six Indians were seen to go into the bushes not far from the garrison at Amesbury; two days before, several men had been killed in the neighborhood, and one woman wounded, whose name was *Quimby.* *Symon* was the alleged leader of the party which committed the depredation. Mrs. *Quimby* was sure that it was he who "knocked her on the head," and she knew many of the names of the rest with him, and named *Andrew, Geoffrey* and *Joseph.* She begged of *Symon* not to kill her. He replied, "*Why, goodwife Quimby, do you think that I will kill you?*" She said she was afraid he would, because he killed all English. *Symon* then said, "I will give quarter to never an English dog of you all," and then gave her a blow on the head, which did not happen to hurt her much; at which, being a woman of great courage, she threw a stone at him; he then turned upon her, and "struck her two more blows," at which she fell, and he left her for dead. Before he gave her the last blows, she called to the garrison for help. He told her she need not do that, for, said he, "I will have that too, by and by." *Symon* was well known to

* Hubbard, *Ind. Wars,* ii. 46.

† *History New England.*

many of the inhabitants, and especially to Mrs. *Quimby*, as he had formerly lived with her father, *William Osgood.** In April, 1677, *Symon* and his companions burnt the house of *Edward Weymouth* at Sturgeon Creek, and plundered the house of one *Crawley*, but did not kill him, because he had shown kindness to *Symon's* grandmother.†

Symon was one of the Christian Indians, as were *Andrew, Jeoffrey, Peter,* and several others of the same company, a circumstance which, with many, much aggravated their offences. The irruption just mentioned is thus related by Mr. *Hubbard*:‡ "*Simon* and *Andrew*, the two brethren in iniquity, with a few more, adventured to come over Pascataqua River on Portsmouth side, when they burnt one house within four or five miles of the town, and took a maid and a young woman captive; one of them having a young child in her arms, with which not willing to be troubled, they gave leave to her that held it, to leave it with an old woman, whom the Indian *Symon* spared, because he said she had been kind to his grandmother; yet one of the two captives escaped from their hands two days after, as did the other, April 22, who gave notice of the Indians, (being not so narrowly looked to as they used to do others.)"

It was on 3 May, 1676, that *Symon, Andrew* and *Peter* fell upon the house of *Thomas Kimbal*, of Bradford, killed him, and carried off his wife and five children into the wilderness. Having on the whole concluded to make peace with the English while they could, did, before the end of six weeks, restore the captives. Instead of improving the opportunity of securing their friendship, the English seized *Symon* and *Andrew*, and confined them in the jail at Dover. This treatment they considered, as very naturally they should, only a precursor of something of a different character; and therefore found means to break jail, and make good their escape. They joined their eastern friends, and hence followed many other cruelties, some of which we have already related. About the first depredation which followed their flight from Dover, was committed at Greenland. One *John Keniston* was killed, and his house burned. A writer of that day, after observing that the perpetrators of the outrage were *Symon, Andrew* and *Peter*, observes that they were the "three we had in prison, and should have killed," and closes with this exclamation, "The good Lord pardon us."§ Thus some considered they had need of pardon for not dealing with more rigor towards the Indians!

We are now to commence upon the recital of one of the most horrid massacres any where recorded—the sacking of Dover by the famous chiefs *Kankamagus* and *Massandowet*, and the barbarous murder of Maj. *Waldron* and many of his people.

Kankamagus, commonly in the histories called *Hogkins, Hawkins*, or *Hakins*, was a Pennakook sachem, and an artful, persevering, faithful man, as long as he could depend upon the English for protection. But when Governor *Cranfield*, of New Hampshire, used his endeavors to bring down the Mohawks to destroy the eastern Indians, in 1684, who were constantly stirred up by the French to commit depredations upon the English, *Kankamagus*, knowing the Mohawks made no distinction where they came, fled to the eastward, and joined the Androscoggins. He had a fort upon that river, where his family and that of another sachem, called *Worombos*, or *Worombo*, lived. But before he fled his country, he addressed several letters to the governor, which discover his fidelity as well as his fears; and from which there is no doubt but he would always gladly have lived in his own country, and on the most intimate and friendly terms with the English, to whom he had become attached, and

* MS. Documents.
† Belknap's *N. Hampshire.*
‡ *Hist. N. England*, 631.
§ Ibid. i. 158.

had adopted much of their manner, and could read and write, but for the reasons just stated. The following letter fully explains the situation of his mind and his feelings, at the time he expected the Mohawks would ravage his country:—

"*May* 15*th*, 1685. *Honor governor my friend. You my friend I desire your worship and your power, because I hope you can do som great matters this one. I am poor and naked, and have no men at my place because I afraid allways Mohogs he will kill me every day and night. If your worship when please pray help me you no let Mohogs kill me at my place at Malamake River called Panukkog and Natukkog, I will submit your worship and your power. And now I want pouder and such alminishon, shatt and guns, because I have forth at my hom, and I plant theare.*"

The above letter is signed by himself and 14 of his principal men. Whether he were among the Pennakooks seized by Major *Waldron* about ten years before, is not certain, or, if he were, it is not probable any resentment remained in his breast against him on that account, as the Pennakooks were all permitted to return home; but it is certain that he was the director and leader in the dreadful calamity which fell upon *Waldron* not long afterward, and which is as much chargeable upon the maltreatment they received from the English, at least, as upon any agency of the French. It may be true that many belonging to the eastward, who were seized with the Pennakooks, and sold or left in foreign countries, had found their way back among their friends again, and were glad of the first opportunity of revenging themselves upon the author of their unjust expatriation.

Major *Waldron* lived at Dover,* New Hampshire, in a strong garrison-house, at which place were also four others. *Kankamagus* had artfully contrived a stratagem to effect the surprise of the place, and had others beside the Pennakooks from different places ready in great numbers, to prosecute the undertaking. The plan was this. Two squaws were sent to each garrison-house to get liberty to stay all night, and when all should be asleep, they were to open the gates to the warriors. *Masandowet*, who was next to *Kankamagus*, went to Major *Waldron's*, and informed him that the Indians would come the next day and trade with him. While at supper with the major, *Masandowet* said to him, with an air of familiarity, "Brother *Waldron*, what would you do if the strange Indians should come?" To which he vauntingly replied, "that he could assemble an hundred men by lifting up his finger." In this security the gates were opened at midnight, and the work of death raged in all its fury. One garrison only escaped, who would not admit the squaws. They rushed into *Waldron's* house in great numbers, and while some guarded the door, others commenced the slaughter of all who resisted. *Waldron* was now 80 years of age, yet, seizing his sword, defended himself with great resolution, and at first drove the Indians before him from room to room, until one getting behind him, knocked him down with his hatchet. They now seized upon, and dragged him into the great room, and placed him in an armed chair upon a table. While they were thus dealing with the master of the house, they obliged the family to provide them a supper, which when they had eaten, they took off his clothes, and proceeded to torture him in the most dreadful manner. Some gashed his breast with knives, saying, "*I cross out my account*;" others cut off joints of his fingers, and said to him, "*Now will your fist weigh a pound?*"

After cutting off his nose and ears, and forcing them into his mouth, he became faint from loss of blood; and some holding his own sword on end upon the floor, let him fall upon it, and thus ended his misery.

* Then called by its Indian name, *Quochecho*.

The Indians had been greatly abused and wronged in their trading with the whites, and it is a tradition to this day all over that part of the country, that Major *Waldron* took great advantage of them in trade, and did not cross out their accounts when they had paid him; and that, in buying beaver, his fist was accounted to weigh a pound. Although he may have taken no more advantage of the Indians than the majority of Indian traders, yet, at this distant day, extenuation will not be looked for in impartial accounts of the transactions of our ancestors with the Indians.

Several were killed at each of the garrison-houses that fell into their hands. They kept the place until the next morning, when, after collecting all the plunder they could carry, took up their march, with 29 captives, into the wilderness towards Canada; where the chief of them were bought by the French, and in time got home to their country again. Twenty-three were killed before they left the place. This affair took place on the night of the 27th of June, 1689. Several friendly Indians informed the English at Chelmsford of the certainty of an attack upon Dover, and they caused a letter to be despatched in season to have notified the people, but on account of some delay at Newbury ferry, the benefit of that information was lost.

Four years after, Col. *Church* took *Worombo's* fort, in which were *Kankamagus's* wife and children. This fort was upon the Androscoggin, about 25 or 30 miles from its mouth. In another place, we have given a history of *Church's* expedition to this fort. The prisoners taken here informed *Church* that there had been lately a great council held there by the Indians, in which "many were for peace and many against it;" but they finally agreed to go with 300 warriors to Wells with a flag of truce, and to offer the English peace, which if not accepted, they would then fall upon them. "If they could not take Wells, then they resolved to attack Piscataqua. The which, says *Church,* when we were well informed of, we left two old squaws that were not able to march, gaue them victuals enough for one week of their own corn, boiled, and a little of our pruisions, and buried their dead, and left them clothes enough to keep them warme, and left the wigwams for them to lye in: gaue them orders to tell their friends how kind we were to them, biding them doe the like to ours. Also if they were for peace to come to goodman *Small's,* att Barwick, within 14 days, who would attend to discourse them; then we came away with our own five captiues, [English that they had delivered,] and nine of theirs."*

In the same letter we are informed that among these prisoners were *Kankamagus's* wife and four children. His brother-in-law was taken, but he "ran away from them." Among the slain was *Kankamagus's* own sister. A girl was brought away whose father and mother had been slain before her eyes. Two of the children of *Worombo* were also among the prisoners, all of whom were carried to Plimouth. This expedition upon the Androscoggin was on Sunday, 14 Sept. 1690.

A few days after this, *Church* landed at Casco, where the Indians fell upon him by surprise, and were not beaten off for some time, and then only by hard fighting. This was on the 21 September. *Church* had seven men killed and 24 wounded, two of whom died in a day or two after. The Indians who made this attack were probably led by *Kankamagus* and *Worombo.*

Hopehood was a chief nearly as celebrated, and as much detested in his time, as the chiefs of which we have just spoken. He was chief of the tribe of the Kennebecks generally known as the Nerigwoks. He was

* Manuscript letter written at the time by *Church*, and sent to Gov. *Hinckley* of Plimouth.

the son of *Robinhood*, a sachem of whom we have spoken in a former chapter. According to one writer, *Hopehood* was also known by the name *Wohawa.** The career of his warlike exploits was long and bloody. Our first notice of him is in *Philip's* war, at the attack of a house at Newichewannok, since Berwick, in Maine. Fifteen persons, all women and children, were in the house, and *Hopehood,* with one only beside himself, *Andrew* of Saco, whom we have before mentioned as an accomplice with Symon, thought to surprise them, and, but for the timely discovery of their approach by a young woman within, would have effected their purpose. She fastened and held the door, while all the others escaped unobserved. *Hopehood* and his companion hewed down the door, and knocked the girl on the head, and, otherwise wounding her, left her for dead. They took two children, which a fence had kept from escaping. One they killed, the other they carried off alive. The young woman recovered, and was entirely well afterwards.

On the 18th of March, 1690, happened a horrid massacre at Salmon Falls. *Hopehood* had joined 22 Frenchmen, under *Hertel,* with 25 of his warriors. They attacked the place, as soon as it was day, in three places. The people defended themselves as well as they were able, in their consternation, until about 30 of their best men were slain, when they gave themselves up to the mercy of the besiegers; 64 men were carried away captive, and much plunder. They burned all the houses, and the barns with the cattle in them. The number of buildings thus destroyed is unknown, but was perhaps about 30, and perhaps 200 head of cattle.

In the same year, *Hopehood* appears again upon our records. In May of that year, at the head of a party, he fell upon Fox Point, in New Hampshire, killed about fourteen persons, and carried away six, after burning several houses. This was as easily done, says Mather,† "as to have spoiled an ordinary *hen roost.*" Two companies of English soon collected and pursued them; came up with them, killed some, and recovered considerable plunder. In this action *Hopehood* was wounded, and lost his gun.‡

Many were the horrid acts of barbarity inflicted on the prisoners taken at this time. Not long after this, *Hopehood* went to the westward, "with a design, says Mather, to bewitch another crew at Aquadocta into his assistance." The Indians of Canada and the Five Nations were then at war, and he being in their country, was met by some of the Canada Indians, who, taking him to be of the Iroquois nation, slew him and many of his companions. He had been once a captive to the English, and served a time in Boston as a slave. There appears to have been another Nerigwok chief of the same name, who treated with Gov. *Dudley* at Casco, in 1703.†

We have, in narrating the events in the life of *Madokawando,* noticed the voyage of Maj. *Waldron* to the eastern coast of Maine, which was at the close of *Philip's* war. How much treachery was manifested at that time by the Indians, which caused the English to massacre many of them, we shall not take upon us to declare; yet this we cannot but bear in mind, that we have only the account of those who performed the tragedy, and not that of those on whom it fell.

Capt. *Charles Frost,* of Kittery, was with *Waldron* upon that expedition, and, next to him, a principal actor in it; and, like him, was killed by the

---

* *Harris,* in his Voyages, ii. 302, who says he was a Huron; but as he cites no authorities, we know not how he came by his information.

† Magnalia Christ. Americana, b. vii. art. ix.

‡ "An heathen Indian would rather part with his head than with his gun." *Loskiel,* ii. 214.

Indians afterwards.* Mr. *Hubbard* gives this account of his taking a noted warrior as follows:—"Capt. *Frost* seized an Indian called *Megunneway,* a notorious rogue, that had been in arms at Connecticut last June, at the falls, and saw that brave and resolute Capt. *Turner,* when he was slain about Green River; and helped to kill *Thomas Bracket* at Casco, August last, [1676.] And with the help of Lieut. *Nutter,* according to the major's order, carried him aboard" their vessel. "By this time," the same author continues, "some of the soldiers were got ashore, and instantly, according to their major's command, pursued the enemy towards their canoes. In the chase, several of the enemy were slain, whose bodies these [soldiers] found at their return, to the number of seven; amongst whom was *Mattahando,* the sagamore, with an old powow, to whom the *Devil* had revealed, as sometimes he did to *Saul,* that on the same day he should be with him; for he had a little before told the Indians, that within two days the English would come and kill them all, which was at the very same time verified upon himself." Here we must acknowledge, notwithstanding our great respect for this author, that his commentary upon that passage was rather gratuitous. He might have considered that *Sauls* among the English would not be wanting, of whom parallels might be made. Indeed, the historian of *Kankamagus* might say the *Devil* was less deceitful in the case of this powow than he was afterwards in the case of Major *Waldron.*

The English took much plunder from the Indians at this time, among which were about a 1000 lbs. of dried beef, and various other commodities. *Megunneway,* after having fallen into their hands as we have stated, was shot without ceremony.

CHAPTER IX.

BOMAZEEN —*Treachery of the whites towards him—Is imprisoned at Boston —Saves the life of a female captive—Captures Saco—Is killed*—ARRUHAWIKWABEMT—*His capture and death*—EGEREMET—*Seized at Pemmaquid—Barbarously murdered—Treachery of Chubb—Its requital—Capt.* TOM—*Surprises Hampton*—DONY—*His fort captured by Col. Church—Events of Church's expedition—Capt.* SIMMO—*Treats with the English at Casco—His speech*—WATTANUMMON —*Capt.* SAMUEL—*His fight at Damaris Cove*—HEGAN—*One of the name barbarously destroyed by the whites*—MOGG—*Westbrook burns Nerigwok—Some account of the Jesuit Rasle—Moulton's expedition to Nerigwok—Death of Mogg—Death of Father Rasle—Notice of Moulton—Charlevoix's account of this affair—Rasle goes out to meet the English, who shoot him down—He falls near the cross which he had raised—Seven Indians shot down by his side—The English burn the church and break its crucifix—Shockingly mangle the body of Rasle*—PAUGUS—*Bounty offered for Indian scalps—Captain John Lovewell's first expedition—His second hunt for Indians—Falls in with* PAUGUS—*Fights him, and is slain—Particulars of the affair—Incidents.*

WE will continue here our catalogue of eminent chiefs of the east, which, though a remote section, has no less claim than any other; and the first of them which we shall introduce was called

* At his native place, 4 July, 1697. *MS. letter of John Farmer, Esq.*

Bomazeen, who was a sachem of a tribe of the Canibas, or Kennebecks, whose residence was at an ancient seat of sagamores, upon a river bearing their name, at a place called *Norridgewock*.* Whether *Bomazeen* were the leader in the attack upon Oyster River in New Hampshire, Groton in Massachusetts, and many other places, about the year 1694, we cannot determine, but *Hutchinson* says he was "a principal actor in the carnage upon the English," after the treaty which he had made with Governor *Phips*, in 1693. In 1694, he came to the fort at Pemmaquid with a flag of truce, and was treacherously seized by those who commanded, and sent prisoner to Boston, where he remained some months, in a loathsome prison. In 1706, new barbarities were committed. Chelmsford, Sudbury, Groton, Exeter, Dover, and many other places, suffered more or less. Many captives were taken to Canada, and many killed upon the way. A poor woman, one *Rebecca Taylor*, who had arrived at the River St. Lawrence, was about to be hanged by her master, an "overgrown Indian," named *Sampson*. The limb of the tree on which he was executing his purpose gave way, and, while he was making a second attempt, *Bomazeen* happened to be passing, and rescued her.

We hear of him just after the death of *Arruhawikwabemt*, in October, 1710, when he fell upon Saco with 60 or 70 men, and killed several people, and carried away some captives. He is mentioned as a "notorious fellow," and yet but few of his acts are upon record. Some time after the peace of 1701, it seemed to be confirmed by the appearance of *Bomazeen*, and another principal chief, who said the French friars were urging them to break their union with the English, "*but that they had made no impression on them, for they were as firm as the mountains, and should continue so as long as the sun and moon endured.*" On peace being made known to the Indians, as having taken place between the French and English nations, they came into Casco with a flag of truce, and soon after concluded a treaty at Portsmouth, N. H., dated 11 July, 1713. *Bomazeen's* name and mark are to this treaty.

When Capt. *Moulton* was sent up to Nerigwok, in 1724, they fell in with *Bomazeen* about Taconnet, where they shot him as he was escaping through the river. Near the town of Nerigwok, his wife and daughter were, in a barbarous manner, fired upon, the daughter killed, and the mother taken.

We purposely omit Dr. C. *Mather's* account of *Bomazeen's* conversation with a minister of Boston, while a prisoner there, which amounts to little else than his recounting some of the extravagant notions which the French of Canada had made many Indians believe, to their great detriment, as he said; as that *Jesus Christ* was a French man, and the Virgin *Mary* a French woman; that the French gave them poison to drink, to inflame them against the English, which made them run mad. And we hear of others, who told the Indians that the English put *Jesus Christ* to death in London.

Arruhawikwabemt, just mentioned, was a sachem of the same tribe, and was said to be of Norridgewock also. We can find but very few particulars of him, but, from the fate he met with, it is presumed he had been very instrumental in continuing or bringing about the eastern war of 1710. In that year, Col. *Walton* made an expedition to the eastern coast of Maine with 170 men. As they were encamped upon an island, the smoke of their fires decoyed some of the Indians into their hands, among whom was *Arruhawikwabemt*. *Penhallow* says, he was "an active, bold fellow,

* *Nerigwok* is believed to be the most proper way of spelling the name of this place, as agreeing best with its orthoepy; at least, with that heard at and in the vicinity of it, at this day, as pronounced by the oldest inhabitants. It is a delightful place, and will be found elsewhere described.

and one of an undaunted spirit; for when they asked him several questions, he made them no reply, and when they threatened him with death, *he laughed at it with contempt!* At which they delivered him up unto our friendly Indians, who soon became his executioners. But when the squaw saw the destiny of her husband, she became more flexible, and freely discovered where each party of them [the Indians] encamped." The savage perpetrators of this act called themselves Christian warriors! and it must be acknowledged that civilization gains nothing in contrasting the conduct of the whites, under *Walton*, and that of *Bomazeen* towards a captive, just related.

Egeremet was of Machias, and, although sometimes called *Moxus,* was, we believe, a distinct sachem. This chief, with five others of like quality, were seized by the English when they came into Pemmaquid Fort to treat with them. *Egeremet* and another were killed. This was 16 February, 1696.* Their seizure could not have been outdone, by the greatest barbarians, for faithlessness; and we shall learn that its author paid for it in due time with his life. We are not disposed to add to transactions which are in themselves sufficiently horrible, but we will venture to give the account as we find it in Dr. C. *Mather's decennium luctuosum:*—†

"Let us, before the year be quite gone, see some vengeance taken upon the *heads in the house of the wicked.* Know then, reader, that Capt. *March* petitioning to be dismissed from his command of the fort at Pemmaquid, one *Chub* succeeded him. This *Chub* found an opportunity, in a pretty *chubbed* manner, to kill the famous *Edgeremet* and *Abenquid*, a couple of principal sagamores, with one or two other Indians, on a Lord's day. Some that well enough liked the thing which was now done, did not altogether like the *manner* of doing it, because there was a pretence of *treaty* between *Chub* and the sagamores, whereof he took his advantage to lay violent hands on them."

Thus the *manner* is seen in which this horrid and cold-blooded act is related!! Few are the instances that we meet with in history, where *Indian treachery,* as it is termed, can go before this. The reverend author adds, "If there were any unfair dealing (which I know not) in this action of *Chub,* there will be another *February* not far off, wherein the *avengers of blood* will take their *satisfaction.*" By this innuendo, what befell Capt. *Chubb* afterwards is understood, and of which we shall presently give an account.

The point of land called *Trott's Neck,* in Woolwich, in the state of Maine, was sold, in 1685, by *Egeremet* and several other sachems. In 1693, he, with 12 other chiefs, treated with Sir *William Phips,* at Pemmaquid, and a treaty was signed by them.‡

Before this, in 1691, "New England being quite out of breath," says Dr. *C. Mather,* a treaty, or truce, was entered into between the eastern sachems and Messrs. *Hutchinson* and *Townsend,* of Boston, and others of the eastern coast, at Sagadahock. Here ten captives were given up by them, and the English gave up eight captive Indians. One was a woman by the name of *Hull,* who had been of great service to them, having written letters on various occasions, such as their affairs required, and with whom they regretted much to part. Another was *Nathaniel White,* who had been bound and tortured in a wretched manner. His ears were cut off, and, instead of food, he was forced to eat them, after which, but for this timely treaty, the sentence of burning would have been executed upon him. This truce stipulated that no hurt should be done the English until May, 1692, and that, on the first of that month, they would deliver,

---

* Manuscript of Rev. John Pike.

† Magnalia, b. vii.

‡ It may be seen in the *Magnalia.*

at Wells, all English captives in their hands, and, in the mean time, would inform of any plots that they might know of the French against the English. *Egeremet* being the chief sachem, and most forward in this business, Dr. *Mather* utters his contempt for him by saying, "To this instrument were set the *paws* of *Egeremet,* and five more of their sagamores and noblemen."*

This treaty may be seen at length in the Massachusetts Collections, but is dated one year earlier than it is in the Magnalia. The fact that it was made upon the water, as Dr. *C. Mather* says, and as we have quoted in the life of *Madokawando,* appears from the last paragraph of that instrument, which is in these words:—

"Signed and sealed interchangeably, upon the water, in canoes, at Sackatehock, *when the wind blew.*"

It was headed, "At a treaty of peace with the eastward Indian enemy sagamores." The other five sachems, beside *Egeremet,* were *Toquelmut, Watumbomt, Watombamet, Walumbe,* [*Worombos,*] and *John Hawkins,* [or *Kankamagus.*] The places for which they stipulated are, according to the treaty, "Pennecook, Winnepisseockeege, Ossepe, Pigwocket, Amosconggen, Pechepscut, Kennebeck River, and all other places adjacent, within the territory and dominions of the above-named sagamores."

The witnesses were, *Dewando,* [the same called *Adiwando* by *Penhallow,* probably,] *Ned Higon, John Alden,* jr. and *Nathaniel Alden.*

The next year, *Egeremet* was with *Madokawando, Moxus* and a body of French under *Labrocre,* and made the notable attack upon the garrison at Wells, which will be found written elsewhere.

We will now inform the reader of the wretched fate of Capt. *Pasco Chub.* It was not long after he committed the bloody deed of killing the Indian sagamores, before he and the fort were taken by the French and Indians. He was exchanged, and returned to Boston, where he suffered much disgrace for his treachery with the Indians.† He lived at Andover, in Massachusetts, where the Indians made an attack in February, 1698, in which he was killed. It was not thought that they expected to find him there; but when they found they had killed him, it gave them as much joy, says *Hutchinson,* "as the destruction of a whole town, because they had taken their beloved vengeance of him for his perfidy and barbarity to their countrymen." They shot him through several times after he was dead.

In his characteristic style, Mr. *Oldmixon* speaks of this event.‡ He says, "Nor must we forget *Chub,* the false wretch who surrendered Pemmaquid Fort. The governor kept him under examination some time at Boston, and then dismissed him. As he was going to his house, at Andover, the Indians surprised him and his wife, and massacred them; a just

---

* Magnalia Christ. Americana, book vii. art. viii.

† *Harris's* Voyages, ii. 305, (ed. 1764.) says *Chub* was arrested by Col. *Gedney,* who was sent east with three ships of war, on hearing of the surrender of the fort, and that no French or Indians could be found; that after he strengthened the garrison, he returned home.

"Col. *Gedney* had been by land with 500 men, to secure the eastern frontiers. Finding the enemy gone, he strengthened the garrisons, which were not taken. He also arrested *Pasco Chubb,* for surrendering Pemaquid Fort, while under his command in July, and had him brought to Boston. Here Capt. *Chubb* was confined, till it was decided that he should lose his commission, and not be eligible for any other. This unfortunate man, with his wife Hannah, and three others, were killed by the Indians at Andover, Feb. 22, 1698." *Rev. Mr. Felt's Annals of Salem.*

A naval force was sent at the same time; hence, the accounts are not altogether irreconcilable. Three men-of-war were sent out in pursuit of the French, "but meeting with contrary winds, they could never get sight of them." *Neal,* Hist. N. Eng. ii. 551.

‡ British Empire in America, i. 77, 78.

reward of his treason." The author, we think, should have added, according to the jurisprudence of savages.

The most favorable account given of the conduct of *Chub*, and indeed the only one, follows: "An Indian sagamore's son appeared with a flag of truce, and Capt. *Chub* went out to them without arms, man for man. An Indian asked for rum and tobacco: the captain said, '*No; it is sabbath day.*' They said, '*We will have rum, or we will have rum and you too.*' Two Indians laid hold on the captain. Then he called to his men, to fall on, for God's sake. Then he made signs to his men, to come from the fort. One of the English had a hatchet under his coat, took it out and killed an Indian; and then ours killed two more Indians, and took another alive, and wounded another, supposed mortally. Then many of the enemy came near to the English, who retreated all safe to the fort."*

There was another sagamore of the same name, noticed in the following wars with the eastern Indians, who was friendly to the whites; it was probably he who sometimes bore the name of *Moxus*.

In the Indian war of 1703, there was a great Indian captain who resided somewhere to the east of Pascataqua River, who made his name dreaded among the settlements in that region, by some bloody expeditions which he conducted. He was called by the English

Captain Tom. On 17 Aug. of this year, this daring war captain, with about 30 others, surprised a part of Hampton, killed five persons, whereof one was a widow *Hussey*, "who was a remarkable speaking Quaker, and much lamented by her sect." After sacking two houses near the garrison, they drew off.†

Many Indians bore the name of *Tom*. Indian Hill, in Newbury, was owned by *Great Tom*. He is supposed to have been the last Indian proprietor of lands in that town. In written instruments, he styles himself, "*I Great Tom Indian.*"‡

We come, in the next place, to an interesting portion of our eastern history. It has been generally supposed that the name *Dony*, or *Doney*, was the name of an Indian chief, but it is now quite certain that he was a Frenchman, who took up his residence among the Indians, as Baron de St. *Casteins* did. There appears in our history, in 1645, a "Monsieur *Dony*," who had some difficulty with Lord *de la Tour*, about their eastern possessions, and he was, doubtless, the same of whom we have an account afterwards, in the war of 1690, with the eastern Indians. At this time, there were two of the name in Maine, father and son. The son, perhaps, like *Casteins* the younger, was half Indian, but of this we are not sure; nevertheless, to preserve our narrative of the events of Col. *Church's* expedition of 1690, we shall notice them among others.

Church landed at Maquait, 12 September, before day, and, after a wet, fatiguing march into the woods of about two days, on the south-west side of the Androscoggin, came into the neighborhood of a fort. They came upon an Indian and his wife who were leading two captives; and immediately pursuing and firing upon them, killed the Indian woman, who proved to be the wife of *Young Doney*.§ We can only hope it was not their design thus to have killed an innocent woman. Which party it was that fired upon them (for they divided themselves into three) is unknown, and we in charity must suppose that, at considerable distance, and in much confusion, it was difficult to know an Indian man from a woman.

---

* Manuscript letter in library Mass. Hist. Soc. written in the following month. As it was written at a great distance from the place, and from a report of the day, little reliance can be placed upon it. It may have been *Chub's* report of the case.

† *Penhallow*, Ind. Wars, 8; *Farmer's Belknap*, i. 167.

‡ Manuscript Hist. Newbury by *J. Coffin*.

§ And the same called in the Magnalia *Robin Doney*.

As *Church* expected, *Doney* ran into one gate of the fort and out at the other, giving the alarm so effectually, that nearly all within it escaped. They found and took prisoners "but two men and a lad of about 18, with some women and children. Five ran into the river, three or four of which were killed. The lad of 18 made his escape up the river." The whole number killed in this action was "six or seven." The English had but one wounded. They took here, at this time,* a considerable quantity of corn, guns and ammunition, and liberated Mrs. *Huckings*, widow of Lieut. *Robert Huckings*, taken at Oyster River, Mrs. *Barnard*, wife of *Benjamin Barnard*, of Salmon Falls, *Anne Heard*, of Cocheco, a young woman, daughter of one *Willis*, of Oyster River, and a boy belonging to Exeter. These captives, says *Church*, "were in a miserable condition." They learned by them that most of their men were gone to Winter Harbor to get provisions for the Bay of Fundy Indians. This information was given by a prisoner taken in the fort, who also said that the Bay of Fundy Indians were to join them against the English, in the spring. "The soldiers, being very rude, would hardly spare the Indian's life, while in examination; intending, when he had done, that he should be executed. But Capt. *Hucking's* wife, and another woman, down on their knees and begged for him, saying, that he had been a means of saving their lives and a great many more; and had helped several to opportunities to run away and make their escape; and that never, since he came amongst them, had fought against the English, but being related to *Hakin's*† wife, kept at the fort with them, having been there two years; but his living was to the westward of Boston. So upon their request, his life was spared."

Two old squaws were left in the fort, provided with provisions, and instructed to tell those who returned who they were, and what they were determined to do. They then put four or five to death, and decamped. Those, we must suppose, were chiefly women and children! "Knocked on the head for an example." We know not that any excuse can be given for this criminal act; and it is degrading to consider that the civilized must be supposed to imagine that they can prevent barbarities by being wretchedly barbarous themselves.

Old Doney was next to be hunted. As they were embarking at Maquait, Mr. *Anthony Bracket* came to the shore and called to them to take him on board, which they did. He learning that an English army was thereabout, made his escape from the Indians, with whom he had been some time a prisoner. The fleet now proceeded to Winter Harbor, from whence they despatched a detachment of 60 men to Saco Falls. When they came near, they discovered *Doney's* company on the opposite side of the river, who chiefly made their escape. A canoe, with three Indians, was observed coming over the river; they did not see the English, and were fired upon, and "all three perished." This gave the first alarm to *Doney's* company. They did not, however, leave their ground without returning the fire of the English, by which Lieut. *Hunnewell* was shot through the thigh.‡ When the parties fired upon each other, *Old Doney*, with an English captive, was higher up the river, who, hearing the firing, came down to see what it meant; and thus he discovered the English time enough to escape. *Doney* fled from the canoe, leaving his captive, who came to the English. His name was *Thomas Baker*, who had lived before at Scarborough.

There were many other movements of the English after this, in which

* Says my record, which is a manuscript letter from *Church*, written at that time.
† The same called *Kankamagus*.
‡ Official letter in MS. from the expedition.

they got much plunder, and which tended to cause an uneasiness among them, and their final determination to return home. *Church* urged a longer continuance, but was out-voted in a council of officers, and thus ended the expedition. Many in the country reproached *Church* with cowardice, and almost every thing but what we should have looked for. If putting to death captives had been the charge, many might have accorded Amen! But we do not find that urged against him.

Two years after this, in 1693, *Robin Doney* became reconciled to the English, and signed a treaty with them at Pemmaquid. But within a year after, he became suspected, whether with or without reason, we know not, and coming to the fort at Saco, probably to settle the difficulty, was seized by the English. What his fate was is rather uncertain, but the days of forgiveness and mercy were not yet.

Among the chiefs which we shall next proceed to notice, there were several of nearly equal notoriety.

Captain *Simmo's* name should, perhaps, stand most conspicuous. We shall, therefore, go on to narrate the events in his life, after a few preliminary observations.

Whenever war commenced between the English and French in Europe, their colonies in America had to fear the worst. This was the aspect which affairs wore in 1703. With the first news, therefore, of its flame, the New Englanders' thoughts were turned towards the Indians. Gov. *Dudley* immediately despatched messengers to most of the eastern tribes, inviting them to meet him in council upon the peninsula in Falmouth, on the 20 June. His object was so to attach them to the English, that, in the event of hostilities between the rival powers on this side of the Atlantic, they would not take arms against them. Agreeably to the wishes of the English, a vast multitude assembled at the time appointed: the chiefs *Adiwando* and *Hegan* for the Pennakooks, *Wattanummon* for the Pequakets, *Mesambomett* and *Wexar* for the Androscoggins, *Moxus* and *Hopehood* (perhaps son of him killed by the Mohawks) for the Nerigwoks, *Bomazeen* and Capt. *Samuel* for the Kennebecks, and *Warrungunt* and *Wanadugunbuent* for the Penobscots. After a short speech to them, in which the governor expressed brotherly affection, and a desire to settle every difficulty "which had happened since the last treaty," Capt. *Simmo* replied as follows:—

"*We thank you, good brother, for coming so far to talk with us. It is a great favor. The clouds fly and darken—but we still sing with love the songs of peace. Believe my words.*—So FAR AS THE SUN IS ABOVE THE EARTH ARE OUR THOUGHTS FROM WAR, OR THE LEAST RUPTURE BETWEEN US."*

The governor was then presented with a belt of wampum, which was to confirm the truth of what had been said. At a previous treaty, two heaps of small stones had been thrown together, near by, and called the *Two-brothers*.† These were considered by the parties in the light of seals to their treaties. They now repaired to these heaps of stones, and each increased their magnitude, by the addition of others. Thus was happily terminated this famous treaty. Some parade and rejoicing now commenced, and a circumstance transpired which threw the English into great fear, and, perhaps, greater suspicion. A grand salute was to be fired upon each side, at parting, and the English, advisedly, and very warily, it must be confessed, but in appearance complimentary, expressed their desire that the Indians would fire first. The Indians received the compliment, and discharged their guns; to their great surprise, the Eng-

* This is Mr. *Williamson's* version of the speech, Hist. Maine, ii. 36.
† The Indians and English.

lish found they had been loaded with bullets. They now considered their treachery certain, and marvelled at their escape. However, it can only be presumed, that, according to the maxim of the whites, the Indians had come prepared to treat or fight, as the case might require; for no doubt their guns were charged when they came to the treaty, otherwise why did they not fire upon the English when they saluted them?

What became of Capt. *Simmo* we have as yet no account. Several of the other chiefs who attended this council were, perhaps, equally conspicuous.

Wattanummon being absent when the council first met on the 20 June, no business was entered upon for several days. However, the English afterwards said it was confirmed that it was not on that account that they delayed the conference, but that they expected daily a reinforcement of 200 French and Indians, and then they were to seize upon the English, and ravage the country. Whether this were merely a rumor, or the real state of the case, we have no means of knowing. *Wattanummon* was supposed to have been once a Pennakook, as an eminence still bears his name about a mile from the state-house in N. Hampshire.*

Capt. *Samuel* was an Indian of great bravery, and one of the most forward in endeavoring to lull the fears of the English at the great council just mentioned. What gave his pretensions the air of sincerity was his coming with *Bomazeen*, and giving some information about the designs of the French. They said,

"*Although several missionaries have come among us, sent by the French friars to break the peace between the English and us, yet their words have made no impression upon us.* WE ARE AS FIRM AS THE MOUNTAINS, AND WILL SO CONTINUE, AS LONG AS THE SUN AND MOON ENDURES."

Notwithstanding these strong expressions of friendship, "within six weeks after," says *Penhallow*, "the whole eastern country was in a conflagration, no house standing nor garrison unattacked." The Indians were no doubt induced to commit this depredation from the influence of the French, many of whom assisted them in the work. And it is not probable that those Indians who had just entered into the treaty were idle spectators of the scene; but who of them, or whether all were engaged in the affair, we know not. A hundred and thirty people were said to have been killed and taken.

Capt. *Samuel* was either alive 20 years after these transactions, or another of the name made himself conspicuous. In June, 1722, this warrior chief, at the head of five others, boarded Lieut. *Tilton*, as he lay at anchor a fishing, near Damaris Cove. They pinioned him and his brother, and beat them very sorely; but, at last, one got clear and released the other, who then fell with great fury upon the Indians, threw one overboard, and mortally wounded two more.† Whether Capt. *Samuel* were among those killed is not mentioned.

There was a Captain *Sam* in the wars of 1745. In the vicinity of St. George's, Lieut. *Proctor*, at the head of 19 militia, had a skirmish with the Indians, 5 Sept. in which two of their leaders were killed, viz. Colonel *Morris* and Capt. *Sam*, and one Colonel *Job* was taken captive; the latter being sent to Boston, he died in prison. To quiet the resentment of his relatives, the government made his widow a valuable present after the peace.‡

We should not, perhaps, omit to speak separately of another chief, who was present at the famous treaty mentioned above; we refer to

Hegan. His name is also spelt *Hegon* and *Heigon*. There were seve-

---

* MS. communication of *J. Farmer*, Esq.

† *Penhallow's* Ind. Wars, 86.

‡ *Williamson*, Hist. Me. ii. 241.

ral of the name. One, called *Moggheigon,* son of *Walter,* was a sachem at Saco, in 1664. This chief, in that year, sold to *Wm. Phillips,* "a tract of land, being bounded with Saco River on the N. E. side, and Kennebunk River on the S. W. side." To extend from the sea up Saco River to Salmon Falls, and up the Kennebunk to a point opposite the former. No amount is mentioned for which the land was sold, but merely "a certain sum in goods."* One *Sampson Hegon* attended the treaty of Pemmaquid, in 1698; *John,* that at Casco, in 1727; *Ned* was a Pennakook; *Walter,* brother of *Mogg;*† which, or whether either of these were the one so barbarously destroyed at Casco, as appears in the following account, we are not informed. The fate of this *Hegon* is remembered among the inhabitants of some parts of Maine to this day. He was tied upon a horse with spurs on his heels, in such a manner that the spurs continually goaded the animal. When the horse was set at liberty, he ran furiously through an orchard, and the craggy limbs of the trees tore him to pieces. *Mather,* in his DECENNIUM LUCTUOSUM,‡ seems to confirm something of the kind, which took place at Casco, in 1694, where the Indians, having taken some horses, made a bridle of the mane and tail of one, on which "a son of the famous *Hegon* was ambitious to mount." "But being a pitiful horseman, he ordered them, for fear of his falling, to tie his legs fast under the horse's belly. No sooner was this *beggar set on horseback,* and the spark, in his own opinion, thoroughly equipped, but the nettlesome horse furiously and presently ran with him out of sight. Neither horse nor man was ever seen any more. The astonished tawnies howled after one of their nobility, disappearing by such an unexpected accident. A few days after, they found one of his *legs,* (and that was all,) which they buried in Capt. *Bracket's* cellar, with abundance of lamentation."

Here we cannot but too plainly discover the same spirit in the narrator, which must have actuated the authors of the deed. He who laughs at crime is a participator in it.

From these, we pass to affairs of far greater notoriety in our eastern history; and shall close this chapter with two of the most memorable events in its Indian warfare.

Mogg, the chief sachem of Norridgewok in 1724, may very appropriately stand at the head of the history of the first event. How long he had been sachem at that period, we have not discovered, but he is mentioned by the English historians, as the old chief of Norridgewok at that time. Notwithstanding *Mogg* was the chief Indian of the village of Nerigwok, or, as Father *Charlevoix* writes it, Narantsoak, there was a French priest settled here, to whom the Indians were all devotedness; and it is believed that they undertook no enterprise without his knowledge and consent. The name of this man, according to our English authors, was *Rallé,* but according to his own historian, *Charlevoix,* it was *Rasle.*§ The depredations of the Abénaquis, as these Indians were called by those who lived among them, were, therefore, directly charged by the English upon Father *Rasle;* hence their first step was to offer a reward for his head.|| The object of the expedition of Col. *Westbrook,* in 1722, was ostensibly to seize upon him, but he found the village deserted, and nothing was effected

* MS. among the files in our state-house.

† MS. letter of *John Farmer,* Esq.

‡ Magnalia, ii. 546.

§ Hist. Gen. de la Nouv. Fr. ii. 380, *et suiv.*

|| *"Après plusieurs tentatives, d'abord pour engager ces sauvages par les offres et les promesses les plus séduisantes à le livrer aux Anglois, ou du moins à le renvoyer à Quabec, et à prendre en sa place un de leurs ministres; ensuite pour le surpendre et pour l'enlever, les Anglois résolus de s'en défaire, quoiqu'il leur en dût coûter, mirent sa tête à prix, et promirent mille livres sterling à celui, qui la leur porteroit." Charlevoix, ut supra.*

by the expedition but the burning of the place. Father *Rasle* was the last that left it, which he did at the same time it was entered by the enemy; having first secured the sacred vases of his temple and the ornaments of its altar. The English made search for the fugitives, but without success, although, at one time, they were within about eight feet of the very tree that screened the object for which they sought. Thus the French considered that it was by a remarkable interposition of Providence, or, as *Charlevoix* expresses it, *par une main invisible*, that Father *Rasle* did not fall into their hands.

Determined on destroying this assemblage of Indians, which was the head quarters of the whole eastern country, at this time, the English, two years after, 1724, sent out a force, consisting of 208 men and three Mohawk Indians, under Captains *Moulton, Harman* and *Bourne*, to humble them. They came upon the village, the 23 August, while there was not a man in arms to oppose them. They had left 40 of their men at Teconet Falls, which is now within the town of Winslow, upon the Kennebeck, and about two miles below Waterville college, upon the opposite side of the river. The English had divided themselves into three squadrons: 80, under *Harman*, proceeded by a circuitous route, thinking to surprise some in their corn-fields, while *Moulton*, with 80 more, proceeded directly for the village, which, being surrounded by trees, could not be seen until they were close upon it. All were in their wigwams, and the English advanced slowly and in perfect silence. When pretty near, an Indian came out of his wigwam, and, accidently discovering the English, ran in and seized his gun, and giving the war-whoop, in a few minutes the warriors were all in arms, and advancing to meet them. *Moulton* ordered his men not to fire until the Indians had made the first discharge. This order was obeyed, and, as he expected, they overshot the English, who then fired upon them, in their turn, and did great execution. When the Indians had given another volley, they fled with great precipitation to the river, whither the chief of their women and children had also fled during the fight. Some of the English pursued and killed many of them in the river, and others fell to pillaging and burning the village. *Mogg* disdained to fly with the rest, but kept possession of a wigwam, from which he fired upon the pillagers. In one of his discharges he killed a Mohawk, whose brother observing it, rushed upon *Mogg* and killed him; and thus ended the strife. There were about 60 warriors in the place, about one half of whom were killed.

The famous *Rasle* shut himself up in his house, from which he fired upon the English; and, having wounded one, Lieut. *Jaques*,* of Newbury,† burst open the door and shot him through the head; although *Moulton* had given orders that none should kill him. He had an English boy with him, about 14 years old, who had been taken some time before from the frontiers, and whom the English reported *Rasle* was about to kill. Great brutality and ferocity are chargeable to the English in this affair, according to their own account; such as killing women and children, and scalping and mangling the body of Father *Rasle*.‡

* Who I conclude was a volunteer, as I do not find his name upon the return made by *Moulton*, which is upon file in the garret, west wing of our state-house.

† Manuscript History of Newbury, by *Joshua Coffin*, S. H. S. which, should the world ever be so fortunate as to see in print, we will ensure them not only great gratification, but a fund of amusement.

‡ As we have confined ourselves chiefly to the English accounts in the relation of this affair, it will, perhaps, be gratifying to many to hear something upon the other side. This we cannot do better than by offering the following extract from Charlevoix. He says,—"*Il n'y avoit alors que cinquante guerriers dans le bourg. Ils prirent les armes, et coururent tumultuairement, non pas pour défendre la place contre un ennemi, qui étoit déja dedans, mais pour favoriser la fuite des femmes, des veillards et des enfans, et leur*

There was here a handsome church, with a bell, on which the English committed a double sacrilege, first robbing it, then setting it on fire; herein surpassing the act of the first English circumnavigator, in his depredations upon the Spaniard's in South America; for he only took away the gold and silver vessels of a church, and its crucifix, because it was of massy gold, set about with diamonds, and that, too, upon the advice of his chaplain. "This might pass," says a reverend author, "for sea divinity, but justice is quite another thing." Perhaps it will be as well not to inquire here what kind of divinity would authorize the acts recorded in these wars, or indeed any wars.

Harman was the general in the expedition, and, for a time, had the honor of it; but *Moulton*, according to Gov. *Hutchinson*, achieved the victory, and it was afterward acknowledged by the country. He was a prisoner, when a small boy, among the eastern Indians, being among those taken at the destruction of York, in 1692. He died about 1759. The township of Moultonborough, in New Hampshire, was named from him, and many of his posterity reside there at the present day.

Under the head *Paugus*, we shall proceed to narrate our last event in the present chapter, than which, may be, few, if any, are oftener mentioned in New England story.

Paugus, slain in the memorable battle with the English under Captain *Lovewell*, in 1725, was chief of the Pequawkets. Fryeburg, in Maine, now includes the principal place of their former residence, and the place where the battle was fought. It was near a considerable body of water, called *Saco Pond*, which is the source of the river of the same name. The cruel and barbarous murders almost daily committed by the Indians upon the defenceless frontier inhabitants, caused the general court of Massachusetts to offer a bounty of £100 for every Indian's scalp. Among the various excursions performed by *Lovewell*, previous to that in which he was killed, the most important was that to the head of Salmon-fall River, now Wakefield, in New Hampshire. With 40 men, he came upon a small company of ten Indians, who were asleep by their fires, and, by stationing his men advantageously, killed all of them. This bloody deed was performed near the shore of a pond, which has ever since borne the name of *Lovewell's Pond*. After taking off their scalps, these 40 warriors marched to Boston in great triumph, with the ten scalps extended upon hoops, displayed in a formal manner, and for which they received £1000. This exploit was the more lauded, as it was supposed that these ten Indians were upon an expedition against the English upon the frontiers; having new guns, much ammunition, and spare blankets and moc-

---

donner le tems de gagner le côté de la riviere, qui n'étoit pas encore occupé par les Anglois. Le P. RASLE *averti par les clameurs et le tumulte du danger, où se trouvoient ses néophytes, alla sans crainte se présenter aux assaillans, dans l'esperance d'attirer sur lui seul toute leur attention, et par-là de procurer le salut de son troupeau au peril de sa vie. Son esperance ne fut pas vaine, à peine eut-il paru, que les Anglois jetterent un grand cri, qui fut suivi d'un grêle de mousquetades, dont il tomba mort aupres d'une croix, qu'il avoit plantée au milieu du village: sept sauvages, qui l'accompagnoient, et qui avoient voulu lui faire un rempart de leurs corps, furent tués à ses côtés. Ainsi mourut ce charitable pasteur, endonant sa vie pour ses ouailles, aprés trente-sept ans d'un pénible apostolat."—"Quoiqu'on eût tire sur eux plus de deux mille coups de fusils, il n'y en eut que trente de tués, et quatorze de blesses:"—"ils n'épargnerent pas l'eglise, mais ils n'y mirent le feu, qu'aprè̀s avoir indignement profané les vases sacrés, et le corps adorable de* JESUS-CHRIST. *Ils, [les Anglois,] retirerent ensuite avec une précipitation,"—"avoient été frappés d'une terreur panique. Les sauvages rentrerent aussi-tôt dans leurs villages; et leur premier soin, tandis que les femmes cherchoient des herbes et des plantes propres à guerir les blessés, fut de pleurer sur le corps de lur S. missionnaire. Its le trouverent percé de mille coups, la chevelure enlevée, le crâne brisé à coups de haches, la bouche et les yeux remplis de bouë, les os des jambes fracassés, et tous les membres mutilés de cent manieres differentes." Hist. Gen.* ii. 382–4.

casons, to accommodate captives. This, however, was mere conjecture, and whether they had killed friends or enemies was not quite so certain as that they had killed *Indians.*

It is said that *Paugus* was well known to many of the English, and personally to many of *Lovewell's* men; and that his name was a terror to the frontiers. In a song, composed after the Pequawket fight, he is thus mentioned, as appearing in that battle:—

"'Twas *Paugus* led the Pequ'k't tribe;
As runs the fox, would *Paugus* run;
As howls the wild wolf, would he howl;
A huge bear-skin had *Paugus* on."

There was another chief, who was second to *Paugus* in this fight, by the name of *Wahwa.* What became of him does not appear.

Capt. *Lovewell* marched upon this expedition against *Paugus,* with 46 men, from Dunstable, about the middle of April, 1725. Their setting out is thus poetically set forth in metre:—

"What time the noble *Lovewell* came,
With fifty men from Dunstable,
The cruel Pequ'k't tribe to tame,
With arms and blood-shed terrible."

They arrived near the place where they expected to find Indians, on the 7 May; and, early the next morning, while at prayers, heard a gun, which they rightly suspected to be fired by some of *Paugus's* men, and immediately prepared for an encounter. Divesting themselves of their packs, they marched forward to discover the enemy. But not knowing in what direction to proceed, they marched in an opposite direction from the Indians. This gave *Paugus* great advantage; who, following their tracks, soon fell in with their packs, from which he learned their strength. Being encouraged by his superior numbers, *Paugus* courted the conflict, and pursued the English with ardor. His number of men was said to have been 80, while that of the English consisted of no more than 34, having left ten in a fort at Ossipee; and one, an Indian, had before returned home, on account of sickness. The fort at Ossipee was for a retreat in case of emergency, and to serve as a deposit of part of their provisions, of which they disencumbered themselves before leaving it.

After marching a considerable distance from the place of their encampment, on the morning of the 8 May, Ensign *Wyman* discovered an Indian, who was out hunting, having in one hand some fowls he had just killed, and in the other, two guns. There can be no probability that he thought of meeting an enemy, but no sooner was he discovered by the English, than several guns were fired at him, but missed him. Seeing that sure death was his lot, this valiant Indian resolved to defend himself to his last breath; and the action was as speedy as the thought: his gun was levelled at the English, and *Lovewell* was mortally wounded by the fire. Ensign *Wyman,* taking deliberate aim, killed the poor hunter; which action our poet describes in glowing terms:—

"*Seth Wyman,* who in Woburn lived,
A marksman he of courage true,
Shot the first Indian whom the saw;
Sheer through his heart the bullet flew.

The savage had been seeking game;
Two guns, and eke a knife, he bore,
And two black ducks were in his hand;
He shrieked, and fell to rise no more."

He was scalped by the chaplain and another; and then they marched again by the way they came, for their packs. This was expected by the wary *Paugus,* and he lay in ambush to cut them off. When they had got completely within the ambush,

> "Anon, there eighty* Indians rose,
> Who'd hid themselves in ambush dread;
> Their knives they shook, their guns they aimed,
> The famous *Paugus* at their head."

When the Indians rose from their coverts, they nearly encircled the English, but seemed loath to begin the fight; and were, no doubt, in hopes that the English, seeing their numbers, would yield without a battle; and, therefore, made towards them with their guns presented, and threw away their first fire. This only encouraged the English, and they rushed toward the Indians, fired as they pressed on, and, killing many, drove the Indians for several rods. But they soon rallied and fired vigorously in their turn, and obliged the English to retreat, leaving nine dead and three wounded, where the battle began. *Lovewell,* though mortally wounded before, had led his men until this time, but fell before the retreat.

> "*John Lovewell,* captain of the band,
> His sword he wav'd, that glitter'd bright,
> For the last time he cheer'd his men,
> And led them onward to the fight.
>
> 'Fight on, fight on,' brave *Lovewell* said;
> 'Fight on, while Heaven shall give you breath!'
> An Indian ball then pierc'd him through,
> And *Lovewell* clos'd his eyes in death."

Being near the shore of Saco Pond, the English made good their retreat to it, which prevented their being surrounded; and but for this motion, none could possibly have escaped. The bank of the pond afforded a kind of breastwork,† behind which the English maintained the fight until night. The Indians drew off about dark, and they saw no more of them. Nine only of the English escaped unhurt, though several that were wounded lived to return home. *Paugus* was killed by one *John Chamberlain,* and is thus mentioned by the poet:—

> "But *Chamberlain,* of Dunstable,
> One whom a savage ne'er shall slay,
> Met *Paugus* by the water-side,
> And shot him dead upon that day."

A son of *Paugus,* after peace was restored, came to Dunstable to revenge his father's death by killing *Chamberlain*; but not going directly to him, his design was mistrusted by some one, and communicated to him, and he kept himself upon guard, and had a hole cut through the door of his house, from which early one morning he discovered an Indian behind a pile of wood, with his gun pointed towards the door, to shoot him, he supposed, as he came out; but making use of his advantage, *Chamberlain* fired upon and killed this son of *Paugus.*

---

* Mr. *Williamson,* Hist. Maine, ii. 137, says "about 63." This number he gets, I suppose, from an average of three authors, thus:— *Penhallow,* 70,—*Hutchinson* and *Syinms,* 80,—and *Belknap,* 41; hence, 70+80+41÷3=63+: But he has missed one of his authorities, for 70+80+80+41÷4=68—; i. e. about 68 would be the accurate average.

† *Penhallow's* Indian Wars, 113.

The English chaplain, *Jonathan Frye*, was mortally wounded during the battle.

"A man was he of comely form,
Polish'd and brave, well learnt and kind.
Old Harvard's learned halls he left,
Far in the wilds a grave to find."

He was of Andover, in Massachusetts, and had, but a short time before, graduated at Harvard college.

"Lieutenant *Farwell* took his hand,
His arm around his neck he threw,
And said, 'Brave chaplain, I could wish
That Heaven had made me die for you.'

The chaplain on kind *Farwell's* breast,
Bloody, and languishing, he fell;
Nor after that, said more but this,
'I love thee, soldier; fare thee well!' "

The following lines apply well here, although they are not in the order of the poet:—

"Then did the crimson streams, that flow'd,
Seem like the waters of the brook,
That brightly shine, that loudly dash,
Far down the cliffs of Agiochook."*

If miracles had not then ceased in the land, we should be induced to pass to their credit the extraordinary escape of several of the wounded Englishmen. *Solomon Keyes*, having received three wounds, said he would hide himself, and die in a secret place, where the Indians could not find him to get his scalp. As he crawled upon the shore of the pond, at some

* The Indian name of the White Mountains, or, as the people of New Hampshire would say, White Hills. The natives believed the summits of these mountains to be inhabited by invisible beings, but whether good or evil we are not informed. Nor is it of much importance, since they reverenced the one as much as the other.

It is always highly gratifying to the curious to observe how people primitively viewed objects which have become familiar to them. We will here present the reader with Mr. *Josselyn's* description of the White Mountains, not for its *accuracy*, but for its curious extravagance. "Four score miles, (upon a direct line,) to the N. W. of Scarborow, a ridge ofmountains run N. W. and N. E. an hundred leagues, known by the name of the White Mountains, upon which lieth snow all the year, and is a landmark twenty miles off at sea. It is a rising ground from the sea shore to these hills, and they are inaccessible but by the gullies which the dissolved snow hath made. In these gullies grow saven bushes, which being taken hold of, are a good help to the climbing discoverer. Upon the top of the highest of these mountains, is a large level, or plain, of a day's journey over, whereon nothing grows but moss. At the farther end of this plain is another hill called the *Sugar-loaf*, to outward appearance a rude heap of massie stones piled one upon another, and you may, as you ascend, step from one stone to another, as if you were going up a pair of stairs, but winding still about the hill, till you come to the top, which will require half a day's time, and yet it is not above a mile, where there is also a level of about an acre of ground, with a pond of clear water in the midst of it, which you may hear run down, but how it ascends is a mystery. From this rocky hill you may see the whole country round about; it is far above the lower clouds, and from hence we beheld a vapor, (like a great pillar,) drawn up by the sun-beams out of a great lake, or pond, into the air, where it was formed into a cloud. The country beyond these hills, northward, is daunting terrible, being full of rocky hills, as thick as mole-hills in a meadow, and cloathed with infinite thick woods." *New England's Rarities*, 3, 4. Sad recollections are associated with the name of these mountains. The destruction of lives, occasioned by an avalanche at the celebrated Notch, in 1826, will not soon be forgotten. Mr. *Moore*, of Concord, has published an interesting account of it in the Col. N. H Hist. Soc. vol. iii.

distance from the scene of action, he found a canoe, into which he rolled himself, and was drifted away by the wind. To his great astonishment, he was cast ashore at no great distance from the fort at Ossipee, to which he crawled, and there met several of his companions; and gaining strength, returned home with them.

Those who escaped did not leave the battle ground until near midnight. When they arrived at the fort, they expected to have found refreshment, and those they had left as a reserve; but a fellow whose name is not mentioned, who deserted the rest when the battle began, so frightened them, that they fled in great confusion and dismay to their homes.

The place where this fight took place was 50 miles from any white inhabitants; and that any should have survived the famine which now stared them in the face, is almost as miraculous as that they should have escaped death at the hands of the courageous warriors of *Paugus;* yet 14 lived to return to their friends.

Fifty men, from New Hampshire, afterwards marched to the scene of action, where they found and buried the dead. They found but three Indians, one of whom was *Paugus*. The rest were supposed to have been taken away when they retreated from the battle.* We will let the poet close the account:—

"Ah! many a wife shall rend her hair,
And many a child cry, ' Woe is me,'
When messengers the news shall bear,
Of *Lovewell's* dear-bought victory.

With footsteps slow shall travellers go,
Where *Lovewell's* pond shines clear and bright,
And mark the place where those are laid,
Who fell in *Lovewell's* bloody fight.

Old men shall shake their heads, and say,
Sad was the hour and terrible,
When *Lovewell,* brave, 'gainst *Paugus* went,
With fifty men from Dunstable."

After *Lovewell's* fight, the Androscoggin and Pequawket Indians retired to the head of Connecticut River. They remained here but two years in peace, at which time the Androscoggins removed to Canada, where they were afterwards known as the St. Francis tribe. The others remained on the Connecticut. Their chief, *Philip,* fought with the Americans in the revolutionary war.†

* For the principal facts in this account, we are indebted to *Symmes's* narrative of the fight, published the same year in which it happened, and lately republished in *Farmer* and *Moore's* Historical Collections, vol. i. The poetry is from vol. iii. of the same work.

† *Rogers's* Reminis. Fr. War. 160.

BOOK IV.

BIOGRAPHY AND HISTORY OF THE SOUTHERN INDIANS.

CHAPTER I.

Preliminary observations respecting the country of the southern Indians— WINGINA, *the first Virginia chief known to the English—Destroys the first colony settled there—*MENATONON— SKIKO— ENSENORE—*Second colony abandons the country—Tobacco first carried to England by them—Curious account of prejudices against it—*GRANGANEMEO—*His kindnesses—His family—His death—*POWHATAN—*Boundaries of his country—Surprises the Payankatanks—Capt. Smith fights his people—Opekankanough takes Smith prisoner—The particulars of that affair—He marches him about the country—Takes him, at length, to Powhatan, who condemns him to be put to death—Smith's life saved at the intercession of Pocahontas—Insolence of Powhatan increased by Newport's folly—Smith brings him to terms—A crown sent over to him from England—Is crowned emperor—Speech—Uses every stratagem to kill Smith—Is baffled in every attempt—Smith visits him—Speeches—Pocahontas again saves Smith and his comrades from being murdered by her father—*TOMOCOMO.

THE difficulty of rightly partitioning between the southern nations and the Iroquois, or Five Nations, can easily be seen by all such as have but very partially taken a survey of them, and considered their wandering habits. Therefore, should we, in this book, not always assign a sachem to his original family or nation, we can only plead in excuse, that we have gone according to our best information. But we have endeavored to draw a kind of natural boundary between the above-mentioned nations, distinguishing those people beyond the Chesapeake and some of its tributaries, as the southern Indians, and those between that boundary and the Hudson by the name Iroquois. To their respective territories inland, we shall not, nor is it necessary to, fix bounds, in our present business. We are aware that some writers suppose that all the Indians, from the Mississippi to the vicinity of the Hudson, and even to the Connecticut, were originally of the same stock. If this were the case, the period is so remote when they spread themselves over the country, that these great natural divisions had long since caused quite a difference in the inhabitants which they separated; and hence the propriety of noticing them according to our plan.

It is said that the territory from the sea-coast to the River Alleghany, and from the most southern waters of James River up to Patuxent, in the state of Maryland, was inhabited by three different nations, and that the language of each differed essentially from the others. The English called these nations by the names *Powhatans, Manahoacs*, and *Monacans*; these were the Tuscaroras. The Powhatans were the most powerful, and consisted of several tribes, or communities, who possessed the country from the sea-coast to the falls of the rivers.*

To give a tolerable catalogue of the names of the various nations of Virginia, the Carolinas, and thence to the Mississippi, would far exceed our plan. We shall, therefore, pass to notice the chiefs of such of those nations as are distinguished in history, pointing out, by the way, their localities, and whatever shall appear necessary in way of elucidation, as we pass, and as we have done in the preceding books.

Wingina was first known to the English voyagers *Amidas* and *Barlow*, who landed in Virginia in the summer of 1584, upon an island called, by the Indians, *Wokokon*. They saw none of the natives until the third day, when three were observed in a canoe. One of them got on shore, and the English went to him. He showed no signs of fear, "but spoke much to them," then went boldly on board the vessels. After they had given him a shirt, hat, wine, and some meat, "he went away, and in half an hour he had loaded his canoe with fish," which he immediately brought, and gave to the English.

Wingina, at this time, was confined to his cabin from wounds he had lately received in battle, probably in his war with *Piamacum*, a desperate and bloody chief.

Upon the death of *Granganemeo*, in 1585, *Wingina* changed his name to *Pemissapan*. He never had much faith in the good intentions of the English, and to him was mainly attributed the breaking up of the first colony which settled in Virginia.

It was upon the return to England of the Captains *Amidas* and *Barlow*, from the country of Wingina, that Queen *Elizabeth*, from the wonderful accounts of that fruitful and delightful place, named it, out of respect to herself, Virginia; she being called the virgin queen, from her living unmarried. But, with more honor to her, some have said, "Because it still seemed to retain the virgin purity and plenty of the first creation, and the people their primitive innocency of life and manners."† *Waller* referred to this country when he wrote this:—

"So sweet the air, so moderate the clime,
None sickly lives, or dies before his time.
Heav'n sure has kept this spot of earth uncurst,
To show how all things were created first."

---

* From a communication of Secretary *Thompson* to Mr. *Jefferson*, and appended to the Notes on Virginia, ed. of 1801.

† Stith, 11.

Sir *Richard Greenvil*, stimulated by the love of gain, next intruded himself upon the shores of *Wingina*. It was he who committed the first outrage upon the natives, which occasioned the breaking up of the colony which he left behind him. He made but one short excursion into the country, during which, by foolishly exposing his commodities, some native took from him a silver cup, to *revenge* the loss of which, a town was burned. He left 108 men, who seated themselves upon the island of Roanoke. *Ralph Lane*, a military character of note, was governor, and Capt. *Philip Amidas* lieut. governor of this colony. They made various excursions about the country, in hopes of discovering mines of precious metals; in which they were a long time duped by the Indians, for their ill conduct towards them, in compelling them to pilot them about. *Wingina* bore, as well as he could, the provocations of the intruders, until the death of the old chief *Ensenore*, his father. Under pretence of honoring his funeral, he assembled 1800 of his people, with the intention, as the English say, of destroying them. They, therefore, upon the information of *Skiko*, son of the chief *Menatonon*,* fell upon them, and, after killing five or six, the rest made their escape into the woods. This was done upon the island where *Wingina* lived, and the English first seized upon the boats of his visitants, to prevent their escape from the island, with the intention, no doubt, of murdering them all. Not long after, "*Wingina* was entrapped by the English, and slain, with eight of his chief men."

Menatonon was king of the Chawonocks, and *Okisko* of the Weopomeokes, "a powerful nation, possessing all that country from Albemarle Sound and Chowan River, quite to the Chesapeakes and our bay."† At this time, *Menatonon* was lame, and is mentioned as the most sensible and understanding Indian with whom the English were at first acquainted. It was he that made *Lane* and his followers believe in the existence of the mine already mentioned. "So eager were they," says Mr. *Stith*, "and resolutely bent upon this golden discovery, that they could not be persuaded to return, as long as they had one pint of corn a man left, and two mastiff dogs, which, being boiled with sassafras leaves, might afford them some sustenance in their way back." After great sufferings, they arrived upon the coast again.

The reason why *Menatonon* deceived the English, was because they made him a prisoner for the purpose of assisting them in making discoveries. After he was set at liberty, he was very kind to them. Two years after, when Governor *White* was in the country, they mention his wife and child as belonging to Croatan, but nothing of him.

White and his company landed at Roanoake, 22 July, 1587, and sent 20 men to Croatan, on Point Lookout, with a friendly native called *Manteo*, to see if any intelligence could be had of a former colony of 50 men left there by Sir *Richard Greenvil*. They learned, from some natives whom they met, that the people of Dassamonpeak, on what is now Alligator River, had attacked them, killed one, and driven the others away, but whither they had gone none could tell. One of their present company, a principal man of their government, had also been killed by the same Indians. This tribe and several others had agreed to come to Roanoake, and submit themselves to the English; but not coming according to appointment, gave the English an opportunity to take revenge for former injuries. Therefore, Capt. *Stafford* and 24 men, with *Manteo* as a guide, set out upon that business. On coming to their village, "where seeing them sit by the fire, we assaulted them. The miserable soules amazed, fled into the reeds, where one was shot through, and we thought to have

---

* *Smith* calls him the "lame king of Moratoc."

† *Stith's* Virginia, 14. By "our bay" is meant *James River Bay*.

been fully revenged, but we were deceived, for they were our friends come from Croatan to gather their corn!" "Being thus disappointed of our purpose, we gathered the fruit we found ripe, left the rest unspoiled, and took *Menatonon,* his wife with her child, and the rest with us to Roanoak."* But to return to *Wingina.*

While the English were upon the errand we have been speaking of, *Wingina* pretended to be their friend, but deceived them on every opportunity, by giving notice to his countrymen of their course and purpose, and urging them to cut them off. He thought, at one time, that the English were destroyed, and thereupon scoffed and mocked at such a God as theirs, who would suffer it. This caused his son *Ensenore* to join their enemies, but on their return he was their friend again. He, and many of his people, now believed, say the voyagers, that "we could do them more hurt being dead, than liuing, and that, being an hundred myles from them, shot, and struck them sick to death, and that when we die it is but for a time, then we return again." Many of the chiefs now came and submitted themselves to the English, and, among others, *Ensenore* persuaded his father to become their friend, who, when they were in great straits for provisions, came and planted their fields, and made wears in the streams to catch fish, which were of infinite benefit to them. This was in the spring of 1586, and, says *Lane,* "we not having one corn till the next harvest to sustain us." What added greatly to their distresses, was the death of their excellent friend *Ensenore,* who died 20th of April following. The Indians began anew their conspiracies, and the colony availed themselves of the first opportunity of returning to England, which was in the fleet of Sir *Francis Drake,* which touched there in its way from an expedition against the Spaniards in the West Indies.†

The conduct of *Lane* and his company in this fruitless attempt to establish themselves in Virginia, was, in the highest degree, reprehensible. They put to death some of the natives on the most frivolous charges, and no wonder they were driven out of the country, as they ought to have been.‡ While they were there, they became acquainted with the use of *tobacco,* and, taking it to England, its introduction into general use soon rendered it a great article of commerce. And here it will not be improper to notice how many different persons have had the credit, or, perhaps, I should say discredit, of introducing this "Indian weed" into England; as, Sir *Francis Drake,* Sir *Walter Ralegh, Ralph Lane,* and some others. Now, as some writer observes, the reader may father it upon whom he pleases, as it is evident Sir Francis Drake took Ralph Lane and tobacco both together into England; and no one will dispute the agency of the gallant knight, Sir *Walter Ralegh,* for he sent out *Lane* in his employ.

Mr. *John Josselyn,* in his "Two Voyages to N. England," has this passage: "Others will have tobacco to be first brought into England from Peru, by Sir *Francis Drake's* mariners."

There were many who affected a violent disgust towards the use of tobacco; the most conspicuous was King *James,* whose mind seems to have been just weak enough to fight windmills. He even wrote a book denouncing its use in the severest terms he could command. Not doubting but the reader will be gratified with a specimen of the opposition with which our Indian plant met, in its transatlantic use, we will offer him a passage from *Winstanley's* Worthies,§ which, he says, is from one of the poets of that day:—

* *Smith's* Hist. Virginia.
† Relation of *Lane,* printed in *Smith's* Virginia.
‡ *Herriot's* Observations, (one of *Lane's* company,) printed in *Smith.*
§ Page 211, 212.

"He's no good fellow that's without the [—]x,
Burnt pipes, *tobacco*, and his tinder box."

He then proceeds, "a folly which certainly had never spread so far, if here had been the same means of prevention used with us, as was in Turky by *Morat Bassa*, who commanded a pipe to be thrust through the nose of a Turk which was found taking tobacco, and so in derision to be led about Constantinople. Take his farewell to it, who once much doted on this heathenish weed:—

'Farewell, thou Indian smoak, barbarian vapor,
An enemy to life, foe to waste paper.
Thou dost diseases in the body breed,
And like a vulter on the purse dost feed.
Changing sweet breaths into a stinking loathing,
And with three pipes turns twopence into nothing.
Grim Pluto first invented it, I think,
To poyson all the world with hellish stink:
Base heathenish weed, how common is grown,
That but a few years past was scarcely known!
When for to see one take it was a riddle,
As strange as a baboon to tune a fiddle.
Were it confined onely to gentlemen,
'Twere some repute to take tobacco then,
But bedlams, tinkers, coblers, water-bearers,
Your common drunkards, and most horid swearers.
If man's flesh be like hogs, as it is said,
Then surely by smoaking thus it's bacon made.
Farewell, foul smoak, good for such things as these,
'Gainst lice, sore heads, scabs, *mange*, or French disease.' "

Tobacco grew spontaneously in Wingandacoa, (Virginia,) and the natives called it *Uppowoc*. It is generally supposed to be called *tobacco* from the island *Tobago*, but this derivation is denied by some.*

But to return to our biography. *Granganemeo* was a chief very favorably spoken of. As soon as the arrival of the English was made known to him, he visited them with about 40 of his men, who were very civil, and of a remarkably robust and fine appearance. When they had left their boat, and came upon the shore near the ship, *Granganemeo* spread a mat and sat down upon it. The English went to him armed, but he discovered no fear, and invited them to sit down; after which he performed some tokens of friendship; then making a speech to them, they presented him with some toys. None but four of his people spoke a word, or sat down, but maintained the most perfect silence. On being shown a pewter dish, he was much pleased with it, and purchased it with 20 deer-skins, which were worth, in England, one hundred shillings sterling!! The dish he used as an ornament, making a hole through it, and wearing it about his neck. While here, the English entertained him, with his wife and children, on board their ship. His wife had in her ears bracelets of pearl, which reached to her middle. Shortly after, many of the people came out of the country to trade, "but when *Granganemeo* was present, none durst trade but himself, and them that wore red copper on their heads as he did." He was remarkably exact in keeping his promise, "for oft we trusted him, and he would come within his day to keep his word." And these voyagers further report, that "commonly he sent them every day a brace of bucks, conies, hares, and fish, and sometimes melons, walnuts, cucumbers, pease and divers roots."

In their wanderings, Capt. *Amidas* and seven others visited the island of Roanoake, where they found the family of *Granganemeo* living in great

* *Stith's* Hist. Virginia, 19.

comfort and plenty, in a little town of nine houses. The chief was not at home, "but his wife entertained them with wonderful courtesy and kindness. She made some of her people draw their boat up, to prevent its being injured by the beating of the surge; some she ordered to bring them ashore on their backs, and others to carry their oars to the house, for fear of being stole. When they came into the house, she took off their cloathes and stockings, and washed them, as likewise their feet in warm water. When their dinner was ready, they were conducted into an inner room, (for there were five in the house, divided by mats,) where they found hominy,* boiled venison, and roasted fish; and, as a desert, melons, boiled roots, and fruits of various sorts. While they were at meat, two or three of her men came in with their bows and arrows, which made the English take to their arms. But she, perceiving their distrust, ordered their bows and arrows to be broken, and themselves to be beaten out of the gate. In the evening, the English returned to their boat; and, putting a little off from shore, lay at anchor; at which she was much concerned, and brought their supper, half boiled, pots and all to the shore; and, seeing their jealousy, she ordered several men, and 30 women, to sit all night upon the shore, as a guard; and sent five mats to cover them from the weather."† Well hath the poet demanded, "Call ye them savage?" If the wife of *Granganemeo* was savage, in the common acceptation of the term, where shall we look for civilization?

Sir *R. Greenvil,* having arrived on the coast in 1685, anchored off the island Wokokon, 26 May, and, by means of *Manteo,* had some intercourse with the inhabitants. At Hatteras, where they staid a short time, soon after, *Granganemeo,* with *Manteo,* went on board their ships. This was the last visit he made to the English.

This must close our account of the excellent family of *Granganemeo,* and would that the *account* of the English would balance as well, but they exhibit their own, and one item more from it, and we close the comparison. For a small kettle they took 50 skins, worth in England £12. 10s. sterling.‡

We have now arrived at the most interesting article in Virginia history. *Powhatan* was, of all the chiefs of his age, the most famous in the regions of Virginia. The English supposed, at first, that his was the name of the country; a common error, as we have seen in several cases in the previous books of our biography, but, in this case, unlike the others, the error prevailed, and a part of his people, ever after the settlement of the English, were called the *Powhatans.* A great river, since called the *James,* and a bay received his name also. He had three brothers, *Opitchepan, Opekankanough* and *Catatanugh,* and two sisters. His principal residence was at a place called *Werowocomoco,* when the English came into the country; which was upon the north side of what is now York River, in the county of Gloucester, nearly opposite the mouth of Queen's Creek, and about 25 miles below the fork of the river.§ He lived here until the English began to intrude themselves into his vicinity, when he took up his residence at Orakakes.

Powhatan was not his Indian name, or rather original name; that was *Wahunsonacock.* He is described as tall and well proportioned—bearing an aspect of sadness—exceedingly vigorous, and possessing a

---

* "A food made of Indian corn, or maize, beaten and carefully husked, something like furmety in England; and is an excellent dish various ways."

† *Stith's* Hist. Virginia, 10, 11.

‡ *Smith's* Hist. Virginia.

§ About two miles below where Richmond now stands. The farm of a gentleman of the name of *Mayo* included the site of a part of his town, in 1813.—*Campbell's Virginia.*

body capable of sustaining great hardships. He was, in 1607, about 60 years of age, and his hair was considerably gray, which gave him a majestic appearance. At his residence, he had a kind of wooden form to sit upon, and his ornamental robe was of raccoon skins, and his head-dress was composed of many feathers wrought into a kind of crown. He swayed many nations upon the great rivers and bays, the chief of whom he had conquered. He originally claimed only the places called Powhatan, (since named Haddihaddocks,) Arrohattock, (now Appomattox,) Youghtanund, Pamunky, Mattapony, Werowocomoco, and Kiskiak; at which time, his chief seat was at Powhatan, near the falls of James River. But when he had extended his conquests a great way north, he removed to Werowocomoco, as a more commodious situation.

At the termination of his warlike career, the country upon James River, from its mouth to the falls, and all its branches, was the boundary of his country, southerly—and so across the country, "nearly as high as the falls of all the great rivers, over Potowmack, even to Patuxent, in Maryland," and some of the nations on the north shore of the Chesapeake. His dominions, according to his law of succession, did not fall to his children, but to his brothers, and then to his sisters, (the oldest first,) thence to the heirs oldest; but never to the heirs of the males.

He usually kept a guard of 40 or 50 of the most resolute and well-formed men about him, especially when he slept; but, after the English came into his country, he increased them to about 200. He had as many, and such women as he pleased; and, when he slept, one sat at his head and another at his feet. When he was tired of any of his wives, he bestowed them upon such of his men as most pleased him. Like the New England chiefs, he had many places where he passed certain seasons of the year; at some of which he had very spacious wigwams, 30 or 40 yards in extent, where he had victuals provided against his coming.

In 1608, he surprised the people of Payankatank, who were his neighbors and subjects. Captain *Smith,* in the account, "*writ with his own hand,*" says, "the occasion was to vs vnknowne, but the manner was thus." He sent several of his men to lodge with them the night on which he meant to fall upon them; then, secretly surrounding them in their wigwams, commenced a horrid slaughter. They killed 24 men, took off their scalps, and, with the woman and children prisoners, returned to the sachem's village. The scalps they exhibited upon a line between two trees, as a trophy, and the *werowance* (their name of a chief) and his wife *Powhatan* made his servants.

From 1585 to 1607, every attempt to settle a colony in Virginia had failed; and, at this time, would have failed also, but for the unexampled perseverance of one man. I need but pronounce the name of Capt. *John Smith.* The colony with which he came did not arrive until the planting season was over; and, in a short time, they found themselves in a suffering condition, from want of suitable provisions. *Smith,* therefore, undertook to gain a supply by trafficking with the Indians back in the country, who, being acquainted with his situation, insulted him and his men wherever they came; offering him but a handful of corn, or a piece of bread, for a gun or a sword. "But seeing by trade and courtesie there was nothing to be had, he made bold to try such conclusions as necessitie inforced, though contrary to his commission." So he fired upon them, and drove them into the woods. He then marched to their village. There they found corn in abundance, which, after some manœuvring, he succeeded in trading for, and returned with a supply to Jamestown.

Smith, soon after, proceeded to discover the source of the Chikahamania. When he had passed up as far as it was navigable for his barge, he left it in a wide place, at a safe distance from the shore, and ordered his men not to go on shore on any condition. Taking two of his own men and two Indians, he proceeded to complete his discovery. As soon as he was gone, his men went on shore; one was killed, and the rest hardly escaped. *Smith* was now 20 miles into the wilderness. *Opekankanough*, with 300 warriors, having learned, from the men they had just taken, which way he was gone, followed after him, and came upon the two Englishmen belonging to his company, and killed them both while asleep, he being absent to shoot some fowls for provisions; they then continued their pursuit after him. He was not far from his canoe, and endeavored to retreat to it, but, being hard pressed, made a shield of one of his Indians, and, in this manner, fought upon the retreat, until he had killed three, and wounded divers others. Being obliged to give all his attention to his pursuers, he accidentally fell into a creek, where the mud was so deep that he could not extricate himself. Even now, none dared to lay hands upon him; and those whom their own numbers forced nearest to him, were observed to tremble with fear. The Indian he had bound to his arm with his garters, doubtless saved him from being killed by their arrows, from which, owing to his Indian shield, he received but very little hurt, except a wound in his thigh, though his clothes were shot full of them.

When he could stand no longer in the mire, without perishing with cold, he threw away his arms, and suffered them to come and take him. After pulling him out of the mire, they took him to the place where his men had just been killed, where there was a fire. They now showed him kindness, rubbing his benumbed limbs, and warming him by the fire. He asked for their chief, and *Opekankanough* appeared, to whom he gave a small compass. This amused them exceedingly. "Much they marvelled at the playing of the fly and needle, which they could see so plainly, and yet not touch it, because of the glass that covered them. But when he demonstrated, by that globe-like iewell, the roundnesse of the earth, and skies, the spheare of the sunne, and moone, and starres, and how the sunne did chase the night round about the world, continually—the greatnesse of the land and sea, the diversity of the nations, varietie of complexions, and how we were to them antipodes, and many other such like matters, they all stood as amazed with admiration!" Yet, notwithstanding he had such success in explaining to them his knowledge of geography and astronomy, (how much of it they understood we will not undertake to say,) within an hour after, they tied him to a tree, and a multitude of them seemed prepared to shoot him. But when their bows were bent, *Opekankanough* held up his compass, and they all laid down their weapons. They now led him to Orapakas, or Orakakes, a temporary seat of *Powhatan*, on the north side of Chikahominy swamp. Here they feasted him, and treated him well.

When they marched him, they drew themselves up in a row, with their chief in the midst, before whom the guns and swords they had taken from the English were borne. *Smith* came next, led by three great men hold of each arm, and on each side six more, with their arrows notched, and ready, if he should attempt to escape. At the town, they danced and sung about him, and then put him into a large house, or wigwam. Here they kept him so well, that he thought they were fatting him to kill and eat. They took him to a sick man to cure him; but he told them he could not, unless they would let him go to Jamestown, and get something with which he could do it. This they would not consent to.

The taking of Jamestown was now resolved upon, and they made great preparations for it. To this end, they endeavored to get *Smith's* assistance, by making large promises of land and women; but he told them it could not be done, and described to them the great difficulty of the undertaking in such a manner that they were greatly terrified. With the idea of procuring something curious, *Smith* prevailed upon some of them to go to Jamestown; which journey they performed in the most severe, frosty and snowy weather. By this means, he gave the people there to understand what his situation was, and what was intended against them, by sending a leaf from his pocket-book, with a few words written upon it. He wrote, also, for a few articles to be sent, which were duly brought by the messengers. Nothing had caused such astonishment as their bringing the very articles *Smith* had promised them. That he could talk to his friends, at so great a distance, was utterly incomprehensible to them.

Being obliged to give up the idea of destroying Jamestown, they amused themselves by taking their captive from place to place, in great pomp and triumph, and showing him to the different nations of the dominions of *Powhatan*. They took him to Youghtannund, since called *Pamunkey* River, the country over which *Opekankanough* was chief, whose principal residence was where the town of Pamunkey since was; thence to the Mattaponies, Piankatanks, the Nautaughtacunds, on Rappahanock, the Nominies, on the Patowmack River; thence, in a circuitous course, through several other nations, back again to the residence of *Opekankanough*. Here they practised conjurations upon him for three successive days; to ascertain, as they said, whether he intended them good or evil. This proves they viewed him as a kind of god. A bag of gunpowder having fallen into their hands, they preserved it with great care, thinking it to be a grain, intending, in the spring, to plant it, as they did corn. He was here again feasted, and none could eat until he had done.

Being now satisfied, having gone through all the manœuvres and pranks with him they could think of, they proceeded to *Powhatan*. "Here more than 200 of those grim courtiers stood wondering at him, as he had been a monster, till *Powhatan* and his trayne had put themselves in their greatest braveries." He was seated before a fire, upon a seat like a bedstead, having on a robe of raccoon skins, "and all the tayles hanging by." On each side of him sat a young woman; and upon each side of the house two rows of men, and with as many women behind them. These last had their heads and shoulders painted red—some of whose heads were adorned with white down; and about their necks white beads. On *Smith's* being brought into the presence of *Powhatan,* all present joined in a great shout. "The queen of Apamatuck was appointed to bring him water to wash his hands, and another brought him a bunch of feathers, instead of a towel, to dry them." Then, having feasted him again, "after their best barbarous manner they could, a long consultation was held, but the conclusion was, two great stones were brought before *Powhatan*—then as many as could lay hands on him, dragged him to them and thereon laid his head, and being ready, with their clubs, to beat out his brains, *Pocahontas,* the king's dearest daughter, when no entreaty could prevail, got his head in her armes, and laid her own upon his, to save him from death."

Powhatan was unable to resist the extraordinary solicitations and sympathetic entreaties of his kind-hearted little daughter, and thus was saved the life of Capt. *Smith;* a character, who, without this astonishing deliverance, was sufficiently renowned for escapes and adventures.

The old sachem, having set the sentence of death aside, made up his mind to employ *Smith* as an artisan; to make, for himself, robes, shoes, bows, arrows, and pots; and, for *Pocahontas,* bells, beads, and copper trinkets. *Powhatan's* son, named *Nantaquaus,* was very friendly to *Smith,* and rendered him many important services, as well after as during his captivity.

"Two days after, *Powhatan,* having disguised himself in the most fearfullest manner he could, caused Captain *Smith* to be brought forth to a great house in the woods, and there, upon a mat by the fire, to be left alone. Not long after, from behinde a mat that divided the house, was made the most dolefullest noyse he ever heard; then *Powhatan,* more like a Devill then a man, with some 200 more, as black as himselfe, came unto him, and told him, now they were friends; and presently he should go to Jamestowne, to send him two great gunnes, and a gryndestone, for which he would give him the country of Capahowosick, [Capahowsick,] and forever esteem him his sonne, *Nantuquond.* So to Jamestowne, with 12 guides, *Powhatan* sent him. That night they quartered in the woods, he still expecting, (as he had done all this long time of his imprisonment,) every hour to be put to one death or another." Early the next morning, they came to the fort at Jamestown. Here he treated his guides with the greatest attention and kindness, and offered *Rawhunt,* in a jesting manner, and for the sake of a little sport, a huge mill-stone, and two demi-culverins, or nine pound cannons, to take to *Powhatan,* his master; thus fulfilling his engagement to send him a grindstone and two guns. This *Rawhunt* was a sachem under *Powhatan,* and one of his most faithful captains, and who, it seems, accompanied *Smith* in his return out of captivity.

"They found them somewhat too heavie, but when they did see him discharge them, being loaded with stones, among the boughs of a great tree loaded with isickles, the yce and branches came so tumbling down, that the poore salvages ran away half dead with fear. But, at last, we regained some conference with them, and gave them such toyes, and sent to *Powhatan,* his women, and children, such presents, and gave them in generall full content."*

* This is Captain *Smith's* own account, which I shall follow minutely; adding occasionally from *Stith,* to illustrate the geography of the country.

King Powhatan commands C. Smith to be slayne, his daughter Pocahontas *beggs his life his thankfulness and how he subjected of their kings reade y history.*

Engraved from the original as Published by CAPT. SMITH *himself.*

Powhatan was now completely in the English interest, and almost every other day sent his daughter, *Pocahontas,* with victuals, to Jamestown, of which they were greatly in need. *Smith* had told *Powhatan* that a great chief, which was Captain *Newport,* would arrive from England about that time, which coming to pass as he had said, greatly increased his admiration of the wisdom of the English, and he was ready to do as they desired in every thing; and, but for the vanity and ostentation of *Newport,* matters would have gone on well, and trade flourished greatly to their advantage. But he lavished so many presents upon *Powhatan,* that he was in no way inclined to trade, and soon began to show his haughtiness, by demanding five times the value of an article, or his contempt for what was offered.

By *Newport's* imprudence and folly, what had cost *Smith* so much toil and pains to achieve, was blown away by a single breath of vanity. Nevertheless, his great mind, continually exercised in difficult matters, brought the subtle chief again to his own terms. Himself, with Newport, and about 20 others, went to *Powhatan's* residence to trade with him. "Wherein *Powhatan* carried himself so proudly, yet discreetly, (in his salvage manner,) as made us all to admire his natural gifts." He pretended that it was far beneath his dignity to trade as his men did. Thus his craft to obtain from *Newport* his goods for whatever he pleased to give in return. *Smith* saw through *Powhatan's* craft, and told *Newport* how it would turn out, but being determined to show himself as dignified as the Indian chief, repented of his folly, like too many others, when it was too late. *Smith* was the interpreter in the business, and *Newport* the chief. *Powhatan* made a speech to him, when they were about to enter upon trading. He said, "Captain *Newport,* it is not agreeable to my greatness, in this peddling manner, to trade for trifles; and I esteem you also a great werowance. Therefore, lay me down all your commodities together; what I like I will take, and in recompense give you what I think fitting their value." Accordingly, *Newport* gave him all his goods, and received in return only about three bushels of corn; whereas they expected to have obtained 20 hogsheads. This transaction created some hard thoughts between *Smith* and *Newport.*

If it add to raise *Powhatan* in our admiration, it can detract nothing from the character of *Smith,* to say, that he was as wily as the great Indian chief. For, with a few blue beads, which he pretended that he had shown him only by accident, and which he would hardly part with, as he pretended, because they were of great price, and worn only by great kings, he completely got his end, at this time, answered. Tantalization had the desired effect, and *Powhatan* was so infatuated with the lure, that he was almost beside himself, and was ready to give all he had, to possess them. "So that, ere we departed," says my relation, "for a pound or two of blew beades, he brought over my king for 2 or 300 bushells of corne."

An English boy was left with *Powhatan,* by Captain *Newport,* to learn the language, manners, customs and geography of his country; and, in return, *Powhatan* gave him *Namontack,* one of his servants, of a shrewd and subtle capacity; whom he afterwards carried to England. *Powhatan* became offended with Captain *Smith,* when *Newport* left the country, in 1608; at whose departure he sent him 20 turkeys, and demanded, in return, 20 swords, which were granted. Shortly after, he sent the same number to *Smith,* expecting the like return; but, being disappointed, ordered his men to seize the English wherever they could find them. This caused difficulty—many of the English being robbed of their swords, in the vicinity of their forts. They continued their depredations until *Smith* surprised a number of them, from whom he learned that *Powhatan* was endeavoring to get all the arms in his power, to be able to massacre the

English. When he found that his plot was discovered, he sent *Pocahontas*, with presents, to excuse himself, and pretended that the mischief was done by some of his ungovernable chiefs. He directed her to endeavor to effect the release of his men that were prisoners, which *Smith* consented to, wholly, as he pretended, on her account; and thus peace was restored, which had been continually interrupted for a considerable time before.

On the 10th of September, 1608, *Smith* was elected governor of Virginia. *Newport*, going often to England, had a large share in directing the affairs of the colony, from his interest with the proprietors. He arrived about this time, and, among other baubles, brought over a crown for *Powhatan*, with directions for his coronation; which had the ill effect to make him value himself more than ever. *Newport* was instructed to discover the country of the Monacans, a nation with whom *Powhatan* was at war, and whom they would assist him against, if he would aid in the business. Captain *Smith* was sent to him to invite him to Jamestown to receive presents, and to trade for corn. On arriving at Werowocomoco, and delivering his message to the old chief, he replied, "*If your king have sent me presents, I also am a king, and this is my land. Eight days I will stay to receive them. Your father* [*meaning* Newport] *is to come to me, not I to him, nor yet to your fort—neither will I bite at such a bate. As for the Monacans, I can revenge my own injuries; and as for Atquanachuck, where you say your brother was slain, it is a contrary way from those parts you suppose it; but, for any salt water beyond the mountains, the relations you have had from my people are false.*" Some of the Indians had made the English believe that the South Sea, now called the Pacific Ocean, was but a short distance back. To show *Smith* the absurdity of the story, he drew a map of the country, upon the ground. *Smith* returned as wise as he went.

A house was built for *Powhatan*, about this time, by some Germans, who came over with *Newport*. These men, thinking that the English could not subsist in the country, wantonly betrayed all the secrets of the English to *Powhatan*, which was again the source of much trouble. They even urged him to put all the English to death, agreeing to live with him, and assist him in the execution of the horrible project. *Powhatan* was pleased at the proposition, and thought, by their assistance, to effect what he had formerly hoped to do by engaging *Smith* in such an enterprise. Their first object was to kill Captain *Smith;* by which act, the chief obstacle to success would be removed; and, accordingly, they took every means in their power to effect it.

In the first place, he invited him to come and trade for corn, hoping an opportunity, in that business, would offer. That his design might not be mistrusted, *Powhatan* promised to load his ship with corn, if he would bring him a grindstone, 50 swords, some muskets, a cock and a hen, and a quantity of copper and beads. *Smith* went accordingly, but guarded, as though sure of meeting an enemy.

In their way, the English stopped at Warrasqueake, and were informed, by the sachem of that place, of *Powhatan's* intentions. That sachem kindly entertained them, and, when they departed, furnished them with guides. On account of extreme bad weather, they were obliged to spend near a week at Kicquotan. This obliged them to keep their Christmas among the Indians, and, according to our authorities, a merry Christmas it was; having been "never more merry in their lives, lodged by better fires, or fed with greater plenty of good bread, oysters, fish, flesh and wild fowl."

Having arrived at Werowocomoco, after much hardship, they sent to *Powhatan* for provisions, being in great want, not having taken but three or four days' supply along with them. The old chief sent them immediately a supply of bread, turkeys and venison, and soon after made a feast for them, according to custom.

Meanwhile, *Powhatan* pretended he had not sent for the English; telling them he had no corn, "and his people much less,"* and, therefore, intimated that he wished they would go off again. But *Smith* produced the messenger that he had sent, and so confronted him; *Powhatan* then laughed heartily, and thus it passed for a joke. He then asked for their commodities, "but he liked nothing, except guns and swords, and valued a basket of corn higher than a basket of copper; saying, he could rate his corn, but not the copper." Capt. *Smith* then made a speech to him, in which he endeavored to work upon his feelings and sense of honor; said he had sent his men to build him a house while his own was neglected; that, because of his promising to supply him with corn, he had neglected to supply himself with provisions when he might have done it. Finally, *Smith* reproached him of divers negligences, deceptions and prevarications, but the main cause of *Powhatan's* refusing to trade seems to have been because the English did not bring the articles he most wanted.

When *Smith* had done, *Powhatan* answered him as follows:—"*We have but little corn, but what we can spare shall be brought two days hence. As to your coming here, I have some doubt about the reason of it. I am told, by my men, that you came, not to trade, but to invade my people, and to possess my country. This makes me less ready to relieve you, and frightens my people from bringing in their corn. And, therefore, to relieve them of that fear, leave your arms aboard your boats, since they are needless here, where we are all friends, and forever Powhatans.*"

In these, and other speeches of like amount, they spent the first day. "But, whilst they expected the coming in of the country, they wrangled *Powhatan* out of 80 bushels of corn, for a copper kettle; which the president seeing him much affect, [value,] he told him it was of much greater value; yet, in regard of his scarcity, he would accept that quantity at present; provided he should have as much more the next year, or the Manakin country," were that condition not complied with.

This transaction will equal any thing of the kind in the history of N. England, but we will leave the reader to make his own comment.

At the same time, *Powhatan* made another speech, in which were some very singular passages, as reported by *Smith*. One was that he had seen the death of all his people three times; and that none of those three generations was then living, except himself. This was evidently only to make the English think him something more than human. The old chief then went on and said,

"*I am now grown old, and must soon die; and the succession must descend, in order, to my brothers,* Opitchapan, Opekankanough *and* Catataugh,* *and then to my two sisters, and their two daughters. I wish their experience was equal to mine; and that your love to us might not be less than ours to you. Why should you take by force that from us which you can have by love? Why should you destroy us; who have provided you with food? What can you get by war? We can hide our provisions, and fly into the woods; and then you must consequently famish by wronging your friends. What is the cause of your jealousy? You see us unarmed, and willing to supply your wants, if you will come in a friendly manner, and not with swords and guns, as to invade an enemy. I am not so simple, as not to know it is better to eat good meat, lie well, and sleep quietly with my women and children; to laugh*

* The reader may wonder how this could be, but it is so in the old history, by Stith, 86.

† Catanaugh, *Stith*.

and be merry with the English; and, being their friend, to have copper, hatchets, and whatever else I want, than to fly from all, to lie cold in the woods, feed upon acorns, roots, and such trash, and to be so hunted, that I cannot rest, eat, or sleep. In such circumstances, my men must watch, and if a twig should but break, all would cry out, 'Here comes Capt. Smith'; *and so, in this miserable manner, to end my miserable life; and, Capt.* Smith, *this might be soon your fate too, through your rashness and unadvisedness. I, therefore, exhort you to peaceable councils; and, above all, I insist that the guns and swords, the cause of all our jealousy and uneasiness, be removed and sent away."*

Smith interpreted this speech to mean directly contrary to what it expressed, and it rather confirmed than lessened his former suspicions. He, however, made a speech to *Powhatan,* in his turn, in which he endeavored to convince him that the English intended him no hurt; urging, that, if they had, how easily they might have effected it long before; and that, as to their perishing with want, he would have him to understand that the English had ways to supply themselves unknown to the Indians; that as to his sending away the arms, there was no reason in that, since the Indians were always allowed to bring theirs to Jamestown, and to keep them in their hands. Seeing *Smith's* inflexibility, and despairing of accomplishing his intended massacre, he spoke again to *Smith* as follows:—

"*Capt.* Smith, *I never use any werowance so kindly as yourself; yet from you I receive the least kindness of any. Capt. Newport gave me swords, copper, clothes, or whatever else I desired, ever accepting what I offered him; and would send away his guns when requested. No one refuses to lie at my feet, or do what I demand, but you only. Of you I can have nothing, but what you value not; and yet, you will have whatsoever you please. Capt.* Newport *you call father, and so you call me; but I see, in spite of us both, you will do what you will, and we must both study to humor and content you. But if you intend so friendly, as you say, send away your arms; for you see my undesigning simplicity and friendship cause me thus nakedly to forget myself."*

Smith now was out of all patience, seeing *Powhatan* only trifled away the time, that he might, by some means, accomplish his design. The boats of the English were kept at a distance from the shore, by reason of ice. *Smith,* therefore, resorted to deception; he got the Indians to break the ice, that his men might come in and take on board the corn they had bought, and, at the same time, gave orders to them to seize *Powhatan; Smith,* in the mean time, was to amuse him with false promises. But *Smith's* talk was too full of flattery not to be seen through by the sagacious sachem; and, before it was too late, he conveyed himself, his women, children, and effects into the woods; having succeeded in his deception better than *Smith;* for two or three squaws amused him while *Powhatan* and the rest escaped. Unwilling, however, to renounce his purpose, *Powhatan* sent *Smith,* soon after, a valuable bracelet, as a present, by an old orator of his, who tried to excuse the conduct of his sachem; he said, *Powhatan* ran off because he was afraid of the English arms, and said, if they could be laid aside, he would come with his people, and bring corn in abundance. At length, finding all artifices vain, *Powhatan* resolved to fall upon the English, in their cabins, on the following night. But here, again, *Pocahontas* saved the life of *Smith* and his attendants. She came alone, in a dismal night, through the woods, and informed *Smith* of her father's design. For this most signal favor, he offered her such articles as he thought would please her; but she would accept of nothing, and, with tears standing in her eyes, said if her father should see her with any thing, he would mistrust what she had done, and instant death would be her reward; and she retired by herself into the woods, as she came.

Powhatan was so exasperated at the failure of his plots, that he threatened death to his men if they did not kill *Smith* by some means or other. Not long after, a circumstance occurred, which gave him security the rest of his administration. One of *Powhatan's* men having, by some means, got a quantity of powder, pretended that he could manage it like the English. Several came about him, to witness his exploits with the strange commodity, when, by some means, it took fire, "and blew him, with one or two more, to death." This struck such a dread into the Indians, and so amazed and frightened *Powhatan,* that his people came from all directions, and desired peace;* many of whom returned stolen articles that the English had never before missed. *Powhatan* would now send to Jamestown such of his men as had injured the English, that they might be dealt with as they deserved. The same year, 1609, he sent them nearly half his crop of corn, knowing them to be in great want.

Captain *Smith,* having, by accident, been shockingly burned by his powder-bags taking fire, for want of surgical aid, was obliged to leave the country and go to England, from whence he never returned. He published the account of the first voyages to Virginia, and his own adventures, which is almost the only authority for the early history of that country. He died in London, in 1631,† in the 52d year of his age.

> "—————— Thou thus admired,
> Didst make proud *Powhatan,* his subjects send,
> To Iames his towne, thy censure to attend:
> And all Virgina's lords, and pettie kings,
> Aw'd by thy vertue, crouch, and presents brings,
> To gain thy grace; so dreaded thou bast beene:
> And yet a heart more milde is seldome seene."‡

The Dutchmen of whom we have spoken, and who had been so assiduous to bring ruin upon the colony, came to a miserable end. One of them died in wretchedness, and two others had their brains beat out by order of *Powhatan*, for their deception.

After *Smith* had left Virginia, the Indians were made to believe that he was dead. *Powhatan* doubted the report, and, some time after, ordered one of his counsellors, named *Uttamatomakin,*§ or *Tomocomo,*|| whom he sent to England, to find out, if possible, where he was. He instructed him, also, to note the number of the people—to learn the state of the country—and, if he found *Smith*, to make him show him the God of the English, and the king and queen. When he arrived at Plimouth, he took a long stick, and began to perform a part of his mission by cutting a notch for every person he should see. But he soon gave up that business. And, when he returned to his own country, his chief asked him, among other things, to give him an account of the number of the inhabitants in England. His answer to that inquiry, we hazard not much in saying, is nearly as extensively known as the golden rule of *Confucius*. It was as follows: "*Count the stars in the sky, the leaves on the trees, and the sand upon the sea-shore,—for such is the number of the people of England.*"

Tomocomo had married a sister of *Pocahontas*, and, probably, accompa-

---

* Did not the English of N. England owe their safety to *Massasoit* and *Miantunnomoh's* fear of the same article?

† Josselyn, N. Eng. Rarities, 106.

‡ Laudatory verses affixed to the first volume of his History of Virginia.

§ Or *Uttamaccomack,* Smith.

|| Purchas.

nied her to England.* While there, the famous antiquary, *Samuel Purchase*, had an interview with him, and from whom he collected many facts relating to the manners and customs of his countrymen; the result of which he afterwards published in his Pilgrims.†

The difficulties were almost perpetual between *Powhatan* and the English; very little time passed, while he lived, but what was full of broils and dissatisfaction, on the one part or the other. Few Indian chiefs have fallen under our notice, possessing such extraordinary characteristics as *Powhatan*. He died at peace with the English, in April, 1618, and was succeeded by *Opitchapan*, his second brother, who was known afterwards by the name *Itopatin*.

Our readers will be compelled to acknowledge that Capt. *Smith* was barbarous enough towards the Indians, but we have not met with any thing quite so horrible, in the course of his proceedings, as was exhibited by his successor, Lord *De La War*. This *gentleman*, instead of taking a mean course between the practices of Smith and Newport, went into the worst extreme. Finding *Powhatan* insolent, on his arrival in the country, he determined, by severity, to bring him to unconditional submission. Having, therefore, got into his hands an Indian prisoner, his lordship caused his right hand to be cut off. In this maimed and horrid condition, he sent him to *Powhatan;* at the same time, giving the sachem to understand that all his subjects would be served in this manner, if he refused obedience any longer; telling him, also, that all the corn in the country should be immediately destroyed, which was just then ripe.‡ This wretched act increased, as reasonably it should, the indignation of *Powhatan*, and his acts were governed accordingly.

CHAPTER II.

Reflection upon the character of Powhatan—POCAHONTAS—*She singularly entertains Capt. Smith—Disaster of a boat's crew—Smith's attempt to surprise Powhatan frustrated in consequence—Pocahontas saves the life of Wyffin—Betrayed into the hands of the English*—JAPAZAWS—*Mr. Rolfe marries Pocahontas*—OPACHISCO—*Pocahontas visits England—Her interview with Smith—Dies at Gravesend—Her son*—OPEKANKANOUGH—*Made prisoner by Smith—Is set at liberty*—NEMATTANOW—*Murders an Englishman—Is murdered in his turn—His singular conduct at his death—Conducts the massacre of 1622—Plots the extirpation of the English—Conducts the horrid massacre of 1644—Is taken prisoner—His conduct upon the occasion—Barbarously wounded by the guard—Last speech, and magnanimity in death—Reflections*—NICKOTAWANCE—TOTOPOTOMOI—*Joins the English against the Rechahecrians—Is defeated and slain.*

IT is impossible to say, what would have been the conduct of the great *Powhatan*, towards the English, had he been treated by them as he ought to have been. The uncommonly amiable, virtuous and feeling disposition of his daughter will always be brought to mind in reading his history; and, notwithstanding he is described by the historians as possessing a sour,

* Mr. *Oldmixon* (Brit. Empire, i. 285.) says, "That when the princess *Pocahontas* came for England, a coucarousa, or lord of her own nation, attended her; his name was *Uttamaccomack*."

† Vol. v. b, viii. chap. vi. page 955.

‡ *Harris*, Voyages, ii. 226.

morose and savage disposition, full of treachery, deceit and cunning—and whose word was never to be depended upon, yet, on the very page that he is thus represented, we shall find the same faults set him as examples by the English themselves.

The first and most memorable events in the life of *Pocahontas* have necessarily been detailed in the account of her father; therefore we shall, under her own name, give those which are more disconnected with his.

Pocahontas was born about the year 1594 or 5, and hence was no more than 12 or 13 years old, when she saved the life of Capt. *Smith,* in 1607. Every particular of that most extraordinary scene has been exhibited. It has also been mentioned, that, at the suggestion of Capt. *Newport, Smith* went with a few men to Werowocomoco, to invite *Powhatan* to Jamestown to receive presents, hoping thereby to influence him to open a trade in corn with them.

When he arrived at that place, *Powhatan* was not at home, but was at the distance of 30 miles off. *Pocahontas* and her women received him, and while he waited for her father, they thus entertained him: "In a fayre plaine field, (says *Smith,*) they made a fire, before which, he sitting upon a mat, suddainly amongst the woods was heard such a hydeous noise and shrecking, that the English betooke themselves to their arms, and seized on two or three old men by them, supposing *Powhatan,* with all his power, was come to surprise them. But presently *Pocahontas* came, willing him to kill her if any hurt were intended; and the beholders, which were men, women and children, satisfied the captain there was no such matter. Then presently they were presented with this anticke; 30 young women came naked out of the woods, onely covered behind and before with a few greene leaues, their bodies all painted, some of one color, some of another, but all differing. Their leader had a fayre payre of bucks hornes on her head, and an otter-skinne at her girdle, and another at her arme, a quiver of arrowes at her backe, a bow and arrows in her hand. The next had in her hand a sword, and another a club, another a pot-sticke, all horned alike; the rest every one with their seuerall devises. These fiends, with most hellish shouts and cryes, rushing from among the trees, cast themselves in a ring about the fire, singing and dancing with most excellent ill varietie, oft falling into their infernall passions, and solemnly again to sing and daunce. Having spent neare an houre in this mascarado, as they entred, in like manner they departed." After a short time, they came and took the English to their wigwams. Here they were more tormented than before, "with crowding, pressing, hanging about them, most tediously crying, 'Love you not me? love you not me?' " When they had finished their caresses, they set before them the best victuals their country afforded, and then showed them to their lodgings.

While Captain *Smith* was upon an expedition into the country, with an intention of surprising *Powhatan,* there happened a melancholy accident at home, to a boat's crew, which had been sent out in very severe weather, by one who was impatient to have the direction of matters. In the boat were Captain Waldo, Master *Scrivener,* the projector of the expedition, Mr. *Anthony Gosnold,* brother of the well-known *Bartholomew Gosnold,* and eight others. By the sinking of the boat, these all perished, and none knew what had become of them, until their bodies were found by the Indians. The very men on whom *Smith* depended to remain at the fort for his succor, in case he sent for them, were among the number. Therefore, to prevent the failure of this expedition, somebody must be sent to apprize *Smith* of the catastrophe. None volunteered for the hazardous service, but Mr. *Richard Wyffin,* who was obliged to undertake it alone. This was a time when *Powhatan* was very insolent, and urged daily the killing of *Smith* upon his men. Nevertheless, after many difficulties,

2*

he arrived at Werowocomoco. Here he found himself amidst preparations for war, and in still greater danger than he had yet been. But *Pocahontas* appeared as his savior. Knowing the intention of the warriors to kill him, she first secreted him in the woods, and then directed those who sought him in an opposite direction from that he had gone; so, by this means, he escaped, and got safe to *Smith* at Pamunkey. This was in the winter of 1609.

We next hear of her saving the life of *Henry Spilman*, who, was one of 30 that went to trade, upon the confidence of *Powhatan*, but who were, all except *Spilman*, killed by his people.

From 1609, the time *Smith* left the country, until 1611, *Pocahontas* was not seen at Jamestown. At this time, she was treacherously taken prisoner by Captain *Argal*, and kept by the English to prevent *Powhatan* from doing them injury, and to extort a great ransom from him, and such terms of peace as they should dictate. At the time she was betrayed into the hands of Captain *Argal*, she was in the neighborhood of the chief of Potomack, whose name was *Japazaws*, a particular friend of the English, and an old acquaintance of Captain *Smith*. Whether she had taken up her residence here, or whether she was here only upon a visit, we are not informed. But some have conjectured, that she retired here soon after *Smith's* departure, that she might not witness the frequent murders of the ill-governed English, at Jamestown. Captain *Argal* was in the Potomack River, for the purpose of trade, with his ship, when he learned that Pocahontas was in the neighborhood. Whether *Japazaws* had acquired his treachery from his intercourse with the English, or whether it were natural to his disposition, we will not undertake to decide here; but certain it is, that he was ready to practise it, at the instigation of *Argal*. And for a copper kettle for himself, and a few toys for his squaw, he enticed the innocent girl on board *Argal's* ship, and betrayed her into his hands. It was effected, however, without compulsion, by the aid of his squaw. The captain had previously promised that no hurt should befall her, and that she should be treated with all tenderness. This circumstance should go as far as it may to excuse *Japazaws*. The plot to get her on board was well contrived. Knowing that she had no curiosity to see a ship, having before seen many, *Japazaws'* wife pretended great anxiety to see one, but would not go on board unless *Pocahontas* would accompany her. To this she consented, but with some hesitation. The attention with which they were received on board soon dissipated all fears, and *Pocahontas* soon strayed from her betrayers into the gun-room. The captain, watching his opportunity, told her she was a prisoner. When her confinement was known to *Japazaws* and his wife, they feigned more lamentation than she did, to keep her in ignorance of the plot; and, after receiving the price of their perfidy, were sent ashore, and *Argal*, with his pearl of great price, sailed for Jamestown. On being informed of the reason why she was thus captivated, her grief, by degrees, subsided.

The first step of the English was to inform *Powhatan* of the captivity of his daughter, and to demand of him their men, guns and tools, which he and his people had, from time to time, taken and stolen from them. This unexpected news threw the old, stern, calculating chief into a great dilemma, and what course to take he knew not; and it was three months before he returned any answer. At the end of this time, by the advice of his council, he sent back seven Englishmen, with each a gun which had been spoiled, and this answer: that when they should return his daughter, he would make full satisfaction, and give them 500 bushels of corn, and be their friend forever; that he had no more guns to return, the rest being lost. They sent him word, that they would not restore her, until he had complied with their demand; and that, as for the guns, they did not believe they were lost. Seeing the determination of the English, or his inability to satisfy them, was, we apprehend, why they "heard no more from him for a long time after."

In the spring of the year 1613, Sir *Thomas Dale* took *Pocahontas*, and went, with a ship, up *Powhatan's* River to Werowocomoco, the residence of her father, in hopes to effect an exchange, and bring about a peace. *Powhatan* was not at home, and they met with nothing but bravadoes, and a disposition to fight, from all the Indians they saw. After burning many of their habitations, and giving out threats, some of the Indians came and made peace, as they called it, which opened the way for two of *Pocahontas's* brothers to come on board the ship. Their joy at seeing their sister may be imagined.

A particular friendship had some time existed between *Pocahontas* and a worthy young Englishman, by the name of *John Rolfe*; which, at length, growing into a sincere attachment, and being mutual between them, he made known his desire to take her for his companion. This being highly approved of by Sir *Thomas Dale*, and other gentlemen of high standing and authority, a consummation was soon agreed upon. Acquainting her brother with her determination, it soon came to the knowledge of her father also; who, as highly approving of it as the English, immediately sent *Opachisco*, her uncle, and two of his sons, to witness the performance, and to act as her servants upon the occasion: and, in the beginning of April, 1613, the marriage was solemnized according to appointment. *Powhatan* was now their friend in reality; and a friendly intercourse commenced, which was, without much interruption, continued until his death.

Pocahontas lived happily with her husband, and became a believer in the English religion, and expressed no desire to live again among those of her own nation. When Sir *Thomas Dale* returned to England, in 1616, *Pocahontas* accompanied him, with her husband, and several other young natives. They arrived at Plimouth on the 12th of June of that year. She met with much attention in that country, being taken to court by the Lord and Lady *Delaware*, and others of distinction. She was, at this time, called the Lady *Rebecca*. Her meeting with Captain *Smith* was affecting; more especially as she thought herself, and very justly, no doubt, too slightly noticed by him, which caused her much grief. Owing to the barbarous nonsense of the times, *Smith* did not wish her to call him father, being afraid of giving offence to royalty, by assuming to be the father of a king's daughter. Yet he did not intend any cause of offence, and did all in his power to make her happy. At their first interview, after remaining silent some time, she said to him, "*You promised my father, that what was yours should be his; and that you and he would be all one. Being a stranger in our country, you called* Powhatan *father; and I, for the same reason, will now call you so. You were not afraid to come into my father's country, and strike fear into every body but myself; and are you here afraid to let me call you father? I tell you, then, I will call you father, and you shall call me child; and so I will forever be of your kindred and country. They always told us that you were dead, and I knew not otherwise, till I came to Plimouth. But* Powhatan *commanded* Tomocomo *to seek you out, and know the truth, because your countrymen are much given to lying.*"

The useful and worthy young *Pocahontas*, being about to embark for her native country, in the beginning of the year 1617, fell sick at Gravesend, and died; having attained only the age of 22 years. She left one son, whose name was *Thomas Rolfe*, very young; and whom Sir *Lewis Steukly*, of Plimouth, desired to be left with him, that he might direct his education. But, from the unmanly part this gentleman took against the unfortunate *Ralegh*, he was brought into such merited disrepute, that he found himself obliged to turn all his attention to his own preservation; and the son of *Pocahontas* was taken to London, and there educated by his uncle, Mr. *Henry Rolfe*. He afterwards came to America, to the native country of his mother, where he became a gentleman of great distinction, and possessed an ample fortune. He left an only daughter, who married Colonel *Robert Bolling*, and died, leaving an only son, Major *John Bolling*, who was the father of Colonel *John Bolling*, and several daughters; one of whom married Col. *Richard Randolph*, from whom are descended those bearing that name in Virginia, at this day.*

Barlow thus notices *Pocahontas*:—

"Blest *Pocahontas!* fear no lurking guile;
Thy hero's love shall well reward thy smile.
Ah, soothe the wanderer in his desperate plight,
Hide him by day, and calm his cares by night;
Tho' savage nations, with thy vengeful sire,
Pursue their victim with unceasing ire—
And tho' their threats thy startled ear assail,
Let virtue's voice o'er filial fears prevail."—*Columbiad.*

Opekankanough has already received our notice. He was a very conspicuous character in his time, and was styled, by the Virginians, King of the Pamunkies. The dreadful massacre, of which he was author, brings to mind his name oftener than almost any other chief of his times.

There seems to be some contradiction, or difference of opinion, with regard to the origin of this chief. Some of the Indians reported that he came from the west, and was not a brother of *Powhatan*; but that story, we judge, is merely a fable, invented and told by some of them, who were his enemies, to influence the English against him, that they might destroy him.

Opekankanough seems to have borne the name of *Mangopeomen* in 1621,† a circumstance unnoticed by most historians, and, therefore, we conclude that it prevailed only among his own tribe, and, perhaps, even among them fell into disuse soon after.

Opitchapan, called also *Oetan*, and lastly *Sasauopeomen*,‡ was the successor of *Powhatan*, but he seems never to have been otherwise noted. "The defects of the new emperor," says Mr. *Burk*, "were aggravated in the minds of the Indians, by a comparison with the accomplished *Opekankanough*, who, in the council and the field, was the most conspicuous warrior amongst the Powhatans; and who, during the life-time of the late emperor, had procured from the free tribe of the Chickahominies, the title of their king." The same author calls *Opitchapan* a "feble and decrepid" chief, who "was little calculated to secure respect, or enforce obedience."§

In 1608, the Indians had become universally at variance with the English, and insulted them whenever they appeared abroad; knowing their miserable, half-starved condition. Insult followed insult, upon both sides, and, but for the never-tiring perseverance of *Smith*, this colony, like the first, would have been soon destroyed. The Indians would promise to trade with them, but when they went to them for that purpose, they only "laughed at their calamities;" sometimes putting jokes upon them, and at others, running away into the woods.

In this extremity of their circumstances, though in the depth of winter, *Smith* resolved to make himself master of some of the Indians' store of provisions, by some means or other. He, therefore, proceeded to Pamunkey, the residence of *Opekankanough*, with 15 men, where he tried to

* *Smith's* Virginia, with additions from *Stith*.
† *Burk's* Va. i. 228. ‡ Ibid. § Hist. Virginia, i. 233.

trade with him for corn; but, not succeeding, he, in a desperate manner, seized upon the chief by his hair, in the midst of his men, "with his pistoll readie bent against his breast. Thus he led the trembling king, neare dead with fear, amongst all his people."* *Smith* told him that he had attempted to murder him, which was the cause of his treating him thus. No one can doubt, on reading the history of those affairs, that the Indians all wished *Smith* dead, but whether they all wanted to kill him, is not quite so plain.

One great end of *Smith's* design was now answered; for *Opekankanough's* people came in loaded with presents to ransom their chief, until his boats were completely filled. News being brought of a disaster at Jamestown, he was set at liberty.

Nemattanow, a renowned warrior, we have to introduce here, as well on account of his supposed agency in bringing about the great massacre of 1622, as for the object of exhibiting a trait of character equally to be admired and lamented. We are not certain that he belonged to the people of *Opekankanough,* but it is storied that a jealousy existed between them, and that the chief had informed Sir *George Yeardley* that he wished *Nemattanow's* throat were cut, some time before the massacre took place, to which we have alluded. However, *Opekankanough* denied it afterwards, and affected great indignation at his murder, and the Indians said the massacre was begun by him, to revenge *Nemattanow's* death. But our present object is to portray the character of *Nemattanow,* who was both eccentric and vain, and "who was wont, out of bravery and parade, to dress himself up, in a strange, antic and barbaric fashion, with feathers, which, therefore, obtained him the name of *Jack-of-the-feather.*" He was even more popular among his countrymen than *Opekankanough,* which, doubtless, was the ground of that chief's jealousy; especially as he was one of the greatest war-captains of his times. He had been in many fights and encounters with the English, always exposing himself to the greatest danger, and yet was never wounded in any of them. This circumstance caused the Indians to believe in his invulnerability, and hence he was by them considered superhuman. Only about 14 days before the massacre, *Jack-of-the-feather* went to the house of one *Morgan,* where he saw many such articles exhibited as were calculated to excite admiration in such people. *Jack,* perhaps, had not the means to purchase, but, it seems, he was resolved, some how or other, to possess them. He, therefore, told *Morgan,* that if he would take his commodities to Pamunkey, the Indians would give him a great price for them. Not in the least mistrusting the design of Nemattanow, the simple Englishman set out for Pamunkey, in company with this Indian. This was the last the English heard of *Morgan.* However, strange as it may seem, *Jack's* ill-directing fate sent him to the same place again, and, what was still more strange, he had the cap of the murdered *Morgan* upon his head. *Morgan's* servants asked him where their master was, who very deliberately answered, that he was dead. This satisfied them that he had murdered him. They, therefore, seized him, in order to take him before a magistrate at Berkeley; but he made a good deal of resistance, which caused one of his captors to shoot him down. The singular part of the tragedy is yet to be related. Though mortally wounded, *Nemattanow* was not killed outright, and his captors, which were two stout young men, got him into a boat to proceed to Mr. *Thorp's,* the magistrate. As they were going, the warrior became satisfied that he must die, and, with the most extraordinary earnestness, besought that two things might be granted him. One was, that it should

* Perhaps the New Englanders followed *Smith's* example, afterwards, in the case of *Alexander, Ninigret,* and others.

never be told to his countrymen that he was killed by a bullet; and the other, that he should be buried among the English, so that it should never be discovered that he had died, or was subject to death like other men. Such was the pride and vanity exhibited by an Indian at his death. The following inference, therefore, is naturally to be drawn; that a desire to be renowned, and held in veneration by posterity, is not confined to the civilized and learned of any age or nation.

Meanwhile, *Opekankanough,* the better to increase the rage of his warriors, affected great grief at *Nemattanow's* death, which had the effect he intended; owing, especially, to the favor in which that warrior had stood among the Indians. But the English were satisfied that this was only pretence, as we have before observed; because they were informed of his trying to engage some of his neighbors against them, and otherwise acted suspiciously, some time before *Nemattanow's* death; of the justice of which, however, the English tried arguments at first, and threats afterwards, to convince him. By his dissimulation, *Opekankanough* completely deceived them, and, just before the massacre, treated a messenger that was sent to him, with much kindness and civility; and assured him that the peace, which had been some time before concluded, was held so firm by him, that the sky should fall sooner than it should be violated on his part. And such was the concert and secrecy among all the Indians, that, only two days before the fatal 22 March, some kindly conducted the English through the woods, and sent one of their youth to live with the English, and learn their language. Moreover, on the morning of that very day, they came unarmed among them, and traded as usual, and even sat down to breakfast with their victims, in several instances. Never, perhaps, was a massacre so well contrived and conducted, to ensure success, as was this of *Opekankanough.* The English were lulled into a fatal security, and even unknowingly assisted the Indians in their design; lending them their boats to communicate with distant tribes, and furnishing them with various utensils, which were converted at once into weapons of death.

The 22 March, 1622, having come, and the appointed hour of that memorable day arrived, with a simultaneousness unparalleled on any former occasion, the Indians rose from their ambushes, and, with the swiftness of the tiger, appeared, in a moment, amidst the English settlements. Age, sex nor condition shielded no one; their greatest benefactors were among their first victims. Thus, in the space of about one hour, fell *three hundred and forty-seven* men, women and children. By this horrid calamity, out of 80 plantations, six only were left uninjured. And these were saved by the timely information of a Christian Indian called *Chanco.*

The ensuing summer was spent, by the surviving English, in strengthening themselves against further attacks, and preparations for taking vengeance on the Indians; wholly neglecting all improvements, works of utility, and even their planting. Every thing was lost sight of in their beloved project of revenge; and the English, in their turn, showed themselves more treacherous, if not more barbarous, than their enemy. For, under the pretence of making peace again with them, they fell upon them at unawares, and murdered many without mercy. This crime was vastly aggravated, in that, to induce the Indians to come forward and make peace, the English had not only solemnly assured them forgiveness, but likewise security and safety in their persons.

It was, for some time, supposed that *Opekankanough* was among the slain, but, if Mr. *Beverley* was not misinformed, the same sachem, 22 years afterwards, executed a still greater massacre upon the English, as, in the next place, we shall relate.

How long *Opekankanough* had been secretly plotting to cut off the intruders of his soil cannot be known; but, in 1644, all the Indians, over a space of country of 600 miles in extent, were leagued in the enterprise. The old chief, at this time, was supposed to be near 100 years of age, and, though unable to walk, would be present in the execution of his beloved project. It was upon the 18 April, when *Opekankanough,* borne in a litter, led his warriors forward, and commenced the bloody work. They began at the frontiers, with a determination to slay all before them, to the sea. After continuing the massacre two days, in which time about 500 persons were murdered, Sir *William Berkeley,* at the head of an armed force, checked their progress. The destruction of the inhabitants was the greatest upon York and Pamunkey Rivers, where *Opekankanough* commanded in person. The Indians now, in their turn, were driven to great extremity, and their old chief was taken prisoner, and carried in triumph to Jamestown. How long after the massacre this happened, we are not informed; but it is said that the fatigues he had previously undergone had wasted away his flesh, and destroyed the elasticity of his muscles to that degree, that he was no longer able to raise the eye-lids from his eyes; and it was in this forlorn condition, that he fell into the hands of his enemies. A soldier, who had been appointed to guard him, barbarously fired upon him, and inflicted a mortal wound. He was supposed to have been prompted to the bloody deed, from a recollection of the old chief's agency in the massacre. Just before he expired, hearing a great bustle and crowd about him, he ordered an attendant to lift up his eye-lids; when he discovered a multitude pressing around, to gratify the untimely curiosity of beholding a dying sachem. Undaunted in death, and roused, as it were, from sleep, at the conduct of the confused multitude, he deigned not to observe them; but, raising himself from the ground, with the expiring breath of authority, commanded that the governor should be called to him. When the governor came, *Opekankanough* said, with indignation, "*Had it been my fortune to have taken* Sir WM. BERKELEY *prisoner, I would not meanly have exposed him as a show to my people*;"* and soon after expired.

It is said, and we have no reason to doubt the fact, that it was owing to the encroachments upon his lands, that caused *Opekankanough* to determine upon a massacre of the whites. These intrusions were, nevertheless, conformable to the grants of the proprietors. He could hardly have expected entire conquest, as his people had already begun to waste away, and English villages were springing up over an extent of country of more than 500 miles, with a populousness beyond any preceding example; still, he was determined upon the vast undertaking, and sacrificed himself with as much *honor,* it will, perhaps, be acknowledged, as did *Leonidas* at Thermopylæ.

Sir *William Berkeley* intended to have sent him, as a present, to the king of England; but assassination deprived him of the wretched satisfaction, and saved the chief from the mortification.†

None of the Virginia historians seem to have been informed of the true date of this last war of *Opekankanough*; the ancient records of Virginia, says Mr. *Burk,* are silent even upon the events of it, (an extraordinary omission.) Mr. *Beverley* thinks it began in 1639, and, although Mr. *Burk* is satisfied that it took place after 1641, yet he relates it under the date 1640. And we are not certain that the real date would ever have been fixed, but for the inestimable treasury of N. England history, *Winthrop's* Journal.

That it took place subsequent to 1641, Mr. *Burk* assures us, upon the evidence of the MS. records; for they relate that, in 1640, one *John Burton* had been convicted of the murder of an Indian, and that his punish-

* *Beverley,* Hist. Virg. 51.

† See British Empire in America, i. 240, 1.

ment was remitted, "at the intercession of *Opekankanough,* and his great men." And that, in the end of the year 1641, *Thomas Rolfe,* the son of *Pocahontas,* petitioned the governor for permission to visit his kinsman, *Opekankanough,* and *Cleopatre,* the sister of his mother. That, therefore, these events happened previous to the war, and death of *Opekankanough.*

Nickotawance succeeded *Opekankanough,* as a tributary to the English. In 1648, he came to Jamestown, with five other chiefs, and brought 20 beaver skins to be sent to King *Charles.* He made a long oration, which he concluded with the protestation, "that the sun and moon should first loose their glorious lights, and shining, before he, or his people, should ever more hereafter wrong the English."

Totopotomoi, probably, succeeded *Nickotawance,* as he was king of Pamunkey in 1656. In that year, a large body of strange Indians, called *Rechahecrians,* came down from the inland mountainous country, and forcibly possessed themselves of the country about the falls of James River. The legislature of Virginia was in session, when the news of their coming was received. What cause the English had to send out an army against them, our scanty records do not satisfactorily show;* but, at all events, they determined at once to dispossess them. To that end, an army of about 100 men was raised, and put under the direction of Col. *Edward Hill,* who was joined by *Totopotomoi,* with 100 of his warriors. They did not find the Rechahecrians unprepared, but what were the particulars of the meeting of the adverse parties we are not informed. The event, however, was, to the allies, most disastrous. *Totopotomoi,* with the most of his men, was slain, and the English suffered a total defeat, owing, it is said, to the criminal management of Col. *Hill.* This officer lost his commission, and his property was taken to defray the losses sustained by the country. A peace seems to have been concluded with the Indians soon after.

---

* By the following preamble and resolve of the legislature, all we possess, touching this matter, is to be gathered:—"Whereas information hath been received, that many western or inland Indians are drawn from the mountains, and lately set down near the falls of James River, to the number of 6 or 700, whereby, upon many several considerations being had, it is conceived great danger might ensue to this colony. This assembly, therefore, do think fit and resolve, that these new come Indians be in no sort suffered to seat themselves there, or any place near us, it having cost so much blood to expel and extirpate those perfidious and treacherous Indians, which were there formerly. It being so apt a place to invade us, and within the limits, which, in a just war, were formerly conquered by us, and by us reserved, at the conclusion of peace, with the Indians." *Burk,* Hist. Virginia, ii. 105.

CHAPTER III.

Settlement of Carolina—The English are kindly receivea by the Indians— TOMOCHICHI—*Holds a council with the English—Its proceedings—Speeches of the chiefs—Tomochichi, with several others, goes to England with Gen. Oglethorpe—Makes a speech to the king—Returns to America—His death*—ATTAKULLAKULLA, MALACHTA, WOLF-KING, *and others, visit Charleston—Some Indians brutally murdered—Proceedings of Attakullakulla in preventing retaliation upon some English in his power—Speech to his warriors—War—Conducted with barbarity on both sides—English murder hostages—Ockonostota takes Fort Loudon—Most of the captives slain*—CHLUCCO, *or the* LONG-WARRIOR.

THE presumption is pretty strongly supported, that Sir *Walter Ralegh* visited the southern shores of North America. When Gen. *Oglethorpe* landed in Georgia, in 1732, O. S., and communicated to the Indians the contents of a journal of Sir *Walter's*, they seemed to have a tradition of him, which they had fondly cherished; although, if the person they meant were *Ralegh*, a hundred years had elapsed since he was there. They pointed out to Mr. *Oglethorpe* a place near Yamacraw bluff, since Charleston, on which was a large mound, in which was buried, they said, a chief who had talked with Sir *Walter Ralegh* upon that spot. The chief had requested his people to bury him there, that the place might be kept in veneration.

Tomochichi was the principal chief, or mico, as chiefs were called; of this region. Several chief men, of various tribes, came to welcome the English, immediately after their arrival. "They were as follows: From the tribe of Coweeta, *Yahan-lakee*, their king, or mico; *Essaboo*, their warrior, the son of *Old-brim*, lately dead, whom the Spaniards called emperor of the Creeks, with eight men and two women attendants. From the tribe of *Cussetas, Cusseta*, their mico; *Tatchiquatchi*, their head warrior, with four attendants. From the tribe of Owseecheys, *Ogeese*, the mico, or war king; *Neathlouthko* and *Ougachi*, two chief men, with three attendants. From the tribe of Cheechaws, *Outhleteboa*, their mico, *Thlautho-thlukee, Figeer, Sootamilla*, war captains, with three attendants.

3

From the tribe of Echetas, *Chutabeeche* and *Robin,* two war captains, (the latter was bred among the English,) with four attendants. From the tribe of Polachucolas, *Gillattee,* their head warrior, and five attendants. From the tribe of Oconas, Oueekachumpa, called by the English *Long-king, Koowoo,* a warrior. From the tribe of Eufaule, *Tomaumi,* head warrior, and three attendants.

"The Indians being all seated, Oueekachumpa, a very tall old man, stood, and made a speech, which was interpreted by Mr. *Wiggan* and Mr. *Musgrove,"* in which he said all the lands to the southward of Savannah River belonged to the Creeks. He said, the Indians were poor, but the same Power that gave the English breath, gave them breath also. That that Power had given the English the most wisdom. That, as they had come to instruct them, they should have all the lands which they did not use themselves. That this was not only his mind, but the minds of the eight towns of Creeks, who had, after consulting together, sent some of their chief men with skins, which was their wealth. At this period of *Oueekachumpa's* speech, some of the chiefs of the eight towns brought each a bundle of buck's skins, and laid them down before Mr. *Oglethorpe.* Then the chief said, "*These are the best things we possess, but we give them with a good heart. I thank you for your kindness to Tomochichi, and his people. He is my kinsman, and, though he was banished from his nation, he is a good man and a great warrior. It was on account of his wisdom and justice, that the banished men chose him their king. I hear that the Cherokees have killed some Englishmen. If you* [addressing Mr. Oglethorpe] *will command us, we will go against them with all our force, kill their people, and destroy their living."*

Tomochichi belonged to Yamacraw, and was sachem of the tribe that resided there. When *Oueekachumpa* had done speaking, *Tomochichi* drew near with his men, and, after making a low bow, said,—

"*I was a banished man, and I came here poor and helpless to look for good land near the tombs of my ancestors, and when you came to this place, I feared you would drive us away; for we were weak and wanted corn. But you confirmed our land to us, and gave us food."* The other chiefs spoke in the same manner as *Oueekachumpa* had, and then agreed upon and executed an amicable treaty.

The next year, 1734, Mr. *Oglethorpe* returned to England. He took along with him, *Tomochichi, Senawki,* his consort, and *Toonakowi,* the prince, his nephew; also, *Hillispilli,* a war captain, and *Apakowtski, Stimalechi, Sintouchi, Hinguithi* and *Umphychi,* five other chiefs, with their interpreter. These were accommodated, while in London, at the Georgia office, Old Palace Yard, where they were not only handsomely entertained, but had great attention showed them. After being dressed suitably, they visited the king's court, at Kensington, where they had an interview with his majesty, King *George* II. Tomochichi presented him with several eagle's feathers, which was considered, by him and his people, the most respectful present they could make. The sachem then delivered the following speech to the king:—

"*This day I see the majesty of your face, the greatness of your house, and the number of your people. I am come for the good of the whole nation of the Creeks, to renew the peace they had long ago made with the English. I am come over in my old days; and, though I cannot live to see any advantage to myself, I am come for the good of the children of all the nations of the Upper and Lower Creeks, that they may be instructed in the knowledge of the English. These are the feathers of the eagle, which is the swiftest of birds, and who flieth all round our nations. These feathers are a sign of peace in our land, and we have brought them over to leave them with you, great king, as a sign of everlasting peace. O! great king, whatsoever* *words you shall say unto me, I will tell them faithfully to all the kings of the Creek nations.*" The king's answer was, in the highest degree, conciliatory, and what was termed gracious.*

Thus are traced the first steps in the history of Georgia, and thus did every thing promise a continuance of that friendship so well begun by Gen. *Oglethorpe*. Nothing was left undone, while the Creek chiefs were in England, to impress upon their minds exalted ideas of the power and greatness of the English nation. The nobility were not only curious to see them, but entertained them at their tables in the most magnificent style. Multitudes flocked around them, conferring gifts and marks of respect upon them. The king allowed them £20 sterling a week, during their stay, and it was computed that, at their return to America, they brought presents to the amount of £400 sterling. After remaining in England four months, they embarked at Gravesend for Georgia. They were conveyed to the place of embarkation in his majesty's carriages.†

We have not met with a record of the death of *Tomochichi,* but as he was, at this time, an old man, he probably died not long after.

In the invasion of Georgia by the Spaniards, in 1743, many Indians were drawn into the controversy, on both sides. Toeanoeowi,‡ or Tooanohowi,§ a nephew of *Tomochichi,* was shot through the right arm, in an encounter with the Spaniards, by a Spanish captain. *Tooanohowi* drew his pistol with his left hand, and shot the captain through the head.

Thus, with the Spaniards upon one hand, and the English upon the other, and the French in the midst of them, the Creeks and Cherokees became subject to every possible evil to which the caprice of those several nations gave rise. Although there were events, in every year, of importance, yet, in this place, we shall take up the period rendered more memorable by the distinguished chiefs *Attakullakulla* and *Ockonostota.*||

The fame of Carolina had, in 1753, drawn a multitude of Europeans to her shores. The same year, on the 26 May, *Malachty,* attended by the *Wolf-king* and the Ottasee chief, with about 20 others, and above a hundred of their people, came to Charleston. They were met, on their way, by a troop of horsemen, who conducted them to the town, by the governor's order, in great state. This was to induce them to make peace and remain their allies, and, to this end, the Gov., *Glenn,* made a very pacific speech, in the Indian manner. *Malachty,* who, at this time, seems to have been the head chief among the Creeks, presented the governor with a quantity of skins, and readily consented to a peace with the English, but, in regard to a peace with the Cherokees, he said, that was a matter of great moment, and he must deliberate with his people, before he could give an answer. The Cherokees were already under the protection of the English, and some of them had, not long before, been killed by the Creeks, in the very neighborhood of Charleston. The party which committed this outrage was led by *Malachty.* Notwithstanding, a cessation of hostilities seems to have taken place, for numbers of each nation joined the English immediately after the capture of Oswego, by the French, in 1756. The Cherokees are particularly named as having rendered essential service in the expedition against Fort Duquesne; but a circumstance happened, while those warriors were returning home from that expedition, which involved them in an immediate war with the Eng-

* *Harris,* Voyages.

† *M' Call's* Georgia, i. 45. ‡ Harris.

§ *M' Call,* who says he accompanied Gen. *Oglethorpe* to England, in 1734, with *Tomochichi.*

|| Ouconnostotah, Ouconnostota, Ouconnostata, *Wynne.*—Occonostota, *Ramsay.*—*Attakullakulla* was generally called the *Little-carpenter.*

lish, in whose service they had been engaged. Having lost their horses, and being worn out with toil and fatigue, on coming to the frontiers of Virginia, they picked up several of those animals, which belonged to the inhabitants of the places through which they travelled. This, Dr. *Ramsay** says, was the cause of the massacre, which they suffered at that time. But Mr. *Adair*,† who lived then among the Indians in those parts, says, "Several companies of the Cheerake, who joined our forces under Gen. *Stanwix*, at the unfortunate Ohio, affirmed that their alienation from us was because they were confined to our martial arrangement, by unjust suspicion of them—were very much contemned,—and half starved at the main camp: their hearts told them, therefore, to return home, as freemen and injured allies, though without a supply of provisions. This they did, and pinching hunger forced them to take as much as barely supported nature, when returning to their own country. In their journey, the German inhabitants, without any provocation, killed, in cool blood, about 40 of their warriors, in different places—though each party was under the command of a British subject." It must be remembered that, upon Braddock's defeat, Virginia had offered a reward for the scalps of hostile Indians. Here, then, was an inducement for remorseless villains to murder, and it was impossible, in many cases, to know whether a scalp were taken from a friend or an enemy. Out of this, then, we have no hesitation in saying, grew the excessive calamities, which soon after distressed the southern provinces. Forty innocent men, and friends, too, murdered in cold blood by the backwoodsmen of Virginia, brought on a war, which caused as much distress and misery among the parties engaged, as any since that region of country was planted by the whites.

At one place, a monster entertained a party of Indians, and treated them kindly, while, at the same time, he caused a gang of his kindred ruffians to lie in ambush where they were to pass, and, when they arrived, barbarously shot them down to a man! The news was forthwith carried to the Cherokee nation, and the effect of it upon the minds of the warriors, was like that of electricity. They seized their tomahawks and war clubs, and, but for the wisdom of *Attakullakulla*, would have murdered several Englishmen, then in their country upon some matters respecting a treaty. As *Attakullakulla* was a chief sachem, he was among the first apprized of the murders, and the design of vengeance. He therefore goes immediately to them, and informed them of their danger, and assisted them to secrete themselves; then, without loss of time, he assembled his warriors, and made a speech to them, in which he inveighed, with great bitterness, against the murderous English, and urged immediate war against them; "*and never* (said he) *shall the hatchet be buried, until the blood of our countrymen be atoned for. Let us not* (he continued) *violate our faith, or the laws of hospitality, by imbruing our hands in the blood of those who are now in our power. They came to us in the confidence of friendship, with belts of wampum to cement a perpetual alliance with us. Let us carry them back to their own settlements; conduct them safely within their confines, and then take up the hatchet, and endeavor to exterminate the whole race of them.*" This council was adopted. Before commencing hostilities, however, the murderers were demanded, but were blindly refused them, and we have *mentioned the consequences.*

The French, it was said, used their influence to enrage the Indians; but,

---

* Hist. South Carolina, i. 169.

† Hist. Amer. Indians, 245. That the Indians' taking horses was no pretext for the murders, even at the time, appears evident. "As (says Capt. *M'Call*, i. 257.) the horses in those parts ran wild in the woods, it was customary, both among the Indians and white people on the frontiers, to catch them and appropriate them to their own use."

if that were the case, we should not deem it worth naming, as it appears to us that nothing more could be necessary to inflame them than the horrid outrages of which we have spoken.

Meanwhile, war parties dispersed themselves along the frontiers of South Carolina, and began the slaughter of the inhabitants with that fury and barbarity which might justly have been expected from an exasperated people. With such tardy steps did the whites proceed, that half a year had passed before a force could be sent against them. Col. *Montgomery*, afterwards Lord *Eglington*, at length marched into their country, but was ambushed at a place called Crows-creek, a dangerous defile between a river and a steep mountain, where he met with a dismal defeat. The colonel and a part of his men escaped.

If we can believe Mr. *Adair*,—and I know not that he is or has been under any impeachment,—the perfidy of the whites, in this war, surpasses, or, at least, is equal to any thing which occurred in New England, regarding the Praying Indians, in the times of *Pometacom*, alias King *Philip*. The following is an instance. A great many of the remote Cherokee towns took no part in the war, in the first place, but, on the contrary, declared themselves the friends of the whites, and even volunteered to fight against whatever people should be found in arms against them; and, as they needed ammunition, a large deputation from those tribes set out for Charleston, to strengthen their friendship and tender their assistance. The principal leader of these Indians was a chief, whom the whites called *Round-O*, "on account of a blue impression he bore in that form;" a brave and aged warrior, and particular friend of the English. The friendly Indians, under *Round-O*, were met by an army under Gov. *Lyttleton*, of 1100 men, at Fort Prince George, in Dec. 1759. This fort was upon the Savannah River, near the Cherokee town called *Keowee*. Here the governor compelled these friendly Indians to sign a treaty, one article of which required them to deliver 22* of their people into his hands, to be kept as hostages for the due fulfilment of all the rest.† Besides the absurdity of detaining hostages from their friends, the English seem to have been miserably blind to their interests in other respects; for the Indians, at this time, knew not the meaning of hostages,‡ but supposed those so retained were doomed to slavery; an office the most unsufferable to Indians of all others. The following are such of the names of the unfortunate Cherokees as we have been able to collect, who, under the name of hostages, were thrown into a dismal, close prison, scarce large enough for six men, where they remained about two months, and were then massacred, as in the sequel we shall show:—

Chenohe, Ousanatanah, Tallichama, Tallitahe, Quarrasattahe, Connasaratah, Kataetoi, Otassite of Watogo, *Ousanoletah* of Jore, *Kataeletah* of *Cowetche, Chisquatalone, Skiagusta* of Sticoe, *Tanaesto, Wohatche, Wyejah, Oucahchistanah, Nicholche, Tony, Toatiahoi, Shallisloske* and *Chistie*.

Both *Attakullakulla* and *Ockonostota*, it appears, were at Fort Prince George at this time, and signed the treaty; and *Otassite, Kitagusta, Oconnocca* and *Killcannokca* were the others on the part of the Indians. Things having been thus settled, Mr. *Lyttleton* returned to Charleston, where he

---

* This was the number of murderers the governor demanded should be delivered to him. Two had been delivered up before the hostages were taken, and when any others were delivered, the same number of hostages were to be released. Treaty, ART. III.

† The treaty is printed at length in the British Empire, by Mr. *Wynne*, (ii. 273.) an author, by the way, of very great merit.

‡ Adair.

was received like a conqueror, although what he had done, it will appear, was worse than if he had done nothing at all.

Ockonostota, for good reason, no doubt, entertained a deep-rooted hatred against Capt. *Cotymore,* an officer of the garrison, and the army had but just left the country, when it was found that he was hovering about the garrison with a large number of warriors. But it was uncertain, for some time, whether they intended to attack the fort, or whether they wished to continue near their friends, who were imprisoned in it. However, it is said, that, by some means, a plan was concerted between the Indians without and those confined within the fort, for surprising it. Be this as it may, *Ockonostota* practised the following wile to effect the object. Having placed a party of his warriors in a dark cane-brake near at hand, he sent a squaw to the garrison to invite the commander to come out, for he had something of importance to communicate to him. Capt. *Cotymore* imprudently went out, accompanied by two of his officers, and Ockonostota appeared upon the opposite bank of the Savannah, with a bridle in his hand, the better to conceal his intentions. He told the captain he was going to Charleston to effect the release of the hostages, and requested that a white man might accompany him; and that, as the distance was great, he would go and try to catch a horse. The captain promised him a guard, and hoped he would succeed in finding a horse. *Ockonostota* then quickly turned himself about, and swinging his bridle thrice over his head, which was the signal to his men, and they promptly obeying it, about 30 guns were discharged upon the officers at the same moment. Capt. *Cotymore* received a shot in his left breast, from which he died in two or three days after, and both the others were wounded. On recovering the fort, an attempt was made to put the hostages in irons. An Englishman, who laid hold on one of them for that purpose, was stabbed and slain; and, in the scuffle, two or three more were wounded, and driven out of the place of confinement. The tragedy in the fort had now only commenced; the miserable prisoners had repelled their assassins for the moment, and doubtless hoped for deliverance from their friends without, who had now closely besieged the place. But unfortunately for these poor wretches, the fort was too strong to be carried by their arts of war, and the dastardly whites found time and means to murder their victims, one by one, in a manner too horrible to relate.

There were few families who did not lose a friend or relation by this massacre, and, as one man, the nation took up the hatchet, and desolations quickly followed.

Meanwhile, singular as it may appear, *Attakullakulla* remained the fast friend of the whites, and used all his arts to induce his countrymen to make peace. But it was in vain he urged them to consider that they had more than revenged themselves; they were determined to carry all before them. *Attakullakulla* was now an old man, and had been in England formerly,* and had become much attached to the English, from several causes. On the other hand, *Ockonostota* was a stern warrior, in the vigor of manhood, and, like the renowned *Pontiac,* was determined to rid his country of his barbarous enemies.

After the unfortunate expedition of Col. *Montgomery,* to which we have before alluded, all communication was cut off between Fort Loudon and the English settlements, and nothing but famine and the worst of deaths stared those who held it in the face. The number of men stationed here was 200, and their situation was truly deplorable. *Ockonostota,* with his numerous warriors, kept strict watch, insomuch that there was no means of escape. At length, the garrison having miserably subsisted, for some time,

* He went over with Sir *Alexander Cumming,* in 1730.

upon poor famished horses, dogs, &c., many became resolved to throw themselves into the power of the Indians, wishing rather to die by their hands, than miserably to perish within their fortress. Capt. *Steuart,* an officer among them, was well known to the Indians, and possessed great address and sagacity. He resolved, at this crisis, to repair to Chote, the residence of *Ockonostota,* and make overtures for the surrender of the garrison. He, accordingly, effected his object, and returned with articles of capitulation agreed upon. Besides the names of *Ockonostota* and *Paul Demere,* the commander of the garrison, the name of another chief was to the articles, called *Cunigacatgoae.* The articles stipulated, that the garrison should march out with their arms and drums, each soldier having as much powder and ball as his officers should think necessary, and that they should march for Virginia unmolested.

Accordingly, on 7 August, 1760, the English took up their march for Fort Prince George. They had proceeded but about 15 miles, when they encamped, for the night, upon a small plain near Taliquo. They were accompanied thus far by *Ockonostota* in person, and many others, in a friendly manner, but at night they withdrew without giving any notice. The army was not molested during the night, but, at dawn of day, a sentinel came running into camp with the information that a host of Indians were creeping up to surround them. Capt. *Demere* had scarce time to rally, before the Indians broke into his camp with great fury. The poor emaciated soldiers made but feeble resistance. Thirty of their number fell in the first onset, among whom was their captain. Those that were able, endeavored to save themselves by flight, and others surrendered themselves upon the place. Among the latter was Capt. *Steuart.* The prisoners were conducted to Fort Loudon, which now became *Ockonostota's* head-quarters.

Attakullakulla, learning that his friend *Steuart* was among the captives, proceeded immediately to Fort Loudon, where he ransomed him at the expense of all the property he could command, and took care of him with the greatest tenderness and affection.

The restless *Ockonostota* next resolved to invest Fort Prince George. He was induced to undertake that project, as fortune had thrown in his way some of the means for such an undertaking, hitherto beyond his reach. Before abdicating Fort Loudon, the English had hid in the ground several bags of powder. This his men had found. Several cannon had also been left behind, and he designed to force his English prisoners to get them through the woods, and manage them in the attack upon Fort Prince George. But *Attakullakulla* defeated these operations, by assisting Capt. *Steuart* to escape. He even accompanied him to the English settlements, and returned loaded with presents.

Ockonostota continued the war until Col. *Grant,* in 1761, traversed the Cherokee country, and subdued his people in several battles; and peace was at last effected by the mediation of *Attakullakulla.* This chief's residence was upon the Tennessee or Cherokee River, at what was called the *Overhill Towns.* In 1773, when the learned traveller, *Bartram,* traveled into the Cherokee country, he met the old chief on his way to Charleston; of which circumstance he speaks thus in his Travels:—"Soon after crossing this large branch of the Tanase, I observed descending the heights, at some distance, a company of Indians, all well mounted on horseback. They came rapidly forward; on their nearer approach, I observed a chief at the head of the caravan, and apprehending him to be the *Little-carpenter,* emperor or grand chief of the Cherokees, as they came up, I turned off from the path to make way, in token of respect, which compliment was accepted, and gratefully and magnanimously returned; for his highness, with a gracious and cheerful smile, came up to me, and clapping his hand on his breast, offered it to me, saying, I am *Ata-cul-culla,* and heartily shook hands with me, and asked me if I knew it; I answered, that the good spirit who goes before me spoke to me, and said, that is the great *Ata-cul-culla.*" Mr. *Bartram* added, that he was of Pennsylvania, and though that was a great way off, yet the name of *Attakullakulla* was dear to his white brothers of Pennsylvania. The chief then asked him if he came directly from Charleston, and if his friend "*John Stewart* were well." Mr. *Bartram* said he saw him lately, and that he was well. This was, probably, the same person whom *Attakullakulla* had assisted to make an escape, as we have just related.

In carrying out the history of the two chiefs, *Attakullakulla* and *Ockonostota,* we have omitted to notice *Chlucco,* better known by the name of the *Long-warrior,* king or mico of the Seminoles. He went out with Col.

Montgomery, and rendered him essential service in his unsuccessful expedition, of which we have spoken. A large band of Creeks accompanied him, and there is but little doubt, if it had not been for him and his warriors, few of the English would have returned to their friends. But, as usual, the English leader, in his time, had all the honor of successfully encountering many difficulties, and returning with his own life and many of his men's. It was by the aid of *Chlucco,* that the army escaped ambush after ambush, destroyed many of the Cherokee villages, and finally his warriors covered its retreat out of one of the most dangerous countries through which an army could pass. *Long-warrior* was what the New-England Indians termed a great powwow. That he was a man possessing a good mind, may fairly be inferred from his ability to withstand the temptation of intoxicating liquors. He had been known to remain sober, when all his tribe, and many whites among them, had all been wallowing in the mire of drunkenness together. In the year 1773, at the head of about 40 warriors, he marched against the Chocktaws of West Florida. What was the issue of this expedition we have not learned. We may have again occasion to notice *Chlucco*.

CHAPTER IV.

MONCACHTAPE, *the Yazoo—Narrative of his adventures to the Pacific Ocean*—GRAND-SUN, *chief of the Natchez—Receives great injustice from the French—Concerts their destruction—700 French are cut off—War with them—The Natchez destroyed in their turn*—GREAT-MORTAR—M'GILLIVRAY—*His birth and education—Visits New York—Troubles of his nation—His death*—TAME-KING — MAD-DOG.

Moncachtape was a Yazoo, whose name signified, in the language of that nation, *killer of pain and fatigue*. How well he deserved this name the sequel will unfold. He was well known to the historian *Du Pratz*, about 1760, and it was owing to his singular good intelligence, that that traveller was able to add much valuable information to his work. "This man (says *Du Pratz**) was remarkable for his solid understanding and elevation of sentiment; and I may justly compare him to those first Greeks, who travelled chiefly into the east, to examine the manners and customs of different nations, and to communicate to their fellow citizens, upon their return, the knowledge which they had acquired." He was known to the French by the name of the *Interpreter*, as he could communicate with several other nations, having gained a knowledge of their languages. Mons. *Du Pratz* used great endeavors among the nations upon the Mississippi, to learn their origin, or from whence they came; and observes concerning it, "All that I could learn from them was, that they came from between the north and the sun-setting; and this account they uniformly adhere to, whenever they give any account of their origin." This was unsatisfactory to him, and in his exertions to find some one that could inform him better, he met with *Moncachtape*. The following is the result of his communications, in his own words:—

"I had lost my wife, and all the children whom I had by her, when I undertook my journey towards the sun-rising. I set out from my village contrary to the inclination of all my relations, and went first to the Chicasaws, our friends and neighbors. I continued among them several days, to inform myself whether they knew whence we all came, or, at least, whence they themselves came; they, who were our elders; since from them came the language of the country. As they could not inform me, I proceeded on my journey. I reached the Wabash, or Ohio, near to its source, which is in the country of the Iroquois, or Five Nations. I left them, however, towards the north; and, during the winter, which, in that country, is very severe and very long, I lived in a village of the Abenaquis, where I contracted an acquaintance with a man somewhat older than myself, who promised to conduct me, the following spring, to the great water. Accordingly, when the snows were melted, and the weather was settled, we proceeded eastward, and, after several days' journey, I at length saw the great water, which filled me with such joy and admiration, that I could not speak. Night drawing on, we took up our

* Hist. Louisiana, ii. 121.

lodging on a high bank above the water, which was sorely vexed by the wind, and made so great a noise that I could not sleep. Next day, the ebbing and flowing of the water filled me with great apprehension; but my companion quieted my fears, by assuring me that the water observed certain bounds, both in advancing and retiring. Having satisfied our curiosity in viewing the great water, we returned to the village of the Abenaquis, where I continued the following winter; and, after the snows were melted, my companion and I went and viewed the great fall of the River St. Lawrence, at Niagara, which was distant from the village several days' journey. The view of this great fall, at first, made my hair stand on end, and my heart almost leap out of its place; but afterwards, before I left it, I had the courage to walk under it. Next day, we took the shortest road to the Ohio, and my companion and I cutting down a tree on the banks of the river, we formed it into a pettiaugre, which served to conduct me down the Ohio and the Mississippi, after which, with much difficulty, I went up our small river, and at length arrived safe among my relations, who were rejoiced to see me in good health.—This journey, instead of satisfying, only served to excite my curiosity. Our old men, for several years, had told me that the ancient speech informed them that the red men of the north came originally much higher and much farther than the source of the River Missouri; and as I had longed to see, with my own eyes, the land from whence our first fathers came, I took my precautions for my journey westwards. Having provided a small quantity of corn, I proceeded up along the eastern bank of the River Mississippi, till I came to the Ohio. I went up along the bank of this last river, about the fourth part of a day's journey, that I might be able to cross it without being carried into the Mississippi. There I formed a cajeux, or raft of canes, by the assistance of which I passed over the river; and next day meeting with a herd of buffaloes in the meadows, I killed a fat one, and took from it the fillets, the bunch, and the tongue. Soon after, I arrived among the Tamaroas, a village of the nation of the Illinois, where I rested several days, and then proceeded northwards to the mouth of the Missouri, which, after it enters the great river, runs for a considerable time without intermixing its muddy waters with the clear stream of the other. Having crossed the Mississippi, I went up the Missouri, along its northern bank, and, after several days' Journey, I arrived at the nation of the Missouris, where I staid a long time to learn the language that is spoken beyond them. In going along the Missouri, I passed through meadows a whole day's journey in length, which were quite covered with buffaloes.

"When the cold was past, and the snows were melted, I continued my journey up along the Missouri, till I came to the nation of the west, on the Canzas. Afterwards, in consequence of directions from them, I proceeded in the same course near 30 days, and at length I met with some of the nation of the Otters, who were hunting in that neighborhood, and were surprised to see me alone. I continued with the hunters two or three days, and then accompanied one of them and his wife, who was near her time of lying in, to their village, which lay far off betwixt the north and west. We continued our journey along the Missouri for nine days, and then we marched directly northwards for five days more, when we came to the fine river, which runs westward in a direction contrary to that of the Missouri. We proceeded down this river a whole day, and then arrived at the village of the Otters, who received me with as much kindness as if I had been of their own nation. A few days after, I joined a party of the Otters, who were going to carry a calumet of peace to a nation beyond them, and we embarked in a pettiaugre, and went down the river for 18 days, landing now and then to supply ourselves with provisions. When I arrived at the nation who were at peace with the Otters, I staid with them till the cold was passed, that I might learn their language, which was common to most of the nations that lived beyond them.

"The cold was hardly gone, when I again embarked on the fine river, and in my course I met with several nations, with whom I generally staid but one night, till I arrived at the nation that is but one day's journey from the great water on the west. This nation live in the woods about the distance of a league from the river, from their apprehension of bearded men, who come upon their coasts in floating villages, and carry off their children to make slaves of them. These men were described to be white, with long black beards that came down to their breast; they were thick and short, had large heads, which were covered with cloth; they were always dressed, even in the greatest heats; their clothes fell down to the middle of their legs, which, with their feet, were covered with red or yellow stuff. Their arms made a great fire and a great noise; and when they saw themselves out-numbered by red men, they retired on board their large pettiaugre, their number sometimes amounting to thirty, but never more.

"Those strangers came from the sun-setting, in search of a yellow stinking wood, which dyes a fine yellow color; but the people of this nation, that they might not be tempted to visit them, had destroyed all those kind of trees. Two other nations in their neighborhood, however, having no other wood, could not destroy the trees, and were still visited by the strangers; and being greatly incommoded by them, had invited their allies to assist them in making an attack upon them, the next time they should return. The following summer I accordingly joined in this expedition, and, after travelling five long days' journey, we came to the place where the bearded men usually landed, where we waited seventeen days for their arrival. The red men, by my advice, placed themselves in ambuscade to surprise the strangers, and accordingly, when they landed to cut the wood, we were so successful as to kill eleven of them, the rest immediately escaping on board two large pettiaugres, and flying westward upon the great water.

"Upon examining those whom we had killed, we found them much smaller than ourselves, and very white; they had a large head, and in the middle of the crown the hair was very long; their head was wrapt in a great many folds of stuff, and their clothes seemed to be made neither of wool nor silk; they were very soft, and of different colors. Two only, of the eleven who were slain, had fire-arms, with powder and ball. I tried their pieces, and found that they were much heavier than yours, and did not kill at so great a distance.

"After this expedition, I thought of nothing but proceeding on my journey, and, with that design, I let the red men return home, and joined myself to those who inhabited more westward on the coast, with whom I travelled along the shore of the great water, which bends directly betwixt the north and the sun-setting. When I arrived at the villages of my fellow travellers, where I found the days very long, and the nights very short, I was advised by the old men to give over all thoughts of continuing my journey. They told me that the land extended still a long way in a direction between the north and sun-setting, after which it ran directly west, and at length was cut by the great water from north to south. One of them added, that, when he was young, he knew a very old man who had seen that distant land before it was eat away by the great water, and that when the great water was low, many rocks still appeared in those parts. Finding it, therefore, impracticable to proceed much farther, on account of the severity of the climate, and the want of game, I returned by the same route by which I had set out; and, reducing my whole travels westward to days' journeys, I compute that they would have employed me 36 moons; but, on account of my frequent delays, it was five years before I returned to my relations among the Yazoos."

Thus ends the narrative of the famous traveller *Moncachtape*. He soon after left Mons. *Du Pratz*, and returned to his own country. It would have been gratifying, could we have known more of the history of this very intelligent man. The same author brings also to our knowledge a chief called *Grand-sun*, chief of the Natchez. Although *Sun* was a common name for all chiefs of that nation, this chief was particularly distinguished in the first war with the French, which exhibits the compass of our information concerning him, and which we purpose here to sketch.

He was brother to the great warrior, known to the French by the name of *Stung-serpent*, and like him was a friend to the whites, until the haughty, overbearing disposition of one man brought destruction and ruin on their whole colony. This affair took place in the year 1729. The residence of the *Grand-sun* was near the French post of Natchez, where he had a beautiful village called the *White Apple*. M. *de Chopart* had been reinstated in the command of the post, whence he was for a time removed by reason of misconduct, and his abominable injustice to the Indians became more conspicuous afterwards than before. To gratify his pride and avarice, he had projected the building of an elegant village, and none appeared to suit his purpose so well as the White Apple of the *Grand-sun*. He sent for the chief to his fort, and unhesitatingly told him that his village must be immediately given up to him, for he had resolved to erect one a league square upon the same ground, and that he must remove elsewhere. The great chief stifled his surprise, and modestly replied, "that his ancestors had lived in that village for as many years as there were hairs in his double cue, and, therefore, it was good that they should continue there still." When this was interpreted to the commandant, he showed himself in a rage, and threatened the chief, that, unless he moved from his village speedily, he would have cause of repentance. *Grand-sun* left the fort, and said he would assemble his counsellors, and hold a talk upon it.

In this council, which actually assembled, it was proposed to lay before the commandant their hard situation, if they should be obliged to abandon their corn, which then was just beginning to shoot from the ground, and many other articles on which they were to depend for subsistence. But, on urging these strong reasons, they met only with abuse, and a more peremptory order to remove immediately. This the *Grand-sun* reported to the council, and they saw all was lost, unless, by some stratagem, they should rid themselves of the tyrant *Chopart*, which was their final decision. The secret was confided to none but the old men. To gain time, an offer was to be made to the avaricious commandant, of tribute, in case he would permit them to remain on their land until their harvest. The offer was accepted, and the Indians set about maturing their plan with the greatest avidity. Bundles of sticks were sent to the suns of the neighboring tribes, and their import explained to them by the faithful messengers. Each bundle contained as many sticks as days which were to pass before the massacre of all the French in the Natchez. And that no mistake should arise in regard to the fixed day, every morning a stick was drawn from the bundle and broken in pieces, and the day of the last stick was that of the execution.

The security of the wicked, in the midst of their wickedness, and their deafness to repeated warnings, though a standing example before them upon the pages of all history, yet we know of but few instances where they have profited by it. I need cite no examples; our pages are full of them.

The breast of women, whether civilized or uncivilized, cannot bear the thoughts of revenge and death to prey upon them for so great a length of time as men. And, as in the last case, I need not produce examples; on our pages will be found many.

A female sun having, by accident, understood the secret design of her people, partly out of resentment for their keeping it from her, and partly from her attachment to the French, resolved to make it known to them. But so fatally secure was the commandant, that he would not hearken to her messengers, and threatened others of his own people with chastisement, if they continued such intimations. But the great council of so many suns, and other motions of their wise men, justly alarmed many, and their complaints to the commandant were urged, until seven of his own people were put in irons, to dispel their fears. And that he might the more vaunt himself upon their fears, he sent his interpreter to demand of the Grand-sun, whether he was about to fall upon the French with his warriors. To dissemble, in such a case, was only to be expected from the chief, and the interpreter reported to the commandant as he desired, which caused him to value himself upon his former contempt of his people's fears.

The 30th of November, 1729, at length came, and with it the massacre of near 700 people, being all the French of Natchez. Not a man escaped. It being upon the eve of St. *Andrew's* day, facilitated the execution of the horrid design. In such contempt was M. *Chopart* held, that the suns would allow no warrior to kill him, but one whom they considered a mean person. He was armed only with a wooden tomahawk, and with such a contemptible weapon, wielded by as contemptible a person, was M. *Chopart* pursued from his house into his garden, and there met his death.

The design of the *Grand-sun* and his allies was, to have followed up their success until all the French were driven out of Louisiana. But some tribes would not aid in it, and the governor of Louisiana, promptly seconded by the people of New Orleans, shortly after nearly annihilated the whole tribe of the Natchez. The Choctaws offered themselves, to the number of 15 or 1600 men, and, in the following February, advanced into the country of the Natchez, and were shortly after joined by the French, and encamped near the old fort, then in possession of the *Grand-sun*. Here flags passed between them, and terms of peace were agreed upon, which were very honorable to the Indians; but, in the following night, they decamped, taking all their prisoners and baggage, leaving nothing but the cannons of the fort and balls behind them. Some time now passed before the French could ascertain the retreat of the Natchez. At length, they learned that they had crossed the Mississippi, and settled upon the west side, near 180 miles above the mouth of Red River. Here they built a fort, and remained quietly until the next year.

The weakness of the colony caused the inhabitants to resign themselves into the hands of the king, who soon sent over a sufficient force, added to those still in the country, to humble the Natchez. They were accordingly invested in their fort, and, struck with consternation at the sudden approach of the French, seem to have lost their former prudence. They made a desperate sally upon the camp of the enemy, but were repulsed with great loss. They then attempted to gain time by negotiation, as they had the year before, but could not escape from the vigilance of the French officer; yet the attempt was made, and many were killed, very few escaped, and the greater number driven within their fort. Mortars were used by their enemies in this siege, and the third bomb, falling in the centre of the fort, made great havoc, but still greater consternation. Drowned by the cries of the women and children, *Grand-sun* caused the sign of capitulation to be given. Himself, with the rest of his company, were carried prisoners to New Orleans, and thrown into prison. An increasing infection caused the women and children to be taken out and employed as slaves on the king's plantations; among whom was the woman who had used every endeavor to notify the commandant, *Chopart,* of the intended massacre, and from whom the particulars of the affair were learned. Her name was *Stung-arm*. These slaves were shortly after embarked for St. Domingo, entirely to rid the country of the Natchez.* The men, it is probable, were all put to death.

Great-mortar, or *Yah-yah-tustanage*, was a very celebrated Muskogee chief, who, before the revolutionary war, was in the French interest, and received his supplies from their garrison at Alabama, which was not far distant from his place of abode, called *Okchai*. There was a time when he inclined to the English, and but for the very haughty and imprudent conduct of the superintendent of Indian affairs, among them, might have been reclaimed, and the dismal period of massacres which ensued averted. At a great council, appointed by the superintendent, for the object of regaining their favor, the pipe of peace, when passing around, was refused to *Great-mortar*, because he had favored the French. This, with much other ungenerous treatment, caused him ever after to hate the English name. As the superintendent was making a speech, which doubtless contained severe and hard sayings against his red-bearers, another chief, called the *Tobacco-eater*, sprung upon his feet, and darting his tomahawk at him, it fortunately missed him, but stuck in a plank just above his head. Yet he would have been immediately killed, but for the interposition of a friendly warrior. Had this first blow been effectual, every Englishman present would have been immediately put to death. Soon after, *Great-mortar* caused his people to fall upon the English traders, and they murdered ten. Fourteen of the inhabitants of Longcane, a settlement near Ninety-six,† next were his victims. He now received a commission from the French, and the better to enlist the Cherokees and others in his cause, removed with his family far into the heart of the country, upon a river, by which he could receive supplies from the fort at Alabama. Neither the French nor *Great-mortar* were deceived in the advantage of their newly-chosen position; for young warriors joined him there in great numbers, and it was fast becoming a general rendezvous for all the Mississippi Indians. Fortunately, however, for the English, the Chickasaws in their interest plucked up this *Bohon upas* before its branches were yet extended. They fell upon them by surprise, killed the brother of *Great-mortar*, and completely destroyed the design. He fled, not to his native place, but to one from whence he could best annoy the English settlements, and commenced anew the work of death. Augusta, in Georgia, and many scattering settlements were destroyed.‡ Those ravages were continued until their united forces were defeated by the Americans under Gen. *Grant*, in 1761, as we shall have occasion to notice in our progress.§ The fate of *Great-mortar*, like many others, is hidden from us.

We have next to notice a chief, king, or emperor, as he was at different times entitled, whose omission, in a biographical work upon the Indians, would incur as much criminality, on the part of the biographer, as an omission of *Buckougehelas, White-eyes, Pipe*, or *Ockonostota;* yea, even more. We mean

* Mons. *Du Pratz*, Hist. de Louisiana, tome i. chap. xii.

† So called because it was 96 miles from the Cherokee. *Adair.*

‡ *Adair's* Hist. N. American Indians, 254, &c.

§ *Wynne's* Brit. Empire, ii. 283.

Alexander M'Gillivray, who was, perhaps, one of the most conspicuous, if not one of the greatest, chiefs that has ever borne that title among the Creeks; at least, since they have been known to the Europeans. He flourished during half of the last century, and such was the exalted opinion entertained of him by his countrymen, that they styled him "king of kings." His mother was his predecessor, and the governess of the nation, and he had several sisters, who married leading men. On the death of his mother, he came in chief sachem by the usages of his ancestors, but such was his disinterested patriotism, that he left it to the nation to say whether he should succeed to the sachemship. The people elected him "emperor." He was at the head of the Creeks during the revolutionary war, and was in the British interest. After the peace, he became reconciled to the Americans, and expressed a desire to renounce his public life, and reside in the U. States, but was hindered by the earnest solicitations of his countrymen, to remain among them, and direct their affairs.

M'Gillivray was a son of an Englishman of that name who married a Creek woman, and hence was a half Indian. He was born about 1739, and, at the age of ten, was sent by his father to school in Charleston, where he was in the care of Mr. *Farquhar M'Gillivruy*, who was a relation of his father. His tutor was a Mr. *Sheed*. He learned the Latin language under the tuition of Mr. *William Henderson*, afterwards somewhat eminent among the critics in London. When young *M'Gillivray* was 17, he was put into a counting-house in Savannah, but mercantile affairs had not so many charms as books, and he spent all the time he could get, in reading histories and other works of usefulness. After a short time, his father took him home, where his superior talents soon began to develop themselves, and his promotion followed, as we have shown. He was often styled general, which commission, it is said, he actually held under *Charles* III., king of Spain. This was, probably, before he was elected emperor.

"The times that tried men's souls" were his times, and the neighborhood of the Spanish, French and English gave him and his people troubles which ended only with their lives.

On the 23 July, 1790, Col. *M'Gillivray*, and 29 of his chiefs and warriors, visited New York, accompanied by Col. *Marinus Willet*. They were conducted to the residence of the secretary of war, Gen. *Knox*, who conducted them to the house of the president of the U. States, and introduced them to him. President *Washington* received them "in a very handsome manner, congratulated them on their safe arrival, and expressed a hope that the interview would prove beneficial both to the U. States and to the Creek nation." They next visited the governor of the state, from whom they received a most cordial welcome. They then proceeded to the City Tavern, where they dined in company with Gen. *Knox*, and other officers of government. A correspondence between Gov. *Telfair*, of Georgia, and "*Alexander M'Gilvary*, Esq." probably opened the way for a negotiation, which terminated in a settlement of difficulties. From the following extract from *M'Gillivray's* letter, a very just idea may be formed of the state of the affairs of his nation previous to his visit to New York. "In answer to yours, I have to observe, that, as a peace was not concluded on between us at the Rock-landing meeting, your demand for property taken by our warriors from off the disputed lands cannot be admitted. We, also, have had our losses, by captures made by your people. We are willing to conclude a peace with you, but you must not expect extraordinary concessions from us. In order to spare the further effusion of human blood, and to finally determine the war, I am willing to concede, in some measure, if you are disposed to treat on the ground of mutual concession. It will save trouble and expense, if the negotiations are managed in the nation. Any person from you can be assured of personal safety and friendly treatment in this country." It was dated at Little Tellassee, 30 March, 1790, and directed to "His Excellency *Edward Telfair*, Esq." and signed "*Alex. M'Gillivray*."

This chief seems afterwards to have met with the censure of his people, at least some of them, in a manner similar to that of *M'Intosh* recently; and was doubtless overcome by the insinuations of designing whites, to treat for the disposal of his lands, against the general voice of his nation. One *Bowles*, a white man, led the councils in opposition to his proceedings, and, for a time, *M'Gillivray* absented himself from his own tribe. In 1792, *M'Gillivray's* party took *Bowles* prisoner, and sent him out of the country, and solicited the general to return to his own nation.* To this he consented, and they became more attached to him than ever. He now endeavored to better their condition by the introduction of teachers among them. In an advertisement for a teacher, in the summer of 1792, he styles himself emperor of the Creek nation. His quiet was soon disturbed, and the famous *John Watts*, the same summer, with 500 warriors, Creeks, and five towns of the Chickamawagas, committed many depredations. The Spaniards were supposed to be the movers of the hostile party. *M'Gillivray died* in April, 1793, and is thus noticed in the Pennsylvania Gazette:—" This idolized chief of the Creeks styled himself king of kings. But, alas, he could neither restrain the meanest fellow of his nation from the commission of a crime, nor punish him after he had committed it! He might persuade or advise, all the good an Indian king or chief can do." This is, generally speaking, a tolerably correct estimate of the extent of the power of chiefs; but it should be remembered that the chiefs of different tribes exercise very different sway over their people, according as such chief is endowed with the spirit of government, by nature or circumstance. There is great absurdity in applying the name or title of king to Indian chiefs, as that title is commonly understood. The first Europeans conferred the title upon those who appeared most prominent, in their first discoveries, for want of another more appropriate; or, perhaps, they had another reason, namely, that of magnifying their own exploits on their return to their own countries, by reporting their interviews with, or conquests over, "many kings of an unknown country."

Contemporary with Gen. *M'Gillivray* was a chief called the *Tame-king*, whose residence was among the Upper Creeks, in 1791; and he is noticed in our public documents of that year, as a conspicuous chief in matters connected with establishing the southern boundary. At this time, one *Bowles*, an English trader, had great influence among the Lower Creeks, and used great endeavors, by putting himself forward as their chief, to enlist all the nations in opposition to the Americans. He had made large promises to the Upper Creeks, to induce them not to hear to the American commissioners. They so far listened to him, as to consent to receive his talk, and accordingly the chiefs of the upper and lower towns met at a place called the *Half-way-house*, where they expected *Bowles* in person, or some letters containing definite statements. When the chiefs had assembled, *Tame-king* and *Mad-dog*, of the upper towns, asked the chiefs of the lower, "whether *they* had taken *Bowles's* talks, and where the letters were which this *great man* had sent them, and where the white man

* In 1791, this *Bowles*, with five chiefs, was in England, and we find this notice of him in the European Magazine of that year, vol. 19, p. 268: "The ambassadors consisted of two Creeks, and of Mr. *Bowles*, (a native of Maryland, who is a Creek by adoption, and the present general of that nation.) and three Cherokees.

was to read them." An Indian in *Bowles's* employ said, "he was to give them the talk." They laughed at this, and said, "they could hear his mouth every day; that they had come there to see those letters and hear them read." Most of the chiefs of the upper towns now left the council, which was about the termination of *Bowles's* successes. He was shortly afterwards obliged to abdicate, as we have already declared in the life of *M'Gillivray*. He returned again, however, after visiting Spain and England, and spending some time in prison.

Mr. *Ellicott* observes,* that, at the close of a conference with sundry tribes, held 15 August, 1799, in which objects were discussed concerning his passage through their country, that "the business appeared to terminate as favorably as could be expected, and the Indians declared themselves perfectly satisfied; but I nevertheless had my doubts of their sincerity, from the depredations they were constantly making upon our horses, which began upon the Coeneuck, and had continued ever since; and added to their insolence, from their stealing every article in our camp they could lay their hands on." Mr. *Ellicott* excepts the Upper Creeks, generally, from participating in these robberies, all but *Tame-king* and his people.

Though we have named *Tame-king* first, yet *Mad-dog* was quite as conspicuous at this time. His son fought for the Americans in the last war, and was mentioned by Gen. *Jackson* as an active and valuable chief in his expeditions. His real name we have not learned, and the general mentions him only as *Mad-dog's* son.

In the case of the boundary already mentioned, the surveyors met with frequent difficulties from the various tribes of Indians, some of whom were influenced by the Spanish governor, *Folch,* of Louisiana. *Mad-dog* appeared their friend, and undeceived them respecting the governor's pretensions. A conference was to be held about the 4 May, between the Indians, Governor *Folch* and the American commissioners. The place of meeting was to be upon Coenecuh River, near the southern estuary of the bay of Pensacola. When the Americans arrived there, *Mad-dog* met them, and informed Col. *Hawkins,* the Indian agent, that two Indians had just gone to the Tallessees with bad talks from the governor. The colonel told him it could not be possible. Shortly after, Mad-dog asked Colonel *Hawkins* and Mr. *Ellicott,* the commissioner, if they supposed that Gov. *Folch* would attend at the treaty; they said, "Most assuredly." "*No,*" returned *Mad-dog,* "*he will not attend, he knows what I shall say to him about his crooked talks. His tongue is forked, and, as you are here, he will be ashamed to show it. If he stands to what he has told us, you will be offended, and if he tells us that the line ought to be marked, he will contradict himself: but he will do neither; he wilt not come.*" It turned out as *Mad-dog* declared. When it was found that the governor would not attend, the chief went to Col. *Hawkins* and Mr. *Ellicott,* and, by way of pleasantry, said, "*Well, the governor has not come. I told you so. A man with two tongues can only speak to one at a time.*" This observation has reference to the governor's duplicity, in holding out to the Indians his determination not to suffer a survey of the boundary, while, at the same time, he pretended to the Americans that he would facilitate it.†

Mad-dog was an upper-town Creek, of the Tuckaabatchees tribe.

---

* In his Journal, 214.

† Ibid, 203, &c.

CHAPTER V.

Weatherford—*His character and country—The corner-stone of the Creek confederacy—Favors the designs of Tecumseh—Captures Fort Mimms—Dreadful massacre—Subjection of the Creeks—Weatherford surrenders himself—His speeches—*M'Intosh—*Aids the Americans—Battle of Autossee—Great slaughter of the Indians—Battle of the Horse-shoe-bend—Late troubles in the Creek nation—M'Intosh makes illegal sale of lands—Executed for breaking the laws of his country*—Menawway—Tustenugge—Hawkins—Chilly M'Intosh, son of William—Marriage of *his sister*—Lovett.

Weatherford, one of the most conspicuous war chiefs of the Creek nation, demands an early attention, in the biographical history of the late war. Mr. *Claiborne,* in his Notes on the War in the South, informs us that, "among the first who entered into the views of the British commissioners was the since celebrated *Weatherford;*" that he was born in the Creek nation, and whose "father was an itinerant pedler, sordid, treacherous and revengeful; his mother a full-blooded savage, of the tribe of the Seminoles. He partook (says the same author) of all the bad qualities of both his parents,* and engrafted, on the stock he inherited from others, many that were peculiarly his own. With avarice, treachery, and a thirst for blood, he combines lust, gluttony, and a devotion to every species of criminal carousal. Fortune, in her freaks, sometimes gives to the most profligate an elevation of mind, which she denies to men whose propensities are the most vicious. On *Weatherford* she bestowed genius, eloquence and courage. The first of these qualities enabled him to conceive great designs, the last to execute them; while eloquence, bold, impressive and figurative, furnished him with a passport to the favor of his countrymen and followers. Silent and reserved, unless when excited by some great occasion, and superior to the weakness of rendering himself cheap by the frequency of his addresses, he delivered his opinions but seldom in council; but when he did so, he was listened to with delight and approbation. His judgment and eloquence had secured the respect of the old; his vices made him the idol of the young and the unprincipled." "In his person, tall, straight, and well proportioned; his eye black, lively and penetrating, and indicative of courage and enterprise; his nose prominent, thin, and elegant in its formation; while all the features of his face, harmoniously arranged, speak an active and disciplined mind. Passionately devoted to wealth, he had appropriated to himself a fine tract of land, improved and settled it; and from the profits of his father's pack, had decorated and embellished it. To it he retired occasionally, and, relaxing from the cares of state, he indulged in pleasures which are but rarely found to afford satisfaction to the devotees of ambition and fame. Such were the opposite and sometimes disgusting traits of character in the celebrated *Weatherford,* the key and corner-stone of the Creek confederacy!"

It is said that this chief had entered fully into the views of *Tecumseh,* and that, if he had entered upon his designs without delay, he would have been amply able to have overrun the whole Mississippi territory. But this fortunate moment was lost, and, in the end, his plans came to ruin. Not long before the wretched butchery at Fort Mimms, Gen. *Claiborne*

* The reader should be early apprized that this was written at a time when *some* prejudice *might* have infected the mind of the writer.

visited that post, and very particularly warned its possessors against a surprise. After giving orders for the construction of two additional block-houses, he concluded the order with these words:—"To respect an enemy, and prepare in the best possible way to meet him, is the certain means to ensure success." It was expected that *Weatherford* would soon attack some of the forts, and Gen. *Claiborne* marched to Fort Early, as that was the farthest advanced into the enemy's country. On his way, he wrote to Maj. *Beasley,* the commander of Mimms, informing him of the danger of an attack, and, strange as it may appear, the next day after the letter was received, (30 Aug. 1813,) *Weatherford,* at the head of about 1500 warriors, entered the fort at noon-day, when a shocking carnage ensued. The gate had been left open and unguarded; but before many of the warriors had entered, they were met by Maj. *Beasley,* at the head of his men, and for some time the contest was bloody and doubtful; each striving for the mastery of the entrance. Here, man to man, the fight continued for a quarter of an hour, with tomahawks, knives, swords and bayonets: a scene there presented itself almost without a parallel in the annals of Indian warfare! The garrison consisted of 275: of these only 160 were soldiers; the rest were old men, women and children, who had here taken refuge. It is worthy of very emphatical remark, that every officer expired fighting at the gate. A lieutenant, having been badly wounded, was carried by two women to a block-house, but when he was a little recovered, he insisted on being carried back to the fatal scene, which was done by the same heroines, who placed him by the side of a dead companion, where he was soon despatched.

The defenders of the garrison being now nearly all slain, the women and children shut themselves up in the block-houses, and seizing upon what weapons they could find, began, in that perilous and hopeless situation, to defend themselves. But the Indians soon succeeded in setting these houses on fire, and all such as refused to meet death without, perished in the flames within!! Seventeen only escaped of all the garrison, and many of those were desperately wounded. It was judged that, during the contest at the gate, near 400 of *Weatherford's* warriors were wounded and slain.

When the news of this affair was circulated through the country, many cried aloud for vengeance, and two powerful armies were soon upon their march into the Indian country, and the complete destruction of the Indian power soon followed. The Indians seeing all resistance was at an end, great numbers of them came forward and made their submission. Weatherford, however, and many who were known to be desperate, still stood out; perhaps from fear. Gen. *Jackson* determined to test the fidelity of those chiefs who had submitted, and, therefore, ordered them to deliver, without delay, *Weatherford,* bound, into his hands, that he might be dealt with as he deserved. When they had made known to the sachem what was required of them, his noble spirit would not submit to such degradation; and to hold them harmless, he resolved to give himself up without compulsion. Accordingly, he proceeded to the American camp, unknown, until he appeared before the commanding general, to whose presence, under some pretence, he gained admission. Gen. *Jackson* was greatly surprised, when the chief said, "*I am Weatherford, the chief who commanded at the capture of Fort Mimms. I desire peace for my people, and have come to ask it.*" *Jackson* had, doubtless, determined upon his execution when he should be brought bound, as he had directed, but his sudden and unexpected appearance, in this manner, saved him. The general said he was astonished that he should venture to appear in his presence, as he was not ignorant of his having been at Fort Mimms, nor of his inhuman conduct there, for which he so well deserved to die. "I ordered," continued the general, "that you should be brought to me bound; and, had you been brought in that manner, I should have known how to have treated you." In answer to this, *Weatherford* made the following famous speech:—

"*I am in your power—do with me as you please—I am a soldier. I have done the whites all the harm I could. I have fought them, and fought them bravely. If I had an army, I would yet fight—I would contend to the last: but I have none. My people are all gone. I can only weep over the misfortunes of my nation.*"

Gen. *Jackson* was pleased with his boldness, and told him that, though he was in his power, yet he would take no advantage; that he might yet join the war party, and contend against the Americans, if he chose, but to depend upon no quarter if taken afterward; and that unconditional submission was his and his people's only safety. *Weatherford* rejoined, in a tone as dignified as it was indignant,—"*You can safely address me in such terms now. There was a time when I could have answered you—there was a time when I had a choice—I have none now. I have not even a hope. I could once animate my warriors to battle—but I cannot animate the dead. My warriors can no longer hear my voice. Their bones are at Talladega, Tallushatches, Emuckfaw and Tohopeka. I have not surrendered myself without thought. While there was a single chance of success, I never left my post, nor supplicated peace. But my people are gone, and I now ask it for my nation, not for myself. I look buck with deep sorrow, and wish to avert still greater calamities. If I had been left to contend with the Georgia army, I would have raised my corn on one bank of the river, and fought them on the other. But your people have destroyed my nation. You are a brave man. I rely upon your generosity. You will exact no terms of a conquered people, but such as they should accede to. Whatever they may be, it would now be madness and folly to oppose them. If they are opposed, you shall find me amongst the sternest enforcers of obedience. Those who would still hold out, can be influenced only by a mean spirit of revenge. To this they must not, and shall not sacrifice the last remnant of their country. You have told our nation where we might go and be safe. This good talk, and they ought to listen to it. They shall listen to it.*" And here we must close our present account of *Weatherford,* and enter upon that of a character opposed to him in the field, and, if we can believe the writers of their times, opposite in almost all the affairs of life. This was the celebrated and truly unfortunate.

Gen. *William M'Intosh*, a Creek chief, of the tribe of Cowetaw. He was, like *M'Gillivray*, a half-breed, whom he considerably resembled in several particulars, as by his history will appear. He was a prominent leader of such of his countrymen as joined the Americans in the war of 1812, 13 and 14, and is first mentioned by General *Jackson*,* in his account of the *battle*, as he called it, of Autossee, where he assisted in the brutal destruction of 200 of his nation. There was nothing like fighting on the part of the people of the place, as we can learn, being surprised in their wigwams, and hewn to pieces. "The Cowetaws," says the general, "under *M'Intosh*, and *Zookaubatchians*,† under *Mad-dog's-son*, fell in on our flanks, and fought with an intrepidity worthy of any troops." And after relating the burning of the place, he thus proceeds:—"It is difficult to determine the strength of the enemy, but from the information of some of the chiefs, which it is said can be relied on, there were assembled at Autossee, warriors from eight towns, for its defence; it being their beloved ground, on which they proclaimed no white man could approach without inevitable destruction. It is difficult to give a precise account of

* *Brannan's* official letters.

† Tuckabatche. *Bartram,* 447.

the loss of the enemy; but from the number which were lying scattered over the field, together with those destroyed in the towns, and the many slain on the bank of the river, which respectable officers affirm that they saw lying in heaps at the waters' edge, where they had been precipitated by their surviving friends,[!!] their loss in killed, independent of their wounded, must have been at least 200, (among whom were the Autossee and Tallassee kings,) and from the circumstance of their making no efforts to molest our return, probably greater. The number of buildings burnt, some of a superior order for the dwellings of savages, and filled with valuable articles, is supposed to be 400." This was on the 29 November, 1813.

M'Intosh was also very conspicuous in the memorable battle of the Horse-shoe-bend, in the Tallapoosie River. At this place the disconsolate tribes of the south had made a last great stand, and had a tolerably regular fortified camp. It was said that they were 1000 strong. They had constructed their works with such ingenuity, that little could be effected against them but by storm. "Determined to exterminate them," says Gen. *Jackson*, "I detached General *Coffee* with the mounted, and nearly the whole of the Indian force, early on the morning of yesterday, [March 27, 1814,] to cross the river about two miles below their encampment, and to surround the bend, in such a manner, as that none of them should escape by attempting to cross the river." "*Bean's* company of spies, who had accompanied Gen. *Coffee*, crossed over in canoes to the extremity of the bend, and set fire to a few of the buildings which were there situated; they then advanced with great gallantry towards the breast-work, and commenced a spirited fire upon the enemy behind it." This force not being able to effect their object, many others of the army showed great ardor to participate in the assault. "The spirit which animated them was a sure augury of the success which was to follow." "The regulars, led on by their intrepid and skilful commander, Col. *Williams*, and by the gallant Maj. *Montgomery*, soon gained possession of the works in the midst of a most tremendous fire from behind them, and the militia of the venerable Gen. *Doherty's* brigade accompanied them in the charge with a vivacity and firmness which would have done honor to regulars. The enemy was completely routed. *Five hundred and fifty-seven** were left dead on the peninsula, and a great number were killed by the horsemen in attempting to cross the river. It is believed that not more than *twenty* have escaped.

"The fighting continued with some severity about five hours; but we continued to destroy many of them, who had concealed themselves under the banks of the river, until we were prevented by the night. This morning we killed 16 who had been concealed. We took about 250 prisoners, all women and children, except two or three. Our loss is 106 wounded, and 25 killed. Major *M'Intosh*, the Cowetau, who joined my army with a part of his tribe, greatly distinguished himself."† Truly, this was a war of extermination!! The friend of humanity may inquire whether all those poor wretches who had secreted themselves here and there in the "caves and reeds," had deserved death. They were first taken prisoners, then murdered!

The most melancholy part of the life of the unfortunate *M'Intosh* remains to be recorded. The late troubles of the Creek nation have drawn forth many a sympathetic tear from the eye of the philanthropist. These troubles were only the consequences of those of a higher date. Those of 1825, we thought, completed the climax of their affliction, but 1832

---

* These are the general's italics; at least, *Brannan* so prints his official letter.

† Brannan, *ut supra*.

must sully her annals with records of their oppression also. It is the former period with which our article brings us in collision, in closing this account. In that year, the government of the U. States, by its agents, seemed determined on possessing a large tract of their country, to satisfy the state of Georgia. *M'Intosh,* and a small part of the nation, were for conceding to their wishes, but a large majority of his countrymen would not hear to the proposal. The commissioners employed were satisfied of the fact, and communicated to the president the result of a meeting they had had for the purpose. He was well satisfied, also, that *M'Intosh* could not convey the lands, as he represented but a small part of his nation, but still the negotiation was ordered to be renewed. A council was called by the commissioners, (who were Georgians,) which assembled at a place called *Indian-springs.* Here the chief of the Tuckaubatcheese spoke to them as follows: "We met you at Broken Arrow, and then told you we had no land to sell. I then heard of no claims against the nation, nor have I since. We have met you here at a very short notice, and do not think that the chiefs who are here have any authority to treat. General *M'Intosh* knows that we are bound by our laws, and that what is not done in the public square, in the general council, is not binding on the nation. I am, therefore, under the necessity of repeating the same answer as given at Broken Arrow, that we have no land to sell. I know that there are but few here from the upper towns, and many are absent from the lower towns. Gen. *M'Intosh* knows that no part of the land can be sold without a full council, and with the consent of all the nation, and if a part of the nation choose to leave the country, they cannot sell the land they have, but it belongs to the nation." "This is the only talk I have for you, and I shall return home immediately." He did so. The ill-advised commissioners informed *M'Intosh* and his party, that the Creek nation was sufficiently represented by them, and that the United States would bear them out in a treaty of sale. The idea of receiving the whole of the pay for the lands among themselves, was doubtless the cause of the concession of *M'Intosh* and his party. "Thirteen only of the signers of the treaty were chiefs. The rest were such as had been degraded from that rank, and unknown persons; 36 chiefs present refused to sign. The whole party of *M'Intosh* amounted to about 300, not the tenth part of the nation." Still they executed the articles, in direct violation to the laws of their nation, which themselves had helped to form. It must be remembered that the Creeks had made no inconsiderable advances in what is termed civilization. They had towns, and even printed laws by which they were to be governed, similar to those of the United States.

"*M'Intosh* was aware, that, after signing the treaty, his life was forfeited. He, and others of his coadjutors, repaired to Milledgeville, stated their fears, and claimed the protection of Georgia, which was promised by Gov. *Troup.*"* It must be observed that the greater part of the purchased territory was within the claimed limits of Georgia;† and that the Georgians had no small share in the whole transaction. It is not stranger that the people of Georgia should conduct as they have, than that the United States' government should place it in her power so to act. To take, therefore, into account the whole merits of the case, it must be remembered, that, by a compact between the two parties in 1802, the former, in consideration of the latter's relinquishing her claim to the Mississippi territory, agreed to extinguish, at the national expense, the Indian title to the lands occupied by them, in Georgia, *whenever it could be done, upon rea-*

---

* Thus far selected from facts published by Mr. *W. J. Snelling.*

† *Perkins,* Hist. U. States, a work, by the way, of great value, and which we are surprised should have issued from the press with little or no notice.

*sonable terms.** Who was to decide *when* the practicable time had arrived, we believe was not mentioned. However, previous to 1825, the United States had succeeded in extinguishing the aboriginal title of 15,000,000 acres, and there were yet about 10,000,000 to be bought off.† The change of life from wandering to stationary, which the arts of civilization had effected among the Indians, made them prize their possessions far more highly than heretofore, and hence their reluctance and opposition to relinquish them.

Thus much it seemed necessary to premise, that the true cause of the fate of *M'Intosh* should be understood. It appears that when the whole of the nation saw that the treaty *M'Intosh* and his party had made could not be abrogated, forty-nine fiftieths of them were violent against them; and therefore resolved that the sentence of the law should be executed upon him. The execution, and circumstances attending it, are thus related:‡ "About two hours before day, on Sunday morning, 1 May,§ the house of Gen. *M'Intosh* was surrounded by *Menaw-way,* and about 100 Oakfuskee warriors. *M'Intosh* was within, as likewise were his women and children, and some white men. *Menaw-way* directed an interpreter to request the whites, and the women and children, to come out, as the warriors did not wish to harm them; that Gen. *M'Intosh* had broken the law that he himself had long since made, and they had come to execute him accordingly. They came out of the house, leaving *M'Intosh* and *Etomi-tustenugge*, one of his adherents, therein. The warriors then set fire to the house; and as *M'Intosh* and his comrade [*Tustenugge*] attempted to come out at the door, they shot them both down. The same day, about 12 o'clock, they hung *Sam Hawkins*, a half breed, in the Huckhosseliga Square. On Monday, the 2 May, a party of Halibee Indians fired on and wounded *Ben Hawkins*, another half breed, very badly. The chiefs stated, at the time, that no danger whatever was to be apprehended by persons travelling through the nation; that they were friends to the whites, and wished them not to be alarmed by this execution, which was only a compliance with the laws that the great chiefs of the nation made at Polecat Spring. *Chilly M'Intosh* escaped from the house with the whites, and was not fired at or wounded." He is now chief among the western Creeks, and some time since increased his notoriety by beating a member of Congress, in Washington.

The great agitation which the execution of the head chiefs of the *M'Intosh* party caused was allayed only by the interference of the United States' government. Gov. *Troup* of Georgia declared vengeance against the Creek nation, denouncing the execution of the chiefs as an act of murder; however, he, by some means, learned that his judgment was gratuitous, and, by *advice* of President *Adams,* desisted from acts of hostility, the survey of the disputed lands, &c.

We have not learned much of the family of *M'Intosh*. On 14 August, 1818, Jenny, his eldest daughter, was married to *William S. Mitchel*, Esq., assistant Indian agent of the Creek nation. They were married at a place called *Theacatckkah* near Fort Mitchel, in that nation.||

Gen. *M'Intosh* participated in the Seminole campaigns, as did another chief of the name of *Lovett* with about 2000 of their warriors. They joined the American army at Fort Scott in the spring of 1818.¶

---

* Amer. An. Regr. i.

† Ibid.

‡ In the Annual Register, *ut supra*.

§ 30 April is mentioned, in another part of the same work, as the date of the execution, and so it is set down by Mr. *Perkins*, in his Hist. U. S.

|| *Niles's* Register, 14, 407.

¶ N. Y. Monthly Mag. iii. 74.

BOOK V.

BIOGRAPHY AND HISTORY OF THE IROQUOIS OR FIVE NATIONS, AND OTHER NEIGHBORING NATIONS OF THE WEST.

CHAPTER I.

Particulars respecting the Iroquois—GRANGULA—*His famous speech to a French general*—ADARIO—*His successful wars against the French*—*Destroys a thousand inhabitants in one expedition*—*His real name*—BLACK-KETTLE—*His wars against the French*—TE-YEE-NEEN-HO-GA-PROW—SA-GA-YE-AN-QUA-PRAH-TON—E-LOW-OH-KA-OM—OH-NEE-YE-ATH-TON-NO-PROW—GAN-A-JOH-HO-RE—*Their visit to England*—*Particulars of their residence there*—*Treated with great attention by the nobility*—*Their interview with the queen*—*Speech to her*—*Their return to America.*

THE great western confederacy of Indian nations has generally been styled by the French, *Iroquois*,* but generally by the English, the *Five Nations*, and sometimes the *Six Nations*; but either of the two latter appellations must be considered *only* as such, because we shall show, as we proceed, that they are not numerically true *now*, if they *ever* were.

* "*Ces barbares ne sont qu'une seule nation, et qu'un seul intérêt public. On pourroit les nommer pour la distribution du terrain, les Suisses de ce continent. Les Iroquois sont partager en cinq cantons, sçavoir les Tsonontoüans, les Goyogoans, les Onnotagues, les Onoyouts, et les Agniés.*" (Lahontan, i. 35.) Thus comprehending in his *five nations* some nations which the English never have, and *vice versa*. By the *Agniés* we are to understand *Mohawks*.

Five may have been the number which originally leagued together, but when that happened, if indeed it ever did, can never be known. It is a tradition that these people came from beyond the lakes, a great while ago, and subdued or exterminated the inhabitants of the country on this side. Even if this were the case, it proves nothing of their origin; for there may have been a time when their ancestors went from this side to the country beyond, and so on. The Mohawks are said to have been the oldest of the confederacy, and that the "Onayauts" (Oneidas) were the first that joined them by putting themselves under their protection. The Onondagos were the next, then the "Teuontowanos, or Sinikers," (Senecas,) then the "Cuiukguos," (Cayugas.) The Tuscaroras, from Carolina, joined them about 1712, but were not formally admitted into the confederacy until about 10 years after that. The addition of this new tribe gained them the name of the Six Nations, according to most writers, but it will appear that they were called the Six Nations long before the last-named period. The Shawanese were not of the confederacy, but were called brothers by them. This nation came from the south, at no very remote period, and the Iroquois assigned them lands on the west branch of the Susquehannah, but looked upon them as inferiors. They occupied, before the French wars, a great extent of country, some of their towns being 80 miles asunder.

The Six Nations did not know themselves by such names as the English apply to them, but the name Aquanuschioni,* which signified *united people*, was used by them.† This term, as is the case with most Indian words, is defined by a knowledge of its etymology. A knowledge of the Indian languages would enable us to know what almost every place in the country has been noted for; whether hill or mountain, brook or river. It is said by *Colden*,‡ that New England was called *Kinshon*, by the Indians, which, he says, means a fish;§ and that the New England Indians sent to the Iroquois a "model of a fish, as a token of their adhering to the general covenant." The waters of New England are certainly abundantly stored with fish. From these cursory observations we must proceed to details in the lives of the most noted men.

Perhaps we cannot present the reader with a greater orator than *Garangula*, or *Grangula*, as *Lahontan* writes his name, and that writer knew him. He was by nation an Onondaga, and is brought to our notice by the manly and magnanimous speech which he made to a French general, who marched into the country of the Iroquois to subdue them.

In the year 1684, Mr. *de la Barre*, governor-general of Canada, complained to the English, at Albany, that the Senecas were infringing upon their rights of trade with some of the other more remote nations. Governor *Dongan* acquainted the Senecas with the charge made by the French governor. They admitted the fact, but justified their course, alleging that the French supplied their enemies with arms and ammunition, with whom they were then at war. About the same time, the French governor raised an army of 1700 men, and made other "mighty preparations" for the final destruction of the Five Nations. But before he had progressed far in his great undertaking, a mortal sickness broke out in his army, which finally caused him to give over the expedition. In the mean time, the governor of New York was ordered to lay no obstacles in the way of the French expedition. Instead of regarding

* *Loskiel*, Hist. Mis. i. 2.

† At a great assemblage of chiefs and warriors at Albany, in Aug. 1746, the chief speaker of the Six Nations informed the English commissioners that they had taken in the Messesagnes as a seventh nation. *Colden*, Hist. F. Nations, ii. 175.

‡ Hist. Five Nations, i. 109.

§ *Kickons*, in Algonkin; *Kegonce*, in Chippeway. *Long's Voyages*, &c. 202. 4to.

this order, which was from his master, the duke of York, he sent interpreters to the Five Nations to encourage them, with offers to assist them.

De la Barre, in hopes to effect something by this expensive undertaking, crossed lake Ontario, and held a talk with such of the Five Nations as would meet him.* To keep up the appearance of power, he made a high-toned speech to *Grangula*, in which he observed, that the nations had often infringed upon the peace; that he wished now for peace; but on the condition that they should make full satisfaction for all the injuries they had done the French, and for the future never to disturb them. That they, the Senecas Cayugas, Onondagos, Oneidas, and Mohawks, had abused and robbed all their traders, and unless they gave satisfaction, he should declare war. That they had conducted the English into their country to get away their trade heretofore, but the past he would overlook, if they would offend no more; yet, if ever the like should happen again, he bad express orders from the king, his master, to declare war.

Grangula listened to these words, and many more in the like strain, with that contempt which a real knowledge of the situation of the French army, and the rectitude of his own course, were calculated to inspire; and after walking several times round the circle, formed by his people and the French, addressing himself to the governor, seated in his elbow chair, he began as follows:—†

"*Yonnondio*;‡ I honor you, and the warriors that are with me likewise honor you. Your interpreter has finished your speech. I now begin mine. My words make haste to reach your ears. Harken to them.

"*Yonnondio*; You must have believed, when you left Quebeck, that the sun had burnt up all the forests, which render our country inaccessible to the French, or that the lakes had so far overflown the banks, that they had surrounded our castles, and that it was impossible for us to get out of them. Yes, surely, you must have dreamt so, and the curiosity of seeing so great a wonder has brought you so far. Now you are undeceived, since that I, and the warriors here present, are come to assure you, that the Senecas, Cayugas, Onondagas, Oneidas and Mohawks are yet alive. I thank you, in their name, for bringing back into their country the calumet, which your predecessor received from their hands. It was happy for you, that you left under ground that murdering hatchet that has been so often dyed in the blood of the French.

"*Hear, Yonnondio*; I do not sleep; I have my eyes open; and the sun, which enlightens me, discovers to me a great captain at the head of a company of soldiers, who speaks as if he were dreaming. He says, that he only came to the lake to smoke on the great calumet with the Onondagas. But *Grangula* says, that he sees the contrary; that it was

---

* As it will gratify most of our readers, we believe, to hear the general in his own words, we will present them with a paragraph of his speech to *Grangula* in his own language:—

"Le roi mon maitre informe que les cinq Nations, Iroquoises contrevenoient depuis long-tems à la paix, m'aordonné de me transporter ici avec une escorte, et d'envoier Akouessan au village des Onnatagues, pour inviter les principaux chefs à me venir voir. L'intention de ce grand monarque est que nous fumions toi et moi ensemble dans le grand calumet de paix; pourvû que tu me promettes au nom des Tsonontouans, Goyogoans, Onnotagues, Onoyouts et Agniés, de donner une entiere satisfaction et dédommagement à ses sujets, et de ne rien faire à l'avenir, qui puisse causer une facheuse rupture," &c. *Lahontan*, i. 58, 59.

† "*Grangula*, qui pendant tout le descours avoit eu les yeux fixament attachez sur le bout de sa pipe, se leve, et soit par une civilité bisarre, ou pour se donner sans façon le tems de méditer sa réponse il fait cinq ou six tours dans nôtre cercle composé de sauvages et de François. Revenu en sa place il resta debout devant le général assis dans un bon fauteuil, et le regarant il lui dit." *Lahontan*, (i. 61, 62.) who was one of those present.

‡ The name they gave the governors of Canada. Spelt in *Lahontan*. *Onnontio*.

to knock them on the head, if sickness had not weakened the arms of the French. I see *Yonnondio* raving in a camp of sick men, whose lives the Great Spirit has saved, by inflicting this sickness on them.

"*Hear, Yonnondio*; our women had taken their clubs, our children and old men had carried their bows and arrows into the heart of your camp, if our warriors had not disarmed them, and kept them back, when your messenger *Akouessan** came to our castles. It is done, and I have said it.

"*Hear, Yonnondio*; we plundered none of the French, but those that carried guns, powder and balls to the Twightwies† and Chictaghicks, because those arms might have cost us our lives. Herein we follow the example of the Jesuits, who break all the kegs of rum brought to our castles, lest the drunken Indians should knock them on the head. Our warriors have not beaver enough to pay for all those arms that they have taken, and our old men are not afraid of the war. This belt preserves my words.

"We carried the English into our lakes, to trade there with the Utawawas and Quatoghies,‡ as the Adirondaks brought the French to our castles, to carry on a trade, which the English say is theirs. We are born free. We neither depend on *Yonnondio* nor *Corlear*.§ We may go where we please, and carry with us whom we please, and buy and sell what we please. If your allies be your slaves, use them as such, command them to receive no other but your people. This belt preserves my words.

"We knock the Twightwies and Chictaghicks on the head, because they had cut down the trees of peace, which were the limits of our country. They have hunted beaver on our lands. They have acted contrary to the customs of all Indians, for they left none of the beavers alive, they killed both male and female. They brought the Satanas into their country, to take part with them, after they had concerted ill designs against us. We have done less than either the English or French, that have usurped the lands of so many Indian nations, and chased them from their own country. This belt preserves my words.

"*Hear, Yonnondio*; what I say is the voice of all the Five Nations. Hear what they answer. Open your ears to what they speak. The Senecas, Cayugas, Onondagas, Oneidas and Mohawks say, that when they buried the hatchet at Cadarackui, in the presence of your predecessor, in the middle of the fort, they planted the tree of peace in the same place; to be there carefully preserved: that, in the place of a retreat for soldiers, that fort might be a rendezvous for merchants: that, in place of arms and ammunition of war, beavers and merchandise should only enter there.

"*Hear, Yonnondio*; take care for the future, that so great a number of soldiers as appear there do not choke the tree of peace planted in so small a fort. It will be a great loss, if, after it had so easily taken root, you should stop its growth, and prevent its covering your country and ours with its branches. I assure you, in the name of the Five Nations, that our warriors shall dance to the calumet of peace under its leaves; and shall remain quiet on their mats, and shall never dig up the hatchet, till their brother *Yonnondio* or *Corlear* shall, either jointly or separately, endeavor to attack the country which the Great Spirit has given to our ancestors. This belt preserves my words, and this other, the authority which the Five Nations have given me."

Then, addressing himself to the interpreter, he said, "Take courage, you

* The name they gave Mr. *Le Maine*, which signified a partridge.

† Iwikties, *Colden*. ‡ Chictaghicks, Colden.

§ The name they gave the governors of New York.

have spirit, speak, explain my words, forget nothing, tell all that your brethren and friends say to *Yonnondio,* your governor, by the mouth of *Grangula,* who loves you, and desires you to accept of this present of beaver, and take part with me in my feast, to which I invite you. This present of beaver is sent to *Yonnondio,* on the part of the Five Nations."

De la Barre was struck with surprise at the wisdom of this chief, and equal chagrin at the plain refutation of his own. He immediately returned to Montreal, and thus finished this inglorious expedition of the French against the Five Nations.

Grangula was at this time a very old man, and from this valuable speech we became acquainted with him; a very *Nestor* of his nation, whose powers of mind would not suffer in comparison with those of a Roman, or a more modern senator. He treated the French with great civility, and feasted them with the best his country would afford, on their departure. We next proceed to notice

Adario, chief of the Dinondadies, a tribe of the Hurons.* About 1687, the Iroquois, from some neglect on the part of the governor of New York, owing, says *Smith,*† to the orders of his master, "King *James,* a poor bigoted, popish, priest-ridden prince," were drawn into the French interest, and a treaty of peace was concluded. The Dinondadies were considered as belonging to the confederate Indians, but from some cause they were dissatisfied with the league with the French, and wished by some exploit to strengthen themselves in the interest of the English. For this purpose, *Adario* put himself at the head of 100 warriors, and intercepted the ambassadors of the Five Nations at one of the falls in Kadarakkui River, killing some and taking others prisoners. These he informed that the French governor had told him that 50 warriors of the Five Nations were coming that way to attack him. They were astonished at the governor's apparent perfidiousness, and so completely did the plot of *Adario* succeed, that these ambassadors were deceived into his interest. In his parting speech to them, he said, "*Go, my brethren, I untie your bonds, and send you home again, though our nations be at war. The French governor has made me commit so black an action, that I shall never be easy after it, till the Five Nations shall have taken full revenge.*" This outrage upon their ambassadors, the Five Nations doubted not in the least to be owing to the French governor's perfidy, from the representations of those that returned. They now sought immediate revenge; and assembling 1200 of their chief warriors, landed upon the island of Montreal, 26 July, 1688, while the French were in perfect security, burnt their houses, sacked their plantations, and slew all the men, women and children without the city. A thousand‡ persons were killed in this expedition. In October following, they attacked the island again with success. These horrid disasters threw the whole country into the utmost consternation. The fort at Lake Ontario was abandoned, and 28 barrels of powder fell into the hands of the confederate Indians. Nothing now saved the French from an entire extermination from Canada, but the ignorance of their enemies in the art of attacking fortified places.

The real name of *Adario* was *Sastaretsi.* He married a woman of his own nation, by whom he had several children. The French nicknamed him the *Rat,* by which he is often mentioned by *Lahontan* and others. Another warrior, though an Iroquois, of nearly equal fame, was

Black-kettle. A war with France, in 1690, brought this chief upon the records of history. In the summer of that year, Major *Schuyler,* of Albany,

* Dionondadies, *Colden*; Tionnontatés, *Charlevoix*. † Hist. N. Y. 56. (4to ed.)

‡ So says *Colden,* but *Charlevoix* says 400, and that 200 of these were burnt afterwards. There can be doubt but that the truth is between them, as there is ample room.

with a company of Mohawks, fell upon the French settlements at the north end of Lake Champlain. *De Callieres*, governor of Montreal, hastily collected about 800 men, and opposed them, but, notwithstanding his force was vastly superior, yet they were repulsed with great loss. About 300 of the enemy were killed in this expedition. The French now took every measure in their power to retaliate. They sent presents to many tribes of Indians, to engage them in their cause, and in the following winter a party of about 300 men, under an accomplished young gentleman, marched to attack the confederate Indian nations at Niagara. Their march was long, and rendered almost insupportable; being obliged to carry their provisions on their backs through deep snow. *Black-kettle* met them with about 80 men, and maintained an unequal fight until his men were nearly all cut off; but it was more fatal to the French, who, far from home, had no means of recruiting. *Black-kettle,* in his turn, carried the war into Canada during the whole summer following, with immense loss and damage to the French inhabitants. The governor was so enraged at his successes, that he caused a prisoner, which had been taken from the Five Nations, to be burnt alive. This captive withstood the tortures with as much firmness as his enemies showed cruelty. He sung his achievements while they broiled his feet, burnt his hands with red hot irons, cut and wrung off his joints, and pulled out the sinews. To close the horrid scene, his scalp was torn off, and red hot sand poured upon his head.

We will close this chapter with an account of the visit of five Iroquois chiefs to England. The English in America had supposed that if they could convince the Indian nations of the power and greatness of their mother country, they should be able to detach them forever from the influence of the French. To accomplish this object, these chiefs were prevailed upon to make the voyage. They visited the court of Queen *Anne* in the year 1710. None of the American historians seem to have known the names of these chiefs, or, if they did, have not thought it proper to transmit them. *Smith*, in his history of New York, mentions the fact of their having visited England, and gives the speech which they made to the queen, and says it is preserved "in *Oldmixon*," perhaps in his BRITISH EMPIRE IN AMERICA,* as nothing of the kind is found in his history of England, although he records the circumstance, and ill-naturedly enough too. We think he would hardly have done even this but for the purpose of ridiculing the friends of the queen. The following is all that he says of them:† "Three weeks after the battle of Sarragossa was fought by Gen. *Stanhope*, whose victory made way for the march to Madrid, the news of the victory was brought to the queen by Col. *Harrison,* the 15 Sept. O. S., at which time the High-church rabble were pelting Gen. *Stanhope's* proxy, and knocking down his friends at the Westminster election. However, for the successes in Spain, and for the taking of Doway, Bethune and Aire, by the duke of *Marlborough* in Flanders, there was a thanksgiving-day appointed, which the queen solemnized in St. James's chapel. To have gone as usual to St. Paul's, and there to have had Te Deum sung on that occasion, would have shown too much countenance to those brave and victorious English generals, who were fighting her battles abroad, while High-church was plotting, and railing, and addressing against them at home. The carrying of four Indian Casaques about in the queen's coaches, was all the triumph of the Harleian administration; they were called kings, and clothed, by the play-house tailor, like other kings of the theatre; they were conducted to audience by Sir

* The edition I use (1708) does not contain it.
† *Hist. England,* ii. 452. (Fol. London, 1735.)

Charles Cotterel; there was a speech made for them, and nothing omitted to do honor to these five monarchs, whose presence did so much honor to the new ministry; which the latter seemed to be extremely fond of, and defrayed all their expenses during their stay here. They were the captains of the four nations, [Five Nations,] in league with the English at New York and New England, and came in person to treat of matters concerning trade with the lords commissioners of plantations; as also of an enterprise against the French, and their confederate Indians in those parts."

Sir *Richard Steele* mentions these chiefs in his Tatler of May 13, 1710, and *Addison* makes them the subject of a number of the Spectator the next year, at a suggestion of Dean *Swift*.* Neither of these papers, however, contain many facts respecting them. In the former it is mentioned that one of them was taken sick at the house where they were accommodated during their stay in London, and they all received great kindness and attention from their host, which, on their departure, was the cause of their honoring him with a name of distinction; which was *Cadaroque*, and signified "*the strongest fort in their country*." In speaking of their residence, Mr. *Steele* says, "They were placed in a handsome apartment at an upholster's in King-street, Covent-garden." There were fine portraits of each of them painted at the time, and are still to be seen in the British Museum.†

The best and most methodical account of these chiefs was published in the great annual history by Mr. *Boyer*,‡ and from which we extract as follows: "On the 19 April *Te Yee Neen Ho Ga Prow*, and *Sa Ga Yean Qua Prah Ton*, of the Maquas; *Elow Oh Kaom*, and *Oh Nee Yeath Ton No Prow*,§ of the river sachem, and the Ganajoh-hore sachem, four kings, or chiefs of the Six Nations|| in the West Indies,¶ which lie between New England, and New France, or Canada: who lately came over with the West India fleet, and were cloathed and entertained at the queen's expense, had a public audience of her majesty at the palace of St. *James*, being conducted thither in two of her majesty's coaches, by Sir *Charles Cotterel*, master of the ceremonies, and introduced by the duke of *Shrewsbury*, lord chamberlain. They made a speech by their interpreter, which Major *Pidgeon*, who was one of the officers that came with them, read in English to her majesty, being as follows:—

"Great Queen—We have undertaken a long and tedious voyage, which none of our predecessors** could be prevailed upon to undertake. The motive that induced us was, that we might see our great queen, and relate to her those things we thought absolutely necessary, for the good of her, and us, her allies, on the other side the great water. We doubt not but our great queen has been acquainted with our long and tedious

---

* "I intended to have written a book on that subject. I believe he [*Addison*] has spent it all in one paper, and all the under hints there are mine too." *Swift's Letter to Mrs. Johnson, dated London*, 28 April, 1711.

† Notes to the *Spectator*, ed. in 8 vols. 8vo. London, 1789.

‡ "The Annals of Queen *Anne's* Reign, Year the IX. for 1710." 189—191. This is a work containing a most valuable fund of information, and is, with its continuation, a lasting monument to its learned publisher. His being dragged into the Dunciad in one of Pope's freaks notwithstanding.

§ We have these names in the Tatler spelt *Tee Yee Neen Ho Ga Row, Sa Ga Yeath Rua Geth Ton, E Tow Oh Koam*, and *Ho Nec Yeth Taw No Row*.

|| *Quere*. If, according to *Colden* and others, the Tuscaroras did not join the Iroquois until 1712, and until that time these were called the Five Nations, how comes it that they were known in England by the name of *Six Nations* in 1710?

¶ No one can be misled by this error, any more than an Englishman would be by being told that London is situated at the foot of the Rocky Mountains.

** None of the Six Nations, must be understood.

war, in conjunction with her children, against her enemies the French: and that we have been as a strong wall for their security, even to the loss of our best men. The truth of which our brother Queder, Col. [*Peter*] *Schuyler*, and *Anadagarjaux*, Col. *Nicholson*, can testify; they having all our proposals in writing. We were mightily rejoiced when we heard by *Anadagarjaux*, that our great queen had resolved to send an army to reduce Canada; from whose mouth we readily embraced our great queen's instructions: and in token of our friendship, we hung up the kettle, and took up the hatchet; and with one consent joined our brother *Queder*, and *Anadagarjaux*, in making preparations on this side the lake, by building forts, store-houses, canoes and batteaux; whilst *Aundiasia*, Col. *Vetch*, at the same time, raised an army at Boston, of which we were informed by our ambassadors, whom we sent thither for that purpose. We waited long in expectation of the fleet from England, to join Anadiasia, to go against Quebec by sea, whilst *Anadagarjaux, Queder*, and we, went to Port Royal by land; but at last we were told, that our great queen, by some important affair, was prevented in her design for that season. This made us extreme sorrowful, lest the French, who hitherto had dreaded us, should now think us unable to make war against them. The reduction of Canada is of such weight, that after the effecting thereof, we should have free hunting, and a great trade with our great queen's children; and as a token of the sincerity of the Six Nations, we do here, in the name of all, present our great queen with the belts of wampum. We need not urge to our great queen, more than the necessity we really labor under obliges us, that in case our great queen should not be mindful of us, we must, with our families, forsake our country, and seek other habitations, or stand neuter; either of which will be much against our inclinations. Since we have been in alliance with our great queen's children, we have had some knowledge of the Savior of the world; and have often been importuned by the French, both by the insinuations of their priests, and by presents, to come over to their interest, but have always esteemed them men of falsehood: but if our great queen will be pleased to send over some persons to instruct us, they shall find a most hearty welcome. We now close, with hopes of our great queen's favor, and leave it to her most gracious consideration."

We cannot but respond *amen* to Mr. *Oldmixon's* opinion of this speech, namely, that it was made *for* instead of *by* the chiefs; still we thought it proper to print it, and that by so doing we should give satisfaction to more than by withholding it. Our account next proceeds: "On Friday, the 21 April, the four Indian princes went to see Dr. *Flamstead's* house, and mathematical instruments, in Greenwich Park; after which they were nobly treated by some of the lords commissioners of the admiralty, in one of her majesty's yachts. They staid about a fortnight longer in London, where they were entertained by several persons of distinction, particularly by the duke of *Ormond*, who regaled them likewise with a review* of the four troops of life-guards; and having seen all the curiosities in and about this metropolis, they went down to Portsmouth, through Hampton Court and Windsor, and embarked on board the Dragon, one of her majesty's ships, Capt. *Martin*, commodore, together with Col. *Francis Nicholson*, commander in chief of the forces designed for an expedition in America. On the 8 May, the Dragon and Falmouth sailed from Spithead, having under convoy about 18 sail, consisting of merchantmen, a bomb-ship and tender, and several transports, with British

* And the chiefs made a speech in return, but our author makes this note upon it: "N. B. The speech which was said to have been made by them, on that occasion, to the duke of *Ormond*, is spurious."

officers, a regiment of marines, provisions and stores of war; and on the 15 July arrived at Boston in N. England."

Little is to be gathered from *Smith's* History of New York relative to those sachems. He gives a speech which they made to the queen, but it is a meagre abridgment of less than half of the one above, and the rest is omitted entirely. "The arrival of the five sachems in England made a great bruit throughout the whole kingdom. The mob followed wherever they went, and small cuts of them were sold among the people."*

CHAPTER II.

TAMANY, *a famous ancient Delaware—His history*—SHIKELLIMUS—*Favors the Moravian Brethren—His reception of Count Zinzendorf—His death*—CANASSATEGO—*Visits Philadelphia—His speech to the Delawares—Anecdotes of him*—GLIKHIKAN—*His speech to Half-king—His attachment to the Christian Indians—Meets with much trouble from Capt. Pipe—Conduct of Half-king—Of Pipe—Glikhikan perishes in the massacre at Gnadenhuetten*—PAKANKE—*His history*—NETAWATWEES—*Becomes a Christian—His speech to Pakanke—His—death*—PAXNOUS—TADEUSKUND—*His history and death*—WHITE-EYES—*His transactions with the missionaries*—SKENANDO—*His celebrated speech—Curious anecdote of him—His death.*

Tamany was a name much in print a fifty years since, but of what nation or country, or whether applied to an imaginary or real personage, by any account accompanying it, no one could determine. The truth respecting this has at length come to light.

He was a Delaware chief, of similar renown to the *Basheba* of Kennebeck, and *Nanepashemet* of Massachusetts; and we infer from *Gabriel Thomas,*† that possibly he might have been alive as late as 1680 or 1690. He wrote the name *Temeny*.

Mr. *Heckewelder*, in his Historical ACCOUNT OF THE INDIAN NATIONS, devotes a chapter to this chief and *Tadeuskund*. He spells the name *Tamaned*. The difficulty of gaining information of deceased individuals among the Indians is well known to those conversant with their history. Mr. *Heckewelder* says, "No white man who regards their feelings, will introduce such subjects in conversation with them." This reluctance to speak of the departed he attributes to "the misfortunes which have befallen some of the most beloved and esteemed personages among them, since the Europeans came among them." It is believed, however, that it had a more remote origin. The same author continues, "All we know of *Tamened* is, that he was an ancient Delaware chief, who never had his equal."‡

It is said that when, about 1776, Col. *George Morgan*, of Princeton, N. J. visited the western Indians by direction of congress, the Delawares conferred on him the name of *Tamany*, "in honor and remembrance of their ancient chief, and as the greatest mark of respect which they could show to that gentleman, who they said had the same address, affability and meekness as their honored chief."§

---

* Hist. New York, 122. ed. 4to. London, 1757.

† "Who resided there [in Pennsylvania] about 15 years," and who published "*An Historical* and *Geographical Account of Pa.* and *W. Jersey*," 12mo. *London*, 1698.

‡ Some will doubtless imagine that this was *knowing* a good deal.

§ Heckewelder, *ut supra*.

"The fame of this great man extended even among the whites, who fabricated numerous legends respecting him, which I never heard, however, from the mouth of an Indian, and therefore believe to be fabulous. In the revolutionary war, his enthusiastic admirers dubbed him a saint, and he was established under the name of St. *Tammany*, the patron saint of America. His name was inserted in some calendars, and his festival celebrated on the first day of May in every year. On that day a numerous society of his votaries walked together in procession through the streets of Philadelphia, their hats decorated with bucks' tails, and proceeded to a handsome rural place out of town, which they called the *wigwam*; where, after a *long talk* or Indian speech had been delivered, and the calumet of peace and friendship had been duly smoked, they spent the day in festivity and mirth. After dinner, Indian dances were performed on the green in front of the wigwam, the calumet was again smoked, and the company separated."

It was not till some years after the peace that these yearly doings were broken up, which would doubtless have lasted longer but for the misfortune of the owner of the ground where they were held. Since that time Philadelphia, New York, and perhaps other places, have had their *Tamany* societies, *Tamany* halls, &c. &c. In their meetings these societies make but an odd figure in imitating the Indian manner of doing business, as well as in appropriating their names upon one another.

Among the multitude of poems and odes to *Tamany,* the following is selected to give the reader an idea of the acts said to have been achieved by him:—

"Immortal *Tamany,* of Indian race,
Great in the field and foremost in the chase!
No puny saint was he, with festing pale;
He climbed the mountain, and he swept the vale,
Rushed through the torrent with unequalled might;
Your ancient saints would tremble at the sight;
Caught the swift boar and swifter deer with ease,
And worked a thousand miracles like these.
To public views he added private ends,
And loved his country most, and next his friends;
With courage long he strove to ward the blow;
(Courage we all respect ev'n in a foe;)
And when each effort he in vain had tried,
Kindled the flame in which he bravely died!
To *Tamany* let the full horn go round;
His fame let every honest tongue resound;
With him let every gen'rous patriot vie,
To live in freedom or with honor die."*

We are next to speak of a chief, concerning whom much inquiry has been made from several considerations. We mean

Shikellimus, the father of the celebrated *Logan*. He was a Cayuga sachem, and styled by Mr. *Loskiel*,† "first magistrate and head chief of all the Iroquois Indians living on the banks of the Susquehannah, as far as Onondago.

He is the same often mentioned by Colden,‡ under the names *Shickcalamy, Shicalamy,* and *Shick Calamy,* and occupies a place next the famous *Canassatego*. His residence was at Conestoga in Pennsylvania. He was present at a great council held in Philadelphia in 1742, with 91 other chiefs, counsellors and warriors of the Six Nations, to consult about the encroachments of some of the Delawares upon the people of Pennsylvania, as will be found mentioned in the history of *Canassatego*. That he

* *Carey's* Museum, v. 104.

† *Hist. Missions,* ii. 119.

‡ *Hist. Five Nations,* ii. 57, 69, 75, 77, 85.

was a man of much consequence among the Five Nations will appear from the fact, that *Canassatego* repeated a speech of his to Gov. *Thomas,* when the assault upon *William Webb* was inquired into, "whereby his [the said *Webb's*] jaw-bone was broke, and his life greatly endangered, by an unknown Indian." This took place upon the disputed lands in the forks of the Delaware. "*Canassatego* repeating the message delivered to the Six Nations by *Shickcalamy*, in the year 1740, with a string of wampum, said in answer: 'The Six Nations had made diligent inquiry into the affair, and had found out the Indian who had committed the fact; he lived near Asopus, [Æsopus,] and had been examined and severely reproved; and they hoped, as *William Webb* was recovered, the governor would not expect any further punishment, and therefore they returned the string of wampum received from their brethren, by the hand of *Shickcalamy*, in token that they had fully complied with their request.'"

When Count *Zinzendorf* visited this country, in 1742, he had an interview with this chief at Shamokin. *Conrad Weiser* was present, and *Shikellimus* inquired with great anxiety the cause of the count's visit. Weiser told him "that he was a messenger of the living God, sent to preach grace and mercy;" to which he answered, "he was glad that such a messenger came to instruct his nation."

Shikellimus was a great friend of the missionaries, and his death was a severe loss to them. He died at his own residence in Shamokin, in 1749. We have already named the chief proper to be proceeded with, on finishing our account of *Shikellimus*.

Canassatego, a chief of the Six Nations, was of the tribe of Onondago. In 1742, there arose a dispute between the Delawares and the government of Pennsylvania, relative to a tract of land in the forks of the Delaware. The English claimed it by right of prior purchase, and the Delawares persisted in their claim, and threatened to use force unless it should be given up by the whites. This tribe of the Delawares were subject to the Six Nations, and the governor of Pennsylvania sent deputies to them to notify them of the trouble, that they might interfere and prevent war. It was on this occasion that *Canassatego* appeared in Philadelphia with 230 warriors. He observed to the governor, "that they saw the Delawares had been an unruly people, and were altogether in the wrong; that they had concluded to remove them, and oblige them to go over the river Delaware, and quit all claim to any lands on this side for the future, since they had received pay for them, and it is gone through their guts long ago. They deserved, he said, to be taken by the hair of the head, and shaken severely, till they recovered their senses, and became sober; that he had seen with his own eyes a deed signed by nine of their ancestors, above fifty years ago, for this very land, and a release signed not many years since, by some of themselves, and chiefs yet living, (and then present,) to the number of 15 and upwards; but how came you (addressing himself to the Delawares present) to take upon you to sell land at all? We conquered you; we made women of you; you know you are women; and can no more sell land than women; nor is it fit you should have the power of selling lands, since you would abuse it. This land you claim is gone through your guts; you have been furnished with clothes, meat and drink, by the goods paid you for it, and now you want it again, like children as you are. But what makes you sell lands in the dark? Did you ever tell us that you had sold this land? Did we ever receive any part, even the value of a pipe shank, from you for it? You have told us a blind story, that you sent a messenger to us, to inform us of the sale; but he never came amongst us, nor did we ever hear any thing about it. This is acting in the dark, and very different from the conduct our Six Nations observe in the sales of land. On such occasions they give public notice, and invite all the Indians of their united nations, and give them all a share of the presents they receive for their lands.

"This is the behavior of the wise united nations. But we find you are none of our blood; you act a dishonest part, not only in this, but in other matters; your ears are ever open to slanderous reports about your brethren. For all these reasons, *we charge you to remove instantly; we don't give you liberty to think about it.* You are women." They dared not disobey this command, and soon after removed, some to Wyoming and Shamokin, and some to the Ohio.*

This is but a part of *one* of *Canassatego's* numerous speeches. In a future chapter we intend to lay before the reader several others.

When *Canassatego* was at Lancaster, in Pennsylvania, in 1744, holding a talk about their affairs with the governor, he was informed that the English had beaten the French in some important battle. "Well," said he, "if that be the case, you must have taken a great deal of rum from them, and can afford to give us some, that we may rejoice with you." Accordingly, a glass was served round to each, which they called a *French glass.*†

Dr. *Franklin* tells us a very interesting story of *Canassatego,* and at the same time makes the old chief tell another. In speaking of the manners and customs of the Indians, the doctor says, "The same hospitality, esteemed among them as a principal virtue, is practised by private persons; of which *Conrad Weiser*, our interpreter, gave me the following instances: He had been naturalized among the Six Nations, and spoke well the Mohawk language. In going through the Indian country, to carry a message from our governor to the council at Onondago, he called at the habitation of *Canassatego,* an old acquaintance, who embraced him, spread furs for him to sit on, placed before him some boiled beans, and venison, and mixed some rum and water for his drink. When he was well refreshed, and had lit his pipe, *Canassatego* began to converse with him; asked how he had fared the many years since they had seen each other; whence he then came; what occasioned the journey, &c. *Conrad* answered all his questions; and when the discourse began to flag, the Indian, to continue it, said, '*Conrad*, you have lived long among the white people, and know something of their customs: I have been sometimes at Albany, and have observed, that once in seven days they shut up their shops, and assemble in the great house; tell me what that is for; what do they do there?' 'They meet there,' says *Conrad*, 'to hear and learn good things.' 'I do not doubt,' says the Indian, 'that they tell you so; they have told me the same; but I doubt the truth of what they say, and I will tell you my reasons. I went lately to Albany, to sell my skins, and buy blankets, knives, powder, rum, &c. You know I used generally to deal with *Hans Hanson*; but I was a little inclined this time to try some other merchants. However, I called first upon *Hans*, and asked him what he would give for beaver. He said he could not give more than four shillings a pound; but, says he, I cannot talk on business now; this is the day when we meet together to learn *good things*, and I am going to the meeting. So I thought to myself, since I cannot do any business to day, I may as well go to the meeting too, and I went with him. There stood up a man in black, and began to talk to the people very angrily; I did not understand what he said, but perceiving that he looked much at me, and at *Hanson*, I imagined that he was angry at seeing me there; so I went out, sat down near the house, struck fire, and lit my pipe, waiting till the meeting should break up. I thought too that the man had mentioned something of beaver, and suspected it might be the subject of their

---

* *Colden* and *Gordon's* Histories.

† *Colden's* Hist. Five Nations, ii. 142.

meeting. So when they came out, I accosted my merchant. "Well, *Hans*," says I, "I hope you have agreed to give more than 4*s*. a pound." "No," says he, "I cannot give so much, I cannot give more than three shillings and sixpence." I then spoke to several other dealers, but they all sung the same song,—*three and sixpence, three and sixpence*. This made it clear to me that my suspicion was right; and that whatever they pretended of meeting to learn *good things*, the purpose was to consult how to cheat Indians in the price of beaver. Consider but a little, *Conrad*, and you must be of my opinion. If they met so often to learn good things, they would certainly have learned some before this time. But they are still ignorant. You know our practice. If a white man, in travelling through our country, enters one of our cabins, we all treat him as I do you; we dry him if he is wet; we warm him if he is cold, and give him meat and drink, that he may allay his thirst and hunger; and we spread soft furs for him to rest and sleep on: we demand nothing in return But if I go into a white man's house at Albany, and ask for victuals and drink, they say, Get out, you Indian dog. You see they have not yet learned those little *good things* that we need no meetings to be instructed in, because our mothers taught them to us when we were children; and therefore it is impossible their meetings should be, as they say, for any such purpose, or have any such effect: they are only to contrive the cheating of Indians in the price of beaver.'"*

The missionary *Frederic Post*, in his journal of an embassy to the Indians on the Ohio, in 1758, mentions a son of *Canassatego*, whom he calls *Hans Jacob*.

We are not to look into the history of Pennsylvania for a succession of Indian wars, although there have been some horrid murders and enormities committed among the whites and Indians. For about 70 years, their historic page is very clear of such records, namely, from 1682, the arrival of William Penn, until the French war of 1755.

There were several chiefs very noted about this period, on account of their connection with the Moravian Brethren. Among the most noted was *Glikhikan*,† or *Glikhickan*,‡ "an eminent captain and warrior, counsellor, and speaker of the Delaware chief [*Pakanke*] in Kaskaskunk." It is said that he had disputed with the French Catholic priests in Canada, and confounded them, and now (1769) made his appearance among the United Brethren for the purpose of achieving a like victory; but as the Brethren's account has it, his heart failed him, and he became a convict to their doctrines. In 1770, he quitted Kaskaskunk, to live with the Brethren, greatly against the minds of his friends and his chief. This occasioned great trouble, and some endeavored to take his life. *Pakanke's* speech to him upon the occasion will be seen when we come to the account of that chief. At the time of his baptism, *Glikhikan* received the name of *Isaac*.

The period of the revolutionary war was a distressing time for the Brethren and those Indians who had adhered to their cause. War parties from the hostile tribes were continually passing and repassing their settlements, and often in the most suspicious manner. It was to the famous chief *Glikhikan* that they owed their preservation on more than one occasion. The Indians about the lakes sent deputies to draw the Delawares into the war against the Americans, but they were not received by them. Shortly after, in the year 1777, 200 Huron warriors, with Half-king at their head, approached the Moravian settlement of Lichtenau, in their way to attack the settlements upon the frontiers, and caused

* The editors of the valuable Encyclopedia Perthensis have thought this anecdote worthy a place in that work, (i. 652.)

† *Loskiel*. ‡ *Heckewelder*.

great consternation among the Brethren; but resolving to show no signs of fear, victuals were prepared for them, and sent out by some of the Christian Indians to meet them. The reception of those sent out was far more promising than was anticipated, and soon after was "sent a solemn embassy to the *Half-king* and other chiefs of the Hurons." *Glikhikan* was at the head of this embassy, and the following is his speech to *Half-king*:—"Uncle! We, your cousins, the congregation of believing Indians at Lichtenau and Gnadenhuetten, rejoice at this opportunity to see and speak with you. We cleanse your eyes from all the dust, and whatever the wind may have carried into them, that you may see your cousin with clear eyes and a serene countenance. We cleanse your ears and hearts from all evil reports which an evil wind may have conveyed into your ears and even into your hearts on the journey, that our words may find entrance into your ears and a place in your hearts. [*Here a string of wampum was presented by Glikhikan.*] Uncle! hear the words of the believing Indians, your cousins, at Lichtenau and Gnadenhuetten. We would have you know, that we have received and believed in the word of God for 30 years and upwards, and meet daily to hear it, morning and evening. You must also know, that we have our teachers dwelling amongst us, who instruct us and our children. By this word of God, preached to us by our teachers, we are taught to keep peace with all men, and to consider them as friends; for thus God has commanded us, and therefore we are lovers of peace. These our teachers are not only our friends, but we consider and love them as our own flesh and blood. Now as we are your cousin, we most earnestly beg of you, uncle, that you also would consider them as your own body, and as your cousin. We and they make but one body, and therefore cannot be separated, and whatever you do unto them, you do unto us, whether it be good or evil." Then several fathoms of wampum were delivered. *Half-king* received this speech with attention, and said it had penetrated his heart, and after he had consulted with his captains, he spoke as follows in answer:—"Cousins! I am very glad and feel great satisfaction that you have cleansed my eyes, ears and heart from all evil, conveyed into me by the wind on this journey. I am upon an expedition of an unusual kind; for I am a warrior and am going to war, and therefore many evil things and evil thoughts enter into my head, and even into my heart. But thanks to my cousin, my eyes are now clear, so that I can behold my cousin with a serene countenance. I rejoice, that I can hear my cousins with open ears, and take their words to heart." He then delivered a string of wampum, and after repeating the part of *Glikhikan's* speech relating to the missionaries, proceeded: "Go on as hitherto, and suffer no one to molest you. Obey your teachers, who speak nothing but good unto you, and instruct you in the ways of God, and be not afraid that any harm shall be done unto them. No creature shall hurt them. Attend to your worship, and never mind other affairs. Indeed, you see us going to war; but you may remain easy and quiet, and need not think much about it, &c." This was rather odd talk for a savage warrior, and verily it seems more like that of one of the European Brethren, but the veracity of Loskiel will not be questioned.

Some time after this, a circumstance occurred which threw *Glikhikan* into much trouble and danger. A band of Huron warriors seized upon the missionaries at Salem and Gnadenhuetten, and confined them, and did much mischief. *Michael Jung*, *David Zeisberger* and *John Heckewelder* were the Brethren confined at this time. The savages next pillaged Schoenbrunn, from whence they led captive the missionary Jungman and wife, and the sisters *Zeisberger* and *Senseman;* and, singing the death-song, arrived with them at Gnadenhuetten, where were the rest of the prisoners. This was Sept. 4, 1781. It appears that the famous Capt. *Pipe* was among these warriors, from what follows. A young Indian woman, who accompanied the warriors, was much moved by the hard treatment of the Brethren, and in the night "found means to get Capt. *Pipe's* best horse, and rode off full speed to Pittsburgh, where she gave an account of the situation of the missionaries and their congregations." This woman was related to *Glikhikan*; on him, therefore, they determined to vent their wrath. A party of warriors seized him at Salem, and brought him bound to Gnadenhuetten, singing the death-song. When he was brought into the presence of the warriors, great commotion followed, and many were clamorous that he should be at once cut to pieces; especially the Delawares, who could not forget his having renounced his nation and manner of living; here, however, *Half-king* interfered, and prevented his being killed. They now held an inquisitorial examination upon him, which terminated in a proof of his innocence, and, after giving vent to their spleen in loading him with the worst of epithets and much opprobrious language, set him at liberty.

The missionaries and their congregations were soon at liberty, but were obliged to emigrate, as they could have no rest upon the Muskingum any longer; war parties continually hovering about them, robbing and troubling them in various ways. They went through the wilderness 125 miles, and settled at Sandusky, leaving their beautiful cornfields just ready to harvest. Their losses and privations were immense. Above 200 cattle and 400 hogs, much corn in store, beside 300 acres just ripening, were among the spoils. "A troop of savages commanded by English officers escorted them, enclosing them at the distance of some miles on all sides." They arrived at their place of destination Oct. 11, and here were left by *Half-king* and his warriors without any instructions or orders.

Many believing Indians had returned to Gnadenhuetten and the adjacent places in 1782. Here, on 8th March of this year, happened the most dreadful massacre, and *Glikhikan* was among the victims. Ninety-six persons were scalped and then cut to pieces. Besides women, there were 34 children murdered in cold blood.* This was done by white men!

Pakanke was a powerful Delaware chief, whose residence, in 1770, was at a place called Kaskaskunk, about 40 miles north of Pittsburgh. He is brought to our notice by the agency of the missionary *Loskiel*, from whom it appears that he was very friendly to the Brethren at first, and invited them into his country, but when *Glikhikan*, his chief captain and speaker, forsook him, and went to live with them, he was so disconcerted, that he turned against them, and for a time caused them much difficulty. Meeting with *Glikhikan* afterward in public, he spoke to him in an angry tone as follows: "And even you have gone over from this council to them. I suppose you mean to get a white skin! But I tell you, not even one of your feet will turn white, much less your body. Was you not a brave and honored man, sitting next to me in council, when we spread the blanket and considered the belts of wampum lying before us? Now you pretend to despise all this, and think to have found something better. Some time or other you will find yourself deceived." To which *Glikhikan* made but a short and meek reply. Some epidemic disease carried off many of the Indians about this time, and they attributed its cause to their obstinacy in not receiving the gospel. *Pakanke* was among the number at last who accepted it as a remedy. He appears not to have been so

* I have been particular in noticing this affair, as it is not found in such extensively circulated works as the *American Annals*

credulous as many of his neighbors; for when the acknowledgment of Christianity was concluded upon by many, he remained incredulous; and when a belt of wampum was sent him, accompanied with a message, declaring that "whosoever refused to accept it would be considered a murderer of his countrymen," he affected not to understand its import, and doubtless would not have acknowledged it, but for the impending danger which he saw threatening him. When he went to hear the Brethren preach, he declared his conviction, and recommended his children to receive the gospel. A son of his was baptized in 1775.

Netawatwees was head chief of the Delawares, and if we are of him from our scanty records, he will appear to the best advantage. "He used to lay all affairs of state before his counsellors for their consideration, without telling them his own sentiments. When they gave him their opinion, he either approved of it, or stated his objections and amendments, always alleging the reasons of his disapprobation." Before the revolution, it was said that he had amazingly increased the reputation of the Delawares; and he spared no pains to conciliate all his neighbors, and reconcile them one to another. His residence, in 1773, was at Gekelemukpechuenk. The Moravian missionaries sent messengers to him, with information of the arrival of another missionary, in July of this year, requesting a renewal of friendship and a confirmation of his former promise of protection. When this was laid before him and his council, they were not much pleased with the information, and the old chief *Netawatwees* said, "*They have teachers enough already, for a new one can teach nothing but the same doctrine.*" He was, however, prevailed upon to give his consent to their request, and afterwards became a convert to their religion. After he had set out in this course, he sent the following speech to his old friend *Pakanke*: "*You and I are both old, and know not how long we shall live. Therefore let us do a good work, before we depart, and leave a testimony to our children and posterity, that we have received the word of God. Let this be our last will and testament.*" *Pakanke* consented, and was at great pains to send solemn embassies to all such tribes as he thought proper, to communicate his determination. *Netawatwees* died at Pittsburgh near the close of 1776. The missionaries felt the great severity of his loss, for his counsel, as they acknowledge, was of great benefit to them upon all trying occasions.

Paxnous was head chief of the Shawanese in 1754. At this time, the Christian Indians of the Moravian settlement, Gnadenhuetten, were oppressed by a tribute to the Hurons. This year, *Paxnous* and *Gideon Tadeuskund*, who had become dissenters, came to them, and delivered the following message: "The great head, that is, the council of the Iroquois in Onondago, speak the truth and lie not: they rejoice that some of the believing Indians have moved to Wajomick, [near Wilksburg and the Susquehannah,] but now they lift up the remaining Mahikans and Delawares, and set them also down in Wajomick; for there a fire is kindled for them, and there they may plant and think of God. But if they will not hear of the great head, or council, will come and clean their ears with a red-hot iron;" that is, set their houses on fire, and send bullets through their heads. The next year, *Paxnous* and 13 others came again, and in the name of the Hurons demanded an answer to the summons he had delivered last year. His wife attended him, and for whom he had great affection, having then lived with her 38 years. She, being touched by the preaching of the Brethren, was no doubt the cause of softening the heart of *Paxnous,* and causing him thenceforth to do much for them. This answer was returned to him to bear to the Hurons: "The Brethren will confer with the Iroquois themselves, concerning the intended removal of the Indians from Gnadenhuetten to Wajomick." *Paxnous,* "being only an ambassador in this business, was satisfyed, and even formed a closer acquaintance with the Brethren." This is sufficient to explain *Paxnous'* partiality for the Brethren. Before they departed, his wife was baptized, and all present, among whom was her husband, were much affected. She declared as she returned home, "that she felt as happy as a child new born." *Paxnous* also had two sons, who did much for the Brethren.

Tadeuskund, a noted chief among the Delawares, may be considered next in importance to those above named. He was known among the English, previous to 1750, by the name *Honest-John*. About this time, he was received into the Moravian community, and after some delay, "owing to his wavering disposition," was baptized, and received into fellowship. His baptismal name was *Gideon*. He adhered to the missionaries just as long as his condition appeared to be better, but when any thing more favorable offered, he stood ready to embark in it.

The Christian Indians at Gnadenhuetten were desirous of removing to Wajomick, which offered more advantages than that place, and this was a secret desire of the wild Indians; for they, intending to join the French of Canada, wished to have them out of the way of their excursions, that they might with more secrecy fall upon the English frontiers. It was now 1754.

Meanwhile *Tadeuskund* had had the offer of leading the Delawares in the war, and hence he had been a chief promoter of a removal to Wajomick. The missionaries saw through the plot, and refused to move; but quite a company of their followers, to the number of about 70, went thither, agreeably to the wishes of *Tadeuskund* and his party, and some went off to other places.

Tadeuskund was now in his element, marching to and from the French in warlike style. When *Paxnous,* as has been related, summoned the remaining believers at Gnadenhuetten to remove to Wajomick, *Tadeuskund* accompanied him. As the interest of the French began to decline, *Tadeuskund* began to think about making a shift again. Having lived a considerable part of the year 1758 not far from Bethlehem, with about 100 of his followers, he gave the Brethren there intimations that he wished again to join them; and even requested that some one would preach on his side of the Lehigh. But the hopes of his reclaim were soon after dissipated. And "he now even endeavored to destroy the peace and comfort of the Indian congregation." From the discouraging nature of the affairs of the French, ten Indian nations were induced to send deputies to treat with the English at Easton, which eventuated in a treaty of peace. *Tadeuskund* pretended that this treaty had been agreed to on condition that government should build a town on the Susquehannah for the Indians, and cause those living with the brethren to remove to it. This his enemies denied. There was some foundation, from their own account, for Tadeuskund's pretending to have received full commission to conduct all the Indians within certain limits, which included those of Bethlehem, to Wajomick; and therefore demanded their compliance with his commands. He was liberal in his promises, provided they would comply; saying, they should have fields cleared and ploughed, houses built, and provisions provided: not only so, but their teachers should attend them, to live there unmolested, and the believers entirely by themselves. But, through the influence of their priests, they would not comply, which occasioned some threats from *Tadeuskund*, and he immediately set off for Philadelphia, considerably irritated.

Tadeuskund went to Philadelphia in consequence of an intended general congress of the Indians and English, including all those who did not attend at Easton. When he returned, he demanded a positive answer, and they replied that they would not remove unless the governor and all the chiefs so determined, for that they could not without the greatest inconvenience. This seemed to satisfy him, and he left them.

The great council or congress of English and Indians at Easton above referred to, being of much importance in Indian history, as also illustrative of other eminent characters as well as that of *Tadeuskund*, we will refer its details to a separate chapter.

Tadeuskund was burnt to death in his own house at Wajomick in April, 1763.

A chief nearly as distinguished as *Tadeuskund* we shall introduce in this place; but will first note that we observe the same errors, if so they may be called, in more modern writers, with regard to the standing of chiefs, as in the very earliest. The New England historians, it will have been noticed, make several chiefs or sachems each the next to a still greater one: thus, *Annawon, Tyasks, Woonashum* and *Akkompoin* were said to have been severally next to *Metacomet*. And authors who have written about the western Indians, mention several who are head chiefs of the same tribes. But, as we have observed in a former book, such misnomers were scarcely to be avoided, and we only mention it here, that we may not be thought remiss in perpetuating them.

White-eyes (or, as though deficient in organs of vision, some write *White-eye*) was "the first captain among the Delawares." There was always great opposition among the Indians against missionaries settling in their country; who, in the language of one of the Moravians, "were a stone of offence to many of the chiefs and to a great part of the council at Gekelemukpechuenk, and it was several times proposed to expel them by force." But "this man [Captain *White-eyes*] kept the chiefs and council in awe, and would not suffer them to injure the missionaries, being in his own heart convinced of the truths of the gospel. This was evident in all his speeches, held before the chiefs and council in behalf of the Indian congregation and their teachers."*

The old chief *Netawatwees* used every art to thwart the endeavors of *White-eyes*, and, as they were rather in a strain bordering upon persecution, were only sure to make the latter more strenuous. He therefore declared "that no prosperity would attend the Indian affairs, unless they received and believed the saving gospel," &c. *White-eyes* was forced about this time to separate himself from the other chiefs. "This occasioned great and general surprise, and his presence being considered both by the chiefs and the people as indispensably necessary, a negotiation commenced, and some Indian brethren were appointed arbitrators. The event was beyond expectation successful, for chief Netawatwees not only acknowledged the injustice done to Captain *White-eye*, but changed his mind with respect to the believing Indians and their teachers, and remained their constant friend to his death."*

At the breaking out of the revolutionary war, the American congress endeavored to treat with the chiefs of the Six Nations, and accordingly invited the Delawares to send deputies. *White-eyes* attended on the part of the Brethren, and his conduct before the commissioners was highly approved by the missionaries.

Towards the close of the year 1676, the Hurons sent a message to the Delawares, "that they must keep their shoes in readiness to join the warriors." *Nettawatwees* being their head chief, to him, consequently, was the talk delivered. He would not accept the message, but sent belts to the Hurons, with an admonition for their rash resolution, and reminding them of the misery they had already brought upon themselves. Captain

---

* *Loskiel*, iii. 101—2.

White-eyes was a bearer of the belts, who in his turn was as unsuccessful as the Huron ambassadors: for when they were delivered to the chiefs in Fort Detroit, in presence of the English governor, he cut them in pieces, and threw them at the feet of the bearers, ordering them, at the same time, to depart in half an hour. He accused *White-eyes* of a connection with the Americans, and told him his head was in danger.

It is not strange that *White-eyes* was treated in this manner, if he took the stand at the commencement of the war, which we suppose from the following circumstance that he did: The Iroquois, being chiefly in the English interest, and considering the Delawares bound to operate with them, ordered them to be in readiness, as has been just related. Upon this occasion, *White-eyes* said "he should do as he pleased; that he wore no petticoats, as they falsely pretended; he was no woman, but a man, and they should find him to act as such."*

We hear nothing more of importance of this chief until 1780, which was the year of his death. He died at Pittsburgh, in Pennsylvania, of the small-pox. Many others died about this time, among whom was a man who must have been very old, perhaps near 120, as he could well remember when the first house was built in Philadelphia, in 1682, being then a boy.

Although *White-eyes* was so friendly to the Brethren, yet he never fully joined them, stating his political station as a reason.

The Delaware nation perpetuated his name; a chief signed a treaty in 1814, at Greenville, in Ohio, hearing it.† *White-eyes'* town is frequently mentioned in history. It was the place of his residence, which was near the falls of the Muskingum.

Skenando, though belonging to a later age, may very properly be noticed here. He was an Oneida chief, contemporary with the missionary *Kirkland,* to whom he became a convert, and lived many years of the latter part of his life a believer in Christianity. Mr. *Kirkland* died at Paris, N. York, in 1808, and was buried near Oneida. *Skenando* desired to be buried near him at his death, which was granted. He lived to be 110 years old, and was often visited by strangers out of curiosity. He said to one who visited him but a little time before his death, "*I am an aged hemlock; the winds of an hundred winters have whistled through my branches; I am dead at the top. The generation to which I belonged has run away and left me.*"

In early life, he was, like nearly all of his race, given to intoxication. In 1775, he was at Albany to settle some affairs of his tribe with the government of New York. One night he became drunk, and in the morning found himself in the street, nearly naked, every thing of worth stripped from him, even the sign of his chieftainship. This brought him to a sense of his duty, and he was never more known to be intoxicated. He was a powerful chief, and the Americans did not fail to engage him on their side in the revolution. This was congenial to his mind, for he always urged the rights of the prior occupants of the soil, and once opposed the Americans on the same principle, for encroachments upon the red men. He rendered his adopted Anglo brethren important services.

From the "Annals of Tryon County,"‡ we learn that *Skenando* died on the 11 March, 1816. He left an only son. And the same author observes that "his person was tall, well made, and robust. His countenance was intelligent, and displayed all the peculiar dignity of an Indian chief. In his youth he was a brave and intrepid warrior, and in his riper years, one of the noblest counsellors among the North American tribes:" and that, in

---

* *Heckewelder,* Hist. 22.

† See Hist. Second War, by *S. R. Brown,* Appendix, 105. ‡ By W. *W. Campbell.*

the revolutionary war, by his vigilance he preserved the settlement of German Flats from being destroyed.

CHAPTER III.

Of several chiefs spoken of by Washington, in his journal of an embassy to the French of Ohio—SHINGIS—MONACATOOCHA—HALF-KING—JUSKAKAKA—WHITE-THUNDER—ALLIQUIPA—CAPTAIN JACOBS—HENDRICK—*His history—Curious anecdote of*—LOGAN—*Cresap's War—Battle of Point Pleasant—Logan's famous speech*—CORNSTOCK —*His history*—RED-HAWK—ELLINIPSICO —*The barbarous murder of these three—Melancholy death of Logan*—PONTIAC—*A renowned warrior—Col. Rogers's account of him—His policy—Fall of Michilimakinak*—MENEHWEHNA—*Siege of Detroit—Pontiac's stratagem to surprise it—Is discovered—Official account of the affair of Bloody Bridge—Pontiac abandons the siege—Becomes the friend of the English—Is assassinated.*

THE expedition of *Washington* to the French on the Ohio, in 1753, brings to our records information of several chiefs of the Six Nations, of the most interesting kind. He was commissioned and sent as an ambassador to the French, by Governor *Dinwiddie* of Virginia. He kept an accurate journal of his travels, which, on his return to Virginia, was published, and, not long after, the same was republished in London, with a map; the substance of this journal was copied into almost every periodical of importance of that day.

Shingis was the first chief he visited, who lived in the forks of the Alleghany and Monongahela rivers, where Pittsburgh now stands. He intended holding a council with the celebrated *Half-king,** already mentioned, at Loggstown, and such others as could be assembled at short notice, to strengthen them in the English interest. He therefore invited *Shingis* to attend the council, and he accordingly accompanied him to Loggstown. "As soon as I came into town," says *Washington,* "I went

* He is called a *Huron* by *Loskiel*, Hist. Missions, iii. 123. He was called by the Delawares *Pomoacan*, which in English means *Sweet-house. Heckewelder,* Nar. 235.

to *Monakatoocha,* (as the *Half-king* was out at his hunting cabin, on Little Beaver Creek, about 15 miles off,) and informed him by *John Davidson,* my Indian interpreter, that I was sent a messenger to the French general, and was ordered to call upon the sachems of the Six Nations to acquaint them with it. I gave him a string of wampum and a twist of tobacco, and desired him to send for the half-king, which he promised to do by a runner in the morning, and for other sachems. I invited him and the other great men present to my tent, where they stayed about an hour, and returned." This place was about 140 miles, "as we went, and computed it," says the great writer, "from our back settlements, where we arrived between sunsetting and dark, the twenty-fifth day after I left Williamsburgh.

Half-king, it seems, had, not long before, visited the same place to which *Washington* was now destined; for as soon as he returned to his town, *Washington* invited him privately to his tent, "and desired him to relate some of the particulars of his journey to the French commandant," the best way for him to go, and the distance from that place. "He told me," says *Washington,* "that the nearest and levelest way was now impassable, by reason of many large miry savannas; that we must be obliged to go by Venango, and should not get to the near fort in less than five or six nights' sleep, good travelling." *Half-king* further informed him that he met with a cold reception; that the French officer sternly ordered him to declare his business, which he did, he said, in the following speech:—

"Fathers, I am come to tell you your own speeches; what your own mouths have declared. You, in former days, set a silver basin before us, wherein there was the leg of a beaver, and desired all the nations to come and eat of it; to eat in peace and plenty, and not to be churlish to one another: and that if any such person should be found to be a disturber, I here lay down by the edge of the dish a rod, which you must scourge them with; and if your father should get foolish, in my old days, I desire you may use it upon me as well as others.—Now, fathers, it is you who are the disturbers in this land, by coming and building your towns; and taking it away unknown to us, and by force.—We kindled a fire, a long time ago, at a place called Montreal, where we desired you to stay, and not to come and intrude upon our land. I now desire you may despatch to that place; for, be it known to you, fathers, that this is our land, and not yours.—I desire you may hear me in civilness; if not, we must handle that rod which was laid down for the use of the obstreperous. If you had come in a peaceable manner, like our brothers the English, we would not have been against your trading with us, as they do; but to come, fathers, and build houses upon our land, and to take it by force, is what we cannot submit to."

Half-king then repeated what was said to him in reply by the French, which, when he had done, *Washington* made a speech to him and his council. He acquainted them with the reason of his visit, and told them he was instructed to call upon them by the governor of Virginia, to advise with them, to assure them of the love of the English, and to ask the assistance of some of their young men, to conduct him through the wilderness, to the French, to whom he had a letter from his governor. *Half-king* made this reply:—

"In regard to what my brother the governor had desired of me, I return you this answer." "I rely upon you as a brother ought to do, as you say we are brothers, and one people." "Brother, as you have asked my advice, I hope you will be ruled by it, and stay until I can provide a company to go with you. The French speech belt is not here; I have it to go for, to my hunting cabin. Likewise the people, whom I have ordered in, are not yet come, and cannot until the third night from this; until which time, brother, I must beg you to stay."

When *Washington* told him that his business would not admit of so much delay, the chief seemed displeased, and said it was "*a matter of no small moment, and must not be entered without due consideration.*" Perhaps it will not be too much, to give this Indian chief credit for some of that character which was so well exemplified by *Washington* in all his after life. And "as I found it impossible," says the narrator, "to get off, without affronting them in the most egregious manner, I consented to stay." Accordingly, *Half-king* gave orders to King *Shingis*, who was present, to attend on Wednesday night with the wampum, and two men of their nation, to be in readiness to set out with us next morning." There was still a delay of another day, as the chiefs could not get in their wampum and young men which were to be sent; and, after all, but three chiefs and one hunter accompanied. "We set out," says *Washington*, "about 9 o'clock, with the *Half-king, Juskakaka,** *White-thunder*, and the hunter; and travelled on the road to Venango, where we arrived the 4th of December." This place is situated at the junction of French Creek with the Ohio. Here the French had a garrison, and another a short distance above it, which was the extent of our discoverer's peregrinations north. The commanders of these posts used all means to entice *Half-king* to desert the English, and it was with great difficulty that *Washington* succeeded in preventing them. They endeavored to weary out the major, by making the chiefs delay their departure from day to day, by means of liquor, so that they should be left behind. At length, having out-generaled his complotters, and "got things ready to set off, I sent for the *Half-king,"* continues the narrator, "to know whether he intended to go with us, or by water. He told me that *White-thunder* had hurt himself much, and was sick, and unable to walk; therefore he was obliged to carry him down in a canoe;" so, notwithstanding the delays, Washington was obliged to go without him; but he cautioned him strongly against believing Monsieur *Joncaire's* pretensions of friendship, and representations against the English. Here ends *Washington's* account of Half-*king*.

He now set out for the frontiers with all expedition. He had, he says, the "most fatiguing journey possible to conceive of. From the 1st to the 15th December, there was but one day on which it did not rain or snow incessantly; and through the whole journey, we met with nothing but one continued series of cold, wet weather."

This expedition of *Washington* has in it great interest, more especially from his superior eminence afterwards. It is pleasing to contemplate the "savior of his country" in every adventure and circumstance of his life; and even gratifying to view him with a gun in one hand, a staff in the other, and a pack upon his back; wading through rivers, encountering storms of sleet and snow, and sleeping upon the ground, thus early, for his country's good. He had some very narrow escapes, and, during part of the way on his return, he had but one attendant. One day, as they were passing a place called *Murdering Town*, they were fired upon by one of a war-party of French Indians, who had waited in ambush for them; and although they were within fifteen paces of him, yet they escaped unhurt. They captured the fellow that fired upon them, and

---

* We hear again of this chief in 1794, when, with 58 others, he signed a treaty with the U. States at Fort Stanwix. His name is there written *Jishkaaga,* which signified a *green grasshopper*. He was sometimes called *Little-Billy*.

kept him until nine at night, then dismissed him, and travelled all night, "without making *any* stop," fearing they should be pursued the next morning by his party. Continuing their course all the next day, they came to the river where they intended to cross. Here the firmness of *Washington* and his companion was thoroughly tried. The river was very high, and filled with floating ice, and there was no way to pass it but by a raft. They had "but one poor hatchet," with the assistance of which, after laboring from morning till sunset, they had a raft ready to launch; on this they set out, but it was soon crushed between the floating ice, and they very narrowly escaped perishing. *Washington* was himself precipitated into the river, where the water was ten feet deep. Fortunately, however, he catched by a fragment of the raft, and saved himself. They finally extricated themselves from their perilous situation, by getting upon the ice which confined their frail bark, and from thence to an island, and finally to the opposite shore. The cold was so intense, that Mr. *Gist* froze his hands and feet. This place was about three miles below the mouth of the Yohogany, where an Indian queen, as *Washington* calls her, lived. He went to see her, he observes, she having "expressed great concern that we passed her in going to the fort. I made her a present of a watch coat, and a bottle of rum, which latter was thought much the best present of the two." Her name was *Alliquippa*. From this place, he pursued his journey home without further accident.

We have mentioned the friendly attention of *Shingis* to our adventurer, who had probably expected he would have attended him on his journey; but *Shingis* went to collect in his men, and did not return. The Indians said it was owing to the sickness of his wife, but *Washington* thought it was fear of the French which prevented him. But this conjecture does not seem well founded, for he ordered *Kustaloga,* who lived at Venango, to proceed to the French and return the wampum, which was as much as to tell them they wished no further fellowship with them.

The massacres which followed *Braddock's* defeat were horrible beyond description. *Shingis* and Capt. *Jacobs* were supposed to have been the principal instigators of them, and 700 dollars was offered for their heads.* It was at this period, that the dead bodies of some that had been murdered and mangled were sent from the frontiers to Philadelphia, and hauled about the streets, to inflame the people against the Indians, and also against the Quakers, to whose mild forbearance was attributed a laxity in sending out troops. The mob surrounded the house of assembly, having placed the dead bodies at its entrance, and demanded immediate succor. At this time the above reward was offered.

Some of the most noted chiefs now fall under our observation.

Hendrick was a gallant Mohawk chief, who took part, with many of his men, against the French, in the year 1755. The French were encouraged by the defeat of Gen. *Braddock,* and were in high expectation of carrying all before them. *Hendrick* joined the English army at the request of Gen. *Johnson,* and met the French, consisting of 200 men, under Gen. *Dieskau,* at Lake George. While the English and Indians were encamped in a slight work, their scouts brought news of the approach of the French, with a great body of Indians upon their flanks. Gen. *Johnson* despatched Col. *Williams* of Massachusetts, with 1000 men, and Hendrick with 200 of his warriors, to give them battle; but falling in with them about four miles from camp, unexpectedly, Col. *Williams* and *Hendrick* were killed, with many other officers and privates of the detachment. The rest fled to the main body with great precipitation, infusing consternation into the whole

* Watson's Annals of Philadelphia, 450.

army.* The French followed closely, and poured in a tremendous fire, which did very little execution, from the precaution of the English in falling flat upon their faces. They soon recovered from their surprise, and fought with bravery, having advantage not only in numbers, but artillery, of which the French had none.† At length the brave *Dieskau* was wounded in the thigh, and his Indians, being terrified at the havoc made by the cannon of the English, fled to the woods, and the regulars were ordered to retreat by their general, which they did in great disorder. Gen. *Dieskau* was found in the pursuit, supporting himself by the stump of a tree. Supposing plunder to be the first object of his captors, as he was attempting to draw his watch to present to them, some one, supposing him to be searching for his pistol, discharged his gun into his hips. Notwithstanding he was thus twice wounded, he lived to reach England, but he died soon after. The French lost 800 men in the attack.

When Gen. *Johnson* was about to detach Col. *Williams,* he asked *Hendrick's* opinion, whether the force was sufficient. To which he replied, "*If they are to fight, they are too few. If they are to be killed, they are too many.*" And when it was proposed to divide the detachment into three parts, Hendrick objected, and forcibly to express the impracticability of the plan, picked up three sticks, and, putting them together, said to the general, "*You see now that these cannot be easily broken; but take them one by one, and you may break them at once.*" But from this valuable counsel very little advantage seems to have been derived.

It was reported at the time, that 38 of *Hendrick's* men were killed, and 12 wounded.‡ Few historians mention the loss of the Indians; probably considering them as unworthy of record! Such historians may be forgotten. At least, they cannot expect to pass under that name in another age.

The Indians were greatly exasperated against the French, "by the death of the famous *Hendrick,*" says the same writer, "a renowned Indian warrior among the Mohawks, and one of their sachems, or kings, who was slain in the battle, and whose son, upon being told that his father was killed, giving the usual Indian groan upon such occasions, and suddenly putting his hand on his left breast, swore his father was still alive in that place, and stood there in his son: that it was with the utmost difficulty, Gen. *Johnson* prevented the fury of their resentment taking place on the body of the French general."§

As soon as the battle was over, the Indians dispersed themselves in various directions, with the trophies of victory. Some to their homes, to condole with the friends of the slain, and some to the English, to carry the welcome news of victory. The different runners brought into Albany above 80 scalps, within a very short time after the fight.|| And thus we are furnished with an early record of the wretched custom which appears to have been fostered, and actually encouraged by all who have employed the Indians as auxiliaries in war. Indeed to employ them, was to employ their practices—they were inseparable. To talk, as some have done, of employing them, and preventing their barbarous customs with the unfortunate captives, all experience shows, is but *to talk* one thing and mean another.

Soon after Sir *William Johnson* entered upon his duties as superintendent of Indian affairs in North America, he received from England some richly embroidered suits of clothes. *Hendrick* was present when they were received, and could not help expressing a great desire for a share in them. He went away very thoughtful, but returned not long after, and called upon Sir *William,* and told him he had dreamed a dream. Sir

* The English lost about 200 in this ambush. *Guthrie's* Universal History, x. 94.
† Ibid. ‡ Gent. *Magazine* for 1755. § Ibid. || Ibid.

William very concernedly desired to know what it was. *Hendrick* very readily told him he had dreamed that Sir *William Johnson* had presented him with one of his new suits of uniform. Sir *William* could not refuse it, and one of the elegant suits was forthwith presented to *Hendrick,* who went away to show his present to his countrymen, and left Sir *William* to tell the joke to his friends. Some time after, the general met *Hendrick,* and told him he had dreamed a dream. Whether the sachem mistrusted that he was now to be taken in his own net, or not, is not certain; but he seriously desired to know what it was, as Sir *William* had done before. The general said he dreamed that *Hendrick* had presented him with a certain tract of land, which he described, (consisting of about 500 acres of the most valuable land in the valley of the Mohawk River.) *Hendrick* answered, "It is yours;" but, shaking his head, said, "Sir *William Johnson,* I will never dream with you again."

John Konkapot, a Stockbridge Indian, was grandson to *Hendrick,* and he informs us that his grandfather was son of the *Wolf,* a Mohegan chief, and that his mother was a Mohawk.* Rev. *Gideon Hawley,* in a letter to Gov. *Hutchinson* (1770) about the Marshpee Indians, has this passage: "Among *Johnson's* Mohawks, *Abraham* and *Hendrick* were the oldest of their tribe, when they died, and neither of them was 70, at their deaths. I saw a sister of theirs in 1765, who appeared to be several years above 70. At Stockbridge, Captain *Kunkapot* was for many years the oldest man in his tribe."† We have now come to one of the most noted chiefs in Indian story.

Logan was called a Mingo‡ chief, whose father, *Shikellimus,* was chief of the tribe of the Cayugas, whom he succeeded. *Shikellimus* was attached in a remarkable degree to the benevolent *James Logan,* from which circumstance, it is probable, his son bore his name. The name is still perpetuated among the Indians. For magnanimity in war, and greatness of soul in peace, few, if any, in any nation, ever surpassed *Logan.* He took no part in the French wars which ended in 1760, except that of a peacemaker; was always acknowledged the friend of the white people, until the year 1774, when his brother and several others of his family were murdered, the particulars of which follow. In the spring of 1774, some Indians robbed the people upon the Ohio River, who were in that country exploring the lands, and preparing for settlements. These land-jobbers were alarmed at this hostile carriage of the Indians, as they considered it, and collected themselves at a place called Wheeling Creek, the site on which Wheeling is now built, and, learning that there were two Indians on the river a little above, one Captain *Michael Cresap,* belonging to the exploring party, proposed to fall upon and kill them. His advice, although opposed at first, was followed, and a party led by *Cresap* proceeded and killed the two Indians. The same day, it being reported that some Indians were discovered below Wheeling upon the river, *Cresap* and his party immediately marched to the place, and at first appeared to show themselves friendly, and suffered the Indians to pass by them unmolested, to encamp still lower down, at the mouth of Grave Creek. *Cresap* soon followed, attacked and killed several of them, having one of his own men wounded by the fire of the Indians. Here some of the family of *Logan* were slain. The circumstance of the affair was exceeding aggravating, inasmuch as the whites *pretended no provocation.*

Soon after this, some other monsters in human shape, at whose head were *Daniel Greathouse* and one *Tomlinson,* committed a horrid murder upon a company of Indians about thirty miles above Wheeling. *Great-*

---

* *Col. Mas. Hist. Soc.* † Ibid. 3. i. 151.

‡ *Mengwe, Maquas, Maqua,* or *Iroquos,* all mean the same.

house resided at the same place, but on the opposite side of the river from the Indian encampment. A party of thirty-two men were collected for this object, who secreted themselves, while *Greathouse,* under a pretence of friendship, crossed the river and visited them, to ascertain their strength; which, on counting them, he found too numerous for his force in an open attack. These Indians, having heard of the late murder of their relations, had determined to be avenged of the whites, and *Greathouse* did not know the danger he was in, until a squaw advised him of it, in a friendly caution, "to go home." The sad requital this poor woman met with will presently appear. This abominable fellow invited the Indians to come over the river and drink rum with him; this being a part of his plot to separate them, that they might be the easier destroyed. The opportunity soon offered; a number being collected at a tavern in the white settlement, and considerably intoxicated, were fallen upon, and all murdered, except a little girl. Among the murdered was a brother of *Logan,* and his sister, whose delicate situation greatly aggravated the horrid crime.

The remaining Indians, upon the other side of the river, on hearing the firing, set off two canoes with armed warriors, who, as they approached the shore, were fired upon by the whites, who lay concealed, awaiting their approach. Nothing prevented their taking deadly aim, and many were killed and wounded, and the rest were obliged to return. This affair took place May 24th, 1774.* These were the events that led to a horrid Indian war, in which many innocent families were sacrificed to satisfy the vengeance of an incensed and injured people.

A calm followed these troubles, but it was only such as goes before the storm, and lasted only while the tocsin of war could be sounded among the distant Indians. On the 12 July, 1774, *Logan,* at the head of a small party of only eight warriors, struck a blow on some inhabitants upon the Muskingum, where no one expected it. He had left the settlements on the Ohio undisturbed, which every one supposed would be the first attacked, in case of war, and hence the reason of his great successes. His first attack was upon three men who were pulling flax in a field. One was shot down, and the two others taken. These were marched into the wilderness, and, as they approached the Indian town, *Logan* gave the scalp halloo, and they were met by the inhabitants, who conducted them in. Running the gauntlet was next to be performed. *Logan* took no delight in tortures, and he in the most friendly manner instructed one of the captives how to proceed to escape the severities of the gauntlet. This same captive, whose name was *Robinson,* was afterwards sentenced to be burned; but *Logan,* though not able to rescue him by his eloquence, with his own hand cut the cords that bound him to the stake, and caused him to be adopted into an Indian family. He became afterwards *Logan's* scribe, and wrote the letter that was tied to a war club, the particulars of which we shall relate farther onward.

The warriors now prepared themselves for open conflict, and, with *Cornstock* at their head, were determined to meet the *Big-knives,* as the Virginians were called, from their long swords, in their own way.

It is necessary to notice a chief rather suddenly introduced here, as, in fact, he was the leader, or commander-in-chief, of the Indians in this war. The name of *Cornstock* we have already mentioned. He was chief of the Shawanese, and in the time of the revolutionary war, was a great friend of the Moravian missionaries. We shall again notice him.

The Virginia legislature was in session when the news of Indian depredations was received at the seat of government. Gov. *Dunmore* immedi-

---

* Facts published in *Jefferson's Notes.*

ately ordered out the militia, to the number of 3000 men, half of whom, under Col. *Andrew Lewis*, were ordered towards the mouth of the Great Kanhawa, while the governor himself, with the other half, marched to a point on the Ohio, to fall upon the Indian towns in the absence of the warriors, drawn off by the approach of the army under Col. *Lewis*.

The Indians met the division under *Lewis* at a place called *Point Pleasant*, on the Great Kanhawa, where a very bloody battle ensued. A detachment of 300 men first fell in with them, and were defeated, with great slaughter; but the other divisions coming up, the fight was maintained during the whole day. Never was ground maintained with more obstinacy. Every step was disputed, until the darkness of the night closed the scene. The Indians slowly retreated, and while the Americans were preparing to pursue and take revenge for their severe loss, an express arrived from Gov. *Dunmore*, that he had concluded a treaty with the Indian chiefs. In this battle, above 140 Americans were killed and wounded, nearly half of which were of the former, among whom was Col. *Charles Lewis*, brother of *Andrew*, and Col. *Field*. These officers led the first division. Of the number of the Indians destroyed, we are ignorant; though very probably they were many, as their numbers engaged were said to have been about 1500.*

After the Indians had been beaten, as we have stated, the Americans encamped on a plain eight miles from Chillicothe, a place appointed for meeting the chiefs to treat of peace. Three days after, *Cornstock*† came to the encampment with eight other chiefs, where a short debate was held between him and Lord *Dunmore*, in which each charged the other with the breach of treaties and injuries committed by their respective countrymen; but finally a peace was settled. It was at this time that the far-famed speech of *Logan* was delivered; not in the camp of Lord *Dunmore*, for, although desiring peace, *Logan* would not meet the Americans in council, but remained in his cabin in sullen silence, until a messenger was sent to him, to know whether he would accede to the proposals. On which occasion, after shedding many tears for the loss of his friends, he said to the messenger, who well understood his language, in substance as follows:—

"*I appeal to any white to say, if ever he entered Logan's cabin hungry, and he gave him not meat; if ever he came cold and naked, and he clothed him not.*

"*During the course of the last long bloody war, Logan remained idle in his cabin, an advocate for peace. Such was my love for the whites, that my countrymen pointed as they passed, and said, 'Logan is the friend of white men.'*

"*I had even thought to have lived with you, but for the injuries of one man. Col.* Cresap, *the last spring, in cold blood, and unprovoked, murdered all the relations of* Logan; *not even sparing my women and children.*

"*There runs not a drop of my blood in the veins of any living creature. This called on me for revenge. I have sought it. I have killed many. I have fully glutted my vengeance. For my country, I rejoice at the beams of peace. But do not harbor a thought that mine is the joy of fear.* Logan *never felt fear. He will not turn on his heel to save his life. Who is there to mourn for* Logan?—*Not one!*"

When Mr. *Jefferson* published his "Notes on Virginia," the facts therein stated implicating *Cresap* as the murderer of *Logan's* family, were

---

* *Campbell's* Virginia.

† Some write *Cornstalk*, but when a word is used for a proper name, there is no harm in adopting a different spelling, and we follow our oldest printed authority.

by *Cresap's* friends called in question. Mr. *Jefferson* at first merely stated the facts as preliminary to, and the cause of, the "Speech of *Logan*," which he considered as generally known in Virginia; but the acrimony discovered by his enemies in their endeavors to gainsay his statement, led to an investigation of the whole transaction, and a publication of the result was the immediate consequence, in a new edition of the "Notes on Virginia."

Among other proofs, that the chief guilt lay upon the head of *Cresap* of bringing about a bloody war, since well known by his name, Judge *Innes* of Frankfort, Kentucky, wrote to Mr. *Jefferson*, 2 March, 1799, that he was, he thought, able to give him more particulars of that affair than, perhaps, any other person; that, in 1774, while at the house of Col. *Preston*, in Fincastle county, Va., there arrived an express, calling upon him to order out the militia, "for the protection of the inhabitants residing low down on the north fork of Holston River. The express brought with him a war club, and a note tied to it, which was left at the house of one *Robertson*, whose family were cut off by the Indians, and gave rise for the application to Col. *Preston*." Here follows the letter or note, of which Mr. *Innes* then made a copy, in his memorandum book:—

"*Captain* Cresap, *What did you kill my people on Yellow Creek for? The white people killed my kin at Conestoga,* a great while ago; and I thought nothing of that. But you killed my kin again, on Yellow Creek, and took my cousin prisoner. Then I thought I must kill too; and I have been three times to war since: but the Indians are not angry; only myself.*"

It was signed, "*Captain* John Logan."

Not long after these times of calamities, which we have recorded in the life of *Logan*, he was cruelly murdered, as he was on his way home from Detroit. For a time previous to his death, he gave himself up to intoxication, which in a short time nearly obliterated all marks of the great man!

The fate of *Cornstock* is equally deplorable, although in the contemplation of which, his character does not suffer, as does that of *Logan*. He was cruelly murdered by some white soldiers, while a hostage among them. And there is as much, nay, far more, to carry down his remembrance to posterity, as that of the tragical death of *Archimedes*. He was not murdered while actually drawing geometrical figures upon the ground, but, while he was explaining the geography of his country by drawings upon the floor, an alarm was given, which, in a few minutes after, eventuated in his death. We will now go into an explanation of the cause and manner of the murder of *Cornstock*. It is well known that the war of the revolution had involved all, or nearly all, of the Indians in dreadful calamities. In consequence of murders committed by the Indians on the frontiers of Virginia, several companies marched to Point Pleasant, where there had been a fort since the battle there in 1774. Most of the tribes of the north-west, except the Shawanese, were determined to fight against the Americans. *Cornstock* wished to preserve peace, and therefore, as the only means in his power, as he had used his powerful eloquence in vain, resolved to lay the state of affairs before the Americans, that they might avert the threatened storm. In the spring of 1777, he came to the fort at Point Pleasant, upon this friendly mission, in company with another chief, called *Redhawk*. After explaining the situation of things with regard to the confederate tribes, he said, in regard to his own, the Shawanese, "*The current sets* [with the Indians] *so strong against the Americans, in consequence of the agency of the British, that they*

* Alluding, I Suppose, to the massacre of the Conestoga Indians in 1763.

[the Shawanese] *will float with it, I fear, in spite of all my exertions.*" Upon this intelligence, the commander of the garrison thought proper to detain him and *Redhawk* as hostages to prevent the meditated calamities. When Captain *Arbuckle,* the commander of the garrison, had notified the new government of Virginia of the situation of affairs, and what he had done, forces marched into that country. A part of them having arrived, waited for others to join them under Gen. *Hand,* on whom these depended for provisions.

Meanwhile the officers held frequent conversations with *Cornstock,* who took pleasure in giving them minute descriptions of his country, and especially of that portion between the Mississippi and Missouri. One day, as he was delineating a map of it upon the floor for the gratification of those present, a call was heard on the opposite side of the Ohio, which he at once recognized as the voice of his son, *Ellinipsico,* who had fought at his side in the famous battle of Point Pleasant, in 1774, of which we have spoken. At the request of his father, *Ellinipsico* came to the fort, where they had an affectionate meeting. This son had become uneasy at his father's long absence, and had at length sought him out in his exile here; prompted by those feelings which so much adorn human nature. The next day, two men crossed the Kanhawa, upon a hunting expedition. As they were returning to their boat after their hunt, and near the side of the river, they were fired upon by some Indians, and one of the two, named *Gilmore,* was killed, but the other escaped. A party of Captain *Hall's* men went over and brought in the body of *Gilmore;* whereupon a cry was raised, "Let us go and kill the Indians in the fort." An enfuriated gang, with Captain *Hall* at their head, set out with this nefarious resolution, and, against every remonstrance, proceeded to commit the deed of blood. With their guns cocked, they swore death to any who should oppose them. In the mean time, some ran to apprize the devoted chiefs of their danger. As the murderers approached, *Ellinipsico* discovered agitation, which when *Cornstock* saw, he said, "*My son, the Great Spirit has seen fit that we should die together, and has sent you to that end. It is his will, and let us submit.*" The murderers had now arrived, and the old chief turned around and met them. They shot him through with seven bullets. He fell, and died without a struggle!

Ellinipsico, though having at first appeared disturbed, met his death with great composure. He was shot upon the seat on which he was sitting when his fate was first pronounced to him.

Red-hawk was a young Delaware chief, and, like *Ellinipsico,* had fought under *Cornstock.* He died with less fortitude: having tried to secrete himself, he was soon discovered and slain. Another Indian, whose name is not mentioned, was mangled and murdered in the most barbarous manner. Suffice it here to say, that this was all that was effected by the expedition, and the forces soon after returned home.

Few, if any, chiefs in history are spoken of in terms of higher commendation than *Cornstock.* Mr. *Withers,* a writer on Indian affairs,* speaks as follows of him:

"Thus perished the mighty *Cornstalk,* sachem of the Shawanees, and king of the northern confederacy, in 1774,—a chief remarkable for many great and good qualities. He was disposed to be at all times the friend of white men, as he ever was the advocate of honorable peace. But when his country's wrongs 'called aloud for battle,' he became the thunderbolt of war, and made her oppressors feel the weight of his uplifted arm." "His noble bearing—his generous and disinterested attachment' to the

* In his "*Chronicles,*" a work, it is our duty to remark, written with candor and judgment.

colonies, when the thunder of British cannon was reverberating through the land—his anxiety to preserve the frontier of Virginia from desolation and death, (the object of his visit to Point Pleasant,) all conspired to win for him the esteem and respect of others; while the untimely and perfidious manner of his death, caused a deep and lasting regret to pervade the bosoms even of those who were enemies to his nation; and excited the just indignation of all towards his inhuman and barbarous murderers."

Col. *Wilson,* present at the interview between the chiefs and Gov. *Dunmore* in 1774, thus speaks of *Cornstock*:—"When he arose, he was in no wise confused or daunted, but spoke in a distinct and audible voice, without stammering or repetition, and with peculiar emphasis. His looks, while addressing *Dunmore,* were truly grand and majestic; yet graceful and attractive. I have heard the first orators in Virginia,—*Patrick Henry* and *Richard Henry Lee,*—but never have I heard one whose powers of delivery surpassed those of *Cornstalk."*

Ten years after the bloody affair above related, an able writer* upon those times says, "The blood of the great CORNSTOCK and of his gallant son was mingled with the dust, but their memory is not lost in oblivion." But how few at this day know of his fate, or even that such a chief ever existed! and, at the same time, the same persons would be indignant, were we to suppose them ignorant of the fate of the monster *Pizarro.*

As great a warrior, perhaps, as any who have lived among the nations of the west, we shall in the next place proceed to give an account of. This was

Pontiac, a chief of the Ottaway nation, whose fame, in his time, was not alone confined to his own continent; but the gazettes of Europe spread it also.

One who knew this chief, and the tribes over whom he had sway, thus speaks of them in 1765:—"The Indians on the lakes are generally at peace with one another, having a wide-extended and fruitful country in their possession. They are formed into a sort of empire, and the emperor is elected from the eldest tribe, which is the Ottawawas, some of whom inhabit near our fort at Detroit, but are mostly further westward, towards the Mississippi. *Ponteack* is their present king or emperor, who has certainly the largest empire and greatest authority of any Indian chief that has appeared on the continent since our acquaintance with it. He puts on an air of majesty and princely grandeur, and is greatly honored and revered by his subjects."†

In 1760, Major *Rogers* marched into his country, in fulfilling his orders of displacing the French, after the fall of Quebec.‡ Apprized of his approach, *Pontiac* sent ambassadors to inform him that their cheif was not far off, and desired him to halt until he could see him "with his own eyes," and that he was lord of the country.

Pontiac soon met the English officer, and demanded his business into his country, and how it came about that he dared enter it without his permission. When the colonel told him he had no design against the Indians, and only wished to remove the French, their common enemy, and cause of all their trouble, delivering him at the same time several belts of wampum, *Pontiac* replied, "I stand in the path you travel in, until to-morrow morning," and gave him a belt. This communication was understood, and "was as much as to say," says the actor, "I must not march further without his leave." The colonel continues: "When he departed for the night, he inquired whether I wanted any thing that

---

* In *Carey's* Museum, iv. 140.

† *Rogers's Account of North America,* extracted in the *Annual Register* for 1765.

‡ *Quebeis* is an Algonquin word, signifying a *Strait. Charlevoix.*

his country afforded, and [if I did] he would send his warriors to fetch it. I assured him that any provisions they brought should be paid for; and the next day we were supplied by them with several bags of parched corn, and some other necessaries. At our second meeting, he gave me the pipe of peace, and both of us by turns smoked with it; and he assured me he had made peace with me and my detachment; that I might pass through his country unmolested, and relieve the French garrison; and that he would' protect me and my party from any insults that might be offered or intended by the Indians; and, as an earnest of his friendship, he sent 100 warriors to protect and assist us in driving 100 fat cattle, which we had brought for the use of the detachment from Pittsburgh, by the way of Presque-Isle. He attended me constantly after this interview till I arrived at Detroit, and while I remained in the country, and was the means of preserving the detachment from the fury of the Indians, who had assembled at the mouth of the strait, with an intent to cut us off. I had several conferences with him, in which he discovered great strength of judgment, and a thirst after knowledge."

This same officer observes, that he discovered much curiosity at their equipage, and wished to know how their clothes were made, and to learn their mode of war. He expressed a willingness to acknowledge the king of England, though not as his superior, but as his uncle, which he would acknowledge, as he was able, in furs. England was much in his thoughts, and he often expressed a desire to see it. This was very natural, and was often observed among other natives. He told Col. *Rogers* that, if he would conduct him there, he would give him a part of his country.

He was willing to grant the English favors, and allow them to settle in his dominions, but not unless he could be viewed as sovereign; and he gave them to understand, that, unless they conducted themselves agreeably to his wishes, "he would shut up the way," and keep them out. Hence it is fair, within the scope of the most reasonable conjecture, to conclude, that his final disaffection to the English was owing to their haughty carriage, and maltreatment of him and his people.

The principal scenes of his prowess were at Michilimakinak and Detroit. The French finally gave up possession in Canada, in 1760; but many of the Indian nations who had become attached to them were taught, at the same time, to hate the English. *Pontiac* was most conspicuous in his enmity, although, until he had united the strength of many tribes to his, he showed great kindness and friendship towards them. The Miamis, Ottawas, Chippewas, Wyandots, Pottowatomies, Mississagas, Shawanese, Ottagamies, and Winnebagoes, constituted his power, as, in after time, they did that of *Tecumseh*.

There was more system employed by this distinguished man than, perhaps, by any other of his countrymen upon any similar undertaking, not excepting even *Metacomet* or *Tecumseh*. In his war of 1763, which is justly denominated "*Pontiac's* war," he appointed a commissary, and began to make and issue bills of credit, all of which he afterwards carefully redeemed. He made his bills or notes of bark, on which was drawn the figure of the commodity he wanted for it. The shape of an otter was drawn under that of the article wanted, and an otter was the insignia or arms of his nation. He had also, with great sagacity, urged upon his people the necessity of dispensing altogether with European commodities, to have no intercourse with any whites, and to depend entirely upon their ancient modes of procuring sustenance.

Major *Gladwin* held possession of Detroit in 1763. Having been despatched thither by General *Amherst,* he had been informed by commissioners who had been exploring the country, that hostile feelings were manifested among the Indians, and he sent men on purpose to ascertain the fact, who, on their return, dissipated all fears.

Major *Roberts* was a messenger to *Pontiac* from Col. *Rogers,* and took with him, for a present, what he thought would be most agreeable to him, which was a quantity of *l'eau-de-vie,* i. e. brandy. When it was presented, his men, thinking it to be a stratagem to poison him, entreated him not to taste of it. But that the English should not in the least apprehend fear or distrust in him, he said to his people present, "*It is not possible that this man, who knows my love for him, who is also sensible of the great favors I have done him, can think of taking away my life;*" and, taking the spirit, drank it with as much apparent confidence of its purity and good effect, as Socrates did his fatal cup. And, adds the historian, "*Cent traits d'une elévation parielle avoient fixé sur Pontheack les yeux des nations sauvages. Il vouloit les reunir toutes sous les memes drapeaux, pour faire respecter leur territoire et leur indépendance. Des circonstances malheureuses firent avorter ce grand project.*"*

Several traders had brought news to the fort at Michilimakinak, that the Indians were hostile to the English. Major *Etherington* commanded the garrison, and would believe nothing of it. A Mr. *Ducharme* communicated the information to the major, who was much displeased at it, "and threatened to send the next person who should bring a story of the same kind a prisoner to Detroit."†

The garrison, at this time, consisted of 90 men, besides two subalterns and the commander-in-chief. There were also at the fort four English merchants.

Little regard was paid to the assembling of sundry bands of Indians, as they appeared friendly; but when nearly 400 of them were scattered up and down throughout the place, "I took the liberty," says Mr. *Henry,* "of observing to Major *Etherington,* that, in my judgment, no confidence ought to be placed in them; in return, the major only rallied me on my timidity."

On the fourth of June, the king's birth day, the Indians began, as if to amuse themselves, to play at a favorite game of ball, which they called *baggatiway,* which is thus described by Mr. *Henry*:—"It is played with a bat and ball, the bat being about four feet in length, curved, and terminated in a sort of racket. Two posts are placed in the ground, at a considerable distance from each other, as a mile or more. Each party has its post, and the game consists in throwing the ball up to the post of the adversary. The ball, at the beginning, is placed in the middle of the course, and each party endeavors as well to throw the ball out of the direction of its own post, as into that of the adversary's." This farce drew many off their guard, and some of the garrison went out to witness the sport.

"The game of baggatiway, (he continues,) as from the description above will have been perceived, is necessarily attended with much noise and violence. In the ardor of contest, the ball, as has been suggested, if it cannot be thrown to the goal desired, is struck in any direction by which it can be diverted from that designed by the adversary. At such a moment, therefore, nothing could be less liable to excite premature alarm, than that the ball should be tossed over the pickets of the fort, nor that, having fallen there, it should be followed, on the instant, by all engaged in the game, as well the one party as the other, all eager, all striving, all shouting, all in the unrestrained pursuit of a rude athletic exercise." And this was their plan, while in the height of their game, to

---

* *Raynal,* Hist. Philos. et Politique, &c. ix. 89. ed. Geneva, 1781.

† Travels in Canada, by *Alexander Henry,* Esq., from which the following account of the destruction of Michilimakinak is taken.

throw their ball within the pickets of the fort, and then all to rush in, and, in the midst of their hubbub, to murder the garrison; and it succeeded to their wishes. They struck the ball over the stockade, as if by accident, and repeated it several times, running in and out of the fort with all freedom, "to make the deception more complete;"* and then, rushing in in every direction, took possession of the place without the least resistance.

They murdered the soldiers, until their numbers were so diminished, that they apprehended nothing from their resistance; many of whom were ransomed at Montreal afterwards, at a great price. Seventy were put to death, and the other twenty reserved for slaves. A few days after, a boat from Montreal, without knowing what had happened, came ashore with English passengers, who all fell into the hands of the Indians. *Pontiac* was not personally concerned in this affair, but it was a part of his design, and, therefore, is very properly here related. A chief named *Menehwehna* was the commander in that affair.†

It was only 15 days from the time the first blow was struck, before *Pontiac* had taken possession of every garrison in the west except three. No less than 10 were, in this short space, reduced. Detroit alone remained in that distant region, and, as will presently be seen, this was brought to the very brink of the most awful precipice of which the imagination can conceive. The names of those captured at this time were Le Boeuf, Venango, Presq' Isle, on or near Lake Erie; La Bay, upon Lake Michigan; St. Joseph's, upon the river of that name; Miamis, upon the Miami River; Ouachtanon, upon the Ouabache; Sandusky, upon Lake Junundat; and Michilimakinak.‡

The garrison at Detroit was closely besieged by *Pontiac,* in person, before the news of the massacre of Fort Michilimakinak arrived there. It was garrisoned by about 300 men, and when *Pontiac* came with his warriors, although in great numbers, they were so intermixed with women and children, and brought so many commodities for trade, that no suspicion was excited, either in the mind of Major *Gladwin,* or the inhabitants. He encamped a little distance from the fort, and sent to the major to inform him that he was come to trade, and, preparatory thereto, wished to hold a talk with him for the purpose of "brightening the chain of peace" between the English and his people. No suspicion was yet entertained, and the major readily consented, and the next morning was fixed upon for the council.

The same evening, a circumstance transpired which saved the garrison from a dreadful massacre. An Indian woman, who had made a pair of moccasins for Major *Gladwin,* out of a curious elk skin, brought them to him, and returned the remainder of the skin. Being much pleased with them, the major wished her to take the skin and make another pair, as he had concluded to give the others to a friend, and what was left to make into shoes for herself. She was then paid for her work, and dismissed. But when those whose duty it was to see that the fort was clear of strangers, and to close the gates for the night, went upon their duty, this woman was found loitering in the area, and, being asked what she wanted, made no reply. The major, being informed of her singular demeanor, directed her to be conducted into his presence, which being done, he asked her why she did not depart before the gates were shut. She replied, with some hesitation, that she did not wish to take away the skin, as he set so great a value upon it. This answer was delivered in such a manner, that the major was rather dissatisfied with it, and asked her why she had not made the same objection on taking it in the first

* *Carver's* Travels, 19, 20. edit. 8vo. Lond. 1784.

† *Henry's* Travels, ut supra.

‡ *Bouquet's* Ohio Expedition, Int. iii.

place. This rather confused her, and she said that if she took it away now, she never should be able to return it.

It was now evident that she withheld something which she wished to communicate, but was restrained through fear. But on being assured by Major *Gladwin* that she should not be betrayed, but should be protected and rewarded, if the information was valuable, she said that the chiefs who were to meet him in council the next day had contrived to murder him, and take the garrison, and put all the inhabitants to death. Each chief, she said, would come to the council, with so much cut off of his gun, that he could conceal it under his blanket; that *Pontiac* was to give the signal, while delivering his speech, which was, when he should draw his peace belt of wampum, and present it to the major in a certain manner; and that, while the council was sitting, as many of the warriors as could should assemble within the fort, armed in the same manner, under the pretence of trading with the garrison.

Having got all the information necessary, the woman was discharged, and Major *Gladwin* had every precaution taken to put the garrison into the best possible state for defence. He imparted the discovery to his men, and instructed them how to act at the approaching council; at the same time sending to all the traders in different directions to be upon their guard.

The next morning having arrived, every countenance wore a different aspect; the hour of the council was fast approaching, and the quick step and nervous exercise in every evolution of the soldiers were expressive of an approaching event, big with their destiny. It was heightened in the past night, when a cry was heard in the Indian encampment different from what was usual on peace occasions. The garrison fires were extinguished, and every man repaired to his post. But the cry being heard no more, the remainder of the night was passed in silence.

The appointed hour of ten o'clock arrived, and also as punctual arrived *Pontiac* and his 36 chiefs, followed by a train of warriors. When the stipulated number had entered the garrison, the gates were closed. The chiefs observed attentively the troops under arms, marching from place to place; two columns nearly enclosing the council house, and both facing towards it. On *Pontiac's* entering it, he demanded of Major *Gladwin* the cause of so much parade, and why his men were under arms; he said it was an odd manner of holding a council. The major told him it was only to exercise them. The Indians being seated upon the skins prepared for them, *Pontiac* commenced his speech, and when he came to the signal of presenting the belt, the governor and his attendants drawing their swords half out of their scabbards, and the soldiers clinching their guns with firmness, discovered to the chiefs, by their peculiar attitudes, that their plot was discovered. *Pontiac,* with all his bravery, turned pale, and every chief showed signs of astonishment. To avoid an open detection, the signal in passing the belt was not given, and *Pontiac* closed his speech, which contained many professions of respect and affection to the English. But when Major *Gladwin* commenced his, he did not fail directly to reproach *Pontiac* with treachery; told him he could not do any thing to ensnare the English, and that he knew his whole diabolical plan. *Pontiac* tried to excuse himself, and to make Major *Gladwin* believe that he had laid no plot; upon which the major stepped to the chief nearest himself, and, drawing aside his blanket, exposed his short gun, which completed their confusion.

The governor, for such was Major *Gladwin,* ordered *Pontiac* to leave the fort immediately, for it would be with difficulty he could restrain his men from cutting him in pieces, should they know the circumstances. The governor was afterwards blamed for thus suffering them to withdraw, without retaining several of them as hostages for the quiet behavior of the rest; but he, having passed his word that they should come and go without hinderance or restraint, merited, perhaps, less censure for keeping it, and respecting his honor, than those who reproached him.

A furious attack was the next day made upon the fort. Every stratagem was resorted to. At one time they filled a cart with combustibles, and run it against the pickets, to set them on fire. At another, they were about to set fire to the church, by shooting fiery arrows into it; but religious scruples averted the execution,—a French priest telling *Pontiac* that it would call down the anger of God upon him. They had frequently, during the siege, endeavored to cut down the pickets so as to make a breach. Major *Gladwin* ordered his men, at last, to cut on the inside at the same time, and assist them. This was done, and when a breach was made, there was a rush upon the outside towards the breach, and at the same instant, a brass four pounder, which had been levelled for the purpose, was shot off, which made a dreadful slaughter among them. After this they merely blockaded the fort, and cut off its supplies, and the English were reduced to the greatest distress, and for some time subsisted upon half rations.

There was great difficulty in throwing succor into the garrison at Detroit, as there was such an extent of country between it and the other most western posts, in possession of the English. Fort Pitt and Niagara had been besieged, and all communication for a long time cut off; the former had been reduced to great extremities, but they were at length relieved by Col. *Bouquet*. Capt. *Dalyell* was at the same time sent for the relief of Detroit, where he arrived on 29 July, 1763.* A bloody scene was shortly to follow. Captain *Dalyell*, with 247 men, went out of the fort to surprise *Pontiac* in his camp; but the wary chief had runners out, who gave him timely notice, and he met them in an advantageous place, and, being vastly superior in numbers, and concealed behind a picket fence, near a bridge where the English were to pass, poured in upon them a dreadful fire. Many fell at the first onset, but they kept their order, and exerted themselves to regain the bridge they had just passed. They effected their purpose, but many fell in the attempt, among whom was Captain *Dalyell*. The famous Major *Rogers*, the second in command, and Lieut. Brehm, with about 200 others, recovered the fort. This bridge, where so many brave men were slain, is called to this day Bloody Bridge.

Pontiac ordered the head of Captain *Dalyell* to be cut off and set upon a post. Between eighty and a hundred dead bodies were counted upon the bridge the next morning, which entirely blocked up its passage.

Having been put in possession of the official return of Sir *Jeffery Amherst*, minutely detailing this affair, we will lay it before the reader, as it appeared at that time:—

"On the evening of the 30th of July, Captain *Dalyell*, aid-de-camp to General *Amherst*, being arrived here with the detachment sent under his command, and being fully persuaded that *Pontiac*, the Indian chief, with his tribes, would soon abandon his design, and retire, insisted with the commandant, that they might easily be surprised in their camp, totally routed, and driven out of the settlement; and it was thereupon determined, that Captain *Dalyell* should march out with 247 men. Accordingly, we marched about half an hour after two in the morning, two deep, along the great road by the river side, two boats up the river along shore, with a patteraro in each, with orders to keep up with the line of march, cover our retreat, and take off our killed and wounded; Lieutenant *Bean*, of the *Queen's Independents*, being ordered, with a rear guard, to convey the dead

* *Bouquet's* Expedition, Introd. iv.

and wounded to the boats. About a mile and a half from the fort, we had orders to form into platoons, and, if attacked in the front, to fire by street-firings. We then advanced, and, in about a mile farther, our advanced guard, commanded by Lieut. *Brown,* of the 55th regiment, had been fired upon so close to the enemy's breastworks and cover, that the fire, being very heavy, not only killed and wounded some of his party, but reached the main body, which put the whole into a little confusion; but they soon recovered their order, and gave the enemy, or rather their works, it being very dark, a discharge or two from the front, commanded by Captain *Gray.* At the same time, the rear, commanded by Captain *Grant,* were fired upon from a house, and some fences about twenty yards on his left; on which he ordered his own and Captain *Hopkins's* companies to face to the left, and give a full fire that way. After which, it appearing that the enemy gave way every where, Captain *Dalyell* sent orders to Captain *Grant,* to take possession of the above-said houses and fences; which he immediately did; and found in one of the said houses two men, who told him, the enemy had been there long, and were well apprized of our design. Captain *Grant* then asked them the numbers; they said, above 300; and that they intended, as soon as they had attacked us in the front, to get between us and the fort; which Captain *Grant* told Captain *Dalyell,* who came to him when the firing was over. And in about an hour after, he came to him again, and told Captain *Grant* he was to retire, and ordered him to march in the front, and post himself in an orchard. He then marched, and about half a mile farther on his retreat, he had some shots fired on his flank; but got possession of the orchard, which was well fenced; and just as he got there, he heard a warm firing in the rear, having, at the same time, a firing on his own post, from the fences and corn-fields behind it. Lieutenant *M'Dougal,* who acted as adjutant to the detachment, came up to him, (Captain *Grant,*) and told him, that Captain *Dalyell* was killed, and Captain *Gray* very much wounded, in making a push on the enemy, and forcing them out of a strong breastwork of cord wood, and an intrenchment which they had taken possession of; and that the command then devolved upon him. Lieut. *Bean* immediately came up, and told him, that Captain *Rogers* had desired him to tell Captain *Grant,* that he had taken possession of a house, and that he had better retire with what numbers he had, as he (Captain *Rogers)* could not get off without the boats to cover him, he being hard pushed by the enemy from the enclosures behind him, some of which scoured the road through which he must retire. Captain *Grant* then sent Ensign *Pauli,* with 20 men, back to attack a part of the enemy which annoyed his own post a little, and galled those that were joining him, from the place where Captain *Dalyell* was killed, and Captain *Gray,* Lieutenants *Brown* and *Luke,* were wounded; which Ensign *Pauli* did, and killed some of the enemy in their flight. Captain *Grant,* at the same time, detached all the men he could get, and took possession of the enclosures, barns, fences, &c. leading from his own post to the fort, which posts he reinforced with the officers and men as they came up. Thinking the retreat then secured, he sent back to Captain *Rogers,* desiring he would come off; that the retreat was quite secured, and the different parties ordered to cover one another successively, until the whole had joined; but Captain *Rogers* not finding it right to risk the loss of more men, he chose to wait for the armed boats, one of which appeared soon, commanded by Lieutenant *Brehm,* whom Captain *Grant* had directed to go and cover Captain Rogers's retreat, who was in the next house. Lieut. *Brehm* accordingly went, and fired several shots at the enemy. Lieut. *Abbott,* with the other boat, wanting ammunition, went down with Capt. *Gray.* Lieutenant *Brown* and some wounded men returned also, which

Captain *Grant* supposes the enemy seeing, did not wait her arrival, but retired on Lieutenant *Brehm's* firing, and gave Captain *Rogers,* with the rear, an opportunity to come off: so that the whole from the different posts joined without any confusion, and marched to the fort in good order, covered by the armed boats on the water side, and by our own parties on the country side, in view of the enemy, who had all joined, and were much stronger than at the beginning of the affair, as was afterwards told us by some prisoners that made their escape; many having joined them from the other side the river, and other places. The whole arrived at the fort about eight o'clock, commanded by Captain *Grant,* whose able and skilful retreat is highly commended.

Return of killed and wounded of the several detachments near the Detroit, July 31, 1763.

55*th Regiment.*—1 serjeant, 13 rank and file, *killed*; 1 captain, 2 lieutenants, 1 drummer, 28 rank and file, *wounded.*
Royal Americans.—1 rank and file, *killed;* 1 rank and file, *wounded.*
80*th Regiment.*—2 rank and file, *killed;* 3 rank and file, *wounded.*
Queen's Rangers.—2 rank and file, *killed*; 1 rank and file, *wounded.*

Names of the Officers.

55*th Regiment.*—Captain *Gray,* Lieutenant *Luke,* and Lieutenant Brown, wounded.
N. B. Captain *Dalyell,* killed, not included in the above.

	killed.	wounded.
Captain,	0	1
Lieutenants,	0	2
Serjeant,	1	0
Drummer,	0	1
Rank and file,	18	38
Total,	19	42"

Hence it appears that the accounts hitherto circulated of this famous action contain material errors; at least, they differ materially from that furnished by those engaged in it.

About this time several small vessels fell into the hands of *Pontiac,* which were destined to supply the garrison, and the men were cruelly treated. The garrison was in great straits, both from the heavy loss of men, as well as from want of provisions and continual watching. In this time of despondency, there arrived near the fort a schooner, which brought them supplies of provisions, but nothing of this kind could be landed without *Pontiac's* knowledge, and he determined, if possible, to seize the schooner; a detachment made the attempt, and, to save herself, the vessel was obliged to tack short about, and proceed in an opposite direction. The Indians followed her in canoes, and, by continually firing into her, killed almost every man, and at length boarded her. As they were climbing up the sides and shrouds in every quarter, the captain, having determined not to fall into their hands alive, ordered the gunner to set fire to the magazine, and blow all up together. This was heard by a Huron chief, who understood enough English to know what was going forward, and instantly communicated it to his followers. They disengaged themselves from the vessel as fast as possible, and fled from her in a great fright, at considerable distance. Meantime the crew took the advantage of a wind, and arrived safe back to the fort. In the pursuit of the vessel, the Indians discovered extreme temerity, often coming so close to the schooner as to be severely burned by the discharge of her guns.

Many other circumstances are related of this famous siege, but it is believed the preceding are all that are well authenticated.

Pontiac having invested Detroit now for about twelve months, and the news having been carried to various parts of the British empire, extensive preparations were made to put down the Indian power. Aware of the movements of General *Bradstreet,* who was proceeding for Detroit with an army of 3000 men, he gave up, and sued for peace, which was granted him, and his warriors retired to their hunting grounds. He seems now to have laid aside all resentment against the English, and became their friend; and to reward his attachment, the government granted him a liberal pension. But it is reported that he became suspected afterwards, and as he was going to hold a council among the Indians in Illinois, as an agent for the English, a spy attended him to observe his conduct; and that, in a speech, he betrayed the English, and discovered his former enmity against them. When he had finished, the Indian who had accompanied him plunged a knife into his breast, and thus ended the days of a chief who has been renowned for singular sagacity, daring courage, great spirit of command, and indeed numerous other qualities, found only in those born to be great.

CHAPTER IV

CAPT. PIPE—*Situation of affairs on the frontiers at the period of the revolution—Sad condition of the Moravian Indians at this period—Half-king engages to take them to Canada—His speech to them—They remonstrate—Half-king inclines not to molest them, but Capt. Pipe's counsel prevails, and they are seized—Pipe's conduct thereupon—Missionaries taken to Detroit and examined—Pipe went to accuse them—Changes his conduct towards them, and they are acquitted—Remarkable deliverance—Capt.* WHITE-EYES, *or Koquethagaeehlon, opposes the conduct of Pipe—His speech to his people—Col. Broadhead's expedition—Brutal massacre of a chief*—PACHGANTSCIHILAS—*Surprises the missionaries—His speech to them—Treats them with great kindness*—GELELEMEND—BUOKONGAHELAS—*Murder of Major Trueman and others disapproved by him—His speech to the murderers—In the battle of Presque-Isle—His death—His great intrepidity—Further particulars of Capt. Pipe—His famous speech—Expedition and defeat of Col. Crawford, who was taken prisoner and burnt at the stake*—CHIKTOMMO—TOM-LEWIS—MESSHAWA—KING-CRANE—LITTLE-TURTLE—*Defeats Gen. St. Clair's army—Incidents in that affair—Little-turtle's opinion of Gen. Wayne—Visits Philadelphia—His interview with C. F. Volney—Anecdotes*—BLUE-JACKET—*Defeated by Gen. Wayne in the battle of Presque-Isle.*

Pipe, or Captain *Pipe,** as he is usually called, from his having been a most conspicuous war-captain among the Delawares, during the period of the revolution, in particular, was chief of the Wolf tribe. His character is a very prominent one, in the memorable troubles among the frontier settlements, at the breaking out of the war. Situated as were the Dela-

* A chief of this name signed a treaty at Fort Greenville, in 1814, with 112 others, by which it seems the Delawares perpetuated it. It followed that of *White-eyes.*

wares between the English of Canada and the Americans, it was hardly to be expected but that they should be drawn into that war. They could not well weigh its merits or demerits upon either side. A speech of the renowned *Corn-plant* contains the best commentary upon this matter. The English stood much the best chance of gaining the Indians to their interest, inasmuch as they were profuse in their presents of what was useful to them, as well as ornamental, whereas the Americans required all their resources to carry on the war. The commanding officer at Detroit, believing that the Moravian Indians upon the Susquehannah favored the Americans, ordered them, dead or alive, with their priests, to be brought into Canada. The Iroquois agreed that it should be done, but, unwilling to do it themselves, sent messengers to the Chippeways and Ottawas, to intimate that if they would do it, "they should have them to make soup of." These two tribes, however, refused, and the *Half-king* of the Hurons undertook it himself. He had been formerly very friendly to the believing Indians, and now pretended that he only concluded to seize upon them, to save them from destruction; and, Mr. Loskiel adds, "even the *Half-king* would certainly never have agreed to commit this act of injustice, had not the Delaware, Capt. *Pipe*, a noted enemy of the gospel and of the believing Indians, instigated him to do it." Pipe and his company of Delawares, joined by *Half-king* and his warriors, and some Shawanese, held a war-feast, roasted a whole ox, and agreed upon the manner of proceeding. The captains only of this expedition knew fully its destination. With such secrecy did they proceed, that the Moravian settlements knew nothing of their approach, until they were in their vicinity. They bore an English flag, and an English officer was among them. It was now 10 August, 1781. *Half-king* sent in a message to Salem, requesting the inhabitants not to be alarmed, for they should receive no injury, and that he had good words to speak to them, and wished to know at which of the settlements they might hold a council with them. Gnadenhuetten being fixed upon, all assembled there upon 11 August.

Meanwhile, the numbers of *Pipe's* expedition had increased from 140 to 300, and about 10 days after, *Half-king* made the following speech to the believing Indians and their teachers:—

"Cousins: ye believing Indians in Gnadenhuetten, Schoenbrunn, and Salem, I am much concerned on your account, perceiving that you live in a very dangerous spot. Two powerful, angry and merciless gods stand ready, opening their jaws wide against each other: you are sitting down between both, and thus in danger of being devoured and ground to powder by the teeth of either one or the other, or both. It is therefore not advisable for you to stay here any longer. Consider your young people, your wives, and your children, and preserve their lives, for here they must all perish. I therefore take you by the hand, lift you up, and place you in or near my dwelling, where you will be safe and dwell in peace. Do not stand looking at your plantations and houses, but arise and follow me! Take also your teachers [priests] with you, and worship God in the place to which I shall lead you, as you have been accustomed to do. You shall likewise find provisions, and our father beyond the lake [the governor at Detroit,] will care for you. This is my message, and I am come hither purposely to deliver it."

The brethren, after taking this into consideration, remonstrated, in feeling language, against such an immediate removal; saying they did not conceive that the danger was so great, as, moreover, they were at peace with all men, and took no part in the war, and that it would bring famine and distress upon them, to set out before their harvest with nothing in their hands, but that they would keep and consider his words, and would answer him the next winter. It was supposed that Half-king was willing to comply, but for the importunity of *Pipe* and the English captain.

This affair eventuated in the seizure of the missionaries and their removal to Sandusky, as has been written in the account of *Glikhikan.*

Capt. *Pipe* now publicly boasted of his exploit, and said the Indians and their priests were his slaves. They had had but a moment's repose at Sandusky, when the governor at Detroit ordered Capt. *Pipe* to conduct them to him. They were glad of an opportunity of seeing the governor face to face, believing they could convince him that they had never assisted the Americans, and accordingly attended *Pipe* thither. Here the missionaries *Zeisberger, Senseman, Heckewelder* and *Edwards* had to await a kind of trial, and Pipe was the evidence against them. On the 9 November, this trial or examination came on, and Capt. Pipe appeared, and spoke as follows: "*Father, you have commanded us to bring the believing Indians and their teachers from the Muskingum. This has been done. When we had brought them to Sandusky, you ordered us to bring their teachers and some of their chiefs unto you. Here you see them before you: now you may speak with them yourself, as you have desired. But I hope you will speak good words unto them, yea I tell you, speak good words unto them, for they are my friends, and I should be sorry to see them ill used.*" The governor then repeated to Pipe the charges he had formerly urged against the brethren, and called on him to prove his assertions. The chief seemed now evidently confused, and said such things might have happened, but they would do so no more, for they were now at Detroit. This did not satisfy the governor, and he peremptorily demanded that Pipe should answer positively to the point. This caused him still greater embarrassment, and he asked his counsellors what he should say, but each held down his head in silence, and this occasioned his choosing the only wise course, and he thus ingenuously spoke: "*I said before, that some such thing might have happened, but now I will tell you the plain truth. The missionaries are innocent. They have done nothing of themselves: what they have done, they were compelled to do. I am to blame, and the chiefs that were with me in Goschachguenk: we have forced them to do it, when they refused.*" The governor now declared them innocent, in the presence of the court, and they were permitted to return to their brethren.

One circumstance, illustrative of savage superstition, we will notice here. When *Pipe's* warriors were about to force the brethren to leave their dwellings, it was almost unanimously concluded at one time by the chiefs, that the white brethren should be put to death. They, however, would not adventure upon such a deed without the advice of one of their common warriors, who was considered a great sorcerer. His answer was, "he could not understand what end it would answer to kill them." Upon this, the chiefs held a council, in which it was resolved to kill not only the white brethren and their wives, but the Indian assistants also. When they made this resolution known to the sorcerer, he said to them, "Then you have resolved to kill my friends; for most of their chief people are my friends: but this I tell you, that if you hurt any one of them, I know what I will do!" This threat deterred them: thus were the missionaries as well as many others saved.

It is stated by Mr. *Heckewelder,* that, notwithstanding Capt. *Pipe* was so eager for the war before its commencement, he soon became sorry for it afterwards. This might have been the case; and yet he was one of the most efficient enemies of the Americans after the peace, as will elsewhere appear. Capt. *White-eyes,* or *Koquethagaeehlon,* which was his Indian name,* was his particular friend, and they were both great men of the

* According to Mr. *Heckewelder.* His residence was at the mouth of the Big Beaver.

Delaware nation, having been nearly alike distinguished by their courage on many occasions. No one could have more at heart the welfare of their country, than Capt. *White-eyes* had that of the Delaware nation, and it is not pretended, but that as much should be said of Capt. *Pipe;* but they were differently circumstanced, and the former was open and fearless in his declarations in favor of the Americans, while the latter secretly favored the British. Thus they were unwillingly opposed to each other, and for about two years, one by his frankness and the other by his clandestine operations, strove to unite and strengthen their respective parties.

Meanwhile a circumstance happened, which Capt. Pipe seized upon for declaring war. *M'Kee, Elliot, Girty,* and several others, had been held at Pittsburg as tories. Early in the spring of 1778, they made an escape, and fled into the Indian country, and, as they went, proclaimed to that people, that the Americans had determined to destroy them; that therefore their only safety consisted in repelling them; that they must fly to arms, and fight them in every place. *Pipe,* being rather inclined to war, believed all that those exasperated fugitives said; while, on the other hand, *White-eyes* would give no credit to them. Having got many of his men together, Capt. *Pipe* addressed them with great earnestness, and with great force of oratory said, "Every man is an enemy to his country, who endeavors to persuade us against fighting the Americans, and all such ought surely to be put to death." Capt. *White-eyes* was not idle, and at the same time had assembled the people of his tribe, and the substance of what he said was, "that if they [any of his warriors] meant in earnest to go out, as he observed some of them were preparing to do, they should not go without him. He had, he said, taken peace measures in order to save the nation from utter destruction. But if they believed that he was in the wrong, and gave more credit to vagabond fugitives, whom he knew to be such, than to himself, who was best acquainted with the real state of things; if they had determined to follow their advice, and go out against the Americans, he would go out with them; but not like the bear hunter, who sets the dogs on the animal to be beaten about with his paws, while he keeps at a safe distance; no! he would lead them on, place himself in the front, and be the first who should fall. THEY only had to determine on what they meant to do; as for his own mind, it was fully made up, not to survive his nation; and he would not spend the remainder of a miserable life, in bewailing the total destruction of a brave people, who deserved a better fate."

This speech was spoken with a pathos and in a manner calculated to touch the hearts of all who listened to it, and its impression was such, that all unanimously came to the determination to obey its instructions and orders, and to hear or receive directions from no other person, of any nation or color, but Capt. *White-eyes.*

At the same time, Capt. *White-eyes,* in order to counteract, as much as possible, the evil counsel of the white men just mentioned, despatched runners to the Shawanese towns on the Scioto, where these impostors had gone, with the following speech: "Grandchildren, ye Shawanese, some days ago, a flock of birds, that had come on from the east, lit at Goschochking, imposing a song of theirs upon us, which song had nigh proved our ruin. Should these birds, which on leaving us, took their flight towards Scioto, endeavor to impose a song on you likewise, do not listen to them, for they lie!"

A knowledge of the proceedings of Capt. *White-eyes* having reached *Pipe,* he knew not what course to take, and, while thus confounded, a kind and conciliatory message was received in the Delaware nation, from the American agent of Indian affairs at Pittsburg. It particularly cautioned the people of that nation "*not to hearken to those wicked and worthless men, who had run away from their friends in the night, and to be assured of the real friendship of the United States.*" This completed *Pipe's* confusion. But after pondering a while upon the wrongs to which his countrymen had for a long time been subjected, like the sachem of the Wampanoags, he permitted his warriors to go out, and surprise, and murder all the Americans they could lay their hands upon.

Blood having now begun to flow, barbarities followed in quick succession. Early in the spring of 1781, Col. *Broadhead* arrived near the Moravian town of Salem, and notified the inhabitants that he was on an expedition against the hostile Indians, and gave them that timely notice that they might collect their people, if any were abroad, that they might not be taken for enemies. "However," says Mr. *Heckewelder,* "whilst the colonel was assuring me that our Indians had nothing to fear, an officer came with great speed from one quarter of the camp, and reported that a particular division of the militia 'were preparing to break off for the purpose of destroying the Moravian settlements up the river, and he feared they could not be restrained from so doing.'" They were, however, by the exertions of the commander in chief, aided by Col. *Shepherd,* of Wheeling, prevented from their murderous design. Thus these Christian Indians were situated precisely like many of those of N. E. in Philip's war. But we have no instance to record, of the latter, equal in extent, for diabolical atrocity, to that of the massacre of Gnadenhuetten, elsewhere mentioned.

Meanwhile Col. *Broadhead* proceeded to Coshocton, a hostile settlement near the forks of the Muskingum; and with such secrecy did he proceed, that not a person escaped. How many fell into the hands of the army is not mentioned; but, not long after, 16 warriors were put to death with shocking manifestations of depravity. There accompanied Col. *Broadhead's* army a Delaware chief named *Pekillon.** Sixteen of the captive warriors were designated by him as perpetrators of murders, and they were forthwith tomahawked and scalped. They were executed pursuant to the decree of a court-martial.

Some extenuation has been urged for this revolting transaction, and that alone in which, perhaps, the mind can find any relief. But a short time before *Broadhead's* expedition, a large Indian force, called by the whites an army, collected, and set out for the destruction of North-western Virginia. This army was divided into two parts, and their expectations were wrought up to a very high degree, which, when suddenly blasted, were changed into rage and fury. Having, in their march, taken a large number of captives, they retreated to a place of safety, and there tied them to trees and put them to death in their barbarous manner. This massacre was, however, confined to their male prisoners. Fathers, in presence of their families, were led forth to execution, amid tears and lamentations, which no creature but infuriated man could withstand. This barbarity was the more aggravating, when it was contemplated that those who fell into their hands had made no resistance! Nothing, therefore, like just retribution was to be expected from an army of frontier militia, when vengeance was the only pursuit.

After every thing had been destroyed in the Indian country through which the Americans passed, they returned to Pittsburg. Before leaving Coshocton, a shocking circumstance occurred, which alone was sufficient to have tarnished the most brilliant exploits. An Indian came to the side of the river over against the encampment, and called to the sentinels, who asked him what he wanted. He answered that he wished to see the big captain, (the name by which Indians commonly designate the commander in chief.) Col. *Broadhead* appeared, and asked him what he wanted,

---

* The same who, afterwards, as I conclude, was a party to *Wayne's* treaty.

who replied, "*To make peace.*" Then, said the colonel, send over some of your chiefs. The Indian interrogatively said, "May be you kill?" No, said the colonel, they shall come and go in safety. Hereupon a chief of most elegant appearance crossed to the encampment, and—I hesitate to relate it—while this chief was conversing with the colonel, a monster, of the militia, came up, and with a tomahawk, which he had concealed in his clothes, laid him dead with a single stroke!* Thus the peace which might have been concluded was unhappily suspended, and the war afterwards might well have been expected to exhibit scenes no less bloody than before.

A chief, called *Pachgantschihilas*, distinguished himself upon the frontiers, immediately upon the retreat of Col. *Broadhead's* army; not as many others have, but by magnanimity and address. He was, according to Mr. *Heckewelder,†* the head war chief of the Delaware nation. And subsequently his name was set to many treaties between his nation and the United States, from that of Gen. *Wayne* at Greenville to that of St. Mary's in 1818: if, indeed, *Petchenanalas, Bokongehelas,* and several other variations, stand for the same person.

Petchenanalas, at the head of 80 warriors, appeared suddenly at Gnadenhuetten, surrounding it before day, allowing no one a chance for escape. Not knowing his object, the people were filled with terror. But he soon dispelled their fears, by telling them that he came to take the chief *Gelelemend*, and a few other head men, whom he would have, either dead or alive. As it happened, not one of those he sought after was there at the time. Having satisfied himself of this fact, the chief demanded that deputies from the three Christian towns should meet to hear what he had to say to them. When the deputies and others had met, he spoke to them as follows:—

"Friends and kinsmen, listen to what I say to you. You see a great and powerful nation divided. You see the father fighting against the son, and the son against the father.—The father has called on his Indian children to assist him in punishing his children, the Americans, who have become refractory. I took time to consider what I should do; whether or not I should receive the hatchet of my father, to assist him. At first I looked upon it as a family quarrel, in which I was not interested. At length it appeared to me, that the father was in the right, and his children deserved to be punished a little.—That this must be the case, I concluded from the many cruel acts his offspring had committed, from time to time, on his Indian children—in encroaching on their lands, stealing their property—shooting at and murdering without cause, men, women, and children:—yes, even murdering those, who at all times had been friendly to them, and were placed for protection under the roof of their father's house;‡ the father himself standing sentry at the door, at the time!—Friends and relatives, often has the father been obliged to settle and make amends for the wrongs and mischiefs done us, by his refractory children; yet these do not grow better. No! they remain the same, and will continue to be so, as long as we have any land left us! Look back at the murders committed by the Long Knives on many of our relations, who lived peaceable neighbors to them on the Ohio! Did they not kill them without the least provocation?—Are they, do you think, better now, than they were then? No! indeed not; and many days are not elapsed, since you had a number of these very men near your doors, who panted to kill

---

* Chronicles of Western Settlements, *passim.*
† Narrative, 216.
‡ Alluding to the murder of the Conestoga Indians, which was as atrocious as that at Gnadenhuetten, and of which we shall in due course give a relation.

you, but fortunately were prevented from so doing, by the Great Sun,* who, at that time, had by the Great Spirit been ordained to protect you!"

The chief then spoke with respect of their peaceable mode of life, and commended their desire to live in friendship with all mankind; but said, they must be aware of their exposed situation—living in the very road the hostile parties must pass over, in going to fight each other; that they had just escaped destruction, from one of these parties; that therefore no time should be lost, but they should go to the country on the Miami, where they would be entirely out of danger.

The Christian Indians replied, that, as they had never injured the Americans, they thought they need not fear injury from them; that if their friends at war wished them well, in truth, they would not make their settlement upon the path they took to go to war, as it would lead their antagonists the same way; and that they could not remove without great detriment; and therefore, as they were then situated, they could not consent to go.

Pachgantschihilas consulted in the mean time with his chief men, and answered very feelingly to what the brethren had said. He observed that he was sorry that they should differ from him in opinion, but that he had no intention to use compulsion, and only requested that those might be permitted to go, whose fears prompted them to it. This was readily assented to, and the council broke up, and the warriors departed. At Salem they made a short stay, where they conducted themselves as they had done at Gnadenhuetten. Here a family of old people joined them, through fear of what *Pachgantschihilas* had predicted, and the event justified the proceeding! The massacre of Gnadenhuetten will ever be remembered with the deepest regret and indignation.

Nothing was feared from the good *Petchenanalas;* but the prowling monsters *M'Kee, Girty, Elliot,* and perhaps others, calling themselves white, were the plotters of the ruin of the innocent people at Gnadenhuetten, which followed not long after.

Our present design makes it expedient that we pass over many events in the chronicles of the frontier wars, that we may be enabled to proceed with more minuteness of detail, in the lives of the eminent chiefs. Although we cannot, by any rule known to us, derive *Buokongahelas* from *Pachgantscihilas* or *Petchenanalas,* yet, as they have as much affinity as *Pometacom* and *Metacomet,* we shall let them pass for the same person, and thus continue our narrative.

Buokongahelas was not only a great, but a noble warrior. He took no delight in shedding blood; and when he raised the hatchet on the side of the British in the revolution, it was for the best of reasons; and would that numerous other allies we could name had acted from as pure motives. Our next notice of *Buokongahelas* is in 1792, when he showed himself no less magnanimous than at Gnadenhuetten and Salem. Col. *Hardin*, Major *Trueman*, and several others, were sent, in May of this year, with a flag of truce, to the Indian nations of the west, particularly the Maumee towns. They having arrived near the Indian town of Au Glaize on the S. W. branch of the Miami of the Lake, fell in with some Indians, who treated them well at first, and made many professions of friendship, but in the end took advantage of them, while off their guard, and murdered nearly all of them. The interpreter made his escape, after some time, and gave an account of the transaction. His name was *William Smally*; and he had been some time before with the Indians, and had learned their manners and customs, which gave him some advantage in being able to save himself. He was at first conducted to Au Glaize, and soon

* Referring to what we have just related of Col. *Daniel Broadhead* and his army.

after to *"Buokungahela,* king of the Delawares, by his captors." The chief told those that committed the murder, *he was very sorry they had killed the men. That instead of so doing, they should have brought them to the Indian towns; and then, if what they had to say had not been liked, it would have been time enough to have killed them then. Nothing,* he said, *could justify them for putting them to death, as there was no chance for them to escape.* The truth was, they killed them to plunder their effects. *Buokongahelas* 'took Mr. *Smally* into his cabin, and showed him great kindness; told him to stay there while he could go safely to his former Indian friends. (He having been adopted into an Indian family, in place of one who had been killed, in his former captivity.) While here with *Buokongahelas,* which was near a month, Mr. *Smally* said the chief would not permit him to go abroad alone, for fear, he said, that the young Indians would kill him. Thus, though we do not meet often with *Buokongahelas,* but when we do, the interview is no less honorable to him, than in the instances we have given.

It is said that the conduct of the British, at the battle of Presque Isle, forever changed the mind of this chief, as it did that of many others, in regard to them. *Buokongahelas* said he would henceforth trust them no more. The fort at Maumee was critically situated, but by its own imprudence. The officers of it had told the Indians that if the battle turned against them, they should have protection in the fort. Immediately after, Gen. *Wayne* informed them, that if they did protect the Indians in that event, he would treat them as though found in arms against him; therefore, thinking their own safety of more consequence than keeping their faith with the Indians, they barred the gates, and were idle spectators of those they had basely betrayed, cut down in great numbers by the swords of the horsemen, under their very ramparts!

It would seem from a passage in the Memoirs of Gen. *Harrison,** that *Buokongahelas* died soon "after the treaty of 1804;" that if he had been alive, Mr. *Dawson* thinks, when *Tecumseh* and the *Prophet* enlisted so many nations against the Americans, he would not have suffered their plans to have been matured. The same author relates an incident of peculiar interest, concerning our subject, which is as follows:—After the fight with *Wayne's* army before mentioned, *Buokongahelas* collected the remnant of his band, and embarked with them in canoes, and passed up the river, to send a flag of truce to Fort *Wayne.* When the chief arrived against the British fort, he was requested to land, which he did. When he had approached the sentinel, he demanded, "*What have you to say to me*?" He was answered that the commandant desired to speak with him. "Then he may come HERE," was the reply. The sentry then said the officer would not do that, and that he would not be allowed to pass the fort, if he did not comply with its rules. "*What shall prevent me*?" said the intrepid chief. Pointing to the cannon of the fort, the sentry said, "Those." The chief replied indignantly, "*I fear not your cannon: after suffering the Americans to defile your spring, without daring to fire on them, you cannot expect to frighten* BUOKONGEHELAS ." He reëmbarked, and passed the fort, without molestation. By "defiling their spring," he meant an ironical reproach to the British garrison for their treachery to the Indians, which has been mentioned.

It is said that Buokongahelas was present at Fort M'Intosh, at the treaty of 1785; but as his name is not among the signers, we suppose he was opposed to it. Gen. *George R. Clark, Arthur Lee,* and *Richard Butler,* were the American commissioners; the former had been a successful warrior against the Indians, which had gained him the respect of *Buokon-*

* By Mr. *Dawson,* page 82.

gahelas; and when he had an opportunity, he passed the others without noticing them, but went and took Gen. *Clark* by the hand, and said, "*I thank the Great Spirit for having this day brought together two such great warriors, as* BUOKONGAHELAS *and* GEN. CLARK."

A separate article in the treaty just named, illustrates the history of several chiefs already mentioned. It is in these words:—"It is agreed that the Delaware chiefs *Kelelamand*, [Gelelemend, Killbuck,] or Col. *Henry*; *Hengue-pushees*, or the *Big-cat*; *Wicocalind*, or Capt. *White-eyes;* who took up the hatchet for the United States, and their families, shall be received into the Delaware nation, in the same situation and rank as before the war, and enjoy their due portions of the lands to the Wyandot and Delaware nations in this treaty, as fully as if they had not taken part with America." We shall have occasion again to consider further some of the characters which we have but incidentally mentioned here. For the present, we will proceed with some matters of deep interest in the life of Capt. *Pipe*.

At one time, after an expedition against the Americans, Capt. *Pipe* went to Detroit, where he was received with respect by the British commandant, who, with his attendants, was invited to the council-house, to give an account of past transactions. He was seated in front of his Indians, facing the chief officer, and held in his left hand a short stick, to which was fastened a scalp. After a usual pause, he arose and spoke as follows:—

"Father, [then he stooped a little, and, turning towards the audience, with a countenance full of great expression, and a sarcastic look, said, in a lower tone of voice,] "I have said FATHER, although, indeed, I do not know WHY I am to call HIM so, having never known any other father than the French, and considering the English only as BROTHERS. But as this name is also imposed upon us, I shall make use of it, and say, [at the same time fixing his eyes upon the commandant,] Father, some time ago you put a war hatchet into my hands, saying, 'Take this weapon and try it on the heads of my enemies, the Long-Knives, and let me afterwards know if it was sharp and good.' Father, at the time when you gave me this weapon, I had neither cause nor inclination to go to war against a people who had done me no injury; yet in obedience to you, who say you are my father, and call me your child, I received the hatchet; well knowing, that if I did not obey, you would withhold from me the necessaries of life, without which I could not subsist, and which are not elsewhere to be procured, but at the house of my father.—You may perhaps think me a fool, for risking my life at your bidding, in a cause too, by which I have no prospect of gaining any thing; for it is your cause and not mine. It is your concern to fight the Long-Knives; you have raised a quarrel amongst yourselves, and you ought yourselves to fight it out. You should not compel your children, the Indians, to expose themselves to danger, for your sakes.—Father, many lives have already been lost on your account!—Nations have suffered, and been weakened!—children have lost parents, brothers, and relatives!—wives have lost husbands!—It is not known how many more may perish before your war will be at an end!—Father, I have said, that you may, perhaps, think me a fool, for thus thoughtlessly rushing on your enemy!—Do not believe this, father: Think not that I want sense to convince me, that although you now pretend to keep up a perpetual enmity to the Long-Knives, you may before long conclude a peace with them.—Father, you say you love your children, the Indians.—This you have often told them, and indeed it is your interest to say so to them, that you may have them at your service. But, father, who of us can believe that you can love a people of a different color from your own, better than those who have a white skin like yourselves? Father, pay attention to what I am going to say. While you, father, are setting me [meaning the Indians in general] on your enemy, much in the same manner as a hunter sets his dog on the game; while I am in the act of rushing on that enemy of yours, with the bloody destructive weapon you gave me, I may, perchance, happen to look back to the place from whence you started me; and what shall I see? Perhaps I may see my father shaking hands with the Long-Knives; yes, with these very people he now calls his enemies. I may then see him laugh at my folly for having obeyed his orders; and yet I am now risking my life at his command! Father, keep what I have said in remembrance.—Now, father, here is what has been done with the hatchet you gave me. [With these words he handed the stick to the commandant, with the scalp upon it, above mentioned.] I have done with the hatchet what you ordered me to do, and found it sharp. Nevertheless, I did not do all that I might have done. No, I did not. My heart failed within me. I felt compassion for your enemy. Innocence [helpless women and children] had no part in your quarrels; therefore I distinguished—I spared. I took some live flesh, which, while I was bringing to you, I spied one of your large canoes, on which I put it for you. In a few days you will recover this flesh, and find that the skin is of the same color with your own. Father, I hope you will not destroy what I have saved. You, father, have the means of preserving that which with me would perish for want. The warrior is poor, and his cabin is always empty; but your house, father, is always full."

After a high encomium upon this speech, which need not be repeated, Mr. *Heckewelder* says, "It is but justice here to say, that *Pipe* was well acquainted with the noble and generous character of the British officer to whom this speech was addressed. He is still living in his own country, an honor to the British name. He obeyed the orders of his superiors in employing the Indians to fight against us; but he did it with reluctance, and softened as much as was in his power the horrors of that abominable warfare. He esteemed Capt. *Pipe,* and, I have no doubt, was well pleased with the humane conduct of this Indian chief, whose sagacity in this instance is no less deserving of praise than his eloquence."

The name of Capt. *Pipe* is unfortunately associated with the history of the lamented Col. *William Crawford,* who perished at the stake, after suffering the most horrible and excruciating tortures possible for Indians to inflict. He was particularly obnoxious to them, from having been many years a successful commander against them. He fell into the hands of the Indians not far from Upper Sandusky, in the latter end of May, 1782. At this time he was arrived there, at the head of a band of about 500 volunteers, who were attacked and put to flight, without having acquitted themselves like soldiers in any degree; except, indeed, some individual instances. At least a hundred were killed and taken, and of the latter, but two are said ever to have escaped.

Capt. *Pipe,* if not the principal, was probably one of the chief leaders of the Indians at this time. When the rout of the army began, instead of retreating in a body, they fled in small parties, and thus fell an easy prey into the hands of their pursuers. Col. *Crawford* became separated from the main body of his soilders, by his extreme anxiety for his son, and two or three other relations, whom he suspected were in the rear, and therefore waited for them an unreasonable time. He at length fled, in company with a Dr. *Knight* and two others. Unfortunately, after travelling nearly two days, they were, with several others, surprised by a party of Delawares, and conducted to the Old Wyandot Town. Here Capt. *Pipe,* with his own hands, painted *Crawford* and *Knight* black in every part of their bodies. A place called the New Wyandot Town was not far off. To this place they were now ordered, and *Pipe* told *Crawford,* that when he arrived there, his head should he shaved; of which, it seems, he did not understand the import. These miserable men were accompanied by

Pipe and another noted Delaware chief, named *Wingenim*. Several other captives had been sent forward; and in the way, as *Knight* and *Crawford* passed along, they saw four of the mangled bodies of their friends, lying upon the ground, dead and scalped. Nine others had been picked up at the same time the two just named were, and four of these were those murdered in the way. The other five met a like fate, from the hands of Indian squaws and boys at the destined village. Here *Crawford* and *Knight* saw *Simon Girty*, of whom no human being since, we apprehend, has spoken or written without indignation. He is represented to have witnessed the torture of *Crawford* with much satisfaction!

After the colonel was tied to the fatal post, Capt. *Pipe* addressed the assembled Indians in an earnest speech, which when he had closed, they all joined in a hideous yell, and fell to torturing the prisoner, which continued for about three hours, when he sunk down upon his face, and with a groan expired.

Dr. *Knight* was reserved for the same fate, and was present, and obliged to hear the agonizing ejaculations of his friend, and at last to see him expire, without being able to render him even the assistance of a consoling word!—Indeed the thoughts of his own condition, and the end that awaited him, were as much, nay, more, perhaps, than a rational mind could bear. There seemed no possibility of a deliverance; but it came in an unexpected hour. He was to be sent to the Sawanee Town, and for this purpose was intrusted to a young warrior, who watched him incessantly. The distance was about 40 miles; and, during their march, he found means to knock down his driver and make good his escape. He was 21 days in the wilderness alone, and was nearly famished when he arrived at Fort M'Intosh. At the place to which he was destined by the Indians, Col. *Crawford's* son, son-in-law, and several others, were put to death about the same time.

The expedition of Col. *Crawford* was not so laudably undertaken as many others, in as far as it was directed against the Moravian towns upon the Muskingum, where *many*, who composed it, were determined that the Christian Indians, which they there expected to find, should glut their vengeance by their blood, as those at Gnadenhuetten had done but a short time before,* as will elsewhere be found noticed. We may again, in a future chapter, extend our account of these affairs, which we pass here, to give place to the events in the life of a noted Shawanese chief, who made himself conspicuous by his successful depredations at this period. This was

Chikatommo. In 1790, he succeeded in capturing many boats upon the Ohio River, killing many of those in them, and taking and destroying a vast amount of property. Among the boats which fell into the hands of *Chikatommo* was one in which was a Mr. *Charles Johnston* of Botetourt county, Virginia, and several others, and from whose narrative we derive much of this information—a book replete with instruction, and one of the most valuable in its kind.† As this company were descending the Ohio, in an unwieldy flat-bottomed boat, in which were a number of horses and considerable merchandise, two white men appeared upon the shore, and called to them, affecting great distress, and begged to be taken

* Our chief authority for these events is the valuable CHRONICLES by Mr. *Withers* before referred to.

† The author appears to have been prompted to its publication by the misinterpretation of his oral communications by the *Duke de Laincourt*; whom, by the way, we do not find to differ so materially, in his account, from the author as one might apprehend from his statement. The chief disagreement appears in such minor points as the spelling of names: thus, in naming the persons captivated, for Skyles he writes *Skuyl;* for Dolly Fleming, *Doly Flamming*; for Flinn, *Phlyn*, &c.

on board. Before these two whites showed themselves however, a smoke was seen above the trees, and for some time held them in doubt on which side of the river it was. They wished to ascertain this fact, as thereby they might keep close in upon the opposite shore, and so escape mischief in the event of an ambushment of Indians. They were thus wary, as the Indians were constantly doing mischief upon the rivers, and had but a short time before destroyed a settlement at a place called Kennedy's Bottom, in Kentucky.

It was before sunrise on the 20 March, that the two white men before mentioned hailed the boat, which was safely out of the reach of fire-arms, having discovered the smoke to be upon the N. W. shore, and therefore they kept upon the S. W. These white men, the more effectually to decoy the boat's crew, said they had been taken prisoners by the Indians at Kennedy's Bottom, and had just escaped from them, and unless they would take them on board they must perish from hunger and cold. The truth was, one or both of them were abandoned wretches, who had leagued with a band of depredators under *Chikatommo,* and thus were the means of destroying many innocent lives in the most atrocious manner. When hailed by them, as we have just said, some in the boat were for listening to them, and some against it. In the mean time, the boat floated fast down the current, and left those on shore considerably in the rear, although they exerted themselves to keep abreast of the boat. Those who were against taking them on board had their objections well grounded; for when these men were asked the occasion of the smoke upon their side of the river, they denied that there had been any, or said they knew of no such thing; and this was urged as a sufficient reason why they should reject the other part of their story. Still, as the boat glided down, those on board debated the subject, and at length concluded, that if there were Indians where they first saw the men, they must then be far up the river, as it was thought impossible that they could have got through the woods so fast as they had floated down; and one of the company, a Mr. *Flinn,* whose kindness of heart brought upon them this calamity, proposed hazarding his own person on shore, without in the least endangering the rest. His plan was as follows: that whereas they must be now out of the reach of the Indians, they should haul in, and barely touch upon the shore, and he would jump out, and the boat should at the same time haul off; so that if Indians should be coming, the boat would have time to get off safe, and as to himself, he could well outrun them, and would get on board the boat again at a certain point below. And thus was the humane plan laid of relieving supposed distress, the sad recompense of which we now proceed to relate.

One circumstance had not been taken into account by this devoted company. The current being rapid, it took them much longer than they had anticipated to gain the shore; and this gave some of the most swift-footed of *Chikatommo's* party time to arrive at the point at the same time with them. Having arrived close to the shore, Mr. *Flinn* had but barely cleared himself from the boat, when a large number of Indians, painted in the most frightful manner, came rushing upon them. Some of the boat's crew seized their guns, and determined to resist, while the others used every means to get their boat from the shore; but every thing seemed to conspire against them. Their boat became entangled in the branches of a large tree, and the whole body of Indians, having arrived, being 54 in number, gave a horrible yell, and poured in their whole fire upon the boat. From the protection afforded by the side of the boat, one only was killed, *Dolly Fleming,* and Mr. *Skyles* wounded. All resistance was vain, and the others lay down upon the bottom of the boat, to prevent being immediately killed. The Indians kept up their fire until all the horses were shot down, which added much to the horror of the situation of those upon the bottom of the boat, as they were great danger of being trampled to death by them before they fell, and afterwards from their strivings. When this was finished, the firing ceased, and Mr. *May* stood up, and held up a white cap in token of surrender; but he fell in a moment after, with a ball shot through his head. Several of the Indians now swam to the boat, and were helped into it by those within. Having now got possession of it, they seemed well pleased, and offered no further violence. All things were now taken on shore, and an immense fire kindled; the dead were scalped, and thrown into the river, and the captives divested of most of their clothes. As several Indians were gathered around Mr. *Johnston* when he was stripped, one, observing that he had on a kind of red vest, approached and said to him in English, "*Oh! you cappatin*?" He said, "No." Then the Indian pointed to his own breast, and said, "*Me cappatin—all dese my sogers.*" This was *Chikatommo*. An Indian, named *Tom Lewis*, discovered much humanity to Mr. *Johnston*, in that he covered him with his own blanket after he had lost his clothes.

Being all stationed about the fire, *Chikatommo* was at one end of it, (it being about 50 feet in length,) who, rising up, made a speech to the multitude. An old Shawanee chief, whose name is not mentioned, made the first speech, at -the. end of which *Chikatommo* conducted *Johnston* to another Shawanee chief, whose name was *Mes-shaw-a*, to whom he was given or assigned, and informed that he was his friend. At the end of *Chikatommo's* speech, another prisoner was disposed of. The same ceremony was repeated with the third and last. *Johnston, Skyle*s and *Flinn* went to the Shawanese, and *Peggy Fleming* to the Cherokees. This band of robbers appears to have been made up of adventurers from the tribes just mentioned, with the addition of a few Delawares. The latter had none of the prisoners, as they did not wish to be known in the business, thinking it might involve their nation in a war with the U. States.

The two white men who had decoyed the boat into the Indians' hands, were still with them, and the next day all the captives were ordered to take a position upon the edge of the river, to decoy the first that should be passing. A boat soon appeared, and, repugnant as such an employment was to the feelings of these captives, yet they were obliged thus to do, or suffer a horrible death. *Divine* and *Thomas* were the names of the two whites so often mentioned: the former was the voluntary agent, and, as Mr. *Johnston* expresses it, the one who "alone had devised and carried into effect their destruction;" and, "ingenious in wicked stratagems, seemed to be perfectly gratified to aid the savages in their views, and to feel no scruples in suggesting means for their accomplishment. He fabricated a tale, that we were passengers down the Ohio, whose boat had suffered so great an injury, that we were unable to proceed until it was repaired; but that for want of an axe, it was impossible for us to do the necessary work. These unsuspecting canoe-men turned towards us; but the current bore them down so far below us, as to preclude all chance of my putting them on their guard. [Mr. *Johnston* having intended by some sign to have given them warning of what awaited them.] The Indians, as they had acted in our case, ran down the river at such a distance from it, and under cover of the woods, that they were not discovered until the canoe was close to the shore, when they fired into it, and shot every one on board. As they tumbled into the water, their little bark was overset. Two, who were not yet dead, kept themselves afloat, but were so severely wounded that they could not swim off. The Indians leaped into the river, and, after dragging them to the shore, despatched them with the tomahawk. The bodies of the four who were killed were also brought to land, and the whole six were scalped. All were then thrown into the river. Nothing I could then learn, or which has since come: to my knowledge, has enabled me to understand who these unfortunate sufferers were."

After various successes and encounters upon the river, *Chikatommo* left it, and met a number of his company at an encampment about five miles from it. Here he left the rest, taking with him a select number and some of the Cherokees, with Miss *Fleming*; and the company with whom *Johnston* remained did not join him again for many days. After much delay and interesting incident, they reached the Indian town of Upper Sandusky. Here they squandered all their rich booty for whiskey, and, as usual, rioted in drunkenness for several days. *Chikatommo* at this time showed himself very savage to the prisoners, and had he not been prevented by the humane and benevolent *Messhawa*,* would have killed some of them. The unfortunate *Skyles* had some time before left them, and gone in an unknown direction with his cruel master.

A French trader at Sandusky, a Mr. *Duchouquet*, had used endeavors to ransom *Johnston*; but his master for some time would hear nothing of it. At length, having dissipated all his booty, and ashamed to return home in such a state, he concluded to sell *Johnston* for the most he could get; and accordingly 600 silver broaches were paid him, equal in value to 100 dollars, the amount agreed upon. *Chikatommo* and his party then took up their march for Detroit. Not long after this, Mr. *Johnston* returned home by way of that place. Before he left Sandusky, he was informed of the burning of the ill-fated *Flinn*: he suffered at the stake at the Miami village, and was eaten by his torturers. The Indian who brought the news to Sandusky, said that he himself had feasted upon him.

King-crane, a Wyandot chief, appears conspicuous in this narrative, and illustrates a valuable trait of character in Indian life. When Mr. *Duchouquet* and *Johnston* had arrived at Lower Sandusky, in their way to Detroit, the town was filled with alarm, and they soon learned the occasion to be from the arrival of some Cherokees in the neighborhood with a female captive. The traders in the place immediately went to their camp, where they found *Peggy Fleming*, who some time before had been separated from *Johnston* and the other captives. Among those who went to see her, was a white man by the name of *Whitaker*, who, having been carried into captivity in his youth, had grown up in all the Indian habits, and being a man of considerable physical powers and enterprise, had become a chief among the Wyandots.† He had been upon the frontiers with the Indians upon trading expeditions, and had lodged at times in Pittsburg in the tavern of Miss *Fleming's* father. She immediately knew him, and besought him, in the most affecting manner, to deliver her from bondage. He went immediately to *King-crane*, and told him that the woman with the Cherokees was his sister,‡ and urged him to use means for her relief. *King-crane* went without loss of time, and urged the Cherokees to restore her to her brother. They were enraged at the request, and there was danger of their murdering her lest she should be taken from them. He next tried to purchase her; but his benevolent offers were indignantly refused, and their rage was still increased. Resolved to rescue her out of their hands, *King-crane* repaired to their camp early the next morning, accompanied with 8 or 10 young warriors. They found the Cherokees asleep, but the captive—it is shocking to humanity to relate—was without the least attire! extended and lashed to the stake!—ready to be burned!—her body painted all over with black.

* Mr. *Johnston*, throughout his narrative, gives him an excellent character. He was alive after the war of 1812 began, and was one of the followers of *Tecumseh*.

† *Hurons* and *Wyandots* are synonymous terms with most writers.

‡ If ever good came out of evil, we should expect it in a case like this.

King-crane silently cut the thongs with which she was bound, then awakened the murderers, and threw down upon the ground the price of a captive in silver broaches, (which are current money among them,) and departed. She was soon after sent forward for her home, disguised in the attire of a squaw. The Cherokees prowled about seeking vengeance upon some white person for a few days, and then disappeared.

The reader may wish to know what became of *Skyles*:—he was taken to a place upon the Miami River, where he was doomed to be burnt, but made his escape the night previous to the day on which he was to have suffered. After enduring the most painful fatigues and hunger, from wandering alone in the wilderness, he met with some traders who conveyed him to Detroit, and from thence home to Virginia.

The sequel of the life of the old hard-hearted *Chikatommo* is as follows: For four years succeeding the events above related, he followed his depredating career, and was concerned in opposing the war parties of Americans until the time of Gen. *Wayne's* famous expedition. As that veteran was advancing into the western region, *Chikatommo* met an advance party of his army at the head of a band of his desperate warriors, who were sent forward as the Indian forlorn hope. A sharp skirmish followed, and *Chickatommo* was slain. This was the action near Fort Defiance. *King-crane* was also in arms to oppose Gen. *Wayne*; but in the last war against England, he fought for the Americans, and is supposed to have died three or four years after its close. He was one of the signers of *Wayne's* famous treaty at Fort Greenville, and several others.

We now pass to a chief by far more prominent in Indian history than many who have received much greater notice from historians. This was *Mishikinakwa*, (a name by no means settled in orthography,) which, interpreted, is said to mean the *Little-turtle*. To the different treaties bearing his name, we find these spellings: *Meshekunnoghquoh*, Greenville, 3 Aug. 1795; *Meshekunnoghquoh*, Fort Wayne, 7 June, 1803; *Mashekanahquah*, Vincennes, 21 Aug. 1805; *Meshekenoghqua*, Fort Wayne, 30 Sept. 1809; and were we disposed to look into the various authors who have used the name, we might nearly finish out our page with its variations.

Little-turtle was chief of the Miamis, and the scenes of his warlike achievements were upon the country of his birth. He had, in conjunction with the tribes of that region, successfully fought the armies of *Harmer* and *St. Clair*; and in the fight with the latter, he is said to have had the chief command; hence a detailed account of that affair belongs to his life.

It is well known that the Americans inveighed loudly against the English of Canada, in most instances, charging them with all the guilt of the enormities committed on their frontiers by the Indians. It is equally well known, at this day, by every judicious inquirer, that they were not so blamable as the Americans represented, nor so innocent as themselves and friends, even long after, represented them. That the British government encouraged depredations upon the frontiers in times of peace, should not too easily be received for truth; still, there is reason to believe that some who held inferior offices under it, were secret abettors of barbarities. In the attack upon Gen. *St. Clair's* army, now about to be related, there was much cause of suspicion against the Canadians, as it was known that many of them even exceeded in that bloody affair the Indians themselves. Mr. *Weld*, the intelligent traveller, says,* "A great many young Canadians, and in particular many that were born of Indian women, fought on the side of the Indians in this action; a circumstance which confirmed the people of the States in the opinion they had pre-

* *Travels in Canada*, 436-7, 8vo. London, (4 ed.) 1800.

viously formed, that the Indians were encouraged and abetted in their attacks upon them by the British. I can safely affirm, however, from having conversed with many of these young men who fought against *St. Clair*, that it was with the utmost secrecy they left their homes to join the Indians, fearful lest the government should censure their conduct."

The western Indians were only emboldened by the battles between them and detachments of Gen. *Harmer's* army, in 1790, and, under such a leader as *Mishikinakwa*, entertained sanguine hopes of bringing the Americans to their own terms. One murder followed another, in rapid succession, attended by all the horrors peculiar to their warfare, which caused President *Washington* to take the earliest opportunity of recommending Congress to adopt prompt and efficient measures for checking those calamities; and 2000 men were immediately raised and put under the command of Gen. *St. Clair*, then governor of the North-Western Territory. He received his appointment the 4th of March, 1791; and proceeded to Fort Washington, by way of Kentucky, with all possible despatch, where he arrived 15 May.* There was much time lost in getting the troops embodied at this place; Gen. *Butler*, with the residue, not arriving until the middle of September. There were various circumstances to account for the delays, which it is unnecessary to recount here.

Col. *Darke* proceeded immediately on his arrival, which was about the end of August, and built Fort Hamilton, on the Miami, in the country of *Little-turtle*; and soon after Fort Jefferson was built, forty miles farther onward. These two forts being left manned, about the end of October the army advanced, being about 2000 strong, militia included, whose numbers were not inconsiderable, as will appear by the miserable manner in which they not only confused themselves, but the regular soldiers also.

Gen. *St. Clair* had advanced but about six miles in front of Fort Jefferson, when 60 of his militia, from pretended disaffection, commenced a retreat; and it was discovered that the evil had spread considerably among the rest of the army. Being fearful they would seize upon the convoy of provisions, the general ordered Col. *Hamtramk* to pursue them with his regiment, and force them to return. The army now consisted of but 1400 effective men, and this was the number attacked by *Little-turtle* and his warriors, 15 miles from the Miami villages.

Gen. *Butler* commanded the right wing, and Col. *Darke* the left. The militia were posted a quarter of a mile in advance, and were encamped in two lines. They had not finished securing their baggage, when they were attacked in their camp. It was their intention to have marched immediately to the destruction of the Miami villages. Of this their movements apprized the Indians, who acted with great wisdom and firmness. They fell upon the militia before sunrise, 4 November, who at once fled into the main camp, in the most disorderly and tumultuous manner: many of them, having thrown away their guns, were pursued and slaughtered. At the main camp the fight was sustained some time, by the great exertions of the officers, but with great inequality; the Indians under *Little-turtle* amounting to about 1500 warriors. Cols. *Darke* and *Butler*, and Major *Clark*, made several successful charges, which enabled them to save some of their numbers by checking the enemy while flight was more practicable.

Of the Americans, 593 were killed and missing, beside *thirty-eight* officers; and 242 soldiers and *twenty-one* officers were wounded, many of whom died. Col. *Butler* was among the slain. The account of his fall is shocking. He was severely wounded, and left on the ground. The well-known and infamous *Simon Girty* came up to him, and observed

* *St. Clair's Narrative*, p. 4.

him writhing under severe pain from his wounds. *Girty* knew and spoke to him. Knowing that he could not live, the colonel begged of *Girty* to put an end to his misery. This he refused to do, but turned to an Indian, whom he told that the officer was the commander of the army; upon which he drove his tomahawk into his head. A number of others then came around, and after taking off his scalp, they took out his heart, and cut it into as many pieces as there were tribes in the action, and divided it among them. All manner of brutal acts were committed on the bodies of the slain. It need not be mentioned for the information of the observer of Indian affairs, that *land* was the main cause of this as well as most other wars between the Indians and whites; and hence it was very easy to account for the Indians filling the mouths of the slain with earth after this battle. This was actually the case, as reported by those who shortly after visited the scene of action and buried the dead.

Gen. *St. Clair* was called to an account for the disastrous issue of this campaign, and was honorably acquitted. He published a narrative in vindication of his conduct, which, at this day, few will think it required. What he says of his retreat we will give in his own words.* "The retreat was, you may be sure, a precipitate one; it was in fact a flight. The camp and the artillery were abandoned; but that was unavoidable, for not a horse was left alive to have drawn it off, had it otherwise been practicable. But the most disgraceful part of the business is, that the greatest part of the men threw away their arms and accoutrements, even after the pursuit, which continued about four miles, had ceased. I found the road strewed with them for many miles, but was not able to remedy it; for, having had all my horses killed, and being mounted upon one that could not be pricked out of a walk, I could not get forward myself, and the orders I sent forward, either to halt the front, or prevent the men from parting with their arms, were unattended to."

The remnant of the army arrived at Fort Jefferson the same day, just before sunset, the place from which they fled being 29 miles distant. Gen. *St. Clair* did every thing that a brave general could do. He exposed himself to every danger, having, during the action, eight bullets shot through his clothes. In no attack related in our records, did the Indians discover greater bravery and determination. After giving the first fire, they rushed forward with tomahawk in hand. Their loss was inconsiderable; but the traders afterwards learned among them that *Little-turtle* had 150 killed and many wounded.* "They rushed on the artillery, heedless of their fire, and took two pieces in an instant. They were again retaken by our troops; and whenever the army charged them, they were seen to give way, and advance again as soon as they began to retreat, doing great execution, both in the retreat and advance. They are very dextrous in covering themselves with trees; many of them however fell, both of the infantry and artillery." "Six or eight pieces of artillery fell into their hands, with about 400 horses, all the baggage, ammunition, and provisions."†

It has been generally said, that had the advice of *Little-turtle* been taken at the disastrous fight afterwards with Gen. *Wayne*, there is very little doubt but he had met as ill success‡ as Gen. *St. Clair*§ did before him.

---

* *Penn. Gazette*, of that year.

† Letter from Fort Hamilton, dated six days after the battle.

‡ *Little-turtle* told Mr. Volney circumstances which gave him that opinion. See his *Travels in America*, ed. Lond. 1804.

§ Gen. *Arthur St. Clair* was of Edinburgh, Scotland. He came to America in the fleet which brought over Admiral *Boscawen*, in 1755, and having served through the revolutionary and Indian wars, died at his farm near Greensburgh, Pa. 31 Aug. 1818. *Amer. Mon. Mag.* ii. 469, (N. Y. 1818.)

He was not for fighting Gen. *Wayne* at Presque Isle, and inclined rather to peace than fighting him at all. In a council held the night before the battle, he argued as follows: "*We have beaten the enemy twice, under separate commanders. We cannot expect the same good fortune always to attend us. The Americans are now led by a chief who never sleeps: the night and the day are alike to him. And during all the time that he has been marching upon our villages, notwithstanding the watchfulness of our young men, we have never been able to surprise him. Think well of it. There is something whispers me, it would be prudent to listen to his offers of peace.*" For holding this language he was reproached by another chief with cowardice, which put an end to all further discourse. Nothing wounds the feelings of a warrior like the reproach of cowardice; but *Little-turtle* stifled his resentment, did his duty in the battle, and its issue proved him a truer prophet than his accuser believed.* His residence was upon Eel River, *about* 20 miles from Fort Wayne, where our government built him a house, and furnished him with means of living, much to the envy of his countrymen. Therefore, what had been bestowed upon *him*, to induce others to a like mode of life by their own exertions, proved not only prejudicial to the cause, but engendered hatred against him in the minds of all the Indians. He was not a chief by birth, but was raised to that standing by his superior talents. This was the cause of so much jealousy and envy at this time, as also a neglect of his counsel heretofore. The same author,† from whom we get the facts in the preceding part of this paragraph, says, "*Meshecunnaqua*, or the *Little-turtle*, was the son of a Miami chief, by a Mohecan woman. As the Indian maxim, with regard to descents, is precisely that of the civil law in relation to slaves, that the condition of the woman adheres to the offspring, he was not a chief by birth," &c.

Little-turtle was alike courageous and humane, possessing great wisdom. "And," says my author, "there have been few individuals among aborigines who have done so much to abolish the rites of human sacrifice. The grave of this noted warrior is shown to visitors, near Fort Wayne. It is frequently visited by the Indians in that part of the country, by whom his memory is cherished with the greatest respect and veneration."‡

The grave of his great opponent was also in the same region; but his remains were not long since removed to the seat of his family. Ever after his successful expedition, the Indians called him the *Big-wind*;§ or *Tornado*; some, however, on particular occasions, called him *Sukach-gook*, which signified, in Delaware, a black-snake; because, they said, he possessed all the art and cunning of that reptile.|| We hear yet of another name, which, though it may not have been his fault that acquired it, is less complimentary than the two just named. It is well known that the British bestowed a great many more presents upon the Indians than the Americans did; but some of the latter made large pretensions about what they would do. Gen. *Wayne*, the Indians said, made great promises to them of goods, but never got ready to fulfil them, (probably from being disappointed himself by the failure of his government in not forwarding what was promised;) therefore they called him Gen. *Wabang*, which signified Gen. *To-morrow*.¶

When the philosopher and famous traveller *Volney* was in America, in the winter of 1797, *Little-turtle* came to Philadelphia, where he then was, and who sought immediate acquaintance with the celebrated chief, for highly valuable purposes, which in some measure he effected. He made

---

* *Schoolcraft's* Travels. † *Dawson*, Mems. Harrison. ‡ *Schoolcraft's* Travels.
§ Pa. Gazette. || *Heckewelder's* Nar. ¶ *Weld's* Travels, 424.

a vocabulary of his language, which he printed in the appendix to his Travels. A copy in manuscript, more extensive than the printed one, is said to be in the library of the Philosophical Society of Pennsylvania.

Having become convinced that all resistance to the whites was vain, *Little-turtle* brought his nation to consent to peace, and to adopt agricultural pursuits. And it was with the view of soliciting Congress, and the benevolent society of Friends, for assistance to effect this latter purpose, that he now visited Philadelphia. While here, he was inoculated for the small-pox, and was also afflicted with the gout and rheumatism.

At the time of Mr. *Volney's* interview with him for information, he took no notice of the conversation while the interpreter was communicating with Mr. *Volney*, for he did not understand English, but walked about, plucking out his beard and eye-brows. He was dressed now in English clothes. His skin, where not exposed, Mr. *Volney* says, was as white as his; and on speaking upon the subject, *Little-turtle* said, "I have seen Spaniards in Louisiana, and found no difference of color between them and me. And why should there be any? In them, as in us, it is the work of the Father of colors, the Sun, that burns us. You white people compare the color of your face with that of your bodies." Mr. *Volney* explained to him the notion of many, that his race was descended from the Tartars, and by a map showed him the supposed communication between Asia and America. To this *Little-turtle* replied, "*why should not these Tartars, who resemble us, have come from America? Are there any reasons to the contrary? Or why should we not both have been born in our own country?*" It is a fact that the Indians give themselves a name which is equivalent to our word *indigene*, that is, *one sprung from the soil*, or natural to it.*

Baron *Lahontan*,† after describing the different dances, or dances for different occasions, among the Indians of Canada, adds the following in a note:—"Toutes ces danses peuvent être comparées à la pyrrhique de Minerve, car les sauvages observent, en dansant d'une gravité singuliére, les cadences de certaines chansons, que les milices Grecques d'Achille, apelloient hyporchematiques. Il n'est pas facile de sçavoir si les sauvages les ont aprises des Grecs, ou si les Grecs les ont aprises des sauvages." It is, perhaps, from such passages that *Lahontan* has been branded with the name of infidel;‡ but truly there can be nothing irreligious in such deductions, inasmuch as it is conceded on all hands that the geological formations of the new world have required as much time for their perfection as those of the old. Mr. *Volney* comes within the same pale, when he compares the Spartans to the five Nations. In contrasting the states of Lacedæmon with modern France, he says, "Maintenant que j'ai vu les sauvages d'Amérique, je persiste de plus en plus dans cette comparaison, et je trouve que le premiere livre de Thucydide, et tout ce qu'il dit des mœurs des Lacédémoniens, convienent tellement aux cinq nations, que j'appellerais volontiers les Spartiates, les Iroquois de l'ancien monde."§

When Mr. *Volney* asked *Little-turtle* what prevented him from living among the whites, and if he were not more comfortable in Philadelphia than upon the banks of the Wabash, he said, "Taking all things together, you have the advantage over us; but here I am deaf and dumb. I do not

---

* See *Volney's* Travels, *ut supra*. † Memoires de L'Amerique, ii. 109.

‡ No one presumes to pronounce Father *Hennepin* an infidel, and he denies, (after living much among the Inians,) that they have any notion, or belief, of what Christians call *Deity*. But Mr. *Beverley* (Hist. Virginia, 169.) says, "Baron *Lahontan*, on the other hand, makes them have such refined notions, as seem almost to confute his own belief of Christianity."

§ Œuvres de C. F. *Volney*, t. 6. 129. (Paris, 1826.)

talk your language; I can neither hear, nor make myself heard. When I walk through the streets, I see every person in his shop employed about something: one makes shoes, another hats, a third sells cloth, and every one lives by his labor. I say to myself, Which of all these things can you do? Not one. I can make a bow or an arrow, catch fish, kill game, and go to war: but none of these is of any use here. To learn what is done here would require a long time." "Old age comes on." "I should be a piece of furniture useless to my nation, useless to the whites, and useless to myself." "I must return to my own country."

At the same time, (1797,) among other eminent personages to whom this chief became attached in Philadelphia, was the renowned *Koskiusko.* This old Polish chief was so well pleased with *Little-turtle*, that when the latter went to take his final leave of him, the old "war-worn soldier" and patriot presented him with a beautiful pair of pistols, and an elegant robe made of sea-otter's skin, of the value of "several" hundred dollars.

Little-turtle died in the spring of 1812, at his residence, but a short time before the declaration of war against England by the U. States. His portrait, by Stewart, graces the walls of the war-office of our nation. The following notice appeared in the public prints at the time of his death: "Fort Wayne, 21 July, 1812. On the 14 inst. the celebrated Miami chief, the *Little-turtle*, died at this place, at the age of 65 years.—Perhaps there is not left on this continent, one of his color so distinguished in council and in war. His disorder was the gout. He died in a camp, because he chose to be in the open air. He met death with great firmness. The agent for Indian affairs had him buried with the honors of war, and other marks of distinction suited to his character." He was, generally, in his time, styled the Messissago chief,* and a gentleman who saw him soon after *St. Clair's* defeat, at Montreal, says he was six feet high, "about 45 years of age, of a very sour and morose countenance, and apparently very crafty and subtle. His dress was Indian moccasins, a blue petticoat that came half way down his thighs; an European waistcoat and surtout; his head was bound with an Indian cap that hung half way down his back, and almost entirely filled with plain silver-broaches, to the number of more than 200; he had two ear-rings to each ear, the upper part of each was formed of three silver medals, about the size of a dollar; the lower part was formed of quarters of dollars, and fell more than 12 inches from his ears—one from each ear over his breast, the other over his back; he had three very large nose jewels of silver, that were curiously painted. The account he gave of the action [with the Americans, 4 Nov.] was, that they killed 1400 of them, with the loss of nine only of their party, one of whom killed himself by accident." The person who gave this account said this chief was in Canada for the purpose of raising all the Indian force he could to go out again in the spring against the whites.

Mr. *Dawson* relates a pleasant anecdote of *Little-turtle*, which happened while he was sitting for his portrait in Philadelphia. A native of the Emerald Isle was sitting for his at the same time, who prided himself upon his ability at joking. *Little-turtle* was not backward in the same business, and they passed several meetings very pleasantly. One morning, *Little-turtle* did not take much notice of his friend, and seemed rather sedate, which was construed by the Hibernian into an acknowledgment of victory on the part of the chief, in their joking game, and accordingly began to intimate as much. When *Little-turtle* understood him, he said to the interpreter, "*He mistakes; I was just thinking of proposing to this*

* Those of this tribe in the vicinity of Lake Ontario, are of a much darker complexion than the other Indians of the west. *Weld*, Travels in America, 451.

man, to paint us both on one board, and there I would stand face to face with him, and blackguard him to all eternity."

Among the chiefs associated in command, in the wars of which we have been speaking with the famous *Mishikinakwa,* was another of nearly equal note, familiarly called *Blue-jacket* by the whites, but by his own nation, *Weyapiersenwaw.* He was the most distinguished chief of the Shawanese, and we hear of him at Fort Industry, on the Miami of the Lake, as late as 1805. By some particular arrangement, the chief command seems to have devolved on him of opposing Gen. *Wayne.* He was more bloody and precipitate than *Mishikinakwa,* and possessed less discrimination and judgment. The tribes which furnished warriors to oppose the Americans were the Wyandots, Miamis, Pottowattomies, Delawares, Shawanese, Chippeways, Ottaways, and a few Senecas. *Blue-jacket* was the director and leader of this mighty band of warriors.

From the time General St. Clair was defeated, in 1791, murders were continued upon the frontier, and all attempts on the part of government to effect a peace, proved of no avail; and lastly the ambassadors sent to them were murdered, and that too while the army was progressing towards their country.

After building Fort Greenville, upon the Ohio, six miles above Fort Jefferson, General *Wayne* took possession of the ground where Gen. *St. Clair* had been defeated, and there erected a fort, to which he gave the name of Recovery, in which the army spent the winter of 1793-4. Many censures were passed upon the general for his slow progress; but he knew much better what he was doing than newspaper writers did what they were writing, when they undertook to censure him, as the event proved.

It was the 8 August, 1794, when the army arrived at the confluence of the rivers Au Glaize and Maumee, where they built Fort Defiance. It was the general's design to have met the enemy unprepared, in this move; but a fellow deserted his camp, and notified the Indians. He now tried again to bring them to an accommodation, and from the answers which he received from them, it was some time revolved in his mind, whether they were for peace or war; so artful was the manner in which their replies were formed.* At length, being fully satisfied, he marched down the Maumee, and arrived at the rapids, 18 August. His army consisted of upwards of 3000 men, 2000 of whom were regulars. Fort Deposit was erected at this place, for the security of their supplies. They now set out to meet the enemy, who had chosen his position, upon the bank of the river, with much judgment. They had a breastwork of fallen trees in front, and the high rocky shore of the river gave them much security, as also did the thick wood of Presque Isle. Their force was divided, and disposed at supporting distances for about two miles. When the Americans had arrived at proper distance, a body was sent out to begin the attack, "with orders to rouse the enemy from their covert with the bayonet; and when up, to deliver a close fire upon their backs, and press them so hard as not to give them time to reload."† This order was so well executed, and the battle at the point of attack so short, that only about 900 Americans participated in it. But they pursued the Indians with great slaughter through the woods to Fort Maumee, where the carnage ended. The Indians were so unexpectedly driven from their strong hold, that their numbers only increased their distress and confusion. And the cavalry made horrible havoc among them with their long sabres. Of the Americans, there were killed and wounded about 130. The loss of the Indians could not be ascertained, but must have been very severe. The American loss was chiefly at the commencement of the action, as

* *Marshall's* Washington, v. 481. ed. 4to.

† *Schoolcraft.*

they advanced upon the mouths of the Indians' rifles, who could not be seen until they had discharged upon them. They maintained their coverts but a short time, being forced in every direction by the bayonet. But until that was effected, the Americans fell fast, and we only wonder that men could be found thus to advance in the face of certain death.

This horrid catastrophe in our Indian annals is chargeable to certain white men, or at least mainly so; for some days before the battle, General *Wayne* sent a flag of truce to them, and desired them to come and treat with him. The letter which he sent was taken to Col. *M'Kee*, who, it appears, was their ill-adviser, and he, by putting a false construction upon it, increased the rage of the Indians: he then informed them that they must forthwith fight the American army. Some of the chiefs, learning the truth of the letter, were for peace; but it was too late. *Little-turtle* was known to have been in favor of making peace, and seemed well aware of the abilities of the American general; but such was the influence of traders among them, that no arguments could prevail. Thus, instances without number might be adduced, where these people have been destroyed by placing confidence in deceiving white men.

The night before the battle, the chiefs assembled in council, and some proposed attacking the army in its encampment, but the proposal was objected to by others; finally the proposition of fighting at Presque Isle prevailed.

In this battle all the chiefs of the Wyandots were killed, being nine in number. Some of the nations escaped the slaughter by not coming up until after the defeat. This severe blow satisfied the western Indians of the folly of longer contending against the Americans; they therefore were glad to get what terms they could from them. The chiefs of twelve tribes met commissioners at Fort Greenville, 3 Aug. 1795, and, as a price of their peace, gave up an extensive tract of country south of the lakes, and west of the Ohio; and such other tracts as comprehended all the military posts in the western region. The government showed some liberality to these tribes, on their relinquishing to it what they could not withhold, and as a gratuity gave them 20,000 dollars in goods, and agreed to pay them 9000 dollars a year forever; to be divided among those tribes in proportion to their numbers.*

CHAPTER V.

Life of THAYANDANECA, *called by the whites,* BRANT—*His education—His being but half Indian an error—Visits England—Commissioned there—His sister a companion to Sir Wm. Johnson—His letter to the Oneidas—Affair with Herkimer at Unadilla—Cuts off Herkimer and 200 men at Oriskana, near Oneida Creek—Anecdote of Herkimer—Burns Springfield—Horrid affair of Wyoming—Incidents—Destroys Cherry Valley—Barbarities of the tories—Sullivan's depredations among the Five Nations—Brant defeated by the Americans at Newtown—Destruction of Minisink, and slaughter of 100 people—Destruction of Harpersfield—Brant's letter to M'Causland—Marriage of his daughter—Her husband killed—*

* The terms of this treaty were the same as were offered to them before the battle, which should be mentioned, as adding materially to our good feelings towards its authors. It is generally denominated *Wayne's* treaty. It is worthy of him.

Brant becomes the friend of peace—Visits Philadelphia—His marriage—Lands granted him by the king—His death—His son John—Traits of character—One of his sons killed by him, in an attempt to kill his father—Account of Brant's arrival in England—Some account of his children.

Col. *Joseph Brant* was an Onondaga of the Mohawk tribe, whose Indian name was *Thayendaneca,** or *Tayadanaga,*† signifying *a brant.*‡ But as he was seldom called by that name after he became known to the whites, it was generally forgotten. He received a very good English education at the "Moor's charity school," at Lebanon, in Connecticut, where he was placed by Sir *William Johnson,* in July, 1761. His age, at this time, we have not learned.

The story that he was but half Indian, the son of a German, has been widely spread, but is denied by his son, and now believed to be a falsehood, ignorantly circulated. This error might have arisen either from the known fact of his being of rather a lighter complexion than his countrymen in general, or from his having married a woman who was half white.

Brant went to England in 1775, in the beginning of the great revolutionary rupture, where he was received with attention, and doubtless had there his mind prepared for the part he acted in the memorable struggle which ensued. He had a colonel's commission in the English army, upon the frontiers, which consisted of such of the Six Nations and tories, as took part against the country. Gen. Sir *William Johnson* was agent of Indian affairs, and had greatly ingratiated himself into the esteem of the Six Nations. He lived at the place since named from him, upon the north bank of the Mohawk, about 40 miles from Albany. Here he had an elegant seat, and would often entertain several hundreds of his red friends, and share all in common with them. They so much respected him, that, notwithstanding they had the full liberty of his house, yet they would take nothing that did not belong to them. The better to rivet their esteem, he would, at certain seasons, accommodate himself to their mode of dress, and, being a widower, took as a kind of companion a sister of *Brant,* by the name of *Molley.* He had received honors and emoluments from the British government, and the Indians received also, through his agency, every thing which, in their opinion, conduced to their happiness. Hence it is not strange that they should hold in the greatest reverence the name of their "great father," the king, and think the *few* rebels who opposed his authority, when the revolution began, most ungratefully wicked, and unworthy all mercy. Sir *William* died in 1774, about a year before the battle of Bunker's Hill.

The *Butlers, John* and *Walter,* whose names are associated with the recollection of the horrid barbarities upon Cherry Valley and Wyoming, lived at Caughnewaga, four miles south-easterly from the village of Johnston, and upon the same side of the Mohawk.

In 1775, in a letter to the Oneidas, our chief subscribes himself "secretary to *Guy Johnson.*" This was early in the summer of that year, and hence he was immediately from England. Col. *Guy Johnson* was son-in-law of Sir *William.* The letter was found in an Indian path, and was supposed to have been lost by the person who was intrusted with it. It was in the Mohawk language, the translation of which commences thus: "*Written at* Guy Johnson's, *May,* 1775. *This is your letter, you great ones* or sachems. Guy Johnson *says he will be glad if you get this intelligence,*

* *Carey's* Museum, v. 18. † Annals Tryon County, 15.

‡ Generally written *Brandt* by those who are unacquainted with the meaning of his Indian name.

you Oneidas, how it goes with him now, and he is now more certain concerning the intention of the Boston people. Guy Johnson *is in great fear of being taken prisoner by the Bostonians. We Mohawks are obliged to watch him constantly,*" &c.

After this, *Brant* accompanied *Guy Johnson* when he fled to Canada. The two *Butlers* were also in the train. Being now in a place of safety, and the means in their hands, plots of destruction were put in execution in rapid succession.

Having had some disagreement with *Johnson, Brant* came again to the frontiers. Some of the peaceable Mohawks had been confined, to prevent their doing mischief, as were some of the Massachusetts Indians in *Philip's* war. *Brant* was displeased at this, for he said, if the distant Indians should come down, they would destroy them indiscriminately with the whites. He was accompanied by a band of 70 or 80 warriors, who, in their rambles, visited Unadilla, where they assembled the inhabitants, and told them that they stood in need of provisions, and if they did not give them some, they should take it by force; a refusal, therefore, would have been worse than useless. *Brant* further observed, "that their agreement with the king was strong, and that they were not such villains as to break their covenant with him." Gen. *Herkimer* marched up to Unadilla, in July, with 380 men, where he found *Brant* with 130 of his warriors. Here he had an interview with him, in which he held the following language: "That the Indians were in concert with the king, as their fathers and grandfathers had been. That the king's belts were yet lodged with them, and they could not falsify their pledge. That Gen. *Herkimer* and the rest had joined the Boston people against their king. That Boston people were resolute, but the king would humble them. That Mr. *Schuyler*, or general, or what you please to call him, was very smart on the Indians at the treaty at German Flatts; but was not, at the same time, able to afford them the smallest article of clothing. That the Indians had formerly made war on the white people all united; and now they were divided, the Indians were not frightened." Col. *Cox*, who accompanied *Herkimer*, said, if war was his determination, the matter was ended. *Brant* then spoke to his warriors, and they shouted, and ran to their place of encampment, seized their arms, fired several guns, and, after giving the war-whoop, returned in warlike array. Gen. *Herkimer* then told *Brant* he did not come to fight, and the chief motioned for his men to remain quiet. Perhaps, as a worthy author observed upon a transaction in *Philip's* war, it is better to omit the cause of the conduct of *Herkimer*, than too critically to inquire into it. His men vastly outnumbered the Indians, and his authority was ample; but his motives were no doubt pure, and his courage must not now be called in question, as will appear from what is to be related. To put the most favorable construction upon his neglecting to break down the power of *Brant*, is to suppose that he was impressed with the belief that the Indians would not join with the English in committing hostilities; if this were the case, he too late discovered the error of his judgment.

After the general had said that he did not come to fight, *Brant*, with an air of importance, said, "If your purpose is war, I am ready for you." A tempest, which came up suddenly, separated the parties, and each retired peaceably. This is said to be the last talk held by any of the Americans with the Six Nations, previous to hostilities, except with the Oneidas; all, except a very few, of whom remained neutral.

Towards the autumn of this year, (1777,) *Brant* was under the direction of Gen. *St. Leger*, who detached him with a considerable body of warriors for the investment of Fort Stanwix. Col. *Butler* was commander in chief, with a band of tories. The inhabitants in the valley of the Mokawk determined to march for the relief of Col. *Ganesvoort*, who commanded the fort, which they did, in two regiments, with Gen. *Herkimer* at their head. As is usual with militia, they marched in great disorder, and when the general ordered scouting parties to march as security against surprise, upon the flanks of the main body, they accused him with cowardice, which, most unwarrantably, had more influence upon his mind, than the safety of his army. A catastrophe ensued, which, though not so momentous in that day, as was that of *Lothrop* in 1676, nor so complete a victory on the part of the Indians, yet it was a severe fight, in which 200 Americans were slain.* The place of attack was selected by *Brant* or *Butler,* and was a ravine of a broad bottom, nearly impassable, except a rough track covered with logs, of from 12 to 15 feet in length, laid transversely,† which extended across it. Gen. *Herkimer* arrived at this place about two hours before mid-day, August 6. He might reasonably have expected an ambush, but his first intimations of the vicinity of an enemy were the terrifying yells of the Indians, and the still more lasting impressions of their rifles. The advanced guard were all cut off. Such as survived the first fire, were hewn down with the tomahawk. The fatal causeway was semicircular, and *Brant* and his forces occupied the surrounding heights. A surgeon, Dr. *Moses Younglove,* was taken prisoner in this battle, and after his return from captivity, he wrote a poem upon the affair, from which we extract the following:—

"The time and place of our unhappy fight,
To you at large were needless to recite:
When in the wood our fierce inhuman foes,
With piercing yell from circling ambush rose,
A sudden volley rends the vaulted sky;
Their painted bodies hideous to the eye,
They rush like hellish furies on our bands,
Their slaughter weapons brandish'd in their hands.
Then we with equal fury join the fight,
E'er Phœbus gain'd his full meridian height:
Nor ceased the horrors of the bloody fray,
Till he had journey'd half his evening way."

Running down from every direction, they prevented the two regiments from forming a junction, one of them not having entered the causeway; and a part of the assailants fell upon those without, and the remainder upon those within it. The former fared worse than the latter, for in such cases a flight has almost always been a dismal defeat. It was now the case. The other regiment, hemmed in as they were, saw, in a moment, that,

To fight, or not to fight, was death.

They, therefore, back to back, forming a front in every direction, fought like men in despair. This, Dr. *Younglove* thus forcibly depicts:—

"Now, hand to hand, the contest is for life,
With bay'net, tom'hawk, sword, and scalping knife:
Now more remote the work of death we ply,
And thick as hail the show'ring bullets fly:
Full many a hardy warrior sinks supine;
Yells, shrieks, groans, shouts and thund'ring volleys join;
The dismal din the ringing forest fills,
The sounding echo roars along the hills."

---

* Their whole loss was about 400, says *Marshall,* Life Washington, v. 261.

† All who have travelled, even within a few years, in this part of the state of New York, cannot but well remember the "*Corduroy*" roads. Such was the *road* over this memorable ravine.

The poet thus presents to our view the attacking parties:–

"Of two departments were the assailing foes;
Wild savage natives lead the first of those;
Their almost naked frames, of various dyes,
And rings of black and red surround their eyes:
On one side they present a shaven head;
The naked half of the vermilion red;
In spots the party-color'd face they drew,
Beyond description horrible to view;
Their ebon locks in braid, with paint o'erspread;
The silver'd ears depending from the head;
Their. gaudry my descriptive power exceeds,
In plumes of feathers, glitt'ring plates and beads."

He thus speaks of the tories:—

"With them of parricides a bloody band,
Assist the ravage of their parent land:
With equal dress, and arms, and savage arts,
But more than savage rancor in their hearts.
These for the first attack their force unite,
And most sustain the fury of the fight;
Their rule of warfare, devastation dire,
By undistinguish'd plunder, death and fire;
They torture man and beast, with barbarous rage,
Nor tender infant spare, nor rev'rend sage."

And *Butler* is noticed in the same poem from which we have made the preceding extracts, as follows:—

"O'er them a horrid monster bore command,
Whose inauspicious birth disgrac'd our land;
By malice urg'd to ev'ry barb'rous art;
Of cruel temper, but of coward heart."

With such bravery did they fight in this forlorn condition, that the Indians began to give way; and, but for a reinforcement of tories, under Major *Watson,* they would have been entirely dispersed.* This reinforcement is thus characterized by the surgeon:—

"The second was a renegado crew,
Who arm and dress as Christian nations do,
Led by a chief who bore the first command;
A bold invader of his native land."

The sight of this reinforcement greatly increased the rage of the Americans. It was composed of the very men who had left that part of the country at the commencement of the war, and were held in abhorrence for their loyalty to the king. The fight was renewed with vigor, and the reinforcement fought also with bravery, until about 30 of their number were killed. Maj. *Watson,* their leader, was wounded and taken prisoner, but left upon the battle ground.

In the mean time, Gen. *Herkimer* had got forward to the fort an express, which informed Col. *Ganesvoort* of his situation. He immediately detached Col. *Marinus Willet* with 207 men, who succeeded in rescuing the remnant of this brave band from destruction. He beat the enemy from the ground, and returned to the fort with considerable plunder. Such were the events of the battle of Oriskana.

* Dr. *Gordon* says the tories and Indians got into a most wretched confusion, and fought one another; and that the latter, at last, thought it was a plot of the whites on both sides, to get them into that situation, that they might cut them off.

Gen. *Herkimer* died of a wound which he received in this fight. Near its commencement, he was severely wounded in the leg, and his horse was killed. He directed his saddle to be placed upon a little knoll, and resting himself upon it, continued to issue his orders. On being advised to remove to a place of greater safety, he said, "*No—I will face the enemy*;" and, adds the historian of Tryon county, "In this situation, and in the heat of the battle, he very deliberately took from his pocket his tinder-box, and lit his pipe, which he smoked with great composure."

The Indians, as well as the Americans, suffered dreadfully in this fight. And our poet writes,

"Such was the bloody fight: and such the foe:
Our smaller force return'd them blow for blow;
By turns successfully their force defy'd,
And conquest wav'ring seem'd from side to side."

Brant's loss being about 100 men; we are inclined to think the loss of the Indians exaggerated in these lines:—

"Not half the savages returned from fight;
They to their native wilds had sped their flight."

The Senecas alone lost 30, and the tories about 100. The regiment which fled suffered severely, but would have suffered still more, had not their pursuers been apprized of the desperate case of their fellows engaged in the ravine, which caused them to abandon the pursuit. The commanding officer, Col. *Cox,* was killed, and the command devolved upon Lieut. Col. *Campbell* and Major *Clyde,* who conducted the retreat.

The scene in the night following the battle is thus strikingly presented by Dr. *Younglove,* the eye-witness:—

"Those that remain'd a long encampment made,
And rising fires illumin'd all the shade:
In vengeance for their num'rous brothers slain,
For torture sundry prisoners they retain;
And three fell monsters, horrible to view,
A fellow pris'ner from the sentries drew;
The guards before received their chief's command,
To not withhold from the slaught'ring band;
But now the sufferer's fate they sympathize,
And for him supplicate with earnest cries.
I saw the general* slowly passing by,
The sergeant, on his knees, with tearful eye,
Implor'd the guards might wrest him from their hands,
Since now the troops could awe their lessen'd bands.
With lifted cane the gen'ral thus replies,
(While indignation sparkles from his eyes:)
'Go! sirrah! mind your orders giv'n before!
'And for infernal rebels plead no more!'
For help the wretched victim vainly cries,
With supplicating voice and ardent eyes;
With horror chill'd, I turn away my face,
While instantly they bear him from the place.
Dread scene!—with anguish stung I inly groan,
To think the next hard lot may be my own"

"When through the grove the flaming fires arise;
And loud resound the tortur'd pris'ners' cries;
Still as their pangs are more or less extreme,
The bitter groan is heard, or sudden scream:
But when their natures fail'd, and death drew near,
Their screeches faintly sounded in the ear."

* *Butler.*

The poet next describes his dream, in which he was carried to the battle-ground; and then thus opens the morning scene:—

"When savages, for horrid sport prepar'd,
Demand another pris'ner from the guard,
We saw their fear'd approach, with mortal fright,
Their scalping-knives they sharpen'd in our sight,
Beside the guard they sat them on the ground,
And view'd, with piercing eyes, the pris'ners round."

"At length, one rising seized me by the hand;
By him drawn forth, on trembling knees I stand;
I bid my fellows all a long adieu,
With answering grief, my wretched case they view.
They led me bound, along the winding flood,
Far in the gloomy bosom of the wood;
There, (horrid sight!) a pris'ner roasted lay,
The carving-knife had cut his flesh away."

After enduring every thing but death in his captivity, Dr. *Younglove* returned home in safety.

In 1778, a fort was built at Cherry-valley, where families for considerable extent about took up their abode, or retired occasionally for safety. *Brant* intended to destroy this, and came into the neighborhood for the purpose. It happened that, at the time he chose to make the discovery of the strength of the garrison, the boys were assembled in a training, with wooden guns, for amusement: not having a clear view of them from the foliage of the trees which intervened, *Brant* thought them to be men. It was his design to have made the attack the following night; but on this discovery, he gave up the design. He still remained in the neighborhood, secreted behind a large rock near the main road to the Mohawk, and about two miles north of the fort in the valley. Here he waited to intercept some unwary passenger, and gain more certain intelligence. Near this place is the little cascade called by the natives, *Tekaharawa*. The inhabitants of the valley were in expectation of a company of soldiers from the Mohawk, to reinforce them, and the same day Lieut. *Wormwood* came from thence, and informed them that Col. *Klock* would arrive the next day with the party. Near night he set out to return, accompanied by one *Peter Sitz*, the bearer of some despatches. He was a young officer, of fine personal appearance, and was to return the next day with one of the companies of soldiers. He had been out of sight but a few minutes, when, as he passed the ambush of *Brant*, his warriors fired upon him, and he fell from his horse. The chief, springing from his hiding-place, tomahawked him with his own hands. *Wormwood* and his companion were ordered to stand, but not obeying, occasioned their being fired upon. *Brant* was acquainted with Lieut. *Wormwood* before the war, and afterwards expressed sorrow at his fate, pretending that he took him to be a continental officer. His horse immediately running back to the fort, with blood upon the saddle, gave some indication of what had happened. His companion, *Sitz*, was taken prisoner.

In June, the same summer, *Brant* came upon Springfield, which he burned, and carried off a number of prisoners. The women and children were not maltreated, but were left in one house unmolested. About this time, great pains were taken to seize the wary chief, but there was no Capt. *Church*, or, unlike *Philip* of Pokanoket, *Brant* had the remote nations to fly to without fear of being killed by them. Capt. *M'Kean* hunted him for some time, and, not being able to find him, wrote an insulting letter for him, and left it in an Indian path. Among other things, he challenged him to single combat, or to meet him with an equal number of

6*

men; and "that if he would come to Cherry-valley, and have a fair fight, they would change him from a *Brant* into a *Goos*." This letter, it is supposed, Brant received, from an intimation contained in one which he wrote about the same time to a tory. To this man (*Parcifer Carr*, of Edmeston) he writes from Tunadilla [Unadilla] under date 9 July, 1778,—"*Sir: I understand by the Indians that was at your house last week, that one Smith lives near with you, has little more corn to spare. I should be much obliged to you, if you would be so kind as to try to get as much corn as* Smith *can spared; he has sent me five skipples already, of which I am much obliged to him, and will see him paid, and would be very glad if you could spare one or two your men to join us, especially Elias. I would be glad to see him, and I wish you could sent me as many guns you have, as I know you have no use for them, if you any; as I mean now to fight the cruel rebels as well as I can; whatever you will able to sent'd me, you must sent'd by the bearer. I am your sincere friend and humble ser't.* JOSEPH BRANT. P. S. *I heard that Cherry-valley people is very bold, and intended to make nothing of us; they called us wild geese, but I know the contrary.*" This we suppose to be a fair specimen of the composition of the chief who afterwards translated the Gospel according to *John* into the Mohawk language, also the Book of Common Prayer; copies of which are in the library of Harvard college.*

The next event of importance in which *Brant* was engaged, was the destruction of Wyoming,† one of the most heart-rending records in the annals of the revolutionary war. In that horrid affair, about 300 settlers were killed or carried into captivity; from the greater part of whom no intelligence was ever obtained.

There were assembled at the fort in Wyoming 368 men. On the 3 July, 1778, a council of war was held among them, upon the propriety of marching in quest of an enemy. While they were holding this council, news was brought that a party had left Niagara, to attack the settlements upon the Susquehannah, and the majority of the people determined upon an expedition of discovery. Accordingly, they issued forth the same day, and ranged up the river, under the command of Col. *Zebulon Butler*, who was cousin to the leader of the tories.‡ The Americans sent forward a scout, who soon discovered the enemies: the tories were in possession of a fort, and the Indians in huts about it.§ Every appearance was now in favor of the Americans, and the spies returned towards their camp with the important intelligence. They had not proceeded far, when they were discovered by two Indians, who were, doubtless, upon the same business. The scouts fired each upon the other, and then hastened to their respective head-quarters. Both parties were immediately in motion, and joined battle near a thick swamp. The Indians and tories, being the more numerous,|| out-flanked the Americans, and *Brant*, at the head of his furious warriors, issuing from the swamp, turned their left flank, and creating thereby a confusion, which greatly favored his kind of warfare, and enabled him to make dreadful havoc among them.

The Americans were in two lines, and it was the line commanded by Col. *Denison* that *Brant* successfully encountered. *Butler*, at the same

* It would seem from Mr. *Weld*, (Travels in America, 485,) that he translated those works before the war.

† This name is said to signify *a field of blood*, from a great battle fought there by the Indians before its settlement by the whites.

‡ Life *Washington*, iii. 556.

§ This was Fort Wintermoot, which, being garrisoned by tories, was treacherously given up on the approach of *Butler* and *Brant*. *Marshall*, ibid. 557.

|| 1600 strong, say the histories of the revolution; but this is believed to exceed their number about 300. The Indians were supposed to be 800.

time, was gaining some advantage over the other line, under his cousin *Zebulon*, which, added to the raging disaster in the left, became immediately a flight. Col. *Denison's* order to fall back, by which he designed to make an advantageous evolution, was distorted, by the terrified troops, into an order for flight; and all was in a few moments lost. And from Judge *Marshall* we add as follows:—"The troops fled towards the river, which they endeavored to pass, in order to enter Fort Wilkesbarre, [in the village of that name on the opposite side of the Susquehannah.] The enemy pursued 'with the fury of devils;' and of the 400 who had marched out on this unfortunate parley, only about 20 escaped," among whom were the commanding officers.*

The fort at Wyoming was now closely besieged, and seeing no chance of escape, Col. *Butler* proposed a parley with his *friend* and namesake, which was assented to. The place of meeting was appointed at some distance from the fort, and the Americans marched out in considerable force, to prevent treachery, to the place appointed; but when they arrived there, they found nobody with whom to parley. The commander of the tories has been branded with gross infamy, for this piece of treachery with his kinsman; for he feigned fear from his approach, and had retired as they advanced, displaying meanwhile the flag of truce. The unwary Americans were, by this treacherous stratagem, led into an ambush in nearly the same manner as were *Hutchinson* and *Wheeler*, at Wickabaug Pond, in *Philip's* war. They were, in a moment, nearly surrounded by *Brant's* warriors, and the work of death raged in all its fury. The tories "were not a whit behind the very chiefest" of them in this bloody day. A remnant only regained the fort out of several hundreds that went forth. They were now more closely besieged than before; and the more to insult the vanquished, a demand was sent in to them to surrender, "accompanied by 196 bloody scalps, taken from those who had just been slain." When the best terms were asked for the besiegers, the "infamous *Butler*" replied in these two words, "the hatchet." This was the only truth we hear of his uttering. It was the hatchet, indeed—a few only fled to the surrounding wilderness, there to meet a more lingering death by famine. These were chiefly women and children.

Thus passed the *fourth of July*, 1778, in the before flourishing settlement of Wyoming, on the eastern branch of the Susquehannah. *Barlow* knew well, in his early day, who was forever to be branded with infamy for the acts of this memorable tragedy. He says,—

"His savage hordes the murderous *Johnson* leads,
Files through the woods and treads the tangled weeds,
Shuns open combat, teaches where to run,
Skulk, couch the ambush, aim the hunter's gun,
Whirl the sly tomahawk, the war-whoop sing,
Divide the spoils, and pack the scalps they bring."
Columbiad, vi. 389, &c.

Having now got full possession of Wyoming, and, observes Dr. *Thacher*, "after selecting a few prisoners, the remainder of the people, including women and children, were enclosed in the houses and barracks, which were immediately set on fire, and the whole consumed together. Another fort was near at hand, in which were 70 continental soldiers; on surrendering without conditions, these were, to a man, butchered in a barbarous manner; when the remainder of the men, women and children were shut up in the houses, and the demons of hell glutted their vengeance in be-

* There are disagreements in the accounts of this affair. I follow partly *Chapman's* history of it, as printed in the Annals of Tryon County.

holding their destruction in one general conflagration." The houses of the tories were spared. As though they could not exercise their cruelty enough upon human beings, they fell upon the beasts in the field—shooting some, wounding and mangling others, by cutting out their tongues, &c. and leaving them alive. Well does *Campbell* make his Oneida chief to say, (who comes as a friend to warn the settlement of the approach of the combined army of tories and Indians,)

"'But this is not a time,'—he started up,
And smote his breast with woe-denouncing hand—
'This is no time to fill thy joyous cup:
The mammoth comes—the foe—the monster *Brandt,*
With all his howling desolating band;—
These eyes have seen their blade, and burning pine,
Awake at once, and silence half your land.
Red is the cup they drink; but not with wine:
Awake and watch to-night! or see no morning shine.

"'Scorning to wield the hatchet for his bribe,
'Gainst *Brandt* himself I went to battle forth:
Accursed *Brandt! he left of all my tribe*
Nor man, nor child, nor thing of living birth:
No! not the dog, that watched my household hearth,
Escaped, that night of blood, upon our plains!
All perished!—I alone am left on earth!
To whom nor relative nor blood remains,
No!—not a kindred drop that runs in human veins!' "

Gertrude of Wyoming.

The tories, as was often the case, were attired like Indians, and, from every account, it appears that they exceeded them in ferocity.

Dr. *Thacher* gives us the following examples of horror which were of notoriety at the time, and "promulgated from authentic sources. One of the prisoners, a Capt. *Badlock,* was committed to torture, by having his body stuck full of splinters of pine knots, and a fire of dry wood made round him, when his two companions, Capts. *Ranson* and *Durkee,* were thrown into the same fire, and held down with pitchforks, till consumed. One *Partial Terry,* the son of a man of respectable character, having joined the Indian party, several times sent his father word that *he hoped to wash his hands in his heart's blood.* The monster, with his own hands, *murdered his father, mother, brothers and sisters,* stripped off their scalps, and cut off his father's head!"*

It was upon such scenes as these, that the mind of the poet just cited had dwelt, which caused him to wield the pen of denunciation with such effect upon the memory of *Brant.* That *Butler* was the far greater savage, none can dispute, and Mr. *Campbell* has long since acknowledged his too great severity upon the character of the former. We should explain here, that a son of Col. *Brant,* a chief Mohawk, of the name of *Ahyonwaeghs,* called by the English *John Brant,* was in London in 1822, and furnished Mr. *Campbell* with documents, which, in the poet's own words, "changed his opinion of his father." This passage was contained in a long and interesting letter upon the subject, to *Ahyoniwaeghs,* which appeared at that time in the newspapers.

With Wyoming were destroyed Wilkesbarre and Kingston, upon the other side of the Susquehannah. Though Wyoming is generally understood to be the place destroyed, it should be remembered that in the valley bearing that name, there were three other towns, which were all destroyed, as well as Wyoming.† These towns were settled by emigrants

* *Thacher's* Journal.

† The settlement of Wyoming consisted of eight townships, each five miles square. *Annual Reg.* for 1779, page 9. "Each containing a square of five miles," is the language of the Register; but it is thought unlikely that these towns were so small.

from Connecticut, and when destroyed contained more than a 1000 families, and had furnished the continental army with more than a 1000 men, who were generally the young and active part of the population.* The opposite sides which the inhabitants took in the great revolutionary question, created the most violent rancor in the bosoms of both parties, and hence the barbarities which ensued.

In November following, Cherry-valley met with a fate similar to Wyoming. At this time, *Brant* was returning to winter-quarters, when he was met by a tory captain, and persuaded to engage in one expedition more. This was *Walter Butler,* son of *John,* the hero of Wyoming. He went to Canada with *Guy Johnson,* in 1775, as has been mentioned; and now some circumstance brought him among the frontier settlements of New York. What his object was, we are not informed; but it was, doubtless, that of a spy. However, he was taken up on suspicion, at least, and confined in jail at Albany; falling sick, he was removed to a private dwelling, from whence he soon found means to escape. Joining his father at Niagara, he succeeded in detaching a part of his regiment upon an incursion. Meeting with *Brant,* as was just mentioned, they returned to the frontier. It is said that *Brant* was at first displeased with the project, understanding that Capt. *Walter* had been put in office over him by his old general, Walter's father, but stifled his resentment. Their whole force was 700 men, 500 of whom were the warriors of *Brant.*

Col. *Ichabod Alden,* of Massachusetts, was in command at Cherry-valley, and to his misguided judgment is to be attributed the disaster which ensued. But, like *Waldron* of Cochecho, he was doomed to escape the disgrace. He was early apprized of the march of *Brant,* and when urged to receive the inhabitants into the fort, observed that there was no danger, as he would keep out scouts who would apprize them of the approach of an enemy in season to remove. Scouts were accordingly sent out; one of which, either forgetting the business they were upon, or what was equally reprehensible, made a large fire and lay down to sleep. *Brant's* warriors were not misled by so luminous a beacon, and the whole were made prisoners. This was on the night of the 9 November, 1778. The prisoners now in the hands of *Brant* were obliged to give the most exact intelligence concerning the garrison. On the morning of the 11, favored by a thick and hazy atmosphere, they approached the fort. Cols. *Alden* and *Stacia* quartered at the house of a Mr. *Wells.* A Mr. *Hamble* was fired upon as he was coming from his house to the fort, by a scout, which gave the first notice of the enemy. He escaped, and gave the alarm to Col. *Alden,* who, strange as it may appear, was still incredulous, and said it was nothing more than some straggling Indians. The last space of time was thus lost!—and, in less than half an hour, all parts of the place were invested at once. Such of the soldiers as were collected being immediately all killed or taken, the poor inhabitants fell an easy prey. Col. *Alden* was among the first victims. Like *Chopart,* in the massacre at Natchez, he fled from his house, and was pursued by an Indian with his hatchet, at whom the colonel endeavored several times to discharge his pistol; but it missing fire, and losing time in facing about for this purpose, the Indian was sufficiently near to throw his tomahawk with deadly effect. He did so. Col. *Alden* fell upon his face, and his scalp was in a moment borne off in triumph. "A tory boasted that he killed Mr. *Wells* while at prayer." His daughter, a young lady of great amiableness, fled from the house to a pile of wood for shelter; but an Indian pursued her, who coming near, composedly wiped his long knife, already bloody, upon his leggins, then returning it to his belt, seized her by the arm, and with a

† *Marshall,* iii. 555.

blow of his tomahawk ended her existence. She could speak some Indian, and begged her murderer to spare her life, and a tory interceded, who stood near, urging that she was his sister; but he would hear to neither. Other transactions in this affair, of still greater horror, we must pass in silence.

Between 30 and 40 prisoners were carried off; but the fort, containing about 200 soldiers, was not taken, although several trials were made upon it.

Brant was the only person engaged in this tragedy of whom we hear any acts of clemency; one of which was the preservation of a poor woman and her children, who, but for him, would have met the tomahawk. He inquired for Capt. *M'Kean,* (who wrote him the letter before mentioned,) saying he had now come to accept his challenge. Being answered that "Capt *M'Kean* would not turn his back upon an enemy," he replied, "I know it. He is a brave man, and I would have given more to have taken him than any other man in Cherry-valley; but I would not have hurt a hair of his head."

Brant had seen and heard so much of what is called *civilized, warfare,* that he was afraid of the traduction of his character, and always said that, in his councils, he had tried to make his warriors humane; and to his honor it is said, (but in proportion as his character is raised, that of the white man must sink,) that where he had the chief command, few barbarities were committed.

The night before *Brant* and *Butler* fell upon Cherry-valley, some of the tories who had friends there, requested liberty to go in secretly and advise them to retire. *Butler,* though some of his own friends were among the inhabitants, refused, saying, "that there were so many families connected, that the one would inform the others, and all would escape. He thus sacrificed his friends, for the sake of punishing his enemies." This, whether reported by *Brant* to magnify his own humanity, by a contrast with the depravity of his associate, is not known, but it may have been the fact.

Various incursions into the Indian country by Gen. *Sullivan,* and others, much damped the spirits of the Indians, although few of them were either killed or taken. When the armies approached their settlements, they fled into swamps and mountains; yet they suffered extremely from the loss of all their crops. It was said that this summer, (1779,) 160,000 bushels of their corn was destroyed. As soon as it was known that Sullivan was, advancing into the country, *Brant* & *Butler,* with 600 Indians, and *Johnson,* with 200 tories, took a position on his route, to cut him off. Sullivan came upon them, August 29, at a place called *Newtown,* where they had entrenched themselves, and immediately attacked them. The battle lasted about two hours, when, by a successful movement of Gen. *Poor,* at the head of his New Hampshire regiment, *Brant's* warriors were thrown into confusion, and the whole were put to flight.* Few were killed, and they made no other stand against the Americans during the expedition.† The historian adds, "They utterly destroyed 40 villages, and left no single trace of vegetation upon the surface of the ground."‡ All their cattle were either killed or brought off, many of which they had be-

---

* Nine only of the Indians were killed; of the Americans, four. It is said to be owing to the sagacity of *Brant,* that his whole force escaped falling into the hands of the Americans. *Annals Tryon* Co. 125.

† *Botta,* Hist. Rev. ii. 206.

‡ Ibid. Some of the officers thought it too degrading to the army to be employed in destroying fruit-trees, and remonstrated to Gen. *Sullivan* against the order. He replied, "The Indians shall see that there is malice enough in our hearts to destroy every thing that contributes to their support." *Gordon,* Amer. Rev. iii. 21.

fore taken from the Americans. "None of the bounties of nature, none of the products of human industry, escaped the fury of the Americans."* Upon this business the same author writes, that "the officers charged with the execution of these devastations, were themselves ashamed of them; some even ventured to remonstrate that they were not accustomed to exercise the vocation of banditti." Gen. *Poor,* doubtless, was the efficient man in this expedition, but the ostentation of *Sullivan* gained him the *honor*! of it. Thus were the Five Nations chastised for acting as they had been taught by the white people; yea, by the Americans themselves.†

The following summer, (23 July, 1779,) Col. *Brant,* with 60 of his warriors and 27 white men, came suddenly upon Minisink, in Orange county, New York, where they killed sundry of the inhabitants and made others captives. They burnt ten houses, twelve barns, a garrison and two mills, and then commenced their retreat. The militia from Goshen and places adjacent, to the number of 149, collected, pursued and came up with them, when a most bloody battle was fought. The Indians were finally victorious, and 30 only, out of the 149 whites, escaped. Some were carried into captivity, and the rest were killed. Not being sufficiently cautious, they fell into an ambush, and so fought at great disadvantage.‡

In 1821, a county meeting was held, by which it was voted that the bones of the slain should be collected, and deposited under a suitable monument, at the same time ordered to be erected.§ In 1822, the committee appointed to collect the bones "which had been exposed to the suns and snows for 43 years," had found those of 44 persons, which were, with much formality, publicly interred.||

In the spring of 1780, *Brant* surprised Harpersfield, with a company of his warrior, and a few tories. He took 19 prisoners, and killed several others. On 2 August following, he fell upon Canajoharrie, with about 400 mixed warriors, killed 16 people, took about 55 prisoners, chiefly women and children; they killed and drove away, at the same time, about 300 cattle and horses, burnt 53 houses, and as many barns, besides out-houses, a new and elegant church, a grist-mill and two garrisons.

Doubtless there were many other warlike scenes in which *Brant* was engaged personally, but we have already dwelt longer upon them than we intended.

European writers, for a long time, contended that the N. American Indians had, naturally, no beards.¶ A Mr. *M'Causland* took the trouble of writing to *Brant,* after the revolution, to get the truth of the matter. The following is *Brant's* letter to his inquiry:—"*Niagara,* 19 *April,* 1783. *The men of the Six Nations have all beards by nature; as have likewise all other Indian nations of North America, which I have seen. Some Indians allow a part of the beard upon the chin and upper lip to grow, and a few of the Mohawks shave with razors, in the same manner as Europeans; but the generality pluck out the hairs of the beard by the roots, as soon as they begin to appear; and as they continue this practice all their lives, they appear to have no beard, or, at most, only a few straggling hairs, which they have neglected to pluck out. I am, however, of opinion, that if the Indians*

---

* *Gordon,* Amer. Rev. iii. 207.

† See the speech of *Big-tree, Corn-plant* and *Half-town,* to which nothing need be added by way of commentary upon such affairs.

‡ *Gordon's* America, iii. 22.

§ *Spafford's* Gaz. 328.

|| *Holmes's* Amer. Annals, ii. 302.

¶ Even the great luminary *Voltaire* fell into this error. He says, "*Les Iroquois, les Hurons, et tous les peuples jusqu'á la Florida, parurent olivâtres et sans aucum poil sur le corps excepté la tête.*" That is, all from the 60° of N. latitude. Voyez *Œuvres complètes,* iv. 708, ed. Paris, 1817, 8vo. See also *Raynal,* viii. 210.

*were to shave, they would never have beards altogether so thick as the Europeans; and there are some to be met with who have actually very little beard.** JOS. BRANT THAYENDANEGA."

A daughter of Col. *Brant* married a Frenchman, who, in June, 1789, was killed by a party of Indians, while peaceably travelling up the Wabash River. He was in company with nine others, four of whom were killed and three wounded. When the hostile party came up to them, and discovered the son-in-law of *Brant,* they assisted in drawing the arrows from the wounded, and then went off.†

When the Indians upon the southern and western frontier were showing themselves hostile, in 1791, Col. *Brant* used his exertions to prevent hostilities, by visiting such tribes as appeared hostile. His name appears in many important transactions of those times. The boundary line between the United States and the Indian nations had not been satisfactorily established, which was the cause of much trouble. A gentleman in Canada wrote to another in the state of New York, under date of 2 August, 1791, wherein Col. *Brant* is thus mentioned: "Capt. *Joseph Brant,* after having attended for some time the councils of the western Indians at the Miami River, set off a few days ago for Quebec, attended with several of the chiefs from that quarter; as they avowedly go to ask Lord *Dorchester's* advice, and as we well know his and government's strong desire for peace, we would gladly hope that it may be the means of bringing on an accommodation."

In 1792, his arrival in Philadelphia is thus publicly noticed in the Gazette of that city:—"Capt. *Joseph Brant,* the principal warrior chief of the Six Nations, arrived in this city on Wednesday evening last, (June 20.) It is said his errand is a visit to a number of his acquaintance residing here, and to pay his respects to the president of the United States." He left there about the beginning of July, upon another peace excursion among the western tribes, which still remained hostile.

When Gen. *Wayne* was marching into the Indian country, in 1793, many of the tribes were alarmed, having heard that his army consisted of 8000 men. Learning, also, that commissioners accompanied the army, authorized to treat of peace, and wishing to know the strength of the Americans, thirty chiefs of different tribes were despatched upon this important business. Col. *Brant* was one of these 30 Indian ambassadors. If the Americans would make the Ohio the boundary, they wished peace. The whole cause of Gen. *Wayne's* war appears to have been about the lands lying west of the Ohio and Alleghany Rivers. We have no doubt *Brant* secretly, if not openly, advocated the establishment of this boundary; yes, and we must acknowledge that if he did, it was from the best of reasons. We know that *Tecumseh* labored incessantly for this boundary. Rightly did they conceive of the mighty wave of population rolling westward, southward and northward. Truly, they must have been blind not to have seen that it was about to engulf them forever! When they had met the commissioners, and found them inflexible in their determination, *Brant,* with most of the chiefs of the Six Nations, gave up the point as hopeless, preferring peace, on any terms, to war. But the Wyandots, Delawares, Shawanees and Miamis would not agree to it.

Mention will be found in the account of *Farmers-brother* of a great council held by the chiefs of most of the western nations, at Niagara, in April, 1793. In this council it was agreed that peace should be maintained; and "they unanimously agreed to meet the Americans in a grand council, to be holden the June following, upon the south side of Lake

---

* This is the case with many of the whites.
† *Carey's* Museum, vi. 178.

Erie; and for the purpose of making the peace more permanent and extensive, they have appointed *Brant*, who is now their king of kings, to go and convene all those tribes who live to the north-west of Lake Ontario. He accordingly, the day after, set out for that purpose." The Indians did not assemble until July, from the difficulty of their journeys and other causes, which is generally the case with meetings of this kind. The council was held at Sandusky, and Col. *Brant* set out from Niagara for that place in May. Before leaving, he had frequent conversations with a gentleman of respectability, to whom he gave it as his opinion, that no peace could take place, until the Ohio and Muskingum should make the boundary between the Americans and the red men. He still expressed good feelings towards the United States, and hoped that they would see it to be their interest to agree to that boundary, as he firmly believed war would ensue should they refuse. He even said, that, in case they would not consent to make these rivers the boundary, he should take part against them. It was not agreed to; but we do not hear that the old chief was actually engaged in the hostilities that followed.

How much the English of Canada influenced the measures of the Indians, it is difficult to determine;* but men like *Pontiac, Brant* and *Tecumseh* could easily see through such duplicity as was practised by a few unprincipled speculators, as *M'Kee, Girty* and *Elliot*. They had, doubtless, conceived that if the Ohio and Muskingum were made the boundary, it would be an easy matter for them to possess themselves of the country from thence to the lakes, and thus enlarge the extent of Canada. They knew well that if the Indians possessed this tract of country, it would be no difficult matter to purchase it from them by means of a few trifling articles, comparatively of no consideration, and that worst of calamities, ardent spirits! In this they were disappointed, and, with the battle of Presque Isle, resigned their hopes, at least for a season. They urged upon the Indians what they must have been well assured of—their destruction!

Much has been said and written of the cold-blooded atrocities of Brant, but which, in our opinion, will be much lessened on being able to come pretty near the truth of his history. Every successful warrior, at least in his day, is denounced by the vanquished as a barbarian. *Napoleon* was thus branded by all the world—we ask no excuse for our chief on this score—all wars are barbarous, and hence those who wage them are barbarians! This we know to be strong language; but we are prepared to prove our assertion. When mankind shall have been cultivated and improved to that extent which human nature is capable of attaining,—when the causes of avarice and dissension are driven out of the human mind, by taking away the means which excite them,—then, and not till then, will wars and a multitude of attending calamities cease.

---

* We will hear a great writer and traveller upon this subject, whose means of forming a correct judgment, it is presumed, will not be questioned. "Je remarquerai à cette occasion sans m'étendre davantage sur ce sujet, que toute la politque de l'Angleterre avec les Indiens est absolument dans les mains des agens, qui seuls en entendent la langue; et qui seuls sont les distributeurs des presens;" &c. *Voyage dans les Etats-unis en* 1795, *etc. Par La Rochefoucauld-Laincourt,* ii. 78. The duke was at Newark, U. C. at this time, where he witnessed a business assemblage of Indians. After a dance, which they held before their audience with the governor of Canada, the duke says that, "Pendant ces jeux, l'agent s'est approché du général avec un des chefs, et lui a dit que sa nation de Tuscorora le consultait pour savoir si elle irait à un conseil tenu par les Indiens Oneydas à Onondago pour vendre leurs terres de reserve, que l'Etat de New Yorck dèsirait acheter. Le gouverneur a répondu trés-vaguement à cett question; l'agent a traduit comme il a voulu cette réponse; mais il a répliqué au gouverneur de la part des Indiens qui comme ils croyaient être plus agréables au roy d'Angleterre en n'y allant pas; ils n'iraient pas." Ibid. 77.

7

As a sample of the stories circulating about Col. *Brant,* while the affairs of Wyoming and Cherry-valley were fresh in the recollections of all, we extract from *Weld's* Travels the following:—*

"With a considerable body of his troops he joined the forces under the command of Sir *John Johnston.*" "A skirmish took place with a body of American troops; the action was warm, and *Brant* was shot by a musket ball in his heel; but the Americans, in the end, were defeated, and an officer with about 60 men were taken prisoners. The officer, after having delivered up his sword, had entered into conversation with Col. *Johnston,* who commanded the British troops, and they were talking together in the most friendly manner, when *Brant,* having stolen slily behind them, laid the American officer lifeless on the ground with a blow of his tomahawk. The indignation of Sir *John Johnston,* as may be readily supposed, was roused by such an act of treachery, and he resented it in the warmest terms. *Brant* listened to him unconcernedly, and when he had finished, told him, that *he was sorry for his displeasure, but that, indeed, his heel was extremely painful at the moment, and he could not help revenging himself on the only chief of the party that he saw taken.*"

Upon this passage the author of the Annals of Tryon County† observes: "I have heard a story somewhat similar told of him, but it was said that the officer was killed to prevent his being retaken by the Americans, who were in pursuit." This we should pronounce very *dis*-similar to the story told by Mr. *Weld.* But there was, no doubt, some circumstance out of which a story has grown, the truth of which, we apprehend, is now past finding out.

Col. *Brant* was married, in the winter of 1779, to a daughter of Col. *Croghan* by an Indian woman. He had lived with her some time, ad libitum, according to the Indian manner, but at this time, being present at the wedding of a Miss *Moore,* at Niagara, (one of the captives taken from Cherry-valley,) insisted on being married himself; and thus his consort's name was no longer Miss *Croghan,* but Mrs. *Brant.* The ceremony was performed by his companion in arms, Col. *John Butler,* who, although he had left his country, yet carried so much of his magistrate's commission with him, as to *solemnize* marriages *according to law.*

King *George* conferred on his famous ally a valuable tract of land situated upon the west shore of Lake Ontario, where he finally settled and lived after the English fashion. His wife, however, would never conform to this mode of life, but would adhere to the custom of the Indians, and on the death of her husband, which happened 24 Nov. 1807, she repaired to Grand River, there to spend her days in a wigwam, with some of her children, while she left behind others in a commodious dwelling.‡ A son, of whom we have spoken, with a sister, lately occupied this mansion of their father, and constituted an amiable and hospitable family. This son, whose name is *John,* is a man of note, and is the same who was in England in 1822, as has been mentioned, and the same, we conclude, who has been returned a member of the colonial assembly of Upper Canada. His place of residence was in the county of Haldiman, in Brantford, so called, probably, in honor of the old chief.§ Several other places are mentioned as having been the residence of *Brant*—Unadilla, or Anaquaqua, (which is about 36 miles south-west from the present site of Cooperstown,) and Niagara. He resided at these places before the Mohawks removed to Canada, which was soon after the war of the revolution was ended. They

* Page 486, octavo ed. London, 1800.

† In the Appendix, page 16.

‡ *Buchanan's* Sketches, i. 36.

§ Mr. *Campbell's* Annals of Tryon County has been one of our main sources of information throughout this account, especially of the revolutionary period.

made their principal residence upon Grand River, which falls into Lake Erie on the north side, about 60 miles from the town of Newark, or Niagara. At one time, he had no less than 30 or 40 negroes, who took care of his horses and lands. "These poor creatures," says Mr. *Weld,* "are kept in the greatest subjection, and they dare not attempt to make their escape, for he has assured them, that if they did so, he would follow them himself, though it were to the confines of Georgia, and would tomahawk them wherever he met them. They know his disposition too well not to think that he would adhere strictly to his word." The same author says that *Brant* received presents, which, together with his half pay as captain, amounted to £500 *per annum.*

An idea of the importance of this chief, in 1795, may be formed from the circumstance, that a gentleman considered himself a loser to the amount of £100, at least, by not being able to arrive at Niagara in season to attend to some law case for him. Contrary winds had prevented his arrival, and the business had been given to another.*

"Whenever the affairs of his nation shall permit him to do so, *Brant* declares it to be his intention to sit down to the further study of the Greek language, of which he professes himself to be a great admirer, and to translate from the original, into the Mohawk language, more of the New Testament; yet this same man, shortly before we arrived at Niagara, killed his own son, with his own hand. The son, it seems, was a drunken, good-for-nothing fellow, who had often avowed his intention of destroying his father. One evening, he absolutely entered the apartment of his father, and had begun to grapple with him, perhaps with a view to put his unnatural threats in execution, when *Brant* drew a short sword, and felled him to the ground. He speaks of this affair with regret, but, at the same time, without any of that emotion which another person than an Indian might be supposed to feel. He consoles himself for the act, by thinking that he has benefited the nation, by ridding it of a rascal."†

With regard to the dress of the sachem, there has been some contradiction. Mr. *Weld,* though he did not see him, says he wore his hair in the Indian fashion, as he also did his clothes; except that, instead of the blanket, he wore a kind of hunting frock. This was in 1796. But it was reported, that, in 1792, *Brant* having waited on Lord *Dorchester,* the governor of Canada, upon some business, his lordship told him, that as he was an officer in the British service, he ought to lay aside the Indian dress, and assume that of an English captain; and that, if he persisted in wearing an Indian dress, he should stop his pay. It is added that thereupon he changed his dress.‡

When Col. *Brant* arrived at any principal city, his arrival was publicly announced in the gazettes with great minuteness. Although we have given some specimens of these, we will add one more:—

"New York, June 20, 1792. On Monday last arrived in this city, from his settlement on Grand River, on a visit to some of his friends in this quarter, Capt. *Joseph Brandt,* of the British army, the famous Mohawk chief, who so eminently distinguished himself during the late war, as the military leader of the Six Nations. We are informed that he intends to visit the city of Philadelphia, and pay his respects to the president of the U. States,"§ Gen. *Washington,* which he did. We have before mentioned his visit to that city.

The very respectable traveller|| *Roshefoucauld* thus notices our chief: "At 24 miles from this place, (Newark, U. C.) upon Grand River, is

* *Weld,* Travels, 487.

† Ibid. 489.

‡ Apollo for 1792.

§ American Apollo, 297.

|| Duke *de Laincourt,* Travels, ii. 81, before cited, from whom we translate this.

an establishment which I had been curious to visit. It is that of Col. *Brant*. But the colonel not being at home, and being assured that I should see little else than what I had already seen among those people, I gave over my intention. Col. *Brant* is an Indian who took part with the English, and having been in England, was commissioned by the king, and politely treated by every one. His manners are half European. He is accompanied by two negro servants, and is in appearance like an Englishman. He has a garden and farm under cultivation; dresses almost entirely like an European, and has great influence over the Indians. He is at present [1795] at Miami, holding a treaty with the United States, in company with the Indians of the west. He is equally respected by the Americans, who extol so much his character, that I regret much not to have seen him."*

The great respect in which *Brant* was held in England will be very apparent from a perusal of the following letter,† dated 12 December, 1785: "Monday last, Col. *Joseph Brant*, the celebrated king of the Mohawks, arrived in this city, [Salisbury,] from America, and after dining with Col. *de Peister*, at the head-quarters here, proceeded immediately on his journey to London. This extraordinary personage is said to have presided at the late grand congress of confederate chiefs of the Indian nation in America, and to be by them appointed to the conduct and chief command in the war which they now meditate against the United States of America. He took his departure for England immediately as that assembly broke up; and it is conjectured that his embassy to the British court is of great importance. This country owes much to the services of Col. *Brant* during the late war in America. He was educated at Philadelphia, [at the Moor's charity school in Lebanon, Connecticut,] is a very shrewd, intelligent person, possesses great courage and abilities as a warrior, and is inviolably attached to the English nation."

It has been denied that *Brant* was in any way engaged in the massacres at Wyoming, but it seems hardly possible that so many should have been deceived at that time; and, moreover, we do not find that it was denied until almost every one of that age had left the stage of action. Those who deny that he was at Wyoming should, at least, prove an alibi, or they cannot expect to be believed.‡

---

* This French traveller seems to have been in advance of history, in as far as he thus early sets in their proper light the characters of the heroes of Wyoming. After speaking of the influence of Indian agents over those people, as we have extracted in a previous note, he thus consigns to Col. *Butler* the place which he is doubtless to hold in all after time in the annals of his country:—"L'agent anglais dont il est ici queston, est le Colonel *Buttler*, fameux par ses incendies, ses pillages et ses meurtres dans la guerre d'Amérique. Il est lui-même Américain d'auprès de Wilkesbarre; [one of the towns in the valley of Wyoming;] son prétendu loyalisme qu'il a su se faire payer de brevets et de traitemens, lui a fait commettre plus de barbaries, plus d'infamies contre sa patrie, qu'à qui que ce soit. Il conduisait les Indiens, leur indiquait les fermes, les maisons à brûler, les victimes à scarpeler, les enfans à déchirer. L'Angleterre a recompensé son loyalisme de 5000 acres de terre pour lui, d'une quantité pareille pour ses enfans, d'une pension de deux à trois cents livres sterlings, d'une place d'agent auprès des Indiens, qui lui en vaut cinq cents autres, avec la facilité de puiser à volonté dans les magasins de présens." *Rochefoucauld*, ut supra, (ii. 78–9.)

† There is no name to this letter; but it was written in Salisbury, Eng. and thence sent to London, where it was published.

‡ In a late criminal trial which has much agitated New England, reasonable people said, the defendant, out of respect to public opinion, ought to make it appear where he was at the time a murder was committed, although in law he was not bound so to do. An advocate for his innocence told the writer, that "he was not *obliged* to tell where he was," and it was nobody's business; and, therefore, we were bound, according to law, to believe him innocent. This we offer as a parallel case to the one in hand. But it happens we are not "bound by law" to believe our chief entirely innocent of the blood shed at Wyoming.

Brant was said to have been 65 years old at his death. A daughter of his married Wm. *J. Ker*, Esq. of Niagara, and he had several other children besides those we have mentioned. The son who visited England in 1822, and another named *Jacob*, entered *Moor's* school at Hanover, N. H. in 1801, under the care of Dr. *Wheelock*. The former son, *John*, died about two years since, in the winter of 1831.

CHAPTER VI.

Facts in the history of the Seneca nation—SAGOYEWATHA, or RED-JACKET—*His famous speech to a missionary—His interview with Col. Snelling—British invade his country—Resolves to repel them—His speech upon the event—Gov. Clinton's account of him—Witchcraft affair—Complains of encroachments—One of his people put to death for being a witch—He defends the executioner—His interview with Lafayette—Council at Canandaigua—Farmers-brother—Red-jacket visits Philadelphia—His speech to the governor of Pennsylvania—Speech of Agwelondongwas, or Good Peter—Narrative of his capture during the revolutionary war*—FARMERS-BROTHER, *or* HONAYAWUS—*Visits Philadelphia*—PETER-JAQUETTE—*Visits France—Account of his death—Memorable speech of Farmers-brother—His letter to the secretary of war—Notice of several other Seneca chiefs*—KOYINGQUAUTAH, *or* YOUNG-KING—JUSKAKAKA, *or* LITTLE-BILLY—ACHIOUT, or HALF-TOWN—KIANDOGEWA, *or* BIG-TREE—GYANTWAIA, *or* CORN-PLANT—*Address of the three latter to President Washington—Grant of land to Big-tree—His visit to Philadelphia, and death—Further account of Corn-plant—His own account of himself—Interesting events in his life—His sons.*

THE Senecas were the most important tribe among the Iroquois, or Five Nations, and, according to *Conrad Weiser*, they were the fourth nation that joined that confederacy. He calls them* "Ieuontowanois or Sinikers," and says, "they are styled by the Mohawks and Onondagos, brothers;" and that their title in councils is Onughkaurydaaug. The French call them Tsonnonthouans, from their principal castle, or council-house, the name of which, according to *Colden*, is Sinondowans.† Other particulars of this nation will be related as we proceed in detailing the lives of its chiefs. Among these, perhaps, the most illustrious was

Sagoyewatha,‡ called by the whites, *Red-jacket*. His place of residence was, for many years previous to his death, (which happened 20 January 1830, at his own house,) about four miles from Buffalo, and one mile north of the road that leads through the land reserved for the remnant of the Seneca nation, called the *Reservation*. His house was a log cabin, situated in a retired place. Some of his tribe are Christians, but *Red-jacket* would never hear to any thing of the kind. He was formerly considered of superior wisdom in council, and of a noble and dignified behavior which would have honored any man. But, like nearly *all* his race, he could not withstand the temptation of ardent spirits, which, together with his age, rendered him latterly less worthy notice. Formerly, scarce a

* American Mag.

† Hist. Five Nations, i. 42.

‡ The common method of spelling. Gov. *Clinton* writes, *Saguoaha*. Written to the treaty of "Konondaigua," (Nov. 1794,) *Soggooyawauthau*; to that of Buffalo Creek, (June, 1802,) *Soogooyawautau*; to that of Moscow, (Sept. 1823,) *Sagouata*. It is said to signify "*One who keeps awake*," or simply, *Keeper-awake*.

traveller passed near his place of residence, who would not go out of his way to see this wonderful man, and to hear his profound observations.

In the year 1805, a council were held at Buffalo, in the state of New York, at which were present many of the Seneca chiefs and warriors, assembled at the request of a missionary, Mr. *Cram,* from Massachusetts. It was at this time that *Red-jacket* delivered his famous speech, about which so much has been said and written, and which we propose to give here at length, and *correctly,* as some omissions and errors were contained in it as published at the time. It may be taken as genuine, at least as nearly so as the Indian language can be translated, in which it was delivered, for *Red-jacket* would not speak in English, although he understood it. The missionary first made a speech to the Indians, in which he explained the object for which he had called them together; namely, to inform them that he was sent by the missionary society of Boston to instruct them "how to worship the *Great Spirit,*" and not to get away their lands and money; that there was but one religion, and unless they embraced it they could not be happy; that they had lived in darkness and great errors all their lives; he wished that, if they had any objections to his religion, they would state them; that he had visited some smaller tribes, who waited their decision before they would consent to receive him, as they were their "older brothers."

After the missionary had done speaking, the Indians conferred together about two hours, by themselves, when they gave an answer by *Red-jacket,* which follows:—

"*Friend and brother,* it was the will of the Great Spirit that we should meet together this day. He orders all things, and he has given us a fine day for our council. He has taken his garment from before the sun, and caused it to shine with brightness upon us; our eyes are opened, that we see clearly; our ears are unstopped, that we have been able to hear distinctly the words that you have spoken; for all these favors we thank the Great Spirit, and him only.

"*Brother,* this council fire was kindled by you; it was at your request that we came together at this time; we have listened with attention to what you have said; you requested us to speak our minds freely; this gives us great joy, for we now consider that we stand upright before you, and can speak what we think; all have heard your voice, and all speak to you as one man; our minds are agreed.

"*Brother,* you say you want an answer to your talk before you leave this place. It is right you should have one, as you are a great distance from home, and we do not wish to detain you; but we will first look back a little, and tell you what our fathers have told us, and what we have heard from the white people.

"*Brother, listen to what we say.* There was a time when our forefathers owned this great island.* Their seats extended from the rising to the setting sun. The Great Spirit had made it for the use of Indians. He had created the buffalo, the deer, and other animals for food. He made the bear, and the beaver, and their skins served us for clothing. He had scattered them over the country, and taught us how to take them. He had caused the earth to produce corn for bread. All this he had done for his red children because he loved them. If we had any disputes about hunting grounds, they were generally settled without the shedding of much blood: but an evil day came upon us; your forefathers crossed the great waters, and landed on this island. Their numbers were small; they found friends, and not enemies; they told us they had fled from their own country for fear of wicked men, and come here to enjoy their religion.

* A general opinion among all the Indians that this country was an island.

They asked for a small seat; we took pity on them, granted their request, and they sat down amongst us; we gave them corn and meat; they gave us poison* in return. The white people had now found our country, tidings were carried back, and more came amongst us; yet we did not fear them, we took them to be friends; they called us brothers; we believed them, and gave them a larger seat. At length, their numbers had greatly increased; they wanted more land; they wanted our country. Our eyes were opened, and our minds became uneasy. Wars took place; Indians were hired to fight against Indians, and many of our people were destroyed. They also brought strong liquors among us: it was strong and powerful, and has slain thousands.

"*Brother*, our seats were once large, and yours were very small; you have now become a great people, and we have scarcely a place left to spread our blankets; you have got our country, but are not satisfied; *you want to force your religion upon us.*

"*Brother, continue to listen.* You say that you are sent to instruct us how to worship the *Great Spirit* agreeably to his mind, and if we do not take hold of the religion which you white people teach, we shall be unhappy hereafter; you say that you are right, and we are lost; how do we know this to be true? We understand that your religion is written in a book; if it was intended for us as well as you, why has not the Great Spirit given it to us, and not only to us, but why did he not give to our forefathers the knowledge of that book, with the means of understanding it rightly? We only know what you tell us about it; how shall we know when to believe, being so often deceived by the white people?

"*Brother*, you say there is but one way to worship and serve the Great Spirit; if there is but one religion, why do you white people differ so much about it? why not all agree, as you can all read the book?

"*Brother*, we do not understand these things; we are told that your religion was given to your forefathers, and has been handed down from father to son. We also have a religion which was given to our forefathers, and has been handed down to us their children. We worship that way. *It teacheth us to be thankful for all the favors we receive; to love each other, and to be united; we never quarrel about religion.*

"*Brother*, the Great Spirit has made us all; but he has made a great difference between his white and red children; he has given us a different complexion, and different customs; to you he has given the arts; to these he has not opened our eyes; we know these things to be true. Since he has made so great a difference between us in other things, why may we not conclude that he has given us a different religion according to our understanding; the Great Spirit does right; he knows what is best for his children; we are satisfied.

"*Brother*, we do not wish to destroy your religion, or take it from you; we only want to enjoy our own.

"*Brother*, you say you have not come to get our land or our money, but to enlighten our minds. I will now tell you that I have been at your meetings, and saw you collecting money from the meeting. I cannot tell what this money was intended for, but suppose it was for your minister, and if we should conform to your way of thinking, perhaps you may want some from us.

"*Brother*, we are told that you have been preaching to white people in this place; these people are our neighbors; we are acquainted with them, we will wait a little while and see what effect your preaching has upon them. If we find it does them good, makes them honest, and less disposed to cheat Indians, we will then consider again what you have said.

---

* Spirituous liquor is alluded to, it is supposed.

"*Brother*, you have now heard our answer to your talk, and this is all we have to say at present. As we are going to part, we will come and take you by the hand, and hope the Great Spirit will protect you on your journey, and return you safe to your friends."

In one version of this speech we find the following passage, which, though very well agreeing with *Red-jacket's* sentiments, we cannot aver to be genuine. It may be mentioned, that the Indians cannot well conceive how they have any participation in the guilt of the crucifixion; inasmuch as they do not believe themselves of the same origin as the whites; and there being no dispute but that they committed that act. What our chief is reported to have said is as follows:—

"*Brother, if you white men murdered the Son of the Great Spirit, we Indians had nothing to do with it, and it is none of our affair. If he had come among us, we would not have killed him; we would have treated him well. You must make amends for that crime yourselves.*"

The chiefs and others then drew near the missionary to take him by the hand; but he would not receive them, and hastily rising from his seat, said, "that there was no fellowship between the religion of *God* and the works of the *Devil*, and, therefore, could not join hands with them." Upon this being interpreted to them, "they smiled, and retired in a peaceable manner."

Red-jacket took part with the Americans in the war of 1812, but was not distinguished for that prodigality of life which marked the character of *Tecumseh*, and many others, but, on all occasions, was cool and collected. He had become attached to Col. *Snelling* during the war, and when he heard that that officer was ordered to a distant station, he went to take his farewell of him. At that interview, he said,

"*Brother, I hear you are going to a place called* Governor's Island. *I hope you will be a governor yourself. I understand that you white people think children a blessing. I hope you may have a thousand. And, above all, I hope, wherever you go, you may never find whiskey more than two shillings a quart.*"*

Grand Island, in Niagara River, just above the famous Niagara Falls, is owned by the Senecas. When it was rumored that the British had taken possession of it, in their last war with the Americans, *Red-jacket* assembled his people, to consult with Mr. *Granger*, their agent. After having stated to him the information, the old chief made the following profound speech:—

"*Brother*, you have told us that we had nothing to do with the war that has taken place between you and the British. But we find the war has come to our doors. Our property is taken possession of by the British and their Indian friends. It is necessary now for us to take up the business, defend our property, and drive the enemy from it. If we sit still upon our seats, and take no means of redress, the British (according to the customs of you white people) will hold it by conquest. And should you conquer the Canadas, you will claim it upon the same principles, as [though] conquered from the British. We, therefore, request permission to go with our warriors, and drive off those bad people, and take possession of our lands." Whereupon, such of the Senecas as had an inclination, were permitted to join the American army.

Gov. *De. Witt Clinton*, in his most valuable discourse before the Historical Society of New York, thus notices *Red-jacket*:—"Within a few years, an extraordinary orator has risen among the Senecas; his real name is *Saguoaha*. Without the advantages of illustrious descent, and with no extraordinary talents for war, he has attained the first distinctions in the na-

* N. E. Galaxy, 13 July, 1883.

tion by the force of his eloquence." *Red-jacket* having, by some means, lost the confidence of his countrymen, in order, as it is reported, to retrieve it again, prevailed upon his brother to announce himself a prophet, commissioned by the Great Spirit to redeem the miserable condition of his countrymen. It required nothing but an adroit and skilful reasoner to persuade the ignorant multitude, given to the grossest superstition, of his infallibility in the pretended art or mystery. If good ever came out of evil, it did at this time. The Onondagas were, at that period, the most drunken and profligate of all the Iroquois. They were now so far prevailed upon as almost entirely to abstain from ardent spirits, became sober and industrious, and observed and respected the laws of morality. This good effect was not confined to the Onondagas, but shed its benign influence through the nations adjacent. But as this reform was begun in hypocrisy, it necessarily ended with its hypocritical author. The greatest check, perhaps, which can be thrown in the way of imposture, is its own exposition. In this case, like witchcraft among us in former times, it was stayed by its own operations. Many were denounced as witches, and some would have been executed but for the interference of their white neighbors. *Red-jacket* was denounced in a great council of Indians, held at Buffalo Creek, as the chief author of their troubles. He was accordingly brought to trial, and his eloquence saved his life, and greatly increased his reputation. His defence was near three hours long. And, in the language of Governor *Clinton*, "the iron brow of superstition relented under the magic of his eloquence: he declared the prophet [his brother] an impostor and a cheat; he prevailed; the Indians divided, and a small majority appeared in his favor. Perhaps the annals of history cannot furnish a more conspicuous instance of the triumph and power of oratory, in a barbarous nation, devoted to superstition, and looking up to the accuser as a delegated minister of the Almighty. I am well aware that the speech of *Logan* will be triumphantly quoted against me; and that it will be said, that the most splendid exhibition of Indian eloquence may be found out of the pale of the Six Nations. I fully subscribe to the eulogium of Mr. *Jefferson*, when he says, 'I may challenge the whole orations of *Demosthenes* and *Cicero*, and of any more eminent orator, if Europe has furnished more eminent, to produce a single passage superior to the speech of *Logan*.' But let it be remembered that *Logan* was a *Mingo* chief," that is, an Iroquois.

The time is not far distant, if not already arrived, when the name of *Red-jacket* will be heard, in the most august assemblies, to give weight to the mightiest efforts of eloquence. In the debate on the Indian bill, in 1830, in Congress, Mr. *Crockett*, of Tennessee, said, "I am forcibly reminded of the remark made by the famous *Red-jacket*, in the rotunda of this building, when he was shown the pannel which represented in sculpture the first landing of the Pilgrims, with an Indian chief presenting to them an ear of corn, in token of friendly welcome. The aged Indian said, '*That was good*.' He said he knew they came from the Great Spirit, and he was willing to share the soil with his brothers. But when he turned round to view another pannel, representing *Penn's* treaty, he said, '*Ah! all's gone now*.' There was a great deal of truth in this short saying."

Nothing seems more to have troubled the peace of *Red-jacket* than the intrusion of missionaries among his people. With the merits or demerits of the manner in which particular creeds have been forced upon the Indians in general, we have nothing to do, but we will refer the reader to Mr. *Buchanan's* Sketches,* where, in our opinion, every sectarian will glean some useful hints upon that head.

---

* Vol. i. chap. ix.

Red-jacket and his council, in 1821, made a formal complaint to the governor of New York, of the arbitrary conduct of some teachers among his people, and of their undue influence generally. Considering it to contain a most important and valuable piece of information, we will give it entire:—

"Brother *Parish*, I address myself to you, and through you to the governor. The chiefs of Onondaga have accompanied you to Albany, to do business with the governor; I also was to have been with you, but I am sorry to say that bad health has put it out of my power. For this you must not think hard of me. I am not to blame for it. It is the will of the Great Spirit that it should be so. The object of the Onondagas is to purchase our lands at Tonnewanta. This and all other business that they may have to do at Albany, must be transacted in the presence of the governor. He will see that the bargain is fairly made, so that all parties may have reason to be satisfied with what shall be done; and when our sanction shall be wanted to the transaction, it will be freely given. I much regret that, at this time, the state of my health should have prevented me from accompanying you to Albany, as it was the wish of the nation that I should state to the governor some circumstances which show that the chain of friendship between us and the white people is wearing out, and wants brightening. I proceed now, however, to lay them before you by letter, that you may mention them to the governor, and solicit redress. He is appointed to do justice to all, and the Indians fully confide that he will not suffer them to be wronged with impunity. The first subject to which we would call the attention of the governor, is the depredations that are daily committed by the white people upon the most valuable timber on our reservations. This has been a subject of complaint with us for many years; but now, and particularly at this season of the year, it has become an alarming evil, and calls for the immediate interposition of the governor in our behalf. Our next subject of complaint is, the frequent thefts of our horses and cattle by the white people, and their habit of taking and using them whenever they please, and without our leave. These are evils which seem to increase upon us with the increase of our white neighbors, and they call loudly for redress. Another evil arising from the pressure of the whites upon us, and our unavoidable communication with them, is the frequency with which our chiefs, and warriors, and Indians, are thrown into jail, and that, too, for the most trifling causes. This is very galling to our feelings, and ought not to be permitted to the extent to which, to gratify their bad passions, our white neighbors now carry this practice. In our hunting and fishing, too, we are greatly interrupted by the whites. Our venison is stolen from the trees, where we have hung it to be reclaimed after the chase. Our hunting camps have been fired into, and we have been warned that we shall no longer be permitted to pursue the deer in those forests which were so lately all our own. The fish, which, in the Buffalo and Tonnewanta Creeks, used to supply us with food, are now, by the dams and other obstructions of the white people, prevented from multiplying, and we are almost entirely deprived of that accustomed sustenance. Our great father, the president, has recommended to our young men to be industrious, to plough and to sow. This we have done, and we are thankful for the advice, and for the means he has afforded us of carrying it into effect. We are happier in consequence of it. *But another thing recommended to us, has created great confusion among us, and is making us a quarrelsome and divided people; and that is, the introduction of preachers into our nation.* These black coats contrive to get the consent of some of the Indians to preach among us, and wherever this is the case, confusion and disorder are sure to follow, and the encroachments of the whites upon our lands are the invariable consequence. The governor must not think hard of me for speaking thus of the preachers. I have observed their progress, and when I look back to see what has taken place of old, I perceive that whenever they came among the Indians, they were the forerunners of their dispersion; that they always excited enmities and quarrels among them; that they introduced the white people on their lands, by whom they were robbed and plundered of their property; and that the Indians were sure to dwindle and decrease, and be driven back, in proportion to the number of preachers that came among them. Each nation has its own customs and its own religion. The Indians have theirs, given to them by the Great Spirit, under which they were happy. It was not intended that they should embrace the religion of the whites, and be destroyed by the attempt to make them think differently on that subject from their fathers.* It is true, these preachers have got the consent of some of the chiefs to stay and preach among us, but I and my friends know this to be wrong, and that they ought to be removed; besides, we have been threatened by Mr. *Hyde*, who came among us as a school-master and a teacher of our children, but has now become a black coat, and refused to teach them any more, that unless we listen to his preaching and become Christians, we will be turned off our lands. We wish to know from the governor if this is to be so, and if he has no right to say so, we think *he* ought to be turned off our lands, and not allowed to plague us any more. We shall never be at peace while he is among us. Let them be removed, and we will be happy and contented among ourselves. We now cry to the governor for help, and hope that he will attend to our complaints, and speedily give us redress.

RED-JACKET."

"This letter was dictated by *Red-jacket*, and interpreted by *Henry Obeal*,† in the presence of the following Indians: *Red-jacket's* son, *Cornplanter, John-cobb, Peter, Young-kings-brother, Tom-the-infant,* [*Onnonggaiheko,*] *Blue-sky,* [*Towyocauna,*] *John-sky, Jemmy-johnson, Marcus, Big-fire, Captain-jemmy.*"

The success this petition met with, it is presumed, was full and satisfactory to him, in respect to one particular; for no ministers are now admitted upon the reservation.

In the spring of 1821, a man of *Red-jacket's* tribe fell into a languishment and died. His complaint was unknown, and some circumstances attended his illness which caused his friends to believe that he was bewitched. The woman that attended him was fixed upon as the witch, and by the law, or custom, of the nation, she was doomed to suffer death. A chief by the name of *Tom-jemmy*, called by his own people *Soo-nong-gise*, executed the decree by cutting her throat. The Americans took up the matter, seized *Tom-jemmy*, and threw him into prison.‡ Some time after, when his trial came on, *Red-jacket* appeared in court as an evidence. The counsel for the prisoner denied that the court had any jurisdiction over the case, and after it was carried through three terms, *Soo-nong-gise* was finally cleared. *Red-jacket* and the other witnesses testified that the woman was a witch, and that she had been tried, condemned and executed in pursuance of their laws, which had been established from time immemorial; long before the English came into the country. The witch doctrine of the Senecas was much ridiculed by some of the Americans, to which *Red-jacket* thus aptly alludes in a speech which he made while upon the stand:—

---

* A happy illustration of the force of education.

† Son of *Cornplanter*, or *Corn-plant*.

‡ Information of a gentleman (*W. J. Snelling*, Esq.) who was on the spot, and saw him brought to Buffalo. This was the next day after the murder, and the blood was yet upon his hands.

"What! do you denounce us as fools and bigots, because we still continue to believe that which you yourselves sedulously inculcated two centuries ago? Your divines have thundered this doctrine from the pulpit, your judges have pronounced it from the bench, your courts of justice have sanctioned it with the formalities of law, and you would now punish our unfortunate brother for adherence to the superstitions of his fathers! Go to Salem! Look at the records of your government, and you will find hundreds executed for the very crime which has called forth the sentence of condemnation upon this woman, and drawn down the arm of vengeance upon her. What have our brothers done more than the rulers of your people have done? and what crime has this man committed by executing, in a summary way, the laws of his country, and the injunctions of his God?" Before *Red-jacket* was admitted to give evidence in the case, he was asked if he believed in future rewards and punishments, and the existence of God. With a piercing look into the face of his interrogator, and with no little indignation of expression, he replied: "*Yes! Much more than the white men, if we are to judge by their actions.*" Upon the appearance of Red-jacket upon this occasion, one observes: "There is not, perhaps, in nature, a more expressive eye than that of *Red-jacket*; when fired by indignation or revenge, it is terrible; and when he chooses to display his unrivalled talent for irony, his keen sarcastic glance is irresistible."*

When *Lafayette*, in 1825, was at Buffalo, among the persons of distinction who called upon him, was *Red-jacket*. Of the old chief, M. *Levasseur* observes:† This extraordinary man, although much worn down by time and intemperance, preserves yet, in a surprising degree, the exercise of all his faculties. He had ever remembered *Lafayette* since 1784, at which time he, with others, met a great council of all the Indian nations at Fort Schuyler, when the interest of all those nations, friends and enemies, was regulated with the United States. He asked the general if he recollected that meeting. He replied that he had not forgotten that great event, and asked *Red-jacket* if he knew what had become of the young chief, who, in that council, opposed with such eloquence the "burying of the tomahawk." *Red-jacket* replied, "*He is before you.*" His speech was a master-piece, and every warrior who heard him was carried away with his eloquence. He urged a continuation of the war against the Americans, having joined against them in the revolution. The general observed to him that time had much changed them since that meeting. "Ah!" said *Red-jacket*, "time has not been so severe upon you as it has upon me. It has left to you a fresh countenance, and hair to cover your head; while to me. . . . . behold. . . . .!" and taking a handkerchief from his head, with an air of much feeling, showed his head, which was almost entirely bald.‡

At this interview, was fully confirmed what we have before stated. Levasseur continues: *Red-jacket* obstinately refuses to speak any language but that of his own country, and affects a great dislike to all others; although it is easy to discern that he perfectly understands the English; and refused, nevertheless, to reply to the general before his interpreter had translated his questions into the Seneca language. The general spoke a few words in Indian, which he had learned in his youth, at which

* Niles's Weekly Register. vol. xx. 359, 411.

† In his *Lafayette en Amérique*, tome ii. 437–8.

‡ "*Les assistants ne purent s'empêcher de sourire de la simplicité de l'Indien, qui semblait ignorer l'art de réparer les injures du temps; mais on se garda bien de détruire son erreur; et peut-être fit-on bien, car il eût pu confondre une perruque avec une chevelure scalpée, et concevoir l'idée de regarnir sa tête aux dépens de la tête d'une de ses voisons.*" *Ibid*. This pleasantry of Mons. *Levasseur* would better have suited the age of the revolution; but even then not so well the character of *Red-jacket*.

Red-jacket was highly pleased, and which augmented much his high opinion of *Lafayette*.

The author of the following passage is unknown to us; but presuming it to be authentic, we quote it. "More than 30 years* have rolled away since a treaty was held on the beautiful acclivity that overlooks the Canandaigua† Lake. The witnesses of the scene will never forget the powers of native oratory. Two days had passed away in negotiation with the Indians for a cession of their lands. The contract was supposed to be nearly completed, when *Red-jacket* arose. With the grace and dignity of a Roman senator, he drew his blanket around him, and, with a piercing eye, surveyed the multitude. All was hushed. Nothing interposed to break the silence, save the gentle rustling of the tree tops, under whose shade they were gathered. After a long and solemn, but not unmeaning pause, he commenced his speech in a low voice and sententious style. Rising gradually with the subject, he depicted the primitive simplicity and happiness of his nation, and the wrongs they had sustained from the usurpations of white men, with such a bold but faithful pencil, that every auditor was soon roused to vengeance, or melted into tears. The effect was inexpressible. But ere the emotions of admiration and sympathy had subsided, the white men became alarmed. They were in the heart of an Indian country—surrounded by more than ten times their number, who were inflamed by the remembrance of their injuries, and excited to indignation by the eloquence of a favorite chief. Appalled and terrified, the white men cast a cheerless gaze upon the hordes around them. A nod from the chiefs might be the onset of destruction. At this portentous moment, *Farmers-brother* interposed. He replied not to his brother chief, but, with a sagacity truly aboriginal, he caused a cessation of the council, introduced good cheer, commended the eloquence of *Red-jacket*, and, before the meeting had reassembled, with the aid of other prudent chiefs, he had moderated the fury of his nation to a more salutary review of the question before them. Suffice it to say, the treaty was concluded, and the Western District, at this day, owes no small portion of its power and influence to the counsels of a savage, in comparison with whom for genius, heroism, virtue, or any other quality that can adorn the bawble of a diadem, not only *George* the IV. and *Louis le Desiré*, but the German emperor and the czar of Muscovy, alike dwindle into insignificance." We can add nothing to this high encomium.

Red-jacket was of the number who visited Philadelphia in 1792, as will be found mentioned in the account of *Jaquette*; at which time he was welcomed by the governor of Pennsylvania to that city, and addressed by him, in behalf of the commonwealth, in the council chamber. The following is the closing paragraph of the governor's speech: "Brothers! I know the kindness with which you treat the strangers that visit your country; and it is my sincere wish, that, when you return to your families, you may be able to assure them, that the virtues of friendship and hospitality are also practised by the citizens of Pennsylvania." He had before observed that the government had furnished every thing to make them comfortable during their stay at Philadelphia. This was upon the 28 March, 1792, and on 2 April following, they met again, when *Red-jacket* spoke in answer to the governor as follows:—

"Brother, Onas‡ Governor, open unprejudiced ears to what we have to

* This writer, I conclude, wrote in 1822. I copy it from *Miscellanies selected from the Public Journals*, by Mr. *Buckingham*.

† Signifying, in the Seneca language, *a town set off*. The lake received its name from the town upon its shore.—*Spafford's* Gaz.

‡ *Onas* was the name the Indians gave *William Penn*, and they continue the same name to all the governors of Pennsylvania.

say. Some days since you addressed us, and what you said gave us great pleasure. This day the Great Spirit has allowed us to meet you again, in this council chamber. We hope that your not receiving an immediate answer to your address, will make no improper impression upon your mind. We mention this lest you should suspect that your kind welcome and friendly address has not had a proper effect upon our hearts. We assure you it is far otherwise. In your address to us the other day, in this ancient council chamber, where our forefathers have often conversed together, several things struck our attention very forcibly. When you told us this was the place in which our forefathers often met on peaceable terms, it gave us sensible pleasure, and more joy than we could express. Though we have no writings like you, yet we remember often to have heard of the friendship that existed between our fathers and yours. The picture* to which you drew our attention, brought fresh to our minds the friendly conferences that used to be held between the former governors of Pennsylvania and our tribes, and showed the love which your forefathers had of peace, and the friendly disposition of our people. It is still our wish, as well as yours, to preserve peace between our tribes and you, and it would be well if the same spirit existed among the Indians to the westward, and through every part of the United States. You particularly expressed that you were well pleased to find that we differed in disposition from the Indians westward. Your disposition is that for which the ancient Onas Governors were remarkable. As you love peace, so do we also; and we wish it could be extended to the most distant part of this great country. We agreed in council, this morning, that the sentiments I have expressed, should be communicated to you, before the delegates of the Five Nations, and to tell you that your cordial welcome to this city, and the good sentiments contained in your address, have made a deep impression on our hearts, have given us great joy, *and from the heart I tell you so. This is all I have to say.*"

When *Red-jacket* had finished, another chief, called *Agwelondongwas,* (and sometimes *Good-peter,*†) addressed the assembly. His speech is much in the style of *Red-jacket's,* and was chiefly a repetition, in other words, of it. It was short, and contained this passage: "What is there more desirable than that we, who live within hearing of each other, should unite for the common good? This is my wish. It is the wish of my nation, although I am sorry I can't say so of every individual in it; for there are differences of opinions among us, as well as among our white brethren."

Since we have here introduced *Dominie Peter*, we will so far digress as to relate what follows concerning him. He was one of those who took part against the Americans in the revolutionary war, and when hostilities commenced, he retired and joined the remote tribes towards Canada. Col. *John Harper* (one of the family from whom Harpersfield, N. Y. takes its name) was stationed at the fort at Schorrie, in the state of New York. Early in the spring of 1777, in the season of making maple sugar, when all were upon the lookout to avoid surprise by the Indians, Col. *Harper* left the garrison and proceeded through the woods to Harpersfield; thence by an Indian path to Cherry-valley. In his way, as he was turning the point of a hill, he saw a company of Indians, who, at the same time, saw him. He dared not attempt flight, as he could expect no other than to be shot down in such attempt. He, therefore, determined to advance and meet them without discovering fear. Concealing his regimentals as well as he could with his great coat, he hastened onward to meet them. Before they met him, he discovered that *Peter* was their chief,

* A fine picture representing Penn's treat with the Indians.

† And often *Domine-peter*. 2 Col. N. Y. Hist. Soc. 74.

with whom he had formerly traded much at Oquago, but who did not know him. *Harper* was the first to speak, as they met, and his words were, "*How do you do, brothers?*" The chief answered, "*Well.—How do you do, brother? Which way are you bound?*" The colonel replied, "*On a secret expedition. And which way are you bound, brothers?*" They answered without hesitation or distrust, thinking, no doubt, they had fallen in with one of the king's men, "*Down the Susquehannah, to cut off the Johnstone settlement.*" This place, since called *Sidney Plains*, consisted of a few Scotch families, and their minister's name was *Johnstone*; hence the name of the settlement. The colonel next asked them where they lodged that night, and they told him, "At the mouth of Scheneva's Creek." After shaking hands, they separated. As soon as they were out of sight, *Harper* made a circuit through the woods with all speed, and soon arrived at the head of Charlotte River, where were several men making sugar. This place was about ten miles from Decatur Hill, where he met the Indians. He ordered them to take each a rope and provisions in their packs, and assemble at Evan's Place, where he would soon meet them: thence he returned to Harpersfield, and collected the men there, which, including the others and himself, made 15, just equal to *Peter's* force. When they arrived at Evan's Place, upon the Charlotte, *Harper* made known his project. They set off, and before day the next morning, came into the neighborhood of the Indians' camp. From a small eminence, just at dawn of day, their fire was seen burning, and *Peter*, amidst his warriors, lying upon the ground. All were fast asleep. *Harper* and his companions each crept silently up, with their ropes in their hands, man to man; and each, standing in a position to grasp his adversary, waited for the word to be given by their leader. The colonel jogged his Indian, and, as he was waking, said to him, "*Come, it is time for men of business to be on their way.*" This was the watchword; and no sooner was it pronounced, than each Indian felt the warm grasp of his foe. The struggle was desperate, though short, and resulted in the capture of every one of the party. When it was sufficiently light to distinguish countenances, *Peter*, observing Col. *Harper*, said, "*Ha! Col. Harper! Now I know you!—Why did I not know you yesterday?*" The colonel observed, "*Some policy in war, Peter.*" To which *Peter* replied, "*Ah! me find em so now.*" These captives were marched to Albany, and delivered up to the commanding officer. By this capital exploit no doubt many lives were saved.*

But to return to *Sagoyewatha*.

We have observed that he was in the war of 1812. In one battle he was particularly named as having distinguished himself. *Farmers-brother* was his equal in command, and, with several others, was also honorably mentioned. When they resolved to take up the hatchet, they did not wish to be under the United States' officers, but desired to retaliate in their own way upon their invaders. This, as far as practicable, was acceded to.

The famous Seneca chief, called the *Farmer's-brother*, is often mentioned in the accounts of *Red-jacket*. His native name was *Ho-na-ya-wus*.

In 1792, *Farmers-brother* was in Philadelphia, and was among those who attended the burial of Mr. *Peter Jaquette*, and is thus noticed in the Pennsylvania Gazette of 28 March, of that year: "On Monday last, the chiefs and warriors of the Five Nations assembled at the state-house, and were welcomed to the city of Philadelphia in an address delivered by the governor. Three of the chiefs made a general acknowledgment for the cordial reception which they had experienced, but postponed their formal answer until another opportunity. The room in which they assembled

* Annals of Tryon Co. 8vo. N. York, 1831.

was mentioned as the ancient council chamber, in which their ancestors and ours had often met to brighten the chain of friendship; and this circumstance, together with the presence of a great part of the beauty of the city, had an evident effect upon the feelings of the Indians, and seemed particularly to embarrass the elocution of the *Farmers-brother.*" This last clause does not correspond with our ideas of the great chief.

Through his whole life, *Farmers-brother* seems to have been a peacemaker. In the spring of the next year, there was a great council held at Niagara, consisting of the chiefs of a great many nations, dwelling upon the shores of the western lakes. At this time, many long and laborious speeches were made, some for and others against the conduct of the United States. *Farmers-brother* shone conspicuous at this time. His speech was nearly three hours long, and the final determination of the council was peace. We know of no speeches being preserved at this time, but if there could have been, doubtless much true history might have been collected from them. He seems not only to have been esteemed by the Americans, but also by the English.*

Of *Peter Jaquette*, whom we have several times incidentally mentioned, we will give some account before proceeding with *Honayawus*. He was one of the principal sachems of the Oneidas. This chief died in Philadelphia, 19 March, 1792. He had been taken to France by Gen. *Lafayette*, at the close of the revolutionary war, where he received an education. Mr. *Jaquette*, having died on Monday, was interred on the following Wednesday. "His funeral was attended from *Oeler's* hotel to the Presbyterian burying-ground in Mulberry-street. The corpse was preceded by a detachment of the light infantry of the city, with arms reversed, drums muffled, music playing a solemn dirge. The corpse was followed by six of the chiefs as mourners, succeeded by all the warriors; the reverend clergy of all denominations; secretary of war, and the gentlemen of the war department; officers of the federal army, and of the militia; and a number of citizens."†

One of the most celebrated speeches of *Farmers-brother* was delivered in a council at Genesee River, in 1798, and, after being interpreted, was signed by the chiefs present, and sent to the legislature of New York. It follows:—

"*Brothers*, as you are once more assembled in council for the purpose of doing honor to yourselves and justice to your country, we, your brothers, the sachems, chiefs and warriors of the Seneca nation, request you to open your ears and give attention to our voice and wishes.—You will recollect the late contest between you and your father, the great king of England. This contest threw the inhabitants of this whole island into a great tumult and commotion, like a raging whirlwind which tears up the trees, and tosses to and fro the leaves, so that no one knows from whence they come, or where they will fall.—This whirlwind was so directed by the Great Spirit above, as to throw into our arms two of your infant children, *Jasper Parrish* and *Horatio Jones*.‡ We adopted them into our families, and made them our children. We loved them and nourished them. They lived with us many years. *At length the Great Spirit spoke to the whirlwind, and it was still.* A clear and uninterrupted sky ap-

* "Le village de Buffalo est habitié par les Senecas. Le chef de cette nation est *Brothers-farmer*, estimé par toutes les tribus comme grand guerrier et grand politique, et fort caressé à ce titre par les agens anglais et les agens Américains. Buffalo est le chef lieu de la nation Seneca." *Rochefoucauld, Voyage dans l' Amérique en* 1795, 6, and 7, t. i. 299.

† Pennsylvania Gazette.

‡ Taken prisoners at the destruction of Wyoming by the tories and Indians under *Butler* and *Brant*.

peared. The path of peace was opened, and the chain of friendship was once more made bright. Then these our adopted children left us, to seek their relations; we wished them to remain among us, and promised, if they would return and live in our country, to give each of them a seat of land for them and their children to sit down upon.—They have returned, and have, for several years past, been serviceable to us as interpreters. We still feel our hearts beat with affection for them, and now wish to fulfil the promise we made them, and reward them for their services. We have, therefore, made up our minds to give them a seat of two square miles of land, lying on the outlets of Lake Erie, about three miles below Black-rock, beginning at the mouth of a creek known by the name of *Scoyguquoydescreek*, running one mile from the River Niagara up said creek, thence northerly as the river runs two miles, thence westerly one mile to the river, thence up the river as the river runs, two miles, to the place of beginning, so as to contain two square miles.—We have now made known to you our minds. We expect and earnestly request that you will permit our friends to receive this our gift, and will make the same good to them, according to the laws and customs of your nation.—Why should you hesitate to make our minds easy with regard to this our request? To you it is but a little thing; and have you not complied with the request and confirmed the gifts of our brothers, the Oneidas, the Onondagas and Cayugas to their interpreters? And shall we ask and not be heard? We send you this our speech, to which we expect your answer before the breaking up our great council fire."

A gentleman* who visited Buffalo in 1810, observes that *Farmers-brother* was never known to drink ardent spirits, and although then 94 years old, walked perfectly upright, and was remarkably straight and well formed; very grave, and answered his inquiries with great precision, but through his interpreter, Mr. *Parrish*, before named. His account of the mounds in that region will not give satisfaction. He told Dr. *King* that they were thrown up against the incursions of the French, and that the implements found in them were taken from them; a great army of French having been overthrown and mostly cut off, the Indians became possessed of their accoutrements, which, being of no use to them, were buried with their owners.

He was a great warrior, and although "eighty snows in years" when the war of 1812 began, yet he engaged in it, and fought with the Americans. He did not live till its close, but died at the Seneca village, just after the battle of Bridgewater, and was interred with military honors by the fifth regiment of U. S. infantry. He usually wore a medal presented him by Gen. *Washington*. In the revolution, he fought successfully against the Americans. Perhaps there never flowed from the lips of man a more sublime metaphor than that made use of by this chief, in the speech given above, when alluding to the revolutionary contest. It is worth repeating: "*The Great Spirit spoke to the whirlwind, and it was still.*"

The following letter will, besides exhibiting the condition of the Senecas, develope some other interesting facts in their biographical history.

"To the Honorable *William Eustis*, secretary at war.

"The sachems and chief warriors of the Seneca nation of Indians, understanding you are the person appointed by the great council of your nation to manage and conduct the affairs of the several nations of Indians with whom you are at peace and on terms of friendship, come, at this

* Dr. *William King*, the celebrated electrician, who gives the author this information verbally.

8 *

time, as children to a father, to lay before you the trouble which we have on our minds.

"Brother, we do not think it best to multiply words: we will, therefore, tell you what our complaint is.—Brother, listen to what we say: Some years since, we held a treaty at Bigtree, near the Genesee River. This treaty was called by our great father, the president of the United States. He sent an agent, Col. *Wadsworth*, to attend this treaty, for the purpose of advising us in the business, and seeing that we had justice done us. At this treaty, we sold to *Robert Morris* the greatest part of our country; the sum he gave us was 100,000 dollars. The commissioners who were appointed on your part, advised us to place this money in the hands of our great father, the president of the United States. He told us our father loved his red children, and would take care of our money, and plant it in a field where it would bear seed forever, as long as trees grow, or waters run. Our money has heretofore been of great service to us; it has helped us to support our old people, and our women and children; but we are told the field where our money was planted is become barren.—Brother, we do not understand your way of doing business. This thing is very heavy on our minds. We mean to hold our white brethren of the United States by the hand; but this weight lies heavy; we hope you will remove it.—We have heard of the bad conduct of our brothers towards the setting sun. We are sorry for what they have done; but you must not blame us; we have had no hand in this bad business. They have had bad people among them. It is your enemies have done this.—We have persuaded our agent to take this talk to your great council. He knows our situations, and will speak our minds.

FARMER'S BROTHER, [*Honayawus*,]	*his*	×	*mark.*
LITTLE BILLY, [*Gishkaka*,]	"	×	"
YOUNG KING, [*Koyingquautah*,]	"	×	"
POLLARD, [*Kaoundoowand*,]	"	×	"
CHIEF-WARRIOR, [*Lunuchshewa*,]	"	×	"
TWO-GUNS,	"	×	"
JOHN SKY,	"	×	"
PARROT-NOSE, [*Soocoowa*,]	"	×	"
JOHN PIERCE, [*Teskaiy*,]	"	×	"
STRONG, [*Kahalsta*,]	"	×	"
WHEELBARROW,	"	×	"
JACK-BERRY,	"	×	"
TWENTY CANOES, [*Cachaunwasse*,]	"	×	"
BIG-KETTLE, [*Sessewa*?]	"	×	"
HALF-TOWN, [*Achiout*,]	"	×	"
KEYANDEANDE,	"	×	"
CAPTAIN-COLD,	"	×	"
ESQ. BLINKNEY,	"	×	"
CAPT. JOHNSON, [*Talwinaha*,]	"	×	"

"N. B. The foregoing speech was delivered in council by *Farmers-Brother*, at Buffalo Creek, 19 Dec. 1811, and subscribed to in my presence by the chiefs whose names are annexed.

ERASTUS GRANGER."

Eight thousand dollars* was appropriated immediately upon receipt of the above.

Little-billy, or *Gishkaka*, is the same of whom we have spoken in a preceding chapter, and called by *Washington*, *Juskakaka*.

Young-king, the third signer of the above talk, was engaged in fighting

* "In lieu of the dividend on the bank shares, held by the president of the U. States, in trust for the Seneca nation, in the bank of the U. States."

for the Americans in the last war with England, and by an act of congress was to be paid yearly, in quarterly payments, 200 dollars, during life. The act states that it was "a compensation for the brave and meritorious services which he rendered" in that war, "and as a provision for the wound and disability which he received in the performance of those services." This was in the spring of 1816.

Of *Pollard*, or Capt. *Pollard*, we shall have occasion elsewhere to say more.

Jack-berry was sometimes interpreter for *Red-jacket*.

Half-town was very conspicuous in the affairs of the Senecas, but as he is generally mentioned, in our documents, in connection with *Corn-plant*, or *Corn-planter*, and *Big-tree*, we had designed to speak of the three collectively.

We find among the acts of the Pennsylvania legislature, of 1791, one "for granting 800 dollars to *Corn-planter, Half-town* and *Big-tree*, Seneca chiefs, in trust for the Seneca nation." At this time much was apprehended from an Indian war. Settlers were intruding themselves upon their country, and all experience has shown that whenever the whites have gone among them, troubles were sure to follow. Every movement of the Indians was looked upon with jealousy by them at this period. *Half-town* was the "white man's friend," and communicated to the garrisons in his country every suspicious movement of tribes of whom doubts were entertained. It is evident that hostile bands, for a long time, hovered about the post at Venango, and, but for the vigilance of *Half-town*, and other friendly chiefs, it would have been cut off. In April this year, (1791,) *Corn-plant* and *Half-town* had upwards of 100 warriors in and about the garrison, and kept runners out continually, "being determined to protect it at all events." Their spies made frequent discoveries of war parties. On the 12 August, 1791, *Half-town* and *New-arrow* gave information at Fort Franklin, that a sloop full of Indians had been seen on Lake Erie, sailing for Presque Isle; and their object was supposed to be Fort Franklin; but the conjecture proved groundless.

The Indian name of *Half-town* was *Achiout*. We hear of him at Fort Harmer, in 1789, where, with 23 others, he executed a treaty with the U. States. The commissioners on the part of the latter were Gen. *Arthur St. Clair, Oliver Wolcut, Richard Butler* and *Arthur Lee*. Among the signers on the part of the Senecas were also *Big-tree*, or *Kiandogewa*, *Corn-planter*, or *Gyantwaia*, besides several others whose names are familiar in history. *Big-tree* was often called *Great-tree*, which, in the language of the Five Nations, was *Nihorontagowa*,* which also was the name of the Oneida nation.† *Big-tree* was with Gen. *Washington* during the summer of 1778, but returned to the Indian nations in the autumn. He proceeded to the Senecas, and used his eloquence to dissuade them from fighting under *Brant* against the Americans. The Oneidas were friendly at this time, and *Big-tree* was received among them with hospitality, in his way, upon this mission. Having staid longer than was expected among the Senecas, the Oneidas sent a messenger to him to know the reason. He returned answer that when he arrived among his nation, he found them all in arms, and their villages, Kanadaseago and Jennessee, crowded with warriors from remote tribes; that they at first seemed inclined to hearken to his wishes, but soon learning by a spy that the Americans were about to invade their country, all flew to arms, and Big-*tree* put himself at their head, "*determined to chastise*," he said, "*the enemy that dared presume to think of penetrating their country*." But we do not

* Or *Kiandogewa, Kayenthoghke*, &c.

† *Benson's* Memoir, before the N. Y. Hist. Soc. page 20. Also Amer. Magazine.

learn that he was obliged to maintain that hostile attitude, and doubtless returned soon after.

In the year 1790, *Big-tree, Corn-plant* and *Half-town* appeared at Philadelphia, and, by their interpreter, communicated to President *Washington* as follows:—

"*Father*: The voice of the Seneca nations speaks to you; the great counsellor, in whose heart the wise men of all the *thirteen fires* [13 U. S.] have placed their wisdom. It may be very small in your ears, and we, therefore, entreat you to hearken with attention; for we are able to speak of things which are to us very great.

"When your army entered the country of the Six Nations, we called you the *town destroyer*; to this day, when your name is heard, our women look behind them and turn pale, and our children cling close to the necks of their mothers."

"When our chiefs returned from Fort Stanwix, and laid before our council what had been done there, our nation was surprised to hear how great a country you had compelled them to give up to you, without your paying to us any thing for it. Every one said, that your hearts were yet swelled with resentment against us for what had happened during the war, but that one day you would consider it with more kindness. We asked each other, *What have we done to deserve such severe chastisement?*

"*Father:* when you kindled your 13 fires separately, the wise men assembled at them told us that you were all brothers; the children of one great father, who regarded the red people as his children. They called us brothers, and invited us to his protection. They told us that he resided beyond the great water where the sun first rises; and that he was a king whose power no people could resist, and that his goodness was as bright as the sun. What they said went to our hearts. We accepted the invitation, and promised to obey him. What the Seneca nation promises, they faithfully perform. When you refused obedience to that king, he commanded us to assist his beloved men in making you sober. In obeying him, we did no more than yourselves had led us to promise." "We were deceived; but your people teaching us to confide in that king, had helped to deceive us; and we now appeal to your breast. *Is all the blame ours*?

"*Father*: when we saw that we had been deceived, and heard the invitation which you gave us to draw near to the fire you had kindled, and talk with you concerning peace, we made haste towards it. You told us you could crush us to nothing; and you demanded from us a great country, as the price of that peace which you had offered to us: *as if our want of strength had destroyed our rights*. Our chiefs had felt your power, and were unable to contend against you, and they therefore gave up that country. What they agreed to has bound our nation, but your anger against us must by this time be cooled, and although our strength is not increased, nor your power become less, we ask you to consider calmly—*Were the terms dictated to us by your commissioners reasonable and just?*"

They also remind the president of the solemn promise of the commissioners, that they should be secured in the peaceable possession of what was left to them, and then ask, "*Does this promise bind you?*" And that no sooner was the treaty of Fort Stanwix concluded, than commissioners from Pennsylvania came to purchase of them what was included within the lines of their state. These they informed that they did not wish to sell, but being further urged, consented to sell a part. But the commissioners said that "*they must have the whole;*" for it was already ceded to them by the king of England, at the peace following the revolution. But still, as their ancestors had always paid the Indians for land, they were willing to pay them for it. Being not able to contend, the land was sold. Soon after this, they empowered a person to let out part of their land, who said Congress had sent him for the purpose, but who, it seems, fraudulently procured a *deed* instead of a *power* to lease; for there soon came another person claiming all their country northward of the line of Pennsylvania, saying that he purchased it of the other, and for which he had paid 20,000 dollars to him, and 20,000 more to the United States. He now demanded the land, and, on being refused, threatened immediate war. Knowing their weak situation, they held a council, and took the advice of a white man, whom they took to be their friend, but who, as it proved, had plotted with the other, and was to receive some of the land for his agency. He, therefore, told them they must comply. "Astonished at what we heard from every quarter," they say, "with hearts aching with compassion for our women and children, we were thus compelled to give up all our country north of the line of Pennsylvania, and east of the Genesee River, up to the great forks, and east of a south line drawn up from that fork to the line of Pennsylvania." For this he agreed to give them 10,000 dollars down, and 1000 dollars a year forever. Instead of that, he paid them 2500 dollars, and some time after offered 500 dollars more, insisting that that was all he owed them, which he allowed to be yearly. They add,

"*Father*: you have said that we were in your hand, and that by closing it you could crush us to nothing. Are you determined to crush us? If you are, tell us so; that those of our nation who have become your children, and have determined to die so, may know what to do. In this case, one chief has said, he would ask you to put him out of his pain. Another, who will not think of dying by the hand of his father, or his brother, has said he will retire to the Chataughque, eat of the fatal root, and sleep with his fathers in peace."

"All the land we have been speaking of belonged to the Six Nations. No part of it ever belonged to the king of England, and he could not give it to you."

"Hear us once more. At Fort Stanwix we agreed to deliver up those of our people who should do you any wrong, and that you might try them and punish them according to your law. We delivered up two men accordingly. But instead of trying them according to your law, the lowest of your people took them from your magistrate, and put them immediately to death. It is just to punish the murder with death, but the Senecas will not deliver up their people to men who disregard the treaties of their own nation."

There were many other grievances enumerated, and all in a strain which, we should think, would have drawn forth immediate relief. In his answer, President *Washington* said all, perhaps, which could be said in his situation; and his good feelings are manifest throughout: still there is something like evasion in answering some of their grievances, and an omission of notice to others. His answer, nevertheless, gave them much encouragement. He assured them that the lands obtained from them by fraud was not sanctioned by the government, and that the whole transaction was declared null and void; and that the persons who murdered their people should be dealt with as though they had murdered white men, and that all possible means would be used for their apprehension, and rewards should continue to be offered to effect it. But we have not learned that they were ever apprehended. The land conveyed by treaty, the president informed them, he had no authority to concern with, as that act was before his administration.

The above speech, although appearing to he a joint production, is believed to have been dictated by *Corn-planter*. It, however, was no doubt the sentiments of the whole nation, as well as those of himself, *Half-town* and *Big-tree.*

In 1791, an act passed the legislature of Pennsylvania, "to empower the governor to grant a patent to *Big-tree*, a Seneca chief, for a certain island in the Alleghany River."

He lamented the disaster of *St. Clair's* army, and was heard to say afterwards, *that he would have two scalps for Gen. Butler's*, who fell and was scalped in that fight. *John Deckard*, another Seneca chief, repeated the same words.

Being on a mission to Philadelphia, in April, 1792, he was taken sick at his lodgings, and died after about 20 hours' illness. Three days after, being Sunday, the 22d, he was buried with all requisite attention. The river *Big-tree* was probably named from the circumstance of this chief having lived upon it. His name still exists among some of his descendants, or others of his tribe, as we have seen it subscribed to several instruments within a few years.

Although *Corn-planter* be but half Indian, we would not throw him out of our book on that account, and will, therefore, proceed again with his memoirs. His Indian name, as we have before noted, was *Kiandogewa*; and most of our knowledge concerning him is derived from himself, and is contained in a letter sent from him to the governor of Pennsylvania; and, although written by an interpreter, is believed to be the real production of *Corn-planter.* It was dated "Alleghany River; 2d mo. 2d, 1822," and is as follows:—

"I feel it my duty to send a speech to the governor of Pennsylvania at this time, and inform him the place where I was from—which was at Conewaugus,* on the Genesee River.

"When I was a child, I played with the butterfly, the grasshopper and the frogs; and as I grew up, I began to pay some attention and play with the Indian boys in the neighborhood, and they took notice of my skin being a different color from theirs, and spoke about it. I inquired of my mother the cause, and she told me that my father was a residenter in Albany.† I still eat my victuals out of a bark dish. I grew up to be a young man, and married me a wife, and I had no kettle or gun. I then knew where my father lived, and went to see him, and found he was a white man, and spoke the English language. He gave me victuals whilst I was at his house, but when I started to return home, he gave me no provision to eat on the way. He gave me neither kettle nor gun, neither did he tell me that the United States were about to rebel against the government of England.

"I will now tell you, brothers, who are in session of the legislature of Pennsylvania, that the Great Spirit has made known to me that I have been wicked; and the cause thereof was the revolutionary war in America. The cause of Indians having been led into sin, at that time, was that many of them were in the practice of drinking and getting intoxicated. Great Britain requested us to join with them in the conflict against the Americans, and promised the Indians land and liquor. I myself was opposed to joining in the conflict, as I had nothing to do with the difficulty that existed between the two parties. I have now informed you how it happened that the Indians took a part in the revolution, and will relate to you some circumstances that occurred after the close of the war. Gen. *Putnam*, who was then at Philadelphia, told me there was to be a council at Fort Stanwix; and the Indians requested me to attend on be-

---

* This was the Iroquois term to designate a place of Christian Indians; hence many places bear it. It is the same as *Caughnewaga.*

† It is said (Amer. Reg. ii. 228) that he was an Irishman.

half of the Six Nations; which I did, and there met with three commissioners, who had been appointed to hold the council. They told me they would inform me of the cause of the revolution, which I requested them to do minutely. They then said that it had originated on account of the heavy taxes that had been imposed upon them by the British government, which had been for fifty years increasing upon them; that the Americans had grown weary thereof, and refused to pay, which affronted the king. There had likewise a difficulty taken place about some tea, which they wished me not to use, as it had been one of the causes that many people had lost their lives. And the British government now being affronted, the war commenced, and the cannons began to roar in our country. General *Putnam* then told me, at the council at Fort Stanwix, that, by the late war, the Americans had gained two objects: they had established themselves an independent nation, and had obtained some land to live upon; the division line of which, from Great Britain, run through the lakes. I then spoke, and said that I wanted some land for the Indians to live on, and General *Putnam* said that it should be granted, and I should have land in the state of New York for the Indians. Gen. *Putnam* then encouraged me to use my endeavors to pacify the Indians generally; and, as he considered it an arduous task to perform, wished to know what I wanted for pay therefor. I replied to him, that I would use my endeavors to do as he had requested, with the Indians, and for pay thereof, I would take land. I told him not to pay me money or dry goods, but land. And for having attended thereto, I received the tract of land on which I now live, which was presented to me by Governor *Miflin*. I told General *Putnam* that I wished the Indians to have the exclusive privilege of the deer and wild game; which he assented to. I also wished the Indians to have the privilege of hunting in the woods, and making fires, which he likewise assented to.

"The treaty that was made at the aforementioned council, has been broken by some of the white people, which I now intend acquainting the governor with. Some white people are not willing that Indians should hunt any more, whilst others are satisfied therewith; and those white people who reside near our reservation, tell us that the woods are theirs, and they have obtained them from the governor. The treaty has been also broken by the white people using their endeavors to destroy all the wolves, which was not spoken about in the council at Fort Stanwix, by General *Putnam*, but has originated lately.

"It has been broken again, which is of recent origin. White people wish to get credit from Indians, and do not pay them honestly, according to their agreement. In another respect, it has also been broken by white people, who reside near my dwelling; for when I plant melons and vines in my field, they take them as their own. It has been broken again by white people using their endeavors to obtain our pine trees from us. We have very few pine trees on our land, in the state of New York; and white people and Indians often get into dispute respecting them. There is also a great quantity of whiskey brought near our reservation by white people, and the Indians obtain it and become drunken. Another circumstance has taken place which is very trying to me, and I wish the interference of the governor.

"The white people, who live at Warren, called upon me, some time ago, to pay taxes for my land; which I objected to, as I had never been called upon for that purpose before; and having refused to pay, the white people became irritated, called upon me frequently, and at length brought four guns with them and seized our cattle. I still refused to pay, and was not willing to let the cattle go. After a time of dispute, they returned home, and I understood the militia was ordered out to enforce the collection of the tax. I went to Warren, and, to avert the impending difficulty, was obliged to give my note for the tax, the amount of which was 43 dollars and 79 cents. It is my desire that the governor will exempt me from paying taxes for my land to white people; and also cause that the money I am now obliged to pay, may be refunded to me, as I am very poor. The governor is the person who attends to the situation of the people, and I wish him to send a person to Alleghany, that I may inform him of the particulars of our situation, and he be authorized to instruct the white people in what manner to conduct themselves towards the Indians.

"The government has told us that when any difficulties arose between the Indians and white people, they would attend to having them removed. We are now in a trying situation, and I wish the governor to send a person, authorized to attend thereto, the fore part of next summer, about the time that grass has grown big enough for pasture.

"The governor formerly requested me to pay attention to the Indians, and take care of them. We are now arrived at a situation that I believe Indians cannot exist, unless the governor should comply with my request, and send a person authorized to treat between us and the white people, the approaching summer. I have now no more to speak."*

Whether the government of Pennsylvania acted at all, or, if at all, what order they took, upon this pathetic appeal, our author does not state. But that an independent tribe of Indians should be taxed by a neighboring people, is absurd in the extreme; and we hope we shall learn that not only the tax was remitted, but a remuneration granted for the vexation and damage.

Corn-plant was very early distinguished for his wisdom in council, notwithstanding he confirmed the treaty of Fort Stanwix of 1784, five years after, at the treaty of Fort Harmer, giving up an immense tract of their country, and for which his nation very much reproached him, and even threatened his life. Himself and other chiefs committed this act for the best of reasons. The Six Nations having taken part with England in the revolution, when the king's power fell in America, the Indian nations were reduced to the miserable alternative of giving up so much of their country as the Americans required, or the *whole* of it. In 1790, *Corn-plant, Half-town* and *Big-tree*, made a most pathetic appeal to Congress for an amelioration of their condition, and a reconsideration of former treaties, in which the following memorable passage occurs:—

"*Father*: we will not conceal from you that the great God, and not men, has preserved the *Corn-plant* from the hands of his own nation. For they ask continually, ' Where is the land on which our children, and their children after them, are to lie down upon? You told us that the line drawn from Pennsylvania to Lake Ontario, would mark it forever on the east, and the line running from Beaver Creek to Pennsylvania, would mark it on the west, and we see that it is not so; for, first one, and then another, come and take it away by order of that people which you tell us promised to secure it to us.' He is silent, for he has nothing to answer. When the sun goes down, he opens his heart before God, and earlier than the sun appears, again upon the hills he gives thanks for his protection during the night. For he feels that among men become desperate by the injuries they sustain, it is God only that can preserve him. He loves peace, and all he had in store he has given to those who have been robbed by your people, lest they should plunder the innocent to repay themselves. The whole season, which others have employed in providing for their

* *Buchanan's* Sketches.

families, he has spent in endeavors to preserve peace; and this moment his wife and children are lying on the ground, and in want of food."

In President *Washington's* answer, we are gratified by his particular notice of this chief. He says, "The merits of the *Corn-plant*, and his friendship for the United States, are well known to me, and shall not be forgotten; and, as a mark of esteem of the United States, I have directed the secretary of war to make him a present of *two hundred and fifty dollars*, either in money or goods, as the *Corn-plant* shall like best."

There was, in 1789, a treaty held at Marietta, between the Indians and Americans, which terminated "to the entire satisfaction of all concerned. On this occasion, an elegant entertainment was provided. The Indian chiefs behaved with the greatest decorum throughout the day. After dinner, we were served with good wine, and *Corn-planter*, one of the first chiefs of the Five Nations, and a very great warrior, took up his glass and said, '*I thank the Great Spirit for this opportunity of smoking the pipe of friendship and love. May we plant our own vines—be the fathers of our own children—and maintain them.*'"*

In 1790, an act passed the legislature of Pennsylvania, for "granting 800 dollars to *Corn-planter, Half-town* and *Big-tree*, in trust for the Seneca nation, and other purposes therein mentioned." In Feb. 1791, *Corn-plant* was in Philadelphia, and was employed in an extremely hazardous expedition to undertake the pacification of the western tribes, that had already shown themselves hostile. The mission terminated unfavorably, from insurmountable difficulties.† There were many, at this time, as in all Indian wars, who entertained doubts of the fidelity of such Indians as pretended friendship. *Corn-plant* did not escape suspicion; but, as his conduct showed, it was entirely without foundation. In the midst of these imputations, a letter written at Fort Franklin says, "I have only to observe that the *Corn-plant* has been here, and, in my opinion, he is as friendly as one of our own people. He has advised me to take care, '*for*,' said he, '*you will soon have a chance to let the world know whether you are a soldier or not.*' When he went off, he ordered two chiefs and ten warriors to remain here, and scout about the garrison, and let me know if the bad Indians should either advance against me, or any of the frontiers of the United States. He thinks the people at Pittsburgh should keep out spies towards the salt licks, for he says, by and by, he thinks, the bad Indians will come from that way."

In 1792, the following advertisement appeared, signed by *Corn-plant*: "My people having been charged with committing depredations on the frontier inhabitants near Pittsburgh, I hereby contradict the assertion, as it is certainly without foundation, and pledge myself to those inhabitants, that they may rest perfectly secure from any danger from the Senecas residing on the Alleghany waters, and that my people have been and still are friendly to the U. States."

About the time *Corn-plant* left his nation to proceed on his mission to the hostile tribes, as three of his people were travelling through a settlement upon the Genesee, they stopped at a house to light their pipes. There happened to be several men within, one of whom, as the foremost Indian stooped to light his pipe, killed him with an axe. One of the others was badly wounded with the same weapon, while escaping from the house. They were not pursued, and the other, a boy, escaped unhurt. (The poor wounded man, when nearly well of the wound, was bitten by a snake, which caused his immediate death.) When *Corn-plant* knew

* *Carey's* Museum, v. 415.

† "Causes of the existing Hostilities," &c. drawn up by the sec'y of war, Gen. *Knox*, in 1791.

what had happened, he charged his warriors to remain quiet, and not to seek revenge, and was heard only to say, "*It is hard, when I and my people are trying to make peace for the whites, that we should receive such reward. I can govern my young men and warriors better than the thirteen fires can theirs.*" How is it that this man should practise upon the maxims of Confucius, of whom he never heard? (*Do ye to others as ye would that they should do unto you;*) and the monster in human form, in a gospel land, taught them from his youth, should show, by his actions, his utter contempt of them, and even of the divine mandate?

In 1816, the Rev. *Timothy Alden*, then president of Alleghany college, in Meadville, Pennsylvania, visited the Seneca nation. At this time, *Corn-plant* lived seven miles below the junction of the Connewango with the Alleghany, upon the banks of the latter, "on a piece of first-rate bottom land, a little within the limits of Pennsylvania." Here was his village,* which exhibited signs of industrious inhabitants. He then owned 1300 acres of land, 600 of which comprehended his town. "It was grateful to notice," observes Mr. *Alden*, "the present agricultural habits of the place, from the numerous enclosures of buck-wheat, corn and oats. We also saw a number of oxen, cows and horses; and many logs designed for the saw-mill and the Pittsburgh market." *Corn-plant* had, for some time, been very much in favor of the Christian religion, and hailed with joy such as professed it. When he was apprized of Mr. *Alden's* arrival, he hastened to welcome him to his village, and wait upon him. And notwithstanding his high station as a chief, having many men under his command, he chose rather, "in the ancient patriarchal style," to serve his visitors himself; he, therefore, took care of their horses, and went into the field, cut and brought oats for them.

The Western Missionary Society had, in 1815, at *Corn-plant's*, "urgent request," established a school at his village, which, at this time, promised success.

Corn-plant receives an annual annuity from the U. States, of 250 dollars, besides his proportion of 9000 divided equally among every member of the nation.

Gos-kuk-ke-wa-na-kon-ne-di-yu, commonly called the *Prophet*, was brother to *Corn-plant*, and resided in his village. He was of little note, and died previous to 1816.† *Corn-plant*, we believe, is yet living, and, like all other unenlightened people, very superstitious. Not long since, he said the Good Spirit had told him not to have any thing to do with the whites, or even to preserve any mementoes or relics they had from time to time given him; whereupon, among other things, he burnt up his belt and broke his elegant sword. He often mentions his having been at *Braddock's* defeat. *Henry Obeale*, his son, he sent to be educated among the whites. He became a drunkard on returning to his home, and is now discarded by his father. *Corn-plant* has other sons, but he says no more of them shall be educated among the whites, for he says, "*It entirely spoil Indian.*" And although he countenances Christianity, he does not do it, it is thought, from a belief of it, but probably from the same motives as too many whites do.‡

Teaslaegee, or *Charles Corn-planter*, was a party to the treaty of Moscow, N. Y. in 1823. He was probably a son of *Koeentwahk*, or *Gyantwaia*.

We find this notice of *Corn-plant* in the Pennsylvania Gazette of 1791: "The Indians in this quarter [Fort Pitt] have been very peaceable for some time, but down the Ohio they are continually doing mischief. There

* Formerly called *Obaletown*. See Pa. Gaz. 1792, and *Stanbury's* Jour.

† Amer. Register for 1816, vol. ii. 226, &c.

‡ Verbal account of E. T. *Foote*, Esq. of Chatauque co. N. Y. who possesses much valuable information upon matters of this kind.

are many conjectures in this country about Col. *Proctor's* business in the Indian country, as it is known he has left Fort Franklin, at French Creek, in company with the *Corn-planter* and many of his people."

Col. *Proctor* was sent to aid *Corn-plant* in his intended mission to the hostile tribes.

CHAPTER VII.

*Tecumseh—His great exertions to prevent the whites from overrunning his country—His expedition on Hacker's Creek—Cooperation of his brother, the Prophet—Rise of the difficulties between Tecumseh and Gov. Harrison—Speech of the former in a council at Vincennes—Fearful occurrence in that council—*WINNEMAK*—Tecumseh visited by Gov. Harrison at his camp—Determination of war the result of the interview on both sides—Characteristic anecdote of the chief—Determines, in the event of war, to prevent barbarities—Battle of Tippecanoe—Battle of the Thames, and death of Tecumseh—Description of his person—Important events in his life—*PUKEESHENO, *father of Tecumseh—His death—Particular account of* ELLSKWATAWA, *or the* PROPHET*—Account of* ROUND-HEAD*—Capture and massacre of Gen. Winchester's army at the River Raisin—*MYEERAH *or the* CRANE, *commonly called* WALK-IN-THE-WATER—TEYONINHOKE-RAWEN, *or* JOHN NORTON — WAWNAHTON — BLACK-THUNDER — ONGPA-TONGA, *or* BIG-ELK— PETALESHARO— METEA.

Tecumseh, by birth a Shawanee, and brigadier-general in the army of Great Britain, in the war of 1812, was born about 1770, and, like his great prototype, *Pometacom,* the Wampanoag, seems always to have made his aversion to civilization appear a prominent trait in his character; and it is not presumed that he joined the British army, and received the red sash and other badges of office, because he was fond of imitating the whites; but he employed them, more probably, as a means of inspiring his countrymen with that respect and veneration for himself which was so necessary in the work of expulsion, which he had undertaken.

The first exploit in which we find *Tecumseh* engaged was upon a branch of Hacker's Creek, in May, 1792. With a small band of warriors, he came upon the family of *John Waggoner,* about dusk. They found Waggoner a short distance from his house, sitting upon a log, resting himself after the fatigues of the day. *Tecumseh* directed his men to capture the family, while himself was engage with *Waggoner.* To make sure work. he took deliberate aim at him rifle; But fortunately he did not even wound him, though the ball passed next to his skin. Waggoner threw himself off the log, and ran with all his might, and *Tecumseh* followed. Having the advantage of an accurate knowledge of the ground, *Waggoner* made good his escape. Meanwhile his men succeeded in carrying off the family, some of whom they barbarously murdered. Among these were Mrs. *Waggoner* and two of her children. Several of the children remained a long time with the Indians.

This persevering and extraordinary man had made himself noted and conspicuous in the war which terminated by the treaty of Greenville, in 1795. He was brother to that famous impostor well know by the name of the *Prophet,* and seems to have joined in his views just in season to prevent his falling into entire disrepute among his own followers. His principal place of rendezvous was near the confluence of the Tippecanoe with the Wabash, upon, the north bank of the latter. This tract of coun–

try was none of his, but had been possessed by his brother the *Prophet,* in 1808, with a motley band of about a 1000 young warriors from among the Shawanese, Delawares, Wyandots, Potowatomies, Ottowas, Kikkapoos and Chippeways. The Miamies were very much opposed to this intrusion into their country, but were not powerful enough to repel it, and many of their chiefs were put to death in the most barbarous manner, for remonstrating against their conduct. The maladministration of the *Prophet,* however, in a short time, very much reduced his numbers, so that, in about a year, his followers consisted of but about 300, and these in the most miserable state of existence. Their habits had been such as to bring famine upon them; and but for the provisions furnished by General *Harrison,* from Vincennes, starvation would doubtless have ensued.* At this juncture, *Tecumseh* made his appearance among them; and although in the character of a subordinate chief, yet it was known that he directed every thing afterwards, although in the name of the *Prophet.* His exertions now became immense, to engage every tribe upon the continent in a confederacy, with the open and avowed object of arresting the progress of the whites.

It will be hard to find excuse for all the proceedings of the government of the United States and its agents towards the Indians at any time. The consciousness of power goes a great way with almost all men.

Agreeably to the direction of the government, Governor *Harrison* purchased of the Delawares, Miamies, and Potowatomies, a large tract of country on both sides of the Wabash, and extending up the river 60 miles above Vincennes. This was in 1809, about a year after the *Prophet* settled with his colony upon the Wabash, as above stated. *Tecumseh* was absent at this time, and his brother, the *Prophet,* was not considered as having any claim to the country, being there without the consent of the Miamies. *Tecumseh* did not view it in this light, and at his return was exceedingly vexed with those chiefs who had made the conveyance; many of whom, it is asserted, he threatened with death. *Tecumseh's* displeasure and dissatisfaction reached Gov. *Harrison,* who despatched a messenger to him, to state "that any claims he might have to the lands which had been ceded, were not affected by the treaty; that he might come to Vincennes and exhibit his pretensions, and if they were found to be solid, that the land would either be given up, or an ample compensation made for it."† This, it must be confessed, was not in a strain calculated to soothe a mighty mind, when once justly irritated, as was that of *Tecumseh,* at least as he conceived. However, upon the 12 August, 1810, (a day which cannot fail to remind the reader of the fate of his great archetype, *Philip, of Pokanoket,*) he met the governor in council at Vincennes, with many of his warriors; at which time he spoke to him as follows:—

"It is true I am a Shawanee. My forefathers were warriors. Their son is a warrior. From them I only take my existence; from my tribe I take nothing. I am the maker of my own fortune; and oh! that I could make that of my red people, and of my country, as great as the conceptions of my mind, when I think of the Spirit that rules the universe. I would not then come to Gov. *Harrison,* to ask him to tear the treaty, and to obliterate the landmark; but I would say to him, Sir, you have liberty to return to your own country. The being within, communing with past ages, tells me, that once, nor until lately, there was no white man on this continent. That it then all belonged to red men, children of the same parents, placed on it by the Great Spirit that made them, to keep it, to traverse it, to enjoy its productions, and to fill it with the same

* Memoirs of *Harrison.*

† *M'Afee.*

race. Once a happy race. Since made miserable by the white people, who are never contented, but always encroaching. The way, and the only way to check and to stop this evil, is, for all the red men to unite in claiming a common and equal right in the land, as it was at first, and should be yet; for it never was divided, but belongs to all, for the use of each. That no part has a right to sell, even to each other, much less to strangers; those who want all, and will not do with less. The white people have no right to take the land from the Indians, because they had it first; it is theirs. They may sell, but all must join. Any sale not made by all is not valid. The late sale is bad. It was made by a part only. Part do not know how to sell. It requires all to make a bargain for all. All red men have equal rights to the unoccupied land. The right of occupancy is as good in one place as in another. There cannot be two occupations in the same place. The first excludes all others. It is not so in hunting or travelling; for there the same ground will serve many, as they may follow each other all day; but the camp is stationary, and that is occupancy. It belongs to the first who sits down on his blanket or skins, which he has thrown upon the ground, and till he leaves it no other has a right."*

How near this is to the original is unknown to us, but it appears too much Americanized to correspond with our notions of *Tecumseh;* nevertheless it may give the true meaning. One important paragraph ought to be added, which we do not find in the author from which we have extracted the above; which was, "that the Americans had driven them from the sea-coasts, and that they would shortly push them into the lakes, and that they were determined to make a stand where they were."† This language forcibly reminds us of what the ancient Britons said of their enemies, when they besought aid of the Romans. "The barbarians (said they) drive us to the sea, and the sea beats us back upon them; between these extremes we are exposed, either to be slain with the sword, or drowned in the waves."‡

Tecumseh, having thus explained his reasons against the validity of the purchase, took his seat amidst his warriors. Governor *Harrison,* in his reply, said, "that the white people, when they arrived upon this continent, had found the Miamies in the occupation of all the country on the Wabash, and at that time the Shawanese were residents of Georgia, from which they were driven by the Creeks. That the lands had been purchased from the Miamies, who were the true and original owners of it. That it was ridiculous to assert that all the Indians were one nation; for if such had been the intention of the Great Spirit, he would not have put six different tongues into their heads, but have taught them all to speak a language that all could understand. That the Miamies found it for their interest to sell a part of their lands, and receive for them a further annuity, the benefit of which they had long experienced, from the punctuality with which the seventeen fires [the seventeen United States] complied with their engagements; and that the Shawanese had no right to come from a distant country and control the Miamies in the disposal of their own property." The governor then took his seat, and the interpreter proceeded to explain to *Tecumseh* what he had said, who, when he had nearly finished, suddenly interrupted him, and exclaimed, "*It is all false*;" at the same time giving to his warriors a signal, they seized their war clubs and sprung upon their feet, from the green grass on which they had been sitting. The governor now thought himself in imminent danger, and, freeing himself from his arm-chair, drew his sword and prepared to defend himself. He was attended by some officers of his gov-

* Hist. Kentucky. † Mem. Harrison. ‡ Seller's England.

ernment, and many citizens, more numerous than the Indians, but all unarmed; most of whom, however, seized upon some weapon, such as stones and clubs. *Tecumseh* continued to make gestures and speak with great emotion; and a guard of 12 armed men stationed in the rear were ordered up. For a few minutes, it was expected blood would be shed. Major G. R. *Floyde,* who stood near the governor, drew his dirk, and Winnemak cocked his pistol, which he had ready primed; he said *Tecumseh* had threatened his life for having signed the treaty and sale of the disputed land. A Mr. *Winas,* the Methodist minister, ran to the governor's house, and taking a gun, stood in the door to defend the family.

On being informed what *Tecumseh* had said, the governor replied to him, that "he was a bad man—that he would have no further talk with him—that he must return to his camp, and set out for his home immediately." Thus ended the conference. *Tecumseh* did not leave the neighborhood, but, the next morning, having reflected upon the impropriety of his conduct, sent to the governor to have the council renewed, and apologized for the affront offered; to which the governor, after some time, consented, having taken the precaution to have two additional companies of armed men in readiness, in case of insult.

Having met a second time, *Tecumseh* was asked whether he had any other grounds, than those he had stated, by which he could lay claim to the land in question; to which he replied, "No other." Here, then, was an end of all arguments. The indignant soul of *Tecumseh* could not but be enraged at the idea of an "equivalent for a country," or, what meant the same thing, a *compensation* for land, which, often repeated, as it had been, would soon *amount to a country*! "The behavior of *Tecumseh,* at this interview, was very different from what it was the day before. His deportment was dignified and collected, and he showed not the least disposition to be insolent. He denied having any intention of attacking the governor, but said he had been advised by white men"* to do as he had done; that two white men had visited him at his place of residence, and told him that half the white people were opposed to Governor *Harrison*, and willing to relinquish the land, and told him to advise the tribes not to receive pay for it; for that the governor would be soon put out of office, and a "good man" sent in his place, who would give up the land to the Indians. The governor asked him whether he would prevent the survey of the land: he replied that he was determined to adhere to the *old boundary*. Then arose a Wyandot, a Kikkapoo, a Pottowattomie, an Ottowas, and a Winnebago chief, each declaring his determination to stand by *Tecumseh,* whom they had chosen their chief. After the governor had informed *Tecumseh* that his words should be truly reported to the president, alleging, at the same time, that he knew the land would not be relinquished, and that it would be maintained by the sword, the council closed.

The governor wished yet to prolong the interview, and thought that, possibly, *Tecumseh* might appear more submissive, should he meet him in his own tent. Accordingly he took with him an interpreter, and visited the chief in his camp the next day. The governor was received with kindness and attention, and *Tecumseh* conversed with him a considerable time. On being asked by the governor, if his determination really was as he had expressed himself in the council, he said, "Yes;" and added, "that it was with great reluctance he would make war with the United States—against whom he had no other complaint, but their purchasing the Indians' land; that he was extremely anxious to be their friend, and if he (the governor) would prevail upon the president to give up the lands

* Memoirs of *Harrison*.

lately purchased, and agree never to make another treaty, without the consent of all the tribes, he would be their faithful ally, and assist them in all their wars with the English," whom he knew were always treating the Indians like dogs, clapping their hands, and hallooing *stu-boy*; that he would much rather join the seventeen fires; but if they would not give up said lands, and comply with his request in other respects, he would join the English. When the governor told him there was no probability that the president would comply, he said, "Well, as the great chief is to determine the matter, I hope the Great Spirit will put sense enough into his head, to induce him to direct you to give up this land. It is true, he is so far off, he will not be injured by the war. He may sit still in his town, and drink his wine, whilst you and I will have to fight it out." He had said before, when asked if it were his determination to make war unless his terms were complied with, "*It is my determination; nor will I give rest to my feet, until I have united all the red men in the like resolution.*"

Thus is exhibited the determined character of *Tecumseh,* in which no duplicity appears, and whose resentment might have been expected, when questioned, again and again, upon the same subject.

Most religiously did he prosecute this plan; and could his extraordinary and wonderful exertions be known, no fiction, it is believed, could scarcely surpass the reality. The tribes to the west of the Mississippi, and those about Lakes Superior and Huron, were visited and revisited by him previous to the year 1811. He had raised in these tribes the high expectation, that they should be able to drive the Americans to the east of the Ohio. The famous *Blue-jacket* was as sanguine as *Tecumseh,* and was his abettor in uniting distant tribes.

The following characteristic circumstance occurred at one of the meetings at Vincennes. After *Tecumseh* had made a speech to governor *Harrison,* and was about to seat himself in a chair, he observed that none had been placed for him. One was immediately ordered by the governor, and, as the interpreter handed it to him, he said, "Your father requests you to take a chair." "*My father*?" says *Tecumseh,* with great indignity of expression, "*the sun is my father, and the earth is my mother; and on her bosom I will repose*;" and immediately seated himself, in the Indian manner, upon the ground.*

The fight at Tippecanoe followed soon after. This affair took place in the night of Nov. 6, 1811, in which 62 Americans were killed, and 126 wounded. *Tecumseh* was not in this fight, but his brother, the *Prophet,* conducted or ordered the attack. During the action, he was performing conjurations on an eminence not far off, but out of danger. His men displayed great bravery, and the fight was long and bloody. *Harrison* lost some of his bravest officers. The late Colonel *Snelling,* of Boston, then a captain, was in this fight, and took prisoner with his own hands an Indian chief, the only Indian taken by the Americans. The name of the captured chief we do not learn, but, from his fear of being taken for a Shawanee, it is evident he was not of that tribe. When he was seized by Capt. Snelling, he ejaculated, with hurried accents, "*Good man, me no Shawanee.*"† The chiefs *White-lion* (*Wapamangwa,*) *Stone-eater* (*Sanamahhonga,*) and *Winnemak,* were conspicuous at this time. The latter had been the pretended friend of the governor, but now appeared his enemy.

Just before hostilities commenced, in a talk Governor *Harrison* had with *Tecumseh,* the former expressed a wish, if war must follow, that cruelty to prisoners should not be allowed on either side. *Tecumseh* assured him that he would do all in his power to prevent it; and it is be-

* Schoolcraft.

† Information of his son, *W. J. Snelling,* Esq. of Boston.

lieved he strictly adhered to this resolution. Indeed, we have one example, which has never been called in question, and is worthy the great mind of this chief. When Col. *Dudley* was cut off, and near 400 of his men, not far from Fort Meigs, by falling into an ambush, *Tecumseh* arrived at the scene of action when the Americans could resist no longer. He exerted himself to put a stop to the massacre of the soldiers, which was then going on; and meeting with a Chippeway chief who would not desist by persuasion nor threat, he buried his tomahawk in his head.*

It is said that *Tecumseh* had been in almost every important battle with the Americans, from the destruction of General *Harmer's* army till his death upon the Thames. He was under the direction of General *Proctor,* in the last great act of his life, but was greatly dissatisfied with his course of proceedings, and is said to have remonstrated against retreating before the Americans in very pointed terms. *Perry's* victory had just given the Americans the command of Lake Erie; and immediately after, *Proctor* abandoned Detroit, and marched his majesty's army up the river Thames, accompanied by General *Tecumseh,* with about 1500 warriors. *Harrison* overtook them near the Moravian town, Oct. 5,1813, and, after a bloody battle with the Indians, routed and took prisoners nearly the whole British army; *Proctor* saving himself only by flight. After withstanding almost the whole force of the Americans for some time, *Tecumseh* received a severe wound in the arm, but continued to fight with desperation, until a shot in the head from an unknown hand laid him prostrate in the thickest of the fight.† Of his warriors 120 were left upon the field of battle.

Thus fell *Tecumseh,* in the forty-fourth year of his age. He was about five feet ten inches in height, of a noble appearance, and a perfectly symmetrical form. "His carriage was erect and lofty—his motions quick—his eyes penetrating—his visage stern, with an air of *hauteur* in his countenance, which arose from an elevated pride of soul. It did not leave him even in death." He is thus spoken of by one who knew him. His dress on the day of the fatal battle was a deerskin coat and pantaloons.

At the battle of the Thames, a chief by the name of *Shane* served as a guide to Col. *Johnson's* regiment. He informs us that he knew *Tecumseh* well, and that he once had had his thigh broken, which not being properly set, caused a considerable ridge in it always after. This was published in a Kentucky newspaper, lately, as necessary to prove that the Indian killed by Col. *Johnson* was *Tecumseh.* From the same paper it would seem, that, even on the day of battle, it was doubted by some whether the chief killed were *Tecumseh,* and that a critical inquest was held over his body; and although it was decided to be he, yet to the fact that the colonel killed him, there was a demur, even then. But, no doubt, many were willing it should so pass, thinking it a matter of no consequence, so long as *Tecumseh,* their most dreaded enemy, was actually slain; and, perhaps, too, so near the event, many felt a delicacy in dissenting from the report of Col. *Johnson's* friends; but when time had dispelled such jealousy, those came out frankly with their opinion, and hence resulted the actual truth of the case.

That the American soldiers should have dishonored themselves, after their victory, by outraging all decency by acts of astonishing ferocity and barbarity, upon the lifeless body of the fallen chief, is grievous to mention, and cannot meet with too severe condemnation. Pieces of his skin were

---

* *James,* i. 291—*Perkins* 221.

† The story that he fell in a personal rencounter with Col. *Johnson,* must no longer be believed. Facts are entirely opposed to such a conclusion. Indeed, we cannot learn that the colonel ever *claimed* the *honor* of the achievement.

taken away by some of them as mementoes!* He is said to have borne a personal enmity to General *Harrison,* at this time, for having just before destroyed his family. The celebrated speech, said to have been delivered by the great "Shawanese warrior" to General *Proctor,* before the battle of the Thames, is believed by many not to be genuine. It may be seen in every history of the war, and every periodical of that day, and in not a few since, even to this. Therefore we omit it here. The speech of *Logan,* perhaps, has not circulated wider. Another, in our opinion, more worthy the mighty mind of *Tecumseh,* published in a work said to be written by one who heard it,† is now generally (on the authority of a public journal‡) discarded as a fiction.

Among the skirmishes between the belligerents, before Gen. *Hull* surrendered the north-western army, *Tecumseh* and his Indians acted a conspicuous part.

Malden, situated at the junction of Detroit River with Lake Erie, was considered the Gibraltar of Canada, and it was expected that Gen. *Hull's* first movements would be to possess himself of it. In a movement that way, Col. *M'Arthur* came very near being cut off by a party of Indians led by *Tecumseh.* About 4 miles from Malden, he found a bridge in possession of a body of the enemy; and although the bridge was carried by a force under Col. Cass,§ in effecting which, 11 of the enemy were killed, yet it seems, that in a "few days afterwards" they were in possession of it again, and again the Americans stood ready to repeat the attack. It was in an attempt to reconnoitre, that Col. *M'Arthur* "advanced somewhat too near the enemy, and narrowly escaped being cut off from his men" || by several Indians who had nearly prevented his retreat.

Major *Vanhorn* was detached from Aux Canards, with 200 men, to convoy 150 Ohio militia and some provisions from the River Raisin. In his second day's march, near Brownstown, he fell into an ambush of 70 Indians under Tecumseh, who, firing upon him, killed 20 men; among whom were Captains *M'Culloch,*¶ *Bostler, Gilcrease*** and *Ubry:* 9 more were wounded.

A British writer upon the late war,†† after having related the battle of the Thames, in which *Tecumseh* fell, says: "It seems extraordinary that Gen. *Harrison* should have omitted to mention, in his letter, the death of a chief, whose fall contributed so largely to break down the Indian spirit, and to give peace and security to the whole north-western frontier of the U. States. *Tecumseh,* although he had received a musket-ball in the left arm, was still seeking the hottest of the fire," when he received the mortal wound in the head, of which he in a few moments expired. The error, which for some time prevailed, of his being shot by Col. *Johnson,* is copied into this author's work. The following descriptions, though in some respects erroneous, are of sufficient value to be preserved.

Tecumseh was endowed "with more than the usual stoutness, possessed all the agility and perseverance, of the Indian character. His carriage was dignified; his eye penetrating; his countenance, which, even in death, betrayed the indications of a lofty spirit, rather of the sterner cast. Had he not possessed a certain austerity of manners, he could never have

---

* We have often heard it said, but whether in truth we do not aver, that there are those who still own razor straps made of it.

† *John Dunn Hunter.* ‡ North American Review.

§ Since governor of Michigan, and now secretary of war.

|| Brackenridge, Hist. War, 31.

¶ In this officer's pocket, it is said, was found a letter written for his wife, giving an account of his having killed an Indian, from whose head he tore the scalp with his teeth. This is the process when the hair is short.

** *Gilchrist,* commonly written. †† *James,* i. 287, &c.

controlled the wayward passions of those who followed him to battle. He was of a silent habit; but, when his eloquence became roused into action by the reiterated encroachments of the Americans,* his strong intellect could supply him with a flow of oratory, that enabled him, as he governed in the field, so to prescribe in the council. Those who consider that, in all territorial questions, the ablest diplomatists of the U. States are sent to negotiate with the Indians, will readily appreciate the loss sustained by the latter in the death of their champion. The Indians, in general, are full as fond as other savages, of the gaudy decoration of their persons; but *Tecumseh* was an exception. Clothes and other valuable articles of spoil had often been his: yet he invariably wore a deerskin coat and pantaloons. He frequently levied subsidies to, comparatively, a large amount; yet he preserved little or nothing for himself. It was not wealth, but glory, that was *Tecumseh's* ruling passion. Fatal day! when the 'Christian people' first penetrated the forests, to teach the arts of 'civilization' to the poor Indian. Till then water had been his only beverage; and himself and his race possessed all the vigor of hardy savages. Now, no Indian opens his lips to the stream that ripples by his wigwam, while he has a rag of clothes on his back, wherewith to purchase rum; and he and his squaw and his children wallow through the day, in beastly drunkenness.† Instead of the sturdy warrior, with a head to plan, and an arm to execute, vengeance upon the oppressors of his country, we behold the puny besotted wretch, squatting on his hams, ready to barter his country, his children, or himself, for a few gulps of that deleterious compound, which, far more than the arms of the United States, [Great Britain and France,] is hastening to extinguish all traces of his name and character. *Tecumseh,* himself, in early life, had been addicted to intemperance; but no sooner did his judgment decide against, than his resolution enabled him to quit, so vile a habit. Beyond one or two glasses of wine, he never afterwards indulged."

It was said not to be from good will to the Americans, that he would not permit his warriors to exercise any cruelty upon them, when fallen into their power, but from principle alone. When Detroit was taken by the British and Indians, *Tecumseh* was in the action at the head of the latter. After the surrender, Gen. Brock requested him not to allow his Indians to ill-treat the prisoners, and to which he replied, "*No! I despise them too much to meddle with them.*"

Some of the English have said that there were few officers in the U. States' service so able to command in the field as *Tecumseh.* This it will not us behove to question; but it would better have become such speechmakers, if they had added, "in his peculiar mode of warfare." That he was a more wily chief than *Mishikinakwa,* may be doubted; that either had natural abilities inferior to those of Gen. *Wayne,* or Gen. *Brock,* we see no reason to believe. But this is no argument that they could practise European warfare as well as those generals. It is obvious, from his intercourse with the whites, that *Tecumseh* must have been more skilled in their military tactics than most, if not all, of his countrymen, whether predecessors or cotemporaries.

A military man,‡ as we apprehend, says, "He [*Tecumseh*] was an excellent judge of position; and not only knew, but could point out the localities of the whole country through which he had passed." "His facility of communicating the information he had acquired, was thus dis played before a concourse of spectators. Previously to Gen. *Brock's* crossing over to Detroit, he asked *Tecumseh* what sort of a country he should

* As though the English of Canada had never been guilty of encroachments!

† This is not true.

‡ Mr. *James, ut supra.*

have to pass through, in case of his proceeding farther. *Tecumseh,* taking a roll of elm-bark, and extending it on the ground by means of four stones, drew forth his scalping-knife, and with the point presently etched upon the bark a plan of the country, its hills, woods, rivers, morasses, and roads; a plan which, if not as neat, was, for the purpose required, fully as intelligible as if *Arrowsmith* himself had prepared it. Pleased with this unexpected talent in *Tecumseh,* also with his having, by his characteristic boldness, induced the Indians, not of his immediate party, to cross the Detroit, prior to the embarkation of the regulars and militia, Gen. *Brock,* as soon as the business was over, publicly took off his sash, and placed it round the body of the chief. *Tecumseh* received the honor with evident gratification; but was, the next day, seen without his sash. Gen. *Brock,* fearing something had displeased the India sent his interpreter for an explanation. The latter soon returned with an account, that *Tecumseh,* not wishing to wear such a mark of distinction, when an older, and, as he said, abler, warrior than himself was present, had transferred the sash to the Wyandot chief *Round-head.*"

The place of this renowned warrior's birth was upon the banks of the Scioto River, near what is now Chillicothe. His father's name was *Pukeesheno,* which means, *I light from flying.* He was killed in the battle of Kanhawa, in 1774. His mother's name was *Meetheetashe,* which signifies, *a turtle laying her eggs in the sand.* She died among the Cherokees. She had, at one birth, three *sons:—Ellskwatawa,* which signifies, *a door opened,* was called the *Prophet; Tecumseh,* which is, *a tiger crouching for his prey*; and *Kumskaka, a tiger that flies in the air.**

Although we have given some important facts in the life of *Ellskwatawa,* there are some circumstances which claim to be related. After the termination of the war of 1812, he received a pension from the government of Great Britain, and resided in Canada. In 1826 he was prevailed upon to leave that country, and went, with others, to settle beyond the Mississippi. At the same time also went the only surviving son of *Tecumseh.*

Much has been said and written about the *Prophet;* and, as is generally the case, the accounts vary, in proportion to their multiplicity. From a well-written article in a foreign periodical,† it is said that, during the first 50 years of his life, he was remarkable for nothing except his stupidity and intoxication. In his 50th year, while in the act of lighting his pipe, he fell back in his cabin, upon his bed; and, continuing for some time lifeless, to all appearances, preparations were made for his interment; and it was not until the tribe was assembled, as usual on such occasions, and they were in the act of removing him, that he revived. His first words were, "*Don't be alarmed. I have seen heaven. Call the nation together, that I may tell them what has appeared to me.*" When they were assembled, he told them that two beautiful young men had been sent from heaven by the Great Spirit, who spoke thus to him:—"The Great Spirit is angry with you, and will destroy all the red men: unless you refrain from drunkenness, lying and stealing, and turn yourselves to him, you shall never enter the beautiful place which we will now show you." He was then conducted to the gates of heaven, from whence he could behold all its beauties, but was not permitted to enter. After undergoing several hours' tantalization, from extreme desire of participating in its indescribable joys and pleasures, he was dismissed. His conductors told him to tell all the Indians what he had seen; to repent of their ways, and they would visit him again. My authority says, that, on the *Prophet's* visiting the neighboring nations, his mission had a good effect on their morals, &c. But this part of his story, at least, is at variance with facts; for none

* *Schoolcraft.*

† The New Monthly Magazine.

would hear to him, except the most abandoned young warriors, of those tribes he visited, and their miserable condition in colonizing themselves upon the Wabash, in 1811, is well known.*

There was an earthquake said to have taken place in the Creek country, in December, 1811.† The *Prophet* visited the Creeks in the previous August, and "pronounced in the public square, that shortly a lamp would appear in the west, to aid him in his hostile attack upon the whites, and, if they would not be influenced by his persuasion, the earth would ere long tremble to its centre. This circumstance has had a powerful effect on the minds of these Indians, and would certainly have led them, generally, to have united with the northern coalition, had it not been for the interposition of travellers." This statement was made by a Mr. *Francis M'Henry*, in the Georgia Journal, to contradict that ever any such earthquake did take place, and by which we learn that that part of the superstitious world really believed that it had, and that places had been actually sunk. The same communicant says, "I have only to state, that I have comfortably reposed in houses where newspapers have announced every disappearance of earth." He states also, upon the authority of "a Mr. *Chadbury*, an English gentleman, from Quebec," that, "at the age of 15, this Indian disappeared from his relatives, and was considered as finally lost. That he strolled to Quebec, and from thence to Montreal, where, taken as a pilot to Halifax, he remained several years; and in this space received an education qualifying him to act the part already known." The comet of 1811 was viewed by many, throughout the country, as a harbinger of evil, and it was upon this seeming advantage that the *Prophet* seized to frighten his red brethren into his schemes.‡

Round-head was a Wyandot, and fought against the Americans in the last war. He was very conspicuous in the battle at Frenchtown, upon the River Raisin. The Indian force in this affair was about 1000.§ Gen. *Winchester's* quarters were at 1 or 200 yards from the main army when the fight commenced, and, in an endeavor to render it assistance, was fallen upon by the Wyandots, and himself and attendants captured. *Round-head* seized upon Gen. *Winchester* with his own hands. It was a severe cold morning, 22 Jan. 1813, and the ground was covered with snow.

Our chief, in a manner truly characteristic, obliged the general to divest himself of his great coat, and all his uniform. With nothing but his shirt to protect him from the cold, *Round-head* conducted him to a fire, but not until he had got on the general's cocked hat, uniform coat, vest, &c. It was in this condition, that Col. *Proctor* found him; and it was not without much persuasion that the stern warrior relinquished his important captive; and it was with still more reluctance, that he gave up the uniform, in which he had had so short a time to strut about and show himself to his countrymen.||

This was a most diastrous expedition for the Americans: 538 were captured, according to the British account, which does not differ materially

---

* This famous vision of the *Prophet* will compare in strangeness with that of *Keposh*, head chief of the Delaware nation, related by *Loskiel*, (ii. 114.) He lay to all appearance dead for three days. In his swoon, he saw a man in white robes, who exhibited a catalogue of the people's sins, and warned him to repent. In 1749, he was about 80 years of age, and was baptized by the name of *Solomon*. We have related in Book III. an account of *Squando's* vision; and others might be mentioned.

† "The earthquakes, which, in 1811, almost destroyed the town of New Madrid of the Mississippi, were very sensibly felt on the upper portion of the Missouri country, and occasioned much superstitious dread amongst the Indians." *Long's Expedition*, I.272.

‡ Halcyon Luminary, i. 205, &c. New York, (June,) 1812.

§ Perkins's Late War, 100.

|| *James*, Milit. Occurrences, i. 188.

from the American;* and 300 killed in the battle and massacred by the Indians immediately after.

In Col. *Proctor's* official account of this affair, he speaks in high terms of the conduct of the Indian chiefs and warriors. His words are: The zeal and courage of the Indian department were never more conspicuous than on this occasion, and the Indian warriors fought with their usual bravery."

Col. *Proctor* has been much censured for his conduct at the River Raisin. It was said that he agreed to the terms asked for by Gen. *Winchester,* and then paid no attention to their observance, but rather countenanced the Indians in their barbarities, thinking thereby to strike the Americans with dread, that they might be deterred from entering the service in future. But the British historians say that "the whereof the left division surrendered at discretion," and not "on condition of their being protected from the savages, being allowed to retain their private property, and having their side-arms returned to them," as stated by Gen. *Winchester:* for, Mr. *James* adds, "had this been the understanding, one may suppose that some writing would have been drawn up; but, indeed, Gen. *Winchester* was not in a condition to dictate terms. Stripped to his shirt and trowsers, and suffering exceedingly from the cold, the American general was found by Col. *Proctor,* near to one of the Indian fires, in possession of the Wyandot chief *Round-head."*

So, according to the judgment of this historian, Col. *Proctor* was under no obligation to keep his word, because there was "no writing" with his name to it. The historian that will even set up a defence for treachery may calculate with certainty upon the value posterity will set upon his work. We want no other than Col. *Proctor's* own account from which to condemn him of, at least, great want of humanity. We do not pretend that the Americans were always free from the same charges; but we would as soon scorn their extenuation as that of their enemies.

Round-head was present with Gen. *Brock* and *Tecumseh* when they took possession of Detroit, on the 15 August, 1812. When about to cross the river to lay siege to Detroit, Gen. *Brock* presented *Tecumseh* with his red sash. This chief had too much good sense to wear it, well knowing it would create jealousy among the other chiefs, who considered themselves equal with him; he therefore presented it to *Round-head,* as has been mentioned in the life of *Tecumseh.*

Whether this chief were more wise than *Tecumseh,* in the last affair in which the latter was engaged, we are unable to say; but it appears highly probable that the conduct of Gen. *Proctor* was the cause of his being abandoned by most, if not all the Wyandots, previous to the battle of the Thames.† As *Round-head* was their chief, to him will be attributed the cause of their wise proceeding.

The following letter, written after the battle of the River Raisin, (we conclude,) is worthy of a place here.

"*The Hurons, and the other tribes of Indians, assembled at the Miami Rapids, to the anhabitants of the River Raisin.—Friends, listen! You have always told us you would give us any assistance in your power. We, therefore, as the enemy is approaching us, within 25 miles, call upon you all to rise up and come here immediately, bringing your arms along with you. Should you fail at this time, we will not consider you in future as friends, and the consequences may be very unpleasant. We are well convinced you*

---

* *Thomson* has 522. Hist. Sketches, 104.

† Gen. *Harrison's* official letter, among *Brannan's Official Doc.* p. 237.

10

have no writing forbidding you to assist us. We are your friends at present.

Round-head ⊰⊱ *his mark.*
Walk-in-the-water ◎ *his mark.**

Walk-in-the-water also signalized himself in these events. His native name is *Myeerah.* He is a Huron, of the tribe of the Wyandots, and, in 1817, resided on a reservation in Michigan, at a village called Maguaga, near Brownstown. Mr. *Brown,* in his valuable WESTERN GAZETTEER, justly styles this famous chief one of "nature's nobles." The unfortunate Gen. *Hull* mention him as one of the principal "among the vast number of chiefs who led the hostile bands" of the west when the war of 1812 commenced. The Kaskaskias Wyandots, in 1814, were nearly equally divided between a chief called *Tarhe,* which signifies the *Crane,* and *Myeerah.* The former was called the grand chief of the nation, and resided at Sandusky. He was a very venerable and intelligent chief. In 1812, *Myeerah* told some American officers who were sent to the Indians to secure their favor, that the American government was acting very wrong to send an army into their country, which would cut off their communication with Canada. The Indians, he said, were their own masters, and would trade where they pleased; that the affair of the Wabash was the fault of Gen. *Harrison* entirely. He commanded the Indian army with *Round-head* at the battle of the River Raisin.

After the battle of the Thames, in which also *Walk-in-the-water* was a eonspicuous commander, he went to Detroit to make peace, or rather to ask it of Gen. *Harrison.* In crossing from Sandwich with a white flag, many were attracted to the shore, to see him, where also were drawn up the Kentucky volunteers. All were struck with admiration at his noble aspect and fearless carriage, as he ascended the bank and passed through the ranks of the soldiers. The greatest firmness attended his steps, and the most dignified *nonchalance* was upon his countenance; notwithstanding his condition was now calculated to discover humiliation and deep depression. Only a few days before, he had fought hand to hand with these same volunteers, whose ranks he now passed through.

We have not heard of the death of the heroic and truly great chief *Myeerah;* but, whether alive or dead, our veneration is the same. It was said of his cotemporary, *Tecumseh,* that in the field he was an *Achilles,* and in the council an *Agamemnon.* At least, we think, as much may in truth be said of *Myeerah.* The sequel of the life of *Tarhe* will be found in a former chapter, where he figures under the name of King Crane. In 1807, a treaty was made at Detroit between the Chippeways, Ottowas, Pottowattomies and Wyandots and the U. States. Two chiefs besides Myeerah signed on behalf of the last-named tribe. His name to that treaty is written *Miere.* The next year, 1808, another treaty was made at Brownstown with the same tribes, with the addition of two delegates from the Shawanees. Three besides *Myeerah* signed at this time. He was also, we believe, a party to the treaty made at Fort Industry in 1805, on the Miami of the Lake.

Less is known of the history of the two next chiefs, of which we shall say something, than of man others less distinguished.

Teyoninhokerawen was a Mohawk chief, who is generally known under the appellation of *John Norton.* "This interesting Indian, about two years ago, [1804 or 5,] visited England, where numerous traits of an amiable disposition and a vigorous intellect produced the most pleasing impressions on all who were introduced to him. A proof of his possessing, in a

---

* *English Barbarities,* 132.

high degree, the qualities of a good temper and great mental quickness, occurred at the *upper rooms*, at Bath, where he appeared in the dress of his country. A young Englishman, who had been in America, accosted the chief with several abrupt questions respecting his place of abode, situation, and the like. To these *Norton* returned answers at once pertinent and modest. The inquirer, however, expressed himself dissatisfied with them, and hinted, in almost plain terms, that he believed him to be an impostor. Still the American suppressed his resentment, and endeavored to convince the *gentleman* that this account of himself might be depended upon. 'Well, but,' returned the other, 'if you really are what you pretend to be, how will you relish returning to the savages of your own country?' '*Sir*,' replied Norton, with a glance of intelligence, '*I shall not experience so great a change in my society, as you imagine, for I find there are savages in this country also.*' Animated with the spirit of genuine patriotism, this generous chieftain was unweariedly occupied, during the intervals of his public business, in acquiring every species of useful knowledge, for the purpose of transporting it to his own country, for the benefit of his people; and what the friends to the happiness of men will hear with still greater admiration and pleasure, he was also engaged, under the auspices of Mr. *Wilberforce* and Mr. *Thornton*, in the laborious employment of translating the Gospel of St. John into his native tongue."* Whether that published by the American Bible Society be the same translation, I am not positive, but believe it is. The following is the 3d of Chap. i. *Yorighwagwegon ne rode weyenòkden, ok tsi nikon ne kaghson yagh oghnahhoten teyodon ne ne yagh raonhah te hayàdare.*

We learn also from Mr. *Jansen* that when *Teyoninhokerawen* was in England, he "appeared to be about 45 years of age;" tall, muscular, and well proportioned, possessing a fine and intelligent countenance. His mother was a Scotch woman, and he had spent two years in Edinburgh, in his youth, namely, from his 13th to his 15th year, read and spoke English and French well. He was married to a female of his own tribe, by whom he had two children. He served in the last war with the English, as will presently be related.

Because this chief spent a few years in Scotland when young, some historians† have asserted that he was not an Indian, but a Scotchman; and a writer‡ of a sketch of the late Canada war, says he was related to the French. Of this we have no doubt, as it is not uncommon for many of those who pass for Indians to have white fathers. We should think, therefore, that, instead of his mother's being a Scotch woman, his father might have been a Frenchman, and his mother an Indian.

Of *Norton's* or *Teyoninhokerawen's* exploits in the last war, there were not many, we presume, as there are not many recorded. When Col. *Murray* surprised Fort Niagara, on the I9 Dec. 1813, *Norton* entered the fort with him, at the head of a force of about 400 men.§ Fort Niagara was garrisoned by about 300 Americans, of whom but 20 escaped. All who resisted, and some who did not, were run through with the bayonet. We only know that *Norton* was present on this occasion.

On the 6 June, 1814, Gen. *Vincent* and *Norton*, with a considerable force,|| attacked an American camp ten miles from Burlington Bay, at a place called Fifty Mile Creek. The onset was made before day on a Sunday morning. The invaders seized upon seven pieces of cannon, and turned them upon their enemies. The night was very dark, and the confusion

* *Janson's* Stranger in America, 278. 4to, London, 1807.

† *James*, Military Occurrences, ii. 16. ‡ Mr. *M. Smith*, who lived then in Canada.

§ Some American historians say, "British and Indians;" but Mr. *James* (ii. 16.) says there was but one "Indian," and he was a Scotchman!

|| The number of rank and file was 704, of the Americans about 3000.

was very great. The American generals *Chandler* and *Winder,* one major, five captains, one lieutenant, and 116 men, were taken prisoners. Nevertheless the Americans fought with such resolution that the attacking party were obliged to abandon their advantage, leaving 150 of their number behind them. They, however, carried off two pieces of cannon and some horses.

The next chief we introduce chiefly to illustrate a most extraordinary mode of doing penance, among the nations of the west.

*Wawnahton,** a bold and fearless chief, of the tribe of Yankton,† (whose name, translated, is "*he who charges the enemy,*") was considerably noted in the last war with Canada. "He had," says my author, "killed seven enemies in battle with his own hand, as the seven war-eagle plumes in his hair testified, and received nine wounds, as was shown by an equal number of little sticks arranged in his coal-black hair, and painted in a manner that told an Indian eye whether they were inflicted by a bullet, knife or tomahawk, and by whom. At the attack on Fort Sandusky, in the late war, he received a bullet and three buck shot in his breast, which glanced on the bone, and passing round under the skin, came out at his back." This, and other extraordinary escapes, he made use of, like the famous *Tuspaquin,* two ages before, to render himself of greater importance among his nation. At this time he was supposed to be about 30 years of age, of a noble and elegant appearance, and is still believed to be living.‡

Major *Long's* company considered *Wawnahton* a very interesting man, whose acquaintance they cultivated with success in the neighborhood of Lake Traverse. They describe him as upwards of six feet high, and

* *Wanotan,* in *Long's* Exped. to St. Peters, i. 448.

† *Yanktoan,* (Long, ib. 404,) which signifies *descended from the fern leaves.*

‡ Facts published by *W. J. Snelling,* Esq. It is said by *Keating,* in *Long's* Exped. i. 448, that he was about 28 years of age. This was in 1823.

possessing a countenance that would be considered handsome in any country. He prepared a feast for the party, as soon as he knew they were coming to his village. "When speaking of the Dacotas, we purposely postponed mentioning the frequent vows which they make, and their strict adherence to them, because one of the best evidences which we have collected on this point connects itself with the character of *Wanotan,* and may give a favorable idea of his extreme fortitude in enduring pain. In the summer of 1822 he undertook a journey, from which, apprehending much danger on the part of the Chippewas, he made a vow to the sun, that, if he returned safe, he would abstain from all food or drink for the space of four successive days and nights, and that he would distribute among his people all the property which he possessed, including all his lodges, horses, dogs, &c. On his return, which happened without accident, he celebrated the dance of the sun; this consisted in making three cuts through his skin, one on his breast, and one on each of his arms. The skin was cut in the manner of a loop, so as to permit a rope to pass between the flesh and the strip of skin which was thus divided from the body. The ropes being passed through, their ends were secured to a tall vertical pole, planted at about 40 yards from his lodge. He then began to dance round this pole, at the commencement of this fast, frequently swinging himself in the air, so as to be supported merely by the cords which were secured to the strips of skin separated from his arms and breast. He continued this exercise with few intermissions during the whole of his fast, until the fourth day about 10 o'clock, A. M., when the strip of skin from his breast gave way; notwithstanding which he interrupted not the dance, although supported merely by his arms. At noon the strip from his left arm snapped off: his uncle then thought that he had suffered enough," and with his knife cut the last loop of skin, and *Wanotan* fell down in a swoon, where he lay the rest of the day, exposed to the scorching rays of the sun. After this he gave away all his property, and with his two squaws deserted his lodge. To such monstrous follies does superstition drive her votaries!

Black-thunder, or *Mackkatananamakee,* was styled the celebrated patriarch of the Fox tribe. He made himself remembered by many from an excellent speech which he made to the American commissioners, who had assembled many chiefs at a place called the Portage, July, 1815, to hold a talk with them, upon the state of their affairs; particularly as it was believed by the Americans that the Indians meditated hostilities. An American commissioner opened the talk, and unbecomingly accused the Indians of breach of former treaties. The first chief that answered, spoke with a tremulous voice, and evidently betrayed guilt, or perhaps fear. Not so with the upright chief *Black-thunder*. He felt equally indignant at the charge of the white man, and the unmanly cringing of the chief who had just spoken. He began:—

"My father, restrain your feelings, and hear calmly what I shall say. I shall say it plainly. I shall not speak with fear and trembling. I have never injured you, and innocence can feel no fear. I turn to you all, red-skins and white-skins—where is the man who will appear as my accuser? Father, I understand not clearly how things are working. I have just been set at liberty. Am I again to be plunged into bondage? Frowns are all around me; but I am incapable of change. You, perhaps, may be ignorant of what I tell you; but it is a truth, which I call heaven and earth to witness. It is a fact which can easily be proved, that I have been assailed in almost every possible way that pride, fear, feeling, or interest, could touch me—that I have been pushed to the last to raise the tomahawk against you; but all in vain. I never could be made to feel that you were my enemy. *If this be the conduct of an enemy, I shall never* *be your friend.* You are acquainted with my removal above Prairie des Chiens.* I went, and formed a settlement, and called my warriors around me. We took counsel, and from that counsel we never have departed. We smoked, and resolved to make common cause with the U. States. I sent you the pipe—it resembled this—and I sent it by the Missouri, that the Indians of the Mississippi might not know what we were doing. You received it. I then told you that your friends should be my friends—that your enemies should be my enemies—and that I only awaited your signal to make war. *If this be the conduct of an enemy, I shall never be your friend.*—Why do I tell you this? Because it is a truth, and a melancholy truth; that the good things which men do are often buried in the ground, while their evil deeds are stripped naked, and exposed to the world.†—When I came here, I came to you in friendship. I little thought I should have had to defend myself. I have no defence to make. If I were guilty, I should have come prepared; but I have ever held you by the hand, and I am come without excuses. If I had fought against you, I would have told you so: but I have nothing now to say here in your councils, except to repeat what I said before to my great father, the president of your nation. You heard it, and no doubt remember it. It was simply this. My lands can never be surrendered; I was cheated, and basely cheated, in the contract; I will not surrender my country but with my life. Again I call heaven and earth to witness, and I smoke this pipe in evidence of my sincerity. If you are sincere, you will receive it from me. My only desire is, that we should smoke it together—that I should grasp your sacred hand, and I claim for myself and my tribe the protection of your country. When this pipe touches your lip, may it operate as a blessing upon all my tribe.—*May the smoke rise like a cloud, and carry away with it all the animosities which have arisen between us.*"‡

The issue of this council was amicable, and on the 14 Sept. following, *Black-thunder* met commissioners at St. Louis, and executed a treaty of peace.

Ongpatonga,§ or, as he was usually called, *Big-elk,* was chief of the Mahas or Omawhaws, whose residence, in 1811, was upon the Missouri.‖ Mr. *Brackenridge* visited his town on the 19 May of that year, in his voyage up that river. His "village is situated about three miles from the river, and contains about 3000 souls, and is 836 miles from its mouth."¶ We shall give here, as an introduction to him, the oration he made over the grave of *Black-buffalo,* a Sioux chief of the Teton tribe, who died on the night of the 14 July, 1811, at "Portage des Sioux," and of whom Mr. *Brackenridge* remarks:** "The *Black-buffalo* was the Sioux chief with whom we had the conference at the great bend; and, from his appearance and mild deportment, I was induced to form a high opinion of him." After being interred with honors of war, *Ongpatonga* spoke to those assembled as follows:—"Do not grieve. Misfortunes will happen to the wisest and best men. Death will come, and always comes out of season. It is the command of the Great Spirit, and all nations and people must obey. What is passed and cannot be prevented should not be grieved

* The upper military post upon the Mississippi, in 1818.

† "This passage forcibly reminds us of that in *Shakspeare*:"

'The evil that men do lives after them;
The good is often interred with their bones.'

‡ Philadelphia Lit. Gazette.

§ *Ongue-pon-we,* in Iroquois, was "men surpassing all others." *Hist. Five Nations.*

‖ "The O' Mahas, in number 2250, not long ago, abandoned their old village on the south side of the Missouri, and now dwell on the Elk-horn River, due west from their old village, 80 miles west-north-west from Council Bluffs." *Morse's* Ind. Rept. 251.

¶ Brackenridge, *ut sup.* 91.

** Jour. up the Missouri, 240.

for. Be not discouraged or displeased then, that in visiting your father* here, [the American commissioner,] you have lost your chief. A mis-

fortune of this kind may never again befall you, but this would have attended you perhaps at your own village. Five times have I visited this land, and never returned with sorrow or pain. Misfortunes do not flourish particularly in our path. They grow every where. What a misfortune for me, that I could not have died this day, instead of the chief that lies before us. The trifling loss my nation would have sustained in my death, would have been doubly paid for by the honors of my burial. They would have wiped off every thing like regret. Instead of being covered with a cloud of sorrow, my warriors would have felt the sunshine of joy in their hearts. To me it would have been a most glorious occurrence. Hereafter, when I die at home, instead of a noble grave and a grand procession, the rolling music and the thundering cannon, with a flag waving at my head, I shall be wrapped in a robe, (an old robe perhaps,) and hoisted on a slender scaffold to the whistling winds,† soon to be blown down to the earth.‡ My flesh to be devoured by the wolves, and my bones rattled on the plain by the wild beasts. Chief of the soldiers, [addressing Col. *Miller*,] your labors have not been in vain. Your attention shall not be forgotten. My nation shall know the respect that is paid over the dead. When I return I will echo the sound of your guns."

Dr. *Morse* saw *Ongpatonga* at Washington in the winter of 1821, and

* Gov. *Edwards* or Col. *Miller*.

† It is a custom to expose the dead upon a scaffold among some of the tribes of the west. See *Brackenridge*, Jour., 186.; Pike's Expedition; *Long's* do.

‡ The engraving at the commencement of Book II. illustrates this passage.

discoursed with him and *Ishkatappa,* chief of the republican Paunees, "on the subject of their civilization, and sending instructers among them for that purpose." The doctor has printed the conversation, and we are sorry to acknowledge that, on reading it, *Big-elk* suffers in our estimation; but his age must be his excuse. When he was asked who made the red and white people, he answered, "The same Being who made the white people, made the red people; *but the white are better than the red people.*" This acknowledgment is too degrading, and does not comport with the general character of the American Indians. It is not, however, very surprising that such an expression should escape an individual surrounded, as was *Ongpatonga,* by magnificence, luxury, and attention from the great.

Big-elk was a party to several treaties, made between his nation and the United States, previous to his visit to Washington in 1821.

Petalesharoo was not a chief, but a brave of the tribe of the Paunees. (A brave is a warrior who has distinguished himself in battle, and is next in importance to a chief.*) He was the son of *Letelesha,* a famous chief, commonly called the *Knife-chief,* or *Old-knife.* When Major *Long* and his company travelled across the continent, in 1819 and 20, they became acquainted with *Petalesharoo.* From several persons who were in *Long's* company, Dr. *Morse* collected the particular of him which he gives in his INDIAN REPORT as an anecdote.

In the winter of 1821, *Petalesharoo* visited Washington, being one of a deputation from his nation to the American government, on a business matter.

---

* *Long's* Expedition, i. 356; and Dr. *Morse's* Indian Report, 247.

This *brave* was of elegant form and countenance, and was attired, in his visit to Washington, as represented in the above engraving. In 1821, he was about 25 years of age. At the age of 21, he was so distinguished by his abilities and prowess, that he was called the "*bravest of the braves.*" But few years previous to 1821, it was a custom, not only with his nation, but those adjacent, to torture and burn captives as sacrifices to the great Star. In an expedition performed by some of his countrymen against the Iteans, a female was taken, who, on their return, was doomed to suffer according to their usages. She was fastened to the stake, and a vast crowd assembled upon the adjoining plain to witness the scene. This *brave*, unobserved, had stationed two fleet horses at a small distance, and was seated among the crowd, as a silent spectator. All were anxiously waiting to enjoy the spectacle of the first contact of the flames with their victim; when, to their astonishment, a *brave* was seen rending asunder the cords which bound her, and, with the swiftness of thought, bearing her in his arms beyond the amazed multitude; where placing her upon one horse, and mounting himself upon the other, he bore her off safe to her friends and country. This act would have endangered the life of an ordinary chief, but such was his sway in the tribe, that no one presumed to censure the daring act.

This transaction was the more extraordinary, as its performer was as much a son of nature, and had had no more of the advantages of education, than the multitude whom he astonished by the humane act just recorded.

This account being circulated at Washington, during the young chief's stay there, the young ladies of Miss *White's* seminary in that place, resolved to give him a demonstration of the high esteem in which they held him on account of his humane conduct; they therefore presented him an elegant silver medal, appropriately inscribed, accompanied by the following short but affectionate address: "Brother, accept this token of our esteem—always wear it for our sakes, and when again you have the power to save a poor woman from death and torture—think of this, and of us, and fly to her relief and her rescue." The *brave's* reply:—"*This* [taking hold of the medal which he had just suspended from his neck] *will give me ease more than I ever had, and I will listen more than I ever did to white men. I am glad that my brothers and sisters have heard of the good act I have done. My brothers and sisters think that I did it in ignorance, but I now know what I have done. I did it in ignorance, and did not know that I did good; but by giving me this medal I know it.*"

Some time after the attempt to sacrifice the Itean woman, one of the warriors of *Letelesha* brought to the nation a Spanish boy, whom he had taken. The warrior was resolved to sacrifice him to Venus, and the time was appointed. *Letelesha* had a long time endeavored to do away the custom, and now consulted *Petalesharoo* upon the course to be pursued. The young *brave* said, "I will rescue the boy, as a warrior should, by force." His father was unwilling that he should expose his life a second time, and used great exertions to raise a sufficient quantity of merchandize for the purchase of the captive. All that were able contributed, and a pile was made of it at the lodge of the *Knife-chief*, who then summoned the warrior before him. When he had arrived, the chief commanded him to take the merchandize, and deliver the boy to him. The warrior refused. *Letelesha* then waved his war-club in the air, bade the warrior obey or prepare for instant death. "*Strike*," said *Petalesharoo*, "*I will meet the vengeance of his friends.*" But the prudent and excellent *Letelesha* resolved to use one more endeavor before committing such an act. He therefore increased the amount of property, which had the desired effect. The boy was surrendered, and the valuable collection of goods sacrificed in his stead.* This, it is thought, will be the last time the inhuman custom will be attempted in the tribe. "The origin of this sanguinary sacrifice is unknown; probably it existed previously to their intercourse with the white traders."† They believed that the success of their enterprises, and all undertakings, depended upon their faithfully adhering to the due performance of these rites.

In his way to Washington, he staid some days in Philadelphia, where Mr. *Neagle* had a fine opportunity of taking his portrait, which he performed with wonderful success. It was copied for Dr. *Godman's* Natural History, and adorns the second volume of that valuable work.

Metea, chief of the Pottowattomies, is brought to our notice on account of the opposition he made to the sale of a large tract of his country. In 1821, he resided upon the Wabash. To numerous treaties, from 1814 to 1821, we find his name, and generally at the head of those of his tribe. At the treaty of Chicago, in the year last mentioned, he delivered the following speech, after Gov. *Cass* had informed him of the objects of his mission.

"My father,—We have listened to what you have said. We shall now retire to our camps and consult upon it. You will hear nothing more from us at present. [This is a uniform custom of all the Indians. When the council was again convened, *Metea* continued.] We meet you here to-day, because we had promised it, to tell you our minds, and what we have agreed upon among ourselves. You will listen to us with a good mind, and believe what we say. You know that we first came to this country, a long time ago, and when we sat ourselves down upon it, we met with a great many hardships and difficulties. Our country was then very large, but it has dwindled away to a small spot, and you wish to pur-

* Long, *ut supra*, 357–8. † *Ibid.*

chase that! This has caused us to reflect much upon what you have told us; and we have, therefore, brought all the chiefs and warriors, and the young men and women and children of our tribe, that one part may not do what the others object to, and that all may be witness of what is going forward. You know your children. Since you first came among them, they have listened to your words with an attentive ear, and have always hearkened to your counsels. Whenever you have had a proposal to make to us, whenever you have had a favor to ask of us, we have always lent a favorable ear, and our invariable answer has been 'yes.' This you know! A long time has passed since we first came upon our lands, and our old people have all sunk into their graves. They had sense. We are all young and foolish, and do not wish to do any thing that they would not approve, were they living. We are fearful we shall offend their spirits, if we sell our lands; and we are fearful we shall offend you, if we do *not* sell them. This has caused us great perplexity of thought, because we have counselled among ourselves, and do not know how we can part with the land. Our country was given to us by the Great Spirit, who gave it to us to hunt upon, to make our cornfields upon, to live upon, and to make down our beds upon when we die. And he would never forgive us, should we bargain it away. When you first spoke to us for lands at St. Mary's, we said we had a little, and agreed to sell you a piece of it; but we told you we could spare no more. Now you ask us again. You are never satisfied! We have sold you a great tract of land, already; but it is not enough! We sold it to you for the benefit of your children, to farm and to live upon. We have now but little left. We shall want it all for ourselves. We know not how long we may live, and we wish to have some lands for our children to hunt upon. You are gradually taking away our hunting-grounds. Your children are driving us before them. We are growing uneasy. What lands you have, you may retain for ever; but we shall sell no more. You think, perhaps, that I speak in passion; but my heart is good towards you. I speak like one of your own children. I am an Indian, a red-skin, and live by hunting and fishing, but my country is already too small; and I do not know how to bring up my children, if I give it all away. We sold you a fine tract of land at St. Mary's. We said to you then it was enough to satisfy your children, and the last we should sell: and we thought it would be the last you would ask for. We have now told you what we had to say. It is what was determined on, in a council among ourselves; and what I have spoken, is the voice of my nation. On this account, all our people have come here to listen to me; but do not think we have a bad opinion of you. Where should we get a bad opinion of you? We speak to you with a good heart, and the feelings of a friend. You are acquainted with this piece of land—the country we live in. Shall we give it up? Take notice, it is a small piece of land, and if we give it away, what will become of us? The Great Spirit, who has provided it for our use, allows us to keep it, to bring up our young men and support our families. We should incur his anger, if we bartered it away. If we had more land, you should get more, but our land has been wasting away ever since the white people became our neighbors, and we have now hardly enough left to cover the bones of our tribe. You are in the midst of your red children. What is due to us in money, we wish, and will receive at this place; and we want nothing more. We all shake hands with you. Behold our warriors, our women, and children. Take pity on us and on our words."

Notwithstanding the decisive language held by *Metea* in this speech, against selling land, yet his name is to the treaty of sale. And in another speech of about equal length, delivered shortly after, upon the same subject, the same determination is manifest throughout.

At this time he appeared to be about forty years of age, and of a noble and dignified appearance. He is allowed to be the most eloquent chief of his nation. In the last war, he fought against the Americans, and, in the attack on Fort Wayne, was severely wounded; on which account he draws a pension from the British government.*

At the time of the treaty of Chicago, of which we have made mention, several other chiefs, besides *Metea*, or, as his name is sometimes written, *Meeteya*, were very prominent, and deserve a remembrance. Among them may be particularly named

Keewagoushkum, a chief of the first authority in the Ottowa nation. We shall give a speech which he made at the time, which is considered very valuable, as well on account of the history it contains, as for its merits in other respects. INDIAN HISTORY by an Indian, must be the most valuable part of any work about them. *Keewagoushkum* began:—

"My father, listen to me! The first white people seen by us were the French. When they first ventured into these lakes they hailed us as children; they came with presents and promises of peace, and we took them by the hand. We gave them what they wanted, and initiated them into our mode of life, which they readily fell into. After some time, during which we had become well acquainted, we embraced their father, (the king of France,) as our father. Shortly after, these people that wear red coats, (the English,) came to this country, and overthrew the French; and they extended their hand to us in friendship. As soon as the French were overthrown, the British told us, 'We will clothe you in the same manner the French did. We will supply you with all you want, and will purchase all your peltries, as they did.' Sure enough! after the British took possession of the country, they fulfilled all their promises. When they told us we should have any thing we were sure to get it; and we got from them the best goods.—Some time after the British had been in possession of the country, it was reported that another people, who wore white clothes, had arisen and driven the British out of the land. These people we first met at Greenville, [in 1795, to treat with Gen. *Wayne*,] and took them by the hand.—When the Indians first met the American chief, [*Wayne*,] in council, there were but few Ottowas present; but he said to them, 'When I sit myself down at Detroit, you will all see me.' Shortly after, he arrived at Detroit. Proclamation was then made for all the Indians to come in.—We were told, [by the general,] 'The reason I do not push those British farther is, that we may not forget their example in giving you presents of cloth, arms, ammunition, and whatever else you may require.' Sure enough! The first time, we were clothed with great liberality. You gave us strouds, guns, ammunition, and many other things we stood in need of, and said, 'This is the way you may always expect to be used.' It was also said, that whenever we were in great necessity, you would help us.—When the Indians on the Maumee were first about to sell their lands, we heard it with both ears, but we never received a dollar.—The Chippewas, the Pottowattomies, and the Ottowas *were, originally, but one nation.* We separated from each other near Michilimackinac. We were related by the ties of blood, language and interest; but in the course of a long time, these things have been forgotten, and both nations have sold their lands, without consulting us."—"Our brothers, the Chippewas, have also sold you a large tract of land at Saganaw. People are constantly passing through the country, but we received neither invitation nor money. It is surprising that the

* *Schoolcraft's* Travels.

Pottowattomies, Ottowas, and Chippewas, who are all one nation, should sell their lands without giving each other notice. Have we then degenerated so much that we can no longer trust one another?—Perhaps the Pottowattomies may think I have come here on a begging journey, that I wish to claim a share of lands to which my people are not entitled. I tell them it is not so. We have never begged, and shall not now commence. When I went to Detroit last fall, Gov. *Cass* told me to come to this place, at this time, and listen to what he had to say in council. As we live a great way in the woods, and never see white people except in the fall, when the traders come among us, we have not so many opportunities to profit by this intercourse as our neighbors, and to get what necessaries we require; but we make out to live independently, and trade upon our own lands. We have, heretofore, received nothing less than justice from the Americans, and all we expect, in the present treaty, is a full proportion of the money and goods."

"A series of misfortunes," says Mr. *Schoolcraft,* "has since overtaken this friendly, modest, and sensible chief. On returning from the treaty of Chicago, while off the mouth of Grand River, in Lake Michigan, his canoe was struck by a flaw of wind and upset. After making every exertion, he saw his wife and all his children, except one son, perish. With his son he reached the shore; but, as if to crown his misfortunes, this only surviving child has since been poisoned for the part he took in the treaty."

The result of this treaty was the relinquishment, by the Ottowas, Chippewas, and Pottowattomies, of a tract of country in the southern part of the peninsula of Michigan, containing upwards of 5,000,000 acres, and for which they received of the United States, in goods, 35,000 dollars; and several other sums were awarded to the separate tribes, to some yearly forever, and to others for a limited term of years. Some of the chiefs who attended to the treaty were opposed to this sale, and hence the reason that *Keewagooshkum's* son was poisoned.

Koange, in the following speech, opposed it in a manly style. He was a chief of mature age, and of a venerable aspect.

"My father, since you heard from our brothers, the Chippewas and Ottawas, we have counselled together. It is now your wish to hear the sentiments of the three Nations. I shall deliver them. Sometimes the Indians have acted like children. When requested they have signed away their lands without consideration. This has always made trouble in the nation, and blood has been spilt in consequence. We wish to avoid such foolish and bad conduct. The last time we sat down in council together, we had not fully consulted each other; and perhaps you drew a wrong conclusion from what we said. We did *not* consent to your request. In times past, when you have asked us for lands, we have freely sold them. At present there are a number of our people opposed to selling, and we have found it very difficult to agree in mind. One point, in particular, we differ much upon; it is the extent of the grant you request. We give you one more proof of our friendship, by meeting you in this council. You know our minds—we now take you by the hand. Look down upon us with compassion and wish us well."

This speech, Mr. *Schoolcraft* says, was rather more favorably rendered by the interpreter, than it should have been, in regard to the disposal of the land. We think, however, that he speaks in very decided terms against it.

There was another chief present at this treaty, a Pottowattomie, whom we will mention, particularly to show the "ruling passion" of the Indians for ardent spirits. This was

Topinabee, or *Thupeneba.* He was a chief much respected, and was venerable now from his age; having been the first chief of his tribe, from before the time of *Wayne's* war. His name stands first to a number of treaties, from that of Greenville, in 1795, to that of Chicago, in 1821. There was a good deal of reluctance with many present, at the latter treaty, to comply with its requisitions, but when it was finally determined that it should be executed, all seemed eager to have it go into effect without delay, from the circumstance, that a certain quantity of whiskey was stipulated to be delivered to them as soon as it was executed. *Thupeneba* said to Gov. *Cass*, "*Father, we are very thirsty for some of that milk you have brought for us. We wish it to be given to us. We can no longer restrain our thirst.*" And when he was told that the goods were not ready to be delivered, he said, "*Give us the whiskey. We care not for the rest.*"

We need not ask, here, whether the tempter or the tempted deserve most our censure in such cases.

CHAPTER VIII.

Of the late war in the west, and the chiefs engaged in it—Black-hawk—Neopope—The Prophet—Keokuk, and others.

IT will be necessary, in this chapter, before detailing events in the lives of chiefs, to give some account of such tribes of Indians as will often be mentioned as we proceed. We shall, however, confine ourselves to such tribes as took part in the late war in the neighborhood of the Lakes Michigan and Superior, more especially; and firstly of the Winnebagoes or Winebaygos. This tribe inhabit the country upon the Ouisconsin, a river that rises between the Lakes Superior and Michigan, and which disembogues itself into the Mississippi, near the S. W. angle of the N. W.

territory. They were found seated here when the country was first visited by whites, about 150 years ago, and here they still remain. In 1820, they were supposed to number 1550 souls, of whom 500 were men, 350 women, and 700 children, and lived in ten towns or villages.* A body of Winnebago warriors was in the fight at Tippecanoe, under the impostor *Ellskwatawa*. *Sanamahhonga*, called *Stone-eater*, and *Wapam*-angwa, or White-loon, were leaders of the Winnebago warriors. The latter was one that opposed Gen. *Wayne* in 1794, but was reconciled to the Americans in 1795, by the treaty of Greenville. He also treated with Gen. *Harrison*, in 1809, at Fort Wayne, and again at Greenville in 1814; but he was active in the war of 1812, and on the British side. Winnebago Lake, which discharges its waters into Green Bay, was probably named from this tribe of Indians, or, what is quite as probable, they received their name from the lake.

Secondly, the Menominies. This tribe inhabits a river bearing their name, and is situated about one degree north of the Winnebagoes, from whom they are separated by a range of mountains. They numbered in 1820, according to some, about 355 persons, of whom not more than 100 were fighters; but this estimate could apply only, it is thought, to the most populous tribe.

Thirdly, the Pottowattomies, or Pouteouatamis. This nation was early known to the French. In the year 1668, 300 of them visited Father *Allouez*, at a place which the French called Chagouamigon, which is an island in Lake Superior. There was among them at this time an old man 100 years old, of whom his nation reported wonderful things; among others, that he could go without food 20 days, and that he often saw the Great Spirit. He was taken sick here, and died in a few days after.†

The country of the Pottowattomies is adjacent to the south end of Lake Michigan, in Indiana and Illinois, and in 1820 their numbers were set down at 3400. At this time the United States paid them yearly 5700 dollars. Of this, 350 dollars remained a permanent annuity until the late war.

Fourthly, the Sacs and Foxes. These are usually mentioned together, and are now really but one nation. They also had the gospel taught them about 1668, by the Jesuits. They live to the west of the Pottowattomies, generally between the Illinois and Mississippi Rivers, in the state of Illinois. The chief of the Sauks, or Sacs, for at least 14 years, has been *Keokuk*. Of him we shall particularly speak elsewhere. The Sacs and Foxes were supposed to amount, in 1820, to about 3000 persons in all; one fifth of whom may be accounted warriors.

Thus we have taken a view of the most important points in the history of the tribes which were engaged in the late border war under *Black-hawk*, and are, therefore, prepared to proceed in the narration of the events of that war. It will be necessary for us to begin with some events as early as 1823; at which period a chief of the Winnebagoes called *Red-bird* was the most conspicuous. This year, the United States' agents held a treaty at Prairie du Chien, with the Sacs or Saques, Foxes, Winnebagoes, Chippeways, Sioux, &c., for the purpose, among other things, of bringing about a peace between the first-named tribe and the others, who were carrying on bloody wars among themselves. To effect the object in view, bounds were set to each tribe. About this time, the Galena lead mines attracted great attention; and the avarice of those concerned drove several thousand miners beyond the limits of the United States, into the

---

* Dr. *Morse* rated them at 5000. *Ind. Report*, Ap. 362.

† *Charlevoix*, Hist. de la Nouv. France, i. 395.

adjacent lands of the Winnebagoes. Whether this great encroachment was the cause of the murder of *M. Methode*, his wife and five children, we are not certain. It is certain that this family lived near Prairie du Chien, and that they were murdered by a party of Winnebagoes; two of whom were afterwards taken and imprisoned in the jail of Crawford county. An article in the treaty just mentioned, provided that any or each of those Indian nations visiting a garrison of the United States, such party or parties should be protected from insult from others by said garrison.

Notwithstanding this, in the summer of 1827, a party of 24 Chippeways, on a visit to Fort Snelling, were fallen upon by a band of Sioux, who killed and wounded eight of them. The commandant of Fort Snelling captured four of them, whom he delivered into the hands of the Chippeways, who immediately shot them, according to their custom.

Red-bird resented the proceedings of the commandant of Fort Snelling, and equally the conduct of the Chippeways, and resolved on retaliation. Accordingly he led a war party against the latter, but was defeated; and upon his return he was derided by his neighbors.

It is said that *Red-bird* had been deceived by the Indians, who told him, that those put to death by the Chippeways were those who had been imprisoned for the murder of *Methode* and family. If this were the case, let it go as far as it will to brighten the character of *Red-bird.*

Enraged at his ill success against the Chippeways, *Red-bird,* with only three desperate companions like himself, repaired to Prairie du Chien, where, about the first July, they killed two persons and wounded a third. We hear of no plunder taken by them, except a keg of whiskey, with which they retired to the mouth of Bad-axe River. Immediately after, with his company augmented, *Red-bird* waylaid two keel-boats that had been conveying commissary stores to Fort Snelling. One came into the ambush in the day-time, and, after a fight of four hours, escaped, with the loss of two killed and four wounded. It was midnight before the other fell into the snare, and, owing to the darkness, escaped without much injury.

Not long after, Gen. *Atkinson* marched into the Winnebago country, with a brigade of troops, regulars and militia, where he succeeded in making prisoners of *Red-bird* and some others of the hostile Winnebagoes. *Red-bird* soon after died in prison. "Some of the other culprits were tried and found guilty, and sentenced to death, but were pardoned by President *Adams,* it is said, on the implied condition of a cession of the mining district."*

In the case of the United States against *Wou-koo-hah* and *Man-na-at-ap-e-kah,* for the murder of *Methode* and family, a *nolle prosequi* was entered, and the prisoners discharged. *Kanonekah,* or *the youngest of* the *Thunders,* and *Karazhonsept-hah,* or *Black-hawk,* had been imprisoned for the attack on the boat above mentioned, and also a son of *Red-bird;* but they were discharged. Two others, at the same court, were found guilty of murders, and sentenced to be executed 26 December following. This was in August, 1828.

Hence, where daily troubles, in kind like what we have related, occurred, no one could expect tranquillity while the parties in them were within hail of each other; and it has often happened that much greater bloodshed has followed far less causes, than existed at the commencement of the present war. Nevertheless, it did not commence, as border wars often do, by a great irruption on the part of the Indians; and it seems as though they were only following up a retaliation, to which, by numerous grievances, they had been actually driven. The complaints on

---

* From a collection of facts published by *W. J. Snelling,* Esq.

the part of the whites are the same as have always been made—that the Indians paid no regard to their engagements. We do not pretend to exonerate them of blame, but we do charge their enemies with much greater. In our present business, it is enough that the whites were the aggressors, which, for once out of hundreds of times, where the facts are well established, we shall not be thought very presumptuous, perhaps, in setting down as granted.

The fact, we apprehend, will not be denied, that many frontier establishments have very little to lose by an Indian war, but much to gain if successful. The settlers are sure that by a war the Indians will be driven farther from them, and be obliged to give up their approximate lands; in which event they are no longer a frontier, but a thoroughfare to one. And hence the flocking in of new settlers raises the value of produce, as well as lands, by creating a demand for them. Thus it is not difficult to see, that the avaricious and wicked have every inducement to bring about an Indian war.

Black-hawk, we have just seen, was, in 1827, suspected, and even imprisoned for an act of alleged hostility; and it is probable that he may have been remotely concerned in the affair charged against him. Be that as it may, *Red-bird* had died in prison, and *Red-bird* was his friend. Indians could be seized, tried and executed, for killing those who aggravated them to do so, but it often happens that when Indians are murdered by whites, the murderers cannot be brought to justice. Sometimes they make an escape, and sometimes are shielded by their friends; therefore the equal administration of justice has never been had. The Indians know and feel the force of these reflections; and it is not strange that, in 1831, the whites of the frontier of Illinois thought that "the Indians, with some exceptions, from Canada to Mexico, along the northern frontiers of the United States, were more hostile to them than at any other period since the last war."* It is not probable, however, that the conjecture was true, to the extent imagined.

A number of the Sac Indians, who, in the war between the U. States and Great Britain, served the latter, which gave them the name of the "British band," was the most conspicuous in opposing the whites. This band of Sacs had rendezvoused at their chief village, on the Mississippi, where they had collected such of their neighbors as wished to engage in the war. Gen. Gaines, joined by Gov. *Reynolds,* and Gen. *Duncan's* brigade of 1400 mounted men, possessed themselves of the Sac village on the 26 June. They did this without opposition; for when the Indians discovered the whites on their march, they fled across the river, and after a short time displayed a white flag for a parley. Meantime their associates had abandoned them, and the Sac band was left alone to manage affairs in the best manner they could. They therefore made peace with the whites, with all due submission; and the latter thought there would be no further cause of alarm. Indeed, such was their deportment, that Gen. *Gaines* was of opinion that they were as completely humbled, as if they had been chastised in battle, and were less disposed to disturb the frontiers than if the other event had taken place; and only a few days before this, Gen. *Gaines* said he was confirmed in the opinion, that, whatever might be their hostile feelings, they were resolved to abstain from the use of their tomahawks and fire-arms, except in self-defence.

Meanwhile a difficulty seems to have arisen between some of the Sacs and the Menominies, and 28 of the latter had been murdered. Agreeably to the 14th article of the treaty of Prairie des Chiens, concluded 19 Aug. 1825, the United States obliged themselves to interpose between these and

---

* Gov. *Reynold's* letter to the secretary of war, 7 July, 1831.

other western tribes in cases of troubles. The Sacs had not only committed the murders just mentioned, but they had recrossed the Mississippi to its east bank, and occupied the country in the spring of 1832, that they had fled from the last year, and by treaty given up. *Black-hawk* was the alleged leader in both cases. Therefore Gen. *Atkinson* set out on an expedition, in which it was hoped he would seize *Black-hawk,* who, it was said, was "the sole fomenter of all these disturbances;" and it was said also that he had little respect for treaties, and that he had, "in former negotiations, so far overreached our commissioners, as to make peace on his own terms." Here we have an early acknowledgment of the abilities of our chief in matters of diplomacy. But to return to the expedition.

Gen. *Atkinson* was at Rock River, at a place called Dixon's Ferry, on 15 May, when he received news from a force which had marched to Sycamore Creek, about 30 miles from Dixon's, that a part of that force had met with a total defeat. There had been various murders committed at Sycamore Creek, which occasioned the march of this force thither. Among the sufferers about that place was the family of a Mr. *Hall,* which, from the circumstance of his two daughters having been carried into captivity, created much sympathy; they being one but 16 and the other 18 years of age. Before they were led away, they saw their mother tomahawked and scalped, and about 20 others (at Indian Creek, which empties into Fox River) treated in like manner. These young women, after they were conveyed out of the reach of the whites, by their captors, were humanely treated, and have since been restored to their friends.

Those who marched to Sycamore Creek were in number about 275, under the command of Maj. *Stillman.* They were encamped at Ogee, or Dixon's Ferry, when the news of the massacre on Indian Creek arrived, at which intelligence Maj. *Stillman* got permission of Gen. *Whitesides* to march in that direction. On Monday, 14 May, they came upon a few Indians, whether enemies or not is not mentioned, nor do we presume the whites stopped to inquire, for "theirs was the march of death," and therefore two of them were shot down, and two others captured. The same day, at evening, when the army had arrived at a convenient place to encamp upon, and after they had made some preparations for encamping, a small band of Indians were discovered bearing a white flag. One company of men went out to meet them, but soon discovered they were only a decoy. How they knew this to be the fact, we are not informed. This detachment, therefore, fell back upon the main body, which, by this time, had remounted; and, as strange as it is true, this misguided band rushed forward, regardless of all order, for several miles, until they had crossed Sycamore Creek, and were completely in the Indians' power. The reader can now expect nothing but a detail almost exactly similar to the Pawtucket fight. The whites had crossed the creek man by man, as they came to it, and all the Indians had to do, was to wait until a goodly number had got within their grasp. It was moonlight when the fight began, and after a few struggles the whites fled in greater disorder, if possible, than they came. The Indians, after making the onset by a discharge of their guns, fell on with their knives and tomahawks, and had not the night and situation of the country favored their flight, nearly all the army must have been cut off. The Indians were reported to have been about 1500 or 2000 strong, and it was said 12 of them were killed in the fight. Of the whites 13 only are reported as having been killed. Their flight was quite equal to that of the army under Gen. *St. Clair.* Immediately after, 1400 men marched to the scene of action, to bury the dead; and their account of barbarities committed on the bodies of the slain adds nothing to those already related in similar events. One soldier only escaped disfiguration, which is not easily accounted for, unless it were the case that he had secreted himself until all the Indians but one had left the scene of action; for he was found side by side with an Indian, each grasping the other, and both in the arms of death. The soldier's head was nearly cut off, and the Indian was shot through the body. Hence it was supposed that these two had exchanged their deadly shafts at the same moment; and from the situation of the Indian it was evident he had died while in the very act of dealing the fatal blow upon his adversary.

An idea of the rapidity with which the Indians convey intelligence of important events may be had from the fact, that a runner from Black-*hawk* and his allies, bearing to the Missouri Indians the news of their victory, arrived at the Des Moines Rapids 24 hours before the express sent by Gov. *Reynolds*.

In July following the cholera ravaged severely among the troops opposed to the Indians, insomuch that several companies were entirely broken up, and many belonging to them perished in a manner too revolting to be described. Of a corps under Col. *Twiggs*, of 208 men, but nine were left alive!

Gen. *Dodge* surprised a party of 12 Indians near Galena, and cut them off to a man. The whites, that they might not be outdone in cruelty by their enemies, scalped the slain. Near this same place Capt. *Stevenson* had what was termed a hard fight with another small party, killing six of them, and losing three of his own men. This fight was severe; knives, bayonets and tomahawks being the weapons employed. What time this affair took place is not mentioned, but it was probably in July.

Black-hawk assembled his forces at a point between Rock and Ouisconsin Rivers, where it was expected he would meet the whites in a general battle. His warriors were supposed to amount to at least 1000. Gen. *Atkinson* had nearly double that number of men, and resolved to meet him as soon as possible; and great hopes were entertained that, in such event, a finishing blow would be put to the war. But the old chief had seen too much experience to fall a prey in this case; he therefore escaped into an interminable wilderness. Gen. *Atkinson*, after almost insurmountable difficulties, arrived at Cashkonong; in this move he was also disappointed in finding any Indians. This was about the middle of July, 1832, and people began to despair of effecting any thing against the old wary chief, but by stratagem.

About the same time, Gen. *Dodge* was in pursuit of a trail of Indians near 40 miles from Fort Winnebago. It appears they were a flying, half-starved band, who made little or no resistance, on being attacked by the whites. It is stated that they were "brought to battle" in the evening; which will account for their not being all cut off. They left 16 dead on the ground where the fight or attack began; and the whites had but one man killed, and four wounded. The condition of the Indians at this period can be well conceived of, when it is understood that the army found many of them dead, as they marched along, emaciated and starved to death! Gen. *Dodge* had pursued this trail of Indians near 100 miles; and the place where he came up with them was upon the Ouisconsin, over against the old Sac village. In the general's official letter, he says, "From the scalps taken by the Winnebagoes, [a part of which tribe were befriending the whites,] as well as those taken by the whites and the Indians carried from the field of battle, we must have killed 40 of them."

It was now uncertain where the Indians were next to be found, but it was supposed they might descend the Ouisconsin, and so escape across the Mississippi in that direction; therefore Gen. *Dodge* recommended the placing a cannon on the river to cut them off, and Gen. *Atkinson* marched for the Blue Mounds with his regular troops, and a brigade of mounted men, in all about 1600 strong.

Meanwhile *Black-hawk*, finding it impracticable to escape with his whole company by way of the Ouisconsin, crossed the country, it appears, and struck the Mississippi a considerable distance above the mouth of the former, and, the better to ensure the escape of his warriors, suffered their women and children to descend the river in boats, by which means a great number of them fell into the hands of the whites. In their passage, some of the boats conveying these poor wretches were overset, (by what means we are not informed,) and many of those in them were drowned. Their condition, on arriving at Prairie du Chien, was doleful in the extreme. Many of the children were in such a famished state that it was thought impossible to revive them. It is humiliating to add, that in speaking of their treatment, it was said, they were "*generally* received and treated with humanity;" if, indeed, *generally* is to be understood in its common import.

Immediately after these transactions, the steamboat Warrior, with a small force on board, was sent up the Mississippi; and on its return the captain of it gave the following account of his expedition:—

"Prairie du Chien, 3 Aug. 1832. I arrived at this place on Monday last, [30 July,] and was despatched, with the Warrior alone, to Wapashaw's village, 120 miles above, to inform them of the approach of the Sacs, and to order down all the friendly Indians to this place. On our way down, we met one of the Sioux band, who informed us that the Indians (our enemies) were on Bad-axe River, to the number of 400. We stopped and cut some wood and prepared for action. About 4 o'clock on Wednesday afternoon, [1 Aug.] we found the *gentlemen* [Indians] where he stated he had left them. As we neared them, they raised a white flag, and endeavored to decoy us; but we were a little too old for them; for, instead of landing, we ordered them to send a boat on board, which they declined. After about 15 minutes' delay, giving them time to remove a few of their women and children, we let slip a six-pounder loaded with canister, followed by a severe fire of musketry; and if ever you saw straight blankets, you would have seen them there. I fought them at anchor most of the time, and we were all very much exposed. I have a ball which came in close by where I was standing, and passed through the bulkhead of the wheel-room. We fought them for about an hour or more, until our wood began to fail, and night coming on, we left and went on to the Prairie. This little fight cost them 23 killed, and, of course, a great many wounded. We never lost a man, and had but one man wounded, (shot through the leg.) The next morning, before we could get back again, on account of a heavy fog, they had the whole [of Gen. Atkinson's] army upon them. We found them at it, walked in and took a hand ourselves. The first shot from the Warrior *laid out three*. I can hardly tell you any thing about it, for I am in great haste, as I am now on my way to the field again. The army lost eight or nine killed, and seventeen wounded, whom we brought down. One died on deck last night. We brought down 36 prisoners, women and children. I tell you what, *Sam*, there is no fun in fighting Indians, particularly at this season, when the grass is so very bright. Every man, and even my cabin-boy, fought well. We had 16 regulars, 5 riflemen, and 20 of ourselves. Mr. *How*, of Platte, Mr. *Hempstead Souilard*, and one of the *Ralettes*, were with us, and fought well."

The place where this fight took place was about 40 miles above Prairie du Chien, on the north side of the Mississippi, nearly opposite the mouth of the Ioway; and the whites were very fortunate in being able, at the same time, to cooperate by land and water. Gen. *Atkinson* having formed a junction with Gen. *Dodge,* the army, consisting of 1300 men, crossed the Ouisconsin on the 27 and 28 July, and soon after fell upon the trail of the Indians, who were flying from the late scene of action on that river, as we have observed above. The country through which the army had to march was a continued series of mountains, covered to their very tops with a thick wood of heavy timber, and much underwood. The valleys were very deep and difficult to be passed; but nothing could damp the ardor of the whites, and they pressed on to overtake *Black-hawk* before he should be able to escape across the Mississippi. This they accomplished, as we have already seen. The place where they were overtaken was very favorable for the Indians, as may be jugded by their being able to maintain a fight of about three hours, in their wretched, half-starved condition, with not more than 300 warriors. They were discovered in a deep ravine, at the foot of a precipice, over which the army had to pass; and they were routed only at the point of the bayonet. Old logs, high grass and large trees covered them until the charge was made, when, as they were driven from one covert, they readily found another, and thus was the fight protracted. At length the whites were able so to dispose of their force, as to come upon them above and below, and also in the centre. No chance remained now to the Indians, but to swim the Mississippi, or elude the vigilance of their enemies by land, who had nearly encompassed them. Many, therefore, undertook the former means of flight, but few escaped by it, as the greatest slaughter was in the river; but a considerable number found means to escape by land. One hundred and fifty of them were supposed to have been killed in this battle.

Black-hawk was among those who escaped, but his precipitation was such, that he left even his papers behind him; one of which was a certificate from British officers, that he had served faithfully and fought valiantly for them in their late war against the United States. The prisoners taken at this time stated that at the battle on the Ouisconsin, with the force under Gen. *Dodge,* 68 of their numbers were killed and many wounded.

It was now thought that the Sacs would be glad to make peace on any terms. Accordingly Gen. *Atkinson* determined to order *Keokuk* to demand a surrender of the remaining principal men of the hostile party. From the battle ground the Generals *Atkinson, Dodge* and *Posey* went down the river to Fort Crawford, (Prairie du Chien,) in the Warrior, and the army followed by land. On the 4 August, Capt. *Price,* with a small company, killed and took 12 Sacs between Cassville and the Ouisconsin.

The fortune of the hostile Indians having now become desperate, enough of their countrymen were ready to volunteer to hunt them in every place. On the 3 August, 100 Sioux had permission to go out after them, and soon after another smaller band set off. News was soon after brought, that these had overtaken the hostile Sacs and Foxes on the south side of the Mississippi, and in a fight had killed about 120 of them.

Keokuk was chief of the friendly Sacs, and, about the same time, caused a nephew of his to be given up to the whites, as being the murderer of one *Martin,* in Warren county, Illinois.

Naopope was second in command to *Black-hawk,* and in all the expeditions against the whites; he was taken prisoner in the fight with the Sioux, and at his examination afterwards by Gen. *Scott,* about the murders which had been committed on the whites, he gave this account of himself:—

"*I always belonged to* Black-hawk's *band. Last summer I went to Malden; when I came back, I found that by the treaty with Gen.* Gaines, *the Sacs had moved across the Mississippi. I remained during the winter with the prophet, on Rock River, 35 miles above the mouth. During the winter, the prophet sent me across the Mississippi, to* Black-hawk, *with a message, to tell him and his band to cross back to his village and make corn: that if the Americans came and told them to move again, they would shake hands with them. If the Americans had come and told us to move, we should have shaken hands, and immediately have moved peaceably. We encamped on Syracuse Creek. We met some Pottowattomies, and I made a feast for them. At that time I heard there were some Americans* [under Major Stillman] *near us. I prepared a white flag to go and see them, and sent two or three young men on a hill to see what they were doing. Before the feast was finished, I heard my young men were killed. This was at sunset. Some of my young men ran out; two killed, and the Americans were seen rushing on to our camp. My young men fired a few guns, and the Americans ran off, and my young men chased them about six miles."*

Naopope further said, that the Pottowattomies of the Village immediately left them, and that no Kickapoos joined them, but those who were originally with *Black-hawk;* but the Winnebagoes did, and brought in scalps frequently; that, at last, when they found the Sacs would be beaten, they turned against them. It was also given in by some of those examined at this time, that *Black-hawk* said, when the steamboat Warrior approached them, that he pitied the women and children, and began to make preparations to surrender to the whites, and for that purpose sent out a white flag to meet the boat, which immediately fired upon them. Then said he, "*I fired too.*" The truth of this will not be questioned, inasmuch as the facts agree with the captain of the Warrior's own account. Hence the inference is clear, that much blood might have been saved, but for the precipitancy of those who only sought revenge.

The bloody scene on the morning of the 2 August may be considered as the last act of hostility of importance between the whites and Indians. Parties of the friendly tribes were so continually on the alert, that it seemed very probable the principal chiefs would soon fall into their hands. These expectations were soon realized; for at 11 o'clock, 27 August, *Black-hawk* and his prophet were delivered to Gen. *Street* at Prairie du Chien. They were brought by two Winnebagoes, *Decorie* and *Chaetar,* and, when delivered, were dressed in a full dress of white tanned deerskins. Soon after they were seated in the presence of the officer, *Decorie,* called the *One-eyed,* rose and spoke thus to him:—

"My father, I now stand before you. When we parted, I told you I would return soon; but I could not come any sooner. We have had to go a great distance, [to the Dalle, on the Ouisconsin, above the Portage.] You see we have done what you sent us to do. These [pointing to the prisoners] are the two you told us to get.—We have done what you told us to do. We always do what you tell us, because we know it is for our good. Father, you told us to get these men, and it would be the cause of much good to the Winnebagoes. We have brought them, but it has been very hard for us to do so. That one, *Mucatamishkakaekq,* [meaning *Black-hawk,*] was a great way off. You told us to bring them to you alive: we have done so. If you had told us to bring their heads alone, we would have done so, and it would have been less difficult than what we have done.—Father, we deliver these men into your hands. We would not deliver them even to our brother, the chief of the warriors, but to you; because we know you, and we believe you are our friend. We want you to keep them safe; if they are to be hurt, we do not wish to see it. Wait until we are gone before it is done.—Father, many little birds have been flying about our ears of late, and we thought they whispered to us that there was evil intended for us; but now we hope these evil birds will let our ears alone.—We know you are our friend, because you take our part, and that is the reason we do what you tell us to do. You say you love your red children: we think we love you as much if not more than you love us. We have confidence in you and you may rely on us.—We have been promised a great deal if we would take these men,—that it would do much good to our people. We now hope to see what will be done for us.—We have come in haste; we are tired and hungry. We now put these men into your hands. We have done all that you told us to do."

Gen. *Street* said in answer:—

"My children, you have done well. I told you to bring these men to me, and you have done so. I am pleased at what you have done. It is for your good, and for this reason I am pleased. I assured the great chief of the warriors, [Gen. *Atkinson,*] that if these men were in your country, you would find them, and bring them to me, and now I can say much for your good. I will go down to Rock Island with the prisoners, and I wish you have brought these men, especially, to go with me, with such other chiefs and warriors as you may select. My children, the great chief of the warriors, when he left this place, directed me to deliver these, and all other prisoners, to the chief of the warriors at this place, Col. *Taylor,* who is here by me.—Some of the Winnebagoes south of the Ouisconsin have befriended the Saukies, [Sacs,] and some of the Indians of my agency have also given them aid. This displeaseth the great chief of the warriors and your great father the president, and was calculated to do much harm.—Your great father, the president at Washington, has sent a great war chief from the far east, Gen. *Scott,* with a fresh army of soldiers. He is now at Rock Island. Your great father, the president, has sent him and the governor and chief of Illinois to hold a council with the Indians. He has sent a speech to you, and wishes the chiefs and warriors of the Winnabagoes to go to Rock Island to the council on the tenth of next month. I wish you to be ready in three days, when I will go with you.—I am well pleased that you have taken the *Black-hawk,* the prophet, and others prisoners. This will enable me to say much for you to the great chief of the warriors, and to the president, your great father. My children, I shall now deliver the two men, *Black-hawk* and the prophet, to the chief of the warriors here; he will take care of them till we start to Rock Island."

Col. *Taylor,* having taken the prisoners into his custody, addressed the chiefs as follows:—

"The great chief of the warriors told me to take the prisoners when you shall bring them, and send them to Rock Island to him. I will take them and keep them safe, but I will use them well, and send them with you and Gen. *Street,* when you go down to the council, which will be in a few days. Your friend, Gen. *Street,* advises you to get ready and go down soon, and so do I. I tell you again I will take the prisoners; I will keep them safe, but I will do them no harm. I will deliver them to the great chief of the warriors, and he will do with them and use them in such manner as shall be ordered by your great father, the president."

Chaeton, the other Winnebago, next spoke, and said, "My father, I am young, and do not know how to make speeches. This is the second time I ever spoke to you before people.—I am no chief; I am no orator; but I have been allowed to speak to you. If I should not speak as well as others, still you must listen to me.—Father, when you made the speech to the chiefs *Waugh-kon-decorie-carramani,* the One-eyed *Decorie* and others 'tother day, I was there. I heard you. I thought what you said to them, you also said to me. You said, if these two [pointing to *Black-hawk* and the prophet] were taken by us and brought to you, there would never more a black cloud hang over your Winnebagoes.—Your words entered into my ear, into my brains, and into my heart. I left here that same night, and you know you have not seen me since until now.—I have been a great way; I had much trouble; but when I remembered what you said, I knew what you said was right. This made me continue and do what you told me to do.—Near the Dalle, on the Ouisconsin, I took Black-hawk. No one did it but me. I say this in the ears of all present, and they know it—and I now appeal to the Great Spirit, our grandfather, and the earth, our grandmother, for the truth of what I say.—Father, I am no chief, but what I have done is for the benefit of my nation, and I hope to see the good that has been promised to us.—That one, *Wa-bo-kie-shiek,* [the *prophet,*] is my relation—if he is to be hurt, I do not wish to see it.—Father, soldiers sometimes stick the ends of their guns into the backs of Indian prisoners when they are going about in the hands of the guard. I hope this will not be done to these men."

On the 7 September, the Indian prisoners and their guards went on board the steamboat Winnebago, and were conveyed down the river to Jefferson Barracks, ten miles below St. Louis. There were, besides *Black-hawk* and the *prophet,* eleven chiefs or head men of the Sacs and Foxes, together with about fifty less distinguished warriors. These were landed just above the lower rapids, on their pledge of remaining peaceable. Two days before, a boat had conveyed to the barracks six or seven warriors, among whom was *Naopope.* On their arrival at the barracks, all of them were put in irons.

Black-hawk is not so old a man as was generally supposed. Some who knew him well said he was not above 48, although the toils of wars had made him appear like one of 70. He was by birth a Pottowattomie, but brought up by the Sacs. His height is about six feet. As to his physiognomy, it is unnecessary for us to add concerning it here, as that may be better had from an inspection of the engraving at the head of this chapter. Our likeness is said, by many who have seen him, to be excellent.

Like other Indian names, his is spelt in as many ways as times used by different writers. At a treaty which he made with the United States in 1829, at Prairie du Chien, it is written *Hay-ray-tshoan-sharp.* In a description of him about the time he was taken, we find him spelt *Mus-cata-mish-ka-kaek*; and several others might be added.

The *prophet,* or *Wabokieshiek,* (white-cloud,) is about 40 years old, and nearly six feet high, stout and athletic. He was by one side a Winnebago, and the other, a Sac or Saukie, and is thus described:—He "has a large broad face, short blunt nose, large full eyes, broad mouth, thick lips, with a full suit of hair. He wore a white cloth head-dress which rose several inches above the top of his head. The whole man exhibiting a deliberate savageness; not that he would seem to delight in honorable war, or fight; but marking him as the priest of assassination or secret murder. He had in one hand a white flag, while the other hung carelessly by his side. They were both clothed in very white dressed deerskins, fringed at the seams with short cuttings of the same." This description, though written long before any painting was made of him, will be found, we think, to correspond very well with the engraving of him on the following page.

It is said by many, that *Wabokieshiek* was the prime mover of this war, and had powwowed up a belief among his people, that he was able to conjure such kind of events as he desired; and that he had made *Black-hawk* believe the whites were but few, and could not fight, and therefore might easily be driven from the disputed lands. It seems, however, rather incredible that *Black-hawk* should have believed that the Americans were *few and could not fight,* when it is known that he was opposed to them in the last war, and must, therefore, have been convinced of the falsity of such a report long before this war.

In September, a treaty was made by the United States with the Winnebagoes, and another with the Sacs and Foxes. The former ceded all their lands south of the Ouisconsin, and east of the Mississippi, amounting to 4,600,000 acres of valuable lands. The treaty with the Sacs and Foxes was on the 21 of that month, and 6,000,000 acres were acquired at that time, "of a quality not inferior to any between the same parallels of latitude." It abounds in lead ore, and the Indians say in others.

For these tracts the United States agreed to make the following considerations:—"to pay an annuity of 20,000 dollars for 30 years; to support a blacksmith and gunsmith in addition to those then employed; to pay the debts of the tribes; to supply provisions; and, as a reward for the fidelity of *Keokuk* and the friendly band, to allow a reservation to be made for them of 400 miles square* on the Ioway River, to include *Keokuk's* principal village."

By the same treaty, *Black-hawk,* his two sons, the *prophet* Naopope, and five others, principal warriors of the hostile bands, were to remain in the hands of the whites, as hostages, during the pleasure of the president of the United States. The other prisoners were given up to the friendly Indians.

A gentleman who visited the captive Indians at Jefferson Barracks, Missouri, speaks thus concerning them:—"We were immediately struck with admiration at the gigantic and symmetrical figures of most of the warriors, who seemed, as they reclined in native ease and gracefulness, with their half-naked bodies exposed to view, rather like statues from some master-hand, than like beings of a race whom we had heard characterized as degenerate and debased. We extended our hands, which they rose to grasp, and to our question, 'How d'ye do?' they responded in the same

---

* So says our authority, (*Niles's* Register,) but we very much doubt this enormous space. 40 miles square gives 1600 square miles, which perhaps might have been the truth. But when 160,000 square miles are considered, all probability is outraged.

words, accompanying them with a hearty shake." "They were clad in leggins and moccasins of buckskin, and wore blankets, which were thrown around them in the manner of the Roman toga, so as to leave their right arms bare." "The youngest among them were painted on their necks, with a bright vermilion color, and had their faces transversely streaked with alternate red and black stripes. From their bodies, and from their faces and eyebrows, they pluck out the hair with the most assiduous care. They also shave, or pull it out from their heads, with the exception of a tuft of about three fingers' width, extending from between the forehead and crown to the back of the head: this they sometimes plait into a queue on the crown, and cut the edges of it down to an inch in length, and plaster it with the vermilion which keeps it erect, and gives it the appearance of a cock's comb."

The same author says, the oldest son of *Black-hawk, Nasinewiskuk,* called *Jack,* but for want of "that peculiar expression which emanates from a cultivated intellect," could have been looked upon by him "as the living personification of his *beau ideal* of manly beauty." He calls *Black-hawk Mack-atama-sic-ac-ac*, and states his height at about 5 feet 8 inches, and that he should judge his age to be 50. Those who have known him for years, say his disposition is very amiable; that he is endowed with great kindness of heart, and the strictest integrity; that, like *Mishikinakwa,* he was not a chief by birth, but acquired the title by bravery and wisdom.

Naseuskuck, or the *Thundercloud*, is the second son of *Black-hawk*, and accompanied him in his captivity. He is said not to be very handsome.

Opeekeeshieck, or *Wabokieshiek*, the prophet, of whom we have already given some particulars, carries with him a huge pipe, a yard in length, with the stem ornamented with the neck feathers of a duck, and beads and ribbons of various colors. To its centre is attached a fan of feathers. He wears his hair long all over his head.

Naopope, Naapope, &c. or *Broth*, of whom we have also several times spoken, was brother to the prophet, and "some years his junior;" and our informant adds, "he resembles him in height and figure, though he is not so robust, and his face is more sharp: in wickedness of expression they are *par nobile fratrum*." "When Mr. *Catlin*, the artist, was about taking the portrait of *Naapope*, he seized the ball and chain that were fastened to his leg, and raising them on high, exclaimed, with a look of scorn, '*Make me so and show me to the great father*.' On Mr. *Catlin's* refusing to paint him as he wished, he kept varying his countenance with grimaces, to prevent him from catching a likeness.

"*Poweeshieck*, or *Strawberry*, is the only Fox among them, the rest being all Sacs. He is the son of the chief *Epanoss*: his parents dying while he was an infant, he was adopted by *Naapope*. He is 19 years of age."

"*Pomahoe*, or *Fast-swimming-fish*, is a short, thick set, good-natured old brave, who bears his misfortunes with a philosophy worthy of the ancients."

The following act of congress we extract, as it throws light upon subsequent details:—"For the expenses of 12 prisoners of war of the Sac and Fox tribes, now in confinement, and to be held as hostages, under the seventh article of the treaty of 21 Sept. 1832, embracing the cost of provisions and clothing, compensation to an interpreter, and cost of removing them to a place of safety, where they may be kept without being closely confined, the sum of 2500."

On the 22 April, (1833,) the captive Indians arrived at Washington, and the next day *Black-hawk* had a long interview with President *Jackson*. The first words with which it is said he accosted the president, were, "I AM A MAN, AND YOU ARE ANOTHER." Before this it was intended to confine the Indians at Fortress Monroe, at Old Point Comfort, Va. but after this interview the president altered his determination, and concluded to send them home on parole, after enforcing upon their minds the folly of contending with the whites in war. To effect this object, it was ordered that they should visit some of the most populous cities in the United States. Accordingly, they visited Baltimore, Philadelphia and New York. From the latter place they took their departure for the west, 26 June, by way of Albany and the lakes. After visiting the Senecas, they proceeded to Detroit, thence to Chicago, near the scenes of the late war.

When Mr. *Durant* was about to ascend in his balloon from the battery in New York, the steamboat in which the Indians came to that city had just arrived in view. They observed with great attention the aeronaut and his machine; and when one asked *Black-hawk* what he thought of them, he said, "*That man is a great brave—don't think he will ever get back.*" Shortly after, when the balloon had attained a vast height, the old chief exclaimed, "*I think he can go to the heavens—to the Great Spirit.*"

www.ingramcontent.com/pod-product-compliance
Lightning Source LLC
Chambersburg PA
CBHW020407100426
42812CB00001B/237

9781582181325